Resilience in Energy, Infrastructure, and Natural Resources Law

Academic Advisory Group (AAG) of the Section on Energy,
Environment, Resources and Infrastructure Law (SEERIL)
of the International Bar Association (IBA).

General Editors

TITLES IN THE SERIES

*Human Rights in Natural Resource Development: Public Participation in the Sustainable
Development of Mining and Energy Resources* (**2002**)

Energy Security: Managing Risk in a Dynamic Legal and Regulatory Environment (**2004**)

Regulating Energy and Natural Resources (**2006**)

Beyond the Carbon Economy: Energy Law in Transition (**2008**)

Property Law in Energy and Natural Resources (**2010**)

Energy Networks and the Law: Innovative Solutions in Changing Markets (**2012**)

*The Law of Energy Underground: Understanding New Developments
in Subsurface Production, Transmission, and Storage* (**2014**)

Sharing the Costs and Benefits of Energy and Resource Activity (**2016**)

Innovation in Energy Law and Technology (**2018**)

*Energy Justice and Energy Law: Distributive, Procedural, Restorative
and Social Justice in Energy Law* (**2020**).

Resilience in Energy, Infrastructure, and Natural Resources Law

Examining Legal Pathways for Sustainability in Times of Disruption

Edited by

CATHERINE BANET, HANRI MOSTERT,
LEROY PADDOCK, MILTON FERNANDO MONTOYA,
AND ÍÑIGO DEL GUAYO

OXFORD
UNIVERSITY PRESS

OXFORD
UNIVERSITY PRESS

Great Clarendon Street, Oxford, OX2 6DP,
United Kingdom

Oxford University Press is a department of the University of Oxford.
It furthers the University's objective of excellence in research, scholarship,
and education by publishing worldwide. Oxford is a registered trade mark of
Oxford University Press in the UK and in certain other countries

Published in the United States of America by Oxford University Press
198 Madison Avenue, New York, NY 10016, United States of America

British Library Cataloguing in Publication Data

Data available

Library of Congress Control Number: 2021924247

ISBN 978–0–19–286457–4

DOI: 10.1093/oso/9780192864574.001.0001

Printed and bound in the UK by
TJ Books Limited

Preface

The image of the sunflower chosen for the cover of this book is deliberate. It conveys the message of encouragement and of standing strong in the face of challenges that this flower has come to symbolize, most recently as part of the medalists' bouquets at the 2021 Olympics in Tokyo, Japan, where the flowers honoured the countless lives lost during the 2011 Tsunami at Miyagi. The depth of the sunflower's message was not lost on us. We remember the devastating cluster of disasters—earthquake, nuclear explosion, and tsunami that shook Japan in 2011, and which caused untold heartbreak and trauma. The sunflower carries the wordless message to take heart and keep moving, and hold on to hope.

In this book, we explore the theme of Resilience. It is the 11th volume in a book series produced by the Academic Advisory Group (AAG) of the Section on Energy, Environment, Resources and Infrastructure Law (SEERIL) of the International Bar Association (IBA). The AAG has been working on an expanding Energy and Natural Resources Law Series with OUP since 2000. The previous books are *Human Rights in Natural Resource Development: Public Participation in the Sustainable Development of Mining and Energy Resources* (2002); *Energy Security: Managing Risk in a Dynamic Legal and Regulatory Environment* (2004); *Regulating Energy and Natural Resources* (2006); *Beyond the Carbon Economy: Energy Law in Transition (2008); Property Law in Energy and Natural Resources* (2010); *Energy Networks and the Law: Innovative Solutions in Changing Markets* (2012); *The Law of Energy Underground: Understanding New Developments in Subsurface Production, Transmission, and Storage* (2014); *Sharing the Costs and Benefits of Energy and Resource Activity* (2016); *Innovation in Energy Law and Technology* (2018); and *Energy Justice and Energy Law: Distributive, Procedural, Restorative and Social Justice in Energy Law* (2020).

Building on the previous and ongoing work of the AAG-SEERIL group, notably in the 2004 book on *Energy Security*,[1] this new volume presents original research on a new topic that will enhance the previous volumes, including the last one that dealt with the law's responses to distributional justice in the energy context.[2]

The 2020 volume on Energy Justice and Energy Law appeared just as the world was heading into the life-altering reality of the COVID-19 pandemic. It was a time to recover from shock, to stabilize and assess, before designing strategies that would facilitate a bounce-back. As a group of thought leaders (and in the spirit of not letting a crisis go to waste), the AAG-SEERIL wanted to embrace the chance to contribute their collective intellectual efforts to facilitate future system designs that will transcend the current crisis. We wanted to be part of the conversation about how not only to bounce back, but to do so in ways that will improve our systems, eliminate from them the parts that no longer serve our

---

[1] B. Barton et al (eds), *Energy Security - Managing Risk in a Dynamic Legal and Regulatory Environment* (Oxford University Press 2004).

[2] I. del Guayo et al (eds), *Energy Justice and Energy Law: Distributive, Procedural, Restorative and Social Justice in Energy Law* (Oxford University Press 2020).

world, and envision new, and better futures for ourselves and generations to come. Within this context, the choice of resilience as a topic of research was obvious.

For the first time since the establishment of the AAG, the conception and development of this project included neither a discussion as part of the SEERIL biennial in 2020, nor by a physical mid-term meeting in 2021. This was due to the pandemic: the Marrakech conference was cancelled and due to travel restrictions, the mid-term meeting took place in virtual mode. We had to adapt around these circumstances, which put a heavier burden on the shoulders of authors and editors, but, at the same time, they also demonstrated the strong links among AAG members. Because we were compelled to develop this book in new ways due to the limitations the COVID-19 pandemic placed on our ability to meet in person, we learned that freedom of thought and of intellectual exchange did not have to be similarly compromised. As a group, we met virtually, across time zones and across several days, to thrash out the details of this volume. This allowed us a greater measure of inclusivity as regards contributors and topics, and the result is a good representation of the issues and questions arising around resilience in the energy, resource, and infrastructure sectors around the world. The editors had the privilege of learning the ropes on new collaborative platforms, and we have seen the advantages of time-efficiency and technological expedience, even as we were working across five different time zones.

We are honoured by the dedication displayed by our contributors who submitted work that withstood the test of the Oxford University Press (OUP) rigorous review process, as well as multiple rounds of editorial review. We are thankful to the OUP editorial staff and to the most helpful input from the OUP book reviewers for their time and effort, which contributed to give the final form to the project. We are, likewise, grateful for the renewed support and collaborative spirit from our colleagues in the IBA SEERIL, on whose counsel we rely.

Assistants have eased the editorial process quite a bit, and we are grateful to Richard Cramer and Bernard Kengni for their input.

We want to extend our greatest appreciation to the editorial staff at OUP. As in previous books written by AAG members and colleagues, on energy law issues, we have benefitted from the help, encouragement, and constant availability of Jack McNichol, Senior Project Editor, Academic & Professional Law at OUP. In particular, we want to highlight his patience in helping and guiding both the editors and authors of the book, so that it was successfully brought to completion. A few weeks before the submission of the manuscript to OUP Jack handed over the editorial contact for the book to his colleague Paulina dos Santos Major, an experienced Project Editor in the Law team. Jack was moving to the Humanities discipline team within OUP. It was sad not to have longer the involvement of Jack, but from the moment Paulina handed over, we have experienced her dedication, energy, and expertise to arrange everything for the production process.

The Editors
September 2021

Contents

PART VI MANAGING DISRUPTION AND RESILIENCE AT CONSUMPTION LEVEL: ACCESS TO ENERGY, DEMAND RESPONSE, EQUITY

PART VII CONCLUSION

List of Abbreviations

AC	Alternating Current
ACER	Agency for the Cooperation of Energy Regulators
ADF	African Development Fund
AEMC	Australia Energy Market Commission
AEMO	Australian Energy Market Operator
AER	Australia Energy Regulator
AfDB	African Development Bank
APEC	Asia-Pacific Economic Cooperation
AUC	Alberta Utilities Commission (Canada)
AWIA	America's Water Infrastructure Act
BBB	Build Back Better
BCP	Business Continuity Plan
BMTA	Bangkok Mass Transit Authority
BRICS	Brazil, Russia, India, China and South Africa
CCGL	Climate Change General Law of 2012 (Mexico)
CCS	Carbon and storage/sequestion
CEC	Clean Energy Certificate (Mexico)
CECs	Citizen Energy Communities
CEER	Council of European Energy Regulators
CEIG	Central Environmental Inspection Group
CER	Canada Energy Regulator
CERA	Canadian Energy Regulator Act
CERM	Coordinated Emergency Response Measures
CES	Clean Energy Standard (United States)
CETA	Comprehensive Economic and Trade Agreement
CEWS	Canada Emergency Wage Subsidy
CFE	Federal Commission of Electricity
CJEU	Court of Justice of the European Union
CLC	1969 International Convention on Civil Liability for Oil Pollution Damage
CNPC	China National Petroleum Corporation
CNS	1997 Convention on Nuclear Safety
COAG	Council of Australian Governments
COP	Conference of the Parties
COVID	Corona Virus Disease
CPTPP	Comprehensive and Progressive Agreement for Trans-Pacific Partnership
CRC	Bushfire and Natural Hazards Collaborative Research Centre (Australia)
CRISTAL	Contract Regarding an Interim Supplement to Tanker Liability for Oil Pollution
CSIRT	Computer Security Incident Response Team
CSP	Curtailment Service Provider
DCG	Distribution Connected Generation
DER	Distributed Energy Resources
DOE	U.S. Department of Energy
DR	Demand Response

DRR	Disaster Risk Reduction
DRRR	Disaster risk reduction and resilience
DSO	Distribution System Operator
ECHR	1950 European Convention for the Protection of Human Rights and Freedoms
ECI	European critical infrastructure
ECLAC	Economic Commission for Latin America and the Caribbean
ECT	Energy Charter Treaty
ECtHR	European Court of Human Rights
EEC	European Economic Community
EGAT	Electricity Generating Authority of Thailand
EIA	Environmental Impact Assessment
EIL	Energy Industry Law (Mexico)
EJ	Exajoule
ENISA	European Network and Information Security Agency
ENTSO-E	European Transmission System Operators for Electricity
ENTSO-G	European Transmission System Operators for Gas
EPAct	Energy Policy Act of 2005 (United States)
ERC	Energy Regulatory Commission (Mexico, Thailand)
ERCOT	Electric Reliability Council of Texas
ESS	Emergency Sharing System
ETL	Energy Transition Law of 2015 (Mexico)
EU	European Union
EV	Electric Vehicle
EWE	Extreme Weather Events
FERC	Federal Energy Regulatory Commission
FTA	Free Trade Agreement between Mexico and the European Union
GAIRS	Generally Accepted International Rules and Standards
GAO	Government Accountability Office (United States)
GATT	General Agreement on Tariffs and Trade
GCC	Gulf Cooperation Council
GDP	Gross Domestic Product
GEI	Global Entrepreneurship Index
GHG	Greenhouse Gas
GSF	Ghana Stabilisation Fund
HL	Hydrocarbons Law
HVDC	High-Voltage Direct Current
IAEA	International Atomic Energy Agency
ICA	Integrated Capacity Analysis
ICJ	International Court of Justice
ICS	Investment Court System
ICT	Information and Communication Technology
IDL	International Disaster Law
IEA	International Energy Agency
ILA	International Law Association
ILC	International Law Commission
ILM	International Legal Materials
IMF	International Monetary Fund
IMO	International Maritime Organisation
IPP	Independent Power Producer
IRENA	International Renewable Energy Agency

ISDR	International Strategy for Disaster Reduction
ISO	Independent System Operator
KIPA	Kyoto Protocol Implementation Act
LEDS	Long-term low GHG Emission Development Strategies
LNG	Liquefied Natural Gas
LOSC	1982 United Nations Convention on the Law of the Sea
LTS	Long-Term Strategy
MARPOL 73/78	1973 International Convention for the Prevention of Pollution from Ships as amended by the 1978 Protocol
ME	Ministry of Energy (Mexico)
MEA	Metropolitan Electricity Authority (Bangkok, Thailand)
MENA	Middle East and North Africa
MS	Member State
NAFTA	North American Free Trade Agreement
NDB	New Development Bank
NDC	Nationally Determined Contribution
NDIA	Natural Damage Insurance
NDP	National Development Plan (Mexico)
NDRC	National Development and Reform Commission
NEA	National Energy Administration (China)
NEBEF	Block Exchange Notification of Demand Response
NECC	National Energy Control Centre (Mexico)
NECP	National Energy and Climate Plan
NEM	National Electricity Market (Australia)
NERC	North American Electric Reliability Corporation
NGM	National Gas Market (Australia)
NGO	Non-Governmental Organization
NHC	National Hydrocarbons Commission
NIS	Network and Information System
NRA	National Regulatory Authority
NREL	National Renewable Energy Laboratory
OECD	Organisation for Economic Cooperation and Development
OES	Operator of Essential Services
OPEC	Organization of Petroleum Exporting Countries
ORE	Offshore Renewable Energy
OSP	Operator Security Plan
OSPAR	Oil Spill Prevention, Administration and Response
OTEC	Ocean Thermal Energy Conversion
PEA	Provincial Electricity Authority (Thailand)
PEMEX	Petróleos Mexicanos
PHMSA	Hazardous Materials Safety Administration
PPs	Plans and Programmes
PPA	Power Purchase Agreement
PPP	Public-Private Partnership
PRMA	Petroleum Revenue Management Act (Ghana)
PUC	Public Utility Commission
PV	photovoltaic
P2P	Peer-to-Peer
RCNNDA	Royal Commission into National Natural Disaster Arrangements (Australia)

RECs	Renewable Energy Communities
REL	Renewable Energy Law (China)
RPS	Renewable Portfolio Standard
RRA	Renewables Readiness Assessment
RTO	Regional Transmission Operator
R4I	Resource-for-Infrastructure
SCADA	Supervisory Control and Data Acquisition
SDG	Sustainable Development Goal
SDR	Special Drawing Right
SEA	Strategic Environmental Assessment
SLO	Security Liaison Officer
SMEs	Small and Medium-Sized Enterprises
SMMEs	Small, Medium, and Micro Enterprises
SOE	State-Owned Enterprise
SPP	Small Power Producer
SWAC	Sea Water Air Conditioning
SWF	Sovereign Wealth Fund
TEN-E	Trans-European Energy Infrastructure
TFEU	Treaty on the Functioning of the European Union
TOVALOP	Tanker Owners Voluntary Agreement Concerning Liability for Oil Pollution
TPA	Third Party Access
TPP	Trans Pacific Partnership
TSO	Transmission System Operator
TSX	Toronto Stock Exchange
TWAIL	Third World Approaches to International Law
TYNDP	Ten-Year Network Development Plan
UAE	United Arab Emirates
UCPTE	Union for the Coordination of Production and Transmission of Electricity
USMCA	United States, Mexico and Canada Trade Agreement
UN	United Nations
UNCITRAL	United Nations Commission on International Trade Law
UNECE	United Nations Economic Commission for Europe
UNEP	United Nations Environment Programme
UNFCCC	United Nations Framework Convention on Climate Change
UNISDR	United Nations Office for Disaster Risk Reduction
UNTS	United Nations Treaty Series
USMCA	United States, Mexico, and Canada Trade Agreement
VAT	Value-Added Tax
VCLT	1969 Vienna Convention on the Law of Treaties
VRE	Variable Renewable Energy
VSPP	Very Small Power Producer
WHO	World Health Organization
WTI	West Texas Intermediate
WTO	World Trade Organization

List of Contributors

Chris Adomako-Kwakye is a Senior Lecturer in Law, Kwame Nkrumah University of Science and Technology, Ghana and a PhD Candidate at the DST/NRF SARCHI Research Chair: Mineral Law in Africa, Faculty of Law, University of Cape Town, South Africa.

Daniela Aguilar Abaunza, LLB, LLM, PhD, is a lecturer and researcher of Energy Law at University Externado of Colombia.

Nadia B. Ahmad, JD, LLM, is an Associate Professor of Law at Barry University School of Law, USA.

Catherine Banet, PhD, is an Associate Professor at the Scandinavian Institute for Maritime Law, Head of the Energy and Resources Law Department, University of Oslo, Norway.

Nigel Bankes is a Professor and Chair of Natural Resources Law, Faculty of Law, at the University of Calgary, Alberta, Canada, and an Adjunct Professor, at the K. G. Jebsen Centre for the Law of the Sea, UiT The Arctic University of Norway.

Barry Barton is a Professor of Law and the Director of the Centre for Environmental, Resources and Energy Law at the University of Waikato, Hamilton, New Zealand.

Anatole Boute is a Professor, Faculty of Law, at the Chinese University of Hong Kong, Hong Kong.

Hans Jacob Bull is Professor Emeritus, Scandinavian Institute for Maritime Law, Faculty of Law, University of Oslo, Norway.

Kangwa-Musole Chisanga is a lecturer of Commercial Law at the National Institute of Public Administration in Zambia. He is a research associate of the DST/NRF SARCHI Research Chair: Mineral Law in Africa, Faculty of Law, University of Cape Town.

Íñigo del Guayo is a Professor of Administrative Law, at the University of Almería, Spain.

Piti Eiamchamroonlarp is a Professor and Program Director of the Master of Laws (Business Law) International Program Faculty of Law, Chulalongkorn University Pathumwan, Bangkok, Thailand.

Louis de Fontenelle is Assistant Professor at Pau University, France.

Isaac Foote is a research assistant, University of Minnesota Law School, Minneapolis, USA.

Lee Godden is a Professor of Law and Director, Centre of Resources, Energy and Environmental Law, Melbourne Law School, The University of Melbourne, Australia.

José Juan González Márquez is a Professor of Law at the Metropolitan Autonomous University, Azcapotzalco, México and the Director of the Mexican Institute for Environmental Law Research, Mexico.

Alexandra B. Klass is a Distinguished McKnight University Professor at the University of Minnesota Law School, Minneapolis, USA.

Alastair R. Lucas is a Professor, Faculty of Law and Adjunct Professor, Faculty of Environmental Design, at the University of Calgary, Alberta, Canada.

Milton Fernando Montoya is a Research Director of the Mining and Energy Law Institute, at the Externado de Colombia University, Bogotá, Colombia.

Hanri Mostert is a Professor of Law, University of Cape Town, South Africa and DST/NRF SARChI Research Chair: Mineral Law in Africa.

Damilola S. Olawuyi is an Associate Professor of Law at HBKU Law School, at the Hamad Bin Khalifa University, Qatar and a Chancellor's Fellow and Director at the Institute for Oil, Gas, Energy, Environment and Sustainable Development, at the Afe Babalola University, Nigeria.

LeRoy Paddock is the Associate Dean of Environmental Law Studies at the George Washington University Law School, Washington DC, United States.

Catherine Redgwell is the Chichele Professor of Public International Law and a Fellow of All Souls College, at the University of Oxford, United Kingdom.

Martha M. Roggenkamp is a Professor of Law and the Director of the Groningen Centre of Energy Law, Faculty of Law, University of Groningen, the Netherlands.

Don C. Smith is an Associate Professor of the Practice of Law, at the Sturm College of Law, University of Denver, Colorado, United States.

Hugo Meyer van den Berg is an Adjunct Associate Professor of the Faculty of Law, University of Cape Town, affiliated with the DST/NRF SARCHI Research Chair: Mineral Law in Africa and a lecturer at the University of Namibia.

Hao Zhang, Faculty of Law, The Chinese University of Hong Kong.

Donald N. Zillman is Godfrey Professor of Law Emeritus at the University of Maine Law School, United States.

PART I
INTRODUCTION

1

Introduction

Catherine Banet, Hanri Mostert, LeRoy Paddock, Milton Fernando Montoya,
and Íñigo del Guayo

I. Introduction

A. Context

This book deals with the law and policy responses to disruptions to energy systems, infrastructures, and natural resources. Extreme weather events including floods, wildfires and hurricanes, and other natural disasters have become both more frequent and more severe. At the
same time the world is facing a once in a century threat to public health that has produced
serious disruptions. The ongoing COVID-19 pandemic is a reminder of the catastrophic effects
such crises and disasters may visit upon the world.

The growing world population and increasing demand for resources alongside rising living
standards have resulted in the unprecedented use of natural resources, increased energy demands, and construction of new infrastructure. In some respects, it has brought humankind
close to the edge of the Earth's 'safe-operating space'.[1] Reports from the Intergovernmental
Panel on Climate Change[2] and the European Environment Agency[3] illustrate that we are
nearing the 'planetary boundaries'[4] in many respects. It is widely known and acknowledged
by now that exceeding the nine 'planetary boundaries' will result in irreversible changes to the
environment, which in some worst-case scenarios could lead to a total collapse of human-sus-
taining systems. Four of the planetary boundaries have already been crossed:[5] climate change,
biosphere integrity, land-system change, and altered biogeochemical cycles.

By the scale of the impacts, frequency, and cumulative effects of such disruptive events,
collapsology[6] and end-of-growth theories may have one questioning whether a point of

---

[1] J. Rockström et al, 'Planetary Boundaries: Exploring the Safe Operating Space for Humanity' (2009) 14(2)
Ecology and Society 32 <http://www.ecologyandsociety.org/vol14/iss2/art32/> accessed 10 September 2021.
[2] 'Climate Change 2021: The Physical Science Basis', Contribution of Working Group I to the Sixth Assessment
Report of the Intergovernmental Panel on Climate Change.
[3] European Environment Agency (EEA)/Federal Office for the Environment (FOEN), 'Is Europe living within
the limits of our planet? An assessment of Europe's environmental footprints in relation to planetary boundaries',
EEA Report No 01/2020.
[4] E.g. climate change, chemical pollution, land-system change, and freshwater use. See T. Häyhä et al, 'From
Planetary Boundaries to National Fair Shares of the Global Safe Operating Space - How Can the Scales be Bridged?'
(2016) 40 Global Environmental Change 62, who distinguish between global and local effects on the planetary
boundaries; D. French and L. J. Kotzé, *Research Handbook on Law, Governance and Planetary Boundaries* (Edward
Elgar 2021), Chapter 2.
[5] W. Steffen et al, 'Planetary Boundaries: Guiding Human Development on a Changing Planet' (2015) (347) 6223
Science <http://science.sciencemag.org/content/early/2015/01/14/science.1259855/tab-pdf> accessed 10 September 2021.
[6] Collapsology is understood as the study of the heralded imminent collapse of our civilization. See P. Servigne
and R. Stevens, *Comment tout peut s'effondrer, Petit manuel de collapsologie* ('How everything can collapse: A

Catherine Banet, Hanri Mostert, LeRoy Paddock, Milton Fernando Montoya, and Íñigo del Guayo, *Introduction* In: *Resilience in Energy,
Infrastructure, and Natural Resources Law*. Edited by: Catherine Banet, Hanri Mostert, LeRoy Paddock, Milton Fernando Montoya, and
Íñigo del Guayo, Oxford University Press. © Catherine Banet, Hanri Mostert, LeRoy Paddock, Milton Fernando Montoya, and Íñigo del
Guayo 2022. DOI: 10.1093/oso/9780192864574.003.0001

no return has already been reached. One may ask whether the causes of disruption can yet be mitigated, alongside necessary adaptation planning. One can also question whether the scale of those disruptive events will delay the energy transition, accelerate it, or broaden its scope towards an ecological transition encompassing natural resources at large. Finally, it can be asked what consequences these events will have on the goals promoted by energy and natural resources law as legal disciplines and legal systems, traditionally focusing on security of supply, sustainability, and affordability.

Given the above, this book focuses on how law and regulation in different legal orders can be reformed or reimagined to make energy and natural resources systems more re-silient in the face of disruptive natural crises or disasters. Addressing these disruptions is critical for a variety of reasons. One reason that stands out is the potential adverse impacts such disruptions may have on states' ability to meet many of the United Nation's Sustainable Development Goals (SDGs).

Disruption of energy systems and infrastructures, and depletion of natural resources, are not new phenomena. However, the nature, intensity, and the frequency of disruptions that have occurred over the last few years is unprecedented, whether they are measured in the number of billion-dollar disasters, the number of people impacted, the types of disruptions that have occurred, or by other standards. The increased frequency and intensity of such disruptions call for a close examination of systems that can mitigate the impacts of disasters and foster resilience to them. Such scrutiny will require a more in-depth and broader reflec-tion than that offered by existing literature on how law can promote resilience. The book also offers a unique approach by looking at the same time at the sectors of energy, infra-structure, and natural resources, three areas that are crucial to meeting the needs of current and future societies and to protecting the natural environment. While resilience may take different forms in each area, we believe it is important to consider how resilience can be en-hanced by considering these areas together.

B. Aim

Considering the disruptive events that the world has faced in the past decade, and that are expected to increase in intensity in the years to come, this book offers a structured and sys-tematic analysis of the challenges such disruptions pose to legal and regulatory systems. Based on this analysis, the book maps and assesses legal responses to disruptive nature-based events, and examines possible legal pathways for more sustainable outcomes, based on its engagement with the concept of 'resilience'.

This book contains a new and differentiated contribution to the existing literature on a highly debated topic. It offers an analytical contribution to the academic discussion on the future of energy and natural resources law in times of more frequent and deeper disrup-tion. In this way it contributes by helping to avoid the worst consequences of disaster and to find ways to prevent disasters where possible. Combining narratives that span many of the world's continents, and that encompass the various facets of energy, infrastructures, and natural resources management, the book identifies lessons from those disruptive events to

brief manual of collapsology') (Le Seuil 2015); C. et R. Larrère, *Le Pire n'est pas certain—Essai sur l'aveuglement catastrophiste* (Premier Parallèle 2020).

inspire the design and building of new, more responsive models of energy, infrastructure, and natural resources law. 'Resilience' is, therefore, seen as a common driver for the interpretation and development of these law and policy frameworks.

A multifaceted approach such as the one encompassed by the collection of chapters in this book is needed to support knowledge-based decisions, as policymakers are required to in most jurisdictions. First, the book provides an in-depth conceptual legal analysis of the concept of resilience and its translation into legal mechanisms. Then, it offers a systematic review of the legal responses provided at international, national, and entity level, structured around the five central parts of the book. Finally, through this analytical frame, the book identifies legal pathways for sustainable development in times of disruption.

C.   Scope

The number of severe, sometimes catastrophic disruptive events has been rapidly increasing. These disruptive events have dramatic consequences on nature and human life, calling for urgent action to mitigate their causes and adapt to their impacts. Some of the most recent incidents include wildfires in Australia and the USA, biodiversity loss (e.g. through the Amazon fires), drought periods (Southern Africa, Middle-East, some parts of the United States), hurricanes (with a record number of hurricanes in the United States including the unprecedented Hurricane Ida in late August 2021), earthquakes (Haiti 2010 and 2021, Sichuan/Wenchuan 2008), floods and landslides (Vargas, Venezuela 1999, Mocoa, Colombia, 2017 and North India, 2013), tsunamis (2004 Indian Ocean earthquake and tsunami), pandemic diseases (COVID-19, H1N1 swine flu, MERS, SARS), and industrial accidents (Deepwater Horizon, Fukushima). Then there are the follow-up or spin-off crises of a more financial and/or budgetary nature, like the global financial crisis of 2008, the 'Great Lockdown Downturn' of 2020, and the drop and then extreme rise in energy prices throughout 2020 and 2021.

Such events, sometimes happening concurrently, have resulted in unprecedented changes in the ecosystems, living conditions, and the global economy. Some of these are naturally occurring events, some directly caused by human activity, and others appear to be caused by a mix of natural events and aggravating human activities.

It is common to distinguish between three categories of threats as sources of disruption: natural, technological, and human-caused threats.[7] Different social and ecological systems will respond differently to these categories of threats, according to their degree of vulnerability.[8] The ability of a system to resist and overcome the disruption will determine its resilience. How to build resilience through changes in law is the subject matter of this book. We bring together experiences and skills from various parts of the world to share narratives that may assist in bridging gaps in policy and law that may stand between a system and its ability to 'bounce back better' from the challenge of multiple, relentless crises.

---

[7] Sherry and L. Jennifer et al, 'Power Sector Resilience Planning Guidebook', Resilient Energy Platform, United States Agency for International Development (USAID)- National Renewable Energy Laboratory (NREL) (2019).
[8] Vulnerabilities are weaknesses within infrastructure, processes, and systems or the degree of susceptibility to various threats. Ibid.

The book addresses energy law, infrastructure law, and natural resources law together. It addresses extreme events arising primarily from natural causes, even though such natural crises and disasters may sometimes have an anthropogenic origin, where human intervention cannot be overlooked. The crises and disasters we focus on here include examples of extreme weather events (EWE) like heat waves, wildfires, drought, hurricanes, and typhoons, but also pandemic illnesses, biodiversity losses, deforestation, and habitat loss, among others.

The book will not address all human causes of disruption directly. As such, events flowing from political instability and wars (Arab Spring, South Sudan), terrorism, digital attacks against networks and companies (Ukraine, Norsk Hydro in Norway), and piracy (against gas/oil pipelines and ships) are excluded, as the nature of these causes differs significantly. However, the book considers in some chapters how the definition of 'resilience' also applies to those human causes of disruption and threats.[9] Some chapters also refer to other human factors when discussing legal responses to disruption.[10]

The energy sector, as a motor of the economy, but also one of the essential elements for welfare and the satisfaction of basic human needs, is affected—sometimes in dramatic ways—by many of these threats. This reality calls for assessing and strengthening its resilience. In a highly regulated sector such as energy, the legal framework can provide essential incentives for ensuring resilience, relying on the involvement of all actors, state entities, private and public companies, and consumers. Similarly, the extractives sector is often implicated as a breeding ground for the kinds of crises and disasters that need resilient responses. The basic principles of access, use and protection of natural resources such as land, minerals, forests, and water, also need to be revisited. They play a central role in balancing ecosystems and ensuring sustainable development for all.

II. Defining Resilience

The concept of 'resilience' has been gaining increased recognition in a broad range of disciplines since the 2000s. However, in the legal and regulatory context, a conceptualization of 'resilience' is still lacking. Very few laws refer to 'resilience' as an objective of legislative intervention; by contrast, many laws will refer to concepts like 'reliability', 'adequacy of supply', or 'security of supply'. Given the increased frequency of disruptive events, and that the concept of resilience is gaining in relevance, it is necessary to ascertain its meaning in legal terms and how it can be used in relation to energy, infrastructure, and natural resources law. This is the core objective and expected outcome of this book.

The noun 'resilience' comes from the latin verb *resilire*, meaning to 'recoil' or 'to rebound', and was used in the 1600s as meaning 'springing back'. In the 1800s–1900s, it took on a more technical understanding and is associated with the qualities of materials and equipment to resist shocks.[11] In social science, where 'resilience' is a well-established concept, it has been defined as 'a system's capacity to absorb disturbance and still remain within the same state

---

[9] Particularly in Chapter 2.
[10] E.g. cybersecurity in Chapter 5.
[11] D. E. Alexander, 'Resilience and Disaster Risk Reduction: an Etymological Journey' (2013) 13 Nat. Hazards Earth Syst. Sci. 2707–2716.

or domain'. Authors like C.S. Holling have further theorized the concept in the context of ecological sciences.[12] They establish that resilience is the ability of a natural system to resist and undergo changes without losing its core structure and function. In the energy context, 'resilience' has notably been defined as 'the ability to withstand and reduce the magnitude and/or duration of disruptive events, which includes the capability to anticipate, absorb, adapt to, and/or rapidly recover from such an event'.[13] Other sub-distinctions are made, such as by Holling, between *engineering resilience*—the time required to return to the pre-disturbance state, and *social-ecological resilience*—as the capacity of an ecosystem to tolerate resilience.[14]

Resilience therefore connotes more than merely resistance to a shock. It also encompasses the ability of a system to deal with change and continue to *develop*. The process of resilience is not linear, but more like a spiral, including a transformative phase. It can be preventive (pre-disaster), but could also follow a disaster, rebounding from it to use the window of opportunity created to introduce resilience as the ability to embrace change, as captured by the term 'Build Back Better' (BBB).[15] As summarized by the Stockholm Resilience Centre: 'Resilience is the capacity of a system, be it an individual, a forest, a city or an economy, to deal with change and continue to develop. It is about how humans and nature can use shocks and disturbances like a financial crisis or climate change to spur renewal and innovative thinking'.[16] This development dimension of resilience is not a synonym of growth, although it could be associated with a growing process for the community or territory encompassed.[17] To align with the sustainability goals, this development dimension of resilience should be associated with the management of ecosystems. Those are some of the interlinkages captured by the notion of social-ecological resilience.[18]

From this general working definition, it is already apparent that 'resilience' is a multi-faceted topic. Engaging with it will require a wide range of assets, resources, actors, and authorities to be involved. In the legal and regulatory context, a multisectoral approach is needed. Cross-sectoral risks and interdependencies must be heeded. Such an engagement will require thinking in terms of local, regional, and global ecosystem approaches. It will also require, as a necessary starting point, a common understanding and taxonomy of the defined types of hazards, threats, and risks to be addressed and the likelihood of their occurrence. In this exercise, a comparison with related concepts, such as disaster risk reduction (DRR) is useful. Further, engagement with the resilience imperative in the legal and

---

[12] C. S. Holling, 'Resilience and Stability of Ecological Systems' (1973) 4 Annual Review of Ecology and Systematics 1–23; C. Folke, S. R. Carpenter, B. Walker et al, 'Resilience Thinking: Integrating Resilience, Adaptability and Transformability' (2010) 15(4) Ecology and Society.

[13] *Grid Reliability & Resilience Pricing Grid Resilience in Regional Transmission Organizations & In-dependent System Operators*, 162 F.E.R.C. para 61,012, 3.

[14] C.S. Holling (n 12).

[15] The Build Back Better (BBB) term has been recognized by the United Nations Sendai Framework for Disaster Risk Reduction (2015–2030) as a key global priority for action for both pre- and post-disaster planning and implementation. See Priority 4: 'Enhancing disaster preparedness for effective response and to "Build Back Better" in recovery, rehabilitation and reconstruction'.

[16] Stockholm Resilience Centre, 'What is resilience', available at <https://www.stockholmresilience.org/research/research-news/2015-02-19-what-is-resilience.html> accessed 10 September 2021.

[17] The suitability of concepts like 'sustainable development' or 'green growth' is often criticized in the literature on resilience.

[18] W. N. Adger, Social and Ecological Resilience: Are They Related? (2000) 24(3) Progress in Human Geography 347–364.

regulatory context requires consideration of a wide range of legal mechanisms and careful assessment of rights and obligations associated with them.

III. Methodology

In response to discourses of collapsology and end-of-growth theories, this book offers an analytical approach to developing legal responses that can help assure that needs of present and future generations can be met through energy systems, infrastructure development, and natural resources management in times of more frequent and intense disruption. 'Resilience' is therefore seen as a common framework for the interpretation and development of energy, infrastructure, and natural resources law.

Within this conceptual framework, the book aims to: first, describe and analyse the legal responses that have developed in the context of recent nature-based disruptive events; and second, advance recommendations for building a legal framework to foster resilience and face future disruptive events.

The methodological approach of the book is based on both thematic chapters and country/regional chapters, integrated into thematic parts as *case studies*. The focus is on the analysis of current *legal responses*, best practices, and development of recommendations. This includes a common reading grid for assessing the content and place given to 'resilience' in the different legal frameworks and its relationship to other concepts (reliability, adequacy, or security of supply). Specific attention is paid to the interplay between 'resilience' and those neighbouring concepts, and conclusions drawn from the analysis in the different chapters.

Finally, the book aims to identify and examine *legal pathways*, taking consideration of the difference in national circumstances and jurisdictions. It identifies the structural *principles* of energy, infrastructure, and natural resources law in the forthcoming new era. It also points out potential pitfalls relating to policy approaches or regulatory choices.

IV. Structure

The book contains 22 chapters and is structured thematically in five parts. The present introduction (Chapter 1) has shortly introduced key concepts for the rest of the book as well as the methodology followed. Joint conclusions from the 20 individual chapters are drawn at the end (Chapter 22).

Part I of the book defines and categorizes disruption and resilience in relation to the energy, infrastructure, and natural resources sectors. It provides an in-depth analytical framework for the rest of book. In Chapter 2, Bankes, Godden, and del Guayo define the origins of the concept of resilience and reviews its application to the field of energy law, infrastructure, and natural resources law. Chapter 3, written by Redgwell, assesses the resilience-building capacity of international law and institutions. In Chapter 4, Banet investigates to which extent energy, climate, natural resources, and spatial planning law has been reflecting the objective of resilience, and puts forward recommendations as to how this objective should be strengthened in the future. Looking at planning as legal mechanism is particularly relevant for ensuring coherence between sectors in a long-term perspective, supported by an increasing duty to integrate planning processes. Chapters 5 and 6 both investigate the regulation of energy networks to face disruption, from the perspective of EU law and US law in turn. While Roggenkamp examines, in Chapter 5, the adequacy of the EU energy infrastructure regime in safeguarding security of energy supply, Klass and Foote discuss in Chapter 6 the extent to which resilience considerations are integrated into energy infrastructure permitting procedures.

Part II analyses the role of the State in the face of disruptive events from the perspective of interventionism by public authorities and the search for the well-being of the community. A wide spectrum of legislative, regulatory, market, and policy responses have been adopted by States and regulatory entities to deal with disruption from natural events. In Chapter 7, Zhang examines the central government response to the impacts of COVID-19 on China's energy sector and how resilience considerations have been integrated into the multi-level regulatory arrangements applicable to the industry. Chapter 8, written by Godden, looks at the impact of both massive forest fires and COVID-19 on the future of both the energy sector and natural resources in Australia. It reviews and analyses the Governments' use of declaratory and emergency powers to control responses. In Chapter 9, Olawuyi examines legal and governance aspects of designing and implementing disaster risk reduction and resilience frameworks to better anticipate, minimize, and address the disruptive impacts of oil and gas volatility in Middle East and North Africa (MENA) markets. Chapter 10 studies the Peruvian and Colombian public policy decisions and effective regulation issued to mitigate, but also boost the mining and electricity industry recovery after the COVID-19 crisis. In this chapter, Montoya and Aguilar Abaunza examine the important link between these two industries in terms of electricity sustainability and energy transition, and what challenges the Peruvian and Colombian energy industries face to support the recovery from a deep COVID-19 crisis. In Chapter 11, Gonzàlez Márquez looks at the ongoing reforms of the energy sector in Mexico, and questions whether the reform process, in the aftermath of the COVID-19 pandemic and drop in oil prices, provides an opportunity to promote a new form of nationalism. Chapter 12, written by Smith and Zillman, examines the 'energy resilience' concept in the US and the impact of the 2020 Presidential and Congressional Elections on forthcoming legal and regulatory initiatives.

Part III examines specific instances of disruption at project level and the legal responses developed by producers, operators, and assets owners to both manage disruptive effects and facilitate more resilient outcomes in the future. Different examples of projects are taken in different jurisdictions. In Chapter 13, Boute looks at the critical issue of how force majeure clauses can impact contracts at a time when circumstances have dramatically increased the assertion that a force majeure incident has occurred. Chapter 14, written by Lucas, studies extreme natural events impacts on the oil and gas sector and its regulation in Canada and North America. Chapter 15 by Paddock discusses the impact of disasters on the movement to low carbon energy in the United States and whether that switch will help create a more or less resilient electric grid where decentralized energy generators and suppliers play a central role.

In Part IV, the focus is on strategic economic, financing, and insurance responses to natural disruptive events. It analyses the influence of such responses on political, economic, and social resilience relating to energy, infrastructures, and natural resources. On the supposition that finance is a critical, global enabler of transformative improvements to achieve systemic resilience, our interest here is to interrogate the manner in which financing and insurance regimes have evolved under the pressure of natural disasters. The question is raised of the nature of choices around the types of projects regarded as deserving support and the governance of the associated support/compensation mechanisms. Notably, those holding the purse strings—the international financing institutions and development banks, for instance—have a decisive influence on the choices being made in response to natural disasters, catastrophes, and pandemics. They also have the leverage to hold weak or failing states—many of whom are resource dependent—to particularly ideologized approaches to responding to natural disasters, catastrophes, and pandemics. The sometimes politicized nature of economic responses to disasters, catastrophes, and pandemics are not limited to the international or even state level. Even in the private sector, financial power has the potential to influence the development of industries and societies. This is illustrated, for instance, in the way insurers choose to frame policy options.

In Chapter 16, Ahmad takes green energy finance as an illustration and looks at the growing phenomenon of transnational law regimes as alternatives or supplementary to international treaties. The author links it to system dynamics theory and offers a deeper analysis of both international organizations like the International Renewable Energy Agency (IRENA) and international agreements like the Energy Charter Treaty (ECT). Chapter 17 analyses the models for financial assistance provided by international institutions to several African countries (South Africa, Namibia, Zambia, and Ghana) to respond to recent crises and disasters. Mostert, Adomako-Kwakye, Chisanga, and van den Berg offer a comparative analysis of the effects this assistance may have on the regulatory and policy choices affecting the resource and energy sectors of these countries. In Chapter 18, Bull looks at natural damage insurance schemes aimed at covering loss and damage suffered by natural perils. The analysis takes the Norwegian scheme as a study case, and puts in perspective its main features and values with some other national schemes. Chapter 19, written by Eiamchamroonlarp, studies the manner in which law can support public-private partnership (PPP) to provide financial support to the reconstruction of the energy sector. It uses the practical example of the reliance on PPP for financing environmentally friendly transportation (EV buses) in Thailand.

Part V of the book examines the role of consumers in helping to avoid disruptions and to soften their consequences when they happen. In doing so, it also explores the 'equity' dimension in managing disruption at consumption level. The world should be moving fast towards a decarbonized system where renewable energies have the main role and where consumers gain a new leadership by means of self-consumption, individually or within communities. In that desirable future, consumers may help to avoid disruptions. The traditional electricity industry, based on few and big productions units, connected with consumers by means of electricity lines, was weak in terms of security since a problem in one of those units or in any of the transport lines would affect a large number of consumers. The more decentralized production is, the stronger becomes the system as a whole. The set of technologies available within the new demand response paradigm (such as storage and the activity of demand aggregation), where consumers have the main say on when and how much energy they consume, will introduce greater flexibility, resilience, and cooperation among agents, thus protecting the system against disruptions. The path towards efficiency in energy consumption, where consumers should also have a leading role, is also the path to the increase of resilience and fight against disruptions, since energy efficiency leads to the reduction of energy consumed and, therefore, to the reduction of perverse consequences of disruptions. In Chapter 20, Barton examines ways to reduce exposure to disruption bottom-up, by the further development of local energy solutions and natural resources supply chains based on circular economy models. Chapter 21, written by de Fontenelle, explores how far the legal norms supporting the energy system have come in enabling energy consumers to contribute to resilience.

Together, these 20 chapters interrogate the appropriateness of resilience as a central consideration of energy, infrastructure, and natural resources law, and they do so in an in-depth and systematic academic manner. They propose a forward-looking analysis of how this concept of resilience could be understood better, so that our world may be strengthened and better prepared for disruptions and disasters that may yet come our way.

PART II
DEFINING RESILIENCE IN ENERGY, INFRASTRUCTURE, AND NATURAL RESOURCES LAW

2

The Role of Law in Fostering or Inhibiting Resilient Energy Systems

Nigel Bankes, Lee Godden, and Íñigo del Guayo

I. Introduction

This chapter reflects on the relevance of resilience and systems theory to the burgeoning challenges that 'disruptors' pose to energy and related systems. Disruption to energy systems can range from COVID-19 pandemic impacts, to hazards and disasters; including those derived from climate change.[1] An early definition identified resilience as, 'the capacity of a system to absorb disturbance and reorganize while undergoing change so as to still retain essentially the same function, structure, identity, and feedbacks.'[2] Ideas of resilience have evolved from its use in engineering, and later in ecology and natural resources management, and now its use by researchers to describe social-ecological systems concepts,[3] including the concept of resilient human and non-human communities. There is growing attention to resilience principles in law, and components of resilience-thinking, such as adaptation to disruption, adaptive governance, and feedback loops are now common in legal analyses.[4] The reach of resilience-thinking to inform legal regulation in energy law and comparable settings is potentially wide-ranging, as resilience could form the basis for developing energy law principles and policy models, and energy law instruments. In addition, resilience and systems thinking has application in examining disruptions in related fields such as infrastructure, including energy infrastructure, and it is well established as a mode of analysis in natural resources management.

This chapter has four further sections. First, it considers the development of resilience theory and its interlinkages with social-ecological systems theory. This analysis identifies key theoretical components such as ecosystems, stability domains, tipping points, and system self-organization. Of particular importance in applying resilience-thinking to energy systems and related fields, is the concept of the 'coupling' between sub-systems or nested systems and the role of resilience at various scales within a system. The coupling of

---

[1] See, for example, US Government Accountability Office (GAO), Electricity Grid Resilience: Climate Change Is Expected to Have Far-reaching Effects and DOE and FERC Should Take Actions (2021) < https://www.gao.gov/assets/gao-21-346.pdf> accessed 9 December 2021.

[2] C. S. Holling, 'Resilience and Stability of Ecological Systems' (1973) 4 Ann Rev Ecology & Systematics 1, 17–19. The GAO Report, (n 1) adopted a definition of Resilience from Presidential Policy, Directive 21, dealing with critical infrastructure. The definition acknowledges human agency insofar as it refers to 'the ability to prepare for and adapt to changing conditions and withstand and recover rapidly from disruptions, including naturally occurring threats or incidents'.

[3] Tracy-Lynn Humby, 'Law and Resilience: Mapping the Literature' (2014) 4 Seattle Journal of Environmental Law 85, 88.

[4] Ibid, 87–88.

Nigel Bankes, Lee Godden, and Íñigo del Guayo, *The Role of Law in Fostering or Inhibiting Resilient Energy Systems* In: *Resilience in Energy, Infrastructure, and Natural Resources Law*. Edited by: Catherine Banet, Hanri Mostert, LeRoy Paddock, Milton Fernando Montoya, and Íñigo del Guayo, Oxford University Press. © Nigel Bankes, Lee Godden, and Íñigo del Guayo 2022. DOI: 10.1093/oso/9780192864574.003.0002

sub-systems can occur within an energy system or for example it could occur within energy and infrastructure sub-systems. Having established the broad features of resilience theory, the chapter considers how resilience concepts can be applied in law (Section II).

In the next section, the chapter considers how resilience and social-ecological systems theory may be applied in the context of energy systems. This section uses the lens of the 'stability domain' concept in resilience and systems theory to examine what systemic factors may trigger a change from one stability domain to another, together with analysing the role of law as a catalyst (Section III).

Next, the chapter applies resilience and social-ecological systems theory as a platform to consider the real world implications of resilience thinking in energy systems. The chapter discusses situations where resilience in energy systems can be demonstrated or found to be lacking, by reference to specific energy law contexts, such as the adoption of flexibility principles in the European Union (EU) energy law system, and resilience thinking in planning energy infrastructure (Section IV, see also Chapter 4 in this book).

Finally, the chapter reflects on the contribution that resilience may make during a period of disruption and change in energy systems and in light of their increasing complexity. This analysis offers some potential pathways in which resilience may be further integrated into energy systems and energy law (Section V).

II. Resilience: Theory and Application

A. Defining resilience

At its core, resilience thinking encapsulates C. S. Holling's propositions from his study of ecosystems. The central model that Holling proposed was that ecosystems had 'multi-stable' states (generally referred to in this chapter as stability domains) rather than an ecosystem's processes working towards a single stable state or equilibrium point, which was the conventional view in ecology. The corollary of the fixed equilibrium model was that ecosystems had a fixed carrying capacity and had to be managed to reduce variability. By contrast, Holling's research suggested that ecosystems could move between various stability domains. As such, ecosystems were complex and adaptive and characterized by unpredictability.[5] Given this central adaptive function of ecosystems, Holling coined the term 'resilience' to refer to the level of disturbance a system could absorb before the processes controlling the ecosystem were 'flipped' to a new set of characteristics, networks, and relationships. When an ecosystem moved to this new mode it was regarded as being in another 'stability region' or stability domain.

A resilient ecosystem however is distinguished by its capacity to absorb disturbance and reorganize while undergoing change so as to still retain essentially the same function, structure, identity, and feedbacks.[6] Holling contrasted the static notion of 'engineering resilience' with the more dynamic, stochastic, and emergent properties that he attributed to

---

[5] Carl Folke, 'Resilience: The Emergence of a Perspective for Social-Ecological Systems Analysis' (2006) 16 Global Environmental Change 253, 254.

[6] Holling (n 2) 17–19. This capacity has been described as the homeostasis of systems: F. González Navarro, *Derecho Administrativo Español*, vol I (2nd edn, EUNSA 1993) 517 .

ecosystems. These features could be ascertained by focusing on the speed and capacity of an ecosystem to return to a steady state or equilibrium (e.g. a climax ecosystem) after disturbance. Importantly, resilience in Holling's terms described the degree of disturbance a system could experience before the system was triggered to dynamically move to a new set of variables and relationships and occupied another 'stability region'.[7] Resilience across a system, 'can be measured in terms of distance from the thresholds of key variables'.[8] If a system is near the threshold of a variable, such as temperature, then it is more likely to be triggered into a new stability domain (i.e. with new structure, function, and feedback characteristics of that system).[9] Warming temperatures that shift arctic ephemeral tundra to permanent grasslands are an example. Researchers have applied these ideas of a shift from one stability domain to another, to the concept of planetary boundaries in environmental and natural resources law. Holling's ecosystem research however suggested that the point at which such change occurs might be random and unpredictable leading to a complex coupling of resilience with non-equilibrium adaptation,[10] and stochastic processes,[11] as central to an evolving social-ecological systems theory.

Resilience is now embedded in systems theory,[12] and researchers have incorporated many of Holling's concepts into social-ecological constructs. Other studies examined how 'complex adaptive systems are constituted of complex structures and patterns of interaction that arise from simple, yet powerful rules guiding change'.[13] 'Panarchy', developed by Gunderson and Holling in 2002, builds on the adaptive cycle model by proposing such cycles as nested at multiple scales in systems.[14] Moreover, as Cosens notes, '[w]hen applied to ecological systems without a human component, resilience theory focuses on both the capacity of the system to return to its prior level of self-organization following a disturbance, and the degree to which that capacity is influenced by or sensitive to changes at smaller and larger scales'.[15] These insights have fostered a range of resource and environmental governance approaches that seek to foster resilience and adaptive management through mechanisms such as feedback loops. Adaptive management concepts have evolved into a more comprehensive adaptive governance model which brings together, 'the reflexive, iterative, scientifically-based learning characteristic of adaptive management',[16] with collaborative governance models that decentre the state and include a wider range of actors across spatial and temporal spheres and institutions and organizations.[17]

---

[7] As cited in Humby, Law and Resilience (n 3) 90.

[8] Humby, Law and Resilience (n 3) 91.

[9] Barbara Cosens, 'Resilience and Law as a Theoretical Backdrop for Natural Resource Management: Flood Management in the Columbia River Basin' (2012) 42 Envtl L 241, 246.

[10] Non-equilibrium adaptation is where a natural system such as a forest does not necessarily return to a steady state after disturbance, e.g. with the same species and communities. These ideas are highly influential in resource management and have been explored in law, A. D. (Dan) Tarlock, 'The Non-Equilibrium Paradigm in Ecology and the Partial Unravelling of Environmental Law' (1994) 27 Loyola of Los Angeles Law Review 1121.

[11] Stochastic refers to non-linear probabilities.

[12] Brian Walker and David Salt, Resilience Thinking: Sustaining Ecosystems and People in a Changing World (Island Press 2006).

[13] Humby, Law and Resilience (n 3) 92.

[14] Lance H. Gunderson and C. S. Holling (eds), Panarchy: Understanding Transformations in Human and Natural Systems (Island Press 2002).

[15] Cosens, Resilience and Law (n 9) 245.

[16] Humby, Law and Resilience (n 3) 98.

[17] Lee Godden, Jacqueline Peel, and Jan McDonald Environmental Law (2nd edn, OUP 2018) 130–135.

B. Social-ecological systems and resilience

Systems theory has a long tradition in the physical sciences, but an important step in developing resilience within social-ecological thinking was the advent of complex (computer) modelling of human and natural systems that gave rise to concepts of bonded social and ecological systems. Theorists began to adopt a social-ecological model to analyse resilience in resource management systems from the 1990s. From that point, research around interlinked human and natural systems has developed as a distinct field that strongly engages interdisciplinary collaboration.[18] Social-ecological systems theory was given general application in the social sciences by theorists, such as Luhmann.[19] The conjoining of the two systems was based on concepts of synergy and a 'fundamental interdependency' between social and environmental sub-systems, 'that determines the condition, function, and response of either subsystem (and thereby the whole system) to a disturbance, or hazard'[20]—i.e. the resilience of the social-ecological system. Ecological systems comprise 'natural' biological elements and processes while social systems are comprised of rules and institutions that mediate human use of resources (including via technologies) as well as the knowledge and value frameworks that construe such natural systems.[21] Luhmann's theory suggests such sub-systems are 'structurally coupled'. Within some forms of social-ecological thinking, human action and behaviour, together with social institutions are regarded as merged with nature, which obviates the distinction between social and natural systems. Other researchers who adopt social-ecological and resilience thinking do maintain a distinction between human and natural systems while seeing them as strongly interlinked.

Notably, social-ecological systems theory acknowledges that social-ecological interaction can augment or diminish ecosystem resilience,[22] thereby linking resilience with sustainability concepts, particularly as expressed in the Sustainable Development Goals (SDGs).[23] Resilience as sustainability can be understood as identifying how and where the tipping thresholds for a given system exist so that the system can be managed to remain sustainably within those bounds. Resilience theory also posits that social-ecological systems strive to reduce natural disruptions and to improve the provision of ecosystem services and the welfare of humans. More recent work has examined the capacity of systems to reorganize while experiencing alteration which allows opportunities for recombined emergent structures and processes that can allow for a renewal of that system. Alternatively, the reorganization may be the pathway for a new system or subsystem to come into existence.

In sum, the resilience of a social-ecological system can be gauged along three linked criteria: the extent to which the system absorbs disturbance but remains within the same stability regime; the degree and quality of the system's self-organization; and the extent of the system's capacity for learning and adaptation.[24]

---

[18] Johan Colding and Stepan Barthel, 'Exploring the social-ecological systems discourse 20 years later' (2019) 24(1) Ecology and Society 1 https://doi.org/10.5751/ES-10598-240102 accessed 9 December 2021
[19] The seminal work here is Nikolas Luhmann, the German sociologist. See e.g. Nikolas Luhmann and Peter Gilgen (tr) *Introduction to Systems Theory* (Polity Press 2012).
[20] Humby, Law and Resilience (n 3) 91.
[21] Humby, Law and Resilience (n 3) 91.
[22] Cosens, Resilience and Law (n 9) 245.
[23] Adopted in 2015, SDGs are part of the of the United Nations' 2030 Agenda for Sustainable Development, see<https://sdgs.un.org/goals> accessed 9 December 2021.
[24] Humby, Law and Resilience (n 3) 94.

C. Resilience and law

From its origins within ecology and social-ecological theory, resilience has evolved into a general 'recovery' or 'survival' discourse, with the term now often denoting the ability of a system to respond to a shock, and maintain stability and durability.[25] Some commentaries therefore suggest that resilience has become a 'fuzzy concept' of variable meaning.[26] Nonetheless, many social science and humanities disciplines, including law, have used resilience as an explanatory model to describe legal systems, particularly institutional responses to impacts and disruptions, and as a proffered solution to failing management and governance approaches that highlight the deficiencies of the relevant law. Resilience, along with adaptive management, offer an alternative framing for thinking about how law can contribute to sustainability in complex systems.

In legal analysis, resilience concepts are regularly employed in studies examining the governance of natural resources,[27] water, the environment, and ecosystems, especially following major perturbation or catastrophe.[28] Cosens, arguing for improved governance to respond to the risk of flooding in the Columbia River Basin, identifies that, '[s]ustainability of social-ecological systems will require careful attention to ecological resilience and the management of ecological systems to enhance that resilience.'[29] In climate change law, resilience is a widely-used concept, although often isolated from its social-ecological underpinnings. There is now a well-established body of scholarship on systems theory and law (e.g. regime interaction), and social-ecological analyses in law are more prevalent. Barnes, for example, has applied resilience theory to property rights, 'mapping out the relationship between social-ecological resilience and the operation of property rights over natural resources.'[30] He examines the degree to which property rights can accommodate or impede social-ecological resilience and suggests that the rich diversity of property rights makes property a highly flexible institution that can readily facilitate social-ecological resilience, particularly at local scales.[31] That said, his review also concedes that private property interests are not always aligned with resilience strategies. By contrast, community-based holdings in natural resources (common property) form a resilient, or at least persistent, form of social organization.[32] The significance of Barnes' work is that he considers both the forms of social organization and law that need to be adaptive and resilient, as well as the resilience qualities in the natural system.

Despite such promising research, there remains a gap in translating social-ecological and law research into concrete legal instruments and in developing governance modes and

---

[25] Gillian Bristow and Adrian Healy, *Handbook on Regional Economic Resilience* (Edward Elgar 2020) Introduction, ch 1.

[26] Ibid.

[27] One of the most comprehensive is Richard Barnes, 'The Capacity of Property Rights to Accommodate Social-Ecological Resilience' (2013) 18(1) Ecology and Society 6.

[28] Humby provides a detailed analysis of the law literature related to resilience. She identifies the main categories of empirical and non-empirical research that employ resilience/socio-ecological thinking in law. This fine study however predates the substantial increase in systems theory work in international law and in the climate change and environment/ natural resources law and regulation literature that has burgeoned since 2014. Humby, Law and Resilience (n 3) 100–124.

[29] Cosens, *Resilience and Law* (n 9) 262.

[30] Barnes, (n 27) 6.

[31] Barnes, ibid, 6.

[32] Barnes, ibid, 12.

policy options beyond an adaptive cycle paradigm. Adaptive governance arrangements nonetheless could be implemented through statutory and non-statutory measures,[33] with clear potential for stronger incorporation of these approaches into existing laws. Whether such laws can be reframed to adopt the pluralistic governance mode deemed necessary to respond to the complexity of the natural world in resilience theory, is yet to be tested. Pivotal to this collection, some resilience theorists indicate that crises may trigger social learning and knowledge generation that can facilitate the adoption of more flexible social-ecological systems. These theories of social learning and resilience have been widely adopted in natural resources systems such as water governance.

To date there is relatively limited use of resilience, as embedded in social-ecological theory, within energy law.[34] This edited collection is an opportunity to widen the application of this significant body of praxis to energy law, infrastructure, and natural resources. Resilience, in its 'engineering' mode is used at times to describe the characteristics of energy systems with many references to the need for 'resilient' energy technologies and resilient infrastructure.[35] Typically, these references are responsive to the need for flexible or better-adapted physical energy infrastructure than that which previously has been destroyed or damaged by hazards so that the physical system will not fail when similar hazards arise in the future.[36] Similarly, the application of resilience in natural resource management emphasizes the need for 'building back better' to ensure the longer term sustainability of resources. The term is less often applied to characterize energy market systems or governing legislation for relevant systems. This gap is surprising as from the vantage of resilience thinking, energy systems clearly can be conceptualized as a social-ecological system or a 'coupled' human/ technological-natural system.

Exploring the insight that energy systems are social-ecological systems opens up many avenues for thinking through how law may facilitate energy system resilience but also how law and legal structures may pose barriers to enhanced resilience within energy systems. Energy law systems are operative at multiple scales that are resilient within certain parameters, although feedback loops are being tested in many countries due to climate change and other disasters such as the COVID-19 pandemic that test the limits of existing energy systems and the governing laws. If we view energy systems as part of wider social-ecological systems, then law will play a critical role in shifting energy 'ecosystems' from one stability domain to another. This triggering to a new regime may be multi-scalar and dynamic as change occurs within the complex, adaptive energy systems where the characteristics that were evident in one stability domain are shifted to a domain with new characteristics, adaptive capacity, and feedback loops.

---

[33] Humby, Law and Resilience (n 3) 98.

[34] For an exception see Humby, Law and Resilience (n 3) 104.

[35] Stephanie Niall and Anne Kallies, 'Electricity Systems between Climate Mitigation and Climate Adaptation Pressures: Can Legal Frameworks for Resilience Provide Answers?' (2017) 34 Environmental and Planning Law Journal 488.

[36] Stephanie Phillips, 'Federal Regulation for a Resilient Electricity Grid' (2019) 46 Ecology LQ 415.

III. Characteristics of Energy Systems

Energy system outcomes do not occur in a vacuum, and are shaped by policy-maker and industry decisions over long periods.[37]

> ... resilience needs to go beyond the electric sector to ensure that critical in-frastructure like water and health services does not fail in a cascading manner.[38]

We define an energy system as an interconnected network of physical infrastructure, or-ganizational and institutional arrangements, and private contractual arrangements that are designed to provide for the delivery (and in some cases storage) of one or more forms of energy from the point of production or generation. The system should aim to be secure, affordable, and sustainable.[39] The physical infrastructure of an energy system may be more or less interconnected depending upon the form of primary or secondary energy.[40] For ex-ample, oil may be readily transported (and stored) in a number of different ways which may or may not involve linear infrastructure (i.e. pipelines). Natural gas may also be moved in small quantities in a variety of different ways, but at scale it will require a network of pipe-lines, and in some cases liquefaction and gasification facilities and purpose-built vessels, as well as physically interconnected storage. Electricity is the most highly interconnected form of energy system. This is in part due to the dominant role of wires and associated infra-structure for the physical delivery of energy, but also due to the technical need to maintain a balance between generation and load,[41] and the inability until recently to cheaply store electricity in large quantities.

In describing different energy systems, it is also important to recognize the increased significance of connections between different energy systems—for example, an electric en-ergy system that depends on significant natural gas generation.[42] In such a case any weak-ness in the natural gas system may have significant knock-on effects for the reliability of the electricity system.[43] The failure of the Texas electricity system to meet load in February 2021 offers a cautionary example of the implications of interconnectedness across energy systems[44] while disruption to the operation of the Colonial Pipeline system a few months

---

[37] Alex Gilbert and Morgan Bazilian, 'The Texas Electricity Crisis and the Energy Transition' *Utility Dive* (19 February 2021) <https://www.utilitydive.com/news/the-texas-electricity-crisis-and-the-energy-transition/595 315/> accessed 9 December 2021

[38] Ibid.

[39] World Energy Council, *World Energy Trilemma Index 2020*, published by the World Energy Council (2020) in partnership with Oliver Wyman.

[40] See generally Donald Z. Zillman et al, 'Energy Networks and the Law: Innovative Solutions in Changing Markets' in Martha M. Roggenkamp et al (eds), *Energy Networks and the Law: Innovative Solutions in Changing Markets* (Oxford University Press 2012).

[41] For references to the technical aspects of grid balancing see LeRoy Paddock and Charlotte Youngblood, 'Demand Response and Infrastructure Development in the United States' in Roggenkamp et al (eds), *Energy Networks and the Law: Innovative Solutions in Changing Markets* (Oxford University Press 2012) 161–179, 163.

[42] International Energy Agency (IEA), Power Systems in Transition: Challenges and opportunities ahead for electricity security (2020) esp. at 32; IEA Net Zero by 2050: A Roadmap for the Global Energy Sector, (2021) esp. at 176–179 referencing also (at 179) the importance of critical minerals such as copper, lithium, nickel, cobalt, and rare earth elements for many clean energy technologies.

[43] The interconnectedness across energy systems becomes particularly apparent as thermal generation selects lower carbon fuels and converts from coal to natural gas. Coal is easy to store at the generation site and generation frequently locates close to mine sites or tidal water both to reduce transportation costs and to enhance security of supply.

[44] See Gilbert and Bazilian (n 37) also noting that the challenges faced by the electricity system also had knock-on effects for water utility systems.

later affecting gasoline and other fuel supplies to the US east coast illustrates the important interconnections between energy systems and communication and cybersecurity systems.[45]

In addition to a greater or lesser degree of direct physical interconnection, energy systems also require a degree of organizational interconnection to ensure the appropriate functional integration of the different activities entailed in delivering energy services. It is common to describe two paradigmatic organizational models: a vertically integrated model and an unbundled model.[46] The following paragraphs discuss these two different models which we posit as two different stability domains within a resilience discourse. The analysis generally focuses on electricity systems as examples, although the same pattern is evident, although perhaps to a lesser extent, in natural gas systems.

A. The vertically integrated model

The vertically integrated model entails a single organization responsible for all elements of the value chain: in the case of electricity, generation, transmission, distribution, and supply or retail. The price of electricity within such an organizational model is generally based on cost of service rather than market pricing on the grounds that at least some elements of the value chain represent a natural monopoly.[47] In some cases, the vertically integrated utility may be investor owned (historically the dominant North American model especially in the US), whereas in other cases the utility may be state owned (the historical model in Canadian provinces (e.g. BC Hydro, Hydro Quebec), Europe (e.g. EDF (Électricité de France S.A.), GDF (Gaz de France), CEGB (Central Electricity Generating Board, England), and Australia[48]). State involvement favoured service areas based on the territory of the state, or, in the case of a federal state, the territory of the sub-unit of the federation. In the vertically integrated model, there is no need for a separate and distinct system operator since dispatch and balancing functions can be discharged by the integrated utility itself.[49] Competition law has little role to play in the vertically integrated model insofar as the economic regulation of a natural monopoly serves as a substitute for competition.[50]

B. The Unbundled Model

The unbundled model begins with the understanding that while some elements of the value chain may best be characterized as natural monopolies (transmission and distribution), other elements (generation and supply/retail) are not and therefore should be subject

[45] David Sanger and Nicole Perlroth, 'Pipeline Attack Yields Urgent Lessons about U.S. Cybersecurity' *New York Times* (21 May 2021) <https://www.nytimes.com/2021/05/14/us/politics/pipeline-hack.html> accessed 9 December 2021.
[46] These are not the only models. Geographically isolated communities may have no grid connection but still require secure supply chains and storage capacity for necessary inputs such as diesel fuel.
[47] Tariff structures may be established by, or require the approval of, an economic regulator such as a public utility commission.
[48] For Australia see Lee Godden and Anne Kallies, 'Electricity Network Development: New Challenges for Australia' in Roggenkamp et al (eds) (n 40) 292–312, 294
[49] IEA, Power Systems in Transition (n 42) 14.
[50] Organisation for Economic Co-operation and Development (OECD), *Regulated Conduct Defence*, (2011) <http://www.oecd.org/regreform/sectors/48606639.pdf> accessed 9 December 2021.

to the discipline of the market. In this model the market sets wholesale and retail prices while transmission and distribution continue to be priced on the basis of cost of service and subject to economic regulation. Unbundling in a jurisdiction that has previously been organized on the basis of a vertically integrated model frequently proceeds incrementally[51] and may involve required divestments as well as restrictions on participation in successive elements of the value chain.[52]

There are different forms of energy markets. While some jurisdictions operate almost exclusively as energy only markets[53] (with small ancillary service markets[54]) other jurisdictions may also establish a capacity market in order to provide a greater assurance of supply.[55] In an energy only market, generation is only compensated when it is actually dispatched in the merit order. It follows from this that the generation must recover all of its fixed and variable costs from those hours when it is on dispatch, and that investors will only build new generation if they have reasonable assurance of such recovery. In a jurisdiction with a capacity market, generation has the opportunity to secure two sources of revenue, a capacity payment in return for the commitment to make a specified amount of capacity available, if needed, and an energy payment when actually dispatched. A capacity market offers greater assurance to generation that it will be able to recover its fixed costs but represents a less 'pure' version of a market insofar as the regulator must assess how much capacity needs to be acquired to provide the desired level of security of supply.

In the unbundled model there will be a much larger number and greater diversity of market participants. In turn this diversity requires government to appoint a system operator(s) with responsibility for the wholesale market and operation of the power pool (i.e. for dispatch according to economic merit, balancing generation and load, and settlement of accounts) and for ensuring non-discriminatory access to the transmission and distribution systems.

Competition law plays a more significant role in the unbundled model because of the risk that a generator may exercise market power by physically or economically withholding[56] a part of its generation thereby driving up the system marginal price and transferring wealth from consumers to generation. Competition or other regulatory authorities may also seek to ensure that market participants only participate in one element of the value chain, or, if they are allowed to participate more broadly, do not abuse their position in one function in

---

[51] Perhaps best illustrated by the EU's successive Directives on Electricity and Natural Gas. See Angus Johnston and Guy Block, *EU Energy Law* (Oxford University Press 2012) ch 3, Unbundling. For the US see Paddock and Youngblood (n 41) 161–179, 162

[52] And as the EU also illustrates and as further discussed in Section IV of this chapter, unbundling may take various forms from full ownership unbundling to various functional mechanisms designed to remove 'conflict of interests between producers, suppliers and transmission system operators', EU Commission Staff Working Paper on the Unbundling Regime (2010) <https://ec.europa.eu/energy/sites/ener/files/documents/2010_01_21_the_un bundling_regime.pdf> accessed 9 December 2021.

[53] For example, ERCOT (the Electric Reliability Council of Texas) and Alberta, Canada.

[54] Ancillary services refer to a package of services required by a system operator including operating reserve and black start services.

[55] EU Commission, Final Report of the Sector Inquiry on Capacity Mechanisms (2016).

[56] Economic withholding refers to the practice of bidding generation into the pool at a price well above the fixed and variable costs of that facility with the expectation that the unit will be out of merit and thus not dispatched and forcing the system operator to move up the merit order. A withholding strategy only makes sense for a generator with a large enough portfolio position that its remaining in merit generation benefits sufficiently from the increase in the system marginal price so as to offset the losses entailed by removing one or more units from the merit order.

the chain to secure an advantage for itself in another part of the chain or foreclose access by others.

C. Effects of the choice of organizational models (for the energy systems) on resilience

Both the vertically integrated model and the unbundled model have proven to be resilient over time and in that sense represent, in resilience theory, different versions of a stable system or stability domain. Each is capable of producing societally desirable outcomes in terms of providing secure, affordable, and sustainable energy services. That said, the last 30 years has seen many jurisdictions move their energy systems from the vertically integrated model to an unbundled model in response to a number of factors. These factors include ideological reasons (reducing the power of the state and its role in the economy), the perceived benefits of competition (cost savings and enhanced consumer choice), and technological developments including new and scalable forms of generation which facilitate entry by a variety of smaller players.[57] But this shift in stability domain is not an organic evolution; it is a result of deliberate political decisions and resulting legislation. Neither has the shift been consistent. For example, vertically integrated Crown corporations continue their dominant role in a number of Canadian provinces (e.g. British Columbia and Quebec) and the trend to deregulation in the United States is far from uniform.[58]

As the epigram to this section of the chapter recognizes, energy systems do not exist in isolation but are nested within, and react with, social-ecological systems including the climate system, information systems,[59] and domestic and international political and legal systems. Both paradigmatic forms of energy system have been able to withstand the disturbances resulting from these interactions and for most part maintain similar levels of functionality even while going through significant change. For example, many if not most energy systems increasingly face the challenge of accommodating significant changes in energy mix including the integration of increased amounts of intermittent or non-dispatchable energy while maintaining system reliability.[60]

Energy systems are also responding to other disruptors.[61] Traditionally, electricity systems have been considered to be unidirectional in the sense that energy moves from generation through the value chain to the ultimate consumer. But technological developments, including a diversity of smaller-scale generation[62] and the availability of storage, has increasingly allowed generation to connect to the distribution system (distribution connected generation (DCG) or more generally and encapsulating demand side contributions, distributed energy resources (DER)). This allows consumers not only to consume but also to

---

[57] Paddock and Youngblood (n 41) 167.

[58] Ibid.

[59] See IEA, Power Systems in Transition (n 42) at 15 noting that the role of digital information technologies is crucial in distributed energy systems but exposes the electricity system to cyber threats as exemplified by the disruption to the Colonial pipeline system in the US in 2021 (n 45).

[60] See IEA, Power Systems in Transition (n 42) discussing six phases in the accommodation of variable renewable energy resources (VRE) and also discussing the need to build cyber resilience and climate resilience.

[61] The focus here is on the disruptive effects of new technologies but natural events (e.g. the Texas cold snap of 2021 (n 44) may also cause disruption and challenge the resilience of energy systems.

[62] For example, roof top solar.

supply power to the distribution system and thus act as prosumers.[63] These innovations require not only smart meters to enable demand response[64] but also smart grids that use 'digital and other advanced technologies to monitor and manage the transport of electricity from all generation sources to meet the varying electricity demands of end-users. Smart grids co-ordinate the needs and capabilities of all generators, grid operators, end-users and electricity market stakeholders to operate all parts of the system as efficiently as possible, minimising costs and environmental impacts while maximising system reliability, resilience and stability.'[65]

The disruption caused by DER may have cascading consequences for an electricity system given the large fixed costs associated with transmission and distribution.[66] Current rate structures may enhance the attractiveness of DER options insofar as net billing mechanisms, for example, may allow consumers to reduce or avoid transmission and distribution costs. This inevitably forces others to assume those costs thereby increasing the incentives for others to also adopt DER options—a form of utility death spiral. This may require proactive tariff redesign to provide greater assurance of the recovery of fixed costs and to avoid the risk of stranded assets and unsustainable transmission and distribution systems.[67] At least some discussions of these issues emphasize the importance of learning from the experiences of others and the need for conscious experimentation through pilot projects, particularly with respect to the use of smart meters.[68]

The increased availability of storage may also have a disruptive effect on energy systems insofar as much energy regulation is premised on a binary distinction between load and generation. Storage resources on the other hand move between a charging mode (in which the battery or other storage acts as load) and discharge (in which the battery or other storage acts as supply). The availability of storage resources may also allow a utility to avoid or at least delay investments in new transmission or distribution assets.[69] On the other hand increased adoption of electric vehicles (EVs) may require reinforcement of distribution systems even though EV batteries may also ultimately be used to supply energy. Proper integration of storage resources within an energy system requires the regulator to recognize the multi-functionality of storage and establish clear rules for the treatment of storage.

Energy systems may also change in scale over time. Isolated communities may be connected to a grid and systems that were organized along national or other jurisdictional boundaries may become increasingly connected across jurisdictional lines. Such connections may offer a number of advantages including a greater diversity of sources of

---

[63] Saskia Lavrijssen and Arturo Carrillo Parra, 'Radical Prosumer Innovations in the Electricity Sector and the Impact on Prosumer Regulation' (2017) 9 Sustainability 1207.

[64] Demand response includes load shifting and peak load shaving. See generally Paddock and Youngblood (n 41).

[65] International Energy Agency (IEA), Technology Roadmap -Smart Grid (2011), 6 <https://www.iea.org/reports/technology-roadmap-smart-grids> accessed 9 December 2021. And for discussion of smart grids see Anita Rønne, 'Smart Grids and Intelligent Energy Systems: A European Perspective' in Roggenkamp et al (eds) (n 40) 141–160 and Paddock and Youngblood (n 41) 174–176.

[66] See generally Alberta Utilities Commission (AUC), Distribution System Inquiry, Final Report, 19 February 2021.

[67] Ibid and Council of European Energy Regulators (CEER), Paper on Electricity Distribution Tariffs Supporting the Energy Transition (2020).

[68] AUC, Distribution System Inquiry (n 66) at para 426.

[69] Sometimes referred to a NWAs or non-wires alternatives to providing energy services. The availability of storage may also allow parties to disconnect entirely from the grid.

generation,[70] but may also pose energy security and coordination challenges. We will also see increased interconnectedness as economies depend increasingly on clean forms of generation especially within the transportation sector. While this will require significant investments in infrastructure it may also lead to savings in primary energy due to the inefficiencies associated with carbon-based transportation and the inexorable application of the second law of thermodynamics which applies to all energy systems.[71]

In sum, this section has provided an overview of the concept of an energy system and in doing so described two paradigmatic organizational forms of such a system or stability domain, each of which appears stable and resilient. The section has also provided some examples of disruptors that threaten the resilience of such systems and require forms of re-organization which in some cases can be characterized as requiring or resulting in moving the energy system from one stability domain to another. In the course of doing so we have also referenced the role of law in any such transformation.

IV. The Role of Law

This section explores the role of law in greater detail by examining three examples from European energy law. The first example focuses on the role of law in achieving unbundling in the European energy sector thereby triggering the move from one stability domain to another (A). The second example focuses on the role of law in infrastructure planning and the contribution of that function to the resilience of energy systems given changes in scale (B). The third example examines the role of law in responding to the opportunities and challenges to energy systems associated with the increased adoption of distributed generation and storage (C).

A. Resilience and unbundling

The creation of an internal market for energy in the EU is based upon two pillars: the unbundling of production and supply from networks businesses (transport and distribution) and third-party access to gas and electricity networks. Both are inextricably united, since unbundling facilitates access and vice versa. The successive EU Directives and Regulations in the field of energy (the first dated 1996) have reinforced this model of unbundling, from accounting and legal, to functional and ownership unbundling. Unbundling in the EU is, in effect, the result of deliberate political decisions and resulting legislation. Unbundling reflects a certain preference for a type of 'coupled' energy legal system, so that the unbundled activities become regulated by distinct but coupled legal regimes.

EU law has yet not imposed upon Member States the obligation to introduce a system of ownership unbundling in transport networks. The exception is the obligation imposed

---

[70] For example, the Nordpool system serves to integrate Norway's 96 per cent hydro system with other Nordpool states with a larger variety of generation. This allows Norway to export surplus power in high water years but also offers it an element of security in low water years.

[71] Liam Denning and Elaine He, 'When the Electric Car Is King, Less Energy Is More' *Bloomberg Opinion* (1 February 2021) <https://www.bloomberg.com/graphics/2021-opinion-renewables-will-power-future-of-us-energy>/ accessed 9 December 2021.

upon those Member States, which at the time of the entry into force of the 2009 Electricity Directive already had a system of ownership unbundling. However, some ownership unbundling adopted by several big EU companies is the indirect result of EU legislation. When ownership unbundling was proposed by the European Commission in 2007, France and Germany firmly opposed requiring companies to divest their networks and as a result the 2009 Directives included a *menu à la carte*, so that Member States could choose from three unbundling models: (i) ownership unbundling (which was compulsory if, at the time of the Directive entered into force, there was already ownership unbundling), (ii) functional unbundling, or (iii) an Independent System Operator (ISO).[72] However, following the passing of the 2009 Directive, most EU energy companies (including those of France and Germany) actually divested their transmission networks, even if they were not obliged to do so because there was no point in keeping them within the company, if their management was subject to the many rules associated with functional unbundling. In other words, it was easier to divest transmission networks than to set up the several and complex Chinese walls to comply with functional unbundling. The need for such rules is a signal of the increasing complexity of systems, but, simultaneously, it incents a simpler and more radical form of unbundling, i.e. ownership unbundling.

Unbundling is an instrument to introduce greater transparency and competition in the energy market, since it facilitates access to third parties. However, that is not the only and main objective of unbundling. Unbundling also has to do with resilience of networks. By imposing the obligation to separately run (or even, own) networks from production and supply, EU institutions facilitate the financial accountability of networks, since costs and revenues are accounted for separately and do not mix with those of the liberalized parts of the industry. This reduces the regulatory burden and removes the possibility for cross-subsidies in favour of more profitable aspects of the industry (supply and production). In light of the above, unbundling emerges as an optimal instrument to guarantee the proper functioning of networks, and, thus, to foster resilience.

B. Resilience and infrastructure planning

The EU embarked on an ambitious programme of liberalization and integration of electricity markets beginning in 1996, within the wider context of efforts to build an Internal Market (for Energy). At that time, most European governments shared the view that markets would provide the necessary signals on where and when to invest in electricity infrastructure. After several years' experience it became clear that markets needed to be refined and reinforced in the areas of production and supply and that in the case of transmission and distribution networks, planning was needed.[73] There were severe blackouts in several EU Member States, e.g. Italy (28 September 2003), Germany (4 November 2006), and Spain (27 July 2007), affecting millions of consumers, due to a lack of robust electricity transport infrastructure and of coordination between TSOs.

The EU reacted to that situation by creating a compulsory association of European TSOs (ENTSO-E) with the task, among others, of drafting and adopting network plans. Since

---

[72] Art 9 Directive 2009/72/EC and Directive 2009/73/EC and Commission Staff Working Paper (n 52).
[73] See C. Banet, Chapter 4 of this volume, on resilience planning.

2009, ENTSO-E must adopt and publish a non-binding Union-wide 10-year network development plan, biennially. Under the 2009 Regulation and its successor the 2019 Regulation, the plan must include the modelling of the integrated network, scenario development, and *an assessment of the resilience of the system.*[74]

Both Regulations (2009 and 2019), require ENTSO-E to produce a resource adequacy assessment. The relevant provisions in the 2009 Regulation were very limited but the provisions in the 2019 Regulation are much more detailed.[75] The ENTSO-E must assess the overall adequacy of the electricity system to supply current and projected demands for electricity at the EU level, at the level of the Member States, and at the level of individual bidding zones, where relevant. It must cover each year for a period of 10 years from the date of that assessment. Resource adequacy is relevant for the resilience of the electricity system since generation infrastructure must satisfy the needs of consumers at any time. The problem is that European governments have been tempted to address problems of resource adequacy with capacity payments which violate or threaten to violate competition law.[76] This potential violation of competition law is why the 2019 Regulation contains joint and detailed provisions on resource adequacy assessment and capacity mechanisms, so that governments address resource adequacy issues (whenever they arise) with mechanisms compatible with competition law.[77] This illustrates how different organizational models (or stability domains in resilience discourse) may trigger interconnections between different elements of a legal system.

C. Flexibility services and resilience within an EU perspective

If resilience refers to 'the capacity of a system to absorb disturbance and reorganize while undergoing change so as to still retain essentially the same function, structure, identity, and feedbacks'[78] the concept is clearly closely related to that of flexibility.

In the context of the creation and development of a European internal energy market, the term resilience ordinarily refers to networks and their ability to continue to provide reliable services for the supply of energy. For example, Recital no 83 of Directive (EU) 2019/ 944 of the European Parliament and of the Council of 5 June 2019 on common rules for the internal market for electricity and amending Directive 2012/27/EU[79], provides as follows:

> Regulatory authorities should ensure that transmission system operators and distribution system operators take appropriate measures to make their network more resilient and flexible.

---

[74] Art 8 (10) of the Regulation (EC) no 714/2009 of the European Parliament and of the Council of 13 July 2009 on conditions for access to the network for cross-border exchanges in electricity and repealing Regulation (EC) no 1228/2003 (OJ L 211, of 14 August, 2009). Hereafter referred as to the 2009 Regulation. And Art 30(1)(b) in relation with Art 48(1), both of the Regulation (EC) no 2019/943 of the European Parliament and of the Council of 5 June 2019 on the internal market for electricity (OJ L 158, of 14 June 2019). Hereafter referred as to the 2019 Regulation.

[75] Chapter IV (Arts 20–27) of the 2019 Regulation.

[76] See discussion of energy and capacity markets in Section III of this chapter.

[77] See, further, L. Hancher, A. De Houteclocque, and M. Sadowska (eds), *Capacity Mechanisms in the EU Energy Market. Law, Policy, and Economics* (Oxford University Press 2015).

[78] Holling, 'Resilience and Stability' (n 2).

[79] OJ L 158, 14.06.19

From a broader perspective, resilience is as an exigency imposed upon the energy system as a whole. Consequently, it would be more accurate to refer to the resilience of the energy system, rather than only to the resilience of networks, and this is indeed reflected in EU law, and energy policy documents in several places,[80] as well as in the specialized literature.[81]

EU energy policy documents refer to resilience when addressing the fight against climate change and, therefore, resilience is an essential element of the response of the energy system to extreme weather conditions and related circumstances, which threaten to disrupt the energy system.[82]

Within the EU, there is a linkage between resilience and flexibility, to the extent that these terms are almost interchangeable. This means that a robust or healthy energy system requires that every phase of the energy chain is flexible, including transmission and distribution networks, but also generation and consumption installations.

The EU seeks to move the entire energy system towards a new system, which is decarbonized (carbon neutral) and electrified, where renewable energies are the main or even exclusive way of producing electricity. Climate change is acting as a disruptor, and the introduction of a climate friendly system, shows the shift towards a new stability domain. The various documents containing the EU energy policy (2015–2021)[83] reflect that aim as well as the fourth energy package of legal norms passed between 2018 and 2019 (Clean Energy Package for All Europeans).[84]

In the current electricity model, developed over the last 90 years, consumers have a passive role. Under this model, flexibility of the electricity system comes from the supply side—generation. In peak hours, some producers would produce more (or the relevant authority ask them to produce more) when needed or when some renewable installations cannot operate because there is no water, sun, or wind. The security of the system is measured by the capacity of producers and networks operators to produce more or to transmit more, respectively, when consumers need it.[85]

---

[80] Article 48 (1), of the 2019 Regulation; and 'A Framework Strategy for a Resilient Energy Union with a Forward-Looking Climate Change Policy. Energy Union', *Communication from the Commission to the European Parliament, the Council, the European Economic and Social Committee, the Committee of the Regions and the European Investment Bank*, COM (2015) 80 final, Brussels, 25 February 2015; and 'The European Green Deal'.

[81] There are proposals to have 'two markets' in Europe (one for conventional production, one for renewables), and in that regard 'System benefits – In the short term, the two-market approach won't make any real difference to the system. As now, renewables will get priority dispatch either by law or because they can bid in at zero cost. However, in the longer term it may encourage demand shifting and use of storage, which helps the overall resilience of the system.' See David Robinson and Malcolm Keay, *Glimpses of the future electricity system? Demand flexibility and a proposal for a special auction* (The Oxford Institute for Energy Studies 2020) 7.

[82] For example, the European Commission 'will also examine how our financial system can help to increase resilience to climate and environmental risks, in particular when it comes to the physical risks and damage arising from natural catastrophes'; 'well-designed tax reforms can boost economic growth and resilience to climate shock'; and the need 'to increase climate and environmental resilience'. These quotations are all excerpted from 'The European Green Deal', *Communication from the Commission to the European Parliament, the European Council, The Council, the European Economic and Social Committee, and the Committee of the Regions*, COM (2019) 640 final, Brussels, 11 December 2019.

[83] See (n 82) and (n 83).

[84] Sometimes referred as to the 'Winter Package'.

[85] Some flexibility can be identified on the demand side, in the form of interruptible contracts, by which consumers were ready to stop or lower consumption when asked for, in exchange of a lower tariff. This interruptibility practice, together with some capacity remuneration pose, in turn, clear and severe problems to competition in the light of EU law on state aid (see n 77).

In the future system, consumers will have an active role[86], in a twofold sense. On the one hand, they will become prosumers, i.e. they will consume the energy they produce.[87] On the other hand, with the decisive help of new technologies, consumers will be active in deciding when they consume and from which source and, even more important for the subject of resilience, they will be able to store and to offer to the market surplus electricity at different times. The EU is committed to organizing electricity markets in a more flexible manner and to integrating within it all market players (including producers of renewable energy, new energy service providers, energy storage, and flexible demand).[88] The promotion of demand flexibility is to take place by reinforcing the demand-side ability to respond to the changing conditions of the market.[89]

With that purpose, the new 2018–2019 EU legislation regulates a number of instruments directed to empower consumers while introducing greater flexibility and resilience in the electricity sector. These instruments include aggregation, storage, self-production, smart networks (including smart metering), energy communities, and dynamic contracts.

Energy communities (both renewable energy communities and citizen energy communities) can play a remarkable role in providing resilience to electricity systems. We are experiencing extreme weather conditions, which impose disruptions and/or blackouts in entire electricity systems. These experiences require us to consider greater decentralization so that energy systems become self-sufficient. There must be a judicious balance between decentralization and interconnection. Energy communities can help to provide more flexibility (for example, by allowing them to participate in local markets).[90]

Flexibility implies that the systems respond quickly and in an effective way to the needs of consumers, and applies to both offer (production) and demand (supply). In the current model, resilience is based exclusively on the availability of big production units and adequate transmission capacity. Investment is directed towards those production and transport facilities. This includes the existence of spare capacity and alternative routes to be used when the ordinary route fails. In the future, resilience will be no longer based on building capacity (production and transmission capacity), but rather on the ability of agents to act simultaneously as producers, consumers, and storers.[91] Technology will allow this, including new and bigger batteries. New businesses will emerge. There will be the need, of course, to execute contingency plans, to allow decentralized units to benefit from the supply of some back-up production, which can function whenever there is not enough renewable production. This new decarbonized and decentralized model presents a challenge to traditional conceptions of resilience, but it must be the case that the more flexible the system is, the more resilient the system becomes.

---

[86] See B. Barton, Chapter 22 and L. de Fontenelle Chapter 23 of this volume, on the role of consumers in resilience.

[87] Lavrijesen and Parra (n 63).

[88] 'Launching the public consultation process on a new energy market design', Communication from the Commission to the European Parliament, the Council, the European Economic and Social Committee, and the Committee of the Regions, COM (2015) 340 final, Brussels, 15 July 2015

[89] On the future role of consumers, see David Robinson, Prices Behind the Meter: efficient economic signals to support decarbonization (The Oxford Institute for Energy Studies November 2019).

[90] See Aura Caramizaru and Andreas Uihlein, Energy communities: an overview of energy and social innovation, the Joint Research Centre of the European Commission's science and knowledge service, Brussels 2020.

[91] On the flexibility component of the new demand response, see I. Herrera-Anchústegui and A. Formosa, Regulation of Electricity Markets in Europe in Light of the Clean Energy Package: Prosumers and Demand Response, 2019, available at SSRN: <https://ssrn.com/abstract=3448434> accessed 9 December 2021.

V. Conclusions

The concept of resilience as applied within social-ecological systems theory offers a way of thinking about energy systems as nested systems, comprised not only of a physical infrastructure but also complex organizational systems operating within markets or subject to economic regulation. Such systems are subject to the physical laws of thermodynamics as well as the (changing) physical environment in which they operate, but they must also conform to (changing) laws and regulations. Indeed, law plays a central role in the organization of energy systems and accordingly can also play a role in fostering or inhibiting the resilience of energy systems. Resilience theory suggests that natural systems may flip from one stable domain to another as a result of perturbations within or affecting the system. Law perhaps rarely plays a central role in such a flip within a natural system, but law surely plays a central role in causing complex interlinked social-physical systems such as an energy system to move from one stability domain to another. Such a shift does not occur organically or naturally but in response to some legal direction. Such legal direction must in turn be responsive to a myriad of other factors including technological developments, environmental objectives, and security concerns. Law also plays a central role in energy system design in fostering or inhibiting resilience within any particular stability domain.

Our analysis of energy systems offers several examples of how law can help energy systems to be more flexible and resilient including infrastructure planning, unbundling the different elements of the value chain, and decentralization of supply. Many jurisdictions are adopting energy policies that seek to move existing energy systems to a new paradigm and perhaps a new stability domain characterized by a dominant use of renewable energies and an active role for consumers via demand response technologies and decentralized supply. This new stability domain will rely more on demand flexibility to achieve resilience by contrast with the existing system in which resilience is achieved principally through supply (generation and transmission).

3

Building Resilience from the Top Down? The Role of International Law and Institutions

Catherine Redgwell

I. Introduction

This chapter assesses the resilience-building capacity of international law and institutions in the context of energy and related fields. Ultimately this is a question of their underlying nimbleness in responding to disruptive change, explored further in this contribution. It is also a question of the capacity to do so: in many contexts building resilience is a response to fragility, with half of the world's poorer populations living in fragile or conflict-affected States. As the Organisation for Economic Co-operation and Development (OECD) 2020 *States of Fragility Report* underscores, lack of resilience can be economic, environmental, political, societal, and security related.[1] Nor is there a one-size-fits-all response to the multi-dimensional problem of building resilience in response to fragility. Further complicating the picture is the reality that disruption can take many forms—slow, or sudden onset for example, or the catastrophic, unforeseen event.[2] This colours the development of international legal norms and principles in response, with an emphasis on the prevention as well as remediation of the impacts of disrupting events.

Resilience can be found embedded in the substantive rules of international law, most notably in the emerging field of International Disaster Law (IDL)—an umbrella concept covering a range of norms and instruments—considered further below. It is also inherent in the nature of the contemporary international legal order, with several general features underscoring the flexibility and responsiveness of the international law-making process in particular. First, international institutions, including the United Nations (UN) and its specialized and regional agencies and programmes, have played a leading role in setting law-making agendas and providing negotiating forums and expertise. This may occur speedily in response to disrupting events, such as the legislative response initiated through the International Atomic Energy Agency (IAEA) following the Chernobyl disaster.[3] Additionally, the use of framework treaties has given the law-making process a dynamic

---

[1] Organisation of Economic Co-operation and Development, *States of Fragility 2020* (OECD Publishing 2020) <https://doi.org/10.1787/ba7c22e7-en> accessed 11 August 2021.

[2] And acknowledged in the International Law Commissions' definition of 'disaster': see text at n 79 below. All are evident in the impacts of the climate emergency: on the legal response see, generally, Dan Bodansky, Jutta Brunnée, and Lavanya Rajamani, *International Climate Change Law* (Oxford University Press 2017).

[3] See the 1986 Vienna Convention on Early Notification of a Nuclear Accident (1986) 25 ILM 1370 (entered in force 27 October 1986) and the 1986 Vienna Convention on Assistance in the Case of a Nuclear Accident or Radiological Emergency (1986) 25 ILM 1377 (entered into force 26 February 1987). For the response to the Fukushima-Daiichi nuclear incident, see n 60 below.

Catherine Redgwell, *Building Resilience from the Top Down? The Role of International Law and Institutions* In: *Resilience in Energy, Infrastructure, and Natural Resources Law*. Edited by: Catherine Banet, Hanri Mostert, LeRoy Paddock, Milton Fernando Montoya, and Íñigo del Guayo, Oxford University Press. © Catherine Redgwell 2022. DOI: 10.1093/oso/9780192864574.003.0003

character through regular meetings of the parties or intergovernmental organizations. These provide a basis for progressive action to be taken as scientific knowledge expands, and as regulatory priorities evolve or change, including in response to disruptive events. Such treaties usually set out broad principles while providing for detailed rules and measures to be elaborated in successive protocols, annexes, and related soft-law instruments. Examples of this framework treaty approach to law-making include the 1992 Framework Convention on Climate Change,[4] the 1985 Vienna Convention for the Protection of the Ozone Layer,[5] the 1979 Geneva Convention on Long-Range Transboundary Air Pollution,[6] and the 1973/78 International Convention for the Prevention of Pollution from Ships (MARPOL) Convention,[7] all of which have been amplified by subsequent instruments.[8] These framework treaties, together with the institutions they create, have become regulatory regimes; as a result, what may begin as a very bare outline agreement can become a complex system of detailed law with its own machinery for ensuring compliance and implementation. Most importantly for present purposes, these successive protocols and annexes are more easily amended and adapted to respond to changing circumstances.

Mindful of these general features of the international law-making process,[9] this chapter considers two aspects of building resilience from the top down. First, it assesses the extent to which binding international norms and principles can dynamically change and evolve in response to disrupting events. This includes consideration of the role and particular agility of (non-binding) soft law in such circumstances. However, given that so many of the relevant rules of energy law and related fields (trade, investment, human rights, environment) are found in treaty law,[10] this forms the principal focus. As will be demonstrated, there is considerable flexibility both in form and in the content of these instruments with evidence of significant capacity to respond to disrupting events. This is not universally the case, however, and is particularly dependent on political will and the capacity to implement agreed norms. Secondly and relatedly is the role of international institutions in this process. Building sustainable institutional structures has been identified as playing a key role in disaster risk reduction and response.[11] Some areas of international law such as IDL and some

---

[4] (1992) 31 ILM 851 (entered into force 21 March 1994).

[5] (1987) 26 ILM 1529 (entered into force 22 September 1988).

[6] 1973 International Convention for the Prevention of Pollution from Ships and 1978 Protocol (MARPOL 73/78) (entered into force 2 October 1983) 1340 UNTS 62.

[7] (1973) 12 ILM 1319 (amended by a 1978 Protocol before it entered into force 2 October 1983).

[8] See also the 1992 OSPAR Convention for the Protection of the Marine Environment of the North-East Atlantic (entered into force 25 March 1998) 2354 UNTS 67, with its annexes and appendices, which is a further excellent example of flexible methods of treaty change and adaptation. For further discussion of the legal implications of such flexible amendment procedures under OSPAR, see Louise de La Fayette, 'The OSPAR Convention Comes into Force: Continuity and Progress' (1999) 14(2) International Journal of Marine and Coastal Law 247–297.

[9] See further Alan Boyle and Christine Chinkin, *The Making of International Law* (Oxford University Press 2007). As they observe, much of international law is the product of an essentially legislative process involving international organizations, conference diplomacy, codification and progressive development, international courts, and a relatively subtle interplay of treaties, non-binding declarations or resolutions (soft law), and customary international law.

[10] Of course a treaty rule may be binding in customary international law and become relevant on that basis. See, for example, the Shrimp-Turtle case where the Appellate Body of the World Trade Organization (WTO) noted that, though the United States was not a party to the 1982 Law of the Sea Convention, it accepted the relevant provisions as customary international law: *Import Prohibition of Certain Shrimp and Shrimp Products*, WTO Appellate Body (1998) WT/DS58/AB/R paras 130–131; see also *EC — Measures Affecting the Approval and Marketing of Biotech Products*, WTO Panel Reports (2006) WT/DS291/2/3/R, paras 7.90–7.96.

[11] International Law Commission, Draft Articles on the Protection of Persons in the Event of Disaster, *Yearbook of the International Law Commission*, 2016 (A/71/10), vol II, Part Two, p 10, para 32.

institutions such as the International Energy Agency (IEA) may be viewed as hard-wired to respond to catastrophic change and emergencies. IDL, for example, focuses on the legal issues arising from the preparation for, response to, and recovery from different natural hazards, such as earthquakes or storms, as well as human-made disasters such as large-scale industrial accidents.[12] Beyond these explicit and even 'normalized' emergency contexts is the complex issue of building response to disruption by international law and institutions designed and grounded in maintaining stability and the rule of law, important factors in the energy context where large-scale energy projects of considerable duration are undertaken.

II. Resilience in Norm-Creation, Evolution, and Change

The extent to which binding international norms and principles can dynamically change and evolve, especially when confronted by disrupting events, is a measure of their resilience. This includes considering the capacity for norm creation where there are gaps, as well as adapting existing rules where these are inadequate, in response to disruption. Such norm creation includes the negotiation of a new stand-alone treaty or of an instrument additional to an existing treaty. Treaties are also the modality for the creation of international organizations and bodies such as the IEA and the IAEA which were designed to respond to emergency situations.[13] So treaty law is both a source of rules and a mechanism for institution-building, some of which are designed for resilience in response to disrupting, even catastrophic, events and their impacts on the energy sector. However, multilateral treaties open to a wide range of States generally take a period of time for entry into force, though there are exceptions such as the very swift entry into force of the 1986 IAEA Conventions on Early Notification of a Nuclear Accident, and on Assistance in the Case of a Nuclear Accident or Radiological Emergency, following the Chernobyl reactor meltdown.[14] One mechanism for the swift application of new treaty norms is through States agreeing on the provisional application of a multilateral treaty pending its entry into force,[15] such as Article 45 of the Energy Charter Treaty on provisional application.[16]

Another approach is for industry standards to be used to 'gap fill' in response to disaster, pending the conclusion and entry into force of the treaty response. An example is the industry-sponsored agreements Tanker Owners Voluntary Agreement Concerning Liability for Oil Pollution (TOVALOP) and Contract Regarding an Interim Supplement to Tanker Liability

---

[12] This is not to suggest that 'natural' and 'human-made' are necessarily easily distinguishable, as the current climate emergency and COVID-19 pandemic so amply illustrate, and as the International Law Commission acknowledges in its definition of 'disaster' (n 79).

[13] 1956 Statute of the International Atomic Energy Agency, 276 UNTS 3 (entered into force 29 July 1957); 1974 Agreement on the International Energy Program, (1975) 14 ILM 1 (entered into force 1976) with the IEA established by OECD Council Decision 14 November 1974.

[14] See (n 3) above. The duty to notify of significant transboundary harm, and to exercise due diligence in the regulation of ultra-hazardous activities, are also found in customary international law. See further Alan Boyle and Catherine Redgwell, 'Nuclear Energy and the Environment' in *Boyle, Birnie, and Redgwell's International Law & the Environment* (4th edn, Oxford University Press 2021) ch 7.

[15] See generally Danae Azaria, 'Provisional Application of Treaties' in Duncan B. Hollis (ed), *The Oxford Guide to Treaties* (2nd edn, Oxford University Press 2020) ch 10. The topic was also taken up by the ILC in 2012: see further Provisional application of treaties—Summaries of the Work of the International Law Commission—International Law Commission (<https://legal.un.org/ilc/guide/1_12.shtml>), accessed 11 August 2021.

[16] 1994 Energy Charter Treaty (entered into force 16 April 1998), <www.energychartertreaty.org> accessed 11 August 2021.

for Oil Pollution (CRISTAL) put in place following high-profile oil tanker casualties.[17] This was pending the anticipated lengthy process of the entry into force of the 1969 International Convention on Civil Liability for Oil Pollution Damage and the supplementary 1971 International Convention on the Establishment of an International Fund for Compensation for Oil Pollution Damage,[18] which in their turn required implementing legislation.

With respect to existing instruments, their flexibility and capacity to adapt over time in response to economic, technical, and environmental changes may occur in a number of ways. One is the 'normal' pathway of treaty amendment in response to change, with most treaty boiler-plate including provision for such change. Adding to existing instruments may be in response to developments, or in their anticipation, such as the precautionary future-proofing amendment to the 1996 Protocol to the London Convention to address potential marine geoengineering responses to the climate emergency.[19] Swift, however, it is generally not, as the threshold to achieve successful treaty amendment is usually set high, requiring a significant number of existing State parties to agree both on the adoption of the amendment and for its entry into force—and then, typically such amendment is binding only on the treaty parties that have expressly accepted it.[20]

However, as with provisional application pending the usually slow process of entry into force requirements being met, there are work-arounds. One is to anticipate the need for flexible and more rapid amendment through the incorporation into the treaty of an expedited amendment or a tacit acceptance amendment procedure such as that employed under various International Maritime Organization (IMO) instruments, though usually reserved for technical annexes or appendices.[21] Another is to ensure the evolution of treaty rules and standards without the need for textual change. This is the technique employed in the 1982 Law of the Sea Convention (LOSC)[22] through the incorporation by reference of other 'generally accepted international rules and standards' (GAIRS) which themselves will change over time.[23] This phrase is inherently evolutionary in character, fostering a dynamic interpretation of the relevant treaty provisions.[24] It facilitates the continued vitality and

---

[17] These industry agreements, concluded in 1969 and 1971 respectively, applied until the entry into force of the international agreements in 1997.

[18] Reprinted in (1970) 9 ILM 45 (entered into force 19 June 1975) and (1971) 11 ILM 284 (entered into force 16 October 1978) respectively; superseded by the 1992 Protocol (entered into force 30 May 1996).

[19] 1972 London Convention on the Prevention of Marine Pollution by Dumping of Wastes and other Matter (entered into force 30 August 1975) (1972) 1 ILM 1294; replaced by the 1996 Protocol (entered into force 24 March 2006) (1997) 36 ILM 7; 2013 Amendment to the 2006 Protocol to the Convention on the Prevention of Marine Pollution by Dumping of Wastes and Other Matter, 1972 to Regulate Marine Geoengineering (not yet in force).

[20] See e.g. Arts 312–314 of the 1982 Law of the Sea Convention (LOSC) (entered into force 16 November 1994) (1982) 21 ILM 1261. Note that this is either through general amendment applicable to all parties, or through *inter se* agreements, with the caveat that the latter must be compatible with 'the effective execution of the object and purpose' of the LOSC: Art 311(3).

[21] A pioneer in this regard was the MARPOL 73/78 (n 7) with its tacit acceptance amendment procedure.

[22] (n 20).

[23] See further Catherine Redgwell, 'The Never Ending Story: The Role of GAIRS in LOSC Implementation in the Offshore Energy Sector' in Richard Barnes and Jill Barrett (eds), *Law of the Sea: UNCLOS as a Living Treaty* (British Institute of International and Comparative Law 2016) ch 6; Walter van Reenen, 'Rules of Reference in the new Convention on the Law of the Sea in particular connection with pollution of the sea by oil from tankers' (1981) XII *Netherlands Yearbook of International Law* 3–44. The LOSC does not explain what GAIRS are, other than occasionally to link these with promulgation by a competent international organization or diplomatic conference, e.g. Art 211(5).

[24] As Boyle observes, many of the terms utilized in the LOSC are potentially inherently evolutionary, using the examples, inter alia, of 'the pollution of the marine environment' and the identification of 'generally accepted international rules and standards': Alan Boyle, 'Further Development of the Law of the Sea Convention: Mechanisms for Change' (2005) 54(3) ICLQ 563–584, at 569. See, generally, Eirik Bjorge, *The Evolutionary Interpretation of Treaties* (Oxford University Press 2014).

resilience of the LOSC[25] without the need to go through the cumbersome and politically difficult process of treaty amendment.[26] Gap-filling is a related function for external rules and standards given that certain technical developments could not have been foreseen, such as the extent of offshore renewables development and the need for related transmission infrastructure, the use of depleted offshore reservoirs for storage of CO_2 and the exploitation of methane hydrates.[27]

A particular feature of treaty resilience is where an evolutionary approach to treaty interpretation may be adopted. Even absent explicit reference to external norms such as GAIRS, the process of treaty interpretation and, in particular, an evolutive approach to interpretation can sustain the relevance and currency of the instrument by incorporating new principles by way of interpretation.[28] The 1969 Vienna Convention on the Law of Treaties (VCLT)[29] sets forth rules on the crucial task of treaty interpretation. The tripartite general approach of Article 31 requires an examination not only of the words used, but their interpretation in context and in the light of the object and purpose of the treaty.[30] In addition, treaty interpretation may take into account any relevant treaty made by the parties, any subsequent practice relating to the interpretation of the treaty, and relevant general international law.[31] Article 32 permits recourse to the *travaux préparatoires* (if extant) of the treaty instrument, which may confirm the interpretation arrived at or resolve ambiguity in the text through recourse to the record of the original negotiations.

An illustration of their application is the *Case concerning the Gabčíkovo/Nagymaros Project (Hungary/Slovakia)*, where the International Court of Justice (ICJ) interpreted a bilateral treaty for the construction and operation of a hydroelectric dam in the light of subsequent developments in international law, particularly the emergence of the concept of sustainable development, observing that 'the Treaty is not static, and is open to adapt to emerging norms of international law'.[32] However, this approach was grounded in the evolutionary language of the treaty text itself, and thus on the face of it the process of evolutionary interpretation was not extended beyond the intention of the parties. In the later *Pulp Mills* case the ICJ emphasized that 'there are situations in which the parties' intent upon conclusion of the treaty was, or may be presumed to have been, to give the terms used or some of them a meaning or content capable of evolving, not one fixed once and for all, so as to make

---

[25] James Harrison, *Making the Law of the Sea* (Cambridge University Press 2011) 171.

[26] David Freestone and Alex G. Oude Elferink, 'Flexibility and Innovation in the Law of the Sea: Will the LOS Convention Amendment Procedures ever be used?' in Alex G. Oude Elferink (ed), *Stability and Change in the Law of the Sea: The Role of the LOS Convention* (Martinus Nijhoff 2005).

[27] See further Catherine Redgwell and Lavanya Rajamani, 'Energy Underground: what's international law got to do with it?' in Donald N. Zillman, Aileen McHarg, Lila Barrera-Hernandez, and Adrian Bradbrook (eds), *The Law of Energy Underground: Understanding New Developments in Subsurface Production, Transmission, and Storage* (Oxford University Press 2014) 101–123.

[28] A particularly striking example of this flexibility over time is the *Iron Rhine Arbitration*, PCA (2005) paras 58–59. So too is the extent to which modern environmental principles may be 'read into' the 1982 LOSC: see Robin Churchill, 'The LOSC regime for protection of the marine environment – fit for the twenty-first century?' in Rosemary Rayfuse (ed), *Research Handbook on International Marine Environmental Law* (Edward Elgar 2015) ch 1.

[29] 1969 Vienna Convention on the Law of Treaties (VCLT) (entered into force 27 January 1980) 1155 UNTS 331.

[30] Art 31(1); see generally Gerald Fitzmaurice, 'The Interpretation of Treaties' (1975) 45 *British Yearbook of International Law* 456.

[31] Art 31(3)(a)–(c).

[32] [1997] ICJ Rep 76–80. See also Iron Rhine Arbitration (n 28) para 80; *Pulp Mills on the River Uruguay (Argentina v Uruguay), Judgment,* [2010] ICJ Reports 14, para 205; and generally, Bjorge *Evolutionary Interpretation* (n 24).

allowance for, among other things, developments in international law.'[33] On that basis it interpreted broadly worded provisions of a river treaty concluded in 1975 to include an obligation of environmental impact assessment derived from current international law.[34] Ambulatory incorporation of the existing law, whatever it may be, thus enables treaty provisions to change and develop as the general law itself changes, without the need for any amendment.[35]

In addition to the ICJ, the World Trade Organization (WTO) Appellate Body has also given an evolutionary interpretation to certain terms in the 1947 General Agreement on Tariffs and Trade (GATT) Agreement, notably of the inherently dynamic term 'natural resources' in Article XX(g) GATT in the *Shrimp-Turtle*[36] and *Reformulated Gasoline*[37] cases. So too has the European Court of Human Rights (ECtHR) which provides one of the best-known illustrations of flexible treaty interpretation by a body authorized to interpret the treaty text. For example, unlike later Latin American and African regional instruments, the European Convention on Human Rights (ECHR)[38] does not contain any express provision relating to environmental rights. This has not prevented recognition by the ECtHR of indirect environmental rights through the interpretation of existing rights such as the right to private, home, and family life (e.g. *Lopez-Ostra v Spain*[39] and *Fadeyeva v Russia*[40]) in Article 8 ECHR.[41] In the context of the right to life, the ECtHR has held that States have not just a negative obligation of non-interference but a positive obligation to act to enforce, for instance, zoning legislation and emission limit requirements that could protect life,[42] and to provide information to protect against the risk even of natural disasters such as mudslides[43] and flash floods.[44]

Beyond the flexibility afforded by treaty interpretation, another aspect of treaty resilience may be afforded in treaty design, where the parties may expressly stipulate the consequences of emergency events. Ultimately this is a matter for States as 'masters of the treaty'. Thus, for example, *force majeure* may be stipulated to release parties from their obligations

---

[33] [2010] ICJ Reports 14, para 204, citing *Dispute Regarding Navigational and Related Rights*, [2009] ICJ Reports 213, para 64.

[34] See also *Iron Rhine* (n 28).

[35] As the ICJ points out in the *Oil Platforms* case, such treaty provisions are not intended to operate independently of general international law: [2003] ICJ Reports paras 40–41. See also *Gabčíkovo-Nagymaros* case (n 32) paras 140–141.

[36] WTO, *Report of the Appellate Body in United States—Import Prohibition of Certain Shrimp and Shrimp Products (Shrimp-Turtle)*, 20 May 1998, reproduced at (1998) 37 ILM 603, taking into account soft law instruments such as the 1992 Rio Declaration and Agenda 21, but also treaty instruments such as the 1992 Convention on Biological Diversity and LOSC. For discussion see Callum Musto and Catherine Redgwell, 'US-Import Prohibition of Certain Shrimp and Shrimp Products (1998)' in Eirik Bjorge and Cameron Miles (eds), *Landmark Cases in Public International Law* (Bloomsbury 2017).

[37] WTO, *Report of the Appellate Body in United States—Standards for Reformulated and Conventional Gasoline (Treatment of Imported Gasoline and Like Products of National Origin)*, 20 May 1996, reproduced at (1996) 35 ILM 603.

[38] European Convention for the Protection of Human Rights and Freedoms (entered into force 3 September 1953) 213 UNTS 221.

[39] ECtHR, Case 41/1993, 9 December 1994 (State has a duty to protect these rights through regulation); confirmed in *Guerra v Italy* (116/1996/735/932), 19 February 1998, para 58.

[40] ECtHR, Case 55723/00, 9 June 2005.

[41] See generally Daniel G. San Jose, *Environmental Protection and the European Convention on Human Rights*, Human Rights Files No 21 (Council of Europe 2005); and Richard Desgagne, 'Integrating Environmental Values into the European Convention on Human Rights' (1995) 89 AJIL 263.

[42] *Fadeyeva v Russia*, ECtHR Case 55723/00 (2005).

[43] *Budayeva v Russia*, ECtHR Case No 15339/02 (2008).

[44] *Kolyadenko v Russia*, ECtHR Case No 17423/05 (2012).

under prescribed conditions, such as under the 1996 Protocol to the London Convention.[45] Or, conversely, the treaty may provide for strict liability for damage even where caused by, inter alia, 'a grave natural disaster of an exceptional character', as is the case in the regional and global nuclear liability conventions.[46] In the absence of express stipulation, the residual rules of the VCLT[47] on vitiating factors will apply. However, these are seldom invoked, with practice and case law sparse.[48] International courts and tribunals will not lightly find a treaty terminated owing to frustrating or vitiating factors as the *Gabčíkovo -Nagymaros* case underscores.[49] This reflects the general tenor of the law of treaties, which is to promote stability and security of treaty relations.[50] This is not to say that it does not contain 'escape valves' in exceptional circumstances which, inter alia, allow the parties to terminate or suspend their treaty obligations, and the invocation of which might be expected to rise with increased risk of climate emergency impacts in particular. Although expressed in purely hypothetical terms at the time, in the ILC's preparatory work for what became the text of Article 61 VCLT it was pertinently observed that while 'easier to imagine than to find in practice' examples of supervening impossibility of treaty performance included 'the submergence of an island, the drying up of a river bed, [or] the destruction of a railway, plant, canal, lighthouse or other installations by an earthquake'.[51]

[45] See, for example, the 1996 Protocol to the London Convention (n 19) where derogation from the general prohibition on dumping, outside the stipulated treaty exceptions, is only permitted 'in cases of force majeure, or in any case which constitutes a danger to human life or a real threat to vessels, aircraft, platforms or other man-made structures at sea, if dumping or incineration at sea appears to be the only way of averting the threat and if there is every probability that the damage consequent upon such dumping or incineration at sea will be less than would otherwise occur' (Art 8(1)). See also the 1992 International Convention on Civil Liability for Oil Pollution Damage (n 18) where a shipowner that can demonstrate that pollution damage resulted from, inter alia, 'a natural phenomenon of an exceptional, inevitable and irresistible character' has no liability for such damage under the Convention (Art III).

[46] See the 1997 Protocol to Amend the 1963 Vienna Convention on Civil Liability for Nuclear Damage (1997) 36 ILM 1462 (entered into force 4 October 2003) Art IV.

[47] N 29, confirmed as reflecting customary international law in the *Gabčíkovo -Nagymaros* case (n 32). See in particular Art 61 (supervening impossibility of performance requiring that such impossibility must arise from 'the permanent disappearance or destruction of the object indispensable for the execution of the treaty') and Art 62 (fundamental change of circumstance, which likewise sets a high threshold, including the requirement that the circumstances existing at the time of conclusion of the treaty were an essential basis for consent; the change was unforeseen by the parties; and that 'the effect of the change is radically to transform the extent of obligations still to be performed under the treaty'). These find an echo in the law of State responsibility, where 'circumstances precluding wrongfulness' include *force majeure*, distress, necessity, and self-defence: see 2001 ILC Articles on State Responsibility *ILC Report* (2001) UNGAOR A/56/10, 43–365.

[48] See, generally, Mark E. Villiger, *Commentary on the 1969 Vienna Convention on the Law of Treaties* (Martinus Nijhoff 2009) 752–761 (Art 61), 762–781 (Art 62); Oliver Dörr and Kirsten Schmalenbach (eds), *Vienna Convention on the Law of Treaties: A Commentary* (2nd edn, Springer 2018) 1127–1142 (Art 61) and 1143–1182 (Art 62); and Malgosia Fitzmaurice, 'Exceptional Circumstances and Treaty Commitments') in Hollis (ed) (n 16) 595.

[49] N 32, paras 95 and 104; see also the *Fisheries Jurisdiction (United Kingdom/Iceland)* case, ICJ Reports 1973 18, paras 38 and 41.

[50] And as reflected in the fundamental principle *pacta sunt servanda*—that States must perform their obligations in good faith for all valid treaties in force: Fitzmaurice (n 52) 595; and see further Sotirios Lekkas and Antonios Tzanakopoulos, '*Pacta sunt servanda* versus Flexibility in the Suspension and Termination of Treaties' in Christian Tams et al (eds), *Research Handbook on the Law of Treaties* (Edward Elgar 2013) 312.

[51] Villiger (n 48) 756, citing the ILC Report 1966, *YBILC 1966* II 254, para 217. A contemporary example is the impact of climate-induced sea level rise, which imperils the very existence of small island developing States, as well as having consequences for delimitation of maritime zones and maritime boundary agreements. See e.g. the last report (2018) of the International Law Association's Committee on International Law and Sea-Level Rise available at <http://www.ila-hq.org/images/ILA/DraftReports/DraftReport_SeaLevelRise.pdf> accessed 11 August 2021; additionally, the topic was taken up by the ILC in 2019 with a 'first issues' paper produced in 2021 (A/CN.4/740 and Corr.1 and Add.1).

In addition to treaty law, soft law[52] can also help build resilience into the norm-creating process. While there is no rigorous and widely accepted definition of soft law,[53] at its most succinct it may simply be described as 'legally non-binding norms'[54] or, more expansively, as consisting 'of written instruments that spell out rules of conduct that are not intended to be legally binding, so that they are not subject to the law of treaties and do not generate the *opinio juris* required for them to be state practice contributing to custom'.[55] Since codes of conduct, standards, and guidelines[56] may well form the basis of national legislation, and/ or be transformed into binding international law through subsequent treaty negotiation or into customary international law as a result of State practice and *opinio juris* (that is to say, 'hardened'), the role of codes of conduct and guidelines as contributors to the international law-making process is potentially a highly significant one. Moreover, as we have seen, treaties may require that such soft law guidelines and standards are to be taken into account in their implementation. These instruments often provide the detailed rules or standards or best practice to be achieved by the parties in implementing their treaty obligations and are essential in giving hard content to the open-textured terms of framework treaties.[57] A good example is Article 60(3) LOSC and its implicit reference to the IMO Guidelines.[58]

Most striking is the ability of soft law to span the divide between inevitably more cumbersome and slow treaty amendment processes and the need to respond to emergency situations. Indeed, soft law may be 'instantly applicable' (at least on a voluntary basis) if States choose to make it so. Consider, for example, the strengthening of the peer review provisions of the Convention on Nuclear Safety (CNS)[59] following the Fukushima Daiichi disaster in 2011,[60] the process of treaty amendment considered to be too time-consuming. With the effectiveness of the CNS under scrutiny following the disaster,[61] an extraordinary meeting of the parties to the Convention, held in 2012 to consider the implications for the CNS, identified several key weaknesses including the non-binding peer review mechanism for national

---

[52] See further Christine Chinkin, 'The Challenge of Soft Law' (1989) 38 ICLQ 850; Dinah Shelton (ed), *Commitment and Compliance: The Role of Non-Binding Norms in the International Legal System* (Oxford University Press 2000); Catherine Redgwell, 'International Soft Law and Globalization' in Barry Barton, Lila K. Barrera-Hernandez, Alistair R. Lucas, and Anita Ronne (eds), *Regulating Energy and Natural Resources* (Oxford University Press 2006); and Alan Boyle, 'Soft Law in International-Law Making' in Evans (ed), *International Law* (4th edn, Oxford University Press 2018) .

[53] Dinah Shelton, 'International Law and "Relative Normativity" ' in Malcolm Evans (ed), *International Law* 159.

[54] Shelton (n 52) uses these synonymously in her introduction 'Law, Non-Law and the Problem of "Soft Law" '.

[55] David Harris and Sandesh Sivakumaran, *Cases and Materials on International Law* (8th edn, Sweet & Maxwell 2015) 55.

[56] Examples include the IMO Guidelines and Standards for the Removal of Offshore Installations and Structures on the Continental Shelf, and the IAEA revised 2003 Code of Conduct on the Safety and Security of Radioactive Sources, and supplementary Guidance on the Import and Export of Radioactive Sources.

[57] See e.g. Daniel Bodansky, 'Rules vs Standards in International Environmental Law' (2004) 98 Proceedings of the American Society of international Law 275.

[58] Art 60(3) LOSC requires States to take into account any generally accepted international standards (here, the Guidelines and Standards) established by the competent international organization (here, the IMO). Thus, whilst the Guidelines and Standards are not directly binding as such, the States parties to UNCLOS have this weak treaty obligation to 'take them into account'. On GAIRS, see further Redgwell IJMCL (2019).

[59] 1994 Convention on Nuclear Safety (entered into force 24 October 1996) (1994) 33 ILM 1518.

[60] Both Chernobyl and Fukushima Daiichi were classified as level 7 (major accident) at the top of the IAEA's International Nuclear Event Scale, which was adopted jointly with the OECD's Nuclear Energy Agency in 1990, though the release of radioactive material to the atmosphere caused by the Fukushima accident was only 10 per cent that of Chernobyl: Fukushima Nuclear Accident Update Log, 12 April 2011, available at <http://www.iaea.org> accessed 11 August 2021.

[61] See Selma Kus, 'International Nuclear Law in the 25 years between Chernobyl to Fukushima and Beyond' (2011) 87 Nuclear Law Bulletin 7.

reports submitted under the Convention. Procedural changes were instituted to strengthen peer review and transparency, which unlike treaty amendment may have immediate effect, with a working group established to consider further strengthening through formal amendment of the Convention.[62] While an 'Action Plan on Nuclear Safety' was adopted by the CNS Ministerial Conference and a comprehensive report on Fukushima was produced in 2014, ultimately no further treaty change occurred in terms of formal amendment of the CNS text.[63]

This illustrates an important role for institutions and bodies: the engine of dynamism and change is often found in interpretation by the bodies established under the treaty, from the Conference of the Parties (COP) to other subsidiary treaty bodies. The task of giving guidance on or amplifying the terms of treaties is performed most frequently by resolutions, recommendations, and decisions of international organizations and treaty bodies. The response by the parties to the CNS to the Fukushima-Daiichi nuclear incident is a good illustration of such dynamism. But it is important not to be too starry-eyed about the potential for rapid response to emergency situations and more long-term adjustments to the working practices and standards of the treaty regime. As the CNS example also illustrates, political will and consensus-building is essential, absent which there was no consensus behind amendment to the CNS requiring greater transparency and oversight of the operation of nuclear installations.

A further illustration of the interplay of treaty law and institutions is the IEA Governing Body's development of Coordinated Emergency Response Measures (CERM)[64] to respond to incidents below the treaty threshold for triggering the emergency sharing system (ESS)[65] of the IEA.[66] Indeed, the creation of the IEA was itself an 'emergency' response to the 1973/ 74 energy crisis and marked a shift from essentially unilateral responses to energy supply disruptions to a multilateral conception of and response to such disruption embedded in a binding treaty.[67] The parties, 'desiring to promote secure oil supplies on reasonable and equitable terms', undertake three principal obligations: oil stockpiling, demand restraint, and data exchange.[68] In practice, both oil stockpiling and demand restraint have become an essential part of the IEA's response to oil supply disruptions, even when the ESS as such has not been triggered. For example, both operated in response to the 1979 oil crisis.[69] A lighter

[62] For the outcome of the second extraordinary meeting of the parties to the Convention on Nuclear Safety, see <http://www-ns.iaea.org/conventions> accessed 11 August 2021.

[63] See further Gunther Handl, 'Transboundary Risks of Harm from Peaceful Nuclear Activities: The Evolving International Legal Regime' in Shunmugam Jayakumar, Tommy Koh, Robert Beckman, and Hao Duy Phan (eds), *Transboundary Pollution: Evolving Issues of International Law and Policy* (Edward Elgar 2015).

[64] Decision on Stocks and Supply Disruptions, 11 July 1984, IEA/GB(84)27, Item 2(a)(ii), Annex I and Appendices. In 1995, the IEA Governing Body formally endorsed more flexible measures, deciding that even where a risk to oil security passes the threshold trigger for application of the ESS (i.e. 7 per cent or higher supply restriction as required under Art 13) consideration would be given in the first instance to 'lighter measures than the oil sharing system'.

[65] The ESS comprises physical sharing of oil stocks which have been established and maintained (stockdraw), short term reduction of demand through demand restraint measures (demand restraint), and the gathering and transmission to the IEA of emergency oil data (data system).

[66] The Agreement on an International Energy Programme was signed by 16 States on 18 November 1974. For background see the two-volume treatment by a former legal adviser to the IEA, Richard Scott, *IEA: The First Twenty Years* (2 vols, 1994), with a 2003 supplement by his successor Craig Bamberger, available at <http://www.iea.org> accessed 11 August 2021.

[67] Ibid.

[68] IEP Agreement (n 66).

[69] See further Scott (n 66) 114–123.

touch CERM-like response has now been employed on three occasions, with coordinated stock releases during the 1991 Gulf War, in response to destruction caused by Hurricanes Katrina and Rita to US Gulf coast rigs, pipelines, and refineries in 2005, and in 2011 owing to prolonged disruption of oil supplies caused by civil war in Libya.[70]

III. 'Resilience' in the Face of What? Disasters in International Law

There is no 'one stop shop' with respect to disaster management and response in international law and no general multinational treaty on disaster law. Nonetheless, as revealed in the sectoral multinational and regional instruments already discussed in fields such as oil pollution casualties[71] and nuclear incidents, prevention and disaster response are already part of the fabric of substantive international law in some contexts.[72] To this may be added a number of regional and bilateral treaties and memoranda of understanding which address specific disaster management and response.[73]

'Protection of Persons in the Event of Disaster' has been one of the work topics of the International Law Commission (ILC) since 2007.[74] This followed from the UN International Decade for Natural Disaster Reduction (1990–1999) which emphasized prevention through disaster risk reduction.[75] In 2016, the ILC produced a set of Draft Articles on Protection of Persons in the Event of Disasters.[76] While their principal focus is on the human impact of disaster and disaster response,[77] this clearly includes the essential infrastructure upon

[70] See, for example, Governing Body Conclusion on the Gulf Situation, 11 January 1991, annexed to the Decision adopting the Coordinated Energy Emergency Response Contingency Plan, IEA/GB(91)1, Item 3 and Annex, para (c). The plan was activated, on 17 January 1991, with the launch of the air campaign against Iraq and terminated on 6 March 1991, less than one week after the cessation of hostilities (IEA/GB(91)19, Item 3).

[71] In addition to those instruments mentioned above, see also 1990 the International Convention on Oil Pollution Preparedness, Response and Cooperation (entered into force 13 May 1995) (1991) 30 *ILM* 735, Art 6 (establishing several measures to prepare for a response to an oil pollution incident); amended by a 2000 Protocol extending to Hazardous and Noxious Substances.

[72] See also, for example, the 1997 Convention on the Law of the Non-navigational Uses of International Watercourses (entered into force 4 October 2003) (1997) 36 *ILM* 1462, which requires watercourse States to 'take all appropriate measures to prevent or mitigate conditions related to an international watercourse that may be harmful to other watercourse States, whether resulting from natural causes or human conduct, such as flood or ice conditions, water-borne diseases, siltation, erosion, salt-water intrusion, drought or desertification'. In addition, watercourse States are to notify other watercourse States of an emergency and take all practicable measures to prevent, mitigate and eliminate the harmful effects (Art 28(2)(3)). 'Emergency' is defined as a 'situation that causes, or poses an imminent threat of causing, serious harm to watercourse States or other States and that results suddenly from natural causes, such as floods, the breaking up of ice, landslides or earthquakes, or from human conduct, such as industrial accidents' (Art 28(1)).

[73] For a survey, see 'Protection of persons in the event of disasters', Memorandum by the ILC Secretariat (2007) A/CN.4/590, Add 2.

[74] First identified in the Commission's long-term programme of work in 2006, the topic was taken up in 2007, with Draft Articles adopted by the ILC at its sixty-eighth session, in 2016, and submitted to the General Assembly as a part of the Commission's report covering the work of that session (A/71/10).

[75] UN General Assembly resolution 44/236 of 22 December 1989, followed by repeated UNGA exhortations to States to adopt disaster reduction policies and strategies. See e.g. UNGA resolutions 45/185 of 21 December 1990 and 56/195 of 21 December 2001.

[76] See ILC, Draft Articles on the Protection of Persons in the Event of Disaster, with commentaries, *Yearbook of the International Law Commission*, 2016 (A/71/10), vol II, Part Two.

[77] As the Commentary to Draft Art 1 ('The present draft articles apply to the protection of persons in the event of disasters.') makes clear, 'The draft articles cover, *ratione materiae*, the rights and obligations of States affected by a disaster in respect of persons present in their territory (irrespective of nationality) or in territory under their jurisdiction or control, and the rights and obligations of third States and intergovernmental organizations and non-governmental organizations and other entities in a position to cooperate, particularly in the provision of disaster relief assistance as well as in the reduction of disaster risk.' Draft Articles (n 76) Art 1, Commentary para 2.

which human life depends and the principles enunciated are of broad application in the disaster context.

The Draft Articles address both human-made and natural disasters.[78] 'Disaster' is defined as 'a calamitous event or series of events resulting in widespread loss of life, great human suffering and distress, mass displacement, or large-scale material or environmental damage, thereby seriously disrupting the functioning of society'.[79] In the accompanying Commentary, two important qualifications are made. The first acknowledges the complex and often inter-related character of 'natural' and 'human-made' events, while the second emphasizes that included within the definition of disaster are sudden onset events such as earthquake or tsunami; slow onset events such as drought or sea-level rise; and frequent small-scale events such as floods or landslides.[80] They also recognize that '[t]he incidence of a "disaster" is a function of the risk process, namely the degree of exposure of people, infrastructure and economic activity to a "hazard",[81] such as an earthquake or hurricane, as well as the vulnerability[82] of those exposed to the hazard.'[83]

Two further features of the Draft Articles stand out for present purposes. The first is the strong preventive flavour of the provisions, and of draft Article 9 in particular. It recognizes the obligation to reduce the risk of disasters through a number of actions to be taken by States—including with the assistance of the international community 'where appropriate and necessary'[84]—ranging from 'putting into place the appropriate policy and legal framework, including through the establishment of sustainable institutional structures, to undertaking risk assessments, developing public awareness campaigns, implementing technical and physical risk mitigation programmes and promoting the sharing of information and knowledge.'[85] The overarching purpose of disaster risk reduction is to minimize vulnerabilities and disaster risks 'in order to avoid (prevention) or to limit (mitigation and preparedness) the adverse impacts of hazards, and facilitate sustainable development'.[86]

The second, related, feature of the Draft Articles is the extent to which they identify core principles underpinning disaster response and resilience. These include 'humanity, neutrality, impartiality, non-discrimination, cooperation, sovereignty and non-intervention, and prevention, mitigation, and preparedness.'[87] These are not novel but rather are found in a wide range of existing treaty provisions and reflected to a large extent in customary

---

[78] See e.g. the Preamble, 'Considering the frequency and severity of natural and human-made disasters and their short-term and long-term damaging impact'.

[79] Art 3(a).

[80] Draft Articles (n 76), Art 3(a) Commentary, para 4.

[81] The UN International Strategy for Disaster Reduction (ISDR) in 2004 defined a hazard as being 'a potentially damaging physical event, phenomenon or human activity that may cause the loss of life or injury, property damage, social and economic disruption or environmental degradation. Hazards can include latent conditions that may represent future threats and can have different origins: natural (geological, hydrometeorological and biological) or induced by human processes (environmental degradation and technological hazards)'. *Living with risk: a global review of disaster reduction initiatives* (ISDR 2004, vol I) 16.

[82] Vulnerability is defined as '[t]he conditions determined by physical, social, economic, and environmental factors or processes, which increase the susceptibility of a community to the impact of hazards': *Living with risk* (n x) 16.

[83] 'Protection of persons in the event of disasters', Memorandum by the ILC Secretariat (2007) A/CN.4/590, 8.

[84] See also the careful approach of the 1986 Vienna Convention on Assistance in the Case of a Nuclear Accident or Radiological Emergency (n 3) which imposes no obligation to request, nor any obligation to receive, assistance without consent: see further Boyle and Redgwell (n 14) 830.

[85] ILC Commentary (n 75), pp 27–28.

[86] See ISDR, *Guidelines: National Platforms for Disaster Risk Reduction* (ISDR 2007) 2.

[87] 'Protection of persons in the event of disasters' (n 82) 1.

international law. To take one example, the well-known principle of prevention[88] entails the duty to be proactive in managing risk and is a reflection of due diligence requiring the adoption of appropriate legislation. Putting in place the necessary institutional and policy frameworks to undertake disaster prevention and mitigation activities is itself a preventive measure and is 'particularly relevant in relation to vulnerable communities where there exists a high exposure to the risk of harm by hazards, such as earthquakes, volcanoes and extreme weather phenomena.'[89]

IV. Conclusion

This chapter considered two aspects of building resilience from the top down. First, it argued that the extent to which binding international norms and principles can dynamically change and evolve, especially when confronted by disrupting events, is a measure of their resilience. The focus was principally on treaty law, given the important normative role treaties perform in the energy and related fields. Their flexibility and capacity to adapt over time in response to economic, technical, and environmental changes occurs in a variety of ways, ranging from more formal and cumbersome treaty amendment to more nimble methods for incorporation of external norms (e.g. GAIRS under the LOSC) and evolutive interpretation of treaty provisions, (e.g. as in the *Gabčíkovo -Nagymaros* case). It was also pointed out that some areas of international law such as IDL and some institutions such as the IEA may be viewed as hard-wired to respond to catastrophic change and emergencies, with treaty bodies and institutions playing a catalytic role in responding to disruption.

But is this building resilience from 'the top down'? The examples considered here rely not only on international consensus and cooperation for norm creation and application, but crucially the effectiveness of these responses turns on national implementation. This is true whether it is building a preventive disaster risk management response or implementing the CNS or CLC and Fund Convention requirements. To be sure, there is evidence of the flexibility of international norms and standards both in their form (hard, soft, or a combination thereof) and content (e.g. evolutive interpretation of treaty provisions; dynamic role of treaty bodies) and in their capacity to anticipate and to respond to disrupting events. However, this is not universally the case and is particularly dependent on political will and the capacity to implement agreed norms. As we saw in the example of the CNS and the response to the Fukushima-Daiichi nuclear incident, while decisions of treaty bodies can bridge an immediate gap—here, in addressing (some of) the inadequacies of the nuclear safety regime—further treaty amendment has foundered on lack of consensus grounded, as is so often the case, in national sovereignty and 'institutional over-reach' concerns.[90]

Nor is there a general international agreement on IDL which might be viewed as a starting point, though not a 'one stop shop', for building resilience as a response to fragility

---

[88] See also the ILC's 2001 Draft Articles on Prevention of Transboundary Harm From Hazardous Activities, *Yearbook of the International Law Commission*, 2001, vol II, Part two, para 97, Draft Art 3. The principle has been recognized in a number of multilateral treaties concerning the protection of the environment, the law of the sea, nuclear accidents, space objects, international watercourses, management of hazardous wastes and prevention of marine pollution: see further Leslie-Anne Duvic-Paoli, *The Prevention Principle in International Environmental Law* (Cambridge University Press 2018).

[89] ILC Commentary (n 75) n 83.

[90] See further Handl (n 63).

in the face of disruption. The ILC's Draft Articles offer some general guidance, especially in distilling principles from existing treaty and customary international law which apply in the disaster context. The recognition that disaster comes in many forms—sudden, slow, and repetitive onsets—and that the necessary institutional and policy frameworks must be put in place to undertake disaster prevention and mitigation activities is well-understood. Lamentably this is more in theory than in practice.[91]

---

[91] As underscored by the recent Intergovernmental Panel on Climate Change report on the climate emergency: Reports—IPCC, <https://www.un.org/climatechange/reports> accessed 11 August 2021.

4

Planning for Resilience

Resilience as a Criterion in Energy, Climate, Natural Resources, and Spatial Planning Law

Catherine Banet

I. Introduction

The need to integrate and monitor different requirements related to energy and climate change has resulted in the adoption of new coordination tools. Among them, planning is experiencing a revival, and particularly the use of 'plans' as distinctive legal instruments. At the international, state and local levels, this is taking the form of so-called 'energy and climate plans'. Even the Paris Agreement is making use of planning through the Nationally Determined Contributions (NDCs). Because global concerns need local implementation measures, the energy and climate plans aim to ensure that energy and climate measures are realized, thereby serving as monitoring tools. They also serve as coordination and integration tools, by merging the different planning processes into one plan. Two additional considerations should be added. First, the energy and climate plans come in addition to other existing plans within spatial and natural resources management, raising the question of interaction and possibly coordination with those planning processes too. Secondly, the increasing occurrence and impacts of disruptive nature-based events affecting energy and ecosystems call for a more transversal application of the objective of resilience across planning processes.

This chapter analyses the extent to which resilience is defined as a criterion in relevant planning processes and how a more coordinated and integrated approach in planning law could be developed to ensure that it is applied in a more consistent manner.

The chapter starts by observing the resurgence of planning as a legal tool to monitor the energy and ecological transition (Section II). It identifies four relevant planning processes related to energy, climate, spatial, and natural resources management. Then, it analyses the extent to which resilience to disruptive nature-based events is defined as an objective or a criterion in the legislation applying to these four planning processes (Section III). Because the relevant plans will need to comply with strategic environmental assessment (SEA) requirements, the chapter examines how SEA legislation could support the integration and consistent application of resilience within the plans. Finally, it analyses how the resilience criterion could be applied in a more consistent manner throughout the different planning processes, both vertically, down the planning documentation hierarchy, and horizontally, across the different planning processes. Beyond coordination requirements, the chapter questions the need for a more integrated approach to planning processes to pursue social-ecological resilience (Section IV).

Catherine Banet, *Planning for Resilience* In: *Resilience in Energy, Infrastructure, and Natural Resources Law.* Edited by: Catherine Banet, Hanri Mostert, LeRoy Paddock, Milton Fernando Montoya, and Íñigo del Guayo, Oxford University Press. © Catherine Banet 2022. DOI: 10.1093/oso/9780192864574.003.0004

The chapter aims to make a theoretical contribution to the integration of resilience thinking into planning law. Methodologically, it is based on the interpretation of planning legislation from the European Union (EU), selected EU Member States and non-EU countries, such as Norway[1] and the United States. It primarily follows a public and administrative law approach, looking at international, EU, and national planning requirements. The chapter identifies good practices and provides recommendations for improving the legal framework.

II. The Revival of Planning as a Legal Mechanism in Monitoring the Energy and Ecological Transition

Planning theorists define planning as 'a continuous process which involves decisions about alternative ways of using available resources with the aim of achieving some particular goals in future'.[2] Planning is not an end in itself. It is a purposeful action. It is both a means and a process to promote development.[3] According to James Galbraith, planning, 'when properly conceived, deals with the use of today's resources to meet tomorrow's needs'.[4] This stresses a development perspective which is common to both planning and resilience thinking.

A more laconic definition of planning is 'the action of organising according to plans',[5] where *plans* are strategic documents. Planning documents can have various names (e.g. strategy, programme, plan) and forms (e.g. text, map). They usually find their legal basis in the legislation (*planning requirement*), but have varying legal value. Legal rules on planning can have both a substantive and a procedural nature. This chapter focuses on plans as standalone strategic documents adopted by a legislative body, a government agency, or local public authorities. Their implementation is usually supported by a planning documentation hierarchy. The plan forms the legal basis for other plans at the lower decision-making level and/or for granting permits. It should be distinguished from the *planning process*, which usually consists of the following phases: risk assessment, solution identification, choice of priority actions and mitigation measures, adoption, and implementation.[6] The plan can be both the starting point of a planning process and one of its results.

Different planning processes will be relevant to ensure resilience of the energy and ecological systems to extreme nature-based events, but their legal framework varies greatly. This section starts by identifying the relevant planning requirements (A). Then, it analyses how the integration of resilience thinking influences planning legislation (B), and how planning is increasingly used as a legal tool to monitor the energy and ecological transition (C).

---

[1] Norway is not a member of the EU but implements EU internal market legislation through the European Economic Area Agreement.

[2] D. Conyers and P. Hills, *An introduction to development planning in the third world* (Wiley 1984) 62.

[3] A. Faludi (ed), *A Reader in Planning Theory* (1973) Part 1.

[4] J. Galbraith, *The Predator State* (Free Press Publishers 2008), 33, 165.

[5] Dictionnaire de l'Académie Française, 9th edn.

[6] K. Anderson et al 'Energy Resilience Assessment Methodology' (2019) 2 National Renewable Energy Laboratory (NREL).

A. Relevant planning requirements

Four types of planning requirements are deemed relevant to the analysis, i.e. in relation to: energy (1), climate (2), spatial (3), and natural resources management (4).

1. Energy planning

Energy planning occurs both at the energy system (a) and the energy infrastructure levels (b).

a) Energy system planning

Energy planning is the process of designing and implementing policies regarding the development of the energy system in all its components (generation, storage, conversion, transport, and consumption). It can be undertaken at a local, national, or regional level. Energy planning can be short-, mid-, or long-term, where long-term corresponds on average to 30 years[7] and mid-term to 10 years.[8] Different timeframes enable plan users to adjust to new targets and circumstances, manage uncertainties (access to natural resources, technologies, prices, policies, demand, natural and political risks), and make energy planning a dynamic exercise. Energy planning processes are heavily influenced by *energy modelling*. Energy modelling involves different disciplines, among them computer engineering, physics, and economics. Governments and operators use different types of energy modelling tools[9] as the basis for making decisions on energy system developments.

While energy modelling is often the basis for energy planning policies and decisions, the need arises quickly to clarify processes, objectives, responsibilities, and scope through legislation. Historically, countries have developed their national energy planning framework differently, in terms of both the legally binding nature of the plans (from a simple guidance document to a binding legal framework) and the content (from a few general objectives and targets to full programming law). The examples of comprehensive legal frameworks on energy planning are rare, however, in particular at the national energy system level. Recently, long-term energy planning has become a more common tool supported by specific legislative requirements that may contribute to spreading good practices and harmonization.

Another preliminary observation should be made as to the effect of the liberalization of energy markets on energy planning processes. The intended consequence of liberalization was to split former incumbents into different entities and to let new competitors enter competitive market segments (while natural monopolies must be regulated). Under pre-liberalization models, energy planning was conducted internally, within companies, and in addition often combined electricity, gas, and heat in their portfolio. The multiplication of market actors, as part of the liberalization reform, has created new challenges for energy

---

[7] Regulation (EU) 2018/1999 of 11 December 2018 on the Governance of the Energy Union requires Member States to prepare and submit a 'Long Term Strategy' (Art 15) with a 30-year perspective, which will supplement the Union's Long Term Strategy for greenhouse gas emissions reduction (Annex IV).

[8] The NECPs elaborated by the Member States cover a 10-year period.

[9] Some of the most used energy models are: Wien Automatic System Planning (WASP); Market Allocation Model (MARKAL); Long Range Energy Alternatives Planning System (LEAP); Prospective Outlook on Long-term Energy Systems (POLES); National Energy Modeling System (NEMS); Price-Induced Market Equilibrium System (PRIMES), Model of Energy Supply Strategy Alternatives and their General Environmental Impacts (MESSAGE). H.-K. Ringkjøb et al, 'A Review of Modelling Tools for Energy and Electricity Systems with Large Shares of Variable Renewables' (2018) 96 Renewable and Sustainable Energy Reviews 440–459, 441–442.

system planning. In many jurisdictions, generation and transport infrastructure planning are conducted individually and separately from each other. This calls for new forms of co-ordination among a larger number of actors.[10]

In the following, examples of legislative frameworks on energy system planning are given. At the EU level, the Electricity Directive (EU) 2019/944[11] and Electricity Regulation (EU) 2019/943[12] contain no reference to energy system planning, and planning require-ments concentrate only on network development. The Gas Directive 2009/73/EC does refer to and even defines 'long-term planning' with the specific meaning of planning supply and transport capacity of natural gas undertakings on a long-term basis, for the purpose of meeting demand, diversification of sources, and security of supply to customers.[13] Member States may also introduce long-term planning as part of the public service obligations that they can impose on gas undertakings, in relation to security of supply, energy efficiency/demand-side management, and for the fulfilment of environmental goals including renew-able energy sources.[14] Although the provision relates to the transport system, it is sufficiently broadly worded to include resilience considerations in long-term planning. However, there is no general, explicit planning obligation for the gas system in the Directive. Finally, the Energy Efficiency Directive (EU) 2018/2002 does refer to 'decisions relating to planning the energy system' in which energy efficiency should be taken into account,[15] but does not con-tain any further provisions on planning.

By contrast, Regulation (EU) 2018/1999 on the Governance of the Energy Union (Governance Regulation) contains several references to the task of 'energy planning', de-fines procedures for the elaboration of the integrated National Energy and Climate Plans (NECPs), and stresses the need for regional cooperation in planning.[16] The NECPs are one of the constitutive elements of the so-called 'governance mechanism'. They cover ten-year periods, provide an overview of the current energy system in each Member State and the list of national objectives, targets, and implementing measures for all the five dimensions of the Energy Union.[17] Even though the Governance Regulation does not impose any general energy planning requirement on Member States, it does define a procedural obligation to describe the measures adopted and planned to meet the different separate targets defined in secondary EU law (i.e. GHG emissions reductions, renewable energy, energy efficiency, and electricity interconnection) and the objectives of the Energy Union. This procedural obligation to transcribe all national measures and the obligation to coordinate the plans re-gionally has the indirect effect of starting a planning process both at Member State level and regional level among neighbouring Member States. This is the same dynamic as the one ob-served under the Paris Agreement, where the procedural obligation to put forward NDCs leads indirectly to starting a climate planning process.

---

[10]   This has been described as 'de-integration' of energy planning. See A. Weber et al, 'Long-term Power System Planning in the Context of Changing Policy Objectives' (2013) Berlin University of Technology 3.

[11]   Directive (EU) 2019/944 of 5 June 2019 on common rules for the internal market for electricity and amending Directive 2012/27/EU (Electricity Directive).

[12]   Regulation (EU) 2019/943 of 5 June 2019 on the internal market for electricity (Electricity Regulation).

[13]   Directive 2009/73/EC of 13 July 2009 concerning common rules for the internal market in natural gas, as amended, Art 2(30) (Gas Directive).

[14]   Ibid, Art 3.2.

[15]   Directive (EU) 2018/2002 of 11 December 2018 amending Directive 2012/27/EU on energy efficiency.

[16]   Annex I-1.4.

[17]   Member States must complete and submit the mandatory template provided in Annex I to the Regulation, pursuant to Art 3.1 of the Governance Regulation.

The French legislation offers an example of detailed energy planning requirements, set forth in the legislation at national level, and supported by a series of subsequent local planning instruments. The Multiannual Programme for Energy (*Programmation Pluriannuelle de l'Energie*, PPE) defines concrete implementation measures and quantitative targets designed to reach the national energy policy objectives defined in Articles L. 100-1, L. 100-2 and L. 100-4 of the Energy Code. The adoption of the PPE is a requirement introduced by the 2015 Energy Transition Law for Green Growth.[18] The PPE is set by decree, covers a five-year period and serves as a steering document, defining targets and trajectories. It covers all energy forms and therefore takes a holistic approach to energy system planning.

The Norwegian legislation offers another example of energy planning requirements, combining energy system and grid development planning. In contrast to the French approach, energy planning requirements are primarily imposed on licensees. Onshore, the Energy Act[19] provides the legal basis for energy planning and requires anyone having a licence to operate electrical and district heating facilities to take part in energy planning. The implementing Energy Act Regulations detail the scope of the energy plans that must include electricity production, transmission, distribution, and use.[20] Further, the licensees are obliged to coordinate their individual energy plans among themselves, in particular if they pertain to the same planning area. Finally, the Norwegian Water Resources and Energy Directorate may require the same licensees to elaborate long-term energy plans. It follows that the Norwegian legislation defines energy planning obligations primarily on licensees, with a duty to cooperate and coordinate their energy plans. The licensees also have a duty to provide information on relevant energy supply to municipalities for the purpose of elaborating local climate and energy plans.[21] In addition to those general energy planning requirements, separate legislation (Regulations on Energy Studies) provides for the elaboration by licensees of 'electricity reports' that, although considering the whole energy system, focus on grid development.

In liberalized markets, energy models and plans have been elaborated separately for the different energy carriers and the different chain segments (generation, infrastructure, supply). The upcoming *energy system integration*[22] calls for a more holistic approach, i.e. a 'system approach', to energy system planning. Several regulatory incentives already exist in the legislation. The EU Governance Regulation calls for moving towards a system approach in energy planning,[23] and makes direct reference to it under the security of supply-dimension of the Energy Union.[24] A second reference is made in the draft revised Regulation on guidelines for trans-European energy infrastructure (TEN-E), where ENTSOs must follow an 'energy-system wide' approach when elaborating their methodologies for cost-benefit analysis to projects of common interest and projects of mutual interest.[25] While those

---

[18] Codified in Art L. 141–1 of the Energy Code.

[19] Act relating to the generation, conversion, transmission, trading, distribution and use of energy (Energy Act), Norway, 1990, ch 7.

[20] Regulations No. 959 concerning the generation, conversion, transmission, trading, distribution, and use of energy (Energy Act Regulations), Section 7.1.

[21] Regulations on Energy Studies, Section 3.

[22] Energy system integration refers to the planning and operating of the energy system 'as a whole', across multiple energy carriers, infrastructures, and consumption sectors.

[23] Governance Regulation, Recitals (3), (23), (25), (39), Art 4.

[24] Ibid, Art 8.2(a).

[25] Council of the EU, Proposal for a Regulation on guidelines for trans-European energy infrastructure and repealing Regulation (EU) No 347/2013, General Approach of 11 June 2021, Draft Art 11.1.

provisions offer an opportunity to promote *integrated energy system planning*, the requirements remain quite general and indirect.

b) Energy infrastructure planning

Energy infrastructure planning relates to the planning of transport network development.
In contrast to energy system planning, it has been regulated for a long time in legislation
and in great detail.

The common approach is to define planning obligations on infrastructure operators.
Under EU law, transmission system operators (TSOs) and distribution system operators
(DSOs) for electricity are required to elaborate network development plans. At least every
two years, TSOs must submit to the regulatory authority a ten-year network development
plan based on existing and forecast supply and demand after having consulted relevant
stakeholders.[26] Network development plans must also be introduced for distribution systems, and DSOs must publish a plan at least every two years.[27] At EU level, the European
TSOs for Electricity (ENTSO-E) are required to elaborate a ten-year network development
plan (TYNDP), which is a pan-European electricity infrastructure development plan of
non-legally binding nature.[28] The newly established EU DSO entity must 'promote' the coordination of distribution networks planning with the transmission network planning.[29]
Similar planning obligations apply to gas TSOs[30] and the European TSOs for Gas (ENTSO-
G) as to the TYNDP.[31] For both electricity and gas, 'network codes' have been adopted, with
relevance to the planning of transmission and distribution networks, with the legal basis in
the Electricity and Gas Regulations.[32]

Looking ahead and offshore, in the context of its Offshore Renewable Energy (ORE)
strategy and based on high ambitions within offshore wind, the European Commission has
announced a 'new approach to infrastructure planning', insisting on the need for a 'more
rational grid planning' in terms of hybrid projects and 'integrated regional grid planning'
at sea basin level.[33] As a first step, the revision of the TEN-E Regulation foresees reinforced
cooperation around grid planning within the listed priority offshore grid corridors.[34]

2. Climate governance planning

Planning has more recently entered the climate governance domain, with an increasingly
more important role in climate legislation at the international, national, and local levels.
Climate planning pursues mainly two purposes.

The first purpose of defining planning requirements in climate legislation is to establish
an *implementation* tool to reach climate objectives based on a list of targets, measures, and
trajectories. It also contributes to increasing transparency, accountability, and investment
confidence. At the international level, under the UNFCCC regime, Article 4.2 of the Paris

---

[26] Electricity Directive, Art 51.1.
[27] Ibid, Recital (61), Art 32.3.
[28] Ibid, Art 51.1. Electricity Regulation, Art 30.1(b).
[29] Electricity Regulation, Art 55.1(a).
[30] Gas Directive, Art 22.1.
[31] Electricity Regulation, Art 8.3(b)
[32] Ibid, Art 59. Gas Regulation, Art 6.
[33] European Commission, An EU Strategy to harness the potential of offshore renewable energy for a climate neutral future, COM(2020)741 final, 19.11.2020, 12–13.
[34] Draft revised TEN-E Regulation, Art 14 and Annex I.2 (Priority Offshore Grid Corridors).

Agreement requires Parties to 'prepare, communicate and maintain successive nationally determined contributions' (NDCs) that they intend to achieve. This procedural requirement to put forward the NDC, i.e. a national climate plan, is supplemented by the obligation to take the necessary domestic mitigation measures to achieve it. Parties are also expected to put forward long-term low GHG emission development strategies (LEDS) for 2050.[35] The same logic applies at the EU level, where Member States must develop and communicate a NECP that describes the national objectives, targets, and measures falling under the decarbonization dimension of the Energy Union. Member States are required to submit Long-Term Strategies (LTSs) that are to serve as a basis for the LEDS. Those national plans are usually supplemented by local climate plans, at the regional and/or city level, often with a cross-sectoral approach. Local authorities are here driven by their competence in urban planning. For example, in France, the regional and local Climate-Air-Energy Plans (*Schéma Régional du Climat, de l'Air et de l'Energie*, SRCAEs; *Plans climat-air-energie territoriaux*, PCAET) seek to guide climate and energy policy in the French regions and inter-municipal entities through 2020–2050.

The second purpose behind climate planning requirements relates to *adaptation*. Both mitigation and adaptation measures are encompassed by climate plans, but specific planning requirements are often needed to address adaptation. Response to adaptation often starts locally, notably in cities, and local-level adaptation planning has been made mandatory in many countries. Those local planning efforts have been strengthened by international requirements. The Paris Agreement requires Parties to engage in adaptation planning processes, including the adoption of national adaptation plans.[36] At EU level, the Energy Union governance mechanism strengthens the reporting requirements on adaptation planning, notably to facilitate reporting requirements under the Paris Agreement.[37] Meanwhile, in the new EU Strategy on Adaptation to Climate Change, the European Commission comments on the shortcomings of adaptation planning requirements. Progress in adaptation planning has remained low, and there is a need to go beyond planning and start rolling out adaptation solutions.[38]

3. Spatial planning

Spatial planning is an instrument of long-term space governance. It relies on a series of management and legal tools traditionally distinguished by the literature according to their strategic or regulatory nature.[39] *Strategic planning tools* refer to non-binding strategies and guidelines for spatial development. *Regulatory planning tools* are rules enshrined in law or binding agreements, project approval decisions like permits, or spatial delineation (zoning) for uses and activities. The *regulatory function* of spatial planning serves the need for the competent planning authority to give approval for diverse activities and to set development commitments, following a common trajectory. Indeed, spatial planning has a strong *developmental dimension*, aiming at territorial cohesion and accessibility, the development

---

[35] Paris Agreement, Art 4.19. By end of 2020, 28 Parties communicated their LEDS, as encouraged by COP Decision 1/CP 21, para 35.

[36] Paris Agreement, Art 7.9.

[37] Governance Regulation, Art 19.1 and Annex VIII.

[38] European Commission, 'Forging a climate-resilient Europe – the new EU Strategy on Adaptation to Climate Change', COM(2021)82 final, 24.2.2021, 12.

[39] United Nations Economic Commission for Europe (UNECE), 'Spatial Planning – Key Instrument for Development and Effective Governance', 2008.

of urban functions and industrial activities, the protection of natural resources, and the prevention of natural disasters. To do so, it addresses interactions between sometimes conflicting activities and interests. Because it is essentially a public sector activity, spatial planning will usually be seen as pertaining to public/administrative law.

Spatial planning is a framework concept with sub-areas covering specific geographic areas (e.g. city, maritime, and coastal zone) or activities (e.g. land-use, landscape, housing, or transport). It applies both onshore and offshore, where the interaction between onshore and offshore ecosystems and activities—and therefore planning tools—needs to be assessed. Integrated coastal zone management is an example of how to promote sustainable management through cooperation and integrated planning. At regional level, cross-border cooperation in planning is often rendered mandatory.

4. Natural resources planning

Natural resources planning is a resource management instrument for planning the work with and use of renewable and non-renewable natural resources such as forests, soils (including agricultural lands), minerals, water, and wildlife. As with spatial planning, it aims at reaching a balance between often competing activities and considerations. The balance between the utilization of resources and the protection of natural ecosystems is a central concern. Good natural resources planning will limit the impacts of extreme nature-based events and support resilience.

Natural resources planning involves the development of a detailed plan for managing natural resources within a particular area or project site. Natural resources plans can be understood as a framework instrument (Resource Management Plan) with sub-areas of planning covering either *specific geographic ecosystem*, like rivers or wetlands, or *specific resources*, like forest, wildlife, waste, or water. It occurs at the local, national, and international levels. It takes into account ecosystems and habitats, and the scope of planning instruments can therefore be limited to a specific area such as coastal resources planning. The management through planning of some natural resources such as water courses often has strong cross-border implications and requires international cooperation.

B. Revising planning theory and planning law in the light of resilience: resilience planning

Social-ecological resilience has its origins in systems ecology in the 1970s[40] and has been a research topic of increasing interest for planning theory since the 2000s. Consequently, the *planning theory* literature has proposed giving a stronger role to social-ecological resilience within the field.[41] In contrast, there has been little research so far on the integration of social-ecological resilience into the legal field in general[42] and planning law in particular.

One key argument promoted by organizations working on 'resilience' (like the Stockholm Resilience Institute)[43] is that humans and nature are strongly coupled to the point that they

[40] C.S. Holling, 'Resilience and Stability of Ecological Systems' (1973) 4 Annual Review of Ecology and Systematics 1–23. See Bankes et al, Chapter 2 of this book.
[41] C. Wilkinson, 'Social-Ecological Resilience: Insights and Issues for Planning Theory' (2012) 11(2) Planning Theory 148–169.
[42] For an exception, see B. Bohman, *Legal Design for Social-Ecological Resilience* (Cambridge 2021).
[43] <https://www.stockholmresilience.org> accessed 10 September 2021.

should be conceived as one *social-ecological system*. Resilience is therefore an attempt to create a new understanding of how humans and nature interact, adapt, and impact each other amid change. Resilience thinking has even been proposed as an alternative to conventional natural resource management. Awareness about the importance of the 'water-food-energy-climate nexus' pertains to the same effort.[44] This argues for the integration of resilience considerations early in the planning process and in an integrated manner across the different parallel planning processes.

This also led to the affirmation of 'resilience planning' as a new methodological approach. Resilience planning is the practical application of resilience thinking to strategic planning.[45] It involves the identification of, for example, urban vulnerabilities and the development of adaptive capacities appropriate to each of those vulnerabilities, leading in that case to 'urban resilience'.[46] Successful implementation increases the level of resilience. Some planning practitioners in Australia have applied this approach since the early 2000s, using resilience planning as a general objective or steering criterion along all stages of the planning process.[47] Resilience planning also developed quickly in Asian-Pacific countries as a response to extreme natural disasters.[48] It was theorized in the Resilience Planning Framework, also called 'the Clouds heuristic'.[49]

National legislators and the legal scholars have traditionally taken a more siloed approach to planning law. Planning law is rarely defined as a separate legal discipline but encompasses a number of related practice areas, predominantly urban and land planning law and building or construction law. In that context, planning law means any applicable law which regulates planning processes and decisions, zoning and authorization of development works, or use of land. Environmental law has been increasingly using planning as a regulatory tool for preserving environmental ecosystems. Recently, as seen above, planning has been promoted in energy law, starting with infrastructure development.

Since the 1990s, many countries have engaged in reforming their planning legislation to improve the elaboration and operation of their planning systems. Sometimes, this move has been motivated by international obligations, such as the Paris Agreement and the EU legislation, with the subsequent adoption of adaptation plans or climate and energy plans, as reviewed above. Another dynamic has been to move away from the focus of planning based on physical land-use regulation to the 'integrative spatial planning approach'.[50]

This chapter argues that a new dynamic is currently taking place, where the criterion of resilience is progressively gaining acknowledgment in the legislation in order to develop integrated planning systems. This influences the manner in which planning law is being harmonized across practice areas, the degree of integration of the different planning procedures, and the coordination process among planning authorities.

---

[44] S. Asadi and B. Mohammadi-Ivatloo (eds), *Food-Energy-Water Nexus Resilience and Sustainable Development* (Springer 2020).

[45] A. Sellberg et al, 'From Resilience Thinking to Resilience Planning: Lessons from practice' (2018) 217 Journal of Environmental Management 906–918.

[46] A. Eraydin and T. Taşan-Kok, *Resilience Thinking in Urban Planning*, (Springer 2013).

[47] A. Sellberg et al (n 45).

[48] E.g, World Bank, 'Building Indonesia's Resilience to Disaster', 2016.

[49] M. Mitchell et al, 'Applying Resilience Thinking to Natural Resource Management Through a "Planning-by-Doing" Framework' (2014) 27 Society & Natural Resources 299–314.

[50] UNECE (n 39) 19.

C. The resurgence of planning as a legal tool: towards a more interventionist approach

The current resurgence of planning instruments, and particularly 'plans', bears witness to a general tendency in favour of a more interventionist approach in regulation of the energy and ecological transition. This contrasts with what has been the predominant approach in the energy sector since the wide adoption of liberalization processes, with its strong reliance on market signals to develop generation, allocate capacity, or manage supply. The regulatory tendency observed today is the reinforcement of integrated planning requirements across supply chains.

The reason for reinforcing planning obligations is the need to monitor the fundamental transformations that our energy systems and society must undergo within a short period of time. The need for long-term planning is reinforced in situations of centrally managed power/gas systems or where energy generation and transmission require cross-boundary coordination.[51] It corresponds to the need for steering the development of the energy system, the development of infrastructures, and the use of natural resources to respond to the different challenges in a coordinated, cost-effective, and resource effective manner. The International Renewable Agency (IRENA) acknowledges the need to further rely on planning in order to enable the large integration of variable renewable energy into the energy system and has developed guidance documents for planners.[52] The need for streamlining planning obligations of Member States in relation to the Union's climate and energy policies was also stressed by the Council in its Conclusions of 26 November 2015 on Energy Union Governance.[53]

In a historical perspective, it represents a revival of the planning initiatives developed under World War I and later in the 1930s in Europe and the United States, where the objective was to compensate market deficiencies and contribute to the 'war effort' by a better management of resources.[54] Right after World War II, this was combined with a reconstruction and modernization effort completed in the 1960s through the achievement of social-economic development and environmental protection objectives.[55] This corresponds to the long-term growth dimension in today's resilience discourses. Interestingly, the current revival of planning in EU legislation is taking place within the framework of 'the EU Green Deal', with clear semantic references to the 'New Deal' of F. Roosevelt, inspired by Keynes. There is no war situation today, but a 'climate and environment emergency' situation as recognized by parliaments and municipal assemblies,[56] that call for rapid action.[57] The regained interest in planning in connection with the COVID-19 pandemic has reinforced the trend. Even in the context of the Recovery and Resilience Facility developed post-COVID-19, EU Member States must prepare National Recovery and Resilience Plans.[58] Historically

---

[51] IRENA, 'Insights on planning for power system regulators', 2018.
[52] IRENA, Planning for the renewable future: Long-term modelling and tools to expand variable renewable power in emerging economies, 2017.
[53] Council of the EU, Council conclusions on the governance system of the Energy Union, 26 November 2015.
[54] D. Agacinski et al, 'La planification: idée d'hier ou piste pour demain?', Point de vue, France Stratégie, 17 June 2020, 2.
[55] E.g. in the Fourth and Fifth Plans in France in the 1960s.
[56] E.g. European Parliament resolution of 28 November 2019 on the climate and environment emergency.
[57] 'Climate Change 2021: The Physical Science Basis', Contribution of Working Group I to the Sixth Assessment Report of the Intergovernmental Panel on Climate Change, 2021
[58] Regulation (EU) 2021/241 of 12 February 2021 establishing the Recovery and Resilience Facility, Art 17.1.

too, even though most jurisdictions have a long tradition of spatial planning, certain countries have longer traditions than others within planning legislation, such as in France.[59]

Several provisions of secondary EU law show signs of a move towards a more prescriptive approach in coordinated energy system planning at national and regional level. The provisions are not very detailed or constraining, but this can be interpreted as a first move, focusing—as in the Paris Agreement—on procedural requirements. The Governance Regulation integrates these obligations in the Energy Union governance mechanism, where planning, reporting, and monitoring obligations in the energy and climate fields are streamlined. Pursuant to Article 15.4(e) of the Regulation, Member States' and the Union's LTSs must cover, among other elements, links to other national long-term planning objectives. As part of the mandatory template for the integrated NECPs (Annex I), Member States must include information on regional cooperation in preparing the plan, and notably 'elements subject to joint or coordinated planning with other Member States.'[60]

Recent EU initiatives under the European Green Deal provide several illustrations of proposals for reinforced planning requirements. At policy level, the EU Energy System Integration Strategy calls for more coordinated planning (and operation) of the energy system as a whole, across multiple energy carriers, infrastructures, and consumption sectors.[61] It calls for the 'cost-effective planning and deployment of offshore renewable electricity', taking into account possible interaction and integration with hydrogen production.

A similar call for strengthened planning obligations on the part of both public authorities and utilities has been raised in the United States. Such is the case for natural gas in an effort to better align regulatory framework with climate goals. The Environmental Defense Fund proposed that State Public Utilities Commissions should require gas utilities to perform holistic and transparent long-term planning that includes a consideration of consistency with state climate goals together with possible remediation actions.[62] Several states have started incorporating such requirements into law. In California, a 2020 Commission rulemaking addressed the need to perform long-term gas system planning, together with the revision of the reliability and compliance standards for gas public utilities mandated by GHG emissions reduction legislation.[63] Gas utilities will need to share data with the Commission to contribute to the planning process, but could also be required to assess their internal supply plans against state-wide climate targets, and to submit to the Commission for approval 'long-range plans' presenting load management projections.

Strengthening planning requirements in sectors that are otherwise largely subject to market-based mechanisms shows the need for a new balance, combining the two approaches, rather than a strict choice between the two. Therefore, there is a general trend of adding more planning requirements in order to monitor more closely the attainment of climate and energy goals, even in liberalized environments.

---

[59] A state organ in charge of planning (*Commissariat général du plan*) was created in France after WWII, replaced today by the *France Stratégie* agency led by a Plan Commissioner.

[60] Governance Regulation, Annex I, Part 1, para 1.4.

[61] COM(2020) 299 final, 10.

[62] Environmental Defense Fund, 'Aligning Gas Regulation and Climate Goals – A Road Map to State Regulators', 2021, 16.

[63] California Public Utilities Commission (CPUC) Rulemaking 20-01-007, Order Instituting Rulemaking to Establish Policies, Processes, and Rules to Ensure Safe and Reliable Gas Systems in California and Perform Long-Term Gas System Planning, 16 January 2020.

III. Definition of Resilience as a Criterion in Plans

This section examines the manner in which resilience is defined as a criterion, first in the legislation on strategic environmental assessment (SEA) of plans and programmes (A), and then in the four categories of plans previously identified (B).

A. Resilience as a criterion in strategic environmental assessment

In most jurisdictions, the elaboration of plans will be subject to SEA requirements. SEA is a process aimed at ensuring that the likely significant environmental effects of plans and programmes (PPs) are identified, assessed through a process that includes public participation, taken into account in the final PPs, mitigated by specific measures, and monitored.[64] It is a systematic and anticipatory process, where the findings are to be integrated into decision making. SEA can also be described as 'a sustainability tool',[65] and indeed, SEA law often refers to the Sustainable Development Goals.

The 2003 UNECE Protocol on Strategic Environmental Assessment to the Espoo Convention on Environmental Impact Assessment in a Transboundary Context (SEA Protocol) is the broadest international law instrument directly addressing SEA. It applies primarily to Parties to the Espoo Convention, but a 2001 amendment enables non-UNECE countries to join as Parties.[66] The SEA Protocol is the only legally binding international instrument ensuring that environmental considerations, including health, are 'thoroughly taken into account' in the development of PPs,[67] and, beyond that, are considered in the preparation of policies and legislation.[68]

All plans previously identified in this chapter will normally fall under the scope of the SEA Protocol, which, sector wise, covers PPs prepared for agriculture, forestry, fisheries, energy, industry, including mining, transport, regional development, waste management, telecommunications, tourism, town and country planning, or land use.[69] In addition, the SEA requirements will apply to PPs that set the framework for future development consent for projects listed in Annex I and any other project listed in Annex II that requires an EIA under national legislation.[70]

Concerning the types of impact, Parties must undertake SEA for PPs that are likely to have significant environmental effects.[71] As in the Espoo Convention, these are defined broadly extending to 'any effect on the environment, including human health, flora, fauna, biodiversity, soil, climate, air, water, landscape, natural sites, material assets, cultural heritage and the interaction among these factors.'[72] Besides procedural aspects,[73] the SEA

---

[64] SEA Protocol, Art 2.6.
[65] UNECE, Resource Manual to Support Application of the Protocol on Strategic Environmental Assessment', 2012, 17.
[66] It entered into force on 11 July 2010 and counted 33 Parties to it in 2021.
[67] SEA Protocol, Art 2.5.
[68] Ibid, Arts 1 and 13.
[69] Ibid, Art 4.2.
[70] Ibid.
[71] Ibid, Art 4.1.
[72] Ibid, Art 2.7.
[73] The Protocol describes the process for carrying out the SEA (scoping, drafting, public participation, consultation, decision and monitoring) in Arts 6–12.

Protocol only refers to a shortlist of information to be included in the environmental report that Parties must prepare,[74] and that the conclusions of that report are taken into account for the adoption of the related PPs.[75] The implementation Manual developed by UNECE,[76] which has no legal value for the interpretation of the Protocol, also does not elaborate on the scope of environmental effects.

Directive 2001/42/EC transposes the SEA Protocol into EU legislation.[77] Similar to the SEA Protocol, the Directive is of a procedural nature[78] and many provisions are equivalent to those of the Protocol. The EU and Member States plans addressed in this chapter will fall, in most cases, under the scope of the Directive, including the NECPs. The scope of application of the Directive, in terms of types of PPs and activities, is very similar to the Protocol.[79] There are therefore few elements in the Directive, or in the non-legally binding guidance on its implementation,[80] specifying the exact content of the SEA. The conclusion as to the coverage of resilience as a criterion in SEA is therefore the same.

The list of sectors and effects to be assessed is consequently broad and many aspects of ecosystems resilience are encompassed, although resilience is not formally mentioned. In practice, national SEA legislation will contain further details, and although SEAs focus on environmental effects, they also cover social effects, and therefore include several aspects of 'social-ecological resilience'.[81] Nevertheless, if resilience is to be promoted as an assessment criterion in the elaboration of PPs, a more explicit reference to it will be instrumental. If not, the application of the resilience criterion will lack harmonization, and some components of social-ecological resilience may not to be covered.

The situation, therefore, appears paradoxical: there is increasing use of planning requirements to steer the energy and ecological transition, and a general call for applying social-ecological resilience to planning theory, while SEA rules do not yet integrate resilience considerations in a sufficiently explicit manner. Even more problematic, the concept of resilience is frequently overlooked in traditional SEA procedures or applied differently at national level. This leads to the conclusion that promoting the concept of resilience in planning law requires a better integration of resilience as a criterion in SEA rules. To ensure consistency, this requires making resilience, in particular social-ecological resilience, a mandatory criterion in SEA legislation. This will also facilitate its enforceability.

Integrating resilience into SEA legislation can be done in mainly two ways. A first alternative is to *integrate* the resilience concept explicitly into the SEA methodology and as early as possible, i.e. during screening and scoping stages, and design of impact management measures. This can result, for example, in the use of a planetary boundaries framework as a guide to establishing safe margins, or the application of the ecosystem approach of the

---

[74] I.e. current knowledge and methods or assessments of the likely environmental and health effects, and reasonable alternatives. SEA Protocol, Art 6 and 7.

[75] Ibid, Art 11.1.

[76] UNECE, Resource Manual (n 65).

[77] Directive 2001/42/EC of 27 June 2001 of 27 June 2001 on the assessment of the effects of certain plans and programmes on the environment (EIA Directive).

[78] Structured around the following SEA steps: screening, scoping, considering alternatives and assessing effects, environmental reporting, decision making, monitoring, and evaluation.

[79] EIA Directive, Art 3.2.

[80] European Commission, Guidance on the implementation of Directive 2001/42/EC on the assessment of the effects of certain plans and programmes on the environment, 2003.

[81] For example, within the water industry, it is common to examine the broader social effects of drought planning, in addition to the environmental effects.

Convention on Biological Diversity for assessing cumulative effects.[82] From a legal view-point, applying this approach would require listing resilience explicitly as a criterion in SEA legislation. A second alternative is to *combine* SEA and a so-called 'resilience assessment', where the latter becomes the fourth stage of the SEA, using it as a filter (a 'resilience filter') that assesses the resiliency of environmental, economic, and social impacts.[83] The output of this filter would be to categorize the impacts into three groups of low, medium, and high resilience. Some EIA authors have opposed this idea of adding resilience assessment as a distinct activity within the IA process, because applying a resilience assessment implies that the entire SEA process is based on resilience thinking.[84]

Applying resilience thinking to SEA processes has been proposed and discussed by the EIA literature since the 2010s,[85] but has only found limited practical application so far.[86] Attempts have been limited to integrating 'climate resilience' into SEA rather than using a holistic approach to resilience.[87] Integrating social-ecological resilience into the SEA legis-lation has found only a limited echo in the legal literature[88] and in national legislation. The fact that new policy initiatives and legislation increasingly refer to the objective of resilience may contribute to the process if sufficiently precisely defined.

B. Resilience as a criterion in the relevant plans

This section examines whether and how resilience is defined in the four pre-identified categories of plans, based on some concrete examples. It is of particular interest to ascertain whether resilience is directly referred to as an objective or as an assessment criterion, and which legal requirements are attached to it. If resilience is not directly mentioned, it could overlap with other objectives already addressed in those plans. The question would then be whether those objectives are sufficient to address resilience concerns in a holistic manner. The focus is on assessment criteria rather than adopted mitigation measures to address identified risks and vulnerabilities, although these measures will contribute to resilience. The analysis is based on the direct interpretation of the plans and related legislation, but the

---

[82] B. Sadler, 'SEA effectiveness in a no-analogue world' in B. Sadler and J. Dusik (eds), *European and international experiences in strategic environmental assessment: recent progress and future prospects* (Routledge 2016), ch 2. Other authors developed a specific resilience framework tool called SPARK, see: F. Teigão dos Santos and M. Rosário Partidário 'SPARK: Strategic Planning Approach for Resilience Keeping' (2011) 19(8) European Planning Studies 1517–1536.

[83] H. Mahmoudi et al, 'Integrating Resilience Assessment in Environmental Impact Assessment (2018) 14(5) Integrated Environmental Assessment and Management 568–569; D. Marchese, et al, 'Resilience and Sustainability: Similarities and Differences in Environmental Management Applications' (2018) Science of The Total Environment, Volumes 613–614, 1275–1283

[84] R. Slootweg and M Jones, 'Resilience Thinking Improves SEA: A Discussion Paper' (2011) 29(4) Impact Assessment Project Appraisal) 272.

[85] Ibid, 263–276; M. Jones, 'Can Resilience Thinking be Integrated into the Strategic Environmental Assessment Process? (2018) 14(5) Integrated Environmental Assessment and Management 573; R. Therivel et al, 'Beyond current SEA practice' in B Sadler and J. Dusik (eds), *European and International Experiences in Strategic Environmental Assessment: Recent Progress and Future Prospects* (Routledge 2016) ch 15.

[86] H. Mahmoudi et al (n 82).

[87] E.g. European Commission, 'Guidance on Integrating Climate Change and Biodiversity into Strategic Environmental Assessment', 2013.

[88] As an exception see: A. Flournoy, 'Protecting a Natural Resource Legacy While Promoting Resilience: Can it be Done?' (2009) 87 Neb. L. Rev. 1008, 1011–1116; A. Flournoy, 'The Case for the National Environmental Legal Act' in A. Flournoy and D. Driesen (eds), *Beyond Environmental Law* (Cambridge 2010), 17.

existence of guidance documents on resilience planning should be noted, corroborating the need for assistance on the matter.[89]

1. Resilience considerations in energy plans

As identified in Section A.1, there are few jurisdictions where energy system plans are required beyond energy infrastructure planning. Where such plans exist, they often address resilience in terms of *energy security* and *security of supply*. Such is the case for the NECPs to be elaborated by EU Member States. The EU Governance Regulation does in fact refer explicitly to the resilience of the regional and national energy systems and links it to the energy security dimension of the Energy Union. In their plan, Member States must define national objectives to address constrained or interrupted supply of energy sources, ensuring the diversification of energy sources and supply from third countries, energy system flexibility, notably through the deployment of domestic energy sources, demand response, and energy storage.[90]

Reliability and *operational flexibility* are other key objectives in energy plans, particularly in energy infrastructure plans. Both cover resiliency aspects. Reliability is often explicitly mentioned, associated with additional planning duties, such as power outage planning coordination.[91] Under EU law, the electricity TSOs must include in their network development plan measures able to guarantee the 'adequacy of the system and the security of supply', to avoid unnecessary system expansion and to anticipate consumption and cross-border trade.[92] At distribution level, the network development plans are expected to support the integration of renewable energy generation plans, facilitate the development of energy storage, demand response and the electrification of the transport sector, as well as provide adequate information to system users on anticipated expansions or upgrades.[93] At EU-wide level, the TYNDP elaborated by ENTSO-E must include the modelling of the integrated network, scenario development and 'an assessment of the resilience of the system.'[94] A similar wording is used in the Gas Regulation, for the TYNDP elaborated by ENTSO-G.[95] Resilience is not further defined in the Electricity and Gas Regulations.

Recently, network development plans have started defining readiness for climate changes, or *climate resilience*, as an objective. Still, it is closely linked to network operability. For example, the 2020 TYNDP developed by ENTSO-G lists 'climate stress' as one of the three types of stressful events to take into account to assess the resilience of the European gas system, next to supply route disruptions and infrastructure disruptions. Climate stress refers here to variation in temperatures that impacts demand and the operability of the network.[96]

---

[89] E.g. in the power sector: E. Hotchkiss et al, 'Resilience Roadmap - A Collaborative Approach to Multi-Jurisdictional Planning', NREL, 2018; S. Stout and J. Leisch, 'Power Sector resilience Planning Guidebook, 2019; Resilient Energy Platform www.resilient-energy.org.

[90] Governance Regulation, Art 4 (c)(1), Anne I—Mandatory template, 2.3—Dimension energy security.

[91] E.g. the Electricity Regulation, Art 37.1(f) carrying out regional outage planning coordination in accordance with the procedures and methodologies set out in the system operation guideline adopted on the basis of Article 18(5) of Regulation (EC) No 714/2009, Annex I to the Regulation.

[92] Electricity Directive, Art 51.1. and 51.3. The Gas Directive uses a similar wording, Art 22.1.

[93] Electricity Directive, Recital (61), Art 32(3)

[94] Electricity Regulation, Art 48.1.

[95] Gas Regulation, Art 8.10.

[96] 2020 TYNDP ENTSO-G, 29.

Since energy modelling tools serve as a basis for making energy planning decisions, resilience should be taken into account in those models too. Ensuring resilience is often seen and calculated in terms of costs for utilities in those models (e.g. price for replacing or repairing a power line after a storm), which represents a barrier to its implementation and financing. A change of approach and method is also required in this domain. For example, researchers at the US National Renewable Energy Laboratory (NREL) have developed a methodology for quantifying the benefits of resilience to energy systems (i.e. quantifying resilience metrics).[97]

2. Resilience considerations in climate plans

The concept of *climate resilience* has gained growing recognition in climate change planning legislation, and is primarily addressed in *climate adaptation plans*. Climate resilience can be defined as the ability of an entity or a community to anticipate, resist, recover from, and continue to develop despite climate-related shocks and stresses.[98]

Climate resilience has become a central objective in *climate adaptation plans*, although it has a broader scope than merely adaptation. At international level, according to the Paris Agreement, the national climate adaptation plans referred to in Article 7 are to contribute towards building 'the resilience of socioeconomic and ecological systems, including through economic diversification and sustainable management of natural resources'.[99] Further guidance is provided by the UNFCCC Adaptation Committee,[100] mostly pertaining to the planning process more than the design of the plans. At EU level, the European Climate Law refers extensively to climate resilience, and consistently links it to the enhancement of adaptive capacity and the reduction of Member States' vulnerability to climate change (as three joint pillars of action), referring to Article 7 of the Paris Agreement. Member States must adopt and implement 'adaptation strategies and plans', the content of which covers many aspects of resilience planning, also in relation to natural resources and sectors like energy.[101] Similarly, the European Commission, in February 2021, adopted an EU Strategy on Adaptation to Climate Change, where climate resilience of the EU society by 2050 and full adaptation to the unavoidable impacts of climate change is set as an objective.[102] Under the 2013 EU Adaptation Strategy, guidance documents and tools have been developed and made available on the Climate-ADAPT Platform. These include a European Resilience Management Guideline that provides guidance to cities and local governments in assessing, but also strengthening their local resilience status. It describes a process that can result in the adoption of a local resilience plan or strategy.[103]

---

[97] K. Anderson et al, 'Integrating the Value of Electricity Resilience in Energy Planning and Operations Decisions' (March 2021) 15(1) IEEE Systems Journal 204–214; C. Murphy et al, 'Adapting Existing Energy Planning, Simulation, and Operational Models for Resilience Analysis', Technical Report NREL/TP-6A20-74241, 2020.

[98] Inter-American Development Bank, 'Identification of Climate Resilience Opportunities and Metrics in Financing Operations', July 2021, 27.

[99] Paris Agreement, Art 7.9(e). Article 7 establishes the global goal on adaptation.

[100] E.g. UNFCCC Adaptation Committee, 'Opportunities and options for enhancing adaptation planning in relation to vulnerable ecosystems, communities and groups', Technical paper, FCCC/TP/2018/3.

[101] Draft European Climate Law, Art 4.2.

[102] European Commission, Forging a climate-resilient Europe—the EU Strategy on Adaptation to Climate Change, COM(2021)82 final, 24.2.2021.

[103] <https://climate-adapt.eea.europa.eu/metadata/guidances/european-resilience-management-guideline> accessed 10 September 2021.

3. Resilience considerations in spatial management plans

Many aspects of spatial planning will contribute to resilience. Resilience considerations have been integrated into spatial management plans earlier than in other planning processes because the local entities are the first ones impacted by the consequences of extreme nature-based events along with the competent authorities for spatial planning. Spatial planning authorities have addressed resiliency aspects from primarily two perspectives: *climate adaptation* and *disaster risk reduction* (DRR).

Resilience is often approached from the perspective of climate change and climate adaptation in particularly highly exposed geographic areas, such as coasts, maritime spaces, and cities. The adoption of coastal management plans in risk areas aims to address the need for climate adaptation planning due to sea level rise and erosion. In sea areas, the EU Maritime Spatial Planning Directive requires Member States, through their maritime spatial plans to preserve, protect, and improve the environment, including resilience to climate change impacts.[104] More recently, resilience has been formally promoted as an objective of local spatial management plans and legislation. The 100 Resilient Cities Program (100RC)[105] started in 2013 to assist cities in applying a stepwise resilience strategy and planning process. In 2021, New Jersey enacted S2607 that requires municipalities to include climate change-related vulnerability hazard assessments in the land-use part of their master plan.[106]

Disaster resilience has been another area of focus in spatial planning, with dedicated national or local plans under DRR frameworks. DRR aims to reduce disaster risks caused by natural hazards like earthquakes, floods, droughts, and cyclones, through systematic efforts to analyse and reduce the causal factors of disasters.[107] The importance of resilience in disaster risk management can be seen from the centrality of the term in the 2005–2015 Hyogo Framework for Action, which was subtitled 'Building the Resilience of Nations and Communities to Disasters'. Building resilience, therefore, is understood as the goal of disaster risk reduction.[108] The Preamble to the Sendai Framework for DRR (2015–2030) insists on the urgent and critical need 'to anticipate, plan for and reduce disaster risk in order to more effectively protect persons, communities and countries, their livelihoods, health, cultural heritage, socioeconomic assets and ecosystems, and thus strengthen their resilience' (para 5). At national level, Indonesia has developed a national programme to support the inclusion of DRR principles in urban development plans.[109]

4. Resilience considerations in natural resources plans

The relationship between resilience and natural resources planning is bidirectional with, in one direction, the need to ensure the resilience of natural ecosystems to extreme

[104] Directive 2014/89/EU of 23 July 2014 establishing a framework for maritime spatial planning, Art 5.2.; N. Soininen and F. Platjouw, 'Resilience and Adaptive Capacity of Aquatic Environmental Law in the EU: An Evaluation and Comparison of the WFD, MSFD, and MSPD' in *The Ecosystem Approach in Ocean Planning and Governance* (Brill 2018) ch 2

[105] Now the Resilient Cities Network.

[106] S2607 1R (state.nj.us).

[107] United Nations Office for Disaster Risk Reduction (UNISDR), 'What is Disaster Risk Reduction', <https://eird.org/esp/acerca-eird/liderazgo/perfil/what-is-drr.html> accessed 10 September 2021.

[108] UNISDR, 'Towards a post-2015 framework for disaster risk reduction', 2012.

[109] N. Wijaya et al, 'Spatial Planning, Disaster Risk Reduction, and Climate Change Adaptation Integration in Indonesia: Progress, Challenges, and Approach' in R. Djalante et al (eds) *Disaster Risk Reduction in Indonesia* (Springer 2017) 235–252.

nature-based events and, in the converse direction, awareness of the potential that natural ecosystems have in fostering resilience. Planning requirements can support both processes.

First, most natural resources management plans include requirements to assess risk and plan emergency response to preserve natural ecosystems such as water from natural hazards. For example, under US law, the America's Water Infrastructure Act of 2018 (AWIA) contains several provisions aimed at assessing and reinforcing the resilience of water resources and infrastructures, including through planning. Section 2013 of AWIA requires community water systems that serve more than 3,300 people to complete a risk and resilience assessment and develop an emergency response plan. Particular emphasis is put on the resilience of physical water infrastructure in ensuring water supply. In the UK, under the Water Industry Act 1991, water companies in England and Wales are required to produce an updated Drought Plan every five years. When performing the SEA screening of the draft Drought Plans, the resiliency of water resources and infrastructures to climate change is part of screening criteria.[110]

Secondly, climate and spatial planning legislations increasingly refer to the need to apply an *ecosystem-based approach* to foster resilience, climate adaptation, or DRR. In its guidance documents on climate adaptation planning, the UNFCCC Adaptation Committee calls for the integration of an *ecosystem-based approach to adaptation planning.*[111] Similarly, the European Climate Law insists on the benefits of promoting nature-based solutions for climate-change mitigation, adaptation, and biodiversity protection.[112] Restoring ecosystems would assist in maintaining, managing, and enhancing natural sinks and in promoting biodiversity while fighting climate change. The triple role of forests as sink, storage, and substitution, is highlighted.[113] Member States must promote nature-based solutions and ecosystem-based adaptation in their adaptation strategies.[114] The EU Strategy on Climate Adaptation stresses the need to integrate nature-based solutions in planning, arguing that they should play a bigger role in land-use management and infrastructure planning to reduce costs, provide climate-resilient services, and improve compliance with Water Framework Directive requirements for good ecological status.[115] At city level, new spatial planning approaches such as water-sensitive urban design (WSUD) and green and blue infrastructures are being developed to increase urban flood resilience. Integrated planning of land and water areas is necessary to ensure coherent and robust green and blue infrastructures beyond the urban/rural divides. This would address the negative impacts of the current fragmentation of ecosystems, which reduces the capacity of ecosystems to deliver valuable services for resilience.

To conclude, resilience is increasingly referred to as an objective or assessment criteria in planning legislation across sectors, although not in a consistent manner. Each planning process relies on its own understanding of resilience, with different degrees of enforcement. However, planning processes to address nature-based disruptions are closely interlinked, with some degree of overlap. There is an underlying risk of inconsistency if not supported

---

[110] Ricardo, Energy & Environment, Strategic Environmental Assessment Report, Draft Drought Plan 2021, Report for Severn Trent Water Ltd, 2021.
[111] E.g. UNFCCC Adaptation Committee, 'Opportunities and options for enhancing adaptation planning in relation to vulnerable ecosystems, communities and groups,' Technical paper, FCCC/TP/2018/3.
[112] Draft European Climate Law, Recital 14(a), Art 4.2.
[113] Ibid, Recital (12d).
[114] Ibid.
[115] European Commission (n 102) 11

by coordination instruments at least, or integration processes at best. Applying a resilience approach requires having a transversal approach to the different planning processes. The question raised below is how to ensure consistency across the relevant planning processes.

IV. Integration and Coordination of Planning Processes and Responsibilities: For a Consistent Application of the Resilience Criterion

Ensuring a consistent application of the criterion of resilience throughout the planning processes needs to take place both vertically, down the planning documentation hierarchy within a same sector (A), and horizontally, across the different relevant planning processes (B).

A. Vertical consistency down the plan hierarchy

The application of the resilience criterion down the planning documentation hierarchy will depend on the level and the legal status of the plans defining it.

All states apply some form of hierarchical structure for planning instruments where the higher tier is binding on the tiers below it. The hierarchy order between the plans is regulated by law and follows the allocation of competences between public planning entities.[116] When resilience is defined as an objective or assessment criterion in planning legislation, it also serves as basis for the granting of permits. The level in the hierarchy and legal status of the plans will strongly influence consistency in the application of the resilience criterion at the lower levels. At the international level, the SEA Protocol provides a useful framework for ensuring a consistent application of resilience considerations vertically, along the planning hierarchy and down to the permit level.[117] At national level, references to resilience could not be identified in national constitutions, but national laws increasing refer to the concept, without necessarily defining it. In 2021, the French parliament passed the 'Climate and Resilience Law'[118] that amended many sectoral pieces of legislation to align objectives and measures (e.g. in the legislative codes on energy, forestry, environment protection, food, city planning, education).

If the planning legislation defines resilience as a mandatory criterion for the elaboration of subsequent plans, the lack of compliance with that requirement may render the lower plans invalid. In contrast, when the upper plans are not legally binding on the lower ones, it will be difficult to ensure consistency. For example, pursuant to the EU Electricity Regulation, the TYNDP elaborated by the ENTSO-E are non-legally binding, but TSOs must nevertheless take the plan into account when elaborating their network plan, and the National Regulatory Authorities (NRAs) will check that the latter plan is consistent with the TYNDP and with the Member State's NECP.[119] In case of inconsistency, the NRA can

---

[116] *The EU Compendium of European planning systems and policies*, Regional Development Studies 28, 1997, 53
[117] SEA Protocol, Art 4.2.
[118] Law no 2021-1104 of 22 August 2021.
[119] Electricity Directive, Art 51.3.

consult the Agency for the Cooperation of Energy Regulators (ACER) that must 'provide an opinion' and 'shall recommend' the TSO to amend its plan.

This argues in favour of defining resilience as a criterion in the upper national plans and SEA legislation. If the plans are legally binding, this can ensure a more consistent approach to resilience down the planning hierarchy.

B. Horizontal consistency across the different planning processes

Ensuring consistency in the application of the resilience criterion requires coordinating both the different planning processes (1) and the work of the respective planning authorities (2). Those processes and tasks often run in parallel, but good practices are emerging.

1. From coordinated to integrated planning processes

The question examined below is how coordination and possibly integration between the different planning processes can be pursued, based on resilience thinking.

First, the plans increasingly refer to each other, and the legislation regulating the planning process often prescribes a duty to 'take into account', be 'consistent with' or be 'fully in line with' other relevant plans.[120] The enforcement of such an obligation is often weak, except when the planning authorities are obliged to describe how the interaction has been ensured. For example, the Governance Regulation requires Member States to 'take into account interlinkages' between the five dimensions of the Energy Union in their NECP (Art 3.3(b)). The extent to which the interlinkages have been taken into account can be a topic for review by the Commission during its assessment of the draft plans (Art 13) and the assessment of progress made (Art 29), and can be the subject of a Commission's Recommendation to the Member States (Arts 31 and 32).[121]

A second and more formal approach would be to merge or integrate the processes. This is what the Governance Regulation intends to achieve, by streamlining and bringing together the separate planning and reporting processes across the climate and energy legislation into the governance mechanism. This results in the elaboration of one single energy and climate plan. The objective pursued is to apply *integrated strategic planning* into the governance system of the Energy Union.[122] This should avoid overlaps in planning and reporting obligations, enable synergies and increase cost-efficiency.[123]

This approach, however, is limited to the climate and energy fields. Social-ecological resilience views the social and ecological systems as intertwined, and applying it to planning would also require integrating the natural resources and social dimensions. It has so far been difficult to integrate all planning processes into one plan, but the example of the EU Governance mechanism and the NECPs could serve as a useful blueprint to be further developed.

---

[120] E.g. draft revised TEN-E Regulation, Art 12.1.
[121] The role of the Committee on Climate Change (Art 44), the Energy Union Committee (Art 44) and the use of the E-platform (Art 28) are much more limited into that respect, but can serve as useful platform for exchange of information.
[122] Council conclusions (n 53).
[123] Governance Regulation, Recital (24).

2. Coordination of planning responsibilities between competent entities

There are 'planning authorities' for different sectors, but their action may not be coordinated, hindering a consistent and cost-effective approach to resilience. Some best practices and legal mechanisms are identified below.

A first alternative would be to define a 'coordination duty' imposed on the different planning authorities as a form of reinforced consultation obligation. Indeed, the 'duty to consult' already exists in most legislation, at the national level but also the cross-boundary level among neighbouring countries sharing the same natural resources or energy infrastructures.[124]

Another alternative would be to establish formal ministerial committees, administrative structures, or even persons in charge of the cross-sectoral coordination. At the regional level, many states already have organizations and mechanisms to coordinate sectoral plans.[125] At city level, this has resulted in the creation of the position of Chief Resilience Officer (CRO), who serves as the connecting point between different decision-making agencies and departments to facilitate the integration of the different planning processes.[126]

V. Conclusions

This chapter illustrates the fact that social-ecological resilience is progressively gaining recognition in the field of planning law, with the increasing reliance on 'plans'. Planning, especially in the energy field, has been downplayed in recent years because of the market liberalization process, but it is seeing a resurgence because of the need to advance quickly and monitor the energy and ecological transition, and to respond to disruption.

The research question has been to ascertain the extent to which resilience was taken into account in the different planning processes. In the four processes deemed relevant for the study—energy, climate, spatial, and natural resources planning—, the definition and role given to resilience as an objective or criterion differ. Resilience is rarely mentioned directly in the relevant planning legislation. Most criteria assessed in the different plans do contribute to resilience, but a holistic approach to it is lacking.

The chapter concludes that it is necessary to address resilience in the upper level of the planning documentation hierarchy, starting with the SEA and sectoral legislation. This will enable the integration of resilience considerations early in the planning and decision-making process and thereby ensure consistency in its application along the planning document hierarchy (vertically). Due to the time necessary to amend upper legislation, and the need to act quickly and cost-efficiently at a time of climate emergency, good coordination

---

[124] E.g. the SEA Protocol defines a consultation obligation, where Parties must provide for the detailed arrangement for informing and consulting the responsible national environmental and health authorities (Art 9), but also neighbouring countries in case of cross-boundary activities (Art 10).

[125] *The EU Compendium of European planning systems and policies* (n 116), 53.

[126] M. Berkowitz, 'What a Chief Resilience Officer Does', The Rockefeller Foundation, 7 September 2014.

mechanisms across planning processes (horizontally) can help build resilience in the short term.

Finally, this chapter has demonstrated that a new legal principle is under definition, namely the integration principle in energy system and natural resources planning. The recognition of such a principle would contribute towards ensuring further resilience within the social-ecological systems.

5

Resilient Energy Systems in the European Union

Critical Infrastructures, Supply Security, and Cybersecurity Regulation

Martha M. Roggenkamp

I. Introduction

Since the 1990s the energy sector in the European Union (EU) has rapidly changed. These changes are triggered by three policy considerations: market governance, climate change, and supply security. Although these are three distinctive policies, they are closely connected and influence each other. The development of an internal energy market entails that market parties have a freedom of choice and thus are able to opt for more sustainable energy sources. This is true for producers, consumers, and more recently also prosumers. Such choice is in line with the EU goal to be carbon neutral by 2050. Increasing use of renewable energy sources may, however, impact supply security as the use of many renewable sources are unpredictable and weather dependent. Moreover, energy supply is to a large extent network bound and in a liberalized energy market these networks are separated (unbundled) from commercial activities like production and supply. Such unbundling makes balancing demand and supply more complicated (balancing rules) as it requires detailed communication between producers, consumers, and network operators. Any imbalance may result in brownouts or blackouts and supply interruptions. Also the grid itself can be the object of damages due to digging or other activities. The reliability of the grid is thus also crucial for ensuring supply security.

More recently another trend can be noted: the increasing digitalization of the energy sector. This digitalization applies to the entire energy sector but is better known as smart grids in the case of the network-bound electricity and gas sector. These smart grids rely on smart meters installed at the premises of consumers and on smart appliances. These smart facilities clearly contribute to the management of the system as they facilitate the alignment of energy production, supply and demand, and thus maintaining network balancing. However, it also means that the traditional grid becomes more and more internet-connected and thus may be prone to similar disadvantages and problems as the internet has in general, i.e. cybercrime. Such cyber criminality may affect regular energy supply as has recently been demonstrated when a cyber attack led to a shutdown in May 2021 of the 5,500 mile Colonial Oil Pipeline running from Texas to New York.[1]

---

[1] David Sanger, Clifford Krauss and Nicole Perlroth, 'Cyberattack Forces a Shutdown of a Top U.S. Pipeline' (New York, 8 May 2021) <https://www.nytimes.com/2021/05/08/us/politics/cyberattack-colonial-pipeline.html> accessed 31 July 2021.

Martha M. Roggenkamp, *Resilient Energy Systems in the European Union* In: *Resilience in Energy, Infrastructure, and Natural Resources Law*. Edited by: Catherine Banet, Hanri Mostert, LeRoy Paddock, Milton Fernando Montoya, and Íñigo del Guayo, Oxford University Press.
© Martha M. Roggenkamp 2022. DOI: 10.1093/oso/9780192864574.003.0005

It follows from the above that energy systems are critical for ensuring regular and reliable energy supply. The EU acknowledges the need to protect critical energy infrastructure. This led to a steadily increasing amount of EU legislation aiming at protecting the physical infrastructure but increasingly also virtual (digital) infrastructure. Protecting both types of infrastructure is essential for safeguarding a regular energy supply. This chapter will first present some key concepts and developments of the EU network-bound energy market (Section II). Thereafter it will examine the legal developments safeguarding EU energy supply (Section III). Then it will discuss how the EU approaches the increasing threat of cybercrime and in particular cyber attacks (Section IV). Finally, it will conclude with a brief assessment on how these developments will be relevant for energy transition (Section V).

II. Energy Systems and Markets

The energy system consists of a series of networks connecting producers and consumers. Traditionally energy networks involved three main categories: distribution systems, transmission systems, and interconnectors. Distribution systems operate under low pressure and/or voltage and have a direct connection to consumers. Each EU Member State (MS) has usually several (regional) distribution systems and each of them is connected to the transmission system. The transmission system is basically the country's 'national energy highway' or main grid. It consists of high pressure or high voltage networks and usually covers the entire territory of a State. In addition, these transmission systems can yet again be interconnected.[2] In the EU, such national energy supply systems have been interconnected for a variety of reasons. In the 1950s, cross-border interconnections were promoted by the Union for the Coordination of Production and Transmission of Electricity (UCPTE) in order to contribute to the development of economic activity and to secure energy supply by providing each other mutual aid and assistance.[3] A decade later a start was made with the interconnection of national gas pipeline systems due to the discovery of the Groningen gas-field in 1959 and the decision of the Dutch government to aim at large-scale exports of natural gas.[4] Since the 1990s, interconnectors have been playing an important role in the establishment of an internal energy market in the EU as they are essential for meeting the basic requirements of free movement of goods (energy) and thus facilitate cross-border trade within the EU. As interconnector capacity around the turn of the millennium proved to be scarce, the EU has set a target of 15 per cent interconnectivity by 2030.[5]

---

[2] Martha Roggenkamp et al (eds), *Energy Networks and the Law: Innovative Solutions in Changing Markets* (Oxford University Press 2012) 9–10.

[3] See UCPTE/UCTE, 'The 50 Year Success Story – Evolution of a European Interconnected Grid' <https://eepublicdownloads.entsoe.eu/clean-documents/pre2015/publications/ce/110422_UCPTE-UCTE_The50yearSuccessStory.pdf> accessed 31 July 2021.

[4] Policy note (Nota de Pous) of 1962, *Kamerstukken II* 1961/62, 6767, nr. 1.

[5] European Commission, 'Electricity interconnection targets' <https://ec.europa.eu/energy/topics/infrastructure/electricity-interconnection-targets_en> accessed 31 July 2021.

A. Liberalized markets and system operations

Since the 1990s the EU energy market drastically changed. Although in 1957 the Treaty establishing the European Economic Community (EEC Treaty) was adopted and the rules of free movement of goods, services, persons, and capital without any hindrance to competition applied to the (then six) MSs, these rules did not, in practice, apply to the network-bound energy sector. Following the introduction of the Single European Act in 1986 and Commission Working Document on the internal market in 1988, the situation changed. Because the Single European Act allowed for majority voting, a large number of directives and regulations have been issued since the early 1990s.[6]

The directives primarily aim at liberalizing the energy markets and have led to a gradual abolishment of existing vertically integrated companies that often acted as national monopolies. Instead, consumers were given a freedom of choice of supplier and energy production was opened to anyone meeting the minimum requirements of the directives. As energy networks are natural monopolies, the directives also stipulated that third parties should have non-discriminatory access to the grid. Since the enactment of the first directives in the 1990s these fundamental rules have constantly been adjusted and it also became clear that non-discriminatory third party access (TPA) is easier to achieve if network operators can act independently from production and supply. Therefore, networks have been unbundled from the vertically integrated company. Where distribution companies are subject to a regime of legal unbundling, MSs have on transmission level either appointed an Independent Transmission Operator or opted for ownership unbundling.[7]

Whereas directives need to be transposed in national law and primarily liberalize national energy markets, regulations apply directly and introduce rules that equally apply to all EU MSs. In order to promote the internal energy market, regulations often deal with interconnectors and cross-border trade. As was the case with the energy market directives, the regulations adopted since 2003 have been replaced with more in-depth provisions. In order to promote cross-border cooperation, Regulation (EC) No 713/2009 provided for the establishment of an Agency for the Cooperation of Energy Regulators (ACER) consisting of representatives of the national energy regulatory authorities. ACER's prime aim is to complete the EU internal energy market by improving the regulatory framework at EU level. In parallel with ACER, Regulations No 714/2009 and 715/2009 provided for the establishment of the European Network of Transmission System Operators (ENTSO); one for electricity (ENTSO-E) and one for gas (ENTSOG). Both ENTSOs represent the electric and gas transmission system operators (TSOs)[8] and have a similar goal: to set fair rules for cross-border exchanges and thus enhancing competition within the internal market. The development of cross-border trade has also been supported by the adoption of several network codes and guidelines for the integration of the electricity and/or gas markets. ACER submits draft framework guidelines upon the request of the Commission which serve as the basis for drafting network codes. The framework guidelines and draft codes are developed

---

[6] See for this historic overview also M.M. Roggenkamp et al (eds), *Energy Law in Europe—National, EU and International Regulation* (3rd edn, Oxford University Press 2016).

[7] Ibid.

[8] See <https://www.entsoe.eu> and <http://www.entsog.eu>.

in consultation with ENTSO. Most network codes and guidelines contain provisions on market rules, system operation, and network connection.

B. Decarbonization

The EU has been committed to climate change goals since the early 1990s as it is one of the parties (next to the individual MS) to the UN Framework Convention on Climate Change (UNFCCC) adopted in 1992. The UNFCCC affects the entire economy but is of special importance for the energy sector. It has resulted in a process of energy transition following the gradual switch from fossil fuels to renewable energy sources and the more efficient use of energy sources. This process of energy transition is facilitated by an increasing set of EU laws governing CO_2 emission allowances, the use of renewable energy sources, and the introduction of several mechanisms to promote energy efficiency. The interlinkage between these instruments became apparent when the EU Commission published the Third Energy Package in 2007 and presented the following goals: 20 per cent reduction of CO_2 emissions, 20 per cent renewable energy consumption and 10 per cent more energy efficiency in 2020. In 2020 these targets have increased to a goal of 40 per cent cuts in CO_2 emissions, 32 per cent renewable energy consumption and 32.5 per cent improvement of energy efficiency by 2030, and even 100 per cent climate neutrality by 2050.[9]

For the energy sector this decarbonization process has led (and will continue to lead) to drastic changes as renewable energy sources and energy efficiency measures will reduce the use of fossil fuels. This effect will be most noticeable in the electricity sector as renewables will be used increasingly for electricity generation and the use of electricity will increase due to the electrification of the energy sector (e.g. electric vehicles). Moreover, power plants making use of renewable sources like wind and solar energy are usually smaller in size and connected to the distribution grid. Depending on their size and capacity, the operators of these installations may be professional energy companies but also small (active) consumers who have installed a solar panel or small wind turbine on their premises. These developments have a direct impact on the networks to which these installations are connected. Most renewable sources are intermittent and their production depends on weather circumstances. Therefore it is difficult to predict the levels of production and this may have a direct impact on network balancing. One of the key features of energy networks is, after all, the balancing requirement. Input and offtake of energy need to be in balance in order to avoid brownouts or blackouts. One of the solutions for maintaining proper balancing can be found in the ongoing digitalization of the sector.

C. Digitalization

Technically, an energy network is no longer merely a pipe or a cable but it includes more and more Information and Communication Technology (ICT). Such technology is necessary

---

[9] European Commission, '2030 Climate and Energy Framework' <https://ec.europa.eu/clima/policies/strategies/2030_en>; European Commission, '2050 Long-term Strategy' <https://ec.europa.eu/clima/policies/strategies/2050_en> both accessed 21 July 2021.

for producers, consumers, and system operators to communicate and to maintain network balancing. While energy companies have been making use of telecommunication technologies for many decades, the market and the technology has rapidly changed since the turn of the century. Market liberalization and the accompanying unbundling process led to more communication challenges between commercial market parties and system operators but at the same time computer and data technology has also advanced and led to the introduction of the concept of smart grids or smart energy systems.

The concept of smart grids was introduced in the 2009 Electricity and Gas Directives. Directive 2009/73/EC stated that:

[i]n order to promote energy efficiency, Member States or [....] the regulatory authority shall strongly recommend that natural gas undertakings optimise the use of gas, for example by providing energy management services, developing innovative pricing formulas or introducing intelligent metering systems or smart grids where appropriate[10].

Directive 2009/72/EC provided that:

Member States should encourage the modernization of distribution networks, such as through the introduction of smart grids, which should be built in a way that encourages decentralized generation and energy efficiency.[11]

The concept of smart grids is thus considered as a means to promote energy efficiency and in case of electricity also decentralized generation. Although smart grids may serve both the electricity and gas markets, the focus seems primarily to be the electricity sector as the only legal definition refers to:

[...] an electricity network that can integrate in a cost efficient manner the behaviour and actions of all users connected to it, including generators, consumers and those that both generate and consume, in order to ensure an economically efficient and sustainable power system with low losses and high levels of quality, security of supply and safety.[12]

Smart grids thus refer to energy networks that can automatically monitor energy flows and adjust to changes in energy supply and demand accordingly. A precondition for developing and operating a smart grid is the availability and access to communication networks, which again requires that all parties connected to the grid have access to a 'smart metering system' that consists of an electronic system that is capable of measuring electricity fed into or consumed from the grid, providing more information than a conventional meter, and that is capable of transmitting and receiving data for information, monitoring, and control purposes, using a form of electronic communication.[13] Unlike major energy producers, small (household) consumers until recently only made use of conventional or analogous meters that work in one direction and measure consumption only. However, this is now

---

[10] Art 3(8) Directive 2009/73/EC.
[11] Recital 36 Directive 2009/72/EC.
[12] Art 2(7) Regulation (EU) No 2013/347.
[13] Art 2(23) Directive 2019/944/EU.

gradually changing as the EU aims at installing smart meters in approximately 80 per cent of all households by 2024.

Because smart meters operate digitally, they enable two-directional communication of the real-time prices of generation, loads, and flexibilities within one system.[14] Hence, smart metering systems coupled with smart grids will enable consumers (prosumers) to access the market and allow for a more precise operation of the system. Given the role of these smart meters in the internal energy market, MSs also need to ensure the interoperability of these metering systems[15] and to have due regard to the use of appropriate standards, best practice and any interoperability requirements issued by the EU Commission.[16] Smart meters also have to comply with EU rules and best-available techniques regarding cybersecurity as well as with relevant EU data protection and privacy rules.[17]

III. Securing Energy Supply by Safeguarding Energy Systems

A. Introduction

Given their network-bound character, electricity and gas supply depend on the availability of proper functioning networks. Supply interruptions are often caused by excavation activities resulting in damages to subsoil energy infrastructure. Damages to subsoil gas pipelines can also lead to personal damages and fatal accidents as was clearly illustrated by an incident in the Belgian town Gellingen in 2004.[18] Another clear illustration of infrastructure dependence is the 2006 and 2009 Russia-Ukraine gas crises. Transit problems with the Ukraine pipeline system had a detrimental effect on the amount of gas supplied to Europe, causing, inter alia, Italian and German gas-fired power plants to shut down.[19] The latter illustrates that a disruption in a strongly interconnected energy system may have cascading effects. In other words, a disruption in one part of a national system may have consequences in several MSs. A typical example of such a cascading effect occurred in 2006 when the German electricity distribution company EON performed a planned switch-off of a high voltage powerline across the Ems River in North-West Germany, which resulted in a power deficit on one side of the river and an overload of the grid on the other side.[20] This led to a serious imbalance of the grid, followed by a blackout in Germany, France, Belgium,

---

[14] Lea Diestelmeier, 'A Legal Framework for Smart Grids' in Martha Roggenkamp et al (eds), *Energy Law, Climate Change and the Environment* (Edward Elgar 2021) 653.

[15] Art 2(24) Directive 2019/994/EU defines interoperability as '*the ability of two or more energy or communication networks, systems, devices, applications or components to interwork to exchange and use information in order to perform required functions*' (emphasis added).

[16] Art 24(2) Directive 2019/944/EU.

[17] Jonida Milaj and Jeane Mifsud Bonnici, 'Privacy Issues in the Use of Smart Meters Law Enforcement Use of Smart Meter Data' in A. Beaulieu et al (eds), *Smart Grids from a Global Perspective: Bridging Old and New Energy Systems* (Springer 2016) 179–196.

[18] Martha Roggenkamp, 'Protecting Energy Infrastructure in the EU: The Impact of External Damages on Supply Security' in Martha Roggenkamp et al (eds), *Energy Networks and the Law: Innovative Solutions in Changing Markets* (Oxford University Press 2012) 118–137.

[19] Jonathan Stern, 'The Russian-Ukraine Gas Crisis of January 2006' (OIES 2006); Simon Pirani, Jonathan Stern, and Katja Yafimava, 'The Russo-Ukrainian gas dispute of January 2009: a comprehensive assessment' (OIES 2009) 27.

[20] Sam Wilson, 'Q&A: Europe's power blackout' (London, 6 November 2006) <http://news.bbc.co.uk/2/hi/europe/6121166.stm> accessed 31 July 2021.

Italy, and Spain and left over 10 million European consumers without electricity for several hours. These examples illustrate that cross-border connections can be beneficial for supply security as MSs do not have to rely only on national production and supply resources, but also that the interconnected system may be a cause of danger as network incidents may spread from one network to another.

B. Safeguarding energy networks and security of energy supply

At the beginning of this century it became clear that market liberalization rules are not sufficient to secure energy supply. Hence, the EU issued Directive 2004/67/EC and Directive 2005/89/EC to safeguard regular gas and electricity supply. These directives have in the meantime been replaced by Regulation (EU) 994/2010 as repealed by Regulation (EU) 2017/1938 and Regulation 2019/941. These EU legislative acts are accompanied by Directive 2008/114/EC on the designation of European Critical Infrastructure (ECI), which enable MSs to identify which parts of the energy infrastructure are critical for supply security. These legal developments will be discussed below.

1. EU legal framework safeguarding energy supply

Regulation (EU) 994/2010 was put into place as an explicit response to the Ukraine-Russia crises.[21] It recognizes the role of reliable infrastructure to secure gas supply and consequently required MSs to ensure that in the event of a disruption of the largest infrastructure, the capacity of the remaining infrastructure is able to satisfy total gas demand. In order to make such an assessment the regulation introduced the N-1 formula, which entails that MSs need to ensure that:

> [i]n the event of a disruption of the single largest gas infrastructure, the capacity of the remaining infrastructure [...] is able [...] to satisfy total gas demand of the calculated area during a day of exceptionally high gas demand occurring within a statistical probability of once in 20 years.[22]

As MSs without sufficient infrastructure connection—so-called 'gas islands'—are the most vulnerable in case of major gas supply disruptions, the regulation specifically requires MSs to develop adequate interconnections.[23] However, the national approach of this regulation was perceived as a shortcoming and was replaced by Regulation (EU) 2017/1938 which aims at identifying specific risk groups and facilitating regional cooperation within each risk group, amongst others by discussing and agreeing on appropriate and effective cross-border measures.

Despite many similarities, some interesting differences can be noted in the regime applying to the electricity sector. Directive 2005/89/EC defined the term security of electricity supply as 'the ability of an electricity system to supply final customers with electricity,

---

[21] Commission, 'The January 2009 Gas Supply Disruption to the EU: An Assessment' SEC (2009) 977 final 7.
[22] Art 6(1) Regulation 994/2010. Annex I of the Regulation provides for a calculation model and also defines what the largest infrastructure is, depending on the specific situation in each MS.
[23] See also Silke Goldberg, 'Regulation 994/2010: A Measure to Improve the Security of Gas Supply in The EU?' in Martha Roggenkamp and Ulf Hammer (eds), *European Energy Law Report VIII* (Intersentia 2011) 61–92.

as provided for under this Directive'.[24] This ability is directly linked to system operations as the directive refers to 'operational network security' as the continuous operation of the transmission and, where appropriate, the distribution network under foreseeable circumstances, and next to the 'balance between supply and demand' as the satisfaction of foreseeable demands of consumers to use electricity without the need to enforce measures to reduce consumption.[25] Its successor, Regulation 2019/941 on risk-preparedness in the electricity sector[26], goes one step further as it specifically deals with electricity crises that have a larger scale and impact and requires MSs to prevent such crises and take sufficient measures should system operation rules alone not suffice. Hence, where provisions governing operational network security and balancing apply under foreseeable circumstances, the security of supply is specifically jeopardized when circumstances are unforeseeable. Consequently, the definition in Regulation 2019/941 has been amended to read 'the ability of an electricity system to guarantee the supply of electricity to customers with a clearly established level of performance, as determined by the Member States concerned'.[27] It seems that any operational network security should be considered as part of 'clearly established level of performance determined by a Member State'. Such temporary imbalances are in practice dealt with by system operators on a regular basis.

Regulation 2019/941 goes a step further as it aims at developing a common understanding among MSs of what constitutes an electricity crisis, which is defined as 'a present or imminent situation in which there is a significant electricity shortage, as determined by the Member States and described in their risk-preparedness plans, or in which it is impossible to supply electricity to customers'.[28] The type of crisis should be described in the national risk-preparedness plans and be based on several crisis scenarios. This approach should ensure that all relevant electricity crises are covered, whilst taking into account regional and national specificities such as the topology of the grid, the electricity mix, the size of production and consumption, and the degree of population density.[29] The above-mentioned cascading effect has been taken into account as these scenarios should be based on the assumption that a crisis can be regional in scope and thus requires some sort of regional cooperation.

2. Regional cooperation in the spirit of solidarity

Article 194 of the Treaty on the Functioning of the European Union (TFEU) provides amongst others that MSs should apply a principle of solidarity to ensure security of energy supply in the EU. In line with this principle, both regulations introduce the concept of risk groups for gas/electricity supply threats and a solidarity mechanism in case of gas and electricity crises if so requested.

Pursuant to Regulation (EU) 2017/1938 risk groups will be established on the basis of gas supply routes, supply country risks, and the cohesion of capabilities to exchange gas.[30]

---

[24] Art 2(1) Directive 2005/89/EC.

[25] Arts 2(2) and (3) Directive 2005/89/EC.

[26] Regulation 2019/941 repealing Directive 2005/89/EC, OJ 2019, L 158.

[27] Art 2(1) Regulation 2019/941.

[28] Art 2(9) Regulation 2019/941; Art 2(10) provides that a 'simultaneous electricity crisis' affects more than one Member State at the same time.

[29] Recital 11 Regulation 2019/941.

[30] European Parliament, 'New rules on security of gas supply November 2017' <http://www.europarl.europa.eu/RegData/etudes/BRIE/2017/608810/EPRS_BRI(2017)608810_EN.pdf> accessed 31 July 2021.

These risk groups are selected on the basis of an assessment whether or not MSs have a common gas supplier and a common gas supply route.[31] Hence, only directly intercon-nected MSs are clustered into four main risk groups (Eastern Gas, North Sea Gas, North African Gas, and South-East Gas) but as MSs can be part of several risk groups across dif-ferent categories/sources (e.g. low calorific and high calorific gas) there are 13 risk groups in total.[32] Each risk group needs to develop a 'common risk assessment' at risk group level.[33] The main task of risk groups is, however, to implement solidarity measures under Article 13 Regulation (EU) 2017/1938, which entails that MSs may request solidarity measures to be applied. If so requested, a MS directly connected to the grid of the requesting MS shall, if possible and without creating unsafe situations, take the necessary measures to assist the re-questing MS. This could result in reduced levels of gas supply to their own customers except for so-called solidarity protected customers, like household customers and protected cus-tomers relying on essential social services.[34] These new mechanisms in fact require MSs to directly interfere with the market and contractual obligations of market players. However, a MS requesting such solidarity should promptly pay fair compensation to the MS that is providing solidarity.[35]

In order to effectively monitor security of electricity supply in the EU as a whole, the Electricity Coordination Group (ECG) was established in 2012 as a forum to exchange in-formation and to foster cooperation among MSs in the area of supply security.[36] More spe-cifically, Regulation 2019/941 requires MSs to cooperate, at the regional level and, where applicable, bilaterally, in a spirit of solidarity. Therefore MSs need to develop regional scenarios that will enable them to compare effectively how well they and their neighbours perform. The regions that are covered by these scenarios consist of groups of MSs whose TSOs share the same regional coordination centre.[37] If necessary, MSs may form subgroups within the regions for the purpose of cooperation regarding concrete regional measures, or to cooperate in existing regional forums, as the technical ability to provide mutual assistance to each other in an electricity crisis is essential. As not all MSs in a larger region will be able to provide electricity to another MS in an electricity crisis, it is not necessary for all MSs in a region to conclude regional agreements on concrete measures. Only those MSs that have the technical ability to provide assistance to each other should conclude such agreements. However, all measures taken should comply with the internal market rules and system op-eration and thus be consistent with Regulation (EU) 2017/1485 establishing a guideline on electricity transmission system operation[38] and Regulation (EU) 2017/2196 providing har-monized rules for emergency situations, including procedures involving black-start serv-ices to the full restoration of the network.[39] Non-market rules can only apply as a last resort and must not unduly distort competition.

---

[31] Recital 12 Regulation 2017/1938.
[32] Art 3(7) Regulation (EU) 2017/1938 and Annex 1 Regulation 2017/1938.
[33] Art 7(1) (2) Regulation (EU) 2017/1938.
[34] Art 2(6) Regulation (EU) 2017/1938.
[35] Ruven Fleming, 'Security of Gas Supply: The New European Approach' in Martha Roggenkamp and Catherine Banet (eds), *European Energy Law Report XII* (Intersentia 2018) 271–291.
[36] Commission Decision of 15 November 2012 setting up the Electricity Coordination Group [2012] OJ C353/2.
[37] See Art 36 Regulation (EU) 2019/943.
[38] Commission Regulation (EU) 2017/1485 [2017] OJ L220/1.
[39] Commission Regulation (EU) 2017/2196 [2017] OJ L312/54.

C. Critical energy infrastructure

Following the terrorist attacks in the USA (2001) and Spain (2004), the Commission launched the concept of critical infrastructure.[40] This resulted in Directive 2008/114/EC on the identification and designation of European critical infrastructure (ECI) and the assessment of the need to improve their protection.[41] The directive applies to the energy sector[42] but only as far as the infrastructure has an impact on the EU as a whole. In particular, it identifies facilities necessary for the production and transmission of energy.[43] In order to identify which parts of the energy infrastructure have a pan-national significance and can be considered as ECI, the directive applies a two-step approach. First, it aims to identify within each MS which infrastructure could be considered as 'critical', i.e. which asset or system is essential for the maintenance of vital societal functions, health, safety, security, economic or social well-being of people, and the disruption or destruction of which would have a significant impact as a result of the failure to maintain those functions.'[44] Secondly, it needs to be assessed whether a critical infrastructure could be qualified as an ECI. The directive requires that a disruption or destruction of a critical infrastructure located in a MS have a significant impact on at least two other MS. The involved MSs shall engage in bilateral and/or multilateral discussions; the Commission may participate in the discussions and the selection procedure if necessary.[45] Ultimately, these discussions need to result in an agreement between the MSs involved. Without such an agreement, an ECI cannot be designated.[46] As a next step, MSs were required to conduct a threat assessment within one year following the designation of an ECI and provide every two years a report presenting generic data on the types of risks, threats, and vulnerabilities encountered per ECI sector.[47] Based on these reports, the Commission and MSs assess whether further protection measures at the Community level should be considered for ECIs.

Entities responsible for investments in, and/or day-to-day operation of an ECI had to establish an 'operator security plan' (OSP).[48] The aim of these OSPs is to identify the critical infrastructure assets of the ECI and which security solutions exist or are being implemented for their protection.[49] In order to liaise with the operators of an ECI, each MS will be required to appoint a Security Liaison Officer (SLO) unless such an officer already is in place or an equivalent exists. The main task of the SLO is to act as the point of contact for security related issues between the owner/operator of the ECI and the relevant MS authority.[50] MSs

[40] Commission, 'Critical infrastructure protection in the fight against terrorism' COM (2004) 702 final.
[41] Council Directive 2008/114/EC on the identification and designation of European critical infrastructures and the assessment of the need to improve their protection [2008] OJ L345/75.
[42] In addition to energy, it also covers the transport sector.
[43] See Annex 1 Directive 2008/114/EC.
[44] Art 2(a) Directive 2008/114/EC. Use is made of following cross-cutting criteria apply: (i) the number of casualties; (ii) the economic impact (including potential environmental effects); and (iii) the public impact (psychological and political impact).
[45] Art 3 Directive 2008/114/EC.
[46] In 2020 some 94 ECIs have been designated; two-thirds are located in three MSs in Central and Eastern Europe, see: COM (2020) 829 final 2.
[47] Art 7 Directive 2008/114/EC. The Commission may develop methodological guidelines for carrying out risk analyses in respect of ECIs. The use of such guidelines shall be optional for the Member States.
[48] See Art 5 Directive 2008/114/EC. Where an equivalent already exists such an arrangement is not required.
[49] The minimum content to be addressed by an OSP procedure is set out in Annex II but includes activities aimed at ensuring the functionality, continuity and integrity of critical infrastructures in order to deter, mitigate, and neutralize a threat, risk or vulnerability.
[50] Art 6 Directive 2008/114/EC.

shall implement appropriate means of communication so that the relevant MS authority and the SLO can exchange information concerning identified risks and threats involving an ECI. In addition to a SLO, each MS should appoint a European critical infrastructure protection contact point (ECIP contact point). The ECIP contact points coordinate ECI protection issues within the MS, with other MSs and with the Commission.[51]

A review conducted in 2012 concluded that the directive primarily fostered bilateral rather than pan-European cooperation on matters relating to critical infrastructure protection but also that insufficient consideration had been given to links between different sectors. This prompted the Commission to pilot a new approach emphasizing interdependencies between sectors because threats to one type of infrastructure can have an impact on actors involved in the operation of other critical infrastructure.[52] This pilot took especially into account the electricity and gas transmission networks given their European dimension. The review also showed that the prevention and response mechanisms of the ECI Directive are in line with Regulation 994/2010 safeguarding gas supply and potential synergies between the energy sector (electricity networks) and ICT technology.[53]

An evaluation of the ECI Directive in 2019 found that the relevance of the directive had diminished due to new and evolving challenges and developments, although the objective of the directive to protect critical infrastructure from natural or man-made hazards, terrorism, and cyber attacks remain relevant but also that the directive does not sufficiently take into account cross-sectoral interdependencies.[54]

D. Assessment

The above has shown that security of supply is of growing importance in the EU. The initial directives governing supply security have been replaced by several lengthy regulations, which have in common the need to take into account cross-border and cascading effects of any serious harm to the physical energy system. This is supplemented by the ECI Directive's attempt to identify which parts of the energy system actually is to be considered critical in the sense that damages to these assets will lead to serious supply disruptions. Such supply interruptions may result from external causes (damages to pipelines and cables due to construction work), internal causes (lack of communication between parties) but increasingly also cybercrime. The latter is acknowledged in the evaluation of the ECI Directive but is also addressed in regulations safeguarding electricity and gas supply.[55] The following section will therefore examine in more detail the governance of cybersecurity and how it affects energy supply.

---

[51] Art 10 Directive 2008/114/EC
[52] Evaluation of Council Directive 2008/114, SWD (2019) 308 final 3.
[53] Ibid, 14–15.
[54] Ibid, 20.
[55] Regulation 2017/1938 and Regulation 2019/941.

IV. Protecting Digital Infrastructure

A. Introduction

With the increasing digitalization of the energy sector, the risk of damages resulting from cybercrime also increases.[56] In the last decade, several examples of supply interruptions due to cyber attacks can be found. In addition, it is not clear how many unsuccessful attempts have been made that are unknown to the outside world. Well known, however, is a series of attacks on the supervisory control and data acquisition (SCADA) systems[57] of three electricity distribution companies in Ukraine in December 2015 as a result of which the circuit breakers of 30 distribution sub-stations were opened. This resulted in massive power outages that left more than 200,000 consumers throughout the country without electricity.[58] In December 2016, another cyber attack took place at a transmission substation in Kiev, which caused an hour-long power outage over one fifth of Ukraine's capital. While the effects were short-lived, the attack was considered a major breach of the country's cybersecurity as it made use of the first malware known to specifically target power systems.[59] In August 2017, a sophisticated cyber attack hit a Saudi petrochemical plant and is the first known attempt to manipulate an emergency shutdown system. If successful the attack could have caused a serious industrial accident. In March 2019, the US grid regulator NERC warned that a hacking group was conducting reconnaissance into the networks of American electrical utilities.[60] The most recent example took place on 7 May 2021 and is the ransomware cyber attack of the Colonial Pipeline's computerized equipment managing the pipeline. After the Colonial Pipeline Company paid the requested ransom ($4.4 million), the hackers sent a software application to restore their network. These examples show that the number of attacks is gradually increasing; it is thus not surprising that the EU is developing some legal instruments specifically addressing the protection of critical infrastructure from cyber attacks.

B. Legal framework

Cybersecurity policy has rapidly evolved over the last decade and is primarily based on a European strategy for an 'Open, Safe and Secure Cyberspace', which aimed at increasing resilience, reducing cybercrime, and developing the necessary resources to ensure

---

[56] The author acknowledges the input of Krastina Razheva, 'Digitalization and energy: a dangerous combination? Assessment of cybersecurity in the energy sector of the European Union' (LLM thesis, University of Groningen 2020).

[57] SCADA is a system of both hardware and software elements that allows the remote operation and monitoring of industrial machinery and is commonly used to manage smart energy grids, see Khairy Sayed, 'SCADA and Smart Energy Grid Control Automation' in Hossam Gabbar (ed), *Smart Energy Grid Engineering* (Elsevier 2017) 481.

[58] Robert Lee, Michael Assante and Tim Conway, 'Analysis of the Cyber Attack on the Ukrainian Power Grid' <https://www.readkong.com/page/analysis-of-the-cyber-attack-on-the-ukrainian-power-grid-6826988> accessed 31 July 2021.

[59] Andy Greenberg, "Crash Override': The Malware That Took down a Power Grid' (New York, 6 December 2017) <www.wired.com/story/crash-override-malware/> accessed 31 July 2021.

[60] European Parliament, 'Cybersecurity of critical energy infrastructure' <https://www.europarl.europa.eu/RegData/etudes/BRIE/2019/642274/EPRS_BRI(2019)642274_EN.pdf> accessed 31 July 2021 3.

cybersecurity. It specifically recognized the significance of ensuring cybersecurity for the energy industry.[61] This policy document is the basis for several legislative developments.

1. Network and Information System Directive

Directive (EU) 2016/1148 on Security of Network and Information Systems (hereafter NIS and NIS Directive) is the first legal instrument to cover the issue of cybersecurity in the EU.[62] The directive defines NIS as 'any device or group of interconnected or related devices, one or more of which, pursuant to a program, perform automatic processing of digital data'.[63] A NIS needs to be operated by an entity identified as an 'operator of essential services' (hereafter OES) as identified in Annex II of the Directive.[64] OES involves undertakings offering services 'essential for the maintenance of critical societal and/or economic activities' and where 'an incident would have significant disruptive effects on the provision of [the] service'.[65] To determine a significant disruptive effect, MSs can take into account the number of users relying on a given service, the dependency of other services, and the impact on public safety and social and economic activities.[66] Considering these criteria, energy undertakings should be considered as an OES as is confirmed by Annex II that basically lists undertakings involved in production, transmission, distribution, and supply of energy. In practice MSs have used different approaches and large fluctuations appear in the numbers of services identified as essential.[67] Within the energy sector, the number varies from 3 to 21 services, involving parts of the energy chain: production, transmission and distribution, operation and maintenance, sale, etc. This may result in an uneven playing field for these energy entities in the internal market.[68]

Next, MSs had to adopt national strategies enabling OES to acquire a high level of security, involving actions regarding risk-preparedness, awareness-raising, and cooperation between the public and private sectors.[69] MSs also need to ensure that OES are taking all necessary technical and organizational measures to ensure a level of security appropriate to build resilience against modern threats and minimize the impact of potential attacks, in accordance with the specific needs of a particular NIS.[70] As part of this process, MSs are required to designate: (i) a national competent authority that will monitor the security of the energy sector; and (ii) one or more Computer Security Incident Response Teams (CSIRTs) that are responsible for risk and incident handling.[71] A CSIRT may be established within a competent authority and is charged with specific tasks, such as monitoring incidents,

---

[61] Commission, 'Cybersecurity Strategy of the European Union: An Open, Safe and Secure Cyberspace' JOIN (2013) 1 final.

[62] Commission, 'NIS Directive' < https://digital-strategy.ec.europa.eu/en/policies/nis-directive > accessed 31 July 2021. Please note that a proposal on measures for a high common level of cybersecurity across the Union has been published on 16 December 2020, see COM (2020) 823 final.

[63] Art 4(1)(b) NIS Directive.

[64] Art 5(1) NIS Directive.

[65] Art 5(2) NIS Directive.

[66] Art 6 NIS Directive.

[67] Commission, 'Report assessing the consistency of the approaches taken by Member States in the identification of operators of essential services in accordance with Art 23(1) of Directive 2016/1148/EU on security of network and information systems' COM (2019) 546 final 10.

[68] Ibid, 11.

[69] Art 7 NIS Directive.

[70] Art 14 NIS Directive.

[71] These CSIRTs shall comply with the requirements set out in point (1) of Annex I and cover at least the sectors referred to in Annex II and the services referred to in Annex III.

establishing mechanisms for early warning and information dissemination for the relevant stakeholders, and rendering resources and expertise in adequate incident response to facilitate the OES.[72] Furthermore, CSIRTs are obliged to participate in an EU-wide network in order 'to promote swift and effective operational cooperation'.[73]

Although energy undertakings identified as NIS would be obliged to take all necessary precautionary measures to strengthen the resilience of its systems, it is still possible that a well-organized cyberattack could disrupt the system's defence mechanisms. If so, the OES has to report the incident to the national competent authority, and the appointed CSIRT would be required to facilitate the company's response. This mechanism brings about two crucial benefits. First, the attacked company has at its disposal its own resources and expertise but also those of the relevant CSIRT to respond to the attack and recover its systems. This may significantly reduce the system's recovery time and thus limit company's financial burden. Moreover, the national CSIRT needs to communicate the incident and the measures taken to the EU CSIRT network as a result of which all MSs and their national competent authorities will be able to learn from the experiences, resulting in higher levels of risk preparedness and an overall enhancement of NIS resilience.

2. Cybersecurity Act

Due to the fast-growing cyber threats, the EU presented in 2017 a Cybersecurity Package to develop a uniform strategy towards enhancing cybersecurity in the EU.[74] Two years later it adopted Regulation (EU) 2019/881 (hereafter Cybersecurity Act), which follows up on the NIS Directive and underlines the need to consider energy as a sector with essential services, and the necessity to reinforce NIS.[75]

The Act grants a permanent mandate to the European Network and Information Security Agency (ENISA) and significantly increases its resources and competences.[76] Although ENISA was already established in 2004[77], it did not award European actors sufficient competences to provide adequate security of NIS.[78] The Security Act, however, obliges ENISA to assist MSs, their competent authorities and relevant CSIRTs in their implementation of the NIS Directive, by issuing opinions and guidelines, as well as by providing expert advice and facilitating cooperation in the form of incident reporting and information sharing.[79] ENISA is thus given a core position in the European CSIRTs network, especially as it already was obliged to act as the network's secretariat.[80] ENISA is also called upon to support and promote the development and use of a cybersecurity certification framework that will lead to tailored certification schemes for specific categories of information and communication technology products, processes, and services. As a result, companies only have to certify

---

[72]   Annex I NIS Directive.

[73]   Art 12(1) NIS Directive.

[74]   Commission, 'Resilience, Deterrence and Defence: Building strong cybersecurity for the EU' JOIN (2017) 450 final.

[75]   Cybersecurity Act, recital 1.

[76]   Art 3 Cybersecurity Act.

[77]   Regulation (EC) No 460/2004 of 10 March 2004 establishing the European Network and Information Security Agency [2004] OJ L77/1.

[78]   Art 2 Regulation 460/2004.

[79]   Art 5(2) Regulation 460/2004.

[80]   Art 12(2) NIS Directive.

their products, processes, or services once and obtain certificates that are valid in the entire EU.[81]

The Act is thus significantly strengthening the foundations of ENISA, effectively inaugurating it as a well-secured agency with a wide range of competences and clearly set objectives to facilitate Member States in strengthening their systems and transforming the European Union into one large, cyber-resilient system. It approaches cybersecurity from an all-encompassing point of view but at the same time recognizes the significance of the individual sectors, among which are energy, transport, and healthcare. However, it may be that there is a need for energy-specific cybersecurity regulation specifically adapted to the needs of the industry.

3. Commission Recommendation on Cybersecurity in the Energy Sector

An attempt of energy specific cybersecurity regulation can be found in Commission Recommendation (EU) 2019/553 issued in April 2019.[82] It presents guidelines that MSs and key stakeholders (particularly energy system operators) should take into account when making decisions about their infrastructure and that should be regularly reviewed depending on the progress made. It stresses the need to consider the specifics of the energy sector, like real-time requirements involving the need to react to commands in few milliseconds (balancing) and the cascading effects of incidents. The guidelines propose measures involving cybersecurity risk analysis and preparedness, including the need to regularly update software and hardware, and establishing an automated monitoring capability for security events.

C. New developments

1. Network code on cybersecurity

Regulation 2019/943 on the Internal Electricity Market entitles the Commission to adopt network codes providing sector-specific rules for cyber security aspects of cross-border electricity flows, including rules on common minimum requirements, planning, monitoring, reporting, and crisis management.[83] This network code will regulate topics that are not specified in the NIS Directive and would be better scoped in specific secondary energy legislation.

As a first step for developing this network code on cybersecurity, the Commission invited ACER on 28 January 2021 to draft a framework guideline (see above Section II.A), taking into account the preparatory works by, amongst others, the Smart Grids Task Force.[84] ACER published the draft framework guideline for public consultation on 30 April 2021.[85] These framework guidelines focus on presenting an early warning system for the

---

[81] Art 8 Cybersecurity Act.
[82] Commission Recommendation (EU) 2019/553 of 3 April 2019 on cybersecurity in the energy sector [2019] OJ L96/50.
[83] Art 59(2)(e) Regulation (EU) 2019/943.
[84] Smart Grid Task Force Expert Group 2 Cybersecurity, 'Recommendations for the European Commission on Implementation of a Network Code on Cybersecurity' <https://ec.europa.eu/energy/sites/ener/files/sgtf_eg2_2nd_interim_report_final.pdf> accessed 31 July 2021.
[85] The consultation ran until 29 June 2021, see <https://ec.europa.eu/info/news/public-consultation-establish-priority-list-network-codes-2020-feb-11_en> accessed 31 July 2021.

energy sector in Europe, cross-border and cross-organization risk assessment, a minimum protection level for energy system operators and a common electricity cybersecurity framework.[86] Based on this framework guideline, ENTSO-E will draft the network code. ACER will then assess the draft code whilst taking into account its degree of compliance with this Framework Guideline.

2. Proposal for a Directive on the Resilience of Critical Entities

On 16 December 2020 the European Commission presented a proposal for a directive on the Resilience of Critical Entities.[87] This new directive will replace the existing ECI Directive and better reflect the increased challenges to critical infrastructure and a closer alignment with the NIS Directive (as will be amended to NIS2).[88] It will present minimum requirements for MSs and critical entities identified under the new framework.

The proposal provides a procedure for the identification of critical entities offering services to or in several (if not all) MSs. It thus aims at ensuring that competent authorities designated under this directive, and under the proposed NIS 2 Directive, will take necessary measures and exchange information regarding cyber and non-cyber resilience. Notably, the physical security of NIS of entities in the digital infrastructure sector is also dealt with in the proposed NIS 2 Directive.[89]

Given the above, the proposal identifies some important changes compared to the existing directives. First, the proposed directive applies to a large group of entities, including transport, energy, health, water, waste, digital infrastructure. Secondly, these critical identities will be identified by means of common criteria on the basis of a national risk assessment. Thirdly, it expands the cross-border impact as critical entities that supply to or in more than one third of all MSs will be subject to special oversight. The directive's implementation will be supported by a dedicated knowledge hub within the Commission and the Commission will establish the Critical Entities Resilience Group, which will act as an expert group to advice the Commission and promote strategic cooperation and an exchange of information. Last, the directive also provides for cooperation with entities outside the EU as interdependencies do not stop at EU external borders.

V. Conclusion

This chapter has analysed the EU legal framework designed since the beginning of this century to safeguard energy systems from external disruptions and secure energy supply. The analysis has shown an evolution in the use of legislative instruments, types of infrastructure involved, and legal measures to protect the infrastructure.

When considering the legislative instruments it becomes clear that increasing use is made of regulations, which have a direct effect rather than directives. As disruptions to

---

[86] ACER, 'Framework Guideline on sector-specific rules for cybersecurity aspects of cross-border electricity flows (Draft)', <https://documents.acer.europa.eu/Official_documents/Public_consultations/PC_2021_E_04/Draft%20Framework%20Guideline%20on%20sector-specific%20rules%20for%20cybersecurity%20aspects%20of%20cross-border%20electricity%20flows.pdf> accessed 31 July 2021.

[87] Commission 2020 (n 46).

[88] Ibid, 1.

[89] Ibid, 4.

the interconnected energy system may have cascading effects, it is beneficial to use one single legal framework that applies equally to all MS. Moreover, gradually the focus has been switching to crises that have a serious impact and thus disregarding smaller interruptions and imbalances with which TSOs are used to dealing. Additionally, the emphasis is no longer limited to physical infrastructures but extended to non-physical (digital) infrastructures. Protecting the latter has become a major challenge as cyber attacks can be a major cause of serious supply interruptions.

The analysis also shows some common features. All legislative instruments show a tendency towards regional cooperation, the need to identify the critical or vulnerable infrastructure, the need to identify who is the operator of the essential service or the security plan, how to deal with risk-preparedness and risk management plans and response mechanisms, and last but not least to appoint a national coordinator and a coordinating body on EU level. Given the interdependencies between the energy and ICT sectors, the result may be that several regimes and coordinating bodies apply jointly, which may cause an additional risk. Integrating and streamlining the procedures is thus a welcome development.

The rapid digitalization of the energy sector requires a common approach on EU level. However, data-driven technology is not limited to traditional market parties and system operators but is increasingly used locally by active consumers (prosumers), energy communities, aggregators, electric vehicles, and charging stations. Although disruptions to these data systems may have less impact on the system as a whole, it may still distort energy supply and should thus be taken into account when drafting an EU legal framework providing for resilient energy systems.

6

Building Resilience into U.S. Energy Transport Infrastructure

Alexandra B. Klass and Isaac Foote

I. Introduction

Since the beginning of the 21st century, the effects of climate change have created increasingly serious threats to the U.S. energy system. Hurricanes Katrina, Sandy, Harvey, Irma, and Maria have knocked out power for tens of millions of people, resulting in loss of life and property;[1] wildfires across the western United States have created blackouts and brownouts resulting in death, property damage, and billions of dollars in losses;[2] and extreme cold weather events have placed significant pressure on state and regional energy systems, most notably during the 2021 deep freeze in Texas and surrounding states, resulting in numerous deaths, devastating property damages, and likely financial losses upwards of $120 billion.[3] All of these threats are expected to become more regular occurrences as climate change and its associated effects accelerate into the future. In the context of these climate-related threats, the ability of the energy system to withstand shocks is a growing concern throughout the United States, with some experts giving the nation low marks for its current investment in critical energy infrastructure.[4]

Not surprisingly, this concern has resulted in a greater focus on building increased energy system 'resilience,' a trend that is reflected in a growing number of laws and regulations nationwide requiring system stakeholders to implement resilience concepts into their planning, investment, and decision-making.[5] This chapter evaluates the meaning of energy system resilience in the context of U.S. energy transport infrastructure—the electric

---

[1] National Academies of Sciences, Engineering, and Medicine (National Academies), 'Enhancing the Resilience of the Nation's Electricity System' (*The National Academies Press*, 2017) 58–66; Jonathan Schneider and Jonathan Trotta, 'What We Talk About When We Talk About Resilience' (2018) 39 Energy Law Journal 353.

[2] Katie Worth and Karen Pinchin, 'After Deadly Fire, Regulators and Consumers Question PG&E Blackouts' (*Frontline*, 15 November 2019) <https://www.pbs.org/wgbh/frontline/article/deadly-paradise-fire-regulators-consumers-pge-blackouts-pge-outage/>; Kavla Balaraman, 'Wildfires Pushed PG&E into Bankruptcy. Should Other Utilities Be Worried?' (*Utility Dive*, 19 November 2020) <https://www.utilitydive.com/news/wildfires-pushed-pge-into-bankruptcy-should-other-utilities-be-worried/588435/>.

[3] Alexandra B. Klass, 'Lessons From the Texas Grid Disaster: Planning and Investing for a Different Future' (*Lawfare*, 22 February 2021) <https://www.lawfareblog.com/lessons-texas-grid-disaster-planning-and-investing-different-future>; Brian K. Sullivan, 'Texas Deep Freeze Could Cost $90 Billion in Losses, Modeler Says' (*Bloomberg Law*, 24 February 2021) <https://www.bloomberg.com/news/articles/2021-02-24/texas-deep-freeze-could-cost-90-billion-in-losses-modeler-says>.

[4] Argonne National Laboratory, 'Front-Line Resilience Perspectives: The Electric Grid' (*Argonne National Lab*, 1 November 2016); American Society of Civil Engineers, 2021 Report Card for America's Infrastructure: Energy (*American Society of Civil Engineers* 2021).

[5] Daniel Shea, 'Hardening the Grid: How States are Working to Establish a Resilient and Reliable Electric System' (*National Conference of State Legislatures*, 24 April 2018); Sara R. Gosman, 'Framing Energy Resilience' (2019) 35 Journal of Land Use and Environmental Law 1, 4–5; U.S. Government Accountability Office, 'Electricity

Alexandra B. Klass and Isaac Foote, *Building Resilience into U.S. Energy Transport Infrastructure* In: *Resilience in Energy, Infrastructure, and Natural Resources Law*. Edited by: Catherine Banet, Hanri Mostert, LeRoy Paddock, Milton Fernando Montoya, and Íñigo del Guayo, Oxford University Press. © Alexandra B. Klass and Isaac Foote 2022. DOI: 10.1093/oso/9780192864574.003.0006

transmission lines, oil and natural gas pipelines, and related networks that support the generation, transportation, and use of energy in U.S. society. In doing so, we explore the use of engineering, ecological, and social-ecological resilience strategies described in Chapter 2, as well as the application of 'anti-resilience' thinking, to the U.S. energy transportation network. Section II discusses resilience in the U.S. electric transmission grid, Section III explores resilience for oil and natural gas pipelines, and Section IV proposes permitting and eminent domain reforms for both electric transmission line and pipeline infrastructure to support a clean energy transition which, in turn, will increase overall system resilience.

II. Building U.S. Electric Grid Resilience

The U.S. electric grid transmits electric energy to homes, businesses, and industries over a complex network of long-distance, high-voltage transmission lines connected to lower voltage distribution lines from over 7,000 large power plants and an even larger number of smaller power generation facilities.[6] This Section explores: (A) the laws governing the U.S. electric grid, (B) efforts of U.S. government regulators to define and address electric grid resilience, and (C) the potential to enhance electric grid resilience through a clean energy transition made possible by (1) the expansion and interconnection of long-distance high-voltage electric transmission lines and (2) expansion of smaller-scale distributed energy resources (DERs).

A. Introduction to U.S. electricity regulation

The regulation of the U.S. electric grid is the primary responsibility of the Federal Energy Regulatory Commission (FERC) and the North American Electric Reliability Corporation (NERC). Under the Federal Power Act of 1935 and the Energy Policy Act of 2005 (EPAct 2005), FERC is charged with regulating the wholesale sale of electricity in interstate commerce, the transmission of electricity in interstate commerce, and the reliability of the U.S. electric grid.[7] After the massive grid failure that led to the 2003 blackouts in the northeast United States, Congress authorized FERC to delegate some of its reliability responsibilities to NERC, which today sets national and regional reliability standards for aspects of the electric grid that are subject to FERC oversight and approval.[8] Many of these standards are carried out by Regional Transmission Organizations (RTOs) and Independent System Operators (ISOs), which are independent, non-profit, sometimes multi-state, entities that

Grid: Opportunities Exist for Department of Energy to Better Support Utilities in Improving Resilience to Hurricanes' (*U.S. Government Accountability Office*, 5 March 2021).

[6] U.S. Department of Energy, 'Staff Report to the Secretary on Electricity Markets and Reliability' (*U.S. Department of Energy*, 16 August 2017) 1.

[7] 16 U.S.C. §§ 824–824w; Energy Policy Act of 2005, Pub. L. No. 109-59 §§ 1201–1221, 119 Stat. 594, 941–946; Federal Energy Regulatory Commission (FERC), 'What FERC Does' (*FERC*) <https://www.ferc.gov/about/what-ferc/what-ferc-does> accessed 20 February 2021.

[8] FERC, 'Federal Energy Regulatory Commission Strategic Plan FY 2018-2022' (*FERC*, September 2018) 13; National Academies, 'The Future of Electric Power in the United States' (*The National Academies Press*, 2021) 107; North American Electric Reliability Corporation (NERC), 'About NERC' (*NERC*) <https://www.nerc.com/AboutNERC/Pages/default.aspx> accessed 20 February 2021.

manage many aspects of the electric transmission system on behalf of electric utilities and other transmission owners serving approximately two-thirds of the U.S. population.[9]

At the state level, public utility commissions (PUCs) regulate the retail sale of electricity within their borders, approve the construction of electric generation facilities (other than nuclear and hydropower facilities), and have jurisdiction over the approval (or 'siting') and construction of electric transmission lines.[10] Thus, with only a few exceptions (e.g. connecting federal hydropower projects to the electric grid and electric transmission lines that cross federal lands), electric utilities and other actors wishing to build a transmission line must obtain a siting certificate from the state PUC in each state in which the line passes, and any use of eminent domain authority to obtain the necessary easements to build the line must come from state law. Accordingly, even if a proposed transmission line spanning multiple states would meet a regional or national need, neither FERC nor any other federal agency generally has authority to approve the line or grant the operator the right to use eminent domain to build it.[11] Thus, while FERC and NERC are responsible for electric grid regulation and reliability, the power to approve the transmission infrastructure necessary to ensure resilience and reliability falls primarily to the states.

B. Contemporary efforts to define electric grid resilience

In 2010, the National Infrastructure Advisory Council performed the first major federal energy system resilience analysis and found the U.S. electricity system was highly resilient but in need of investment in extra-high-voltage transformers, regulatory reforms allowing for additional cost recovery for resilience investment, increased information sharing between agencies and utilities, and improved disaster response planning.[12] These results were broadly replicated in later federal studies by the Department of Homeland Security,[13] Argonne National Laboratory,[14] and the National Academies of Sciences, Engineering, and Medicine (National Academies).[15] These agencies and organizations began to define the role of resilience in the context of infrastructure broadly and the electricity sector specifically. For instance, the National Academies report stated:

> Resilience is not the same as reliability. While minimizing the likelihood of large-area, long-duration outages is important, a resilient system is one that acknowledges that such outages can occur, prepares to deal with them, minimizes their impact when they occur, is able to restore service quickly, and draws lessons from the experience to improve performance in the future.[16]

---

[9] FERC, 'Electric Power Markets' (*FERC*, 23 October 2020) <https://www.ferc.gov/industries-data/market-assessments/electric-power-markets>.

[10] James W. Coleman and Alexandra B. Klass, 'Energy and Eminent Domain' (2019) 104 Minnesota Law Review 659, 700.

[11] Ibid.

[12] National Infrastructure Advisory Council, 'A Framework for Establishing Critical Infrastructure Resilience Goals: Final Report and Recommendations by the Council' (*National Infrastructure Advisory Council*, 19 October 2010).

[13] U.S. Department of Homeland Security (DHS), 'National Infrastructure Protection Plan: Partnership for Critical Infrastructure Security and Resilience' (*DHS*, 2013) 6.

[14] Argonne National Laboratory, 'Front-Line Resilience Perspectives' (n 4)

[15] National Academies, 'Enhancing Resilience' (n 1).

[16] Ibid, 10.

In 2018, during the Trump Administration, FERC opened a regulatory docket to consider the resilience of the U.S. electric grid. This was prompted by a request from the U.S. Department of Energy (DOE), which has authority to propose rules and policies for expedited consideration by FERC.[17] The request reflected then-Energy Secretary Rick Perry's concern that federal environmental regulations were making 'baseload' (i.e. coal and nuclear) electric generation plants less competitive in RTO/ISO wholesale electricity markets, leading to the early retirement of those plants and adversely impacting electric grid resilience.[18]

It was clear from the beginning that DOE's proposed rule would provide significant financial subsidies to coal and nuclear facilities.[19] The DOE proposal was opposed by environmental groups; state regulators; utilities; RTOs/ISOs; and renewable, hydroelectric, and natural gas industry groups.[20] They viewed the proposed rule as a massive subsidy to the affected plants and entirely ineffective at increasing system resilience.[21] FERC rejected the proposed rule in 2018 on grounds that it did not satisfy the requirement of showing that existing RTO/ISO tariffs and practices were 'unjust and unreasonable' under Section 206 of the Federal Power Act.[22] Commissioner Richard Glick, in a concurring statement, declared that '[t]he proposed rule had little, if anything to do with resilience and was instead aimed at subsidizing certain uncompetitive electric generation technologies.'[23]

Significantly though, in its order rejecting the DOE proposed rule, FERC recognized the need for increased focus on resilience in the electricity sector and opened a new docket to 'explore resilience issues in the RTOs/ISOs.'[24] In this order, FERC defined resilience as 'the ability to withstand and reduce the magnitude and/or duration of disruptive events, which includes the capability to anticipate, absorb, adapt to, and/or rapidly recover from such an event.'[25] The definition drew heavily from reports by the National Infrastructure Advisory Council and National Academies described above.

In February 2021, FERC closed the resilience docket.[26] In terminating the docket, FERC recognized that resilience 'could encompass a range of attributes, characteristics, and services that allow the grid to withstand, adapt to, and recover from both naturally occurring and man-made disruptive events' and that, 'at the most basic level, ensuring resilience requires that we both (1) determine which risks to the grid we are going to protect against, and (2) identify the steps, if any, needed to ensure those risks are addressed.'[27] However, FERC

---

[17] 42 U.S.C.A. § 7173; Sharon Jacobs, 'The Statutory Separation of Powers' (2019) 179 Yale Law Journal 378, 415–418.

[18] Memorandum to the Chief of Staff from U.S. Energy Secretary Rick Perry, Study Examining Electricity Markets and Reliability (14 April 2017); U.S. Department of Energy, Notice of Proposed Rulemaking, Grid Resiliency Pricing Rule, 82 Fed. Reg. 46940 (10 October 2017).

[19] Schneider and Trotta (n 1) 377.

[20] Jacobs (n 17) 377; Shalanda H. Baker, 'Anti-Resilience: A Roadmap for Transformational Justice Within the Energy System' (2019) 54 Harvard Civil Rights & Civil Liberties Law Review 1, 34–37.

[21] Stephanie Phillips, Note, 'Federal Regulation for a Resilient Electricity Grid' (2019) 46 Ecology Law Quarterly 415, 431.

[22] Order Terminating Rulemaking Proceeding, Initiating New Proceeding, and Establishing Additional Procedures, Grid Reliability & Resilience Pricing; Grid Resilience in Regional Transmission Organizations & Independent System Operators, 162 FERC ¶ 61,012, P 8 (8 January 2018); 16 U.S.C. § 824e.

[23] Ibid, P 1.

[24] Ibid, P 10.

[25] Ibid, P 13.

[26] Order Terminating Proceeding, Grid Resilience in Regional Transmission Organizations and Independent System Operators, 174 FERC ¶ 61,111 (18 February 2021).

[27] Ibid, P 24.

also stated that, based on the record it compiled over the three years comment period, it did not believe any 'generic action' was in order because of significant regional differences, both with regard to threats to the grid, such as hurricanes, heat waves, or extreme cold, as well as the solutions to those challenges.[28]

C. Building ecological and social-ecological resilience in the U.S. electric grid in the face of climate change through grid expansion and DER investment

There is a growing consensus that climate change will 'affect every aspect of the electricity grid, from generation, to transmission, to end-user demand.'[29] As a result, the National Academies argues that, to ensure a resilient and reliable electric grid, the United States must accelerate its clean energy transition in a way that can 'expand the system's ability to generate and move power so as to make abundant electricity available to support the deep decarbonization of all parts of the economy.'[30] Yet, as discussed above, FERC and other electric grid regulators are only beginning to address how to define and implement resilience in the electricity sector. This creates a moment of opportunity for policymakers and regulators to ensure that investing in resilience is not limited to the 'physical resilience' of grid infrastructure. Instead, they must mandate that the actors building and operating the U.S. electric grid support the 'system resilience' of the grid through decarbonizing the electric system.

The remainder of this section identifies two pathways to concurrently increase the physical and system resilience of the U.S. electric grid: (1) by investing in a more interconnected 'macrogrid' that spans the United States and (2) by enhancing more localized DERs to complement that expansion. These pathways are innovative in their ability to combine ecological and social-ecological resilience strategies to simultaneously insulate the grid against climatic shocks and use the threat of those shocks to transition to a decarbonized electric system.

1. Building a U.S. 'macrogrid'

Proponents of a macrogrid buildout argue that to address the dual goals of increasing physical grid resilience and supporting system resilience through decarbonization, we must pursue a massive investment in our existing long-distance electric transmission system.[31] This strategy will involve (i) reinvesting in existing transmission capacity and (ii) expanding the transmission system itself. To advocates, this approach will increase redundancy and integration across the grid, maximize the efficiencies of utility-scale renewable generation, and ensure renewable generation can reach customers everywhere in the United States.[32]

---

[28] Ibid, PP 4–5.
[29] U.S. General Accountability Office (GAO), 'Electric Grid Resilience: Climate Change is Expected to Have Far-Reaching Effects and DOE and FERC Should Take Action' (*GAO*, March 2021).
[30] National Academies, 'The Future of Electric Power' (n 8); Andlinger Center for Energy and the Environment, 'The Net-Zero America Project' (*Princeton University*) <https://acee.princeton.edu/rapidswitch/projects/net-zero-america-project/> accessed 27 June 2021.
[31] James H. Williams et al, 'Carbon-Neutral Pathways for the United States', 2 AGU Advances e2020AV00284 (2021); Americans for a Clean Energy Grid (ACEG), 'Planning for the Future: FERC's Opportunity to Spur More Cost-Effective Transmission Infrastructure' (*ACEG*, 19 January 2021).
[32] Aaron Bloom et al, 'The Value of Increased HVDC Capacity Between Eastern and Western U.S. Grids: The Interconnections Seams Study' (*National Renewable Energy Lab (NREL)*, Preprint, October 2020); Alexandra B. Klass, 'Transmission, Distribution and Storage: Grid Integration' in Michel B. Gerrard and John C. Dernbach (eds),

To accomplish this, grid researchers argue that the United States must build a network of long-distance, high-voltage direct current (HVDC) transmission lines and more long-distance alternating current (AC) lines. The National Renewable Energy Laboratory's Interconnection Seams Study issued in 2020 is one model that would accomplish this goal,[33] while the Climate Institute's 'North American Supergrid' proposal would provide a different means of achieving a similar outcome.[34]

An expansion of the grid footprint can simultaneously increase physical grid resilience and facilitate the decarbonization of the American economy. Today's grid was built on a hub-and-spoke model, centred around large fossil-fuel and nuclear generation plants: forms of generation that are relatively flexible in terms of siting requirements.[35] Renewable energy generation today, however, is far more geographically dependent: wind energy capacity is most abundant in the Midwest and Plains states while the strongest solar resources are in the Southeast and Southwest.[36] Increasing long-distance transmission line connections between regions has the dual advantages of increased grid resilience[37] and facilitating the transition to renewable power.[38] This investment in redundancy and diversity of power supply is very consistent with ecological resilience principles as electric generation failures in one region can be compensated for with sufficient connections to others.

The extreme cold weather that set off the Texas electric grid disaster in February 2021 demonstrates the value of this form of resilience. The United States has three electric grids that operate in relative autonomy from each other—the Eastern Interconnection, the Western Interconnection, and the Electric Reliability Council of Texas, or ERCOT.[39] Texas is the only state in the continental United States that is isolated in this way. While Texas' independence has allowed it to engage in a range of innovative forms energy development and market-based solutions, including significant wind and transmission line buildout, the 2021 winter storm turned Texas's independent grid into a liability.[40] When the storm brought extremely low temperatures to the entire state, it caused failures across multiple forms of energy generation and took nearly half of the state's electric power plants offline. At the same time, demand skyrocketed as residents turned on electric heaters to heat their homes. Facing insufficient electricity to meet residents' needs and limited transmission

---

Legal Pathways to Deep Decarbonization in the United States (Washington D.C., Environmental Law Institute 2019) 529–531; Brattle, 'Unlocking The Queue With Grid-Enhancing Technologies' (*Brattle*, 1 February 2021) 57–58.

[33]   NREL, 'Interconnections Seams Study' (n 32).

[34]   Climate Institute, 'North American Supergrid' (12 December 2017).

[35]   Alexandra B. Klass, 'Future-Proofing Energy Transport Law' (2017) 94 Washington University Law Review 827, 847.

[36]   Dennis Elliott et al, '80 and 100 Meter Wind Energy Resource Potential for the United States' (*NREL*, May 2010); U.S. Department of Energy, Solar Energy Potential, (*U.S. Department of Energy*) <http://energy.gov/maps/solar-energy-potential>; Catherine Morehouse, 'Xcel Proposes $1.7B Transmission Investment in Colorado to Unlock Nearly 5.5 GW New Renewables' (*Utility Dive*, March 4, 2021) <https://www.utilitydive.com/news/xcel-proposes-17b-transmission-investment-in-colorado-to-unlock-nearly-5>.

[37]   U.S. Energy Information Administration (EIA), 'Assessing HVDC Transmission For Impacts of Non-Dispatchable Generation' (*EIA*, 27 June 2018) 24.

[38]   NREL, 'Interconnections Seams Study' (n 32) 5–7; Climate Institute (n 34) 40–43; Karen Uhlenhuth, 'Power from the Prairie Aims to Link West Coast Sun with Midwest Wind' (*Energy News Network*, 24 November 2020) <https://energynews.us/2020/11/24/power-from-the-prairie-aims-to-link-west-coast-sun-with-midwest-wind/>.

[39]   Klass, 'Future-Proofing Energy Transport Law' (n 35) n. 207.

[40]   Clifford Krauss et al, 'How Texas' Drive for Energy Independence Set It Up for Disaster' (*The New York Times*, 21 February 2021) <https://www.nytimes.com/2021/02/21/us/texas-electricity-ercot-blackouts.html>.

connections to unaffected parts of the country, ERCOT resorted to sustained blackouts for millions of residents to avoid a total grid collapse, resulting in numerous deaths and billions of dollars in property damage. Part of this outage was a failure of ecological resilience; by limiting their balancing area, Texas was susceptible to any disaster that impacted the entire state at once.[41]

2. Electric grid resilience through expanding distributed energy resources

In moving away from a hub-and-spoke grid and towards a grid adapted to accommodate two-way energy flows and a broader range and type of energy generation plants, the opportunity for DERs emerges. 'DERs are physical and virtual assets that are deployed across the distribution grid, typically close to load, and usually behind the meter, which can be used individually or in aggregate to provide value to the grid, individual customers, or both.'[42] They include distributed renewable energy generation such as rooftop solar,[43] distributed battery storage,[44] microgrids,[45] and smart grid enabled demand side management.[46] Each serves to manage energy production and consumption at levels far below what typical grid operators address and attempts to increase efficiency, use of renewables, and resiliency.[47] Thus, DERs represent a fundamental shift in how energy is used and consumed in the United States and are an example of a developing social-ecological resilience strategy.

Each of the component technologies of DERs will have a direct impact on the resilience of the grid. First, by moving from a centralized to a decentralized generation system, distributed generation and battery storage will enable a level of response diversity impossible under the tradition system of generation.[48] Rolling blackouts in California in 2020 and Texas in 2021 were caused, in part, from failures at large-scale generation plants and/or large-scale electric transmission.[49] By moving the system away from reliance on a few sub-system parts, an electric grid with fully integrated DERs may be able to better withstand sub-system failures without threatening the grid as a whole.[50] Second, smart grid integration can increase the resilience of the electric grid through changing the adaptive capacity of the system. Smart grid technologies enable demand response at levels far greater than currently available.[51] This means that when the grid is under significant strain, a grid

[41] Edward Klump et al, 'Blackout Crisis: Fallout, Furor, and Fact Checks' (*Energywire*, 17 February 2021) <https://www.eenews.net/stories/1063725271>.

[42] Smart Electric Power Alliance, 'Beyond the Meter: Recommended Reading for a Modern Grid' (*Smart Electric Power Alliance*, June 2017).

[43] Richard L. Revesz and Burcin Unel, 'Managing the Future of the Electricity Grid: Distributed Generation and Net Metering' (2018) 41 Harvard Environmental Law Review 43, 44.

[44] Richard L. Revesz and Burcin Unel, 'Managing the Future of the Electricity Grid: Energy Storage and Greenhouse Gas Emissions' (2017) 42 Harvard Environmental Law Review 139, 155–172.

[45] Dan T. Ton and Merrill A. Smith, 'The United States Department of Energy's Microgrid Initiative' (2012) 25 Electricity Journal 84, 84.

[46] Eity Sarker et al, 'Progress on the Demand Side Management in Smart Grid and Optimization Approaches' (2019) 45 International Journal of Energy Research 36, 37.

[47] Revesz and Unel, 'Distributed Generation and Net Metering' (n 43) 79.

[48] Ibid, 149; U.S. Department of Energy Office of Energy Policy and Systems Analysis, 'Climate Change and the Electricity Sector: Guide for Climate Change Resilience Planning' (*U.S. Department of Energy*, September 2016).

[49] California ISO, 'Final Root Cause Analysis Mid-August 2020 Extreme Heat Wave' (*California ISO*, 13 January 2021); Catherine Morehouse, 'Power Experts Cite Gas Constraints as Main Cause of ERCOT Outages, but System Planning Questions Remain' (*Utility Dive*, 18 February 2021) <https://www.utilitydive.com/news/power-experts-cite-gas-constraints-as-main-cause-of-ercot-outages-but-syst>.

[50] National Association of Regulatory Utility Commission (NARUC), 'Advancing Electric System Resilience with Distributed Energy Resources: A Review of State Policies' (*NARUC*, April 2020) 7.

[51] Pierluigi Siano, 'Demand Response and Smart Grids-A Survey' (2014) 30 Renewable & Sustainable Energy Review 461, 461–464.

sufficiently integrated into the 'internet-of-things' will be able to push down demand far more aggressively than grid operators can today.[52]

Professor Shalanda Baker argues that properly implemented DERs can meet the goals of facilitating the energy transition, increasing traditional concepts of resilience, *and* addressing energy justice consistent with an anti-resilience strategy.[53] She points out the inherent contradiction between energy resilience (which is meant to entrench the existing energy system) and energy justice (which seeks to disrupt a status quo in energy that both concentrates negative externalities in communities of colour and centralizes economic control of the system outside these communities) and describes a way forward that addresses both concerns with community energy models.[54] One example of this in practice is the microgrid proposed in the historic African American Bronzeville neighbourhood of Chicago. This collaboration between the city, the electric utility, and community is attempting to put this vision of resilience and racial justice into action through targeted microgrid development.[55] Another example of this approach is a 2021 proposal to convert Puerto Rico's centralized, fossil fuel based electric grid to one in which every home on the island is equipped with solar power and battery storage, resulting in lower electricity prices, eliminating centralized fossil fuel generation, and making the island's energy system more resilient to severe weather threats like the hurricane that destroyed the island's electric grid in 2017.[56]

III. Building Oil and Natural Gas Pipeline Resilience

Private oil and natural gas pipeline companies own and operate approximately three million miles of natural gas pipelines and nearly 200,000 miles of petroleum pipelines that transport and distribute these fossil fuel resources from extraction sites to refineries to end use consumers.[57] Unlike in the electricity sector, regulators have not addressed the role of resilience—as opposed to reliability or safety—in the context of oil and natural gas pipelines. Thus, this Section begins by introducing the laws and regulations governing the construction, operation, and safety of the U.S. oil and natural gas pipeline network. It then discusses how increased safety regulations of existing pipelines coupled with a retreat from investing in new, long-lived fossil fuel pipeline infrastructure is a way to build both engineering resilience and social-ecological resilience in that system.

[52] Michael Panfil, 'Resiliency+: Demand Response Can Help Prevent Blackouts in the Northeast' (*Environmental Defense Fund*, 30 June 2014) <https://blogs.edf.org/energyexchange/2014/06/30/resiliency-demand-respo nse-can-help-prevent-blackouts-in-the-northeast/>; Seulbi Lee et al, 'Impact of Demand-Side Response on Community Resilience: Focusing on a Power Grid After Seismic Hazards' (2020) 36 Journal of Management in Engineering 04020071-1, 04020071-10.11.

[53] Baker (n 20) 25–27.

[54] Ibid, 25–31.

[55] Kari Lydersen, 'Chicago Shines in a New Global Study of Cities' Resiliency and Clean Energy Plans. But Can It Keep Its Promises?' (*Energy News Network*, 30 January 2020) <https://energynews.us/2020/01/30/chicago-shi nes-in-a-new-global-study-of-cities-resiliency-and-clean-energy-plans-but-can-it-keep-its-promises/>.

[56] Cathy Kunkel and Ingrid Vila Biaggi, 'IEEFA: Puerto Rico Can Provide Resiliency to 100% of Homes Through Solar Expansion' (*Institute for Energy Economics and Financial Analysis*, 12 March 2021) <https://ieefa.org/ieefa-puerto-rico-can-provide-resiliency-to-100-of-homes-through-solar-expansion/>.

[57] EIA, *Natural Gas Pipelines*, (EIA, 3 December 2020) <https://www.eia.gov/energyexplained/natural-gas/natu ral-gas-pipelines.php>.

A. U.S. Regulation of oil and natural gas pipelines

The siting and regulation of natural gas pipelines differs significantly from the siting and regulation of electric transmission lines. FERC has authority under the Natural Gas Act of 1938 to grant a certificate of public convenience of necessity to a natural gas pipeline company proposing to build an interstate natural gas pipeline; this carries with it the power of eminent domain.[58] Although states can provide input on the certificate process and ensure their water quality protection regulations are met, they do not have direct veto power over interstate natural gas pipelines as they do with interstate electric transmission lines. FERC also has extensive regulatory authority over natural gas pipeline rates and charges.[59]

As for interstate oil pipelines, it is the states, not FERC or any other federal agency, that have jurisdiction to grant a siting permit and eminent domain authority, similar to the regulatory regime for interstate electric transmission lines. Thus, an interstate oil pipeline needs siting approval and eminent domain authority from each state in its path, although most states by statute do not make that process particularly burdensome.[60] Federal agencies become involved in oil pipeline approval to the extent they require river crossing or other environmental permits, or if they cross an international border.[61]

In terms of operating regulations for both oil and natural gas pipelines, the U.S. Department of Transportation is primarily responsible for pipeline safety and reliability through the Pipeline and Hazardous Materials Safety Administration (PHMSA) and the Office of Pipeline Safety.[62] PHMSA has not addressed resilience in any regulations[63] and, instead, generally regulates through an incremental approach that emphasizes private regulation and cooperation with states.[64] This incremental approach is reflected in PHMSA's implementation of the Pipeline Safety, Regulatory Certainty, and Job Creation Act of 2011; as of the writing of this chapter (10 years after the passage the 2011 Act), PHMSA had not completed all of the mandates from the 2011 Act, with key regulations on automatic shut-off valves yet to be issued.[65] In fact, as Professor Sara Gosman has noted, 'PHMSA has found it difficult to defend the benefits of reducing low-probability, high consequence risks' and has steered away from such regulations.[66] FERC does retain some reliability authority over oil pipelines, but this is limited to requiring reports from operators after 'serious disruptions of service.'[67]

---

[58] Alexandra B. Klass, 'Eminent Domain Law as Climate Policy' (2020) 2020 Wisconsin Law Review 49, 59–60.
[59] 15 U.S.C § 717c. FERC, 'Staff Report: Winter Energy Market and Reliability Assessment 2020/2021' (*FERC*, 15 October 2020).
[60] Coleman and Klass (n 10) 688.
[61] Klass, 'Future-Proofing' (n 35) 834.
[62] Hazardous Liquid Pipeline Safety Act of 1979, Pub. L. No. 96–129, §§ 201-11, 93 Stat. 989, 1003–1016 (codified as amended in scattered sections of 49 U.S.C.); Sara Gosman, 'Justifying Safety: The Paradox of Rationality' (2018) 90 Temple Law Review 155,172–175.
[63] PIPES Act of 2020, S.2299, 116th Congress § 10 (2020).
[64] Gosman, 'Justifying Safety' (n 62) 206.
[65] Pipeline & Hazardous Materials Safety Administration (PHMSA), 'Pipeline Safety, Regulatory Certainty, and Job Creation Act of 2011: Progress Tracker' (*PHMSA*, 10 December 2020) <https://www.phmsa.dot.gov/legislative-mandates/pipeline-safety-act/pipeline-safety-regulatory-certainty-and-job-creation-act> (accessed 7 March 2021); Lincoln L. Davies et al, Energy Law and Policy 412–434 (2nd edn, St. Paul, West Academic Publishing 2018).
[66] Ibid.
[67] 318 C.F.R. § 260.9(a)(1)(ii).

B. Building engineering and social-ecological resilience in the oil and natural gas pipeline system through increased safety regulations for existing pipelines and retreat from new pipeline investment

While *increasing* the use of electricity in the U.S. economy through a decarbonized grid coupled with increased electrification of transportation and buildings is widely accepted as key to fighting climate change,[68] the role of oil and natural gas in an energy system disrupted by climate change is more fraught.[69] Should we reinforce oil and natural gas transportation system resilience through expansion and reinvestment? Or should we take a wider view of 'resilience' and engage in managed retreat from these fossil fuel industries? As set forth below, we propose that the most resilient solution for the entire energy system is to (1) reinforce the physical resilience of the *existing* oil and natural gas pipeline network to reduce spills and leaks while (2) resisting efforts to expand that system to avoid investing additional billions of dollars in long-lived fossil fuel assets that serve to hinder a clean energy transition.

1. Enhancing pipeline safety regulation

Regardless of where the U.S. energy system is headed, the United States today is heavily reliant on natural gas for heating and electricity and on oil for transportation: 40 per cent of U.S. electricity is provided by natural gas generation,[70] 47 per cent of homes are heated by natural gas furnaces,[71] and nearly 97 per cent of vehicles sold in 2018 still run on petroleum.[72] Due to the interconnected nature of the U.S. energy system, failures in oil and natural gas transportation have the potential to cascade and threaten systems across the economy.[73] As a result, hardening this system against the impacts of climate change as well as leaks, spills, and ruptures can prevent even short-term disruptions that threaten devastating systemic harm.

In a sub-system as diverse and complex as oil and natural gas transportation, there are numerous vulnerabilities and, as a result, numerous opportunities for infrastructure hardening in line with engineering resilience strategies.[74] As discussed above, PHMSA has struggled to justify the expense of low-probability disruption investments under cost-benefit analyses.[75] As a result, many investments in oil and gas transportation infrastructure have either been left up to state regulators or voluntarily enacted by industry stakeholders.[76] The Texas blackouts of 2021 exposed the weaknesses of this reliance on state action and voluntary investment after FERC recommendations around wellhead insulation went unheeded

---

[68] David Roberts, 'The Key to Tackling Climate Change: Electrify Everything' (*Vox*, 27 October 2017); Williams (n 31).

[69] Robert J. Johnson et al, 'The Role of Oil and Gas Companies in the Energy Transition' (*Atlantic Council*, 2 January 2020) 17.

[70] EIA, 'Electricity in the United States' (*EIA*, 18 March 2021) <https://www.eia.gov/energyexplained/electricity/electricity-in-the-us.php>.

[71] EIA, 'U.S. Households' Heating Equipment Choices Are Diverse and Vary by Climate Region' (*EIA*, 6 April 2017).

[72] USA Facts, 'How Many Electric Cars are on the Road in the United States?' (*USA Facts*, 22 October 2020).

[73] Brian Dakss et al, 'Texans Face Drinking Water Shortage as Power Grid Returns to Normal' (*CBS News*, 20 February 2021) <https://www.cbsnews.com/live-updates/texas-drinking-water-power-grid/>.

[74] U.S. Department of Energy, United States Fuel Resilience Volume III (*U.S. Department of Energy*, 2014).

[75] Gosman, 'Justifying Safety' (n 62) 206.

[76] Jacquelyn Pless, 'Making State Gas Pipelines Safe and Reliable: An Assessment of State Policy' (*National Conference of State Legislatures*, 2011).

and gas generation failed in cold weather.[77] Just as in the electricity sector, where small investments in vegetation clearance can increase resilience to storms, similar 'hardening' in the pipeline context through insulation and other weatherization investments can be highly effective engineering resilience strategies.[78] Doing so will help keep energy systems operational during severe heat, cold, and storms, and will also significantly reduce catastrophic oil pipeline spills, like the Enbridge oil pipeline which leaked 850,000 million gallons of Canadian oil sands into the Kalamazoo River in Michigan in 2010.[79]

2. Retreat from new oil and natural gas pipeline investments

To this point, this chapter has generally treated climate change as an exogenous threat to the U.S. energy system. However, this ignores the fact that oil and natural gas account for 46 per cent and 33 per cent of U.S. carbon emissions respectively.[80] Professor Sara Gosman contends that '[g]rouping extreme weather events with intentional attacks, accidents, and other 'natural' events frames the policy problem as external to energy systems ... The frame even treats climate change as a threat to the sustainability of the energy supply—a claim that heightens the sense of danger, but in reality reverses the causal effect.'[81] As a result, Gosman argues, discussions of energy system resilience must be reframed around protecting people, addressing climate change, and halting investment in fossil fuel infrastructure.[82] This approach is consistent with President Biden's energy plan which, in attempting to achieve 100 per cent carbon free electricity generation by 2035 and economy-wide net zero emissions by 2050, departs from President Obama's earlier embrace of natural gas as a 'bridge fuel' and challenges oil's dominance in the transportation sector through a major commitment to electric vehicles.[83]

The conflict between sub-system engineering resilience and the social-ecological resilience of the energy system as a whole is already playing out in debates over new oil and gas pipelines. Pipeline projects like Keystone XL,[84] Enbridge Line 3,[85] and Dakota Access[86] have all faced fierce legal and political opposition from local communities, national environmental groups, property rights advocates, Native American tribes, and celebrities. Opponents often point to local reliability and environmental protection concerns as a primary motivation, but they are part of a much larger system resilience-based resistance

---

[77] Ari Natter and Jennifer A. Dlouhy, 'Texas Was Warned A Decade Ago Its Grid Was Unready for Cold' (*Bloomberg Green*, 14 February 2020); Benjamin Storrow, 'Why the Deep Freeze Caused Texas to Lose Power' (*Scientific American*, 18 February 2021).

[78] U.S. Department of Energy, 'United States Fuel Resilience Volume III' (n 74) 53–55.

[79] Klass, 'Future-Proofing' (n 35) 891–893.

[80] EIA 'Where Greenhouse Gases Come From' (*EIA*, 21 May 2021).

[81] Sara R. Gosman, 'Framing Energy Resilience' (2019) 35 Journal of Land Use and Environmental Law 1, 9.

[82] Ibid, 13; Baker (n 20) 6.

[83] 'President Biden Sets 2030 Greenhouse Gas Pollution Reduction Target Aimed at Creating Good-Paying Union Jobs and Securing U.S. Leadership on Clean Energy Technologies' (*Office of the President*, 22 April 2021) <https://www.whitehouse.gov/briefing-room/statements-releases/2021/04/22/fact-sheet-president-biden-sets-2030-greenhouse-gas-pollution-reduction-target-aimed-at-creating-good-paying-union-jobs-and-securing-u-s-leadership-on-clean-energy-technologies/>.

[84] Harvard Environmental & Energy Law Program, 'Keystone XL Pipeline' (*Harvard Environmental & Energy Law Program*) <https://eelp.law.harvard.edu/2018/02/keystone-xl-pipeline/> accessed 20 February 2021.

[85] Minnesota Public Utility Commission, 'Enbridge Line 3 Replacement Project' (Minnesota Public Utility Commission) <https://mn.gov/puc/line3/> accessed 20 February 2021.

[86] Devika Krisha Kumar, 'Tribes Say Dakota Access Pipeline Review Is Biased' (*Reuters*) https://www.reuters.com/world/us/tribes-say-dakota-access-oil-pipelines-environmental-review-is-biased-2021-09-22/ accessed 22 September 2021.

movement that frames new investment in oil and gas infrastructure as a barrier to a clean energy transition.[87] In Michigan, this resistance has extended to a demand by Governor Gretchen Whitmer that Enbridge (a Canada-based corporation that transports 25 per cent of crude oil and 20 per cent of natural gas in the United States)[88] remove its pipeline underneath the Straits of Mackinac between Michigan's Upper and Lower Peninsulas.[89] The state argues that it has the power to revoke a 1953 easement 'based upon Defendants' persistent and incurable violations of the terms and conditions of the easement' and upon the public trust doctrine.[90] These fundamental challenges to the status quo in energy transportation are all quintessential social-ecological resilience strategies in that they recognize the weaknesses of the energy system as currently constructed and understand that to actually address these weaknesses, the system must fundamentally change and rapidly divest from fossil fuel generation and transportation.

IV. Reimagining Energy System Resilience Through Permitting and Eminent Domain Reforms

System failures in Texas and California demonstrate the need for increased resilience in U.S. energy transport systems. Solutions for increased grid and pipeline engineering resilience are already available to utilities and regulators. Executing on these solutions requires engaged regulators, cooperative utilities, and sufficient funding but, generally, no change in law or authorization for supervising entities. Ecological, social-ecological, and anti-resilience strategies that restructure the energy system in the face of climate change disruptions, however, will need process innovations for effective implementation. Embracing ecological resilience in electric transmission is limited today by fragmented siting authority that makes necessary interstate transmission line projects extremely challenging to execute. Permitting for DERs and their associated technologies is slow and still structured around incumbent entities, limiting their social-ecological and anti-resilience potential. Current regulatory regimes governing the siting of oil and natural gas pipelines assumes there is a continuing 'need' for new pipelines rather than considering whether broader energy system resilience favours phasing out this long-lived fossil fuel infrastructure. Below we discuss permitting and siting reforms for electric transmission lines and oil and natural gas pipelines that meet the dual goals of physical and system resilience in a world increasingly disrupted by climate change.

A. Permitting and eminent domain reforms to enhance and expand the electric grid

As discussed in Section II, to decarbonize the U.S. economy, we will need to move large amounts of onshore wind and solar power from regions of the country rich in renewable

---

[87] Stop Line 3, 'Introduction' (*Stop Line 3*) <https://www.stopline3.org/#intro> accessed 20 February 2021.
[88] Enbridge, 'Enbridge Quick Facts' (*Enbridge*) <https://www.enbridge.com/media-center/enbridge-quick-facts> accessed 20 February 2021.
[89] Complaint at 2–3, *Michigan v Enbridge Energy Ltd.*, (Mich. Circuit Ct.) (No. 20-646-CE).
[90] Ibid, 7.

energy resources to urban areas that may be several states away.[91] To accomplish this, grid researchers argue that the United States must build a network of long-distance, high-voltage direct current (HVDC) lines and more long-distance alternating current (AC) lines. However, as also discussed in Section II, there is very limited federal authority to issue siting permits or authorize eminent domain authority to build such lines. Instead, project proposers are forced to spend decades attempting to secure multiple state siting approvals and exercise eminent domain authority from regulators that often have jurisdiction to consider only the more limited, local costs and benefits of such projects.[92]

Russell Gold's 2020 book *Superpower* details the decade-long effort of the company Clean Line Energy Partners to build a series of HVDC lines to integrate substantial amounts of wind energy into the nation's electric grid. One of those lines, the Plains & Eastern Clean Line, was a proposed 720-mile, 3.5GW HVDC transmission line that would bring wind power from the Oklahoma Panhandle to the east by connecting with the Tennessee Valley Authority (TVA). Despite help from DOE through a partnership authorized by Section 1222 of EPAct 2005 and a federal court decision upholding the authority of DOE to partner with Clean Line,[93] the project ultimately foundered due to objections of the state of Arkansas, opposition from TVA, and ultimately a withdrawal of the partnership by the Trump-era DOE.[94]

Experts have long proposed permitting remedies for the mismatch between state authority over transmission line siting authority and the regional and national scope of the nation's electric grid. Proposals include granting additional siting authority to FERC, as was done in the early 20th century for interstate natural gas pipelines,[95] granting greater authority to RTOs to approve lines to provide a more regional focus to permitting that ties to existing regional grid planning,[96] enhanced efforts by FERC and DOE to use existing authority in EPAct 2005 to help support grid expansion,[97] and increased financial incentives to the private sector to spur investment in the lines themselves.[98] Reforms such as these are critical to increasing resilience in the electric grid and should be a priority for Congress and the Biden Administration.

---

[91] Alexandra B. Klass and Elizabeth J. Wilson, 'Interstate Transmission Challenges for Renewable Energy: A Federalism Mismatch' (2013) 65 Vanderbilt Law Review 1801, 1857.

[92] Klass, 'Future-Proofing' (n 35) 872–874.

[93] 42 U.S.C. § 16421; Section 1222 of the Energy Policy Act of 2005 (42 U.S.C § 16421).

[94] Robert Walton, 'Department of Energy Terminates Partnership with Clean Line Energy Partners' (*Utility Dive*, 26 March 2018).

[95] Klass and Wilson (n 91); Klass, 'Transmission, Distribution and Storage' (n 33) 540–542.

[96] Alexandra B. Klass, 'The Electric Grid at a Crossroads: A Regional Approach to Siting Transmission Lines' (2017) 48 University of California Davis Law Review 1895.

[97] Avi Zevin et al, Building a New Grid Without New Legislation: A Path to Revitalizing Federal Transmission Authorities (*Columbia Center on Global Energy Policy*, 14 December 2020) <https://www.energypolicy.columbia.edu/research/report/building-new-grid-without-new-legislation-path-revitalizing-federal-transmission-authorities>.

[98] ACEG (n 31).

B. Permitting and eminent domain reforms for the oil and gas pipeline sector to discourage new fossil fuel infrastructure

While the prior subsection (IV.A) discussed *expanding* permitting and eminent domain authority to support resilience in the electricity sector and the energy system more broadly, this subsection suggests doing the opposite when it comes to fossil fuel pipelines. Specifically, we argue regulators and lawmakers should revise existing laws to reduce investment in new, long-term fossil fuel infrastructure.[99] This proposal does not address the required implementation of engineering resilience techniques for *existing* pipelines as discussed in Section III. Instead, it prioritizes the resilience of the energy system as a whole by recognizing continued reliance on fossil fuels in electricity generation and transportation is inconsistent with a truly resilient energy system. It also emphasizes that an energy system that seriously engages with anti-resilience thinking cannot continue to rely on fossil fuel energy sources.

Currently, state and federal laws make it relatively easy for new oil and natural gas pipelines to satisfy necessary permit, certificate of need, and eminent domain requirements, at least as compared to electric transmission lines.[100] Such laws provide extremely broad definitions of what is in the 'public interest' for permitting and certificates,[101] and what constitutes a 'public use' for exercising eminent domain.[102] State legislatures and Congress should amend these laws to make it more difficult and, in some cases, impossible for new fossil fuel projects to fall within these definitions given the need to fully decarbonize the U.S. economy. Doing so will bring state laws governing siting and eminent domain in line with the broader climate policies of many states, which are increasingly adopting aggressive, clean energy mandates. Likewise, as the Biden Administration makes decarbonization and clean energy a centrepiece of its economic and energy agendas, Congress and federal agencies should revise federal statutes and regulations that currently favour fossil fuel infrastructure like oil and gas pipelines.

Some may argue that reducing or eliminating new oil pipelines will result in a less resilient energy system, because (i) oil will continue to be produced and used; (ii) it now will travel by rail instead of by pipeline; and (iii) rail is a less reliable and resilient form of oil transportation.[103] The evidence, however, does not entirely support that position. In terms of the physical resilience of pipeline transport of fossil fuels, as described above, pipelines often leak and spill resulting in significant environmental harm and property damage, and federal regulators have had little success in improving that reliability.[104] Additionally,

---

[99] Hiroko Tabuchi and Brad Plumer, 'Is This the End of New Pipelines?' (*The New York Times*, 8 July 2020)<https://www.nytimes.com/2020/07/08/climate/dakota-access-keystone-atlantic-pipelines.html>.

[100] Jacob Hileman, 'Mountain Valley Pipeline is a Prime Example of National Permitting Failure (*Virginia Mercury*, 17 July 2020) <https://www.virginiamercury.com/2020/07/17/20008/>; Sharon Kelly, 'Pipeline Permit Scandal Highlights Confusion Amid Push to Build Plastics Plants' (*Resilience*, 4 September 2019) <https://www.resilience.org/stories/2019-09-04/pipeline-permit-scandal-highlights-confusion-amid-push-to-build-plastics-plants/>; Klass, 'Eminent Domain Law' (n 58) 72–73.

[101] Klass and Coleman (n 10) 682–683. Cf Arianna Skibell, 'FERC Pipeline Eminent Domain Fight Heats Up' (*Energywire*, 4 March 2021) <https://www.eenews.net/energywire/2021/03/04/stories/1063726595>.

[102] See Klass and Coleman, (n 10) 689–692.

[103] Karen Clay et al, 'The External Costs of Transporting Petroleum Product by Pipelines and Rail: Evidence From Shipments of Crude Oil from North Dakota' (*National Bureau of Economic Research*, Working Paper No. 23852, 2017); Kenneth P. Green and Taylor Jackson, 'Safety in the Transportation of Oil & Gas: Pipelines or Rail?' (*Fraser Institute*, August 2015).

[104] Mike Soraghan, 'Giant N.C. Spill Shows Gaps in Pipeline Safety' (*Energywire*, 25 February 2021).

there is arguably a greater regulatory capacity to increase the engineering resilience our rail system, by improving tracks, train cars, and related infrastructure.[105]

But beyond the engineering resilience of the infrastructure in question, there is a powerful system resilience argument that greater investment in new fossil fuel infrastructure like pipelines makes it more difficult to shift to cleaner energy sources as billions of dollars in investment have been spent and these assets will be used for decades.[106] By contrast, a more resilient rail system can be used not only to transport oil but also a wide range of agricultural and other commodities, as well as passengers, making investment in that infrastructure more broadly in the public interest and consistent with clean energy transition.[107] Finally, oil is more expensive to ship by rail than by pipeline and if the United States wants to achieve a more resilient, decarbonized future, it should arguably be placing additional costs on fossil fuel resources and reducing costs on renewable energy resources, not the opposite.[108]

V. Conclusion

The U.S. energy system is in the midst of what is potentially the largest disruption it has ever faced. Climate change is challenging both the physical resilience of energy transportation infrastructure—as it was not designed for a world with increasingly severe weather—and the resilience of the energy system itself. On the latter point, rapid decarbonization of the economy is forcing energy transportation stakeholders to reconsider how energy is, and should be, produced and delivered to consumers. Unfortunately, permitting regimes built for 20th century problems are interfering with the engineering, ecological, and social-ecological resilience solutions that are needed for the U.S. energy system of today. To meet these challenges, the United States must overcome the constraints of the existing system and re-think how legislators and regulators use permitting systems and eminent domain authority for electric grid and pipeline infrastructure. By re-evaluating and revising these permitting and eminent domain regimes, the U.S. energy system can leverage disruption caused by climate change and emerge with a more resilient and equitable system in the future.

---

[105] Klass, 'Future-Proofing' (n 35) 887–896.

[106] Geoffrey Morgan, 'Enbridge Sets High Bar to Build Pipelines as Big Projects Get Riskier' (*Financial Post*, 9 December 2020) <https://financialpost.com/commodities/enbridge-sets-high-bar-to-build-pipelines-as-big-projects-get-riskier>; California Energy Commission, 'The Challenge of Retail Gas in California's Low-Carbon Future' (*California Energy Commission*, 2020).

[107] Association of American Railroads, 'Freight Railroads & Climate Change' (*Association of American Railroads*, March 2021), Robinson Meyer, 'A Major but Little-Known Support of Climate Denial: Freight Railroads' (*The Atlantic*, 13 December 2019) <https://www.theatlantic.com/science/archive/2019/12/freight-railroads-funded-climate-denial-decades/603559/>.

[108] Michael Lazarus and Harro Van Asselt, 'Fossil Fuel Supply and Climate Policy: Exploring the Road Less Taken' 150 Climatic Change 1 (2018); Klass, 'Future-Proofing' (n 35) 838.

PART III
STATE LEGAL RESPONSE TO DISRUPTION

7

Resilience and Energy Law in China in an Era of Energy Decarbonization

Hao Zhang

I. Introduction

China's development in the energy sector has been an enigma to the rest of the world: it is the largest greenhouse gas (GHG) emitter due to its vast consumption of coal, but meanwhile, it is the pioneer of the energy transition with more renewable energy deployment than any other country in the world.[1] Since the announcement of China's first domestic carbon intensity target which was then included in the Copenhagen Accord in 2009,[2] the Chinese central government has steered the energy transition through instituting policy and regulatory incentives to attract low-carbon investments and decentralizing, permitting authority to lower-level governments to facilitate and accelerate the construction of clean energy projects.[3] This development has created multi-level regulatory processes and spaces in which governments at various levels and state-owned enterprises (SOEs) can influence the energy sector transition and its outcomes, including energy resilience.[4]

In the context of increasing natural and man-made disasters, such as the global pandemic caused by the COVID-19, demands on the energy system and its underlying legal regime are intense.[5] As the biggest energy consumer and producer, China is facing increasing pressure to balance the regulatory demands of energy security, environmental protection, and climate mitigation through regulating the energy sector, which is the major source of air pollutants and GHG emissions in the country.[6] These regulatory demands pose some significant challenges to the existing systems and processes in China's energy law and regulation. The most prominent challenges include, for example, integrating renewable energy

---

[1] International Energy Agency (IEA), 'World Energy Outlook 2020' (October 2020) <https://www.iea.org/reports/world-energy-outlook-2020> accessed 20 February 2021.
[2] Letter from Director General of Department of Climate Change, National Development and Reform Commission, China, to Executive Secretary, UNFCCC Secretariat, Germany, 28 January 2010 <https://unfccc.int/files/meetings/cop_15/copenhagen_accord/application/pdf/chinacphaccord_app2.pdf> accessed 20 February 2021.
[3] Sara Schuman and Alvin Lin, 'China's Renewable Energy Law and its Impact on Renewable Power in China: Progress, Challenges and Recommendations for Improving Implementation' (2012) 51 Energy Policy 89; Anatole Boute and Hao Zhang, 'The Role of the Market and Traditional Regulation to Decarbonise China's Energy Supply' (2018) 30(2) J of Environmental L 261–284
[4] Edward A. Cunningham, 'The State and the Firm: China's Energy Governance in Context' (Boston University GEGI Working Paper) 1, 2015) <http://ash.harvard.edu/files/chinas-energy-working-paper.pdf> accessed 20 February 2021; Adrian Lema and Kristian Ruby, 'Between Fragmented Authoritarianism and Policy Coordination: Creating a Chinese Market for Wind Energy' (2007) 35 Energy Policy 3879–3890.
[5] Don C. Smith, 'COVID-19 and the Energy and Natural Resources Sectors: Little Room for Error' (2020) 38(2) J of Energy & Nat Res Law 125–129.
[6] Hao Zhang, 'Antinomic Policy Making under the Fragmented Authoritarianism: Regulating China's Electricity Sector through the Energy-Climate-Environment Dimension' (2019) 128 Energy Policy 162–169.

Hao Zhang, *Resilience and Energy Law in China in an Era of Energy Decarbonization* In: *Resilience in Energy, Infrastructure, and Natural Resources Law.* Edited by: Catherine Banet, Hanri Mostert, LeRoy Paddock, Milton Fernando Montoya, and Íñigo del Guayo, Oxford University Press. © Hao Zhang 2022. DOI: 10.1093/oso/9780192864574.003.0007

into the grid network, increasing natural gas consumption to replace the use of coal, and adopting an effective carbon pricing mechanism to drive low-carbon investments.[7] Some commentators and practitioners have raised some strong concerns about whether the relevant legal and regulatory systems in China are resilient and adaptive enough to address these challenges.[8]

Legal scholars have appropriated the theory on resilience, which has its roots in the study of ecological systems, to critically examine whether the existing law and governance structure is up to the task of managing the natural and man-made problems that have become variable, multi-scalar and increasingly unpredictable.[9] The looming challenges and problems such as climate change and the recent global pandemic caused by the COVID-19 have exerted relentless pressure on the resilience and adaptive capacity of the legal systems, laws, and governance in countries and jurisdictions around the globe. The two concepts, resilience and adaptive capacity, are essential for understanding how the legal system and law can respond to these looming challenges.[10]

Despite the increasing number of scholarly articles on this topic, conceptualizing resilience and adaptive governance in the area of energy law is still lacking.[11] Energy law is at the forefront of energy market reform and its low-carbon transformation, of which the latter has posed some formidable threats to most countries' energy systems and operations that are still largely dominated by concepts such as reliability and energy security.[12] For example, integration of renewable energy to the grid network requires a flexible and adaptive electricity system and the concept of resilience, in this regard, connotes both reliability of supply and adaptability to embrace the intermittency of renewable energy generation. However, the stagnation of energy market reform in most developing countries, including China, is accompanied by the loss or lack of resilience in energy system operation, leading to system inefficiency and vulnerability to natural and man-made disasters and unpredictable changes. As pointed out by Humby, the existing scholarly legal articles on law and resilience, as well as the related concepts such as adaptive governance, have mostly concentrated on countries in the Global North.[13] There is a clear need to bring together the two concepts of resilience and adaptive capacity within the context of developing countries.

---

[7] See e.g. Sufang Zhang, Philip Andrews-Speed and Sitao Li, 'To What Extent will China's Ongoing Electricity Market Reforms Assist the Integration of Renewable Energy?' (2018) 114 Energy Policy 165–172; Eric Yep and Cindy Liang, 'China's Rationalized Coal-to-Gas Policy Crimps Winter Gas Demand Growth' (*S&P Global*, 7 November 2019) <https://www.spglobal.com/platts/en/market-insights/latest-news/natural-gas/110719-china-rationalized-coal-to-gas-policy-crimps-winter-gas-demand-growth> accessed 22 February 2021; Alex Y. Lo, 'Challenges to the Development of Carbon Markets in China' (2016) (16)1 Climate Policy 109–124.

[8] Ibid; see also, Laszlo Varro and An Fengquan, 'Post Covid-19, Further Reform is Necessary to Accelerate China's Clean Energy Future' (IEA, 22 July 2020) <https://www.iea.org/articles/post-covid-19-further-reform-is-necessary-to-accelerate-china-s-clean-energy-future> accessed 22 February 2021

[9] J.B. Ruhl, 'General Design Principles for Resilience and Adaptive Capacity in Legal Systems – With Applications to Climate Change Adaptation' (2011) 89 North Carolina L Rev 1373–1403; Craig Anthony Arnold and Lance H. Gunderson, 'Adaptive Law and Resilience' (2013) 43 ELR: News and Analysis 10426–10443.

[10] Ibid.

[11] The article by Jonathan Schneider and Jonathan Trotta is one of the very few on energy law resilience and it discusses how the U.S. state and federal governments 'grapples with the challenges of grid resilience'. See Jonathan Schneider and Jonathan Trotta, 'What We Talk About when We Talk About Resilience' (2018) 39 Energy L J 353–400.

[12] See e.g. Zhang et al (n 7) on the challenges faced by China to address the significant problem of renewable energy curtailment.

[13] Tracy-Lynn Humby, 'Law and Resilience: Mapping the Literature' (2014) 4(1) Seattle J of Env't L 85–130.

Through the lens of scholarly discussion on law, resilience, and adaptive capacity, this chapter aims to first identify the central themes that are essential to the field of energy law under the banner of resilience and adaptive capacity. The central themes, discussed in Section II, will take into consideration the theory on resilience and adaptive capacity in the relevant legal scholarship, as well as the specific regulatory demands placed on regulators in China's energy sector. Section III briefly introduces the law and governance in China's energy sector, focusing on the system and structure which involves multi-level regulation and is featured by fragmentation and authoritarianism. Due to the different types of energy supply (such as electricity, oil, and natural gas) and the various regulatory frameworks governing them in China, this section pays more attention to China's electricity sector which consumes the most primary energy (i.e. coal) and is now undergoing some significant changes in terms of its structure and processes towards better resilience. The electricity sector in China provides a highly relevant case to understand resilience and adaptive capacity in the sphere of energy law and a developing country's specific context. Section IV critically examines to what extent the core components of energy resilience which has been discussed in Section II have been incorporated in the multi-level regulatory arrangements and processes that underlie electricity law and regulation in China. Given the profound impact of COVID-19 on China's energy sector and its implication for energy resilience, this section also briefly elaborates on the measures undertaken by the main stakeholders in China (government and SOEs) to cope with disruptions caused by the pandemic and the impact of these measures on China's energy transition and resilience. Section V concludes the chapter with some suggestions for future research.

II. Resilience, Adaptive Capacity, and Energy Law

With its roots in studying ecological systems, the theory of resilience has been increasingly used to understand how social-ecological systems manage complexity and maintain their functionality in the event of shocks and disturbance.[14] Ecologists and social scientists highlight two aspects of the resilience theory which are conceptual to comprehend the dynamics of ecological and social systems. The first aspect relates to a system's capacity to maintain its structure and function after absorbing shocks and disturbance.[15] This basic definition is often described as the engineering resilience of a system to return to its equilibrium state.[16] Appreciating the limits of predictability of how systems will respond to change and the multiple stable states of systems makes it obvious that resilience is more than just about being persistent and stable to withstand disturbance, and the capacity to conserve the existing structure and function.[17] The resilience theory also emphasizes the capacity of a system, while responding to shocks and undergoing a shift, to renew, reorganize and develop,

---

[14] Crawford Stanley Holling, 'Resilience and Stability of Ecological Systems' (1973) 4 Annual Rev of Ecology and Systematics 1–23; Andreas Duit et al, 'Introduction: Governance, Complexity, and Resilience' (2010) 20 (3) Global Environmental Change 363–368, 364. Carl Folke, 'Resilience: The Emergence of a Perspective for Social-Ecological Systems Analyses' (2006) 16(3) Global Environmental Change 253–267.

[15] Ibid.

[16] Lance H. Gunderson, 'Ecological Resilience – In Theory and Application' (2000) 31 Annual Rev of Ecology & Systematics 425–439.

[17] Carl Folke et al, 'Adaptive Governance of Social–Ecological Systems' (2005) 30 Annual Rev of Environment and Resources 441–473.

in order to evolve with change.[18] In this sense, the other aspect of resilience theory is intrinsically reflective of adaptive capacity.[19] This aspect, also known as transformability[20], recognizes that shocks and disturbance may generate new opportunities, enabling regime shift towards 'recombination of evolved structures and processes, renewal of the system and emergence of new trajectories'.[21]

A. Legal perspective of the resilience theory

For legal scholars, resilience and adaptive capacity are two important properties to comprehend and critically examine whether the legal system, like any other systems, can withstand the shock and disturbance, and undergo regime shift to become more adaptive.[22] Some earlier studies generally regarded resilience as a positive quality of a legal system to withstand and resolve the trouble by being able to evolve and adapt.[23] While this view reflects the general appreciation of a resilient legal system to remain consistent in its structure and processes from a general point of view, scholars working in the areas of environmental and climate law have increasingly leaned towards a more nuanced view of resilience as being descriptive rather than normative.[24] This nuanced view also includes the notion that a legal system might be too resilient to evolve (which is not necessarily reflecting that being resilient is good or bad), and generalization of an overall legal system as being resilient or not carries the risk of ignoring the major differences that could affect the resilience and adaptability of the sub-areas of law, such as constitutional law, criminal law, and environmental, and energy law.[25]

Indeed, to what extent resilience and adaptive capacity of a specific area of law are desirable depends on the processes and structure of the specific area of law and, more importantly, what specific issues and systems the particular legal discipline aim to address and deal with. Despite its close relationship and sometimes overlapping jurisdictions with environmental law, the area of energy law and regulation is still largely driven and determined by the essential facets of the energy system itself, such as reliability of energy supply and making energy affordable at all economic levels. These facets are often considered as the underlying importance for resilience and adaptive capacity of the energy law and regulation. As observed by the Asia-Pacific Economic Cooperation (APEC) Energy Working Group, APEC member economies attain energy resilience as an action agenda and according to the APEC Energy Ministers in the Cebu Declaration, energy resilience is defined as 'the ability

---

[18] Ibid.

[19] Ibid.

[20] Brian Walker et al, 'Resilience, Adaptability and Transformability in Social-Ecological Systems' (2004) 9 (2) Ecology and Society 5–14.

[21] Folke (n 14) 259.

[22] See particularly, Ruhl (n 9); Arnold and Gunderson (n 9).

[23] Janet C. Neuman, 'Drought Proofing Water Law' (2003) 7(1) Univ of Denver Water L Rev 92–110; Oren Perez, 'Purity Lost: The Paradoxical Face of the New Transnational Legal Body' (2007) 33 (1) Brooklyn J of Int'l L 1–59, 48.

[24] See Ruhl (n 9); Arnold and Gunderson (n 9); Humby (n 13).

[25] Ibid.

or quality of energy infrastructure to withstand natural and man-made disasters, to recover and return to normal conditions in a timely and efficient manner and to build back better'.[26]

B. Defining resilience in energy law

Like any system, the energy law system is defined by its structure and processes which shape its resilience to absorb, accommodate, and recover from impacts of hazardous events in a timely and efficient manner. The definition of energy resilience, as put forward by the APEC Energy Ministers, strongly reflects its focus on ensuring engineering resilience of energy infrastructure, which has been a common objective for all energy systems.[27] Crucial to this definition of energy resilience is ensuring the availability of stable energy supply through expansion and investments in key components of energy infrastructure.[28] Equally important is the goal to reduce the dependence of the energy system on fossil fuels to curb pollution and greenhouse gas emissions.[29] As discussed in Chapter 2 of this book, the configuration of the energy system and the outcome of energy services are shaped and determined by the energy law, regulation, and its governance arrangements and political system in a country's specific context; accomplishing these objectives largely depends on the extent to which the domestic energy law system can gauge the two aspects of resilience theory to enable the sustainability of energy supply and decarbonization of the energy system. Different design configurations of the energy system and its corresponding structures and processes in energy law result in various outcomes of engineering resilience and affect the adaptive capacity of the system towards transformability.

As discussed in the section below, China's energy law system is now under intense pressure to develop both engineering resilience and adaptive capacity to steer transformability. The intense pressure is manifested through China's existing regulatory and governance framework in the energy sector, which features the fragmented authoritarianism model.[30] The framework is designed to manage and mediate the regulatory demands of energy security, environmental protection, and climate mitigation.

III. China's Energy Law and Governance in the Context of Energy Resilience

Understanding the Chinese perception of energy resilience requires the appreciation of the energy legal system and governance in China. As the world's biggest energy producer and consumer, China ranks first globally in terms of power generation capacity and coal use,

---

[26] APEC Energy Working Group, Promoting Resilience in the Energy Sector. Final Report (August 2018) <https://www.apec.org/Publications/2018/11/Promoting-Resilience-in-the-Energy-Sector> accessed 22 February 2021.

[27] Cebu Declaration on East Asian Energy Security (Cebu, Philippines, 15 January 2007) <https://asean.org/?static_post=cebu-declaration-on-east-asian-energy-security-cebu-philippines-15-january-2007-2> accessed 22 February 2021.

[28] Ibid.

[29] Ibid.

[30] Kenneth G. Lieberthal, 'Introduction: the "Fragmented Authoritarianism" Model and its Limitations' in Kenneth G. Lieberthal and David M. Lampton (eds), *Bureaucracy, Politics, and Decisions Making in Post-Mao China* (University of California Press, 1992) 1–31.

with the fast increasing consumption of natural gas and oil.[31] The various types of energy supply and their different industry characteristics concerning domestic supply and import have led to perpetual political sensitivity on China's energy security.[32] Over the past two decades of fast economic development in the country, China's energy sector governance has been largely decentralized, with the primary goal of sustainable energy supply.[33] This overall trend of decentralization in the energy sector has enabled diversification of ownership and stakeholders, which has, to a large extent, weakened the ability of central government to shape energy outcomes, and rendered the energy governance in China highly fragmented, with regulatory powers assigned to lower-level governments and central energy SOEs.[34]

In this sense, China's energy governance is best captured by both fragmentation and authoritarianism. As pointed out by existing studies, the overall decentralization of regulatory power has seen more public regulators enter the regulatory space of China's energy sector, leading to multi-level regulation and fragmentation of authority, the latter of which naturally occurs when different regulators pursue different and often competing regulatory objectives, notably appreciation of state-owned energy-related assets and environmental mandates.[35] Despite the overall trend of energy sector liberalization, public regulators at various levels of government (the provincial governments in particular) and the central energy SOEs have retained key aspects of direct influence under the authoritarian model through nesting in various lines of authority in shaping China's energy development. On a general note, it is very difficult to tell which institutions have more authority over others.[36]

With the improved political will to sustain the energy supply that is climate and environmentally friendly, China has prioritized the transition to a more sustainable energy system.[37] China's energy policy agenda highlights the importance of developing an energy system that is clean, low carbon, safe, and efficient.[38] To achieve the policy objectives, increasing mandates on energy efficiency and experimentations with various decarbonization tools have been devised and implemented.[39] This diversification of policy objectives and the increasing regulatory demands on public regulators to reduce pollution and mitigate carbon emissions have supported the reform of China's energy sector. China's energy system has been undergoing some significant changes, with various progress of reform in the electricity, coal, oil, and natural gas sectors.[40] Due to the lack of effective and comprehensive energy laws, policy instruments are frequently used by Chinese government agencies to regulate and manage the energy sector. Both energy laws and policy, therefore,

---

[31] IEA (n 1).
[32] Gaye Christoffersen, 'The Role of China in Global Energy Governance' (2016) 2 China Perspectives 15–24.
[33] Philip Andrews-Speed, *The Governance of Energy in China: Transition to a Low-Carbon Economy* (Palgrave Macmillan 2012); Boute and Zhang (n 3).
[34] Cunningham (n 4).
[35] Qimin Chai and Xiliang Zhang, 'Technologies and Policies for the Transition to a Sustainable Energy System in China' (2010) 35(10) Energy 3995–4002; H.W. Ngan, 'Electricity Regulation and Electricity Market Reforms in China' (2010) 38 Energy Policy 2142–2148; Zhang (n 6).
[36] Cunningham (n 4); Zhang (n 6).
[37] State Council, 'The 13th Five-year Plan for Economic and Social Development of the People's Republic of China' (2016) ch 30.
[38] National Development and Reform Commission (NDRC) and China National Renewable Energy Centre (CNREC), 'China Renewable Energy Outlook 2018: Executive Summary' (2018) <https://ens.dk/sites/ens.dk/files/Globalcooperation/gr_china_-_creo_2018_ex_summary.pdf> accessed on 22 February 2021.
[39] Genia Kostka and William Hobbs, 'Local Energy Efficiency Policy Implementation in China: Bridging the Gap between National Priorities and Local Interests' (2012) 211 The China Quarterly 765–785; Boute and Zhang (n 3).
[40] Cunningham (n 4); Zhang (n 6).

provide the perspectives to understand how and to what extent energy resilience is defined and institutionalized in China.

A. Chinese perspectives on energy resilience

Reliability of energy supply is a core part of energy resilience in China and this objective of China's energy sector governance is to meet projected energy demand through various means, such as increased volume of domestic production and diversification of import channels. The underlying consideration of sustaining energy supply has influenced the major energy-related laws in China. The core provisions of China's Electric Power Law are built upon the fundamental principles of investment recovery and regulated electricity pricing, to attract investment into upstream generation.[41] The Coal Industry Law is promulgated to promote and guarantee the development of coal mines and coal supply.[42] The major law in the oil and gas sector centres on the protection of oil and gas pipelines[43] and it has been criticized for its narrow focus which protects the interest of one of the three national oil companies—the CNPC (China National Petroleum Corporation) because of its oligopoly in owning and operating the pipeline assets before the establishment of an independent pipeline corporation in China in 2019.[44] In the draft version of Energy Law which was released for public comments in 2020, Article 73 stipulates that the state bears the responsibility of 'guaranteeing the effective supply of energy to meet the basic needs of the national economy and people's livelihood.'[45] In the context of decentralized energy governance, the local governments at or above the county level are also to be assigned with tasks to 'support the construction of energy infrastructure, protect energy infrastructure, ensure unimpeded energy transportation, and improve energy supply capacity.'[46] Due to the increasing occurrence of man-made or natural disasters which affect the reliability of energy systems in China, the draft Energy Law has also emphasized improving the energy reserve and storage capacity for coal, oil, and gas, establishing and further developing the forecasting system on energy supply and demand, as well as enhancing the energy system resilience to respond to energy-related emergency incidents such as energy supply shortage and disruption.[47]

In the event of a man-made or natural disaster affecting the energy system, China's Emergency Response Law has laid down the following basic principles for the emergency response management system: centralized leadership (by the National Energy Administration (NEA)), integrated coordination (involving multiple government agencies depending on the sectors affected), categorized management (based on different types of energy supply), and level-based responsibility and localized management (according to the

---

[41] Electric Power Law of the People's Republic of China (Adopted in December 1995 and amended in 2009, 2015 and 2018 respectively).

[42] Coal Industry Law of the People's Republic of China (Adopted in August 1996 and amended in 2011, 2013 and 2016 respectively).

[43] Oil and Natural Gas Pipeline Protection Law of the People's Republic of China (Adopted in June 2010).

[44] Kefei Tan, 'Analysis and Countermeasures of Legal Issues in the Utilisation of Underground Space in China's Oil and Gas Industry' (2016) 24(4) Journal of Petroleum and Petrochemical Industry 10–14.

[45] Energy Law of the People's Republic of China (Draft for Solicitation of Comments), 3 April 2020 <http://www.nea.gov.cn/2020-04/10/c_138963212.htm> accessed on 22 February 2021.

[46] Ibid, Art 51.

[47] Ibid, Arts 75–77.

scale of disturbance and its impact).[48] China's Emergency Response Law was enacted in 2007, which was part of the reform triggered by the outbreak of SARS in 2003.[49] The definition of 'emergency incidents' in this Law includes a shortage of energy supply which is considered an essential resource.[50] The COVID-19 pandemic has accelerated the revival and promulgation of the updated emergency response plans, especially at the provincial level.[51] Local governments at or above the county level are required to form specialized emergency response command teams to restore supply and related services on a timely basis after the occurrence of an emergency incident affecting the energy sector.[52] This overall emergency management system is aligned with China's energy governance, which is featured by sector and provincial-based regulation.

Reliability of the energy system and its reflection in major energy laws in China manifests the traditional but long-lasting view about the essential facet of energy resilience, which is the ability of an energy system to perform its basic function, even in the event of disruption and disturbance.[53] The focus on energy security is primarily driven by China's high dependence on energy import (i.e. coal, oil, and gas), given China's emergence as a net crude oil importer as early as in the 1990s and surpassing the U.S. as the largest crude oil importer in 2017.[54] As the engine and bloodline of the economy and people's livelihood, the electricity sector has received some particular attention on its capacity to withstand and recover rapidly from disruptions. In the Action plan for Emergency Capacity Building in the Power Industry, the NEA has explicitly set the targets on capacity building and institutional and policy development, intending to enhance the resilience of China's power sector.[55] The specific targets and their major highlights include:

1) *Institutional support*: allocating responsibility between provincial, municipal and county governments in the event of large-scale power outage; adopting an emergency management plan for electric power enterprises and their corresponding capacity assessment system; developing a standard system on electric power emergency management.
2) *Emergency preparedness*: improving risk assessment for power enterprises and hydro dams; institutionalising and normalising emergency drills in the power sector and establishing a national training and drill base.
3) *Prevention and early warning system*: increasing the capacity of the electric grid to absorb disturbance and resist disasters; appropriately enhancing the grid reliability

[48] Emergency Response Law of the People's Republic of China (Adopted in August 2007).
[49] Zhe Wang et al, 'The Disaster and Emergency Management System in China' (The Chinese University of Hong Kong Policy Brief, May 2016) <http://ccouc.org/_asset/file/policybrief-disaster-andemergmxsysinchina-final20161020.pdf> accessed on 23 February 2021.
[50] Lan Xue and Kaibin Zhong, 'Classification, Staging and Grading of Public Emergencies: Basis of Emergency Management System' (2005) 2 Chinese Public Administration 102–107.
[51] Several provinces promulgated their emergency response plans following the outbreak of COVID-19. Jiangsu Province was among the first to release its plan in January 2020. Jiangsu Provincial Government, The Overall Response Plan for Emergency in Jiangsu Province, 20 January 2020.
[52] Ibid, Part 5.
[53] NDRC, Guiding Opinions on Safeguarding Energy Security in 2020, 12 June 2020.
[54] Cunningham (n 4) 20; U.S. Energy Information Administration, 'China Surpassed the United States as the World's Largest Crude Oil Importer in 2017' (February 2018) <https://www.eia.gov/todayinenergy/detail.php?id=34812#> accessed on 23 February 2021.
[55] NEA, Action Plan for Emergency Capacity Building in the Power Industry (2018-2020), 30 July 2018.

standards and constructing inter-and cross-provincial grids, especially in disaster-prone areas; improving disaster monitoring and warning.

4) *Rescue and handling capacity*: promoting communication and coordination with government agencies and enterprises in the power sector; establishing professional teams at national, local and enterprise levels, encompassing professionals and experts from industry and professional agencies; establishing a rescue base for hydropower projects in the southwestern region.

5) *Recovery and reconstruction*: developing a post-disaster assessment mechanism, utility restoration planning and black-start capability; promoting research and application of new technologies to enhance power grid recovery; identifying key power users in the region; and conducting a risk assessment of power supply to key users by grid enterprises, so as to prepare them in case of a power outage.

6) *Industry development*: developing critical equipment to deal with power supply disruption and outages, such as modular power equipment, mobile transformer substations and smart power supplies.[56]

More specifically, the NEA has laid down some concrete and binding criteria to assess the preparedness of targeted government agencies and energy SOEs.[57] All governments at the provincial, municipal, and county levels are required to institute an emergency response plan in case of major power failures. Provincial and municipal governments are responsible for setting up designated electric power emergency response management units. The electric power enterprises (including grid companies and companies owning coal-fired generation units with a capacity of 300 MW and above) must establish similar units and conduct personnel training and risk assessment. In the event of power supply contingencies and outages due to disasters, the responsible government agency and enterprises must restore the supply with the minimum threshold of 80 per cent in major power blackout areas and 90 per cent in key regions and urban areas in less than 7 days.

Clearly, these performance objectives are crafted to ensure an adequate level of reliability in China's power sector, which corresponds to the underlying components of engineering resilience. In the wake of increasing natural and man-made disasters threatening the energy sector, the reliability of sustaining supply is central to the evaluation of resilience risks faced by the energy sector in China and the measures that are adopted in response.[58] However, given the recency of these measures to enhance resilience in China's power sector, its implementation and effectiveness are still unknown. Moreover, the focus on power system reliability does not eliminate the concern of whether the existing energy law and system in China can accommodate the transformation, as China's energy mix continues to become more diverse.

[56] Ibid.
[57] Ibid.
[58] Yuejun Zhang and Wei Wang, 'Capability of [China's] Energy Sector to Ensure Supply during Emergency Needs to be Improved' (China Energy Newspaper, 22 March 2020) <http://paper.people.com.cn/zgnyb/html/2020-03/02/content_1974234.htm> accessed on 23 February 2021.

B. Energy transition and adaptive capacity of China's energy law

Being the world's pioneer in deploying renewable energy, China's energy mix is now transforming from one that is dominated by coal-fired generation to one that is featured by an increasing portfolio of renewable energy generation.[59] Unlike other countries whose focus is to meet the demand from distributed renewable energy sources, China's growing fleet of renewables is still largely concentrated and geographically diverse.[60] This means that the flexibility of China's electric power system is urgently needed to complement renewable energy generation, with more interconnection of transmission networks and some fundamental changes in how the existing power generation is operated and managed. Integration of renewable energy is a test of the adaptive capacity of China's power sector, for the simple reason that accommodating increasing renewables to the grid system requires the adoption of new technologies and improved regulatory structures and processes to operate the power system that is still dominated by coal thermal power generation. China's Renewable Energy Law (REL), promulgated in 2005 and amended in 2009, aims to achieve this transformation of the energy mix. The REL includes some key objectives such as 'promoting development and utilisation of renewable energy and advancing environmental protection.'[61] More specifically, the REL has adopted some essential mechanisms to achieve these goals, namely: (i) a national target for renewable energy development; (ii) mandatory connection and priority access for renewable energy to the grid network; (iii) an obligation for grid enterprises to purchase the full amount the electricity generated by renewable energy resources; and (iv) a national feed-in tariff system, supported by a cost-sharing mechanism.[62]

Unfortunately, the rapid increase in renewable energy capacity led to very high levels of curtailment in some provinces of China in the mid-2010s, creating a significant problem for the further development of renewable energy. According to the NEA, the average curtailment rate of wind power across the country was 17.2 per cent.[63] Provinces with abundant wind resources have witnessed extraordinarily high curtailment rates, including Gansu (43 per cent, 10,400 GWh), Xinjiang Autonomous Region (38 per cent, 13,700 GWh), and Inner Mongolia Autonomous Region (21 per cent, 12,400 GWh).[64] Similarly, the curtailment of solar power across China was 6,620 GWh, accounting for 10.3 per cent of the total solar power produced nationwide.[65] The highest curtailment occurred in Gansu Province and Xinjiang Autonomous Region, with 30.45 per cent and 32.23 per cent, respectively.[66] Hydropower had also witnessed a total curtailment of 51,500 GWh in 2017, with most occurring in Yunnan and Sichuan.[67] It is estimated that, in 2016 alone, the curtailment of wind power in China reached 49,700 GWh, which is more than the total electricity

---

[59]   IEA (n 1); Schuman and Lin (n 3).

[60]   Ibid.

[61]   Renewable Energy Law of the People's Republic of China (Adopted in February 2005 and amended in 2009), Art 1.

[62]   Schuman and Lin (n 3).

[63]   NEA, 'Accessing to the Grid Network by Wind Power in 2016' (January 2017) <www.nea.gov.cn/2017-01/26/c_136014615.htm> accessed on 23 February 2021.

[64]   Ibid.

[65]   NEA, 'Press Conference of NEA on Performance of China's Electricity Sector in 2017' (January 2018) <www.nea.gov.cn/2018-01/24/c_136921015.htm> accessed on 23 February 2021.

[66]   Ibid.

[67]   Ibid.

consumption of Bangladesh's 163 million population in 2016 (49,000 GWh).[68] The curtailment rate was reduced in 2018 and 2019 following the implementation of some policy mandates on minimum purchase hours for local grids and a temporary ban on new project approvals. Nonetheless, the NEA acknowledges that the effects of these mandates may be short-lived because they are relatively effective and easy to implement.[69] Urgently needed is to properly manage the adjustment of benefits caused by the policy change among power generators at the provincial level and to overcome local protectionism and resistance.[70]

Laws and regulations which underpin grid interconnection are a crucial component of broader power sector reform and market factors affecting the penetration of renewable energy into the grid system.[71] Despite successful efforts to separate power generation from transmission and distribution,[72] and the ongoing reforms, including experimentations to unbundle the retail market and liberalize electricity prices,[73] China's dispatch regulation has yet to be fundamentally updated to reflect the transformation of the energy mix.[74] In order to ensure investment recovery for investors owning generation assets, the basic principle of dispatch regulation in China is so-called equal dispatch which allocates the operating hours for baseload equally among generators in the same technological class.[75] Equal dispatch ensures fairness among generators in the same technological class towards investment recovery but overall, it inhibits low-carbon transformation of China's power sector and its improvement towards cost-effectiveness. According to the International Energy Agency, the level of renewable energy capacity in China's western provinces is already comparable to Germany or the UK, which has significantly challenged the existing dispatch regulation and required much more power system flexibility than the current practice can provide.[76]

As one of the major reform efforts to improve the dispatch regulation, the energy efficiency dispatch (also commonly known as green dispatch) was initiated in 2007 as an experiment in some selected Chinese provinces including Henan, Sichuan, Jiangsu, Guizhou, and Guangdong.[77] The green dispatch aimed to establish the dispatch sequence based on the level of energy efficiency of each generating unit and the amount of pollutants discharged. Subject to the requirement that it does not pose a threat to stable operation and reliability of the grid system, the green dispatch prioritizes renewable energy to access the grid network in the dispatch order.[78] There was high hope that the green dispatch experiment would reform the dispatch regulation towards better efficiency and flexibility.[79] However, its implementation and the subsequent rollout to other provinces have encountered significant

---

[68] Ye Qi et al, 'Deepening Reform of Electric Power System and Resolving the Issue of Wind Power Curtailment' (Brookings-Tsinghua Center for Public Policy, 2018).
[69] NEA, Notice on Matters related to Reducing the Burden on Enterprises in the Field of Renewable Energy, 2 April 2018.
[70] Ibid.
[71] Fredrich Kahrl et al, 'Challenges to China's Transition to a Low Carbon Electricity System' (2011) 39 Energy Policy 4032.
[72] Ngan (n 35).
[73] State Council, Opinions of the State Council on Further Reforming the Electric Power System, 15 March 2015.
[74] Kahrl (n 71); Hao Zhang, 'Prioritizing Access of Renewable Energy to the Grid in China: Regulatory Mechanisms and Challenges for Implementation' (2019) 3(2) Chinese J of Environmental L 167.
[75] Ibid.
[76] IEA, 'China Power System Transformation. Assessing the Benefit of Optimised Operations and Advanced Flexibility Options' (2019) <https://www.iea.org/reports/china-power-system-transformation> accessed on 23 February 2021.
[77] State Council, Workplan for the Pilot Programs on Energy Efficiency Dispatching, 2 August 2007.
[78] Ibid, Part 2.
[79] Kahrl (n 71); Zhang (n 74).

barriers and resistance from the provincial authorities. For instance, the NEA discovered and reported that the Hunan provincial government deliberately linked the electricity generation quota with purchasing of local coal when formulating and implementing the annual plan of electricity generation, and the Hubei provincial government prioritized selected medium-sized coal-fired generation units, regardless of their efficiency level, in determining the dispatch sequence.[80]

The barriers also reflect the lack of effective regulation and clear definition of some key concepts in the relevant legal framework. First of all, the complex legal and policy regime governing renewable energy development in China has weakened the authority of the law itself because the provisions are vague and lack enforceability, while the supplementing policy documents face the challenge of maintaining stability and predictability of industrial stakeholders.[81] Secondly, the lack of definition on circumstances affecting power grid stability and security is another major barrier in practice.[82] Since Article 14 of the REL explicitly allows curtailment of renewable energy when its integration poses danger to grid security and stability, this absence of a definition in the law has granted the authority of interpretation to grid enterprises in the event of renewable energy curtailment.[83] When concluding the power purchase agreement with renewable energy generators, the grid company has often abused its bargaining power to include an exemption clause that prevents the grid company from being responsible in the event of curtailment due to the concerns over grid stability and security.[84] To date, this gap in the law is yet to be addressed properly, which reflects the inadequate update on the technical standards applying to new connections such as renewable energy generators. Failure of the green dispatch reform in China provides useful insights to understand to what extent the existing legal system governing China's power sector can accommodate or drive energy transformation. It also reflects the inability of the current law to effectively drive the transformation of the system.

IV. Regulatory Fragmentation and its Impact on Energy Resilience in China

Integration of the principles of the resilience theory in the area of energy law will require the legal and regulatory system to be up to the task of preparing and managing the energy system to withstand and absorb shocks and disturbances and enabling the system to transform due to increasingly diverse regulatory demands on system reliability, pollution control, and climate mitigation. Practising resilience theory in energy law will also require the government agencies to continuously review and update the energy-related laws and the structure and processes of the energy system over time. Through the analysis of the Chinese energy law and governance in the context of resilience theory, the strong focus on energy security encapsulates the drawbacks and deficiencies of the existing energy-related

[80] NEA, 'Supervision Report on Electricity Dispatch for Energy Efficiency and Emissions Reduction' (2015) <http://zfxxgk.nea.gov.cn/auto92/201506/t20150612_1937.htm> accessed on 23 February 2021.
[81] Junxia Liu, 'China's Renewable Energy Law and Policy: A Critical Review' (2019) 99 Renewable and Sustainable Energy Rev 212–219.
[82] Zhang (n 74).
[83] Fredrich Kahrl, James H Williams, and Junfeng Hu, 'The Political Economy of Electricity Dispatch Reform in China' (2013) 53 Energy Policy 361–369.
[84] Ibid.

legal, regulatory, and governance arrangement in China, which demonstrates that the current regime is deeply rooted in the engineering resilience paradigm. China's energy law-making and energy sector reform have been largely driven by the underlying consideration of increasing energy supply and some efforts are being made to enhance the capacity of the power sector to withstand disturbances and recover quickly from the impacts of disasters. During the COVID-19 pandemic, the provincial-based management system was able to respond quickly to demand drop and there was no severe incident of energy shortage across the country.[85] However, as pointed out by commentators, the seemingly resilient energy system, as a result of stringent top-down order, reflects the general lack of a formal and institutionalized system in China's energy sector to deal with unexpected shocks and disturbances.[86] At the provincial level, only a small number of provinces have instituted emergency response plans in case of energy supply interruption.[87] Considering the sector and provincial-based energy governance in China, there is a real need to establish emergency management systems for each type of energy supply to enhance energy resilience.[88]

In China, however, the extent to which the adaptive capacity of the energy law and system can be improved to facilitate energy transformation is largely uncertain under the energy governance featured by regulatory fragmentation. On the one hand, the provincial authorities and the energy SOEs are increasingly powerful to determine the outcomes of energy sector development. The NEA, on the other hand, has been strained between enforcing national energy laws and regulations and being resisted and pushed back by provincial authorities against undesired new laws and regulations (e.g. green dispatch as discussed in Section III.B). In January 2021, the NEA came under harsh criticism. In a move that shocked commentators and stakeholders, China's Central Environmental Inspection Group (CEIG) openly criticized the NEA for failing to limit the expansion of coal power plants and falling behind on promoting the development of low-carbon energy.[89] Observers described the tone of criticism as 'unprecedented' in China's modern history and '[n]ever before has a high-level central government agency been inspected and openly criticised for multiple "failures" related to energy development'.[90] The basic features of the Chinese energy law and governance that are maladaptive can be categorized into the following: too much focus on the reliability of the energy sector under the prevailing goals of political and economic stability; fragmented governance and regulatory structure and arrangements which make the Chinese energy law system resistant to change; and lack of effective regulatory tools that transcend provincial boundary in China's energy governance. From the energy law perspective, the drawbacks and deficiencies of the Chinese regime in the context of enhancing resilience and adaptive capacity can be further understood through the lens of substantive goals and the structure of governing authority and processes of decision making.

[85] Shengjie Zhang and Jinmeng Zhang, 'Modernising Urban Energy Emergency Management Needs to be "On the Agenda" (Protecting Urban Energy Security)' China Energy Newspaper (2 March 2020) <http://paper.people.com.cn/zgnyb/html/2020-03/02/content_1974477.htm> accessed on 23 February 2021.
[86] Ibid.
[87] Based on the available information, only Guangdong (on crude oil), Chongqing (on natural gas), Hunan and Jiangxi (on refined oil) have adopted formal rules to deal with energy supply interruption.
[88] Zhang and Zhang (n 85).
[89] NEA, CEIG's Feedback to the NEA on the Inspection Results (January 2021) <http://www.nea.gov.cn/2021-01/29/c_139707466.htm> accessed on 23 February 2021.
[90] Echo Xie, 'China's Energy Watchdog under Fire over Pollution Failures' (South China Morning Post, 1 February 2021) <https://www.scmp.com/news/china/politics/article/3120111/chinas-energy-watchdog-under-fire-over-pollution-failures> accessed on 23 February 2021.

A. Substantive goals

Arnold and Gunderson's argument on how the legal regime is maladaptive due to its systematically narrow focus to advance stability and security of supply of single systems provides a useful perspective to understand the importance of substantive goals in energy law and the deficiencies faced by the Chinese system.[91] The resilience theory points out that too much focus on optimization is most likely to weaken the system itself over the long term, increasing its vulnerability to both internal and external shocks.[92] In China, the long-standing focus of sustaining energy supply, which is intrinsically related to the goal of economic development, has trumped other objectives and goals that are essential to the transformability of the energy system itself. For instance, despite the liberalization of the coal market in China, some downstream coal users, especially the coal power generation sector which is dominated by the SOEs, have long been protected through a dual-track pricing system through which coal supply to these generators is kept at a much lower level than the market price.[93] Governments at various levels have intervened in the coal market by overseeing coal companies and coal-fired generation companies entering into long-term contracts.[94] The intervention has taken various forms until recent years, although the NEA has explicitly ordered 'the local governments to avoid being at arm's length from the business and operation of the coal power generators'.[95] The consequence of such intervention is that transformation of the power sector has been delayed because inefficient generators are absolved from retirement or elimination. Energy resilience recognizes the fundamental role of the energy system to ensure reliability, which is central to the primary goal of energy law. This substantive goal should also recognize and embrace the diversification of the energy mix and a commitment to low-carbon development and energy system transformability through clearer goals for regulatory and institutional improvement. The majority of energy laws in China, however, have little recognition of this form of value. As discussed in below Section IV.B, given that the substantive goals are closely dependent on the existing structure and processes of China's energy governance especially governing authority and decision making, the place of these goals in the energy law system is still unsettled.

B. Governing authority and decision making

Governing authority and decision making constitute two essential aspects in assessing the adaptive capacity of energy law because these two issues affect how the substantive goals of energy reliability and transformability are implemented and materialized. The case of China suggests that a decentralized energy governance framework, in which governing authority and decision making are largely diffused to provincial authorities and central energy SOEs, is driven by energy security consideration and it has been proved to be rather effective.[96]

---

[91] Arnold and Gunderson (n 9) 10428–10429.
[92] Humby (n 13) 108–109.
[93] Energy Security and National Development Research Center and National School of Development of Peking University, 'Report of China's Energy System Reform' (May 2014) <http://www.ccer.pku.edu.cn/attachments/0b533bf4700f4397954e077ec1b99cc2.pdf> accessed on 23 February 2021.
[94] Ibid.
[95] State Council, Directive Opinions of the General Office of the State Council on Deepening the Market-oriented Reform for Thermal Coal, 20 December 2012, Part 1.
[96] Cunningham (n 4); Boute and Zhang (n 3).

Proponents of decentralized energy governance in China contend that a centralized frame-work was proven to be rather ineffective because of the lack of systematic planning, expertise and local knowledge.[97] However, in the pursuit of energy sector decarbonization, this decentralized and often fragmented governing authority and decision-making power in China are insufficiently flexible to properly manage the adjustment of benefits among stakeholders, which has been caused by the development of the energy law system which advances renewable energy and energy efficiency. The integration of renewable energy in China relies on the pre-existing structures and processes of the electricity sector constituted by law, government policies, and institutions, and in practice, these factors have constrained the efficacy of relevant policy and experimentations to support higher renewable energy penetration. The governing authority and decision-making power in China's energy sector are misaligned with the responsibilities of institutions. In the recent move towards power sector decarbonization, the NEA has increasingly resorted to command-and-control regulations (such as risk warning on coal-fired capacity and energy efficiency standards on coal power) but these measures are rather ineffective. Misalignment of managing power and decision-making authority in China has increased the likelihood of local protectionism towards the pre-existing structure and processes in the energy sector and weakened the adaptive capacity of its energy system towards transformability.

V. Conclusion

As the energy system evolves to become less fossil fuel dependent, the resilience theory provides a useful perspective to understand whether energy law manifests the dynamics and core components of a resilient legal system discussed in the literature, including engineering resilience, and adaptive capacity. This chapter critically examines to what extent engineering resilience and adaptive capacity have been incorporated in the multi-level regulatory arrangements and processes that underlie energy law and governance in China. The focus on energy security and the fear of disruption of energy supply due to severe weather conditions have enabled some incremental development to enhance resilience in China's power sector, while other types of energy supply are still facing the reliability challenge due to the lack of measures that need to be taken to enhance resilience. In pursuit of energy decarbonization, the current energy regulatory and governance system in China has been rather maladaptive, largely due to its existing framework of governing authority and decision making which is fragmented and authoritarian. Provincial governments and central energy SOEs are empowered to resist or push back undesirable new regulations or measures that drive energy transformation. China's energy law system is now under intense pressure to develop both engineering resilience to withstand disturbances and adaptive capacity to enable transformability. Increasing natural and man-made disasters, the evolving nature of the energy system towards diverse supply and decarbonization, and the important role of energy services in sustaining economic development and people's livelihood all urge us to improve energy security and responsiveness of the legal system to support a resilient energy sector.

---

[97] Barry Naughton, 'Claiming Profit for the State: SASAC and the Capital Management Budget' (2006) 18 China Leadership Monitor 1–9; Andrews-Speed (n 33).

8

Law, Resilience, and Natural Disaster Management in Australia

The 'Bushfire Summer' and Critical Energy Networks

*Lee Godden**

I. Introduction: The Bushfire Disaster Summer in Australia

In the summer of 2019–2020 bushfires raged across many parts of Australia, and the world media carried images of burning houses, forests, roads cut off by fires, wildlife that perished or was seeking to escape the flames, and desperate efforts to save communities by weary firefighters. The Cities were wreathed in a smoke hazard from the fires that engulfed major metropolitan areas for weeks on end.[1] The 2019–2020 fires displaced thousands of people and burned approximately 19.4 million hectares across Australia.[2] The area that was burnt was 'larger than the Amazon and California combined'.[3] The extent of the disaster was on a scale that was unprecedented, with areas never previously exposed to the threat of bushfires, burning with an intensity that had not been experienced to date. The scale, speed, and rapidity of the fire spread, while not encountered before, had been the subject of predictions from climate scientists and fire ecologists who had warned of the increasing risk of climate change greatly exacerbating the severity of the bushfire threat.[4]

While not attracting the same degree of media attention, the fires also destroyed major energy infrastructure,[5] with some communities cut off from power supplies due to loss of transmission and network capacity for days, weeks, and sometimes months. The security of the national energy infrastructure and the restoration of electricity supply to communities in remote and rural communities following the bushfires remains a major concern for governments in the aftermath of the bushfires. The bushfire summer added impetus

---

* The author acknowledges the assistance provided by the Australian Research Council, DP190101373 'Property as habitat: reintegrating place, people, and law'.

[1] Australian Government, *Royal Commission into National Natural Disaster Arrangements* (Report, 2020) 22 (hereafter Australian Government, 'Disaster Royal Commission') <https://naturaldisaster.royalcommission.gov.au/publications/html-report/overview> accessed 14 May 2021.

[2] Ben Huf and Holly Mclean, '2019-20 Bushfires Quick Guide' (Research Note No. 1, Parliamentary Library and Information Service, Parliament of Victoria) (2020) 2.

[3] Ibid, 1.

[4] Climate Council 'This is Not Normal': Climate change and escalating bushfire risk' (Briefing Paper) (12 November 2019) <https://www.climatecouncil.org.au/resources/bushfire-briefing-paper/> accessed 12 December 2020.

[5] Energy Networks Australia, 'Bushfire Impacts on Electricity Networks' (Media Release) (4 Feb 2020) (hereafter Energy Networks Australia, 'Bushfire Impacts') <https://www.energynetworks.com.au/news/media-releases/2020-media-releases/bushfire-impacts-on-electricity-networks/> accessed 5 September 2020.

Lee Godden, *Law, Resilience, and Natural Disaster Management in Australia* In: *Resilience in Energy, Infrastructure, and Natural Resources Law*. Edited by: Catherine Banet, Hanri Mostert, LeRoy Paddock, Milton Fernando Montoya, and Íñigo del Guayo, Oxford University Press. © Lee Godden 2022. DOI: 10.1093/oso/9780192864574.003.0008

to existing adaptation planning to increase the resilience of energy infrastructure given the increased risk of disasters.[6] Against the backdrop of resilience concepts and systems theory, this chapter examines the measures adopted at a national and provincial government level in Australia to respond to the combined risk that climate change and natural disasters pose to the resilience of energy infrastructure. It is vital also to realize that electricity infrastructure itself poses a significant risk to human and non-human species and natural systems.[7] Energy infrastructure, such as ageing or poorly maintained electricity transmission systems may exacerbate fire risk, as occurred in the Black Saturday fires in Victoria in 2009.[8]

The government measures to enhance the resilience of energy infrastructure and energy systems as a whole, draw on a complex interplay of legislation, policy, institutional arrangements (regulatory systems), and project-based initiatives that cross disaster and emergency management legislation, the national electricity market, and gas laws and regulation, together with natural disaster and climate adaptation legislation and policy platforms across the federal spectrum. The laws, regulation, and policy operate within a climate change mitigation policy vacuum at the national government level. Efforts to address climate change in a comprehensive way have been stifled by conflicts within the party in power. Those interparty conflicts produce a bizarre situation where climate change adaptation and emergency-based responses to 'natural disasters' are subject to a federal strategic planning focus, while the national government limits the reduction of fossil fuel dependency through minimal climate mitigation efforts. National climate mitigation measures largely rely on a fund that supports voluntary projects, typically land-use-sector focused, while the country remains a major coal and fossil fuel exporter.[9] State (provincial) governments are more proactive in pursuing decarbonization of the electricity sector.

This chapter argues that a more systemic legal approach is required to build a resilient energy infrastructure system to respond to the challenges posed by escalating climate change risks, and the increase in natural disasters. Accordingly, this chapter examines the 2020 Royal Commission's recommendations to reduce bushfire hazards to critical electricity and gas infrastructure; and their potential effectiveness in enhancing electricity system resilience. A systemic approach must include targeted legal obligations for generation, network, and distribution sectors to effectively translate 'fuzzy resilience' concepts into specific outcomes, together with enforcement measures. In turn, the tightening of the regulation of energy systems, especially transmission networks will reduce the probability of electricity caused fires, and the resulting human and ecological impacts.

---

[6] Australian Government, 'National Climate Resilience and Adaptation Strategy 2015' (2015) <https://www.environment.gov.au/climate-change/adaptation/publications/national-climate-resilience-and-adaptation-strategy> accessed 12 December 2020.

[7] Danielle Celermajer and others, 'The Australian bushfire disaster: How to avoid repeating this catastrophe for biodiversity' (First published: 3 March 2021) WIRES Climate Change <https://doi.org/10.1002/wcc.704> accessed 14 May 2021.

[8] State of Victoria, *Victorian Bushfires Royal Commission Final Report Summary* (July 2010) 12 <http://royalcommission.vic.gov.au/finaldocuments/summary/PF/VBRC_Summary_PF.pdf> accessed 12 December 2020.

[9] Simon Anderson, 'A Case Study of Incentive Regulation in Electricity Transmission Networks for the Uptake of Renewable Energy: Build It and They Will Come' (2020) 37 Environmental and Planning Law Journal 153, 155 (hereafter Anderson 'Incentive Regulation').

II. Resilience in Australian Energy Systems

A. Determining what is resilience?

If the objective is to increase the resilience of energy systems and critical energy infrastructure,[10] in Australia, a working definition of resilience is required—a term that has multiple meanings within Australian legal and policy settings. Drawing on Chapter 2 in this volume, resilience can be understood as 'the capacity of a system to absorb disturbance and reorganize while undergoing change so as to still retain essentially the same function, structure, identity, and feedbacks.'[11] Chapter 2 noted the transition from engineering-based concepts of resilience to wider use of the term as a characteristic of social-ecological systems.[12] Given the strong, early alignment between resilience and critical infrastructure in Australian policy settings and law, the physical impact, disturbance oriented model of resilience has tended to be the implicit benchmark against which to asses legislative reforms to enhance resilience.[13]

Niall and Kallies (2017) noted that climate adaptation policies increasingly have adopted resilience as a 'lead term' in relation to man-made and natural environments but there had been little thinking about how resilience is interpreted in a legal context.[14] These authors explore legislation introduced by Victoria that expressly incorporates resilience. The Climate Change Act 2017 (Vic) contains a resilience-related legislative objective, and the Emergency Management Amendment (Critical Infrastructure Resilience) Act 2014 (Vic) provides a framework for achieving critical infrastructure resilience.[15]

Niall and Kallies consider how the policy objective of resilience can be applied in legal frameworks using the example of electricity infrastructure as 'critical infrastructure'. They conclude that resilience can constitute, 'a valuable bridging concept, able to support the transition to a decarbonised as well as climate-proof electricity system'.[16] The authors place a significant rider on the use of resilience though, arguing that its potential, 'can only be realised once issues around scale and definition have been addressed'.[17] They highlight the importance of careful examination of the context in which the term is applied, 'otherwise it risks locking in unintended consequences, such as outdated ways of using and producing electricity'.[18]

---

[10] See Security of Critical Infrastructure Act 2018 (C'th).
[11] C.S. Holling, 'Resilience and Stability of Ecological Systems' (1973) 4 Annual Review of Ecology, Evolution and Systematics 1, 17–19 (hereafter Holling 'Resilience and ecological systems').
[12] Tracy-Lynn Humby, 'Law and Resilience: Mapping the Literature' (2014) 4 Seattle Journal of Environmental Law 85, 88 (hereafter Humby 'Law and Resilience').
[13] Commonwealth of Australia, 'Independent Review into the Future Security of the National Electricity Market: Blueprint for the Future Final Report' (June 2017). (Finkel Review after Chief Scientist of Australia). Among other objectives, it aims to make the National Electricity Market more resilient (i.e. secure and reliable).
[14] This book elaborates the legal translation of resilience. See Stephanie Niall and Anne Kallies, 'Electricity Systems between Climate Mitigation and Climate Adaptation Pressures: Can Legal Frameworks for "Resilience" Provide Answers?' (2017) 34 EPLJ 488, 488–489 (hereafter Niall and Kallies 'Electricity Systems and Resilience').
[15] Ibid, 488.
[16] Ibid.
[17] Ibid.
[18] Ibid.

B. Resilience and critical energy infrastructure

The Niall and Kallies' research identifies a trend toward designating electricity and gas networks as critical infrastructure. Recently, there has been a clear national security focus around building resilience in critical infrastructure, including energy networks. The trend is exemplified by the Security of Critical Infrastructure Act 2018 (C'th). In terms of electricity market design, a similar energy security focus is aligned to resilience outcomes with growing reliance on gas-fired generation in the electricity market.

The Australian Government defines critical infrastructure as:

> those physical facilities, supply chains, information technologies and communication networks which, if destroyed, degraded or rendered unavailable for an extended period, would significantly impact the social or economic wellbeing of the nation or affect Australia's ability to ... ensure national security.[19]

Under the Act, critical infrastructure refers to: critical electricity assets, critical gas assets, critical ports, and critical water assets, as well as designated assets. Critical electricity assets include certain electricity generation assets, and systems, networks, and interconnectors involved in the transmission and distribution of electricity.[20] The Act applies to electricity transmission networks that ultimately service at least 100,000 customers. Under the Act, a critical gas asset is one which ensures the security and availability of gas to the domestic markets, and/or those that meet Australia's export demands.[21] These national categorizations of critical energy infrastructure overlap with state government classifications of essential electricity infrastructure, that are oriented to emergency management and disaster impacts.

In Australia, there is mounting attention given to strengthening protections for critical energy infrastructure, both from a national security and disaster resilience standpoint. Yet, Niall and Kallies suggest a more stringent assessment of the use of resilience is required.[22] These authors argue that the differences between resilience definitions (e.g. engineering, natural resource management, and socio-ecological) are not merely semantic but have significant implications from an applied policy perspective. Drawing on the analysis by Davoudi,[23] they suggest that various meanings for resilience, 'provide distinct objectives that, if pursued in a particular system, would produce different outcomes'. For example, Niall and Kallies suggest that, 'a bridge that absorbs and adapts to a disturbance would look quite different to one that is designed to resist that disturbance'.[24] Niall and Kallies promote a third approach, evolutionary resilience.[25] This framing emphasizes that complex systems evolve and change, and such dynamics cannot be captured by a single, unambiguous policy

---

[19] Australian Government, Department of Home Affairs 'Coverage of the Security of Critical Infrastructure Act 2018' <https://www.homeaffairs.gov.au/nat-security/files/cic-factsheet-coverage-of-security-of-critical-infrastructure-act-2018.pdf>.

[20] Ibid, 1.

[21] Ibid, 2.

[22] Niall and Kallies 'Electricity Systems and Resilience' (n14) 489.

[23] Simin Davoudi, 'Resilience: A Bridging Concept or a Dead End?' (2012) 13 Planning Theory and Practice 299.

[24] Niall and Kallies 'Electricity Systems and Resilience' (n14) 491.

[25] Ibid. For problem framing and socio-ecological theory in water governance, see Lee Godden and Ray Ison, 'Community Participation: Exploring Legitimacy in Socio-Ecological Systems for Environmental Water Governance' (2019) 23(1) Australasian Journal of Water Resources 45–57.

objective. Therefore, for any given policy context, what is required is a careful analysis of the problem being addressed—the level of complexity of the relevant system, the outcomes sought and the level of agency of the system participants, 'to ensure that the precise framing or construction of resilience adopted is appropriate for the context and will produce the desired outcomes'.[26]

Accordingly, a comprehensive concept of resilience, embedded in socio-ecological thinking should be adopted. Otherwise, the reforms to give effect to resilience will not have the necessary degree of adaptive capacity to deal with 'multi-stable' domains states and escalating disaster risks into the future. In a similar way, Holling's research situated resilience in an evolutionary model related to the level of disturbance a system could absorb before the ecosystem is 'flipped' to a new set of characteristics, networks, and relationships—another 'stability domain'.[27] In Australia, we are yet to develop a fully effective governance model to deal with the 'flip' that is occurring. Natural disaster and adaptation law and policy has incorporated some socio-ecological resilience thinking, but mitigation-based governance is lagging. To assist in developing holistic governance, Niall and Kallies identify three critical factors in the translation of resilience from a normative or policy objective into a legal obligation or regulatory outcome that has clarity and precision. The three stages are:

(1) For any given system, the definition of resilience used, how this will manifest in the particular system and whether resilience is even a desirable objective are highly context dependent and often politically contested;

(2) Care needs to be taken to ensure that an emphasis on resilience does not mask the need for more transformational change either within or around a system; and

(3) Adopting resilience into different disciplines without critical analysis can potentially drive unintended consequences.[28]

In turn, Lyster and Verchick offer a resilience objective relevant to climate change and electricity infrastructure: 'To improve the resilience of the grid is to give weight to durability and flexibility.'[29] For an electricity system to be resilient to climate change it must quickly adapt physically and legally.

Situations of extreme disturbance triggering a 'flip' to new system characteristics are now predicted to confront Australia as a result of climate change.[30] Climate change will precipitate a change in the frequency, intensity, spatial extent, duration, and timing of extreme events—as well as the rise of unprecedented events.[31] This is evident in the bushfire summer. Such changes will increase the community's exposure (both people and assets) and

[26] Niall and Kallies 'Electricity Systems and Resilience' (n 14) 491.

[27] Holling 'Resilience and Ecological Systems' (n 11) 17–19.

[28] Niall and Kallies 'Electricity Systems and Resilience' (n 14) 492–493.

[29] Rosemary Lyster and Robert Verchick, 'Protecting the Power Grid from Climate Disasters' in Rosemary Lyster and Robert Verchick (eds), *Research Handbook on Climate Disaster Law* (Edward Elgar Publishing Ltd 2018) 267, 268.

[30] Ray Ison and Ed Straw, *The Hidden Power of Systems Thinking: Governance in a Climate Emergency* (Routledge 2020).

[31] IPCC (Working Group II Contribution to the Fifth Assessment Report), *Climate Change 2014: Impacts, Adaptation, and Vulnerability Part A: Global and Sectoral Aspects* (Cambridge University Press 2014) <https://www.ipcc.ch/site/assets/uploads/2018/02/WGIIAR5-PartA_FINAL.pdf> accessed 12 December 2020>.

vulnerability to disasters.[32] Exacerbation of the existing high risk of disasters in Australia will challenge the adaptability of decision-makers in disaster management and strategic planning. It will require the incorporation of resilience of a different order to those models already developed in the laws and specific rules that govern energy systems in Australia.[33] The ramifications of not adopting a more evolutionary model of resilience are apparent in the escalating climate change risks for energy systems, with bushfires, the major, but not the only threat to Australia's energy systems. Indeed, the International Energy Agency identifies the Asia Pacific region, including Australia, as particularly prone to natural disasters that threaten energy security.[34]

C. Disaster adaptation and resilience

Australia has included electricity system resilience in its disaster-related adaptation planning for over a decade, as the country has been impacted so severely. These measures were in place before the Paris Agreement established a goal designed to enhance adaptive capacity, strengthen resilience, and reduce vulnerability to climate change.[35] Nonetheless, the Paris Agreement is an important reminder of the centrality of adaptation in protecting people, livelihoods, and ecosystems, and that adaptation should be integrated into relevant socio-economic and environment policies and actions.[36]

In 2009 the Council of Australian Governments (COAG) referenced resilience as the goal for recovery following the devastating Black Saturday bushfires and major floods. These cascading disasters were the impetus for a National Disaster Resilience Statement,[37] followed by a National Disaster Resilience Strategy in 2011 which sought to enhance resilience of government, businesses, and individuals in response to climate risks.[38] The focus was on building resilient communities. The strategy had a similar orientation to a National Adaptation plan that had an emphasis on community resilience, and risk reduction through information management.[39] Since the initial strategy, the policy focus has shifted to include the resilience of critical infrastructure,[40] including electricity networks. As this policy trajectory indicates, different understandings of resilience do lead to disparate approaches to disaster recovery.[41]

---

[32] IPCC (Special Report), *Managing the Risks of Extreme Events and Disasters* (Cambridge University Press 2012) 7 <https://www.ipcc.ch/report/managing-the-risks-of-extreme-events-and-disasters-to-advance-climate-change-adaptation/> accessed 12 December 2020>.

[33] Simon Anderson, 'A Study of the National Energy Guarantee and Federal Governance Frameworks within the Power Generation Industry' (2019) 36 Environmental and Planning Law Journal 7, 11.

[34] International Energy Agency *Energy Security in Asean + 6* (IEA, Paris 2019) 2 <https://doi.org/10.1787/6f431256-en> accessed 13 December 2020> (hereafter IEA Energy Security).

[35] United Nations *Framework Convention on Climate Change* (opened for signature 9 May 1994) 1771 UNTS 107 art. 14(2); Paris Agreement (12 December 2015) C.N.92 2016. TREATIES-XXVII.7.d art. 7(1).

[36] Ibid 'Paris Agreement' (2015) Art 7(5).

[37] Council of Australian Governments, 'Communique' (Brisbane 7 December 2009) Attachment C. <https://www.coag.gov.au/meeting-outcomes/coag-meeting-communiqu%C3%A9-7-december-2009> accessed 12 December 2020.

[38] Council of Australian Governments, *National Strategy for Disaster Resilience* (2011) <https://www.homeaffairs.gov.au/emergency/files/national-strategy-disaster-resilience.pdf> accessed 13 December 2020.

[39] Lee Godden et al, 'Law, Governance and Risk: Deconstructing the Public/Private Divide in Climate Change Adaptation' (2013) 36 University of New South Wales Law Journal 224.

[40] Niall and Kallies 'Electricity Systems and Resilience' (n 14).

[41] Thomas Duck, 'Improving Resilience: Electricity Law, Microgrids and Solar in the Context of Climate Change' (2020) 37 EPLJ 443, 444 hereafter Duck 'Improving Resilience'; Anne Siders, 'Resilient Incoherence – Seeking

Similarly, adaptation can cover planned, public, private, reactive and anticipatory adaptation.[42] Australia developed a National Climate Resilience and Adaptation Strategy in 2015 (to be updated in 2021) which:

- sets out how Australia is managing the risks of a variable and changing climate;
- identified principles to guide effective adaptation practice and resilience building; and
- outlined the government's vision for a climate-resilient future.[43]

This strategy is high level and aspirational in its resilience objectives rather than providing concrete (and enforceable) measures. A clear policy direction is the sharing of responsibility for 'resilience' across the public and private sectors and the community. Such partnership models are evident in much adaptation planning in Australia and reflect a normative rather than regulatory governance agenda. It is designed, in part, to defuse the still politically volatile concept of climate change in Australian society. The plans stress the need for anticipatory and inclusive adaption to enable both electricity system and community resilience.[44] Yet without a specific legal framework in place this adaptation process relies heavily on government funding and project initiatives. Changes to electricity laws and associated strategic and land use planning could markedly strengthen the adaptation of communities to climate change and disasters. These measures can be assisted by electricity off-grid technologies and systemic changes such as distributed energy systems.[45] As yet, legal responses have been muted. It will require a new vision for energy networks with adaptive capacity sufficient to respond to the future risks that characterize the socio-ecological system in which electricity supply is embedded.

III. Disasters in Australia: Triggers for Resilient Approaches

A. 2019-2020 bushfires and climate change: crossing a threshold?

Significantly, according to resilience theory, resilience across a system, 'can be measured in terms of distance from the thresholds of key variables'.[46] If a system is near the threshold of a systemic variable then it is more likely to be triggered into a new regime (i.e. with new structure, function, and feedback characteristics).[47] There is an urgency of developing resilient systems for bushfire threat to electricity networks to deal with the potential 'flip' into new regimes as energy system risk thresholds are exceeded. These views about crossing a risk threshold find resonance in the 2019–2020 Royal Commission into National Natural

Common Language for Climate Change Adaptation, Disaster Risk Reduction, and Sustainable Development' in Jacqueline Peel and David Fisher (eds), *The Role of International Environmental Law in Disaster Risk Reduction* (Koninklijke Brill NV, Leiden 2016) 101, 103.

[42] IPCC, *Climate Change 2001: Impacts, Adaptation, and Vulnerability* (Cambridge University Press 2001).
[43] Australian Government, 'National Climate Resilience and Adaptation Strategy 2015' (2015) <https://www.environment.gov.au/climate-change/adaptation/strategy> accessed 13 December 2020.
[44] Duck, 'Improving Resilience' (n 41) 445.
[45] Ibid.
[46] Humby 'Law and Resilience' (n 12) 91.
[47] Barbara Cosens, 'Resilience and Law as a Theoretical Backdrop for Natural Resource Management: Flood Management in the Columbia River Basin' (2012) 42 Environmental Law 241, 246.

Disaster Arrangements (RCNNDA) that investigated the adequacy of Australia's response to the summer bushfire disaster.[48] The Royal Commission noted, '[t]he 2019-2020 bushfires and the conditions leading up to them were unprecedented. They are no longer unprecedented.'[49] The Commission drew attention to the changing nature of disaster risk:

> Natural disasters have changed, and it has become clear ...that the nation's disaster management arrangements must also change.[50]

Climate change is predicted to increase the frequency of extreme events in Australia.[51] With 'further global warming over the next 20 to 30 years ... Australia will have more hot days and fewer cool days.'[52] Consequently, 'bushfires are expected to become more frequent and more intense.'[53] The increase in 'catastrophic fire conditions'[54] may mean that historical 'bushfire prediction models and firefighting techniques'[55] become 'less effective.'[56] Accordingly, planning for the design, location, installation, and maintenance of energy critical infrastructure will need to be more adaptive and to consider that due to the ferocity of the bushfires, firefighting and fire prevention and containment are likely to become less effective over time. Further, in accordance with systems theory that predicts increasing systemic complexity, the RCNNDA found that '[n]atural disasters are expected to become more complex, more unpredictable, and more difficult to manage.'[57]

There is likely to be an increase in 'compounding disasters on a national scale with far-reaching consequences.'[58] The RCNNDA reported that:

> Compounding disasters may be caused by multiple disasters happening simultaneously, or one after another. Some may involve multiple hazards - fires, floods and storms. Some have cascading effects – threatening not only lives and homes, but also the nation's economy, critical infrastructure and essential services, such as our electricity, telecommunications and water supply, and our road, railways and airports.[59]

The finding about the compound character of disasters in Australia, and adverse socio-economic effects between physical and social systems is mirrored in socio-ecological resilience research.[60] Socio-ecological theory posits the synergy between physical and social systems, as well as a 'fundamental interdependency' between social and environmental sub-systems, 'that determines the condition, function, and response of either subsystem (and thereby the whole system) to a disturbance, or hazard'.[61] Acknowledging these interdependencies

---

[48] Australian Government, 'Disaster Royal Commission' (n 1) Interim Observations, 5.
[49] Ibid 6.
[50] Australian Government, 'Disaster Royal Commission' (n 1) 22.
[51] See Australian Government, 'The State of the Climate Report 2020' (Bureau of Meteorology and CSIRO) <http://www.bom.gov.au/state-of-the-climate/> accessed 8 January 2021.
[52] Australian Government, 'Disaster Royal Commission' (n 1) 22.
[53] Ibid.
[54] Ibid.
[55] Ibid.
[56] Ibid.
[57] Ibid.
[58] Ibid, 23.
[59] Ibid, 23.
[60] See e.g. Nikolas Luhmann and Peter Gilgen (trs) Introduction to Systems Theory 2012 (Wiley 2012).
[61] Humby 'Law and Resilience' (n 12) 91.

in translating resilience from a policy objective into substantive legal form will be an important indicator of the dynamic resilience of energy networks in social-ecological systems.

Climate change research on adaptation risk has a similar trajectory with a move from an understanding of climate change as posing a physical threat, e.g. the destruction of electricity infrastructure,[62] to climate change as socio-economic risk, e.g. where a failure to address climate risk posed to assets by companies can lead to economic loss.[63] Ultimately, there may also be a climate change 'transition risk' where a failure to transition to new, e.g. renewable energy technologies and disaster 'proof' networks and transmission systems may result in significant financial risk, not just for the immediate energy producers but those entities that invest and finance such energy systems, especially distribution.[64] These transition risks conventionally are seen as relevant for energy generation (the stranded assets problem). The bushfire summer in Australia reveals the possibility of a transition risk for existing transmission and distribution systems for electricity and gas that cannot withstand future impacts.[65] The following section outlines the nature of the risk to energy systems in Australia posed by disasters, focusing primarily, but not exclusively on bushfires.

B. The disruption threat to the electricity and gas grids

In the 2019–2020 bushfire season in Australia there were significant losses to the electricity grid and transmission system with the destruction of, '... more than 5,000 power poles across Victoria and NSW and entire sections of electricity networks [had to be] rebuilt from the ground up'.[66] As a physical threat, bushfires have direct impacts such as the destruction of 'wires and poles', transmission lines, but also due to indirect impacts such as the fire causing overheating at electricity substations.[67] In the bushfire summer there was resort to emergency power back-ups,[68] as bushfires destroyed electricity distribution systems. This situation highlighted the vulnerability of the electricity networks in urban areas as bushfires burned close to the edge of major metropolitan areas such as Sydney and Canberra. The Australian Energy Market Operator (AEMO) noted that:

Increasing extreme temperatures from climate change and urban population growth and development means increased health and safety risks from non-supply during these events...'.[69]

---

[62] Niall and Kallies, 'Electricity Systems and Resilience' (n 14) 493

[63] See, Susan Shearing 'Climate Governance and Corporations: Changing the Way "Business does Business?"' in R. Lyster and P.R. Lyster (eds), *In the wilds of climate law* (ProQuest Ebook Central 2010) 175.

[64] Chris Barrett and Anna Skarbek, *Climate Risk and the Financial System: Lessons for Australia from international experience* (Monash Sustainable Development Institute 2019).

[65] Duck, 'Improving Resilience' (n 41) 443.

[66] Energy Networks Australia, 'Bushfire Impacts'.

[67] Ibid.

[68] Nick Toscano, "Like New York after Sandy': Bushfires a 'Wake-up Call' for Power Grid' *The Sydney Morning Herald* (10 January 2020).

[69] Australian Energy Market Operator, AEMO Observations: Operational and Market Challenges to Reliability and Security in the NEM, Report (2018) 5.

In addition to the bushfire threat that is acute in south-eastern and south-western Australia, electricity networks are susceptible to floods, cyclones and storms.[70] Major flooding around Brisbane, Queensland in 2011 led to catastrophic floodwater releases from the Wivenhoe dam, resulting in deaths and extensive property damage, as well as significant disruption to power supplies in the metropolitan and regional areas.[71] Long-term droughts as a slow onset disaster can affect the functioning of electricity networks that depend on hydroelectricity generation.[72] Severe droughts are frequent in southern Australia, and in many areas burnt in the summer bushfires, drought preceded the fires, making the countryside tinder dry, and thus more susceptible to bushfire risk (i.e. a compound disaster). The compound disasters in the summer bushfire season were preceded by several earlier extreme events that had impacted the electricity supply in the national grid. These events were not as widespread or as catastrophic as the bushfires, but they sounded a warning about the vulnerability of the electricity system where climate change was increasing the risk of extreme events.

C. Electricity network vulnerability to extreme events

In September 2016, an extreme storm event resulted in large-scale damage to electricity transmission infrastructure, resulting in a subsequent electricity blackout in the State of South Australia.[73] The storm and network damage disrupted power supply to around 850, 000 customers.[74] There were conflicting claims about the cause of the blackout with some attributing it to the high level of renewable energy in the South Australian electricity system. Other commentators identified the increased likelihood of extreme weather events due to climate change as the reason for the damage.[75] AEMO published a final incident report, which included recommendations for actions to avoid future blackouts.[76] The incident highlighted the security of supply challenges for Australian electricity systems in an era of increased risk of disasters and extreme events, while a transition was occurring to a more decarbonized and decentralized electricity system.[77]

In February 2017, rolling blackouts during heatwaves in South Australia and New South Wales triggered load-shedding measures in the electricity system which drew attention to the need for greater resilience to extreme events. These events also occurred against the backdrop of the transition in the electricity system as some fossil fuel generation is being retired while renewables are increasing. As a result, gas-fired plants are required to balance

---

[70] Rosemary Lyster and Robert Verchick, 'Protecting the Power Grid from Climate Disasters' in Lyster and R., Verchick, *Research Handbook on Climate Disaster Law: Barriers and Opportunities* (Edward Elgar Publishing 2018) 269–270

[71] See Maurice Blackburn Lawyers, Queensland Floods Class Action 2021 <https://www.mauriceblackburn.com.au/class-actions/current-class-actions/queensland-floods-class-action/>.

[72] Lyster and Verchick, 'Protecting the Power Grid' (n 70), 270–271.

[73] IEA 2019 50.

[74] AEMO Black System in South Australia 28 September 2016 - Final Integrated Report, 201 (hereafter AEMO Final Report).

[75] The Climate Institute, 'SA Blackout: Climate Change Readiness Will Be Lost if We Fall for the Blame Game' (Media Release, 29 September 2016) <http://www.climateinstitute.org.au/articles/sa-blackout.html> accessed 12 December 2020.

[76] AEMO Final Report (n 74).

[77] Niall and Kallies, 'Electricity Systems and Resilience' (n 14) 488.

peak load in the electricity grid in certain situations. In these blackouts, the balance could not be achieved, partly due to the unavailability of gas-fired electricity generation capacity. Subsequently, the Australian government introduced the Australia Domestic Gas Security Mechanism, to ensure availability of supply for domestic gas users, including generators.[78]

D. Electricity caused fires: Black Saturday

Ironically while bushfires pose a significant risk to energy networks, the electricity distribution system at a local level can cause fires. This risk has seen increased safety regulation develop for electricity networks.[79] Electricity can start bushfires when infrastructure is damaged or foreign objects contact powerlines. This can cause arcing and generate sparks that can ignite dry vegetation.[80] The Energy Networks website notes, that while, 'the number of bushfires ignited by electricity is very low, once started they have the potential to burn large areas'.[81] This statement underestimates risk factors as Duck notes, 'critically with respect to an increase in bushfire risk due to climate change – although fires caused by electricity infrastructure are low (about 1.5% in normal circumstances) on days of extreme fire danger the percentage of fires linked to electrical assets rises dramatically'.[82] Moreover, the Energy Networks statement does not canvass the problem of ageing infrastructure (electricity conductors and inefficient fuses caused major bushfires in 1969 and 1977). Inadequate maintenance of electricity infrastructure such as the failure to clear vegetation from power lines has caused large fires.[83]

The Black Saturday bushfires comprised approximately 400 bushfires that either ignited or were already burning across Victoria on Saturday, 7 February 2009. The Victorian Bushfire Royal Commission in 2010 found that five of eleven bushfires were started as a result of electricity infrastructure in the Black Saturday fires. As the Bushfire Royal Commission concluded, 'electricity-caused fires are most likely to occur when the risk of a fire getting out of control and having deadly consequences is greatest'.[84] The fires, which rank as one of the worst disasters in Australia (highest loss of life), occurred during an extreme weather event where temperatures in the capital city, Melbourne, broke existing temperature records for consecutive days of heatwave. On the Saturday, as wind speeds and temperature were at their highest, and humidity at its lowest, an incorrectly-rigged SWER (single-wire earth return) mains power cable was dislodged in central Victoria. The resulting bushfire was the most intense firestorm experienced to that date in Australia.

The bushfire disaster risk was clearly recognized, with the Commission recommending, 'progressive replacement of all SWER power lines in Victoria with aerial bundled cable, underground cabling or other technology that delivers greatly reduced bushfire risk'.[85]

[78] IEA Energy Security (n 44).
[79] On grid safety regulation, see Catherine Banet and Astrid Skjønborg Brunt 'Regulating High Voltage Power Lines: Electromagnetic Fields and Safety' in Martha Roggenkamp et al, *Energy Law, Climate Change and the Environment* (Edward Elgar 2021) ch 52, 691,
[80] Energy Networks Australia, 'Bushfire Impacts' (n 5).
[81] Ibid.
[82] Duck 'Improving Resilience' (n 41) 446.
[83] State of Victoria, Royal Commission Report into the 2009 Victorian Bushfires, Final Report (July 2010) Vol 2, Electricity-caused Fire, 148.
[84] State of Victoria, Royal Commission into the 2009 Victorian Bushfires, Final Report Summary (July 2010) 12.
[85] State of Victoria, Royal Commission Report into the 2009 Victorian Bushfires, (n 83) 148

Greater safety measures were recommended, including effective maintenance and clearing of lines by distributors. The cost disincentives for network operators of SEWR replacements have limited progress toward updated infrastructure. The Commission also advocated a more strategic approach to managing bushfire disasters in Victoria. Subsequent reforms included adoption of a coordinated disaster management framework in the Emergency Management Act 2014.

Victims of the Black Saturday electricity caused fires pursued a successful class action[86] against the electricity network utility companies involved and the Victorian government. A class action was initiated in the Supreme Court of Victoria on 13 February 2009, and handled by the well-known plaintiff law firm, Maurice Blackburn.[87] In 2016, the Supreme Court of Victoria, 'approved final costs in the Kilmore East-Kinglake and Murrindindi bushfire class actions, paving the way for distribution of almost $700 million to thousands of victims of the 2009 Black Saturday disaster.[88] The devastation and loss of the Black Saturday fires were to find parallels in the bushfire summer of 2019-2020, although loss of human life was not as extreme as 2009.

E. Bushfire and disaster economic impacts

Victoria also provides an instructive case study on the estimated costs of climate-related disaster impacts such heatwaves, droughts, floods, and more severe fire conditions. The Black Saturday bushfires in 2009 are estimated to have cost the Victorian state economy AUD $7 billion. The 2019–2020 bushfires, are estimated to have had national costs of AUD $10 billion—with more than 1.2 million hectares burnt in Victoria, (the 2019–2020 bushfires are the largest in Victoria since 1939), with additional smoke-related health costs estimated at AUD $486 million for Victoria.[89] While identifying the specific causes for these events is complex, research identified that climate change exacerbates the probability of the occurrence of such extreme events.[90] As Victoria is already experiencing climate change, the urgency is growing to have a resilient electricity system that can address mitigation through decarbonization, and pursue adaptation through new technologies and operating models such as decentralized microgrids. Such transformations however must address the complex, interconnected physical, social economic, and political factors that produce 'vulnerability' in energy systems.

The situations that produce vulnerability are captured by the Bushfire and Natural Hazards Collaborative Research Centre, (CRC)[91] in research for developing resilience in

---

[86] For an overview of the class action see the Maurice Blackburn website at <https://www.supremecourt.vic.gov. au/sites/default/files/2018-11/kilmore_east_-_kinglake_murrindindi_-marysville_black_saturday_class.pdf> accessed 5 February 2021.

[87] Ibid.

[88] Supreme Court of Victoria, Media Release 7 December 2016 <https://www.supremecourt.vic.gov.au/court-approves-distribution-of-almost-700m-in-2009-black-saturday-bushfire-class-actions>.

[89] State of Victoria, Climate Change Strategy May 2021, 4 <https://www.climatechange.vic.gov.au/victorias-climate-change-strategy> accessed 5 May 2021.

[90] Ibid, 5.

[91] Australian Government, Australian electricity networks: A Statement on National Research Priorities for Natural Hazards Emergency Management and Resilience, May 2019, (hereafter Australian Government,

Australian electricity networks. As the CRC notes, '[e]ffective disaster resilience thinking acknowledges the complexities and interconnections that exist at all levels across society, including that of a variety of different critical lifeline utility services that contribute to a complex web of risk ownership and management'.[92]

The CRC report recognizes the centralized regulated nature of the electricity networks while identifying specific risk factors, such as the need for transformation to a more decentralized electricity distribution system.[93] The report acknowledges the risks posed by extreme events, but we are yet to see specific changes within the National Electricity Market rules or a national policy strategy that comprehends the systemic risk to energy networks posed by bushfires. The policy and legal response to date has been to develop a system that is oriented to reliability rather than resilience at a systemic level, in part due to the commercial orientation of rules for the national electricity market,[94] and the guiding function of the Energy Security Board.[95]

The CRC report identifies shared vulnerabilities that transcended individual network exposure, and 'which need to be managed in parallel to ensure the reliability and resilience of the collective systems that are required to deliver electricity to consumers'.[96] The report indicated that greater clarity was needed on, 'acceptable decision points for future investment to reduce risk exposure. This includes risk mitigation and maintenance of assets such as powerlines'.[97]

While the push for whole of system reform is compelling, legal reform to, 'electricity generation, distribution and consumption has been made complex by the number of State and private interests, the different, sometimes competing incentives of private and State actors – profit seeking vs carbon reduction for example – and by the types, size and nature of generation – from large State-owned coal and gas generators to home solar'.[98] This heterogeneous mix is overlain by a complex policy, regulatory, and institutional structure for governing energy systems highly influenced by Australia's federal system of government.[99] The energy governance system draws on liberalized markets and competition policy that may not be well suited to meeting the resilience challenges now facing energy networks from climate change and disaster impacts.

'Australian electricity networks'). The Bushfire and Natural Hazards CRC from 2016–2018 examined major issues in natural hazards management to build a more disaster resilient Australia.

[92] Ibid, 4
[93] Australian Government, 'Australian electricity networks' (n 90) 3.
[94] The sector is incentivized for reliability under the Australian Energy Regulator's Service Target Performance Incentive Scheme. See Anne Kallies, 'A Barrier for Australia's Climate Change Commitments: Law, the Electricity Market and Transitioning the Stationary Electricity Sector' (2015) 39 UNSWLJ 1547, 1556.
[95] 'The ESB will also provide whole of system oversight for energy security and reliability to drive better outcomes for consumers', Australian Government Energy Ministers, Overview of the Energy Security Board <https://energyministers.gov.au/market-bodies/energy-security-board> accessed 5 February 2021.
[96] Australian Government, 'Australian electricity networks' (n 90) 4.
[97] Ibid.
[98] Duck, 'Improving Resilience' (n 41) 444.
[99] Lee Godden and Anne Kallies 'Governance of the Energy Market in Australia', in Martha Roggenkamp et al (eds), *Energy Law, Climate Change and the Environment* (Edward Elgar 2021) ch 18, 204, 205.

IV. Electricity Governance, Energy Security and Systemic Resilience

A. Governing the energy system in Australia

Energy is generated, distributed, and regulated in various systems across Australia. To simplify, the focus here is the national energy markets for gas and electricity. Neither the National Electricity Market (NEM) nor the National Gas Market (NGM) extend across the country but instead are concentrated in the highly urbanized parts of southern Australia. The NEM and NGM describe the physical systems (generation, transmission, distribution, and energy retailing) and related legal and institutional governance frameworks. Energy law and governance is characterized by a centralization of policymaking due to cooperative federalism arrangements. The national government has no direct legislative competence for energy, but it can use indirect legislative powers to regulate. Under intergovernmental agreements, it works in conjunction with state and territory governments as these governments have plenary constitutional powers that allow them to regulate energy. Under this arrangement, facilitated as of 2020 by a National Cabinet, energy ministers from each jurisdiction agree national energy policy, which is implemented by participating governments. Climate policy and laws are concurrent responsibilities of the Australian national and state governments.[100] The laws governing the electricity market are comprised of the National Electricity (South Australia) Act 1996, which are adopted via mirror legislation in all jurisdictions participating in the NEM.

The NEM operates within an unbundled energy market paradigm with divided responsibilities between government policies, third party regulators, and private operators which can limit systemic resilience as it defers energy system adaptability to cost imperatives. The market includes a wholesale spot market for selling electricity and an associated transmission grid transporting electricity to customers.[101] Electricity and gas production, transport, and supply across state borders rely on a national cooperative scheme.[102] Fossil fuel generators produce most electricity in the NEM, although there is a transition to renewable generation and increasing battery storage capacity.

Australia's NEM comprises 40,000 kilometres of transmission and distribution lines. Given the physical extent of the electricity grid it is highly exposed to bushfire risk and disasters, such as a flood and cyclone. Australian cities obtain electricity primarily from large generators located some distance from urban centres, although residential solar penetration in south-eastern Australia is rapidly increasing. Without strategic planning and changes to the NEM rules to facilitate more distributed electricity supply, these communities will remain highly dependent upon the transmission grid.[103]

---

[100] Lee Godden, Jacqueline Peel, and Jan MacDonald *Environmental Law* (Oxford University Press, 2018) 108–122.

[101] Australian Energy Regulator, State of the Energy Market 2018 (1st edn, Australian Competition and Consumer Commission 2018) 75.

[102] Ibid, 28.

[103] Duck, 'Improving Resilience' (n 41) 445.

B. Gas grids

While gas supply is less vulnerable to bushfire threat, enhancing resilience in gas-related energy networks is still needed. A similar national model to the NEM is in place for gas supply, with the gas market covering conventional (natural) gas and LNG for the domestic market and large exports. Production from gas and coal seam gas wells is transported through high-pressure pipelines to large industrial customers, LNG plants, gas powered electricity generators, and 'city gates'. Following the NEM model, the National Gas Law was adopted by the participating jurisdictions.[104] Together with the National Gas Rules, it sets up a similar system to the electricity market of 'high-level policy direction, economic regulation, rule-making and rule enforcement'.[105]

The Australian gas and the national electricity markets are governed under the same institutional structure of statutory agencies—the Australian Energy Market Operator (AEMO), the Australia Energy Regulator (AER) and the Australia Energy Market Commission (AEMC). Both sectors are guided by similar legislated objectives focusing on efficiency, reliable, safe, and secure supply, and the long-term interests of consumers with respect to price, quality, and safety.[106] These narrowly conceived objectives that prioritize reliability over flexibility are a barrier to more rapid decarbonization of the electricity market,[107] and to adopting a more adaptive electricity network system more responsive to climate change mitigation and disaster-adaptation imperatives.[108] The emphasis on reliability and security ironically has been driven in part by the perceived need for an engineering/ security response to extreme event threats to the system.[109]

C. Extreme events and energy security

The South Australian blackout of 2016 prompted reviews, 'to identify measures that can promote power sector resilience',[110] given the increased severity of extreme weather events. The major initiative was the Independent Review into Australia's Energy Security (Finkel Review) by the COAG.[111] The Finkel Review recommended a strategy to improve the integrity of the energy infrastructure, and the accuracy of supply and demand forecasting. Review recommendations included: a Generator Reliability Obligation for intermittent sources of generation; Energy Security Obligations; a requirement for large generators to give three years notice before closing; and an Energy Security Board to oversee the NEM.[112] The Board added to the institutional complexity of energy market regulation in a fragmented, unbundled system where the rates of decarbonization and adaptation to disasters in the distribution sector are not uniform across the system—typically due to differing

---

[104] National Gas (South Australia) Act 2008 (SA), with mirror legislation in all states.
[105] S. Hepburn, *Mining and Energy Law* (1st edn, Cambridge University Press 2015) 147.
[106] For electricity see NEL, s 7; for gas see National Gas (South Australia) Act 2008 (SA) s 23. For discussion Godden and Kallies 'Energy Market Australia' (n 98) 208–209.
[107] Anderson, Incentive regulation (n 9) 154.
[108] Niall and Kallies, 'Electricity Systems and Resilience' (n 14) 495.
[109] International Energy Agency, *Energy Security* (n 34) 44.
[110] Ibid.
[111] Commonwealth of Australia, Finkel Review (n 13) 66.
[112] Ibid.

political commitments around climate change and energy transition at a federal and state government level. Several state governments have now initiated public security investments in emergency generation and large battery storage to provide additional system flexibility. The International Energy Agency endorsed these technical responses, which should, 'improve the country's ability to respond to electricity security issues in the short and longer term'.[113] These measures were seen as enhancing the resilience of the energy system, but arguably the response was primarily a technological and engineering form of resilience that was, 'rigid but robust'.[114]

By contrast, the underlying structural problem limiting a more systemic, socio-ecological response is identified by Niall and Kallies who suggest that regulatory frameworks entrench a fragmented ownership structure that limits system-level transformation. Such fragmentation resulted from the introduction of competition rules into state-based energy monopolies, via the adoption of market frameworks designed to separate different functions of the electricity system. 'In this situation, integrated whole-of-system solutions for the future energy system cannot easily be implemented.'[115]

Fundamental political and legal reform of the Australian energy system, particularly rapid decarbonization is unlikely as a short-term response to the bushfire summer, given entrenched political positions by the national government. Yet there is already significant economic and technological momentum shifting the network and distribution profile for electricity and gas. For gas, for example, the Victorian Government has shifted policy on the extent to which it favours gas as a 'bridging' generation source for electricity. While these climate mitigation efforts are a longer-term way to address bushfire risks (and other disasters) in Australia, a short-term response, more closely targeted to bushfires is the promotion of microgrids, solar, and batteries to mitigate escalating risks. At the same time, we are seeing stronger national policy momentum and institutional reorganization in the disaster management and adaptation space as a response to the summer bushfires.

D. Institutional coordination of disasters

Australia has a relatively well-developed legal and institutional framework for emergency and natural disaster management at a state and territory level. Until recently the national government saw its role in disasters primarily in policy development and institutional coordination– in part due to specific federal constitutional arrangements. Central to that coordination by the Australian Government was Emergency Management Australia. Its mission spans disaster risk reduction, disaster preparedness and capability development, critical incident planning, crisis and security management, and disaster recovery.[116] The Royal Commission into National Natural Disaster Arrangements (RCNNDA) set up after the summer bushfires made a series of recommendations aimed at facilitating a more proactive role in meeting the challenges of bushfires and other disasters. The RCNNDA looked

---

[113] Ibid.

[114] Duck (n 41) 444.

[115] Niall and Kallies, 'Electricity Systems and Resilience' (n 14) 501.

[116] Australian Government, Department of Home Affairs, Emergency Management <https://www.homeaffairs.gov.au/about-us/our-portfolios/emergency-management> accessed 5 May 2021.

specifically at disasters and critical infrastructure and made recommendations for essential services such as electricity. Recommendation 9.4 is illustrative:

'The Australian Government, working with state and territory governments and critical infrastructure operators, should lead a process to:

1. identify critical infrastructure
2. assess key risks to identified critical infrastructure from natural disasters of national scale or consequence
3. identify steps needed to mitigate these risks
4. identify steps to make the critical infrastructure more resilient, and
5. track achievement against an agreed plan.[117]

The RCNNDA also recommended improving coordination arrangements between critical infrastructure sectors and government.[118] While such recommendations are appropriate where the goal is greater coordination, they stop short of more substantive measures such as targeting what specific reforms are necessary to make critical infrastructure such as electricity distribution more resilient. Instead, they rely on a consensus driven model. By contrast, a Royal Commission instigated by the New South Wales government following the summer bushfires was more focused on implementing measures. It recommended a zoning model of protecting critical assets by prohibiting certain activities, including controlled burning of vegetation near such assets.[119]

Of more substance, although still pitched at a national coordination level were the RCNDA recommendations for overhauling institutional arrangements for disaster management. The suggested model reflected the strengthening of executive government during the COVID-19 pandemic by the adoption of a National Cabinet. RCNNDA suggested that the 'functions of the National Cabinet, or a similar peak intergovernmental decision-making body, could be adopted for the national management of future natural disasters'.[120] The RCNNDA argued that, '[t]here may be benefit in a single, scalable standing body responsible for natural disaster recovery and resilience at the Australian Government level. Such a body would be responsible for Commonwealth recovery coordination, prioritisation, policy and collation of relevant data'.[121]

Once again exemplifying the aspirational objectives typically attached to resilience, the RCNDA noted that:

The body could also provide national leadership for broader resilience policy and national programs. It would support the development of skills and expertise in recovery, and foster consistent approaches to recovery and lessons management, including by building resilience in communities. It would work closely with governments and organisations

---

[117] Ibid, 38, 240.
[118] Ibid, 38, 244.
[119] New South Wales, NSW Bushfire Inquiry, Final Report of the NSW Bushfire Inquiry (2020) 159.
[120] Australian Government, 'Disaster Royal Commission' (n 1) para 39.
[121] Ibid, para 43.

at the state, territory and local levels. This body would require a strong connection with Australian Government preparation and response capabilities and policy making.[122]

The RCNNDA expressly recommended that the Australian Government establish a standing entity to enhance national natural disaster resilience and recovery, focused on long-term disaster risk reduction.[123] The national government has since acted upon this recommendation recently establishing such an overarching agency.[124] It has announced a number of resilience oriented initiatives such as 'Resilience Services', a climate and disaster risk information service.[125] Notably though, these initiatives in the disaster management space are not paired to national climate change policy on mitigation that would then carry through to regulation of electricity systems. The Australian government instead has taken a stance that its climate change policy will be technology led, with much policy attention to the potential of hydrogen.

V. Conclusion: systemic resilience in energy networks

The bushfire summer had devastating consequences in Australia, although the impetus for policy reform was overtaken by the COVID-19 pandemic as executive governments scrambled to put into effect containment measures. Somewhat belatedly, the national government has put into effect the RCNDA recommendations on building resilience in the natural disaster management system—ironically enough drawing inspiration from the strengthening of executive government emergency decision making in the pandemic. While this governance platform might suggest a stronger position for the national (and state and territory) government to institute major transformations in the electricity and gas sector to translate 'resilience' into specific legal measures, that has not occurred at any appreciable scale. The national government after abandoning its National Energy Guarantee designed to secure energy security primarily by shoring up fossil fuels later introduced legislation which as Pan argues, 'has limited energy security merit and is illustrative of the government's lack of vision in delivering energy security.'[126] It represents hard-edged technological rather than flexible resilience.

Resilience discourse is now firmly entrenched in the disaster management institutional profile in Australia, but it too remains more of a fuzzy concept than a substantive position. Australian state governments, such as Victoria and South Australia with firm legislative targets for emissions reductions and long-term support for renewable energy transition are translating resilience in electricity systems into concrete mitigation and transition measures around generation and battery storage. There is however little cross sectoral integration.

---

[122] Australian Government, 'Disaster Royal Commission' (n 1) para 44.

[123] Ibid, 109.

[124] 'The Commonwealth Government will establish a new resilience, relief and recovery agency by 1 July 2021, to coordinate and align Australia's national capability to build resilience, better prepare for natural disasters, and recover from all hazards', Australian Government, *A national approach to national disasters: The Commonwealth Government response to the Royal Commission into National Natural Disaster Arrangements*, November 2020, Foreword.

[125] Ibid.

[126] Fragmentation of ownership and operational control due to privatization of electricity assets under an unbundled energy market is a problem for effective system-wide responses to disasters.

Substantial reforms to the electricity distribution system which are hyper-critical in terms of disaster responses to bushfires are still lagging. The emphasis on resilience in disaster response coordination in some ways entrenches a piecemeal, reactive position on climate change risk and continues the potential for disasters in the electricity network and distribution system.[127]

To ensure a more systemic, socio-ecological resilience governance model in the distribution and network electricity sector will require more fundamental change to the governing rules of the National Electricity Market and the National Gas Market. The Finkel Review recognized the problem of fragmentation, divided responsibility and the need for system-wide coordination of the entities that participate in these unbundled markets, arguing that better integration of generation and transmission investment was needed.[128] Niall and Kallies' perceptive analysis indicates that the complex regulatory environment characterized by private and public actors, when aligned with high political sensitivity of climate change, makes it difficult to drive system-level resilience of the electricity system.[129] As they conclude:

> We can adapt to increased climatic extremes to a certain extent within the boundaries of our existing system, but ultimately transformation in its design will be required to retain the essential services delivered by the critical infrastructure system. More distributed generation is a necessary component of this transformation; given it is associated with a greater ability to withstand disruptions, improved demand-side management and energy efficiency to help manage disruptions and a shift to renewable energy.... As such, the benefit of "resilience" as a bridging objective for the electricity sector can only be realised if it is applied at the system level and in a manner that allows the system to transform and adapt – consistent with ecological framings.[130]

[127] Duck, 'Improving Resilience' (n 41) 445.
[128] Commonwealth of Australia, Finkel Review (n 13) ch 5.
[129] Niall and Kallies, 'Electricity Systems and Resilience' (n 14) 501.
[130] Niall and Kallies 'Electricity Systems and Resilience' (n 14) 496 (footnotes omitted).

9

Advancing Resilience to Price Volatility in Oil and Gas Markets

Current Challenges and Ways Forward in the MENA Region

Damilola S. Olawuyi

I. Introduction

This chapter examines oil price volatility, and its associated financial and budgetary crises, as a major disruptive event that impacts energy security—the availability, affordability, and accessibility of energy resources—in the Middle East and North African (MENA) region.[1] It discusses law and governance aspects of designing and implementing disaster risk reduction and resilience (DRRR) frameworks to anticipate, minimize, and address the disruptive impacts of oil and gas price volatility in MENA countries.[2]

Endowed with half of the world's known oil and gas reserves, the economy of the MENA region is highly dependent on rents and revenue from the oil and gas industry.[3] Accordingly, oil revenue is directly responsible for over 50 per cent of national gross domestic products (GDPs) in several MENA countries, especially the Gulf countries—Kuwait, Iran, Bahrain, Oman, Qatar, Saudi Arabia, and the United Arab Emirates (UAE).[4] Outside of the Gulf, Maghreb countries such as Algeria, Egypt, and Libya also have similar statistics, reflecting the dominant role of oil and gas in catalysing economic development in several low- to middle-income MENA countries.[5]

Given the prevailing dependence on oil and natural gas as a driving force of MENA economies, oil price volatility often triggers significant macro-economic effects and cyclical swings in MENA countries.[6] For example, the sharp drop in oil prices since the latter half of

---

[1] Oil price volatility is defined as 'the risk that oil prices may change rapidly, substantially, and unpredictably.' see James Daniel, 'Hedging Government Oil Price Risk' in Jeffrey Davis, Annalisa Fedelino, and Rolando Ossowski (eds), *Fiscal Policy Formulation and Implementation in Oil-Producing Countries* (IMF 2003) 359.

[2] Twenty countries are typically included as part of the MENA Region: Algeria, Bahrain, Djibouti, Egypt, Iran, Iraq, Israel, Jordan, Kuwait, Lebanon, Libya, Malta, Morocco, Oman, Qatar, Saudi Arabia, Syria, Tunisia, United Arab Emirates, and Yemen. Similarly, The State of Palestine, a *de jure* sovereign state is also part of the MENA region. See World Bank, Middle East and North Africa, <https://Data.Worldbank.Org/Region/Middle-East-And-North-Africa> accessed 27 June 2019.

[3] D. Olawuyi, 'Advancing Innovations in Renewable Energy Technologies as Alternatives to Fossil Fuel Use in the Middle East: Trends, Limitations, and Ways Forward' in D. Zillman, M. Roggenkamp, L. Paddock, and L. Godden, (eds), *Innovation in Energy Law and Technology: Dynamic Solutions for Energy Transitions* (Oxford University Press 2018) 354–370.

[4] Ibid.

[5] In Libya for example, oil resources account for approximately 69 per cent of export earnings, 75 per cent of government receipts, and about 60 per cent of the GDP. See OPEC Annual Statistical Bulletin 2020,<https://www.opec.org/opec_web/en/about_us/166.htm>

[6] K.C. Ulrichsen, *Insecure Gulf: The End of Certainty and the Transition to the Post- Oil Era* (Columbia University Press 2011).

Damilola S. Olawuyi, *Advancing Resilience to Price Volatility in Oil and Gas Markets* In: *Resilience in Energy, Infrastructure, and Natural Resources Law*. Edited by: Catherine Banet, Hanri Mostert, LeRoy Paddock, Milton Fernando Montoya, and Íñigo del Guayo, Oxford University Press. © Damilola S. Olawuyi 2022. DOI: 10.1093/oso/9780192864574.003.0009

2014, and the ensuing collapse of several industries, factories, and institutions in the region, brought to the fore the high vulnerabilities of MENA economies to cyclical swings associated with oil price volatility.[7] Since 2014, the price of a barrel of oil has fallen more than 70 per cent, wiping out over US$360 billion of revenue from Gulf countries in 2015 alone, about 21 per cent of GDP in the region.[8] Official forecasts by the Organization of Petroleum Exporting Countries (OPEC) already indicate that a return to US$100 per barrel price of oil may not be until after 2040.[9] Consequently, advancing resilience to oil price volatility and cyclical downturns has become high on the legislative and policy agenda in several oil- and gas-dependent countries of the MENA region. The uncertain levels of finance for energy projects during the 'boom or bust' cycles of the oil and gas sector and the resulting disruptions to regional investment, trade, and infrastructure development activities across the region, have accentuated calls for holistic legal and economic reforms to increase the resilience of MENA oil and gas markets to the impacts of oil price volatility.[10]

The paralysing disruptions to MENA oil and gas markets in light of the COVID-19 pandemic have further exacerbated these concerns.[11] Significant declines in demand for oil and gas during the pandemic have resulted in the collapse of oil and gas prices from a peak of US$115 a barrel in August 2014 to a record low of US$25 at the peak of the COVID-19 pandemic.[12] According to World Bank estimates, addressing the impact of the sharp drop in the prices of oil due to the COVID-19 pandemic will cost MENA countries approximately USD 116 billion, almost 4 per cent of the region's combined 2019 GDP.[13] Moreover, there is already evidence of increasing reversal or postponement of energy infrastructure projects in many MENA countries due to the economic downturn resulting from the COVID-19 pandemic.[14] Furthermore, the deployment of low-carbon and renewable energy technologies such as wind turbines, solar panels, and batteries, across the MENA region have faced increased uncertainty due to pandemic-related delays and disruptions.[15]

The COVID-19 pandemic accentuates the need for innovative law and governance approaches to anticipate and manage the short- and long-term impacts of oil price volatility in MENA countries. However, despite the high susceptibility of MENA economies to oil

---

[7] Olawuyi (n 3)

[8] IMF, 'Global Implications of Lower Oil Prices, International Monetary Fund' (2015), <https://www.imf.org/external/pubs/ft/sdn/2015/sdn1515.pdf>; also A. Ghafar, 'Will the GCC Be Able to Adjust to Lower Oil Prices' (2016), <https://www.brookings.edu/blog/markaz/2016/02/18/will-the-gcc-be-able-to-adjust-to-lower-oil-prices/>.

[9] 'OPEC: Oil Won't Be Worth $100 a Barrel Until After 2040', <https://www.businessinsider.com/opec-oil-wont-be-worth-100-a-barrel-until-after-2040-2015-12.>

[10] See M. Al Asoomi, 'Time for Change in Gulf's Energy Policy' Gulf News (22 July 2015), <https://gulfnews.com/business/energy/time-for-change-in-gulfs-energy-policy-1.1553842>.

[11] See Hanen Keskes, How Cheap Oil and The Pandemic Threaten Economies And The Energy Transition In The Middle East And North Africa (Natural Resource Governance Institute 2020)

[12] Lizzy Gurdus, 'Crude Prices Plunge to Lowest Level in History - What Cramer and Others Are Watching' (2020), <https://www.cnbc.com/2020/04/20/crude-prices-plunge-to-record-lows-cramer-others-on-whats-next.html>, accessed 16 August 2020.

[13] R. Arezki and H. Nguyen, 'Coping with a Dual Shock: COVID-19 and Oil Prices' <https://www.worldbank.org/en/region/mena/brief/coping-with-a-dual-shock-coronavirus-covid-19-and-oil-prices>, also 'MENA Economies Face $116 Billion Hit From Virus, Oil Slump: World Bank' https://www.arabnews.com/node/1656236/business-economy.

[14] For example, in April 2020, Algeria announced a 30 per cent cut in public spending, in response to the two shocks—the spread of COVID-19 and the sharp decline in oil prices. This cut is projected to derail Algeria's solar energy project. See International Monetary Fund, Policy Responses to Covid-19, <https://www.imf.org/en/topics/imf-and-covid19/policy-responses-to-covid-19>; also Keskes (n 11).

[15] Keskes (n 11).

price volatility, the conceptualization of DRRR planning in the MENA region has focused mainly on physical energy infrastructure risks. Although the importance of DRRR has been generally well elaborated in the MENA region with respect to urban resilience, infrastructure development, climate change, and disaster management, its practical application and implications have not been discussed exhaustively in the oil and gas context. This chapter fills a gap in this regard.

Building resilience and stabilizing oil and gas industries in the MENA region have to go beyond ad hoc production quotas and cuts. Without mainstreaming DRRR frameworks into resource development and planning, sustaining progress on economic diversification, energy access, and the decarbonization agenda in the MENA region will be difficult in times of reduced demand and low oil and gas prices.

After this introduction, Section II explores the significance and contours of the DRRR discourse and its implications for addressing the high susceptibility of MENA oil and gas markets to oil price volatility. Common and multi-scalar threats that heighten the susceptibility of MENA oil and gas markets to disruptive oil shocks are examined in Section III. Section IV assesses the main legal and institutional barriers to mainstreaming DRRR into resource development and planning in the MENA region. Section V discusses how extant legal barriers to holistic DRRR planning could be addressed in MENA oil and gas markets. Section VI is the concluding section.

II. The DRRR Discourse and its Implications for MENA Oil and Gas Markets

Over the last decade, DRRR frameworks have been promoted by the United Nations Office for Disaster Risk Reduction (UNISDR) as a holistic approach for building resilience and reducing disaster and hazard risks in key sectors and industries.[16] DRRR frameworks include pre-disaster measures that aim to anticipate, prevent, and reduce the occurrence or frequency of disruptive events. At the same time, post-disaster measures aim to provide timely, effective, and cost-efficient recovery from disruptive events as they occur, to reduce their adverse impacts and ensure early response, recovery, and reconstruction.[17] An example is to have rapid response systems, emergency aid, and regulatory incentives in place that can accelerate recovery.

Since the release of the Sendai Framework for Disaster Risk Reduction 2015–2030 (Sendai Framework),[18] MENA countries have increasingly elaborated plans to integrate

---

[16] Hazard is defined as: 'a potentially damaging physical event, phenomenon or human activity that may cause the loss of life or injury, property damage, social and economic disruption or environmental degradation...'. Given that oil price volatility results in social and economic disruptions to the economies of MENA countries, DRRR frameworks are essential to manage such risks. UNISDR, 'Disaster Risk Reduction And Resilience In The 2030 Agenda For Sustainable Development' <https://www.preventionweb.net/files/46052_disasterriskreductioninthe2030agend.pdf>,

[17] I. Kelman, 'Linking Disaster Risk Reduction, Climate Change, and the Sustainable Development Goals' (2017) 26(3) Disaster Prevention And Management: An International Journal 254–258; also M. Roggenkamp, 'Protecting Infrastructure in order to Guarantee Supply Security: Critical Infrastructure in the EU' in Martha M. Roggenkamp, Lila Barrera-Hernandez, Donald N. Zillman, and Inigo del Guayo, *Energy Networks and the Law: Innovative Solutions in Changing Markets* (Oxford University Press 2012).

[18] The Sendai Framework was adopted at the Third United Nations World Conference on Disaster Risk Reduction, held from 14–18 March 2015 in Sendai, Miyagi, Japan, <https://www.preventionweb.net/files/43291_sendaiframeworkfordrren.pdf> accessed 14 December 2021.

DRRR frameworks into national planning to effectively anticipate and prevent risks from disruptive events.[19] In addition, the guiding principles for resilience planning have been elaborated on in several key documents at the regional level. For example, in 2012, the League of Arab States adopted the Arab Strategy for Disaster Risk Reduction 2020, which calls on all Arab countries to develop measures and plans to reduce disaster risks and strengthen the resilience of public infrastructure to natural hazards by the year 2020.[20] Similarly, in 2013, the Gulf Cooperation Council (GCC) undertook to develop a risk reduction road map that will strengthen the resilience of public infrastructure and individuals across the GCC to natural hazards.[21] These documents emphasize the importance of designing and implementing national DRRR frameworks to effectively manage disaster risks.

However, although the importance of DRRR has been generally well elaborated in urban resilience, infrastructure, climate change, and disaster management literature, its practical application and implications have not been exhaustively discussed in the oil and gas context. Despite the economic dependence of MENA countries on their oil and gas revenues, comprehensive legal and institutional frameworks that address the extreme susceptibility of MENA countries to cyclical disruptions posed by oil price volatility have not been easily forthcoming.[22]

The social and economic disruptions caused by oil price volatility makes it a leading cause of environmental vulnerability and energy insecurity in the MENA region.[23] For example, oil price volatility and its associated financial squeeze make it difficult for MENA countries to advance infrastructure projects needed to attain all SDGs. Ranging from SDG 7 on sustainable energy for all, to SDG 8 on sustainable economic growth and productive employment work for all, and SDG 13 on climate change mitigation and adaptation, significant and sustained financing will be required to advance the targets and goals. Hence, the Sendai Framework calls on countries to promote and integrate 'disaster risk reduction considerations and measures into financial and fiscal instruments'.[24]

Though not legally binding, the Sendai Framework highlights the importance of mainstreaming DRRR frameworks into fiscal policies and instruments that underpin susceptible economic sectors, such as the oil and gas industry, to enhance resilience to disruptive events. MENA countries must conceptualize the drivers of—and sustainability risks posed by—oil price volatility and establish pre-disaster and post-disaster frameworks to manage such risks.[25] This will help address the extreme susceptibility of MENA countries to oil price volatility.

[19] See for example, Qatar's Climate Change Risk Management Strategy for the Urban Planning and Development Sector Government of Qatar (2018) <https://www.mme.gov.qa/QatarMasterplan/English/strategicplans.aspx?panel=ccs> accessed 14 December 2021.
[20] Council of Arab Ministers Responsible for the Environment, Resolution # 345, adopted in its 22nd session held at the League of Arab States 19–20 December 2010.
[21] UNISDR (n 16). See also the Arab Strategy for Housing and Sustainable Urban Development 2030 (2016) <https://unhabitat.org/arab-strategy-for-housing-and-sustainable-urban-development> accessed 14 December 2021.
[22] R. Arezki and H. Nguyen (n 13), see T. Mitro, 'Understanding and Mitigating COVID-19 Oil Price Impacts' (10 May 2020), <http://ccsi.columbia.edu/2020/05/22/understanding-and-mitigating-covid-19-oil-price-impacts/> accessed 14 December 2021.
[23] Keskes (n 11), Moawad Ahmed Sayed (2016) 'The Impact of Oil Prices on the Economic Growth and Development in the MENA Countries' MPRA Paper No. 89073, online at <https://mpra.ub.uni-muenchen.de/89073/> accessed 14 December 2021.
[24] Para 30 (m), Sendai Framework.
[25] Mitro (n 22).

III. Drivers of Oil Price Volatility

There are four key drivers of the extreme susceptibility of MENA countries to oil price volatility. First is the nature of the oil and gas commodity itself. The price of oil and gas as a commodity is mainly dependent on forces of demand and supply. When oil demand is high, the prices go very high, and when demand is low, investors look to sell at any reasonable price, leading to a drop in the price of the commodity.[26] Given that oil traders buy and sell oil, based on future expectations of demand and supply, any shift in demand expectations reflects changes in the real price of oil. Consequently, oil demand has played a key role in all major oil price shocks that have occurred since the 1970s, including the recent shock caused by reduced demand for oil during the COVID-19 pandemic.[27]

In addition to natural disasters, pandemics, and economic slowdowns that reduce demand for oil, the excessive supply of oil, driven largely by unexpected growth of unconventional oil production in the United States, also often trigger a supply glut which could also weaken the price of oil.[28] The recent landmark agreements reached by OPEC members to limit oil production in response to oil price volatility demonstrate OPEC's ongoing relevance in stabilizing global oil markets.[29] Such production cuts can provide temporary and ad hoc responses to oil shocks. Even so, there is a need for holistic anticipatory frameworks that could help oil and gas producing countries to anticipate, prevent, and reduce the short- and long-term impacts of oil price fluctuations. Mainstreaming DRRR frameworks into energy policies can help MENA countries develop long-term mechanisms to anticipate and minimize the impacts of future 'bust' cycles.

A second driver of the extreme susceptibility of MENA countries to oil price volatility and fluctuations is the slow pace of economic diversification across the region.[30] Several studies have shown the need for MENA countries to shift from excessive dependence on fossil fuels by promoting growth in other sectors such as tourism, healthcare, education and sports, amongst others.[31] Having mono-industry economies that depend on oil and gas significantly increases the occurrence and frequency of social and economic disruptions resulting from oil price volatility.

The sharp drop in oil price due to the COVID-19 pandemic has triggered renewed calls for robust economic diversification.[32] While some countries in the region have made progress in economic diversification efforts, the economies of several MENA countries remain

---

[26] J. Baffes, M. Ayhan, F. Ohnsorge, and M. Stocker, 'The Great Plunge in Oil Prices: Cause, Consequences, and Policy Responses' World Bank Group, p.4; see also Lutz Kilian, 'Oil Price Volatility: Origins and Effects' (2010) <https://www.wto.org/english/res_e/publications_e/wtr10_forum_e/wtr10_kilian_e.htm> accessed 14 December 2021.

[27] Kilian, ibid.

[28] Baffes et al (n 26), Mitro (n 22).

[29] Europa (2016), Europa 'Impact of the November 2016 OPEC Agreement on the Oil Market' ECB Economic Bulletin, Issue 8 / 2016 <https://www.ecb.europa.eu/pub/pdf/other/eb201608_focus01.en.pdf?84e6b1f5356e5 3c615d6e8e5af195007> accessed 14 December 2021.

[30] A. Kireyev, 'Diversification in The Middle East: From Crude Trends to Refined Policies' (2021) 8(2) The Extractive Industries and Society 100701.

[31] R. Cherif, F. Hasanov, and M. Zhu, 'Breaking the Oil Spell: The Gulf Falcons' Path to Diversification' (IMF 2016); M. Hvidt, 'Economic and Institutional Reforms in the Arab Gulf Countries' (2011) 65(1) Middle East Journal 85–102.

[32] M. Hvidt, 'Economic Reforms in the Arab Gulf Countries: Lip Service or Actual Implementation?' in M. Legrenzi and B. Momani (eds), *Shifting Geo-Economic Power of the Gulf: Oil, Finance and Institutions* (Ashgate 2011) 39–54.

intricately tied to oil and gas.[33] With the rise of climate change mitigation measures —primarily those targeted at reducing global dependence on fossil fuels—economic diversification is no longer an option; it is necessary for all MENA countries.[34] Integrating DRRR thinking into energy policies across the region will require MENA countries to reduce the excessive dependence on oil and gas revenue.[35] Preventive measures in this context will include actively promoting a diversified economic base with a wide range of investment and employment opportunities in diverse sectors. It also includes establishing required legal frameworks to encourage entrepreneurship and private sector participation in the domestic economy, especially in the energy sector. Economic diversification can serve as a tool for incentivizing and facilitating small- and medium-scale entrepreneurial ventures (SMEs) to unlock locally made technologies, tools, and products needed to advance energy security and export diversification in the region.[36] By promoting eco-entrepreneurship and energy citizenship, MENA countries can advance homegrown energy solutions and technologies needed to expand energy access and resilience to several of the complex environmental vulnerabilities facing the region.[37]

Third, and related to economic diversification, is the slow pace of energy diversification and green economy transition in MENA countries. Energy diversification through the use of different energy sources—conventional, unconventional, and renewables—can help countries to reduce dependence on a single resource, thereby promoting energy security, especially in energy importing MENA countries.[38] For example, in countries such as Jordan, Lebanon, and Morocco, the dependence rate on energy import is more than 90 per cent.[39] In such countries, geopolitical instability, conflicts, and cyclical changes in oil and gas prices tend to affect the affordability, availability, and accessibility of energy resources.[40]

Diversifying the energy mix, by investing in renewable and low carbon energy innovation and technology, especially solar energy, can help energy-importing countries in the region to achieve resilience and address energy insecurity associated with cyclical swings in the price of imported oil and gas. For energy-exporting countries, such as the Gulf Countries, diversifying the energy mix can help them advance decarbonization and low carbon transition objectives, that have been widely expressed in national visions and policies.[41] Mainstreaming DRRR thinking into energy policies across the region will require MENA countries to put in place projects, investments, and measures to reduce the excessive dependence on hydrocarbons as the dominant source of energy.

[33] For example, through infrastructure spending on healthcare, tourism, and sports, Qatar has prioritized economic diversification policies. See E. Tok, M. Koç, and C. D'Alessandro, 'Entrepreneurship in a Transformative and Resource-Rich State: The Case of Qatar' (2021) 8(2) The Extractive Industries and Society 100708.
[34] Damilola Olawuyi, 'Can MENA Extractive Industries Support the Global Energy Transition? Current Opportunities and Future Directions' (2021) 8(2) The Extractive Industries and Society 100685.
[35] C. S. Hendrix, 'Kicking a Crude Habit: Diversifying Away from Oil and Gas in the Twenty-First Century' (2019) Int. Rev. Appl. Econ. 33(2), 188–208.
[36] See Damilola Olawuyi, 'From Energy Consumers to Energy Citizens: Legal Dimensions of Energy Citizenship' in K. Hunter et al (eds), Sustainable Energy Democracy and the Law (Brill 2021) 101–123.
[37] Ibid; also G. O'Brien and A. Hope, 'Localism and Energy: Negotiating Approaches to Embedding Resilience in Energy Systems' (2010) 38(12) Energy Policy 7550–7558.
[38] See Olawuyi (n 3).
[39] See OME/Observatoire Méditerranéen de l'Energie, Mediterranean Energy Perspectives 2015 (OME 2015).
[40] Hendrix (n 35), also A. Sutrisno, Ö. Nomaler, and F. Alkemade, 'Has the Global Expansion of Energy Markets Truly Improved Energy Security? (2020) 148 Energy Policy 111931.
[41] See for example, the Qatar National Vision 2030, Bahrain National Vision 2030, Saudi Arabia National Vision 2030, Oman National Vision 2020, and the United Arab Emirates (UAE) National Vision 2021. Olawuyi (n 3).

A fourth driver of the extreme susceptibility of MENA countries to oil price volatility is the prevalence of fiscal incentives such as subsidies and zero taxation which generally reduce the revenue base for governments. Across the MENA region, especially in Gulf countries, there is a low focus on tax revenue collection.[42] Similarly, governments across the region heavily subsidize electricity costs to maintain relatively very low prices for citizens.[43] However, while these arrangements have worked well for decades, especially in a high oil price economy, the sustainability of such fiscal incentives are now under threat.[44] For instance, in 2016, Gulf countries agreed to introduce value-added tax (VAT) on goods and services as a way of increasing the government's revenue base in a low oil price world.[45] However, the full-scale implementation of this plan has been impacted by the COVID-pandemic. As Ezenagu notes, there is now a need for MENA countries to implement robust and effective tax regimes to build resilience for boom or bust cycles of oil and gas prices.[46] MENA countries will need to develop long-term plans on how existing fiscal incentives can be gradually reformed to advance resilience to current and future oil price volatility.[47]

Given these main drivers and the low-price environment triggered by the COVID-19 pandemic, the appetite for implementing structural reforms to improve resilience to oil price volatility is very high across the MENA region. It could remain sustained for the next decade. However, to mainstream DRRR effectively into energy policies across the region, there is a need to establish law and governance frameworks that address legal barriers to holistic DRRR planning. Section IV assesses the main legal and institutional barriers to mainstreaming DRRR into resource development and planning in the MENA region.

IV. Advancing Resilience in Energy Planning: Survey of Legal Barriers and Limitations

DRRR planning requires implementing a wide range of fiscal and economic measures to enhance the resilience of MENA countries to cyclical disruptions and vulnerabilities posed by oil price volatility. Legal and institutional gaps in extant energy regimes that heighten susceptibility will have to be carefully examined and addressed. This will be through the expansion of complementary pre-hazard and post-hazard measures to anticipate, prevent, and reduce the impacts of oil price volatility on energy security in MENA countries.

Pre-hazard measures will include advancing economic diversification to expand the economic and revenue bases of oil and gas-dependent MENA countries; eliminating unsustainable subsidies and fiscal incentives to benefit from additional and diversified revenue base; and diversifying the energy mix to reduce excessive reliance on oil and gas, therefore advancing supply reliability in importing countries and promoting decarbonization

---

[42] A. Ezenagu, 'Boom or Bust, Extractives Are No Longer Saviours: The Need for Robust Tax Regimes in Gulf Countries' (2021) 8(2) The Extractive Industries and Society 100848. See also International Monetary Fund (IMF), 'Trade and foreign investment-keys to diversification and growth in the GCC' (IMF 2018) 3–6; IMF, 'Tax Policy Reforms in the GCC Countries: Now and How?' (IMF 2015).

[43] Olawuyi (n 3)

[44] See Ezenagu (n 42).

[45] See Unified VAT Agreement for the Cooperation Council for The Arab States of the Gulf (GCC Vat Treaty).

[46] Ezenagu (n 42), IMF 2018 (n 42).

[47] A. Malik, *Diversification of Middle Eastern Economies Is More a Political than an Economic Challenge* (Policy Brief/The Lebanese Center for Policy Studies 2016).

objectives. Furthermore, post-hazard measures will include a wide portfolio of wealth management systems (such as sovereign wealth funds and budget stabilization funds) needed to provide timely, effective, and cost-efficient responses that will minimize impacts of future bust cycles and promote a speedy recovery. Such response funds will also need to reflect wider policy objectives such as decarbonization of investment portfolio and assets.

Despite the increasing commitment by national authorities across the MENA region to increase pre-hazard and post-hazard frameworks relating to oil price volatility risks, some legal and institutional barriers will need to be addressed to promote resilience in energy governance and decision making across the region. This section develops a profile of legal barriers and institutional gaps that must be addressed to advance the resilience of oil and gas markets in the region to disruptive events.

A. Regulatory complexities and administrative barriers to entrepreneurship

All MENA countries have elucidated national visions and plans that underscore the importance of entrepreneurship and citizen-led energy investments as ways to promote economic diversification and reduce perennial dependence on oil and gas revenue. However, the diversification of goods, services, and exports across various sectors remains weak, resulting in a near-total dependence on oil and gas exports.[48] One key reason for the slow pace of economic diversification across the MENA region is the absence of comprehensive legal frameworks required to stimulate entrepreneurship and investment across diverse underdeveloped sectors.[49]

For example, in the 2018 Global Entrepreneurship Index (GEI), virtually all MENA countries were ranked low in terms of having robust and adequate legal frameworks that foster entrepreneurship. A positive exception is Qatar, which has the highest rank for any country in the MENA region and is currently ranked 23 out of 138 countries in the GEI.[50] The GEI reflects challenges that remain across the MENA region in terms of creating a supportive legal order for the licensing and registration of energy ventures. Across the region, commencing any energy project or investment require licences and approvals issued by various ministries such as those responsible for energy, industry, and economy.[51] However, the procedures for obtaining such licences are often complicated by administrative delays and layers of regulatory requirements.[52]

The foregoing raises the need for MENA countries to continue to streamline the process of registering and formalizing entrepreneurial ventures, especially energy start-ups,

[48] Ibid.
[49] Olawuyi (n 36); also IMF (2008) (n 42).
[50] Global Entrepreneurship and Development Institute (GEDI) (2018), 'Global Entrepreneurship Index 2018' <http://thegedi.org/2018-global-entrepreneurship-index-data/> accessed 12 December 2021; also T. B. Hassen, *Entrepreneurship, ICT and Innovation: State of Qatar Transformation to a Knowledge-Based Economy* (Nova Science Publishers, Inc. 2019).
[51] Olawuyi (n 36).
[52] See World Bank, 'Doing Business 2020: Middle East And North Africa', which notes significant reform and progress in some countries such as Qatar and the UAE, but administrative delays and regulatory burdens in several others, Available at <https://Espanol.Doingbusiness.Org/Content/Dam/Doingbusiness/Media/Profiles/Regional/Db2020/Mena.Pdf> accessed 9 December 2020.

to make them less cumbersome.[53] It is important for MENA countries to reform laws, regulations, and financial access requirements that hinder broad-based participation in registering and formalizing energy investments and projects. Examples include laws in many parts of the MENA region that stipulate that more than 50 per cent of a business venture must be owned by a government entity or laws that stipulate that energy infrastructure can only be managed and maintained by the national authority.[54] Furthermore, stringent local laws on repatriation of earnings, investment taxation, insurance, and dispute resolution may disincentivize private sector participation and investment in energy projects. It is, therefore, necessary for countries to review and reform extant investment laws and institutions that limit the ability of private citizens and residents to register energy ventures. For example, Qatar, in recognition of the need to expand private participation, recently enacted a new investment law that allows foreign companies and private individuals to invest directly in almost all of the key economic sectors in Qatar without the need for a local partner.[55] Similarly, in 2020, Oman issued a new law that established an SME Authority that will serve as a one-stop shop for streamlining the process of establishing SMEs in the country.[56]

Such reforms to allow for broad-based public participation in energy innovation, as well as streamlining the process of venture registration to address delays, will be key to promoting the development of energy SMEs.

B. Unclear or inadequate legal frameworks on taxation

As earlier noted, one of the key limitations to revenue diversification across the MENA region is the absence of robust legal frameworks on taxation. Resource curse studies show that rentier countries that receive large revenues from oil and gas tend to focus less on raising revenue from domestic taxation, and this has been the case across the MENA region.[57] As Ezenagu notes, due to prevailing governance models that prioritize the distribution of fiscal incentives, such as competitive tax-free salaries, tax waivers for enterprises owned by citizens, energy subsidies, as well as other financial benefits to citizens, several MENA countries 'have not been inclined to tax the citizens and residents'.[58] Consequently, while virtually all MENA countries have tax laws, a survey of extant tax laws across the region show lack of comprehensiveness and depth needed to achieve the central aims of a functional and effective taxation system, namely fairness (proportional, regressive, progressive); certainty; efficiency; and convenience.[59] As MENA countries increasingly consider

[53] Olawuyi (n 36), also See E. Tok, M. Koç, and C. D'Alessandro, 'Entrepreneurship in a Transformative and Resource-Rich State: The Case of Qatar' (2021) 8(2) The Extractive Industries and Society 100708.
[54] See OECD, 'Renewable Energies in the Middle East and North Africa: Policies to Support Private Investment' (OECD 2013) 1–10.
[55] Qatar Law No. 1 of 2019 Regulating the Investment of Non-Qatari Capital in Economic Activity.
[56] Sultanate of Oman, Royal Decree No. 107/2020 establishing the Authority of Small and Medium Enterprises, defines its specializations and endorses its organizational structure.
[57] J. A. Fuinhas and A. C. Marques, 'Rentierism, Energy and Economic Growth: The Case of Algeria and Egypt (1965–2010)' (2013) 62 Energy Policy 1165–1171. A. M. Álvarez, 'Rentierism in the Algerian Economy based on Oil And Natural Gas' (2010) 38 Energy Policy 6338–6348.
[58] Ezenagu (n 42). For example, although Qatar has a corporate income tax at the rate of 10 per cent, entities wholly owned by Qataris and other Gulf nationals are exempt from corporate income tax. Qatar also levies no tax on personal income of residents and citizens. See Qatar Income Tax Law no. 24 of 2018.
[59] H. Almutairi, 'Competitive Advantage through Taxation in GCC Countries' (2014) 13(4) International Business & Economics Research Journal 769–778.

the need to diversify government revenue base through taxation in the aftermath of the recent oil shock, there is an urgent need to develop functional and effective tax systems backed by a comprehensive legal framework.

Taxation laws are a very important means of providing legal certainty and clarity to residents and citizens on their emerging taxation obligations. Furthermore, investors will want to have a clear knowledge of the guiding principles and goals of a country's taxation policies and legislation. By specifying and clarifying obligations under a wide range of taxes such as corporate income tax, value-added tax, stamp duty, amongst others, a comprehensive taxation framework can help boost the sources of revenue required for infrastructure development and social services in a country. Similarly, tax laws can be used to redistribute wealth in society by specifying higher taxation for a certain income threshold and a lower rate for those in need of government support, especially low-income residents and citizens.

Taxation laws can also be designed with the aim of influencing behavioural change, for example, through levying 'sin taxes' for environmentally damaging technologies or activities in key sectors such as the oil and gas sector. Similarly, a comprehensive legal framework on taxation can help a country to achieve greater fiscal transparency and accountability in the management of revenue from the oil and gas sector. Tax laws provide important statutory and legislative foundations for the implementation of these and other aims of taxation. The legal framework will also need to specify clear timeframes, procedures, and processes for meeting tax obligations, and the penalties for non-compliance. These are practical questions that must be carefully laid out in a legal framework designed to clarify and govern tax obligations.

C. Unclear or inadequate legal frameworks on energy diversification and decarbonization

As noted earlier, there is already a clear impetus for the diversification of energy mixes across the MENA region as a way of promoting energy security while also achieving low carbon energy transition.

Despite the growing levels of renewable energy investments in clean technology projects, corresponding law and governance frameworks on alternative energy generation and supply have not been clearly deliberated. For example, while climate awareness and action are increasing across the region, a comprehensive review of global climate change laws reveals that many of the countries in the region do not have specific legislation on climate change.[60]

Similarly, clear and comprehensive legal frameworks on the requirements and procedure for integrating electricity generated from decentralized renewable energy sources into national electricity grids have yet to be developed across the region.[61] Although Gulf countries such as Saudi Arabia, Kuwait, and the UAE have at different times announced plans to develop national renewable energy laws, this has yet to come to fruition.[62] Enacting renewable

[60] Olawuyi (n 3).
[61] Only a few MENA countries have passed renewable energy laws: See League of Arab States, *Pan-Arab Renewable Energy Strategy 2030: Roadmap of Actions for Implementation* (LAS 2014) 36–37.
[62] Ibid.

energy laws could help send positive signals to investors about the political recognition, interest, and commitment to accelerating low-carbon investment and infrastructure development across the region.[63] The adoption of renewable energy laws by Algeria, Jordan, Morocco, Palestine, Syria, and Tunisia is a positive signal that other MENA countries may increasingly begin to back national visions on low-carbon transition with clear and transparent legislative frameworks.[64] Such legal frameworks can pave the way for ensuring coherence and clarity in energy diversification efforts and could enable MENA countries to remove barriers to achieving grid integration, balancing, storage, interconnection, and smart communication, amongst others.

MENA countries can also strengthen their resilience to ongoing transformations occasioned by the energy transition, by leveraging oil and gas stabilization funds and sovereign wealth fund (SWFs) to invest in green assets and projects worldwide.[65] The need for portfolio decarbonization in SWF investments is obvious, with SWFs in New Zealand, Norway, South Korea, and France already announcing various plans to divest from high carbon industries.[66] Similarly, SWFs from the MENA region, such as the Qatar Investment Authority (QIA), Kuwait Investment Authority, the Public Investment Fund of the Kingdom of Saudi Arabia, and the Abu Dhabi Investment Authority, are founding members of the One Planet SWF Working Group, which aims to finance 'the smooth transition to a more sustainable, low-carbon economy'.[67] Despite these commitments, however, decarbonization of investment portfolios will need to be strengthened across the MENA region.[68] By decarbonizing SWF investments and promoting low carbon research and technology development, MENA countries can improve their resilience to future social and economic transformations and energy transition risks, especially stranded assets risks that are projected to increase as countries embrace low carbon transition.[69]

D. Gaps in contractual risk management

Studies have shown a direct correlation between the impact of oil price volatility in a country and the gaps in the overall contractual framework used in the country's oil and gas industry.[70] Failure to effectively introduce risk mitigation techniques and hedging clauses that deal with unexpected changes in the price of oil could have a significant impact on the

[63] Olawuyi (n 3).

[64] League of Arab States (n 61).

[65] OECD, *Managing and Spending Extractive Revenues for Sustainable Development: Policy Guidance for Resource-Rich Countries*, (OECD Policy Dialogue on Natural Resource Based Development 2019).

[66] J. Capapé and M. Santiváñez, *Sovereign Wealth Funds: Sustainable and Active Investors?* (The Case of Norway 2018). <https://sites.tufts.edu/sovereignet/files/2018/06/SustainableActiveInvestors_Capape.pdf> accessed on 30 August 2019.

[67] B. Caldecott and E. Harnett, 'One Planet Sovereign Wealth Funds: Turning Ambition into Action', <https://www.smithschool.ox.ac.uk/research/sustainable-finance/publications/One-Planet-Sovereign-Wealth-Funds-Turning-Ambition-into-Action.pdf> accessed on 30 August 2019.

[68] A. Mazarei (2019), *Efforts of oil exporters in the Middle East and North Africa to diversify away from oil have fallen short*, Peterson Institute for International Economics, <https://www.piie.com/system/files/documents/pb19-6.pdf> accessed on 30 August 2019.

[69] D. Manley, J. Cust, and G. Cecchinato (2017), 'Stranded Nations? The Climate Policy Implications for Fossil Fuel-Rich Developing Countries', *OxCarre Policy Paper*, No. 34, University of Oxford.

[70] K. A. Auzer, *Institutional Design and Capacity to Enhance Effective Governance Of Oil and Gas Wealth: The Case of Kurdistan Region* (Springer 2017); C. R. Blitzer, D. R. Lessard, and J. L. Paddock, 'Risk-Bearing and the Choice of Contract Forms for Oil Exploration and Development' (1984) 5 The Energy Journal 1–28.

resilience of a country to such frequent changes in the price of oil.[71] Consequently, while MENA countries may not be able to do anything to change the volatile and unstable nature of the price of oil, the applicable contractual framework can be reinforced to anticipate and provide different forms of risk mitigation remedies to deal with unexpected changes in the price of oil. For example, a recent study identified the prevalence of ambiguous production-sharing contracts that do not clearly conceptualize risk-bearing options as a key factor for rentierism in Iraq.[72] While the form and nature of contracts adopted across the region are diverse and will require specific examination, this example shows that MENA countries can anticipate and reduce risks of social and economic disruptions resulting from oil price volatility through contractual forms that effectively anticipate, manage, and address the impacts of price fluctuations.

The contract negotiation stage provides a great opportunity to carefully include flexible review clauses and adaptation provisions that could help a country promptly address the impacts of oil shocks.[73] Furthermore, given the long-term nature of oil and natural gas contracts, there is a need for clarity on how unforeseen risks in terms of oil pricing will be allocated and dealt with throughout the contract. As Sauvant and Wells have rightly argued, resource contracts need mechanisms to cover for prospects of future events such as unanticipated price changes and windfalls.[74] For example, the last decade has seen a geometric rise in the number of investor-state arbitration and disputes resulting from attempts by governments across the world to alter fiscal arrangements and contractual performance in the aftermath of price fluctuations.[75] In several such cases, failure to integrate clear automatic price adjustment mechanisms in the contract has significantly weakened the positions of resource-producing countries to cope with changes in circumstances such as price fluctuations.

MENA countries can anticipate and manage adverse changes in circumstances in long-term petroleum contracts by integrating risk mitigation tools that address short- and long-term price volatility risks. This will include inserting detailed price review mechanisms, force majeure, and hardship clauses in petroleum contracts.[76] Irrespective of the contractual clauses selected, the most important step is to put in place a comprehensive contractual framework that allows the host state to mitigate risks in unforeseeable disruptive events, including oil price volatility that could fundamentally weaken the economic equilibrium and position.

The mentioned legal and institutional barriers to resilience planning in oil and gas industries across the region can be addressed through an integrative approach that

---

[71] James A. Daniel, 'Hedging Government Oil Price Risk' (2002) 27(2) Journal of Energy and Development 167–178.

[72] Qaraman Hasan, 'Production Sharing Contracts and Rentierism in Kurdistan Region of Iraq: A Model that Fosters Rentier Economy' (2021) 8(2) Extractives Industry and Society.

[73] D. N. Smith and L. T. Wells, *Negotiating Third World Mineral Agreements* (Basic Books 1975).

[74] K. P. Sauvant and L. T. Wells, 'Obsolescence of The Obsolescing Bargain: Why Governments Must Get Investor-State Contracts Right' (Columbia FDI Perspectives No. 298, 22 February 2021). See also K. Berger 'Renegotiation and Adaptation of International Investment Contracts: The Role of Contracts Drafters and Arbitration' (2003) 36 Vanderbilt Journal of Transnational Law 1347, 1352.

[75] See for example, Juan Carlos Boué, *Enforcing Pacta Sunt Servanda? Conoco-Phillips and Exxon-Mobil versus the Bolivarian Republic of Venezuela and Petróleos de Venezuela* (Cambridge, University of Cambridge Centre of Latin American Studies, Work Paper Series 2(1), 2013).

[76] See Anatole Boute, Chapter 13 of this book.

mainstreams DRRR into energy planning. Section V discusses future directions and steps for mainstreaming DRRR into energy law and policy across the region.

V. Improving Law and Governance Frameworks on DRRR in the MENA Oil and Gas Industries

As countries step up efforts to achieve decarbonization goals under the Paris Agreement, MENA oil and gas exporting countries may have to grapple with a permanently reduced demand for their commodities. While natural gas, especially Liquified Natural Gas, will continue to play an important role in the low carbon transition, the potential glut of supply of various forms of energy sources, particularly renewables, could impact the price of oil and gas and reduce their long-term competitiveness.[77] Therefore, MENA countries must strategically evolve and assume roles that reflect current broader oil market conditions and scenarios to remain relevant in the emerging order.

Improving resilience to oil price volatility risks requires a legal, fiscal, and institutional reform agenda aimed at mainstreaming DRRR measures into energy law and policy across the region. This would be done by infusing energy policies and programmes with incentives, support programmes, and institutional safeguards that promote entrepreneurship and diversification across the energy sector value chain. A starting point is for governments to reform and update licensing procedures and requirements for business registration and formalization to address administrative and regulatory challenges: especially challenges to the registration of companies by non-nationals.

By streamlining the requirements and reducing the time and cost of business registration and project licensing, more citizens and residents will be incentivized to develop energy projects and ventures. Accelerator programmes that enable energy citizens to launch energy start-ups and move their energy innovations and projects from development to implementation are very important aspects of promoting energy and economic diversification. Similarly, regulations, rules, and procedures that act as barriers to foreign participation in energy projects or limit the participation of non-nationals should be reformed to unlock broad-based participation and inclusive access to resources for all, which are the essential hallmarks of energy citizenship and democracy. Furthermore, improving coordination among the various ministries responsible for contract negotiation and fiscal coordination, such as national oil companies, central banks, and national investment authorities, is also essential. Such inter-ministerial coordination will significantly streamline business formalization processes, while also mainstreaming risk reduction thinking into all aspects of the energy value chain, especially contract negotiation, policy development, and investment decision making.[78]

Second, MENA countries can improve their social and economic resilience to disruptive oil price shocks by providing clear and comprehensive legal frameworks that accentuate the importance of taxation. A key starting point here will be for MENA countries

---

[77] See Damilola Olawuyi, 'International Cooperation in Oil and Gas' in M. M. Roggenkamp, K. J. de Graaf, and R. C. Fleming (eds), *Encyclopedia—Energy Law and the Environment* (Edward Elgar) 68–78.

[78] See IMF (2018) (n 42), which highlights the need to improve efficiency and coordination among the fiscal authorities to respond effectively to oil price volatility risks.

to develop active consultations and engagements with citizens and residents to elaborate clear and functional objectives to be achieved by the taxation regime. Such engagement will also examine a fair and predictable process and timelines of implementation to allow for sustained implementation. Having achieved a comprehensive stakeholder engagement process, countries can then reform existing laws or enact more comprehensive legal frameworks on tax administration and governance.

Furthermore, rather than maintaining oil and gas subsidies that do not advance energy transition and economic efficiency, subsidies and incentives can be reformed to support energy diversification goals. For example, by providing fiscal and tax incentives for renewable energy and low carbon projects, domestic capacity and expertise in energy transition projects will be improved over time, thereby increasing the capacity and competitiveness of homegrown energy citizens and actors. Such legal and fiscal reform will also generate additional government savings that can help improve resilience to future oil price shocks.

Third, adopting clear and comprehensive laws on decarbonization and renewable energy investments can help MENA countries to address barriers to energy diversification. As earlier noted, the absence of legal frameworks on renewable energy has not fostered a coherent implementation of energy transition plans and visions. For example, having a renewable energy law that mandates utilities and electricity suppliers to integrate electricity from small-scale producers through feed-in tariff schemes could provide long-term demand and price certainty needed to spur the development and finance of renewable energy investments.

Furthermore, clear laws can provide a basis for SWF regulators to integrate decarbonization into investment consideration and planning. If sustained and backed by appropriate legal and institutional frameworks, renewable energy investments and projects can provide a platform for MENA countries to become part of the emerging new group of renewable world powers. There are significant opportunities for MENA countries to invest oil and gas income into renewable energy projects at home and abroad and acquire lithium, copper, and other mineral assets that are key to wind, hydro, solar, and biofuel production. This way, MENA countries could truly achieve the vision of moving from hydrocarbon-based economies to diversified and knowledge-based economies. Such transition will contribute to the global goals of achieving drastic cuts to GHG emissions and could accelerate global responses to climate change.

Fourth is the need to improve local capacity for fiscal coordination and risk mitigation, especially at contract negotiation phases. One of the key factors that heighten contractual risks in oil and gas markets in the MENA region is weak domestic capacity, especially during contract negotiation phases.[79] While MENA countries have increasingly outsourced contract negotiation work to law firms to match the expertise of international investors, there is a need to expand the domestic capacity of energy sector officials through local content development initiatives. The rise of local content development programmes across the MENA region provide timely tools for MENA countries to incorporate capacity development programmes in areas relating to contract negotiation and development to progressively improve the in-house expertise of national oil companies and entities that are involved in contract negotiation, procurement, and management.[80] Implementing clear local content

---

[79] Damilola S. Olawuyi, 'Local Content and the Sustainable Development in Middle East and North Africa: Current Legal Approaches and Future Directions' in D. Olawuyi, *Local Content and Sustainable Development in Global Energy Markets* (Cambridge University Press 2021) 228–244.
[80] Ibid.

policies that strengthen the abilities of local industries and individuals to actively participate in energy investments remain important tools that can help MENA countries stimulate
domestic value creation, economic diversification, and energy innovation.

VI. Conclusion

The oil supply glut, as well as the increasing competition from renewables and other new
forms of energy, has and may continue to increase the frequency and susceptibility of
MENA oil and gas markets to oil price volatility and its associated socio-economic disruptions. As the world transitions to a low carbon economy order, MENA countries must strategically evolve legal, fiscal, and energy transition policies that reflect current broader oil
market conditions and scenarios to build resilience to the risks of cyclical price volatility.

Legal barriers that stifle economic diversification and structural energy reforms must be
addressed to effectively anticipate and address oil price volatility risks and enhance DRRR
planning in oil and gas law and policy across the region. The lack of clear and supportive
legal frameworks on entrepreneurship and economic diversification is exacerbated by the
absence of robust legal and institutional frameworks on taxation, decarbonization, and renewable energy development across the MENA region. By infusing energy policies and programmes with incentives, support programmes, and institutional safeguards that promote
entrepreneurship and diversification across the energy sector value chain, MENA countries
can reduce their high susceptibility to disruptive oil price volatility risks.

Similarly, great emphasis should be placed on increasing the capacity of citizens and
residents to actively participate in energy investment and activities to stimulate domestic
energy innovation. The rise of local content laws and policies across the region provides
opportunities to increase domestic capacity for risk assessment, contract negotiation, and
fiscal coordination in the oil and gas sector.

10

Reaction from Public Policy and Regulation after COVID-19 Crisis in Latin America

The Cases of Colombia and Peru in Mining and Electrical Industry

Milton Fernando Montoya and Daniela Aguilar Abaunza

I. Introduction

The COVID-19 pandemic as a global health crisis has created an economic and social emergency all around the world. By June 2021, there were around 175 million confirmed cases and 3.8 million confirmed deaths.[1] To stop or at least reduce the massive propagation, countries worldwide executed full or partial lockdowns that affected the international and national economy, together with, of course, the labour market.

The COVID-19 pandemic has generated deep economic crises in all corners of the world and Latin America is not an exception. Especially, and naming only some of its impacts, there were repercussions in terms of employment, exports, public and private debt, in the development of infrastructure projects, and in the mining and electrical sector.

After an extensive quarantine period (almost six months in 2020 and various brief confinements quarantine during 2021 in countries such as Colombia and Peru) the virus left Peru with over 2 million confirmed cases, around 188 thousand deaths and 4.8 million vaccine doses administered.[2] In Colombia, so far, there have been almost 3.7 million confirmed cases, 95 thousand deaths, and more than 12 million vaccine doses administered.[3]

Both the Colombian and Peruvian governments have sought to stimulate the electricity industry's strength as an essential axis of this extended economic and social recovery process. Of course, in both cases, public policy and regulation have become essential instruments issued during the quarantine period, which drew attention to the close relationship that exists, today more than ever before, between the mining and electricity sectors in terms of sustainability and energy transition. At the same time, the Peruvian and Colombian's energy industries will play a role in supporting the Covid crisis recovery.

This chapter studies the Peruvian and Colombian public policy decisions and regulatory choices that sought to mitigate the effects of the pandemic and boost the mining and electricity industries' recovery beyond the immediate crisis.

---

[1] WHO, *Coronavirus Dashboard: Overview* <https://covid19.who.int/>accessed 16 June 2020.
[2] WHO, *Peru, Overview* <https://covid19.who.int/region/amro/country/pe> accessed 16 June 2020.
[3] WHO, *Colombia, Overview* <https://covid19.who.int/region/amro/country/co> accessed 16 June 2020.

Milton Fernando Montoya and Daniela Aguilar Abaunza, *Reaction from Public Policy and Regulation after COVID-19 Crisis in Latin America* In: *Resilience in Energy, Infrastructure, and Natural Resources Law*. Edited by: Catherine Banet, Hanri Mostert, LeRoy Paddock, Milton Fernando Montoya, and Íñigo del Guayo, Oxford University Press. © Milton Fernando Montoya and Daniela Aguilar Abaunza 2022. DOI: 10.1093/oso/9780192864574.003.0010

II. COVID-19's Impact on the Latin America Economy: The Cases of Colombia and Peru

According to the IEA,[4] countries that implemented full lockdowns had a decline of about 25 per cent in energy demand per week. Countries in partial lockdown had an average decline of 18 per cent in energy demand. Moreover, global coal demand was hit strongly by falling 8 per cent compared to the same period in 2019. There were multiple reasons for such decline. One was that in the first quarter of the year, China was first affected by the pandemic freezing its economy. Another reason was the presence of cheap gas and increased renewable share affecting coal imports.[5]

Two moments within the broader crisis disrupted the economy in Latin American countries: first, the general lockdown heavily restricted people's freedoms and activities. Second, once the restrictions gradually began to be lifted, economic activity remained suppressed. People could work more in this stage, but the demand and consumption of products were still reduced. Such a stage was followed by various but shorter and less restricted lockdowns than those in April to May, and general restrictions affected the economy in lesser but still significant levels.[6]

In the Latin American region, according to the United Nations Economic Commission for Latin America and the Caribbean (ECLAC),[7] the COVID-19 pandemic affected the region in at least five external ways: first, the more a country depends on exports, the more it would have been negatively affected. Second, the reduction of international demand for primary products affected the prices of primary products. These prices fell. Also, oil prices saw a phenomenal reduction, for geopolitical reasons, in March 2020. Third, the interruption of the international supply chain affected exports. Fourth, the reduction in tourism affected many countries' primary incomes, especially in the Caribbean. Fifth, currency depreciation was a real challenge.

According to the Peruvian Institute of Economics, the Peruvian economy contracted by 30 per cent in the first semester of 2020, and unemployment increased by almost 40 per cent: six million people lost their jobs.[8] Colombia saw economic repercussions from the COVID-19 pandemic in relation to employment, income, and poverty. The levels of extreme poverty were doubled, and the moderate poverty levels increased by 60 per cent. In real terms, those who qualify as 'poor' increased by 7.9 million, which will add up to the already existing 13.4 million, reaching more than 23 million.[9] In the second trimester of 2020, Colombia experienced its worst fall of gross domestic product in recent history. The economic activity decreased by 15.7 per cent compared to the same period the previous

---

[4] IEA, *Global Energy Review 2020: The impacts of the COVID-19 crisis on global energy demand and CO2 emissions* (April 2020). <https://www.iea.org/reports/global-energy-review-2020> accessed 27 March 2021.

[5] Ibid.

[6] Miguel Jaramillo Banante and Hugo Ñopo Aguilar, 'The Impact of Covid-19 on the Peruvian Economy' (2020) 17(51) Journal of Economic Literature 136–147.

[7] CEPAL, *América Latina y el Caribe ante la pandemia del COVID-19: Efectos económicos y sociales* (April 2020) <https://repositorio.cepal.org/bitstream/handle/11362/45337/S2000264_es.pdf?sequence=6&isAllowed=y> accessed 26 March 2021.

[8] Instituto Peruano de Economia. Boletín IPE, *Impacto del COVID-19 en Perú y Latinoamérica* (October 2020). <https://www.ipe.org.pe/portal/boletin-ipe-impacto-del-covid-19-la-economia-peruana-y-latinoamerica/> accessed 26 March 2021.

[9] Jairo Nuñez Mendez, *Impacto de los aislamientos obligatorios por covid19 sobre la pobreza total y extrema en Colombia* (Fedesarrollo 2020).

year. The worst of the decline was in April 2020. Economic activity improved incrementally after the restrictions were gradually lifted, although the economy could only function at a reduced capacity. The most affected economic activities were tourism, services, entertainments, and arts.[10]

In the following sections, we explore the different regulatory measures that the Peruvian and Colombian government took to address the impacts in the mining and electricity sector during the Covid pandemic.

Covid repercussions and responses in the electricity sector of Colombia

The Colombian electrical industry, as an essential service, was not affected by the lockdown and confinement restrictions, and hence the service's offer was not affected. The employment in the electrical sector was not affected considerably by the pandemic. First, the jobs are formal jobs that continued because of the industry's essential character. Second, the sector is not as relevant in terms of employment generation as other sectors like agriculture or manufacture.[11]

The sector nevertheless was affected by changes in demand. There was less demand for electricity from other economic sectors such as trade, restaurants, hotels, and manufacturers. By the end of May 2020, energy production decreased by 16 per cent and demand for energy by 17 per cent.[12] The market operator confirmed that demand for electricity was reduced by 5.3 per cent from residential or small consumers and by 17.5 per cent from larger users.[13]

The electricity industry in Colombia is liberalized, in which there is a correlation between the free market, free enterprise, and state intervention to promote the public interest. Natural monopolies are regulated by the state (transmission and distribution), promoting competition where possible (generation and retail). The state guarantees quality and aims to ensure a non-interrupted and continuous supply of electricity.[14]

During the COVID-19 Crisis, the Colombian government took different measures to guarantee the continuity of electricity supply and access to energy, especially by vulnerable customers affected strongly by the economic crisis. In terms of assuring the security

---

[10] Universidad Nacional de Colombia, *Impact of the COVID-19 pandemic on the Colombian economy: A temporary pandemic with permanent effects* (August 2020) <http://www.fce.unal.edu.co/media/files/CentroEditorial/documentos/documentosEE/documentos-economia-108.pdf> accessed 26 March 2021.

[11] Instituo Peruano de Economia, *Mercado laboral peruano: impacto por covid-19 y recomendaciones de política* (October 2020) <https://www.ipe.org.pe/portal/wp-content/uploads/2021/02/Informe-Mercado-laboral-peruano-Impacto-de-COVID-19-y-recomendaciones-de-politica.pdf> accessed 27 March 2021

[12] OLADE, *Análisis de los impactos de la pandemia del COVID-19 sobre el Sector Energético de América Latina y el Caribe* (May 2020) <http://biblioteca.olade.org/opac-tmpl/Documentos/old0452.pdf> accessed 27 March 2021.

[13] Universidad Nacional de Colombia (n 10).

[14] The authorities in charge of electricity issues in Colombia are: (i) The Ministry of Mines and Energy (MME), responsible for developing national energy policies; (ii) The Mining and Energy Planning Unit (UPME), which is responsible for determining energy needs and ways to satisfy domestic demand considering available resources and socio-economic aspects, prepare National Energy Plans and Electricity Expansion Plans; (iii) The Energy and Gas Regulatory Commission (CREG) is an independent regulatory authority in charge of overseeing the electricity and gas sector regarding quality, cost, and promotion of competition; (iv) The Planning and Promotion Institute for Energy Solutions to non-interconnected zones (IPSE) is in charge of developing programmes to provide electricity in remote or off-grid areas; (v) Superintendence of Industry and Commerce (SIC) promotes competition in all the economic sectors, including electricity, through regulation, conflict resolution, and enforcing consumer protection laws.

of electricity supply, although the Decree 457 of 22 March 2020 ordered a mandatory lock-down and restricted multiple economic activities, it also established a list of 34 exceptions, one of which was include the supply of electricity. The Circular 4007 of 2020 established that to guarantee the supply of electricity, related or connected activities also form part of the exception. These activities include: generating power, transmission, distribution, self-generation, operation and maintenance of grids and infrastructure related to the electricity industry.

To guarantee access to energy, especially for the more vulnerable, the national government issued the Legislative Decree 517 of 4 April 2020. This provided for flexibility in utility payments and further financial support. The national government, further, established discounts for the utility bills and a series of other measures, through the Decree 798 of June 2020. Such measures included a prohibition to cut electricity supply to vulnerable customers and the possibility to pay bills by instalments.[15]

However, the measure affected grid operators and retailers' finances because of the reduction in demand and the freeze on the payment of utilities to alleviate vulnerable customers, decreasing their capital flow.[16] The government assured the companies they would pay for the delays. Still, the electricity companies are waiting for the government to pay the amount they promised for supplying electricity to vulnerable customers who have not been able to pay their utilities bills, including electricity. By December 2020, the government had already been defaulting for three consecutive months.[17]

Also, energy projects are being delayed because Prior Consultation was frozen in the first semester of the pandemic. Prior Consultation is an essential procedure for some projects located in indigenous and afro-descendent lands as a vital requirement to start the projects' execution.[18] Furthermore, the application for environmental license decreased by 50 per cent in the first semester of 2020, delaying projects' initiation.[19]

B. Covid repercussions and responses in the mining sector of Colombia

In April 2020, the OECD called government, civil society organization, financial institutions, international organizations to action, to safeguard the due diligence in the minerals supply chains.[20] Such safeguard was jeopardized because miners have been severely affected by the pandemic in terms of disruption of their economic activity, livelihoods, and

---

[15] For the first months of the lockdown low-income customers could pay their utility bills from March to April by instalments for up to 36 months. Ariel Yépez-García et al., *COVID-19 y el sector eléctrico en América Latina y el Caribe ¿Cómo ayudar a los grupos vulnerables durante la pandemia?* BID (August 2020) <https://publications.iadb.org/publications/spanish/document/COVID-19-y-el-sector-electrico-en-America-Latina-y-el-Caribe-Como-ayudar-a-grupos-vulnerables-durante-la-pandemia.pdf> accessed 28 March 2021.

[16] Portafolio, *El impacto del Covid en el mercado eléctrico colombiano* (July 2020) https://www.portafolio.co/economia/el-impacto-del-covid-en-el-mercado-electrico-colombiano-542780 accessed 29 March 2021.

[17] Ibid.

[18] Bnamericas, *El impacto del COVID-19 en proyectos energéticos de Colombia en etapa inicial* (July 2020) https://www.bnamericas.com/es/noticias/el-impacto-del-covid-19-en-proyectos-energeticos-de-colombia-en-etapa-inicial accessed 29 March 2021.

[19] Portafolio (n 16).

[20] OECD, *COVID-19—Call to Action for Responsible Mineral Supply Chains By the Multi-Stakeholder Steering Group of the implementation programme for the OECD Due Diligence Guidance for Responsible Mineral Supply Chains* https://mneguidelines.oecd.org/COVID-19-Call-to-Action-for-Responsible-Mineral-Supply-Chains.pdf accessed 26 March 2021

low demand for minerals. In this disruptive situation, illicit actors and non-state armed groups, e.g. guerrilla movements, were positioning themselves in the production and trade of minerals, benefiting themselves from the situation. Such behaviour is a constant in Latin American.[21] The OECD highlighted the vulnerability of a large part of the population that depends on the informal economy, such as informal mining. Such stakeholders had no guarantees against the interruption of activities.[22]

In Colombia, the mining activity experienced a significant impact in April 2020, but later recovered, reaching the same production levels as before the COVID-19 crisis. Even though the production was not highly compromised, mineral exploitation was differently impacted. The confinement measures forced Glencore (a coal mining company) to close two mines, one at Cerrejon in the Guajira region and the other one at Prodeco in the Cesar region. Consequently, in the first semester of 2020, the production of coal by Cerrejon declined by 36 per cent and in Prodeco by 48 per cent compared to previous year levels. This contrasts with the situation for gold mining, which experienced a growth by 24 per cent because of its exportation to the Emirates, United States, and Italy. The increase in the international gold prices occurred because of the panic that weak economies created in different countries, thus central banks' intention of increasing golds reserves made gold more stable and desirable as a commodity.[23] Other kinds of minerals, i.e. those used for the building sector, were highly impacted because there was insufficient demand for building materials, reducing the demand by 35.9 per cent.[24]

In the international context, the shortage of energy demand worldwide and less industrial production decreased coal exportation.[25] Colombia is the world's fifth largest exporter of thermal coal and the tenth largest exporter of metallurgical coal. Coal represents more than 60 per cent of the gross internal product and 19 per cent of the total exportation. The economic impact of the COVID-19 pandemic on this sector is not hard to deduce.

On the other hand, the Colombian mining sector is characterized by high informality and has developed multiple strategies to encourage artisanal miners to legalize and formalize their activity. In the COVID context, the formalization process played a vital role to reactivate the sector gradually and have a better relationship with the community. For instance, the government encouraged traditional miners to register to different programmes and require technical assistance to ease and facilitate procedures with the mining authority.[26]

The current Mining Minister highlighted the importance of the mining sector for the reactivation of the Colombian economy, who also highlighted how vital is the diversification

---

[21] Ibid.
[22] Alliance for responsible mining, Impact of COVID-19 on artisanal and small-scale mining (April 2020) <https://www.responsiblemines.org/en/2020/04/impact-covid-19-artisanal-small-scale-mining/> accessed 26 March 2021.
[23] EITI, *Estudio sobre el papel de la industria extractive ante la crisis del COVID-19 en Colombia y sus implicaciones en el territorio* (October 2020) http://www.eiticolombia.gov.co/media/filer_public/5e/fe/5efeaa54-876b-4375-9d8e-84983d68855c/documento_papel_ie_covid.pdf accessed 26 March 2021.
[24] Universidad Nacional de Colombia (n 10).
[25] EITI (n 23).
[26] Ibid.

of the minerals that are currently exploited. Such diversification is also crucial for bringing more opportunities to the country in the international energy transition context.[27]

The government took different regulatory measures to address the impacts of COVID-19 and the strict lockdowns in the mining sector. Such measures can be classified into four groups: formalization, safety and security, royalty's investments, and procedures before the Mining Agency.

The Decree 457 of March 2020 established the lockdown and social distancing and also set up some exceptions, including mining and related activities, such as the supply chain, importation, exportation, or supply of minerals. However, miner cooperatives or organizations in different areas of the country had to close or suspend operations because they struggled with mobility restrictions. Hence, workers were not able to go to work. Miners working for small-scale companies with reduced financial capacity struggled because they could not receive their salaries. According to the Mining and Energy Ministry data, out of the current 75,000 mining titles, one-fifth belong to small-scale miners[28] who were one of the most affected for their economic fragility. Then, the Decree 1378 of October 2020 set up a flexible procedure for informal miners[29] to be granted a mining title and formalize their activity.

The Law 2045 of August 2020 established the criteria for prioritizing utility supply within the plans or programmes of social investment of the exploration and exploration contracts, and therefore the importance that the private sector helps to guarantee essential services in areas where the project is developed. For instance, energy generation or construction of infrastructure to supply public services, and, in this sense, also helping government for the economic recovery after the pandemic.

In terms of destination of royalties, the Decree 574 of 2020 postponed the payment of ground rent. It also allocated the royalties that result from minerals without origin certain for the management of the Covid response. Regarding the health and safety of mining sites, Resolution 797 of 2020 established the biosecurity protocol for the management and control of COVID-19 in the mining and energy sector.

Finally, regarding the procedure before the Mining National Agency, Resolution 096, 174, 192, 197 of 2020 established the suspension of some procedures, which meant the suspension of terms or filing of appeals before the Agency. It also established some exceptions to such suspension: the transfer of rights, transfer, integration or return of mining areas, and extensions. Also, there was no suspension for the payment of royalties or other economic obligations, rents, or the inspection visits only for areas that represent a high impact on security and sanity. Also, the Mining Agency increased the possibilities of making online enquires and procedures.

---

[27] Pais Minero News, *La minería se proyecta como un eje de reactivación productiva pospandémica: presidente ANM en PDAC* (March 2021) <https://paisminero.co/mineria/mineria-colombiana/22922-la-mineria-se-proyecta-como-un-eje-de-reactivacion-productiva-pospandemica-presidente-anm-en-pdac> accessed: 28 March 2021.

[28] According to the Technical Mining Glossary of Colombia, small-scale mining consists of small exploitation, which is not deep in the ground, that uses simple tools, only using human force, and extracting no more than 250 tons of annual minerals.

[29] Informal miners are those who exploit a mine without a mining title. Also, their exploitation and performance do not take account of proper conditions regarding safety management, operation, health, employment conditions. Consequently, they do not make part of the mining governance and cannot be granted benefits from the government.

C. Covid repercussions and responses in the mining sector of Peru

On March 15 2020 the Peruvian government declared a State of Emergency and, among other measures, imposed a strict lockdown and multiple restrictions on different economic activities, including mining. The lockdown lasted until May, and during this time the mining sector decreased around 40 per cent. Also, in the first semester of 2020, the mining sector's investment decreased by 28 per cent.[30] Later in May, when restrictions began to be lifted gradually, the mining sector was one of the first to reactivate operations and recover production levels.

The Decree 044-2020-PCM declared a State of Emergency. Mining companies were only allowed to carry out vital activities with minimum personnel during March and April to avoid the spread of COVID-19. The Peruvian mining sector's employment in March and April 2020 decreased by 38 per cent and the mineral exports by 22 per cent.

However, from June 2020, the sector has been gradually recovering.[31] By July the whole mining sector was fully activated and operational.[32] However, by Legislative Decree No. 1488 of 2020, one of the measures that formed part of the economic reactivation was the establishment of a special tax regime. It allows—in respect of any economic activity, including mining—an economic depreciation of the 20 per cent annual of the machinery and devices acquired during 2020–2021, which was not allowed before. This measure aimed to promote investments during the pandemic.

D. Covid repercussions and responses in the electricity sector of Peru

As from 1992, the Peruvian electricity sector was reformed to introduce more competition and therefore the unbundling of some activities. It created a wholesale market, the electricity generation is competitive, and transmission and distribution are monopolies. Then the distribution companies supply energy to the consumers, and therefore there is no retail market.[33]

The Peruvian electricity sector witnessed a decrease in the production of energy of 32 per cent and demand for energy of 36 per cent by May 2020.[34] In the Decree of Urgency 026-2020 the national government established that during the State of Emergency, the supply

---

[30] Instituto Peruano de Economía, *Contribución de la minería a la economía nacional* (February 2021) https://www.ipe.org.pe/portal/contribucion-de-la-mineria-a-la-economia-nacional/ accessed 28 March 2021.

[31] The Economic Peruvian Institute (IPE) states that even though the Covid-19 crisis affected the mining sector mainly during the first semester of 2020, the sector has been recovering from the second semester, reaching similar levels than in 2019. Ibid.

[32] Ministerio de Minas y Energia Peru, *Actualización de La cartera de proyectos de exploración minera. Boletin Estadístico Minero* (January 2021) <http://www.minem.gob.pe/minem/archivos/file/Mineria/PUBLICACIONES/VARIABLES/2021/BEM-01-2021.pdf> accessed: 28 March 2021.

[33] The authorities in charge of electricity issues in Peru are: (i) The Ministry of Energy and Mines (MINEM), responsible for developing national energy policies and granting concession to the energy companies; (ii) The Regional Direction of Energy and Mining (DREM), responsible for granting concession to energy project with an installed capacity of less than 10 MW; (iii) Supervisory Agency of the investment in Energy and Mining (OSINERGMIN) is an independent regulatory authority in charge of overseeing the electricity sector, setting tariffs, and resolving conflicts among sector participants; (iv) Council for Electrical System Economic Operating in Peru (COES) in charge of coordinating the operation of the electricity system; (v) The National Institute for the Defence of Competition and Intellectual Property (INDECOPI) oversees promoting competition in all the economic sectors, including electricity.

[34] OLADE (n 12).

of electricity, gas, and fuel was guaranteed because they are considered essential services.[35] The Decree DU-035 of 2020 established complementary measures to reduce the impact that the lockdown and the social distancing had on the economy, focusing its approach on guaranteeing the security of the supply of utilities such as electricity. This decree established that vulnerable customers could pay their utility bills by instalments for up to 24 months. This arrangement provided a reprieve for residential consumers with usage of less than 100 kWh per month and also for off-grid customers in rural areas.[36]

The decree contained some commercial measures to other kinds of customers, such as suspension on the sending and delivery of receipts, sending online receipts, suspension of on-site metering reading and authorization to emit receipts applying an average of consumption.[37] Such measures generally did not alleviate the financial pressure of paying utilities for medium and high-income consumers but instead refer to the payment and delivery method, highlighting the use of online bills and online payments.

The Urgency Decree 074- 2020 further issued extraordinary measures to guarantee access to energy by residential consumers. This decree created an electricity subsidy called 'Bono Electricidad', which aimed to cover the electricity bills pending payment between March 2020 and December 2020. The maximum subsidy was in average US$ 41, which will be granted only once per residential consumer who complies with one of the following requirements: (i) the residential consumer had to have a consumption cap of 150 kWh between March 2019 and February 2020; (ii) the residential consumer had to be resident outside of high-income or medium-income areas or; (iii) for residential consumers who live in rural areas and supply energy to themselves through solar energy. The distribution companies were placed in charge of reporting the list of users who fulfil such conditions to the electricity authority Osinergmin.

The Legislative Decrees 1455 and 1457 of 2020 created the programme 'Reactivated Peru' to respond to the needs of cash flow for different companies, including power companies, affected by the COVID-19 crisis. This programme offered credits to pay the workforce and providers.[38]

III. Conclusions

In both Peru and Colombia, regulatory responses to the COVID-19 pandemic highlight the importance of strengthening the mining and electricity sectors for the effective recovery of the economy. This is important in both these countries because they are export-oriented and popular locations for mining and electricity projects. Colombia and Peru definitely had challenges that complicated accomplishing new goals. Even so, they managed to return to the same levels of production, transformation, and distribution as in 2019. With the electricity sector being an essential service, it was a high-risk decision to keep their companies

---

[35] Ariel Yépez-García et al (n 15)

[36] Fredy Saravia Poicon, *Impact of COVID-19 Pandemic on Electricity Demand and the Chain of Payments of the Peruvian Regulated Market* https://www.researchgate.net/publication/341392173 accessed 29 March 2021.

[37] Ibid.

[38] Ministerio de Economia y Finanzas Peru, *Programa de Garantías "Reactiva Perú* <https://www.mef.gob.pe/es/?option=com_content&language=es-ES&Itemid=102665&lang=es-ES&view=article&id=6429> accessed 29 March 2021.

and their workers operating while fulfilling with biosecurity protocols when the pandemic started.

Nevertheless, both countries' mining operations were highly impacted because of mobility restrictions. The most affected mine workers were those working informally and without the benefit of being able to draw social security. Furthermore, the governments had to devise a short-term solution alongside a long-term one to confront these problems, highlighting the importance of formalization to improve the labour conditions of workers. In the electricity sector, these plans had a wide range that went from the government covering the energy bills for people in a state of vulnerability (low income) who could not afford their basic needs, to helping electricity companies pay off their debts and reactivate the commercial market to increase the demand that reduced during the pandemic (tourism, shopping malls, local enterprises, etc).

The paragraphs above demonstrated how both Peru and Colombia established an alleviation regime for low-income groups' energy needs. What was absent from such strategies was relief for medium-income groups who were also affected by the crisis. In both cases, statistics showed that the increase of poverty and unemployment was probably one of the biggest impacts that the virus left us with.

The lesson enveloped in the COVID-19 crisis is that governments should recognize some of these temporal measures and solutions and consider them as new issues and considerations on the policy and regulatory agenda. This is the case for the special protection of vulnerable customers in terms of payment assistance, or the continued use of subsidies. However, what is urgently needed is the creation of economic and job opportunities to decrease the number of users who need subsidy support.

In addition, the COVID-19 crisis brought more attention to social issues that it is important to be address. In the mining sector, the importance of formalizing artisanal or small-scale miners is highlighted and should be continued. This is not only in terms of the state being able to monitor the activity, but also in creating economic opportunities for those who formalize, such as access to finance and loans to create growth for the communities to which they belong.

11

The New Nationalism of the Mexican Energy Policy in a Turbulent International Context

José Juan González Márquez

I. Introduction

This chapter aims to analyse the new Mexican Energy Transition boosted by the government of the so-called Fourth Transformation of the National Public Life (*4th Transformation*), which took the chair in 2018. The chapter is divided into seven sections. After this introductory section, the second section analyses the interruption of the double energy transition that Mexico had begun during the second decade of the 20th century. Section III discusses the new energy policy promoted by the government of the 4th Transformation. Section IV explains the measures adopted by the 4th Transformation in response to the effects of the COVID-19 pandemic and the international oil price crisis. Section V analyses the legal reforms promoted by the new government to give legal support to its energy policy. Section VI discusses the impacts of the 2021 reforms to the Electricity Industry Law and the Hydrocarbons Law on the international arena. Finally, the last section highlights some conclusions derived from the analysis carried out in this research.

II. The Interrupted Energy Transitions

By 2018, the Mexican Energy Sector was in the middle of two major simultaneous transformations. The first consisted of opening the energy sector to private investment,[1] while the second addressed promoting more significant participation of clean energies within the energy matrix.[2]

In that context, the 2013 Constitutional reform in energy matters drove the Mexican energy sector's liberalization. The new energy laws passed in 2014,[3] and other legal bodies

---

[1] According to one author, there are two reasons for this energy transition. On the one hand, the process of climate change. On the other hand, the physical limits that characterize fossil energy sources, as oil, gas, and coal reserves were beginning to run out. Martínez Camarero C, and López V, 'Transición Energética Y Productiva Justa: ¿De Qué Estamos Hablando?' [2015] *Daphnia* <http://www.daphnia.es/revista/63/articulo/1242/Transicion-energetica-y-productiva-justa-de-que-estamos-hablando> accessed 9 March 2021.

[2] According to Vaclav Smil, the energy transition is a gradual change in the way an economy procures the primary energy it needs to function. Villareal and Tornel point out that energy transition is the process that transforms a centralized, fossil fuel-dependent energy system into a decentralized, environmentally more sustainable, low-carbon, and socially more inclusive system, Villareal J, and Tornel C, *La Transición Energética En México: Retos Y Oportunidades Para Una Política Ambientalmente Sustentable Y Socialmente Inclusiva* (Fundación Friedrich-Ebert-Stiftung 2017)

[3] The new laws are: (i) Law on Hydrocarbons; (ii) Law on the Electricity Industry; (iii) Law on Geothermal Energy; (iv) Law on the Coordinated Regulatory Bodies in Energy Matters; (v) Law on the National Agency for Industrial Safety and Environmental Protection in the Hydrocarbons Sector; (vi) Law on Petróleos Mexicanos;

José Juan González Márquez, *The New Nationalism of the Mexican Energy Policy in a Turbulent International Context* In: *Resilience in Energy, Infrastructure, and Natural Resources Law.* Edited by: Catherine Banet, Hanri Mostert, LeRoy Paddock, Milton Fernando Montoya, and Íñigo del Guayo, Oxford University Press. © José Juan González Márquez 2022. DOI: 10.1093/oso/9780192864574.003.0011

relating to the energy sector approved in the same year established the legal mechanisms charged to achieve that aim.[4]

The constitutional reform also concerned the energy transition. Transitory Articles 17, 18, and 19 of the 2013 constitutional amendment provided a specific foundation to more relevant participation of clean energies into the energy matrix.[5] Under such a constitutional basis, in 2014, the Federal Congress passed the Geothermal Energy Law. The transition towards a low-carbon economy was also a concern shared by the Climate Change General Law of 2012 (CCGL)[6] and the Energy Transition Law of 2015 (ETL).[7] In this regard, one of the objectives of the CCGL is to promote transition to a competitive, sustainable, and low-carbon economy, resilient to extreme hydro-meteorological events associated with climate change.[8] In the same direction, the ETL pursues promoting a progressive increase of clean energies in the electricity sector. In CCGL, Mexico committed to reducing carbon emissions by 30 per cent by 2020 and 50 per cent by 2050.[9] ETL assumed increasing clean energies by 25 per cent by 2018, 30 per cent by 2021, and 35 per cent by 2024.[10]

The double energy transition described above was beginning to deliver results. According to the Clean Energy Progress Report, by the end of the first half of 2018, generation from clean sources had reached 23.4 per cent, less than two percentage points below the 25 per cent clean energy generation target established by ETL and CCGL.[11] Clean technologies that showed the highest growth were photovoltaic, wind, and co-generation.[12]

However, before the two previous transitions consolidated, a third energy sector transition began to occur. This new transition is part of the 4th Transformation. For the current government, the first Transformation of Mexico's public life was independence from Spain; the second was the separation between the Church and the State in the 19th century; and the third was the Mexican Revolution of 1910. The 4th Transformation established as one of the cornerstones of its government strategy the rescue of energy sovereignty through the re-foundation and strengthening of the public monopolies on the electricity and hydro-carbon industries (Federal Commission of Electricity (CFE) and Petroleos Mexicanos

---

(vii) Law on the Federal Electricity Commission; (viii) Law on Hydrocarbon Revenues, and (ix) Law on the Mexican Petroleum Fund for Stabilization and Development. All these laws were published in the DOF on 11 August 2014.

[4] The laws that were reformed are (i) Law on National Waters; (ii) Organic Law of the Federal Public Administration; (iii) Law on Foreign Investment; (iv) Mining Law; (v) Law on Public-Private Partnerships; (vi) Federal Law on Parastatal Entities; (vii) Law on Procurement; Leasing; and Public Sector Services; (viii) Law on Public Works and Related Services; (ix) Federal Law on Duties; (x) Law on Fiscal Coordination; Federal Law on Budget and Fiscal Responsibility; and (xi) General Law on Public Debt. All these reforms were published in the Official Gazette of the Federation on 11 August 2014.

[5] The Electricity Industry Law of 2014 (EIL) was designed to 'promote the sustainable development of the electricity industry and to guarantee its continuous, efficient and safe operation for the benefit of users, as well as compliance with principles of public and universal service, clean energies and pollutant emission reduction obligations'; this law contains just an incipient regulation on clean energies promotion.

[6] Published in the Official Gazette of the Federation on 6 June 2012.

[7] Published in the Official Gazette of the Federation on 24 December 2015.

[8] Article two, section VII of the Climate Change Law.

[9] Second Transitory Provision of Climate Change Law

[10] Third Transitory Provision of Energy Transition Law.

[11] Secretaría de Energía, 'Reporte De Avance De Las Energías Limpias. Primer Semestre De 2018' (SENER 2018). <https://www.gob.mx/cms/uploads/attachment/file/418391/RAEL_Primer_Semestre_2018.pdf> accessed 9 March 2021

[12] Update of the Transition Strategy to Promote the Use of Cleaner Technologies and Fuels, published in the Official Gazette of the Federation on 7 February 2020.

(PEMEX), respectively).[13] However, as analysed below, the energy policy underlying the 4th Transformation is not in line with Mexico's international commitments nor the national energy legal framework currently in force. Moreover, the new energy policy blocked private investment in the energy sector and returned the country to a carbon-based economy.

III. The Government of the 4th Transformation's Energy Policy

The National Development Plan 2019–2024 (NDP) clearly describes the rescue of energy sovereignty boosted by the 4th Transformation.[14] In addition, the NDP points out various arguments that justify that rescue: (i) the energy reform imposed by the previous regime caused severe damage to PEMEX and CFE; (ii) over the past six years, oil production has fallen so steadily that Mexico has gone from being an exporter to an importer of crude oil and refined fuels; and (iii) the total output of the private entities was insignificant, despite the advantageous conditions under which they received the corresponding concessions.

The NDP stresses the strategic purpose of the 4th Transformation's energy policy that PEMEX and CFE should again operate as levers of national development. To achieve this objective, the Plan states that it is necessary to rehabilitate Mexico's six existing refineries, which, according to the document, are in a deplorable situation of abandonment and looting.[15]

The Plan also envisages the construction of a new refinery and the modernization of state-owned electricity generation facilities.[16] It is important to note that the NDP refers mainly to thermoelectric plants that operate with coal, fuel oil, and gas and are therefore highly polluting. However, in light of the 2013 energy reform, the document does not consider that PEMEX and CFE no longer have the monopoly on oil refining or electricity generation that they had in the past. As amended in 2013, regarding the electricity industry, the United Mexican States' Political Constitution (the Constitution) reserved to the State only two strategic activities: transmission and distribution of electricity, whereas, in the case of hydrocarbons industry, the Constitution reserves to the State only activities of exploration and exploitation. The principle of free competence governs any other stages of the electricity and hydrocarbons industries. Consequently, the implementation of the NDP objectives necessarily implies modifying the rules established by the Constitution in 2013.

Regarding clean energies, the NDP only refers to hydroelectric power plants[17] and states that these will receive additional resources for their modernization, together with the old thermoelectric[18] plants. Wind and solar energies are not in the perspective of the 4th Transformation's energy policy.

---

[13] See: National Development Plan 2019–2024, available at <http://www.dof.gob.mx/nota_detalle.php?codigo=5565599&fecha=12/07/2019> accessed 13 December 2021.

[14] Published in the Official Gazette of the Federation on 12 August 2019.

[15] Six refineries currently operate in Mexico: Salamanca, Guanajuato; Minatitlán, Veracruz; Tula, Hidalgo; Cadereyta, Nuevo León; Salina Cruz, Oaxaca; and Ciudad Madero, Tamaulipas.

[16] See National Development Plan 2019–2024, available at <http://www.dof.gob.mx/nota_detalle.php?codigo=5565599&fecha=12/07/2019> accessed 13 December 2021.

[17] There are currently 64 hydroelectric power plants in Mexico, all of them under the control of the Federal Electricity Commission (Comisión Federal de Electricidad). Twenty are large, 44 are small; 57 produce electricity and 7 are out of operation. Leonardo de Jesús Ramos-Gutiérrez and Montenegro Fragoso, 'Manuel La generación de energía eléctrica en México' (octubre–diciembre 2012) III(4) Tecnología y Ciencias del Agua 197–211.

[18] There are 30 thermoelectric plants in the country.

In addition to the above, the only reference that the NDP includes to the decarbonization of the energy matrix is in the sense of stating 'the new energy policy of the Mexican State will promote sustainable development through the incorporation of populations and communities to the production of energy with renewable sources'.[19] Therefore, the NDP also contradicts Mexico's commitments in favour of clean energies.

The new government has not (yet) repealed the constitutional reform of 2013 and its secondary laws of 2014. However, in practice, energy reform was halted and reversed almost immediately after the new presidential term started.

In 2019, the government of the 4th Transformation adopted the following measures against the energy reform:

(i)   The National Hydrocarbons Commission suspended bids for awarding exploration and extraction contracts to private companies.
(ii) On 30 January 2019, the National Energy Control Centre (NECC) cancelled the 2018 long-term auction SLP-1/2018, which allowed the acquisition of energy from clean and renewable sources.[20]
(iii) The CFE proposed renegotiating contracts for gas transport by pipeline between the government and the private sector during 2019.

On these bases, the 4th Transformation moved forward on the NDP's terms in two ways. On the one hand, it reversed the energy transition, and on the other, it took PEMEX and CFE's competitors out of the market. However, because both the constitutional reform of 2013 and the new secondary legislation of 2014 were still in force, all the mentioned decisions were illegal.

IV. The 4th Transformation' energy policy in COVID times

In 2020, two global events triggered the advance of the nationalist energy policy postulated by the NDP:

(i)   The world crisis of oil oversupply and the fall of oil demand, resulting in a negative impact on international oil prices;[21] and
(ii) The COVID-19 pandemic paralysed economic activities worldwide and harmed the market for hydrocarbons and their derivatives.[22]

---

[19] Official Gazette of the Federation, 'Plan Nacional De Desarrollo 2019-2024' (2019) <http://dof.gob.mx/nota_detalle.php?codigo=5565599&fecha=12/07/2019> accessed 9 March 2021.
[20] This auction had already been temporarily suspended in December 2018 to review its objectives and scope.
[21] Analysts point to the cause of this crisis as the coronavirus outbreak in China and its rapid spread dented the global economy, reducing oil demand in the first weeks of 2020. Mentado P, 'Historia De Las Caída De Los Precios Del Petróleo Y La OPEP' (Energía Hoy, 2020) <https://energiahoy.com/2020/03/12/historia-de-las-caidas-de-los-precios-del-petroleo-y-la-opep/> accessed 9 March 2021
[22] According to the International Monetary Fund, the economic crisis caused by the CONORAVIRUS will be 30 times worse than that of 2009. The Mexican economy will fall by 6.6 per cent. Mendoza Escamilla V, 'Esta Crisis Será 30 Veces Peor Que La De 2009; La Economía De México Caerá 6.6 per cent: FMI' [2020] Forbes México <https://www.forbes.com.mx/economia-finanzas-fmi-coronavirus-covid19-recesion-mexico/> accessed 9 March 2021.

Due to the mentioned events, in 2020, the Mexican government faced several problems: (i) a poor health sector infrastructure to deal with the health crisis; (ii) the fall in income from declining oil production and exports; (iii) the lack of economic and human resources to care for the infected and prevent mass deaths; and (iv) the lack of funds to maintain the social programmes implemented since the beginning of the 4th Transformation. Despite this, the government continued building a new airport, a train in the south of the country, and a new refinery and strengthened the market position of PEMEX and CFE.

The decisions made by the 4th Transformation at this juncture seem to indicate that neither attention to the COVID pandemic nor the oil price crisis were at the core of the government's concerns. Instead, the government saw these problems from at least two points of view: as an opportunity to expose the structural flaws of neoliberalism and as an obstacle to the transformation process of the country's public life. In the context of the complexity described above, the 4th Transformation's government adopted other measures that disrupt the energy sector structure, which is analysed below.

A. Changing the rules for awarding Clean Energy Certificates

A Clean Energy Certificate (CEC) is, per Article 3, section VIII of the Energy Industry Law (EIL), a certificate issued by the Energy Regulatory Commission (ERC) that certifies the production of a certain amount of electricity from clean energy sources. CECs serve to meet the requirements associated with the consumption of load centres.[23] According to Article 83 of the EIL Regulation, these certificates are disruptive to achieving electricity generation participation from clean energy sources at the lowest possible cost based on market mechanisms.

The obligation to acquiring CECs was first established by Article 121 of the EIL[24] and later reaffirmed by Article 68 of the ETL.[25] According to the EIL, all electricity suppliers are obliged to cover a certain percentage of their demand with clean energies, and CECs certify compliance with this obligation. Article 123 of the EIL states that the following are obliged to acquire these certificates: (i) Suppliers; (ii) Qualified Market Participant Users; (iii) Final Users supplied by isolated electricity supply; and (iv) Holders of Legacy Interconnection Contracts[26] that include Load Centres, whether public or

---

[23] A load centre is defined by Art 3 section VII of EIL as those 'Facilities and equipment that, at a given site, allow an final user to receive the electricity supply. The load centres will be determined at the metering point of the energy supplied'.

[24] Under Art 121 of the EIL, 'The Ministry shall implement mechanisms to comply with the policy on diversification of energy sources, energy security and the promotion of Clean Energy sources. The Ministry shall establish the obligations for acquiring Clean Energy Certificates and shall implement other mechanisms required to comply with the policy in this area and may enter into agreements that allow its homologation with the corresponding instruments of other jurisdictions'.

[25] In this sense, Art 68 of the ETL states, 'To promote the growth of Clean Energy referred to in this Law and under the terms established in the Electricity Industry Law, the Secretariat will establish obligations to acquire Clean Energy Certificates. To maintain equal competition, these obligations shall apply to goods consumed in a national territory whose production process is energy-intensive'.

[26] The Electricity Industry Law of 2014 created two parallel legal regimes: (i) a so-called 'legacy' or 'grand-fathered' regime granting vested rights to projects holding a power permit or an application filed with the Mexican Energy Regulatory Commission (the 'CRE') before the enactment of the Electricity Industry Law, and (ii) an 'electricity market' regime under which projects are subject to burdensome regulations affecting congestion, financial transmission rights, and transmission and distribution fees. So, a legacy interconnection contract is the interconnection contract or power purchase commitment contract for small producers concluded or to be concluded under the conditions in force before the entry into force of this Law.

private.[27]

According to its energy production, every clean energy generator is entitled to CECs and can subsequently sell them to suppliers on a free-market basis. In this way, the price of a certificate depends on supply and demand.

The mandatory minimum percentage of certificates that a supplier must hold increases year by year: for 2019, the rate was 5.8 per cent, and for 2020 it was 7.4 per cent. In addition, non-compliance is punished to a fair of US$47 to US$357 for each MW/h of non-compliance in the procurement of CECs.

In October 2014, the Ministry of Energy (ME), based on Articles 121, 122, 123, 125, and 126 of the EIL, issued the *Guidelines establishing the criteria for granting clean energy certificates and the requirements for their acquisition.*[28] According to this document, those clean power plants that came into operation after 11 August 2014, would be entitled to receive CECs for 20 years. Then, legacy plants, that is to say, plants that started operations before this date,[29] would not be eligible for CECs unless they had made investments to increase their clean energy production. Furthermore, CFE was obliged to purchase CECs in the market or pay the corresponding fine under this rule.

This rule changed on 28 October 2019, when the ME published in the Official Gazette of the Federation the *Agreement amending the Guidelines that establish the criteria for the granting of Clean Energy Certificates and the Requirements for their acquisition, published on October 31, 2014.*[30] According to sections I and II, of numeral 4 of the new Guidelines:

4. Eligible to receive CECs for a period of up to twenty years shall be clean generators representing:
   i. Clean Power Plants that entered into operation after August 11, 2014.
   ii. Legacy Power Plants, as provided for in the Electricity Industry Law, generate electricity from Clean Energy sources.

Under the new wording of the provision mentioned above, clean legacy power plants can receive CECs for their energy production. However, since the CECs requirements for 'obligated participants' were not increased, this modification will cause an oversupply of these instruments in the market.[31] In other words, this change allowed CFE's hydropower plants to issue CECs, which would devalue prices to almost zero and discourage clean generation. Therefore, CFE no longer needs the auctions and no longer must pay penalties.

---

[27] CECs can also be acquired voluntarily by registering as a Voluntary Entity in the Clean Energy Certificates and Compliance Management System.

[28] Published in the Official Gazette of the Federation on 31 October 2014.

[29] A Legacy Power Plant is a Power Plant that, at the entry into force of the EIL, is not included in a permit to generate electricity under the modality of self-supply, cogeneration, small production, independent production or own continuous uses, and: (i) Is owned by State agencies, entities or companies and is in operating conditions; or (ii) Whose construction and delivery has been included in the Federal Expenditure Budget in the modality of direct investment.

[30] Published in the Official Gazette of the Federation on 28 October 2019. This Agreement in turn was amended by another Agreement of 10 December 2019.

[31] Vazquez Perez J, 'Cambio De Reglas En La Adquisición De Certificados De Energías Limpias: Consecuencias De La Política Eléctrica' (Ciep.mx, 2021) <https://ciep.mx/cambio-de-reglas-en-la-adquisicion-de-certificados-de-energias-limpias-consecuencias-de-la-politica-electrica/> accessed 9 March 2021.

The change also decreases the return on investment in clean technologies, restricting the clean electricity industry's development. Furthermore, the guidelines' shift creates uncertainty for investors, which does not help reverse the economy's stagnating trend.

B. The Resolution to Guarantee the Efficiency, Quality, Reliability, Continuity, and Stability of the National Electric Grid of Mexico during the COVID-19 Pandemic

In April 2020, the National Energy Control Centre (NECC) issued a *Resolution to Guarantee the Efficiency, Quality, Reliability, Continuity, and Stability of the National Electric Grid of Mexico during the SARS-CoV2 Virus (COVID-19) Epidemic*. The Resolution implemented temporary technical and operational measures purportedly to mitigate the effects of the COVID-19 pandemic on the National Electrical Grid of Mexico.[32] In that direction, the document ordered the suspension of functional tests for new wind and photovoltaic power plants as of 3 May 2020. Furthermore, it stated that those plants that have not yet been in commercial operation would not be authorized. Thus, this Resolution displaces private generators, creates barriers to competition, and affects consumers in the commercial and industrial sectors. NECC justified the *Resolution* by saying that, 'Intermittent generation from wind and photovoltaic power plants affects the National Electricity System's reliability in terms of sufficiency, quality, and continuity of electricity supply'.[33] However, behind this Resolution was the intention of eliminating clean energy sources from the market.

C. Resolution for issuance of the Policy on Reliability, Stability, Continuity, and Quality in the National Electric Grid

In May 2020, the ME published in the Official Gazette of the Federation the *Resolution for the Policy on Reliability, Stability, Continuity, and Quality in the National Electric Grid*.[34] The ME's policy aimed at tilting the Mexican power sector to disfavour wind and solar power plants and favours conventional power, which the CFE predominantly provides. From our view, the Resolution's purpose is to increase the market share of CFE, which lost the monopoly on power generation because of the 2013 energy reform. The Resolution affected 44 clean energy generation projects (wind and solar) located in 18 states.[35]

---

[32] The document is dated 29 April 2020 and signed by the Director-General of NECC, available at <https://www.cenace.gob.mx/Docs/MarcoRegulatorio/AcuerdosCENACE/> accessed 9 March 2021.

[33] Solís A, 'Los Tres Golpes A La Industria De Energías Renovables Por Las Medidas Del Gobierno De AMLO, Según Moody'S' [2020] Forbes México <https://www.forbes.com.mx/negocios-golpes-industria-energias-renovables-gobierno-moodys> accessed 9 March 2021.

[34] This document was published in the Official Gazette on 5 May 2020.

[35] These projects are located in Yucatán, Jalisco, Tamaulipas, Sonora, Auascalientes, Tlaxcala, Nuevo León, Guanajuato and Baja California Sur. 'México: 44 Proyectos De Energía Renovable En Riesgo Por La Suspensión De Obras Por Parte Del Gobierno En La Etapa De Contingencia Por Covid-19 - Business & Human Rights Resource Centre' (*Business & Human Rights Resource Centre*, 2021) <https://www.business-humanrights.org/es/%C3%BAltimas-noticias/m%C3%A9xico-44-proyectos-de-energ%C3%ADa-renovable-en-riesgo-por-la-suspensi%C3%B3n-de-obras-por-parte-del-gobierno-en-la-etapa-de-contingencia-por-covid-19/> accessed 9 March 2021.

The Resolution raised a series of fundamental legal issues. First, it contradicted Articles 4, section I; 8, 9, 27, section III; 68; 107; and 140, section I of the EIL. Similarly, the obligation to acquire clean energy certificates referred to in Articles 121 to 129 of the Law mentioned above was infringed. Then, the measure confronts the human right to an adequate environment and the principle of sustainability enshrined in the Constitution. The Regulation also affects the economic structure of the electricity sector. It eliminates competition conditions in energy, contradicts the principles of *open* and *non-discriminatory* access to transmission and distribution networks, and modifies the economic dispatch criterion that governs the wholesale electricity market's operation. Moreover, the Regulation grants advantages favouring individual participants and diminishes others' ability to compete. It also establishes barriers to electricity generation dispatch.

D. The goal of building a new refinery

In 2020, the Federal Executive published in the Official Gazette of the Federation the *Executive Decree Establishing Austerity Measures to be Observed by the Agencies and Entities of the Federal Public Administration Under the Criteria Indicated Therein*. This Decree orders budget cuts in all government areas to allocate more economic resources to alleviate the COVID-19 pandemic but maintains the government's decision to build a new refinery. The new refinery in Dos Bocas, Tabasco, will have a capacity of 340,000 barrels per day. According to the government, this project aims to achieve self-sufficiency in gasoline and diesel production in the medium future and offer better prices for these fuels to consumers. However, for many experts on the subject, the construction of this refinery has more political than economic motivations. Additionally, in May 2021, the Mexican government acquired 100 per cent of the shares of the refinery Deer Park in Houston, Texas.

E. The new transmission tariffs

In May 2020, the seven commissioners of the ERC approved an adjustment to tariffs that the CFE charges to private renewable energy producers for the right to use the transmission grid. The CFE requested such tariff adjustment under the argument that interconnection tariffs should reflect the actual transmission cost.[36]

Notably, the new fees will apply to holders of legacy interconnection contracts with electricity generation plants from renewable energy sources or efficient co-generation and conventional sources. This measure violates the principle of *non-discriminatory* access to the distribution network recognized by EIL. Furthermore, it contradicts Article 27 of the Constitution, limiting free competition in generation and supplying activities.

As can be seen, during the first two years in government, 4th Transformation insistently tried to return to the CFE and PEMEX the monopoly that the 2013 constitutional reform

---

[36] Comisión Reguladora de Energía, 'The CRE Unanimously Approved the Tariffs for the Electricity Transmission Service to be Applied to Holders of Legacy Interconnection Contracts with Electricity Generation Plants, with the Aim of Creating Equal Conditions and Benefits for End Users' (2020) <https://www.gob.mx/cre/prensa/comunicado-de-la-cre-respecto-a-la-sesion-extraordinaria> accessed 9 March 2021.

had taken away from them. The insistent attempts to modify the structure of the energy sector disturb its proper functioning and, above all, have stopped the energy transition. However, all these attempts failed. The judicial branch of the federation suspended their effects, considering that they violated currently in force energy legislation. Due to the preceding, the government of President López Obrador changed its strategy. To give foundation to its nationalizing policy, he proposed that Congress modify EIL and Hydrocarbons Law (HL).

V. The Reforms to the Energy Sector Laws passed by the Federal Congress

The Mexican energy sector has been resilient to the 4th Transformation government's attempts to re-establish the State monopoly on electricity and hydrocarbons industries. Even though the Judiciary has suspended the legal effects of such unconstitutional policies, the 4th Transformation has not ceased to insist on modifying the constitutional and legal energy framework defined by the constitutional reform of 2013.

With that aim, on 1 February 2021, the President of Mexico sent to the Federal Congress an initiative to reform the EIL. The law initiative puts into the legal text all those rules postulated by the *Policy on Reliability, Stability, Continuity, and Quality in the National Electric Grid of 2020*, already declared unconstitutional by the National Supreme Court of Justice. In addition, following this reform, electricity generated by CFE has priority access to the distribution grid, although it is more expensive and polluting than renewable energies. Unfortunately, the legislature approved it without any discussion and analysis on its constitutionality.[37]

However, since the legal reform contradicts the currently in force constitutional text, it affected private investors, environmental organizations, and even autonomous government agencies; they challenged this reform through various *Amparo* lawsuits and Constitutional controversies. As a result, the judges suspended the effects of the reform.

In the same vein, in April 2021, the Federal Congress passed two modifications to the HL. Following this amendment, the ME and the ERC can cancel granted permits in cases of imminent danger for national security, energy security or the national economy. But, again, the problem is that the reform uses vague concepts whose meaning is left to the authorities' interpretation, leaving private investors defenceless.

The second amendment eliminates the asymmetric Regulation of first-hand sales of hydrocarbons and petrochemicals. Asymmetric Regulation in the energy sector refers to rules that aim to create a level playing field between private companies and PEMEX. According to this reform, the ERC will no longer have the power to determine the price of hydrocarbons, petroleum products and petrochemicals offered by PEMEX in first-hand sales. Instead, PEMEX will set those prices, which places it in a dominant position in the market that affects free competition protected by the Constitution.

The Federal Judiciary already suspended the effects of both legal reforms because, as analysed below, they contradict the constitutional energy reform of 2013.

---

[37] The reform to EIL was Published in the Official Gazette of the Federation on 9 March 2021.

A. The test of constitutionality

The 2013 constitutional reform established the guiding principles for energy policy and legislation in Mexico. First, in electricity matters, transmission and electricity distribution are considered strategic and reserved for the nation. Secondly, concessions will not be granted in these activities, notwithstanding that the State may enter into contracts with private parties under the terms established by law. Finally, no strategic activities are open to private investment, and the law must determine how private parties may participate in the electricity industry's other activities.

Regarding the hydrocarbon industry, the constitutional reform of 2013 only reserved for the national monopoly exploration and exploitation activities, while private investment was allowed to conduct any other actions of the hydrocarbons industry chain of value.

On the other hand, the Constitution sets the principles guiding economic development. According to Article 26, economic growth must be integral and sustainable. Finally, Article 4 of the Constitution guarantees to all Mexicans the right to a healthy environment. Both constitutional provisions provide the basis for an energy policy based on renewable energies.

Besides, articles Transitory Seventeenth and Eighteenth of the above-mentioned constitutional reform grant supremacy to renewable energies over traditional sources or electricity.

The 4th Transformation's government pretends that the EIL and HL reforms' grant constitutional support to its energy policy. However, considering all modifications introduced, these reforms of 2021 are unconstitutional because:

(i) They pretend to extend the constitutional monopoly over transmission and distributions activities to generation and supply activities that the Constitution does not reserve to the State.
(ii) They pretend to extend the Constitutional monopoly over exploration and exploitation to refining, storage, transport and first-hand sales of hydrocarbons that the Constitution does not reserve to the State.
(iii) They violate the mandate of incorporating renewables into the energy matrix set up by transitory articles of the 2013 constitutional reform.
(iv) They eliminate the legal mechanism to protect the human right to a healthy environment and the Constitution's sustainability principles.

B. The role of the judiciary

So far, the Federal Judiciary has acted as a counterweight to the enormous presidential power by declaring unconstitutional every attempt to modify the constitutional rules by issuing administrative regulations or modifications to secondary legislation.

Private companies, environmental organizations, and even autonomous bodies of the federal government have filed legal actions against the energy policy of

4th Transformation, including the so-called *Amparo* Trial[38] and 'Constitutional Controversies'.[39]

Each of these actors has made different arguments. For private investors, the 4th Transformation reforms contradict currently in force constitutional provisions on energy matters. For the Federal Economic Competition Commission, these reforms are contrary to free competition in the sector. Finally, for environmental organizations, the change back to traditional energy carbon sources violates the right to a healthy environment and the principle of sustainability recognized by the Constitution and the international commitments assumed by Mexico regarding the transition to a more environmentally friendly economy.

The judges have suspended the application of the reforms promoted by the 4th Transformation. However, trials are still in process, and the possibility of a ruling that recognizes the constitutionality of the challenged reforms is latent.

The Federal Executive has indicated that if the courts declare their reforms unconstitutional, they will promote a reform of the Constitution. However, a constitutional overhaul requires a qualified majority[40] in Congress that the 4th Transformation does not have.

On the other hand, a ruling favouring the 4th Transformation or the constitutional reform would lead the Mexican government to an international commercial conflict. The next section analyses this issue.

VI. The Mexican Energy Policy in the Context of the Multilateral Trade System

Mexico is part of the multilateral trade system and therefore bound by the *more favoured nation* and *national treatment* principles not to discriminate against foreign investment in the energy sector. Moreover, various regional trade agreements signed by Mexico protect foreign investment in this area.

In light of the International Commercial Agreements signed by Mexico, restoring an obsolete electricity production system could have severe consequences for Mexico. The Comprehensive and Progressive Agreement for Trans-Pacific Partnership (CPTPP), the United States, Mexico, and Canada Trade Agreement (USMCA), and the trade agreements with the European Union protect the 2013 Mexican energy reform.

Most of the private investment in the Mexican energy sector comes from foreign countries (United States, Canada, Spain, Japan, among others).[41] Thus, any obstacle to private

---

[38] The *Amparo* Trial is an autonomous constitutional trial, which is initiated by the action exercised by any person before the courts of the Federation against any general rule, acts or omissions of authority (claimed act), in the hypotheses provided for in Art 103 of the United Mexican States' Political Constitution and that is considered a violation of their human rights and their guarantees, recognized in the Constitution or in International Treaties. Its objective is the declaration of unconstitutionality of the act that is challenged, invalidating or nullifying itself in relation to the aggrieved and restoring him in full enjoyment of his rights.

[39] The Constitutional Controversy is a trial that is promoted before the Supreme Court of Justice of the Nation to resolve conflicts that arise between federal powers, powers of the states, government bodies of the Federal District (today Mexico City), or between levels of the federal, state, municipal, or Mexico City government, for invasion of powers or for any type of violation of the Federal Constitution, by the designated bodies. It is considered a procedure to control constitutional regularity.

[40] Qualified Majority requires three-quarters of the votes on the Congress.

[41] Mexico has received US$17.415 billion in foreign direct investment in electric power since 1999, moreover, from 2013 to 2019, the foreign direct investment in electric power that Mexico received had a 56 per cent average growth year over year. 'México Recibió 14.600 Millones De Inversión Extranjera en Energía Eléctrica' (El periodico

investors participation could lead Mexico to a trade dispute under the multilateral trading system set up by World Trade Organization (WTO) agreements and other regional free trade treaties signed by Mexico.

Mexico has concluded many international trade agreements that guarantee national treatment and allow the free flow of investments. Therefore, the reforms to EIL and HL could generate frictions between the federal legal order and the international trade system's rules.

We have to analyse these agreements under the premise that 'All constitutional reforms and legal or regulatory changes must be compatible with Mexico's international commitments', and 'Mexico cannot adopt more restrictive measures than those it has already adopted in other treaties'.

Similarly, Mexico has committed to the international community to move towards a low-carbon economy, so the 4th Transformation energy reforms jeopardize the fulfilment of Mexican government goals in this area. The following sections discuss these two issues.

A. NAFTA

The North American Free Trade Agreement signed by Mexico, the United States, and Canada (NAFTA) in 1992[42] led to the reorganization of Mexico's energy sector. In Annex 620 (3) to Chapter Six of NAFTA, Mexico entered several reservations on strategic activities that concern, among others, the trade and investment in the energy sector. However, some exemptions to this reservation are possible.[43] The Mexican State reserves the right to supply electricity as a public service in Mexico, including generation, transmission, transformation, distribution, and electricity supply. NAFTA does not permit private investment in any of the activities listed except under the conditions provided in Annex 602 (3) paragraph 5.[44] However, the Annex allows private investment in the following areas: electricity production for own use, co-generation and independent power production.

Own use producers must sell their surplus of electricity production to CFE. Besides, independent power producers (IPP) located in Mexico must sell all generated electricity to the CFE. CFE is obligated to buy such electricity under the terms and conditions agreed with the IPP. IPPs located in Mexico are allowed to export electricity to other NAFTA Parties.

Despite the conditions imposed on Mexico's investment by electricity producers from NAFTA countries, Mexico does not prohibit electricity imports by NAFTA suppliers. Mexico has entered exceptions to Article 603 on import and export restrictions. Under these exemptions, Mexico may restrict import and export licences in certain goods listed in the Annex. Market access, however, is limited due to the reservations on the distribution of electricity established by Annex 602 (3) since the importer of electricity will likely have to sell directly to CFE.[45]

---

de la energia, 2021) <https://elperiodicodelaenergia.com/mexico-recibio-14-600-millones-de-inversion-extranj era-en-energia-electrica/> accessed 9 March 2021.

[42] NAFTA came into force on 1 January 1994.
[43] Horlick G and Schuchhardt C, 'NAFTA Provisions and Electricity Sector' (Commission for Environmental Cooperation of North America 2002).
[44] Ibid.
[45] Ibid.

As a result of NAFTA's negotiations, in 1992, the Mexican Congress reformed the Public Service of Electricity Law.[46] The reform allowed domestic and foreign private investment in small-scale production, the export of electricity from co-generation, import of energy exclusively for own use, and generation of power for emergency use. The reform also allowed the participation of independent electricity producers for exclusive sale to CFE. Due to NAFTA, the electricity industry organization in Mexico changed from a state monopoly model vertically integrated into all industry phases to a single buyer model. However, NAFTA did not include specific rules on private investment in the hydrocarbons industry.

B. CPTPP

In NAFTA's case, an amendment to the Public Service Electricity Law incorporated the trade agreement commitments assumed by Mexico into the national legal system. In contrast, the CPTPP embodies the Mexican 2013 energy reform in the text of Annex I of the trade agreement.

In the CPTPP, Mexico included several specific energy-related reservations. Such reservations allow foreign investment in the Mexican energy industry under the conditions set out by the constitutional reform of 2013, excluding any less favourable treatment.[47] Thus, Mexico can liberalize foreign investment restrictions established by the mentioned energy reforms and Annex I without violating the CPTPP (incorporated through Article 32.11). In contrast, it cannot make the rules more restrictive.

This means that the United States and Canada, as USMCA members, must receive treatment in the energy sector that is no less favourable than Mexico's accord to the other CPTPP members, even though the United States did not ratify TPP.[48] The government of the 4th Transformation cannot make the rules under which foreign investment is allowed in the energy sector more restrictive than those set out in the CPTPP annexes.

C. USMCA

Unlike NAFTA, the USMCA does not have a specific energy chapter.[49] However, different branches of the Agreement contain references to the energy sector. For their part, Canada and the United States negotiated a side letter to the USMCA on energy.[50]

Chapter 8 of USMCA recognizes the Mexican State property over hydrocarbons. This property is direct, inalienable, and imprescriptible. This chapter holds:

---

[46] Published in the Official Gazette of the Federation on 23 December 1992.

[47] Mexican energy reform of 2013 is directly incorporated into CPTPP Annex I-Mexico (page 17) through Annex I-Mexico (page 27).

[48] TPP negotiations concluded on 5 October 2015. It is not a traditional free trade agreement; it is a form of 'economic constitution' that provides the foundational rules for the governance of cross-border trade and investment in the Pacific region.

[49] This agreement replaced the North American Free Trade Agreement (NAFTA), which in 1994 created the world's largest free-trade region. The new Free Trade Agreement between Mexico, the United States, and Canada, known as USMCA, came into force on 1 July 2020.

[50] Letter from Robert Lighthizer to Chrystia Freeland (30 November 2018) <https://www.international.gc.ca/trade-commerce/assets/pdfs/agreements-accords/cusma-aceum/letter-energy.pdf>accessed 6 February 2020.

2.   In the case of Mexico, and without prejudice to their rights and remedies available under this Agreement, the United States and Canada recognise that: (a) Mexico reserves its sovereign right to reform its Constitution and its domestic legislation; and (b) Mexico has the direct, inalienable, and imprescriptible ownership of all hydrocarbons in the subsoil of the national territory, including the continental shelf and the exclusive economic zone located outside the territorial sea and adjacent thereto, in strata or deposits, regardless of their physical conditions pursuant to Mexico's Constitution (*Constitución Política de los Estados Unidos Mexicanos*).

However, Chapter 8 does not provide the basis for an energy policy that prevents private investment in the energy sector. In addition to the rules established in Chapter 8, the USMCA contains other regulations that prevent Mexico from modifying the structure of the energy sector. The USMCA includes a kind of 'most favoured nation' clause, which obliges Mexico to grant the United States and Canada treatment no less favourable than it does to other countries. The key provision of the USMCA is as follows:

Article 32.11: Specific Provision on *Cross Border Trade in Services, Investment, and State-Owned Enterprises and Designated Monopolies* for Mexico
      Concerning the obligations in Chapter 14 (Investment), Chapter 15 (Cross-Border Trade in Services), and Chapter 22 (State-Owned Enterprises and Designated Monopolies), Mexico reserves the right to adopt or maintain a measure for a sector or sub-sector 32-12 for which Mexico has not taken a specific reservation in its Schedules to Annexes I, II, and IV of this Agreement, only to the extent consistent with the least restrictive measures that Mexico may adopt or maintain under the terms of applicable reservations and exceptions to parallel obligations in other trade and investment agreements that Mexico has ratified before entry into force of this Agreement, including the WTO Agreement, without regard to whether those other agreements have entered into force.

Under this clause, Mexico must afford treatment to the Canadian and United States investors in sectors covered by the three chapters of USMCA listed in Article 32.11 that is no less favourable than Mexico's treatment in parallel trade and investment agreements. In addition, this clause refers to the rules established by the TPP. Therefore, in general terms, the USMCA locks in Mexico's energy reform.

D. Free Trade Agreement between Mexico and the European Union

In addition to the mentioned Commercial Agreements, the Economic Partnership, Political Coordination and Cooperation Agreement between the United Mexican States and the European Community and its Member States (2000) protects European investment in the Mexican energy sector due to the *parity principle*.[51]
      Two Chapters of NAFTA established the possibility of participation of foreign companies in the domestic electricity industry. Like many other clauses, these chapters automatically

---

[51] Adopted on 16 June 2000.

apply to the E.U.-Mexico Free Trade Agreement (FTA) based on the principle 'NAFTA parity'. NAFTA parity means matching NAFTA's benefits in terms of liberalization of capital and commodities, under terms that could be similar or better than those established in NAFTA but never inferior.[52] The EU achieved through the EU-Mexico FTA the same treatment and similar relief conditions Mexico granted to the United States and Canada under NAFTA. Mexico should recognize to EU any future preferences given to NAFTA members.

The same rule applies to USMCA. This commercial Treaty has already repealed NAFTA, but the *parity principle* also applies to the rules established by the TTP. In other words, in line with TTP, it is impossible to modify the United Mexican States' Political Constitution or the energy sector laws to prevent European companies' participation without confronting the trade dispute settlement system provided by the trade treaties between Mexico and the European Union. Recently Mexico and the European Union renegotiated the free trade agreement. Negotiations finished in 2020. The text of the new Agreement ratifies the principle of parity.

E. The Paris Agreement

In its Nationally Determined Contribution under the Paris Agreement, Mexico committed that 35 per cent of the energy generated by 2024, and 43 per cent by 2030, would be clean. These targets and others, such as reducing short-lived Greenhouse Gasses by 25 per cent and black carbon emissions by 51 per cent, require incentives.[53]As previously mentioned, the 2013 energy reform brought Mexico closer to these goals, but the 4th Transformation halted such an energy transition.

One of the critical elements to meet the targets is to generate economic mechanisms to produce clean energy. To this end, Mexico designed three auctions between 2015 and 2017, resulting in 90 contracts equivalent to an investment of US$9 billion to develop solar, wind, and geothermal energy.[54] These projects would reduce emissions by 54 million tonnes of CO_2 by 2030. Thus, Mexico was moving in the right direction, but everything changed in 2018 when the government of the so-called 4th Transformation took power.

The 4th Transformation's energy policy postulates the return to a carbon-based economy. The idea of building a new refinery and rehabilitating the six old ones illustrates this argument. The various measures to strengthen CFE and PEMEX's position in the energy market also reflect the 4th Transformation's nostalgia for Mexico's oil boom years. All this even though the world is moving towards a low-carbon emissions economy. One of the most questionable steps backwards that the 4th Transformation has taken is modifying rules to grant clean energy certificates.

---

[52] This equalization stems from a bill that was extensively debated during five legislative periods in the US Congress between 1995 and 2002. The initiative, known as the Caribbean Basin Interim Trade Program/NAFTA Parity, was passed by both chambers and signed by President Clinton on 18 May 2000, and authorized for implementation on 2 October 2000 in Presidential Proclamation 7351. Gutierrez Haces M, 'Incidencia Del TLCAN y De Los Acuerdos De Protección A La Inversión Extranjera Sobre Las Relaciones De México Con La Unión Europea' [2014] Economía UNAM.

[53] Nevertheless, the Mexican government has recently launched two projects that directly contradict the Paris agreement: the construction of a refinery in Dos Bocas, Tabasco, and a thermoelectric plan in Huexca, Morelos.

[54] K. Garcia, 'El Gobierno de AMLO desoye a la IP y tira Subasta Eléctrica' (2019), available at <https://www.eleconomista.com.mx/empresas/Gobierno-de-AMLO-desoye-a-la-IP-y-tira-subasta-electrica-20190205-0019.html> accessed 13 December 2021.

As analysed, the reform to EIL of 2021 allows the ME to grant CECs for old power plants that the CFE already had in operation before the Regulation that endorsed the use of these instruments came into force in 2014.[55] This legal change indicates that Mexico has given up on its international commitments to clean energy and climate change.

VII. Conclusions

The reforms to EIL and HL of 2021 contradict several United Mexican States' Political Constitution provisions. Precisely, the reform pretends to extend the electricity and hydrocarbons industries state monopoly to other areas without reserve by the Constitution to the nation. The 4th Transformation's energy policy also prevents free competition in the energy sector postulated by the Mexican Constitution. For these reasons, the 4th Transformation's energy policy is seen as unconstitutional and contrary to Mexico's international commercial and environmental commitments.

The solution to this dilemma could be a constitutional amendment that repeals the energy reform of 2013. However, the Executive does not have enough votes in Congress to succeed. Moreover, unlike legal reforms, constitutional modifications require a qualified majority of ballots in Congress that the president's party does not have. What is more, if the constitutional reform were possible, it could result in inconsistency with environmental and commercial international commitments assumed by Mexico.

During the last three years, the President of Mexico has been disrupting the functioning of the Mexican energy sector, trying to modify the legal framework that governs it. Despite this, and even under the effects of the COVID-19 pandemic, the energy sector has not collapsed. Notwithstanding brief episodes of fuel shortages, the economy has not halted for reasons attributable to the energy sector. The energy sector has been resilient to the changes proposed by the Federal Executive. This resilience is due, in significant part, to the role played by the division of powers in Mexico. The Federal Judiciary has acted as a counterweight to the Executive and the Legislative decisions, and that counterweight is the backbone of the Mexican energy sector's resilience.

---

[55] The Document highlights that, since 2019, Mexico is the second country to allocate more subsidies to fossil fuels, after China, as it has allocated US$17 billion in subsidies to fossil fuels such as oil and gas, mainly through Petróleos Mexicanos and the Federal Electricity Commission.

12

Energy Resilience in the United States

Impact of the 2020 Presidential and Congressional Elections

Don C. Smith and Donald N. Zillman

I. Introduction

The term 'resilience' originates from two Latin words: *resilio* or *resiliere*, meaning to 're-bound' or 'bounce'.[1] Resilience, and the related concept of robustness have prompted in the last 30 years 'rising interest' in specific fields including environmental policy, climate change, and risk management.[2] The study of resilience and robustness has attracted researchers because the terms refer 'to the ability of policies to persist over time by overcoming relevant external shocks and internal perturbations'.[3] The concept of energy resilience has been described as 'a compelling policy quest'.[4]

Resilience in the face of disruptions at the scale many countries including the United States have faced in recent years requires a resilient governance structure to effectively respond to the disruptions. Events in the U.S. in the last decade have raised serious questions about whether its governance model is sufficiently strong to respond effectively to disruptions caused by climate change and other system challenges.

While energy resilience now features more prominently in political discussions,[5] particularly in the context of the international development agenda,[6] the U.S. path forward is far from clear. Since a primary notion underpinning resilience involves policymaking,[7] this chapter considers how the U.S. has (or has not) addressed energy resilience by analysing the results of the 2020 elections for president and Congress to discern what they foretell for future American policy.

Following these introductory comments, the chapter proceeds as follows. Section II explains the extraordinary years of 2020 and 2021 when the nation faced natural and human-caused challenges that demanded resilient responses to preserve an America as it has been known. Section III considers how the election of President Joe Biden changed the tenor of

---

[1] Giliberto Capano and Jun Jie Woo, 'Resilience and robustness in policy design: a critical appraisal' (2017) 50 Policy Sci 399–426, 401 <https://ash.harvard.edu/files/ash/files/resilience_and_robustness.pdf> accessed 8 August 21 (hereafter Capano, 'Resilience and robustness').

[2] Ibid, 400

[3] Ibid, 401

[4] Andrea Gotto and Carlo Drago, 'A taxonomy of energy resilience' (2020) 136 Energy Policy 111006, 111006 (hereafter Gotto and Drago, 'Taxonomy of energy resilience').

[5] Ayyoob Sharifi and Yoshiki Yamagata, 'Principles and criteria for assessing urban energy resilience: A literature review' (2016) 60 Renewable and Sustainable Energy Reviews 1655, 1654–1677, <https://www.sciencedirect.com/science/article/pii/S136403211600263X> accessed 8 August 2021.

[6] Gotto and Drago, 'A taxonomy of energy resilience' (n 4) 111006.

[7] Ibid.

Don C. Smith and Donald N. Zillman, *Energy Resilience in the United States* In: *Resilience in Energy, Infrastructure, and Natural Resources Law*. Edited by: Catherine Banet, Hanri Mostert, LeRoy Paddock, Milton Fernando Montoya, and Íñigo del Guayo, Oxford University Press.
© Don C. Smith and Donald N. Zillman 2022. DOI: 10.1093/oso/9780192864574.003.0012

the energy resilience policy discussion. Meanwhile, Section IV describes the impact of the 2020 congressional election. Looking ahead at the resiliency of the U.S. political system itself and its capacity to effectively deliver energy resilience is addressed in Section V. Finally, Section VI provides conclusory remarks.

II. The Trump Presidency and the Extraordinary years of 2020 and 2021

A. Overview

Over the last several years much has been written about former President Donald Trump's administration and its political opposition as their actions involved energy, environment, infrastructure, and climate change law.[8] Divisions between Democrats and Republicans have been extremely sharp and a study issued a few days after the November 2020 election said, 'Americans have rarely been as polarized as they are today'.[9] Both sides have addressed resiliency issues directly and indirectly.

In 2019 Trump and Congressional Republicans backed policies stressing an 'America First' philosophy that supported increased production of fossil fuels, scepticism about climate change and policies to control it, rejection of half a century of American environmental protection laws, general scepticism of scientific and medical knowledge, rejection of multilateral and international agreements, support for autocratic governments, and challenges to the rule of law and American Constitutional separation of powers.[10]

Opponents of the Trump-Republican agenda included virtually the entire Democratic Party. Opposition also came from many state and local governments, important parts of the business and financial communities, and supporters of environmental protection, renewable energy, and advocacy groups focused on climate change. Opponents generally supported international collaborative efforts to promote resiliency in handling these and other efforts.[11]

Richard Haass, president of the Council on Foreign Relations and keen U.S. political observer, has reflected on Trump's limited perspective about the country's ability to deal with adversity and yet simultaneously prosper, two classic resiliency elements:

> Missing from this worldview is any appreciation of what, from a U.S. perspective, was remarkable about the previous three quarters of a century: the absence of great-power war,

---

[8] See e.g. Don C Smith and Donald Zillman, 'Trump's America and its Impacts on Energy Justice' in Iñigo del Guayo et al (eds), *Energy Justice and Energy Law* (Oxford University Press 2020) 273 (hereafter Smith and Zillman 'Trump's America'; and Donald Zillman and Don Smith, 'The Brave New World of Energy and Natural Resources Development (2019) 37 Journal of Energy and Natural Resources Law 3.

[9] Michael Dimock and Richard Wike, 'America is exceptional in the nature of its political divide' (13 November 2020) Pew Research Center <https://www.pewresearch.org/fact-tank/2020/11/13/america-is-exceptional-in-the-nature-of-its-political-divide/> accessed 8 August 2021.

[10] Smith and Zillman, 'Trump's America and its Impacts on Energy Justice' (n 8) 276–278; see also Samantha Gross, 'What is the Trump administration's track record on the environment'? (4 August 2020) Policy 2020 Brookings Institution <https://www.brookings.edu/policy2020/votervital/what-is-the-trump-administrations-track-record-on-the-environment/> accessed 8 August 2021.

[11] Lisa Friedman, 'Trump Serves Notice to Quit Paris Climate Agreement' *The New York Times* (published 4 November 2019; updated 19 February 2021) <https://www.nytimes.com/2019/11/04/climate/trump-paris-agreement-climate.html> accessed 8 August 2021.

the extension of democracy around much of the world, a 90-fold growth in the size of the U.S. economy, a ten-year increase in the lifespan of the average American. Also missing is a recognition that the Cold War, the defining struggle of that era, ended peacefully, on terms that could hardly have been more favourable to the United States.[12]

B. 2020: Natural disasters

From the late spring through autumn of 2020 another challenge to American resilience—a record setting period for natural disasters occurred. The southern U.S., Central America, and the Caribbean were struck with a record number of hurricanes that brought death and billion-dollar property damage to the regions.[13] The U.S. National Oceanic and Atmospheric Administration estimated that in 2020 alone there were a record 22 weather/climate related events that caused individual losses of over US$1 billion.[14] Over the same period wildfires burned large portions of California and Colorado.[15] A major windstorm-derecho-tornado that struck Iowa received only limited national attention.[16] The first months of 2021 proved similarly impactful in terms of weather-related disasters. The cold wave that occurred in the Midwest in February caused damage losses of more than US$10 billion, making it the 'most costly winter storm event on record for the U.S'.[17] Meanwhile, Kathleen Johnson, a paleoclimatoglist at the University of California at Irvine, predicted in mid-year that the drought affecting much of the American West 'is potentially on track to become the worst that we've seen in at least 1,200 years. And the reason is linked directly to human caused climate change'.[18]

Meanwhile, Trump and most Republicans continued to express doubt about scientific evidence of climate change.[19] Most Democrats, while avoiding directly connecting single hurricanes, wildfires, or tornados, and specific human-caused climate consequences, did proclaim a medium to long-term connection.[20]

---

[12] Richard Haass, 'Present at the Disruption: How Trump Unmade U.S. Foreign Policy' (2020) 99 Foreign Affairs 24, 26, 24–34 (hereafter Hass 'Present at the Disruption: How Trump Unmade U.S. Foreign Policy')

[13] See < https://www.noaa.gov/media-release/record-breaking-atlantic-hurricane-season-draws-to-end> accessed 8 August 2021.

[14] 'Billon-Dollar Weather and Climate Disasters: Overview', NOAA National Centers for Environmental Information <https://www.ncdc.noaa.gov/billions/> accessed 8 August 2021.

[15] See <https://www.thecalifornian.com/story/news/2020/10/01/heat-fire-warnings-issued-monterey-co-ca-wildfires-spew-smoke/5881276002/> accessed 8 August 2021; and Wilson Beese, 'Looking back at Colorado's historic 2020 wildfire season' 9news.com (2 May 2021) <https://www.9news.com/article/news/local/wildfire/colorado-2020-historic-wildfire-season/73-c9458147-c945-45e6-bea9-a1d426cca102> accessed 8 August 2021.

[16] Bob Henson, 'Iowa derecho in August was most costly thunderstorm disaster in U.S. history' The Washington Post (17 October 2020) <https://www.washingtonpost.com/weather/2020/10/17/iowa-derecho-damage-cost/> accessed 8 August 2021.

[17] 'Assessing the U.S. Climate in March 2021' (8 April 2021) National Centers for Environmental Information <https://www.ncei.noaa.gov/news/national-climate-202103> accessed 8 August 2021.

[18] Maanvi Singh, '"Potentially the worst drought in 1,200 years": scientists on the scorching US heatwave' The Guardian (18 June 2021) <https://www.theguardian.com/us-news/2021/jun/18/us-heatwave-west-climate-crisis-drought> accessed 8 August 2021.

[19] Jonathan Lemire et al, 'Trump spurns science on climate' Associated Press (14 September 2020) <https://apnews.com/article/climate-climate-change-elections-joe-biden-campaigns-bd152cd786b58e45c61bebf2457f9930> accessed 8 August 2021.

[20] John Muyskens and Kevin Uhrmacher, 'Where 2020 Democrats stand on Climate change' The Washington Post (8 April 2020) <https://www.washingtonpost.com/graphics/politics/policy-2020/climate-change/> accessed 8 August 2021.

C. Formal withdrawal from Paris Climate Accord

Trump achieved a headline environmental/energy objective in November when the U.S. formally quit the Paris Climate Accord agreement.[21] The formal leaving date was 4 November 2020, one year from the date when the Trump administration notified the United Nations that the U.S. would withdraw from the agreement. Former U.S. Secretary of State Mike Pompeo announced the notification on 3 November 2019 saying that the agreement would place an intolerable burden on the U.S. economy. 'The U.S. approach incorporates the reality of the global energy mix and uses all energy sources and technologies cleanly and efficiently, including fossil fuels, nuclear energy, and renewable energy', Pompeo said.[22]

Despite having withdrawn from the agreement, just weeks later Trump continued railing against the agreement. 'To protect American workers, I withdrew the United States from the unfair and one-sided Paris climate accord, a very unfair act for the United States', he said adding it was 'not designed to save the environment. It was designed to kill the American economy'.[23]

D. 2020: Presidential campaign and election

The topic of energy resiliency was not a particular priority for either candidates' campaign, it was the candidate's thinking that was very different. The closest that Trump got to the subject of energy resilience happened at his administration's mid-point. In the first instance, the Trump administration sought to 'prop up financially struggling coal and nuclear power plants to ensure the electricity grid is resilient and reliable'.[24] However, the proposal to improve grid stability and resilience through this means was rejected unanimously in January 2018 by the Federal Energy Regulatory Commission (FERC).[25] Even Trump-appointed FERC member Richard Glick disputed the wisdom of the proposal saying it 'had little, if anything, to do with resilience, and was instead aimed at subsidizing certain uncompetitive electric generation technologies', adding that it was 'a multi-billion dollar bailout targeted at coal and nuclear generating facilities'.[26] In the second instance, on 26 March 2019, Trump signed an Executive Order on Coordinating National Resilience to Electromagnetic Pulses,[27] which the U.S. Department of Homeland Security described as 'the first-ever

---

[21] Rebecca Hersher, 'U.S. Officially Leaving Paris Climate Agreement', National Public Radio (3 November 2020) <https://www.npr.org/2020/11/03/930312701/u-s-officially-leaving-paris-climate-agreement> accessed 8 August 2021.

[22] Lisa Friedman, 'Trump Serves Notice to Quit Paris Climate Agreement' The New York Times (4 November 2019; updated 19 February 2021) <https://www.nytimes.com/2019/11/04/climate/trump-paris-agreement-climate.html> accessed 8 August 2021.

[23] Deb Reichmann and Aya Batrawy, 'Trump slams global climate agreement Biden intends to rejoin' The Associated Press (22 November 2020) <https://apnews.com/article/joe-biden-donald-trump-climate-climate-change-saudi-arabia-5e425ce92e26d34561d629331461289d> accessed 8 August 2021.

[24] Amy Harder, 'Trump's electricity solution in search of a problem' Axios (23 April 2018) <https://www.axios.com/trumps-electricity-solution-in-search-of-a-problem-287efa7b-181f-44a2-85f2-40625e9e22d0.html> accessed 8 August 2021.

[25] Robinson Meyer, 'Trump's Coal Bailout Is Dead' The Atlantic (9 January 2018) <https://www.theatlantic.com/science/archive/2018/01/trumps-coal-bailout-is-dead/550037/> accessed 8 August 2021.

[26] Ibid.

[27] See <https://www.govinfo.gov/content/pkg/DCPD-201900176/pdf/DCPD-201900176.pdf> accessed 8 August 2021.

comprehensive whole-of-government policy to build resilience and protect against electro-magnetic pulses … which are temporary electromagnetic signals that can disrupt, degrade, and damage technology and critical infrastructure systems across large areas'.[28]

Meanwhile, Biden emphasized the word 'resilient' in his campaign materials, but it was carefully linked with phrases such as 'resilient infrastructure and sustainable clean energy economy', 'climate resilience', and 'climate resilient campuses'.[29] That said, the Biden campaign's climate initiative proposed 'an irresistible path to achieve net-zero emissions, economy-wide, by no later than 2050'.[30] In explaining his plan, Biden referred to climate change and said, 'When Donald Trump thinks about climate change, the only word he can muster is "hoax". When I think of climate change, the word I think about is "jobs" – good-paying union jobs that'll put Americans to work'.[31]

Despite the paucity of effort to directly address energy resilience, there was a huge divide when it came to discussing climate change. Put succinctly, during the campaign there was 'sharp disagreement' between Biden and Trump regarding climate change.[32] *The Wall Street Journal* reported the month before the November vote, 'The 2020 presidential election pits one candidate making climate change integral throughout his platform against another who dismisses its importance and pledges to keep pushing a deregulatory agenda'.[33] Reuters reported that while Trump was focusing on further dismantling climate policy implemented by his predecessor Barack Obama, Biden was advocating for more green infrastructure to tackle climate change.[34]

The election's outcome was watched closely not only by Americans, but by the world as well. As one observer noted, 'In a world where the effects of climate change pervade every aspect of our society, from the socio-economic to the humanitarian and ethical, the elections for the president of the United States have enormous value for the future of our planet'.[35] Before the election ClearView Energy Partners[36] director Kevin Book predicted that 'given the nation's significant role in global energy markets any change to U.S. demand could have long-term international implications', adding that a Biden win would introduce a 2030 world that would look considerably 'different from an energy perspective'.[37]

---

[28] See <https://www.dhs.gov/news/2019/03/27/secretary-nielsen-statement-executive-order-protect-us-elec tromagnetic-pulse-attacks> accessed 8 August 2021.

[29] 'The Biden Plan to Build a Modern, Sustainable Infrastructure and an Equitable Clean Energy Future' https:// joebiden.com/clean-energy/ accessed 8 August 2021.

[30] Ibid.

[31] Alana Wise, 'Biden Outlines $2 Trillion Climate Plan', National Public Radio (14 July 2020) <https://www. npr.org/2020/07/14/890814007/biden-outlines-2-trillion-climate-plan> accessed 8 August 2021.

[32] Dino Grandoni, 'The Energy 202: The U.S. just left the Paris climate accord, even as the presidential race is undecided' *The Washington Post* (4 November 2020) <https://www.washingtonpost.com/politics/2020/11/04/ene rgy-202-us-just-left-paris-climate-accord-even-presidential-race-is-undecided/> accessed 8 August 2021.

[33] Timothy Puko, 'Where Trump and Biden Stand on Climate and Energy Policy' *The Wall Street Journal* (4 October 2020) <https://www.wsj.com/articles/where-trump-and-biden-stand-on-climate-and-energy-policy-11601809200> accessed 8 August 2021.

[34] Timothy Gardner and Valerie Volcovici, 'Factbox: On climate, it's Biden's green revolution versus Trump's war on regulations' *Reuters* (29 October 2020) <https://www.reuters.com/article/us-usa-election-climate-change-fact box/factbox-on-climate-its-bidens-green-revolution-versus-trumps-war-on-regulations-idUSKBN27E1J3> ac-cessed 8 August 2021.

[35] Marco Tedesco, 'As of Today, the U.S. Is No Longer Part of the Paris Agreement' *Columbia Climate School State of the Planet* (5 November 2020) <https://news.climate.columbia.edu/2020/11/05/u-s-leaves-paris-agreem ent/> accessed 8 August 2021.

[36] ClearView Energy Partners, a Washington, DC-based independent research and analysis firm, focuses on macro energy trends. See <http://site.cvenergy.com> accessed 8 August 2021

[37] Molly Christian and Ellie Potter, 'Update: President-elect Biden's climate, energy plans may hinge on Senate races', S&P Global Market Intelligence (9 November 2020) <https://www.spglobal.com/marketintelligence/en/

When the votes were tallied the result was a 306–232 electoral vote Biden victory, backed by a nearly 7 million vote advantage.[38] Several days after the outcome, the *Financial Times* reported 'President-elect Joe Biden will take office with a plan to adopt tough new climate targets for the U.S. and reverse many of the environmental actions of the Trump administration in a stance that was welcomed by world leaders'.[39]

Meanwhile, *The New York Times* said that Biden 'will use the next four years to try to restore the environmental policies that [Trump] has methodically blown up, but the damage done by the greenhouse gas pollution unleashed by President Trump's rollbacks may prove to be one of the most profound legacies of his single term'.[40] But a headline in *Energy and Environment News* perhaps captured it best: 'Biden win ushers in seismic energy policy shift'.[41]

E. 6 January 2021 and Trump impeachment II

While not directly related to energy, the first weeks of January raised fundamental questions about the resiliency of American democracy. First, in a display never witnessed in U.S. history, Trump loyalists stormed and occupied the capitol building in 'a shocking display of violence that shook the core of American democracy'.[42] The rioters breached the capitol building's security and injured 150 people following Trump's speech at the Washington Ellipse where he urged supporters to convene at the capitol while the Congress was certifying the November 2020 election results.[43] In the speech Trump said 'We fight like hell. And if you don't fight like hell, you're not going to have a country anymore', adding that the election had been rigged 'like they've never rigged an election before'.[44] Meanwhile, on the very same day of the riot, *USA Today* reported that of 62 lawsuits filed on behalf of the Trump effort challenging the election, 61 failed and the remaining one did not call into question the legitimacy of the election results.[45]

Despite the events of 6 January, however, in the early morning hours of the following day Congress reconvened, the electoral votes were counted, and former Vice President Mike

news-insights/latest-news-headlines/update-president-elect-biden-s-climate-energy-plans-may-hinge-on-senate-races-61035993> accessed 8 August 2021.

[38] See <https://www.nytimes.com/interactive/2020/11/03/us/elections/results-president.html> accessed 8 August 2021.
[39] Leslie Hook, 'Biden shifts on climate change welcomed by world leaders' *Financial Times* (8 November 2020) <https://www.ft.com/content/5ce99af6-e776-43af-9c74-593d49dc5125> accessed 8 August 2021.
[40] Coral Davenport, 'What Will Trump's Most Profound Legacy Be? Possibly Climate Damage' *The New York Times* (published 9 November 2020; updated 3 December 2020) <https://www.nytimes.com/2020/11/09/climate/trump-legacy-climate-change.html> accessed 8 August 2021.
[41] Lesley Clark, 'Biden win ushers in seismic energy policy shift' *E&E News* (9 November 2020) <https://www.eenews.net/energywire/stories/1063718013/most_read> accessed 8 August 2021.
[42] Nicholas Fandos and Emily Cochrane, 'After Pro-Trump Storms Capitol, Congress Confirms Biden's Win' *The New York Times* (6 January 2021) <https://www.nytimes.com/2021/01/06/us/politics/congress-gop-subvert-election.html> accessed 8 August 2021.
[43] Brian Naylor, 'Read Trump's Jan. 6 Speech, A Key Part of Impeachment Trial, National Public Radio (10 February 2021) <https://www.npr.org/2021/02/10/966396848/read-trumps-jan-6-speech-a-key-part-of-impeachment-trial> accessed 8 August 2021.
[44] Ibid
[45] William Cummings, Joey Garrison, and Jim Sergent, 'By the numbers' *USA Today* (6 January 2021) <https://www.usatoday.com/in-depth/news/politics/elections/2021/01/06/trumps-failed-efforts-overturn-election-numbers/4130307001/> accessed 8 August 2021,

Pence declared Biden the winner.[46] On 7 January, Jason Brumet, president of the Bipartisan Policy Center,[47] observed that 'The abhorrent attack on the Capitol broke more than windows. The violence also shattered the premise that our nation's leader can denigrate our democracy without consequences … While fragile, our democracy has once again proven its resilience' in the form of Congress certifying the electoral results.[48]

Subsequently, Democrats in the House of Representatives introduced and passed—notably with 10 Republican votes—a resolution impeaching Trump for his incitement of insurrection on 6 January.[49] The resolution was referred to the Senate for trial where Trump was ultimately acquitted on 13 February by a 57–43 vote,[50] short of the constitutionally required two-thirds vote for conviction.

III. Bidden/Harris Administration and Energy Resiliency

A. Overview

On 27 January 2021 Biden spoke about the fundamental approach of his administration towards climate change emphasizing that it would be a 'whole-of-government approach … it's not time for small measures; we need to be bold'.[51] During the first year of his presidency, Biden began to implement this approach with a combination of initiatives including global pronouncements and domestically focused measures including executive orders, potential regulations, and legislative ideas.

Of particular importance in Biden achieving his climate change-related goals specifically and energy resilience more broadly is the president's administrative powers involving executive orders and regulation. 'For nearly 30 years, every American president from Bill Clinton to Donald Trump has relied on administrative powers rather than fresh legislation', Professor Barry Rabe of the Brookings think-tank has written.[52] 'This achieved new heights during the Barack Obama presidency, and the succeeding Trump administration has largely eviscerated all of the major Obama climate policy efforts via executive orders, regulatory revisions, and administrative stalling, designed to make it as difficult as possible for any successor to shift gears again'.[53] On the other hand, Andrew Grossman, an attorney who challenged an Obama-era regulation to reduce GHGs, said 'When you are talking about

---

[46] John Wagner et al, 'Pence declares Biden winner of the presidential election after Congress finally counts electoral votes' *The Washington Post* (7 January 2021) <https://www.washingtonpost.com/politics/2021/01/06/congress-electoral-college-vote-live-updates/> accessed 8 August 2021,

[47] The Washington, DC-based organization 'actively fosters' political bipartisanship. See <https://bipartisanpolicy.org/about/> accessed 8 August 2021,

[48] 'Statement by Bipartisan Policy Center President Jason Grumet on the Capitol assault and challenges ahead', Bipartisan Policy Center (7 January 2021) <https://bipartisanpolicy.org/press-release/statement-by-bipartisan-policy-center-president-jason-grumet-on-the-capitol-assault-and-challenges-ahead/> accessed 8 August 2021.

[49] See <https://www.congress.gov/bill/117th-congress/house-resolution/24/text> accessed 8 August 2021.

[50] See <https://www.senate.gov/legislative/LIS/roll_call_lists/roll_call_vote_cfm.cfm?congress=117&session=1&vote=00059> accessed 8 August 2021.

[51] See <https://www.whitehouse.gov/briefing-room/speeches-remarks/2021/01/27/remarks-by-president-biden-before-signing-executive-actions-on-tackling-climate-change-creating-jobs-and-restoring-scientific-integrity/> accessed 8 August 2021.

[52] Barry G Rabe, 'The limitations of a climate change presidency' Brookings (23 June 2020) <https://www.brookings.edu/blog/fixgov/2020/06/23/the-limitations-of-a-climate-change-presidency/> accessed 8 August 2021 (hereafter Rabe, 'The limitations of a climate change presidency').

[53] Ibid.

sweeping changes to the economy, that's supposed to come from Congress. Congress wields the legislative power. And the executive may have some discretion to fill in the details. But when you're talking about major national policies, you're not talking about details'.[54]

Bearing these ideas in mind, the success or failure of the Biden agenda will include difficult choices about whether and how to use executive orders, regulations, and legislation to fulfil his goals.

B. Initiatives

1. Global agenda

America's commitment to global climate change efforts was given priority during the early months of the Biden presidency. The effort began in earnest just hours after taking office on 21 January 2021, when Biden returned the U.S. to the Paris Agreement through an executive order.[55] At a minimum, Biden's action 'signals to the world that the U.S. is serious about addressing climate change again, and that it will have a seat at the table' during the upcoming November 2021 COP 26 meeting, one observer noted.[56]

Subsequently, Biden convened an April climate summit of world leaders. In opening remarks, Biden pledged to slash U.S. greenhouse gas emissions by 50 to 52 per cent by 2030 as compared to 2005 levels—an ambitious target that was characterized as 'staggering'.[57] Biden encouraged nations to follow suit and announce new climate change-related commitments and described the gathering as 'a start of a road that will take us to Glasgow for the U.N. Climate Change Conference in November where we're going to make these commitments real, putting all of our nations on path to a secure, prosperous and sustainable future'.[58] Biden never used the phrase 'energy resiliency' in his summit remarks, referring instead to investing in 'climate resilience and infrastructure' that create 'opportunities for everyone.…That's at the heart of my Jobs Plan that I proposed here in the United States. It's how our nation intends to build an economy that gives everybody a fair shot'.[59]

However, to reach that pledge will likely take a 'herculean effort from Congress'[60] in terms of legislative enactments, and assumes that future administrations or courts will not reverse any Biden-era regulations (see discussion below) targeting GHG emissions.[61] In contrast, Heather Reams, the executive director of Citizens for Responsible Energy Solutions that has

---

[54] Timothy Cama, 'What Biden can do if Congress balks at his green agenda' (28 May 2020) *E&E News* <https://www.eenews.net/special_reports/campaign_2020/stories/1063251345> accessed 8 August 2021.

[55] 'Paris Climate Agreement', The White House (20 January 2021) <https://www.whitehouse.gov/briefing-room/statements-releases/2021/01/20/paris-climate-agreement/> accessed 8 August 2021.

[56] Nathan Rott, 'Biden Moves to Have U.S. Rejoin Climate Accord', National Public Radio (20 January 2021) <https://www.npr.org/sections/inauguration-day-live-updates/2021/01/20/958923821/biden-moves-to-have-u-s-rejoin-climate-accord> accessed 8 August 2021.

[57] Nick Sobczyk, 'Biden made the world a bold promise. Here's Congress' role' *E&E News* (23 April 2021) <https://www.eenews.net/eedaily/2021/04/23/stories/1063730803> accessed 28 June 2021 (hereafter Sobczyk 'Biden made the world a bold promise. Here's Congress' role').

[58] 'Remarks by President Biden at the Virtual Leaders Summit on Climate Session 5' (23 April 2021) https://www.whitehouse.gov/briefing-room/speeches-remarks/2021/04/23/remarks-by-president-biden-at-the-virtual-leaders-summit-on-climate-session-5-the-economic-opportunities-of-climate-action/ accessed 8 August 2021.

[59] Ibid.

[60] Sobczyk, 'Biden made the world a bold promise. Here's Congress' role' (n 57).

[61] Brady Dennis and Juliet Eilperin, 'Biden plans to cut emissions at least in half by 2030' *The Washington Post* (20 April 2021) <https://www.washingtonpost.com/climate-environment/2021/04/20/biden-climate-change/> accessed 8 August 2021.

been described as a 'conservative group' that has worked with the House Republican leadership, said that Biden was 'radically impacting our already battered economy' by pledging to reduce U.S. carbon emissions dramatically by 2030.[62]

2. Executive orders

Presidential executive orders are written, signed, and published directives that involve federal government management. While having the force of law, they require no Congressional authorization and thus are not equivalent to legislation and a sitting president may revoke a prior president's executive order without Congressional involvement.[63] Because executive orders can be easily revoked, they are not a durable type of law.[64] Nevertheless because they are entirely within a sitting president's discretion, they have often been used in recent presidencies particularly in policy goals related to the environment.[65]

Early in his presidency Biden availed himself of the use of climate change-related executive orders. Four were most prominent. The first, the Executive Order on 'Protecting Public Health and the Environment and Restoring Science to Tackle the Climate Crisis',[66] noted that one of his administration's policies would be to 'bolster resilience to the impact of climate change'. The order, described as a 'sweeping executive order …to review former President Trump's environmental rollbacks across the federal government',[67] provided that the federal government under his administration would 'be guided by the best science' and ordered federal agencies to identify Trump administration initiatives that reduced or eliminated efforts to address climate change and propose measures to rectify their impacts. The order included specific reference to 'some of the most notorious actions of the Trump administration that undermined regulations designed to reduce GHG emissions'.[68] The order also 'prioritized an affirmative approach to environmental justice'[69] by requiring agencies to integrate 'achieving environmental justice as part of their missions'.[70]

The second major order, 'Tackling the Climate Crisis at Home and Abroad',[71] proclaimed that 'The United States and the world face a profound climate crisis. We have a narrow moment to pursue action at home and abroad to avoid the most catastrophic impacts of that crisis and to seize the opportunity that tacking climate change presents'. In particular, the order stated that addressing climate change was at the centre of U.S. national security and

---

[62] Oliver Milman, 'Republicans' climate credibility hit by make-believe "war on burgers" claim' *The Guardian* (28 April 2021) https://www.theguardian.com/environment/2021/apr/28/joe-biden-climate-crisis-republicans-meat accessed 8 August 2021.

[63] 'What Is an Executive Order? American Bar Association (25 January 2021) <https://www.americanbar.org/groups/public_education/publications/teaching-legal-docs/what-is-an-executive-order-/>   accessed   8 August 2021.

[64] Rabe, 'The limitations of a climate change presidency' (n 52).

[65] Ibid.

[66] See <https://www.whitehouse.gov/briefing-room/presidential-actions/2021/01/20/executive-order-protecting-public-health-and-environment-and-restoring-science-to-tackle-climate-crisis/> accessed 8 August 2021.

[67] Kelsey Brugger, 'Biden orders sweeping review of Trump regulations' *E&E News* (20 January 2021) <https://www.eenews.net/greenwire/2021/01/20/stories/1063723041> accessed 8 August 2021.

[68] Hana Vizcarra and Harran Perls, 'Biden's Week One: Mapping Ambitious Climate Action' (3 March 2021) p 13 <http://eelp.law.harvard.edu/wp-content/uploads/Bidens-Week-One-Report_030321.pdf> accessed 8 August 2021 (hereafter Vizcarra and Perls, 'Biden's Week One: Mapping Ambitious Climate Action')

[69] Ibid, 6.

[70] See <https://www.whitehouse.gov/briefing-room/presidential-actions/2021/01/20/executive-order-protecting-public-health-and-environment-and-restoring-science-to-tackle-climate-crisis/> accessed 8 August 2021.

[71] See   <https://www.whitehouse.gov/briefing-room/presidential-actions/2021/01/27/executive-order-on-tackling-the-climate-crisis-at-home-and-abroad/> accessed 8 August 2021.

foreign policy, noting that 'The United States will work with other countries and partners, both bilaterally and multilaterally, to put the world on a sustainable climate pathway'. In addition, the order created several new bodies to elevate and inform environmental priorities government-wide.

The third major order, the 'President's Council of Advisors on Science and Technology', stated that 'it is the policy of my Administration to make evidence-based decisions guided by the best available science and data'.[72] The Biden policy 'marks a sharp departure from the Trump administration, particularly at the EPA where leadership replaced qualified experts on the agency's advisory committees, finalized a rule excluding critical science from agency decision-making processes, and limited the scientific information EPA shared with the public'.[73]

The first three orders were signed in Biden's first eight days in office, leading Dan Lashof, director of environmental advocacy organization the World Resources Institute, to remark, 'President Biden has accomplished more on climate change in his first eight days than most presidents accomplish in their entire terms in office'.[74]

The fourth order on 'Climate-Related Financial Risk' called for development in 2021 of a 'comprehensive government-wide [climate-risk] strategy'[75] to 'identify and disclose climate-related financial risks to the federal government and its assets'.[76] Additionally, the order requested that U.S. 'financial regulators analyze climate-related threats to the U.S. financial system' and directed the U.S. Secretary of Labor to contemplate suspending or rescinding 'any Trump administration rules that would prohibit investment firms from considering environmental, social and governance factors, including climate-related risks, in their investment decisions for workers' pensions'.[77]

Although not an executive order per se, one outcome of the Tackling the Climate Crisis at Home and Abroad order, discussed above, was the April 2021 announcement of a U.S. International Climate Finance Plan, a first of its kind federal government document.[78] The plan was another aspect of Biden's 'all-of-government approach to climate change and climate finance'.[79] The plan stated that 'The case for providing and mobilizing climate finance on an international level is compelling ... Climate finance can help unlock deep reductions in other countries' emissions by supporting the deployment of existing clean energy technologies abroad ... while building resilience and helping countries adapt to the impact of climate change'.[80] According to the plan, '[T]he U.S. by 2024 will double the amount of

[72] See <https://www.federalregister.gov/documents/2021/02/01/2021-02176/presidents-council-of-advisors-on-science-and-technology> accessed 8 August 2021.

[73] Vizcarra and Perls, 'Biden's Week One: Mapping Ambitious Climate Action' (n 68) 11

[74] Dan Lashof, 'Will Biden's Climate Blitz Sack the Climate Crisis?', World Resources Institute (2 February 2021) <https://www.wri.org/insights/will-bidens-climate-blitz-sack-climate-crisis> accessed 8 August 2021.

[75] See <https://www.whitehouse.gov/briefing-room/presidential-actions/2021/05/20/executive-order-on-climate-related-financial-risk/> accessed 8 August 2021.

[76] Molly Christian and Ellie Potter, 'Biden issues order to guard US from climate-related financial risks' S&P Global Market Intelligence (20 May 2021) <https://www.spglobal.com/marketintelligence/en/news-insights/latest-news-headlines/biden-issues-order-to-guard-us-from-climate-related-financial-risks-64431412> accessed 28 June 2021.

[77] Ibid.

[78] See <https://www.whitehouse.gov/wp-content/uploads/2021/04/U.S.-International-Climate-Finance-Plan-4.22.21-Updated-Spacing.pdf> accessed 8 August 2021.

[79] Avery Ellfeldt, 'Biden doubles climate spending abroad, disappointing greens' E&E News (23 April 2021) <https://www.eenews.net/stories/1063730797> accessed 28 June 2021 (hereafter Ellfeldt 'Biden doubles climate spending abroad, disappointing greens').

[80] (n 78) 1.

public climate finance that it provides to developing countries'.[81] While the plan did not set a precise funding amount, one estimate was that the U.S. would annually provide for climate adaption about US$1.5 billion and about US$5.7 billion in climate finance.[82] Despite the plan's announcement, not everyone was satisfied with its level of commitment. World Resources Institute representative Joe Thwaites said that regardless of how the final amount was calculated, 'The U.S. is still really lagging' adding that the amount would not be sufficient for the county to claim a climate finance leadership position.[83]

3. Regulatory agenda

Another form of presidential authority involves the issuance of regulations by executive branch agencies.[84] While public policy principles are the basis of legislation, the principles are implemented by regulations that bring the legislation into effect.[85] Consequently, 'Over the past several decades, regulation has become one of the most powerful tools a president has for setting policy'.[86]

The importance of the Biden administration promoting regulatory actions is underscored by the observation that, 'The polarized atmosphere in Washington is such that it is difficult for a Republican to support anything proposed by the Biden administration, lest they be demonized by right-wing media and the party's activist base'.[87]

In preparing for the role regulations will play in his presidency, Biden issued the Modernizing Regulatory Review[88] memo on the day he took office. The memo included the proviso that the nation faced 'serious challenges, including ... the undeniable reality and accelerating threat of climate change' and that 'It is the policy of my Administration to mobilize the power of the Federal Government to rebuild our Nation'.[89] The memo emphasized that 'Regulations that promote the public interest are vital for tackling national priorities'.

Biden's first regulatory 'to-do' list[90] detailed a considerable expansion of the government's role in the environment.[91] With a narrowly divided Congress, 'Biden will be forced to advance many of his goals by regulatory action rather than legislation'.[92] In particular, the list revealed 'plans to continue unraveling the Trump administration's environmental rollbacks on climate'.[93] Sharon Block, acting administrator of the Office of Information and

---

[81] Ellfeldt, 'Biden doubles climate spending abroad, disappointing greens' (n 79).

[82] Ibid.

[83] Ibid.

[84] Nir Kosti et al, 'Legislation and regulation: three analytical distinctions' (2019) 7(3) The Theory and Practice of Legislation 169–178, 171 <https://www.tandfonline.com/doi/pdf/10.1080/20508840.2019.1736369?needAccess=true> accessed 8 August 2021.

[85] Ibid.

[86] Stuart Shapiro, 'What new presidents can (and cannot) do about regulation' (23 December 2015) The Hill <https://thehill.com/blogs/pundits-blog/presidential-campaign/264084-what-new-presidents-can-and-cannot-do-about> accessed 8 August 2021.

[87] Samantha Gross, 'Republicans in Congress are out of step with the American public on climate' (10 May 2021) Brookings < https://www.brookings.edu/blog/planetpolicy/2021/05/10/republicans-in-congress-are-out-of-step-with-the-american-public-on-climate/> accessed 23 June 2021.

[88] See <https://www.whitehouse.gov/briefing-room/presidential-actions/2021/01/20/modernizing-regulatory-review/> accessed 8 August 2021.

[89] Ibid.

[90] See <https://www.reginfo.gov/public/do/eAgendaMain> accessed 8 August 2021.

[91] Courtney Rozen, 'Biden Regulatory Playbook Revives More Active Government (3)' (11 June 2021) Bloomberg Law.

[92] Kelsey Brugger, 'Biden releases his first regulatory agenda' (11 June 2021) E&E News <https://www.eenews.net/stories/1063734797> accessed 8 August 2021.

[93] Ibid.

Regulatory Affairs, said, 'Federal agencies plan to work together to reduce greenhouse gas emissions, strengthen fuel economy standards, and thoughtfully manage natural resources development on public lands and waters. Recognizing the disproportionate harm climate change poses to communities of color and low-income communities, Federal agencies will also prioritize environmental justice as part of this work'.[94]

However, there are limitations to the use of regulations not least of which involve judicial oversight of actions brought by industry,[95] 'red-state' attorneys general,[96] and conservative advocacy groups.[97] In this regard, the Administrative Procedure Act provides the most significant vehicle for challenging federal agency actions.[98] For example, courts will consider the statutory authority for an action and invalidate it if the action exceeds that authority. Additionally, a court may review discretionary agency decisions. And finally, courts may review agency compliance with procedural requirements set forth in the authorizing statute.[99] Moreover, the federal judiciary, who would hear such challenges, has been called 'not overly friendly to environmental administration efforts' undertaken during the George W Bush and Obama presidencies and federal courts may be even less inclined to support agency action considering that some 200 new judges were appointed by Trump.[100] Furthermore, it has been suggested that two consecutive presidential terms 'are essential to have a credible chance to launch and sustain executive-based policies, with a third highly preferable'.[101] The Obama era administrative efforts were 'based on an implicit assumption of a hand-off to an allied successor who would finish the job, putting prior efforts into operation and building upon them'.[102] Trump's election negated that.

4. Legislative proposals

To achieve Biden's ambitious goals, it is likely that Congressional support in passing legislation is necessary. Broadly speaking, 'Government initiatives enacted through legislation are generally more durable because they have attracted broader political support and are less susceptible to unfavourable court judgements'.[103] In the early part of the Biden administration the strategy was to link energy resilience and climate-related ideas to infrastructure investment. Senate Majority Leader Chuck Schumer (D-NY) said as much in April 2021. 'The best way to achieve this ambitious goal is through bold action by this Congress through legislation to reduce carbon pollution, while creating millions of jobs and economic prosperity in a new clean energy economy', Schumer said adding, 'Any legislation without a serious and bold climate component will make it much, much harder to achieve President's Biden's goal'.[104]

---

[94] See <https://www.whitehouse.gov/omb/briefing-room/2021/06/11/an-agenda-to-continue-powering-a-robust-and-equitable-economic-recovery/> accessed 8 August 2021.

[95] Jennifer Epstein and Jennifer Dlouhy, 'Biden Rejoins Climate Fight, Vows Aid as Poor Nations Make Pleas' (22 April 2021) *Bloomberg Law* <https://news.bloomberglaw.com/environment-and-energy/biden-pushes-carbon-plan-to-world-burned-by-trump-leery-of-risk> accessed 8 August 2021.

[96] Rachel Frazin, '12 states sue Biden over "social cost" calculation of greenhouse gases' The Hill (8 March 2021) <https://thehill.com/policy/energy-environment/542149-12-states-sue-biden-over-calculation-of-climate-impacts-in> accessed 8 August 2021.

[97] Jacob Schlesinger, 'Biden's Hurdle: Courts Dubious of Rule by Regulation' *The Wall Street Journal* (2 March 2021).

[98] Jared P Cole, 'An Introduction to Judicial Review of Federal Agency Action' (7 December 2016) Congressional Research Service p 2 <https://fas.org/sgp/crs/misc/R44699.pdf> accessed 8 August 2021.

[99] Ibid.

[100] Rabe, 'The limitations of a climate change presidency' (n 52).

[101] Ibid.

[102] Ibid.

[103] Schlesinger, 'Biden's Hurdle: Courts Dubious of Rule by Regulation' (n 97).

[104] Sobczyk, 'Biden made the world a bold promise. Here's Congress' role' (n 57).

The Biden infrastructure plan, as laid out in 2021, included a federal clean energy standard (CES), which has been described as 'the tool he really wants and needs for his climate plan – a national clean energy standard ... that would achieve a 100 per cent carbon-free electric grid by 2035 and would go economywide by 2050'.[105] Congressional approval of such a measure would transform 'Biden's climate vision from a goal into a mandate ... [and make] it that much harder for a future administration to undue'.[106]

Currently the U.S. annually delivers to the grid an additional 2 per cent of clean energy.[107] Passage of the CES, combined with a build out of the grid, would add nearly 5 per cent annually, University of California Professor and climate change expert Leah Stokes has said noting, 'With the federal government providing financial support to the industry and to ratepayers, this is something we can get done at the pace and scale necessary'.[108]

However, passing such a measure in the Senate during Biden's first two years in office may be impossible. Two ways to pass such a measure are to either garner 60 votes in order to overcome the filibuster, or the measure can be inserted into a bill that could pass in the reconciliation process that only requires a simple majority.[109] That said, it is not entirely certain that Biden could count on all 50 Democratic votes in the Senate to pass legislation by reconciliation.[110] An alternative might be to make the standard more flexible by, for example, mandating a goal but then allowing states to keep nuclear generation in place and even continuing natural gas-generated power combined with carbon capture.[111]

Even if a CES fails, the mere introduction of the concept 'may drive industry response even if it doesn't get enacted', Mike O'Boyle of the non-partisan Energy Innovation think-tank said.[112] He pointed to the impact of Obama's Clean Power Plan regulation that was influential despite the fact it was never implemented.[113] Another 'plan B' idea might include providing incentives to utilities to expand renewable-generated power combined with tax credits targeted to clean energy to accelerate deployment.[114]

Currently the District of Columbia and 30 states have CES's, 'but Biden's proposal outlines a radical shift for the federal government that would see far more solar, wind and other renewable sources come online'.[115] On the other hand, over the past 20 years many efforts to pass similar measures have failed.[116]

[105] Peter Behr and Lesley Clark, 'Biden lays foundation for energy overhaul' (26 April 2021) E&E News <https://www.eenews.net/energywire/2021/04/26/stories/1063730915> accessed 8 August 2021.

[106] Scott Waldman, 'Biden's climate bet rests on a clean electricity standard' (10 May 2021) E&E News <https://www.eenews.net/stories/1063732089> accessed 8 August 2021 (hereafter Waldman, 'Biden's climate bet rests on a clean electricity standard').

[107] Scott Waldman, 'Biden's infrastructure plan would make electricity carbon-free by 2035' (1 April 2021) E&E News https://www.scientificamerican.com/article/bidens-infrastructure-plan-would-make-electricity-carbon-free-by-2035/ accessed 8 August 2021.

[108] Ibid.

[109] Sobczyk, 'Biden made the world a bold promise. Here's Congress' role' (n 57).

[110] Ibid.

[111] Waldman, 'Biden's climate bet rests on a clean electricity standard' (n 106).

[112] Ibid.

[113] Ibid.

[114] Scott Waldman, 'How Dems still might get a clean electricity standard' (23 June 2021) E&E News <https://www.eenews.net/stories/1063735571> accessed 8 August 2021.

[115] Scott Waldman, 'Biden sets 2035 as goal to decarbonize U.S. electricity', (1 April 2021) E&E News <https://www.eenews.net/climatewire/2021/04/01/stories/1063728989> accessed 8 August 2021.

[116] Jim Tankersley, 'Biden Details $2 Trillion Plan to Rebuild Infrastructure and Reshape the Economy' The New York Times (published 31 March 2021, updated 8 June 2021) <https://www.nytimes.com/2021/03/31/business/economy/biden-infrastructure-plan.html> accessed 8 August 2021.

IV. 117th United States Congress

While Biden was winning the presidency, Democrats retained control of the House[117] and took control of the Senate.[118] In the aftermath of the Congressional elections it was suggested that the party might 'potentially advance more aggressive climate and clean energy legislation in the 117th Congress'.[119] However, it was noted at the beginning of this Congressional session that the reality is probably less sanguine bearing in mind the extremely narrow majorities in both houses of Congress and the fact that party unanimity on climate legislation might not hold should more moderate Democrats oppose such legislation.[120]

Notwithstanding narrow Democratic majorities in both houses, Democrats in the Senate will face the challenge of surmounting the filibuster, a procedural delaying tactic that is a long-standing Senate rule and tradition. Under the filibuster, legislation may be delayed or a floor vote prevented unless three-fifths of senators vote in favour of ending the filibuster.[121] Thus, in a full Senate of 100 members, a vote of 60 in favour of ending a filibuster is necessary to continue consideration of a bill. There has been talk of ending or revising the filibuster rule,[122] but unanimous Democratic support will be necessary to make the change and that unanimity has yet to materialize.[123] In the absence of filibuster reform, Democrats could use a procedure called 'budgetary reconciliation' that avoids the requirement of 60 votes, but has its own limitations.[124] Climate change-related legislation is one of the policy initiatives that seems unlikely to draw 60 votes in the Senate, but might potentially pass if all Democratic Senators voted in favour of the legislation under the reconciliation procedure.[125]

Despite the continuation of the filibuster, it has been suggested that its increasing use to stop legislation has troubling consequences for democracy. In one regard, the use of the filibuster 'magnifies the problems of representation endemic to the Senate, where small and large states alike are each represented by two senators ... Today, the 26 least populous states

---

[117] See <https://www.nytimes.com/interactive/2020/11/03/us/elections/results-house.html?action=click&pgt ype=Article&state=default&module=styln-elections-2020&region=TOP_BANNER&context=election_recirc> accessed 8 August 2021.

[118] See <https://www.nytimes.com/interactive/2020/11/03/us/elections/results-senate.html?action=click&pgt ype=Article&state=default&module=styln-elections-2020&region=TOP_BANNER&context=election_recirc> accessed 8 August 2021.

[119] Ellie Potter, 'Blue Congress will still face hurdles to passing climate, energy bills', S&P Global Market Intelligence (6 January 2021) https://www.spglobal.com/marketintelligence/en/news-insights/latest-news-headlines/blue-congress-will-still-face-hurdles-to-passing-climate-energy-bills-61063620 accessed 8 August 2021.

[120] Ibid.

[121] See <https://www.senate.gov/about/powers-procedures/filibusters-cloture.htm> accessed 8 August 2021.

[122] Molly E Reynolds, 'What is the Senate filibuster, and what would it take to eliminate it?' Policy 2020 Brookings (9 September 2020) <https://www.brookings.edu/policy2020/votervital/what-is-the-senate-filibuster-and-what-would-it-take-to-eliminate-it/> accessed 8 August 2021.

[123] Giovanni Russonello, 'Will Democrats Nix (or Weaken) the Filibuster'? *The New York Times* (published 15 March 2021; updated 27 March 2021) <https://www.nytimes.com/2021/03/15/us/politics/democrats-filibuster-manchin-sinema.html> accessed 8 August 2021.

[124] See 'The Budget Reconciliation Process: The Senate's 'Byrd Rule", Congressional Research Service (updated 4 May 2021) <https://fas.org/sgp/crs/misc/RL30862.pdf> accessed 8 August 2021.

[125] Anthony Zurcher, 'Filibuster: The biggest obstacle to Biden getting his way', BBC News (26 April 2021) <https://www.bbc.com/news/world-us-canada-56893296> accessed 8 August 2021.

are home to just 17 per cent of the U.S. population. This means that a group of senators representing a small minority of the country can use the filibuster to prevent the passage of bills with broad public support'.[126] Moreover, the abuse of the filibuster threatens the checks and balances between the executive and legislative branches in particular because 'The relative stagnancy of Congress – which is in large part due to the filibuster – has pushed presidents to increase their use of executive power, which in turn often goes unchecked because of Congress's inability to act'.[127]

V. Looking Ahead: U.S. Governmental Resilience

The capacity of the U.S. federal government to promote energy resiliency necessarily raises the question of the overall resiliency of the same government. Is it preprepared to successfully address the necessary issues that have prevented the county thus far from addressing fundamental matters such as energy resiliency and the stress that climate change is putting on the U.S. economy and society?

The inability of the federal government to take meaningful action on climate change, for example, is hardly accidental. One observer has suggested two reasons for this. '[T]here has been a concerted effort by economic elites in the fossil fuel industry, and their friends, to delegitimize the issue by questioning the science of climate change: "We don't need policy because there is nothing happening and there is no problem"', he claims the industry has promoted.[128] In addition the industry has also taken the position that 'climate change policy will destroy jobs and impair the economy: "Maybe global warming is real, but it's not worth sacrificing my [sports utility vehicle] for"'.[129]

Moreover, there is a concern that the county is simply not prepared to protect its economy in many settings. 'Whether the next crisis is another pandemic [or] … a climate shock … , the United States lacks a comprehensive strategy to ensure its economic resilience. The government does not even have an office equipped to develop such a plan,' it has been observed.[130] This situation was emphasized by two 'futurists' who have written 'If the United States is to remain a well-functioning republic and a prosperous nation, the government cannot rely indefinitely on crisis management, no matter how adroit. We must get ahead of events or we risk being overtaken by them. In short, we must improve our management system to meet today's accelerating and complex challenges'.[131]

[126] Tim Lau, 'The Filibuster, Explained', Brennan Center for Justice (26 April 2021) https://www.brennancenter.org/our-work/research-reports/filibuster-explained accessed 8 August 2021.

[127] Ibid.

[128] Steve Cohen, 'Climate Change and the American Political Agenda', (24 August 2021) State of the Planet Columbia Climate School https://news.climate.columbia.edu/2020/08/24/climate-change-american-political-agenda/ accessed 8 August 2021 (hereafter Cohen, 'Climate Change and the American Political Agenda').

[129] Ibid.

[130] Ganesh Sitaraman, 'A Grand Strategy of Resilience: American Power in the Age of Fragility' (September/October 2020) Foreign Affairs 165, 171 (hereafter Sitaraman, 'A Grand Strategy of Resilience: American Power in the Age of Fragility').

[131] Leon S. Fuerth with Evan M.H. Faber, 'Anticipatory Governance: Winning the Future', (July-August 2013) 47(4)The Futurist 42–49, 42

The need to look ahead is coming none too soon. '[I]n a world where climate risks rarely interact, governments are already inadequately planning for potential disasters', an observer has written, adding 'As those risks compound one another, governments will lag even further behind the threat.'[132] Furthermore, public opinion may be forcing the end of 'climate non-decision-making'.[133]

What the U.S. needs to deal with future major disruptions 'is an economy, a society, and a democracy that can prevent [such] challenges when possible and endure, bounce back, and adapt when necessary'.[134] In addition, a U.S. strategy must also include 'healthy working relationships and frequent cooperation' with other countries.[135] Yet democracy itself will not be resilient 'if people do not believe in it … Americans' trust in government has been stuck near historic lows for years, and surveys show that startling numbers of citizens do not think democracy is important'.[136]

Even assuming the U.S. might successfully achieve more governmental and energy resilience, the degree to which it can be a model for others will be an enormous challenge. Council on Foreign Relations president Richard Haass has written, '[T]he standing of the United States in the world has fallen, thanks to its inept handling of COVID-19 [and] its denial of climate change' among other things.[137]

Notwithstanding the past, today the U.S. is at 'a pivotal moment' one observer has noted.[138] 'Ideas that dominated for decades have been exhausted' and the need for a new approach is essential.[139] 'The precise challenges ahead are not yet known, but they are coming, and they are certain to require planning, adaptation, and durability. In this new era, a grand strategy of resilience can act as a North Star for policymakers. It will make the United States stronger, freer, and more equal, and it will preserve, protect, and strengthen democracy for the next generation.'[140]

Perhaps one place to begin is with a White House resiliency tsar, Rana Foroohar, a *Financial Times* columnist has written, 'someone who answers directly to the president and can cut through public sector bureaucracy, think across agencies and start to focus the [Biden] administration even more sharply on what it is already doing'.[141]

VI. Conclusion

The term 'resilience' underscores many of the challenges facing the U.S. in the years ahead. In particular, one key related to energy resilience, the changing climate, is a 'crisis multiplier' that threatens to initiate the 'collapse of everything that gives us our security' including food

[132] Michael Oppenheimer, 'As the World Burns: Climate Change's Dangerous Next Phase' (2020) 99 Foreign Affairs 34, 39.
[133] Cohen, 'Climate Change and the American Political Agenda' (n 128).
[134] Sitaraman, 'A Grand Strategy of Resilience: American Power in the Age of Fragility' (n 130) 165.
[135] Ibid, 173–174.
[136] Ibid, 168.
[137] Haass, 'Present at the Disruption: How Trump Unmade U.S. Foreign Policy' (n 12).
[138] Sitaraman, 'A Grand Strategy of Resilience: American Power in the Age of Fragility' (n 130) 174.
[139] Ibid.
[140] Ibid.
[141] Rana Foroohar, 'Washington needs a resiliency tsar' (24 May 2021) *Financial Times*

production, ocean food chains, access to clean water, and profoundly impacts world stability and international peace, António Guterres, UN Secretary General, said in 2021.[142]

While the term 'energy resilience' was not always found in the campaigns during the 2020 U.S. general election, the difference in approach to the topics associated with it was never far from the discussion. The differences between how the two major parties, and their presidential candidates, addressed climate change were stark. 'The two parties have long been locked in a culture war over how to address the escalating emergency', *The Guardian* reported in the run up to the elections.[143]

The presidential election results delivered a strong popular vote majority and the electoral college for Biden. In the Senate, Democrats gained a majority by the slimmest margin possible while holding control of the House but losing seats in the process. Meanwhile post-election, Trump engaged in a multi-months long process to overturn the election, despite not a hint of legitimacy to his electoral fraud claims.

Biden took office on 20 January 2021 and began to 'undo the work of [his] predecessor in many ways. But the most striking – and likely most consequential – reversal is on climate'.[144] Meanwhile the Republican Party was beset with internal divisions and in mid-year removed its third highest ranking House member, Congresswoman Liz Cheney, from her leadership position as a result of her rejection of the fictional dream that Trump won the election.

Looking back at 2020 and 2021 and ahead to 2022 and beyond, *New York Times* columnist Ezra Klein in an opinion piece titled 'What if American Democracy Fails the Climate Crisis'? observed that it was possible to consider COVID-19 a 'test run for how our political [system] would handle the disruptions of climate change. It was a crisis that experts had warned about for years and years. And we didn't really prepare at all. And then it hit'.[145] He wondered whether the experience sharpened 'our catastrophic imagination' in preparing for such a disaster or whether it was simply a 'scary lesson in how much external destruction the rich countries, if they can protect themselves, will get used to'.[146]

The 2022 mid-term U.S. election campaigns have begun. Americans will again confront the fundamental issues of whether energy resilience should be a priority and perhaps more importantly, whether their democracy will endure.

[142] 'Climate Change "Biggest Threat Modern Humans Have Ever Faced"' (23 February 2021) United Nations <https://www.un.org/press/en/2021/sc14445.doc.htm> accessed 8 August 2021.

[143] Emily Holden, 'Democrats say they have a bold climate plan – but Republicans have other plans' (30 June 2020) *The Guardian* <https://www.theguardian.com/environment/2020/jun/30/democrats-climate-stymied-political-divide> accessed 8 August 2021.

[144] Ishaan Tharoor, 'The U.S. embarks on a huge climate reset' (18 April 2021) *The Washington Post* <https://www.washingtonpost.com/world/2021/04/19/us-embarks-huge-climate-reset/> accessed 8 August 2021.

[145] Ezra Klein, 'What if American Democracy Fails the Climate Crisis?' *The New York Times* (22 June 2021) <https://www.nytimes.com/2021/06/22/magazine/ezra-klein-climate-crisis.html> accessed 8 August 2021.

[146] Ibid.

PART IV
PROJECT DEVELOPERS' LEGAL RESPONSE TO DISRUPTION

13

Force Majeure and the COVID-19 Energy Market Crash

Lessons for the Peak Oil Era

Anatole Boute[*]

I. Introduction

The COVID-19 pandemic, and in particular government and market reactions to it, in combination with a price war between the major oil producers, triggered one the largest recorded collapses of the global energy market, 'a shock like no other in its history.'[1] Oil prices reached negative levels, and energy buyers struggled to take delivery of purchased cargoes as storage capacity reached maximum levels and government-imposed lockdown measures neutralized unloading facilities. As in previous energy and economic crises, the collapse of prices and demand has encouraged buyers of fossil fuels to seek relief from their long-term purchase obligations and producers from their high-cost investment commitments.[2] Force majeure clauses—a key flexibility provision in energy contracts—have been at the centre of these attempts to obtain relief from fossil energy obligations.[3] This chapter focuses on the COVID-19 oil and gas crash, examining whether the collapse of demand and prices and government responses to the pandemic can provide force majeure relief from long-term sale-purchase agreements.

The possibility to obtain force majeure relief directly concerns the resilience that contracts provide in times of crisis. On the one hand, contracts play an important role in stabilizing the investment conditions in the capital intensive, long-term and risky energy industry.[4]

---

[*] This chapter builds on Anatole Boute, 'Environmental Force Majeure: Relief from Fossil Energy Contracts in the Decarbonisation Era' (2021) 33 Journal of Environmental Law 339–364.

[1] International Energy Agency (IEA), 'The Global Oil Industry Is Experiencing a Shock Like No Other in Its History' (2020), <https://www.iea.org/articles/the-global-oil-industry-is-experiencing-shock-like-no-other-in-its-history> accessed 28 June 2021.

[2] See e.g. A. Ason and M. Meidan, 'Force Majeure Notices from Chinese LNG Buyers: Prelude to a Renegotiation?' (2020) Oxford Institute for Energy Studies, <https://www.oxfordenergy.org/publications/force-majeure-notices-from-chinese-lng-buyers-prelude-to-a-renegotiation/> accessed 28 June 2021.

[3] See e.g. Volterra Fietta, 'Covid-19 and Force Majeure Under Oil and Gas Contracts', 30 April 2020, <https://www.volterrafietta.com/virtual-seminar-Covid-19-and-force-majeure-under-oil-and-gas-contracts/> accessed 28 June 2021; Sidley, Energy Contracts: Inoculating Against Five Misconceptions Regarding Covid-19Covid-19 Force Majeure Claims, March 16, 2020, <https://www.sidley.com/en/insights/newsupdates/2020/03/inoculating-against-five-misconceptions-regarding-covid19-force-majeure> accessed 28 June 2021. Dentons, 'Covid-19 and Force Majeure Positions on Oil & Gas Industry Standard Agreements' (2020), <https://www.dentons.com/en/insights/articles/2020/march/30/Covid-19-and-force-majeure-positions-on-og-industry-standard-agreements> accessed 28 June 2021.

[4] See e.g. L. Mistelis, 'Contractual Mechanisms for Stability in Energy Contracts' in M. Scherer (ed), *International Arbitration in the Energy Sector* (Oxford University Press 2018) 153, 154 ('overall the practice has been, for many years, for contracting parties to use contract drafting as a means of achieving the objective of

Anatole Boute, *Force Majeure and the COVID-19 Energy Market Crash* In: *Resilience in Energy, Infrastructure, and Natural Resources Law*. Edited by: Catherine Banet, Hanri Mostert, LeRoy Paddock, Milton Fernando Montoya, and Íñigo del Guayo, Oxford University Press. © Anatole Boute 2022. DOI: 10.1093/oso/9780192864574.003.0013

According to the principle of sanctity of contracts, 'a contract is binding and shall be performed as such, regardless of the burden it may impose on the parties.'[5] On the other hand, contracts integrate a certain degree of flexibility to reflect the impact that challenging natural conditions, extreme weather events, and sudden geopolitical changes can have on complex energy operations. A force majeure clause typically releases a party from liability for the failure to perform the contract to the extent that, and as long as this failure results from an event beyond the reasonable control of the party, and provided the effects could not have been reasonably avoided by the party.[6] Does the COVID-19 energy market crash constitute a force majeure event that releases or suspends the buyer from its contractual obligations, or is the buyer required to perform regardless of insufficient demand and negative prices following market meltdown?

The analysis is of broader relevance than the immediate effects of the COVID-19 pandemic on the energy industry. It has been argued that the 2020 energy market crash 'serves as a warning for the industry of what is to come' in the peak oil era.[7] The crisis is said to have accelerated peak oil demand as fossil energy consumption dropped, producers cut upstream investments, and decarbonization was placed at the centre of governments postpandemic recovery plans, at least in some jurisdictions.[8] In this context, does force majeure contribute to facilitating the adjustment to decarbonization, or does it contribute to locking the parties in their long-term carbon-intensive obligations, despite the collapse of fossil energy markets?

This chapter answers these questions by briefly introducing the 2020 energy market crash before examining force majeure clauses in energy sale-purchase agreements and their application to previous energy market crises. Contractual disputes in the energy sector are commonly brought to commercial arbitration. Given limited public awards, the following analysis builds on national decisions by English and U.S. courts on force majeure clauses in energy contracts.

II. The 2020 Energy Market Crash

In 2020, in the context of the COVID-19 pandemic, and a price war between major producers, oil and gas markets collapsed. The parties to energy contracts faced a combination of

---

stability'). See also P. Cameron, 'Stability of Contract in the International Energy Industry' (2009) 27 Journal of Energy & Natural Resources Law 305–332.

[5] Final Award in Case 15051 (Extract) (2014) 25 (2) ICC International Court of Arbitration Bulletin, para 349.

[6] See e.g. Art 15.1, BP Master Ex-Ship LNG Sale and Purchase Agreement (2019) <https://www.bp.com/en/global/bp-global-energy-trading/features-and-updates/technical-downloads/lng-master-sales-and-purchase-agreement.html> accessed 28 June 2021 (hereafter 'BP Master Ex-Ship LNG SPA'); Art 12, Trafigura LNG Master Sale and Purchase Agreement (2017) <https://www.trafigura.com/press-releases/trafigura-presents-standard-master-sales-and-purchase-agreement-mspa-for-the-lng-industry-during-gastech> accessed 28 June 2021 (hereafter 'Trafigura Master LNG SPA').

[7] D. Sheppard, 'Pandemic Crisis Offers Glimpse Into Oil Industry's Future' *Financial Times* (2 May 2020) <https://www.ft.com/content/99fc40be-83aa-11ea-b872-8db45d5f6714> accessed 28 June 2021; M. McCormick, 'Coronavirus Will Hasten 'Peak Oil' by Three Years' *Financial Times* (19 June 2020) <https://www.ft.com/content/37551636-4d8e-4334-a7b0-64a474ba055e> accessed 28 June 2021.

[8] European Commission, 'Boosting the EU's Green Recovery: Commission Invests €1 Billion in Innovative Clean Technology Projects', (Press Release, 3 July 2020) <https://ec.europa.eu/commission/presscorner/detail/en/IP_20_1250> accessed 28 June 2021.

interrelated shocks, including the sudden collapse of demand and prices, full storage facilities, and government-imposed lockdown restrictions.

A. Demand and price collapse

The general economic slowdown, together with travel restrictions, triggered a 'precipitous decline in consumption' of energy products.[9] In the U.S., for instance, demand for finished oil products reached the lowest level in decades. From March to April, the supply of finished motor gasoline and jet fuel decreased to reach the lowest monthly value since the mid-1970s.[10] Similarly, the economic crisis and quarantines imposed to combat the COVID-19 crisis caused 'the largest recorded demand shock in the history of global natural gas markets', according to the International Energy Agency.[11]

In the wake of much lower demand, energy prices collapsed, led by crude oil, which suffered a 70 per cent drop from January to April 2020.[12] In April, West Texas Intermediate (WTI) crude oil futures were traded at negative prices for the first time ever, as traders who held futures contracts close to expiration struggled to find buyers to take physical delivery and storage capacity.[13] Negative prices were limited to oil traded on the financial market. Prices of other crude oil benchmarks (e.g. Brent) also suffered a significant drop but remained positive, as did longer-term WTI prices. The collapse of oil prices impacted liquefied natural gas (LNG) transactions that continue to be indexed to oil. Spot LNG prices also fell to a record low[14] before a strong recovery at the end of the year, particularly in Asia.[15]

B. Storage crisis

As a result of the collapse of demand, oil and gas markets faced a storage crisis. As oil refineries operated at significantly lower capacity, and production did not fall quickly enough to match reductions in demand, utilization of storage capacity reached record levels. In May, storage capacity at Cushing reached 83 per cent, with much of the remaining capacity

---

[9] U.S. Energy Information Administration, 'Low Liquidity and Limited Available Storage Pushed WTI Crude Oil Futures Prices Below Zero' (2020), <https://www.eia.gov/todayinenergy/detail.php?id=43495> accessed 28 June 2021.

[10] U.S. Energy Information Administration, 'Drop in Petroleum Demand Led to Rise in Crude Oil Inventories and Low Refinery Utilization' (2020), <https://www.eia.gov/todayinenergy/detail.php?id=44316> accessed 28 June 2021.

[11] International Energy Agency, 'Gas 2020', <https://webstore.iea.org/download/direct/3005> accessed 28 June 2021.

[12] World Bank, Commodity Markets Outlook (2020), 19 <https://openknowledge.worldbank.org/bitstream/handle/10986/33624/CMO-April-2020.pdf> accessed 28 June 2021.

[13] U.S. Energy Information Administration, 'Low Liquidity' (n 9); D. Brower, D. Sheppard and A. Raval, 'What Negative US Oil Prices Mean for the Industry' *Financial Times* (21 April 2020) <https://www.ft.com/content/88997d67-bf69-409e-8155-911fc1f2fd6f> accessed 28 June 2021 .

[14] J. Jaganathan, 'Global LNG –Asian Prices Drop to Record Low as Coronavirus Slams Gas Demand' *Reuters* (3 April 2020)< https://www.reuters.com/article/global-lng/global-lng-asian-prices-drop-to-record-low-as-coronavirus-slams-gas-demand-idUSL4N2BR2MG> accessed 28 June 2021 .

[15] International Energy Agency, 'Gas Market Report Q1-2021', <https://www.iea.org/reports/gas-market-report-q1-2021> accessed 28 June 2021.

already leased or otherwise committed.[16] In April 2020, U.S. commercial oil inventories increased by 10 per cent, which was the largest monthly increase ever recorded by the U.S. Energy Information Administration.[17] In India, refineries were unable to store the excess oil resulting from significantly lower volumes of crude processing.[18] In April, 95 per cent of fuel storage capacity was full, leading refineries to dump the purchased oil on the market and seek force majeure relief from their contracts.[19] Similarly, in the gas sector, available storage space shrank rapidly. In Europe, storage peaked at record levels.[20] In China, the 'majors' decision to declare force majeure on some of their LNG cargoes in February and March, combined with injections into storage in mid-March, suggest that 'storage capacity is now close to full.'[21]

C. Government-imposed lockdown

Government orders to stay-at-home to limit the spread of coronavirus contributed to the collapse of energy demand by limiting travelling and industrial activity. At the same time, lockdown measures impacted the functioning of off-loading facilities at LNG and oil re-ceiving terminals. As government-imposed quarantines prevented workers from reaching their working place, ports experienced logistical difficulties that allegedly impacted the ability of buyers to take timely delivery of the energy they purchased based on contracts concluded before the crisis.[22]

D. Force majeure notices

Energy buyers, for example in China, issued force majeure notices seeking to cancel nat-ural gas imports, invoking the collapse of energy demand and logistical obstacles for the off-take of natural gas, including full storage capacity at the receiving terminals.[23] Force

---

[16] International Energy Agency, 'Gas 2020' <https://webstore.iea.org/download/direct/3005>; U.S. Energy Information Administration, 'Drop in Petroleum Demand Led to Rise in Crude Oil Inventories and Low Refinery Utilization' (2020) <https://www.eia.gov/todayinenergy/detail.php?id=44316> accessed 28 June 2021.

[17] U.S. Energy Information Administration, 'Drop in Petroleum' (n 10); U.S. Energy Information Administration, 'U.S. Commercial Crude Oil Inventories Reach All-time High' (2020) <https://www.eia.gov/todayinenergy/detail.php?id=44256> accessed 28 June 2021.

[18] N. Verma, 'Two Indian Refiners Declare Force Majeure to Curb Mideast Oil Supply' Reuters (28 March 2020) <https://www.reuters.com/article/us-health-coronavirus-india-refineries-e/exclusive-two-indian-refiners-decl are-force-majeure-to-curb-mideast-oil-supply-idUSKBN21E2W5> accessed 28 June 2021 .

[19] S. Sundria and D. Chakraborty, 'India's Oil Tanks Are 95% Full as Refiners Hastily Dump Fuel' BloombergQuint (2020) <https://www.bloombergquint.com/markets/oil-tanks-are-95-full-in-india-as-refiners-dump-fuel-in-haste> accessed 28 June 2021

[20] J. Henderson, 'Quarterly Gas Review: The Impact of Covid-19 on Global Gas Markets' (2020) Oxford Institute for Energy Studies <https://www.oxfordenergy.org/publications/quarterly-gas-review-issue-9/> accessed 28 June 2021 .

[21] Ibid.

[22] See e.g. Ason and Meidan (n 2).

[23] Ibid; S. Stapczynski and A. Shiryaevskaya, 'China's Natural Gas Buyer Cancels Imports After Epidemic Hurts Demand', Bloomberg, 5 March 2020, <https://www.bloomberg.com/news/articles/2020-03-05/china-s-cnpc-iss ues-lng-force-majeure-amid-virus-slowdown> accessed 28 June 2021. See also Reuters, 'Wescoal Says Eskom Declares Force Majeure on Coal Supply Agreements' Reuters (21 April 2020) <https://www.reuters.com/article/us-health-coronavirus-safrica-eskom/wescoal-says-eskom-declares-force-majeure-on-coal-supply-agreements-idUSKCN2231WS> accessed 28 June 2021.

majeure notices were also issued for pipeline gas imports from Central Asia, and exports to China were reduced by 20–25 per cent.[24] Similarly, in India, oil refiners issued force majeure notices to their suppliers in the Middle East alleging that the collapse in fuel demand, lockdown measures, and the lack of storage capacity forced them to reduce significantly crude processing capacity. Thus, the basis for force majeure notices was a combination of government-imposed lockdown, logistical obstacles affecting off-take, and falling demand. At the same time, the difference between depressed LNG prices on the spot market and much higher long-term contract prices likely incentivized the buyers to seek force majeure relief from their purchase obligations. Total has been reported to have rejected force majeure notices by referring to the fact that not all receiving terminals were not adversely impacted by the pandemic and emphasizing that, with lower spot prices, 'there is a strong temptation from some long-term customers to try to play with the force majeure concept'.[25]

III. Force majeure in energy sale-purchase agreements

Before examining the drafting of force majeure clauses in energy contracts, it is necessary to briefly introduce the contractual obligations the parties can seek to avoid based on force majeure, with a focus on LNG contracts.

A. Sale-purchase agreements

With sale-and-purchase agreements, the seller undertakes to sell and deliver, and the buyer agrees to purchase, take, and pay for a certain quantity of energy of a certain quality. For a free-on-board delivery of LNG, the LNG cargo shall be deemed to be delivered (with the transfer of title and risk of loss) as the LNG is loaded into the LNG tanker at the loading port. The buyer is responsible for transporting the LNG to the unloading port and therefore shall maintain the LNG tanker in good working order and ensure that the ship is manned with skilled operators, officers, and crew who are suitably qualified, trained, and experienced in international LNG tanker operations.[26] The seller shall maintain appropriate loading (including liquefaction) facilities and berthing facilities capable of receiving the buyer's LNG tanker.[27] With delivery-at-place (or ex-ship) contracts, title and risk of loss shall pass from seller to buyer as the LNG at the unloading port. The buyer shall therefore

---

[24] Reuters, '1-Kazakhstan Cuts Gas Supplies to China by 20-25%' *Reuters* (11 March 2020) <https://www.reuters.com/article/kazakhstan-gas-china/update-1-kazakhstan-cuts-gas-supplies-to-china-by-20-25-idUSL8N2B41HT> accessed 28 June 2021.

[25] B. Felix and J. Jaganathan, 'France's Total Rejects Force Majeure Notice from Chinese LNG Buyer' *Reuters* (6 February 2020), <https://www.reuters.com/article/us-china-health-total/frances-total-rejects-force-majeure-notice-from-chinese-lng-buyer-idUSKBN2001XQ> accessed 28 June 2021; Ason and Meidan (n 2) at 7.

[26] Art 5, International Group of Liquefied Natural Gas Importers (GIIGNL) Master FOB LNG Sales Agreement 2011 <https://giignl.org/system/files/111231_giignl_fob_msa2011_final_.pdf> accessed 28 June 2021 (hereafter 'GIIGNL Master FOB LNG Sales Agreement'); Art 11, AIPN Master LNG SPA 2009.

[27] Art 5, GIIGNL Master FOB LNG Sales Agreement 2011.

maintain berthing, unloading, storage, and regasification facilities in good working order and of appropriate design and sufficient capacity to take delivery of the LNG cargo.[28]

LNG contracts are characterized by an increasing degree of flexibility, reflecting the increasing liquidity of the global LNG market. Short-term contracts are replacing long-term arrangements, initially aimed at providing investment certainty to investors in gas production and LNG infrastructure. Hub-based prices replace oil-indexation, and contracts can contain price review clauses enabling the parties (or an arbitral tribunal) to adjust the price formula to reflect changes to the energy market conditions and the level of market prices.[29] Destination clauses, preventing the buyer from redirecting its cargo to other markets, and profit-sharing clauses, requiring the buyer to share with the seller the profits made of a rediverted cargo, are being removed from LNG contracts. The parties can agree to reschedule the delivery of the LNG Cargo as soon as it anticipates that it will not be able to receive or deliver the cargo.[30]

B.   Force majeure clause

The purpose of a force majeure clause in commercial contracts is to release a party from liability for the failure to perform any of its contractual obligations in case of external disruption.[31] Depending on the applicable law, the parties are free to define the conditions, scope, and consequences of force majeure.[32] The events which trigger the force majeure clause 'are specifically and relatively narrowly confined. They do not comprehend events which might be treated as force majeure in other contracts'.[33] However, given the widespread use and influence of model agreements in the energy industry,[34] contracts tend to adopt comparable definitions of force majeure, with key variables available to the parties.

A force majeure event must usually be beyond the reasonable control of a party and could not have been avoided by that party, acting as a 'reasonable and prudent operator'.[35] This normally implies that the event occurred after the contract was concluded, as 'a party undertaking an obligation assumes the risk of any conditions pre-existing the entry into of the contract'.[36] It can also imply that the event was unforeseeable at the time of concluding the contract, taking into account that the parties should have taken steps to address

---

[28]   Art 8.1, BP Master Ex-Ship LNG SPA.
[29]   J. Freeman and M. Levy (eds), Gas and LNG Price Arbitrations: A Practical Handbook (2nd edn, Globe Law and Business 2020); G. Block, 'Arbitration and Changes in Energy Prices: A Review of ICC Awards with Respect to Force Majeure, Indexation, Adaptation, Hardship and Take-or-pay Clauses' (2009) ICC International Court of Arbitration Bulletin 51.
[30]   See e.g. Art 6, Trafigura LNG Master SPA; Art 3, GIIGNL Master FOB LNG Sales Agreement.
[31]   C. Brunner, Force Majeure and Hardship under General Contract Principles: Exemption for Non-performance in International Arbitration (Wolters Kluwer 2008) 383.
[32]   See e.g. Wisconsin Electric Power Co. v Union Pacific Railroad Co., 557 F.3d 504 (7th Cir. 2009); Great Elephant Corporation v Trafigura Beheer BV, The Crudesky [2013] EWCA Civ 905 [25]. On English law in energy contracts, see e.g. P. Roberts, Petroleum Contracts: English Law and Practice (Oxford University Press 2013).
[33]   Transocean Drilling UK Ltd v Providence Resources plc (The Arctic III), [2014] EWHC 4260 (Comm), 2012 Folio 1560, at 52.
[34]   See e.g. K. Talus, S. Looper, and S. Otillar, 'Lex Petrolea and the Internationalization of Petroleum Agreements' (2012) 5(3) JWELB 181.
[35]   Art 15.1, BP Master Ex-Ship LNG SPA; Art 12, Trafigura LNG Master SPA.
[36]   Final Award in Case 19149 (Extract) ICC Dispute Resolution Bulletin 2015 No. 2, para 353.

a foreseeable event.[37] Once the force majeure event occurs, the affected party is usually required to take all 'reasonable measures' to remove its inability to fulfil the terms of the contract with a minimum of delay and impact.[38] The payment of money is usually excluded from the scope of force majeure clauses, but this exception can be limited to payments that are due so as to enable the buyer to escape its payment obligation if the delivery or off-take of the energy is impeded by force majeure.

Epidemics can be explicitly listed as force majeure events, besides 'acts of God', such as fire, flood, storm, typhoon, hurricane, and earthquake.[39] However, the outbreak of an epidemic is on its own insufficient to justify the non-performance of the contract. The general conditions of force majeure still have to be met, such as a disruption preventing performance, that is beyond the reasonable control of the party.

Force majeure can excuse performance for the period of time during which the party was unable to perform its obligation as a result of force majeure. In sale-and-purchase agreements, force majeure clauses can require the parties to use 'reasonable efforts' to reschedule the delivery if, as a result of force majeure, the buyer is not able to receive or the seller is not able to deliver the LNG cargo.[40] If these efforts fail, either party can be entitled to cancel the LNG cargo without any liability.[41] Alternatively, the sale and purchase or exploration and production obligations can be terminated without liability if force majeure prevents the affected party from performing its obligations for a number of days or months, as determined in the contract.[42]

Economic changes, if covered in the contract, are rarely listed as force majeure but under a specific 'economic hardship' clause.[43] In contrast to force majeure, typical economic hardship clauses do not suspend the contract but require renegotiation to restore its economic balance.[44] Energy contracts can explicitly exclude economic hardship, or the 'loss of buyer's market' and the 'changes in market conditions', from the definition of force majeure.[45] In more exceptional cases, force majeure clauses can excuse performance if it would place an unreasonable economic burden on the affected party.[46]

---

[37] *Great Elephant Corporation* (n 32) ('It does not seem to me that the word "unforeseeable" adds much to the concept of "within reasonable control" '). See, however, *Sabine Corp. v ONG Western, Inc.,* 725 F. Supp. 1157, 1162, 1989 U.S. Dist. LEXIS 13425, *1-4, 11 U.C.C. Rep. Serv. 2d (Callaghan) 83, 107 Oil & Gas Rep. 292 (W.D. Okla. August 9, 1989) ('Nowhere does the force majeure clause specify that an event or cause must be unforeseeable to be a force majeure event. The focus of the clause is upon a party's ability to control rather than its ability to foresee the alleged cause.'); and Final Award in Case 19149 (Extract) ICC Dispute Resolution Bulletin 2015 No. 2, para 353.

[38] See e.g. Art 22. 4, Petroleum Agreement by and among the Government of the Republic of Ghana, Ghana National Petroleum Corporation, GNPC Exploration and Production Company Limited, A-Z Petroleum Products Ghana Limited, Eco Atlantic Oil and Gas Ghana Limited, Petrogulf Limited Concerning the Deepwater Cape Three Point West Offshore Block, July 2014.

[39] Art 12, Trafigura LNG Master SPA; Art 13, AIPN Master LNG SPA 2012; Art 15, BP Master Ex-Ship LNG SPA; Art 18.2.1, Long-term Sale and Purchase Agreement between Pakistan State Oil Company Limited and Qatar Liquified Gas Company Limited, 10 February 2016.

[40] Art 15.9, BP Master LNG SPA; Art 13, AIPN Master LNG SPA 2012.

[41] Art 15.9, BP Master LNG SPA.

[42] Art 12(7), GIIGNL Master FOB LNG Sales Agreement 2011; Art 22.8 Deepwater Cape Three Point West Offshore; Art 24.4, Petroleum Agreement between the Government of the Cooperative Republic of Guyana and Esso Exploration and Production Guyana Limited, CNOOC Nexen Petroleum Guyana Limited, Hess Guyana Exploration Limited, 2016.

[43] Block (n 29).

[44] See e.g. Block (n 29) at 55.

[45] See e.g. Art 13, AIPN Master LNG SPA 2012.

[46] See e.g. Art 10 'Accord-cadre pour l'accès régulé à l'électricité nucléaire historique', defining force majeure as a party's inability to perform its obligations 'under reasonable economic conditions' (Arrêté du 12 mars 2019

Besides 'acts of god', force majeure events can also cover 'acts of government', for example the 'compliance by the Affected Party with an act, regulation, order or demand of a Competent Authority'.[47] To avoid the risk of collusion between the government and national energy companies, energy contracts can exclude from the scope of force majeure regulations that specifically target the transaction. For instance, BP's Master Ex-Ship LNG Sale Purchase Agreement excludes from the scope of force majeure the 'compliance by the Affected Party with an act, regulation, order or demand of a Competent Authority ... in circumstances where such act, regulation, order or demand affects solely or primarily the Affected Party and is not generally applicable to Persons doing business in the same country'.[48] This is particularly relevant for contracts concluded by state-owned enterprises, taking into account the interest of the government in protecting the commercial interest of companies in which it has a stake.

IV. Take or pay and force majeure

Force majeure has been invoked by parties to energy supply agreements, seeking relief from their sale-purchase obligations following sudden and drastic changes to energy commodity prices and transportation costs. In take-or-pay contracts, a first question is how strictly tribunals interpret the buyer's obligation to take and pay for the energy and whether there is at all scope for force majeure under a strict interpretation of take-or-pay.

A literal interpretation of the inability to take delivery of energy can 'lead to absurd results', taking into account that a buyer 'could never be "unable" to take gas; [it] could always take the gas and vent it into the air, even if its facilities were completely destroyed'.[49] To avoid this absurd result, tribunals in the U.S. have accepted that performance by the buyer could be excused 'when made impracticable'.[50]

Furthermore, the buyer in a take-or-pay agreement in principle always has the possibility of paying for the energy, even if it is prevented from taking delivery. Although a strict interpretation of the requirement to pay would neutralize the relevance of a force majeure clause, tribunals have rejected force majeure when the buyer faced obstacles to taking the energy but could still pay for it.[51] However, it has also been accepted that force majeure does not require the buyer to prove that it was both unable to take and pay for the gas, as this interpretation would 'render the force majeure clause nugatory'.[52]

---

portant modification de l'arrêté du 28 avril 2011 pris en application du II de l'article 4-1 de la loi n° 2000-108 relative à la modernisation et au développement du service public de l'électricité <https://www.legifrance.gouv.fr/eli/arrete/2019/3/12/TRER1907101A/jo/texte> accessed 28 June 2021.

[47] Art 15.1, e), BP Master LNG SPA. See also Art 20, Crude Oil Sales Agreement between PDVSA-Petroleo S.A. and Nustar Marketing LLC, 1 March 2008 <https://www.sec.gov/Archives/edgar/data/1110805/00011931250 8064276/dex101.htm> accessed 28 June 2021, referring to 'any Government measure ('Sovereign Acts').'
[48] Art 15.2, c), BP Master LNG SPA. See also Art 13, AIPN Master LNG SPA 2012.
[49] See *International Minerals and Chemical Corp. v Llano, Inc.*, 770 F.2d 879, 886 (10th Cir. 1985).
[50] Ibid.
[51] For instance, U.S. courts refused to recognize that the closure of power plants constituted force majeure, as the buyer could pay shortfall fees if the minimum volumes of energy could not be used. See *Drummond Coal Sales, Inc. v Norfolk S. Ry. Co.*, 2018 U.S. Dist. LEXIS 143047 (W.D. Va. Aug. 22, 2018). See also *International Minerals and Chemical Corp. v Llano, Inc.*, 881.
[52] *Sabine Corp.* (n 37). See also P. Roberts, *Gas and LNG Sales and Transportation Agreements: Principles and Practice* (Sweet & Maxwell 2017), at 310.

V. Demand and price collapse as force majeure

Based on previous arbitral and judicial practice, the collapse of demand and price in the context of the 2020 energy market crash is unlikely to trigger the application of force majeure, unless economic hardship was included in the definition of force majeure.

A. Market meltdown

In previous energy crises, courts have refused to consider market meltdown as a force majeure event.[53] Lower prices and falling market demand do not prevent buyers of energy from purchasing and using that energy, even if this becomes unprofitable.[54] For instance, the general deterioration of the oil market in the context of the 1973 Oil Shock was seen as a foreseeable risk that did not have a catastrophic impact on social conditions, as a war or earthquake would have.[55] Even the closure of the Suez Canal in 1956—one of the most significant disruptions of the global energy industry—did not excuse shippers from performing their contractual obligation. Although the route round the Cape of Good Hope was more than twice as long and increased transportation expenses by one-third, it was a well-recognized alternative that enabled transportation of the cargo to the agreed destination.[56]

In *United States v Panhandle Eastern Corp.*, a case concerning the performance of an LNG purchase agreement concluded at high prices in the context of the 1973 oil crisis, the U.S. buyer sought to obtain relief from its purchase obligation by presenting the 'unprecedented reduction in prices' that followed the crisis as force majeure events that threatened the company's financial viability.[57] Force majeure was limited to events that affected the LNG facilities and could not be overcome by 'the taking of reasonable measures at a reasonable cost.' However, the clause did not expressly provide that adverse economic or market conditions may constitute force majeure. On this basis, the court excluded the alleged economic hardship resulting from market fluctuations from the ambit of the force majeure clause and ruled that 'ordinarily, only when a force majeure clause specifically includes the event alleged to have prevented performance, will a party be excused from performance. This maxim is especially true where the event relied upon to avoid performance is a market fluctuation.'[58]

---

[53] G. Treitel, *Frustration and Force Majeure* (Sweet & Maxwell 2014).

[54] *Northern Illinois Gas Co. v Energy Cooperative, Inc.*, 461 N.E.2d 1049.

[55] *Hungarian State Enterprise v Jugoslavenski naftovod* (6 July 1983), in International Council for Commercial Arbitration, *Yearbook, Commercial Arbitration IX* (1984), Kluwer Law International, 69; ICC Case No. 2478 (1974), in Jarvin and Derains, pp 25–27. See also M. Reza Firoozmand and J. Zamani, 'Force Majeure in International Contracts: Current Trends and How International Arbitration Practice Is Responding' (2017) 33 *Arbitration International* 410.

[56] See e.g. *American Trading & Production Corp. v Shell International Marine, Ltd.*, 343 F. Supp. 91, 1971 U.S. Dist. LEXIS 12334 (S.D.N.Y. July 22, 1971) United States District Court for the Southern District of New York; *Glidden Co. v Hellenic Lines, Ltd.*, 275 F.2d 253, 1960 U.S. App. LEXIS 5276 (2d Cir. N.Y. February 26, 1960), United States Court of Appeals for the Second Circuit; *Tsakiroglou & Co Ltd v Noblee Thorl GmbH*, [1962] AC 93, [1961] 2 All ER 179, [1961] 2 WLR 633, [1961] 1 Lloyd's Rep 329, House of Lords; *Ocean Tramp Tankers Corpn v V/O Sovfracht, The Eugenia*, [1964] 2 QB 226, [1964] 1 All ER 161, [1964] 2 WLR 114, [1963] 2 Lloyd's Rep 381, Court of Appeal; *Société Franco Tunisienne d'Armement v Sidermar SpA, The Massalia*, [1961] 2 QB 278, [1960] 2 All ER 529, [1960] 3 WLR 701, [1960] 1 Lloyd's Rep 594, Queen's Bench Division.

[57] *United States v Panhandle Eastern Corp.*, United States District Court for the District of Delaware, August 15, 1988, 693 F. Supp. 88, 1988 U.S. Dist. LEXIS 10024.

[58] Ibid.

Similarly, in *Langham-Hill Petroleum, Inc. v Southern Fuels Co.*, a U.S. oil trader unsuccessfully invoked the 'dramatic drop in world oil prices' in 1986 to evade its obligation to purchase significant quantities of oil at a fixed price according to a 1985 contract. As the collapse of the price of oil resulted from Saudi Arabia's attempt to regain market share, the buyer relied on its 'helplessness in the face of Saudi Arabian action and its inability to remain in business if it had satisfied the contract'. However, the court rejected this force majeure defence by declining to consider Saudi Arabia's influence on the market as an event that was 'outside the control' of the buyer.[59]

Given the volatility of energy markets, sudden and drastic price changes are a normal phenomenon in the energy industry.[60] Parties to major energy agreements are usually specialized companies with expertise in energy trading.[61] Price changes are a foreseeable risk, which the parties as professionals should know and are expected to have properly allocated in the contract.[62] In fact, the 'uncertainty of future market prices is often the motivation for entering into a long-term contract.'[63] Long-term energy contracts, by contrast to spot trading, aim to stabilize price and volume conditions and so avoid the risk of price fluctuation. Furthermore, large energy companies are capable of spreading the risk of price fluctuations and even turning price increases to their general advantage.[64]

B. Economic hardship and force majeure

However, in *Kodiak 1981 Drilling Partnership v Delhi Gas Pipeline Corp*, the U.S. Court of Appeals of Texas accepted that the 'drastic decline' in the gas market in 1982, caused by the economic recession, a plummeting crude oil price, weather conditions, and a decline of the drilling market, amounted to force majeure. A determining element in this decision was the broad definition of force majeure in the applicable gas supply agreement, as the 'partial or entire failure to gas supply or market ... not reasonably within the control' of the affected party.[65] More recently, in the context of COVID-19, the Tribunal de commerce de Paris ruled that the impact of COVID-19 on the French electricity market constituted force majeure for energy buyers, taking into account the inclusion of 'unreasonable economic conditions' in the contractual definition of force majeure.[66]

Accordingly, an appeal for force majeure relief based on market collapse, of the type seen in the context of the COVID-19 pandemic, is only likely to be successful if economic

---

[59] *Langham-Hill Petroleum, Inc. v Southern Fuels Co.*, 813 F.2d 1327, 1328, 1987 United States Court of Appeals for the Fourth Circuit LEXIS 3590, *1, 7 Fed. R. Serv. 3d (Callaghan) 321 (4th Cir. Md. March 19, 1987).

[60] Firoozmand and Zamani (n 55) at 413.

[61] Ibid, at 40.

[62] See e.g. *Valero Transmission Co. v Mitchell Energy Co.*, 743 S.W.2d 658, 660 (Tex. App.—Houston [1st Dist.] 1987, no writ) ('An economic downturn in the market for a product is not such an unforeseeable occurrence that would justify application of the force majeure provision.') See also Final Award in Case 11253 (Extract) ICC International Court of Arbitration Bulletin Vol. 21 No. 1.

[63] *Valero Transmission Co. v Mitchell Energy Co* (n 62).

[64] Treitel (n 53) at 263 and 268; *Eastern Air Lines, Inc. v Gulf Oil Corp.*, 415 F. Supp. 429.

[65] *Kodiak 1981 Drilling P'ship v Delhi Gas Pipeline Corp.*, 736 S.W.2d 715 (Tex. App. 1987), writ refused NRE (Oct. 7, 1987) 724.

[66] *Total Direct Energie SA and Association Française Indépendente de l'Electricité et du Gaz v Electricité de France SA*, Tribunal de commerce de Paris, Ordonnance de référé, 20 May 2020.

hardship (or performance under unreasonable economic conditions) has been included in the contract's definition of force majeure.[67]

C. COVID-19 as sole and proximate cause to the market crash

To excuse performance under a force majeure clause, the event relied upon must have been the sole[68] or proximate[69] cause of the failure to perform. Where two causes operate to prevent a party from performing its contractual obligations, 'a force majeure notice has to be given in respect of each of them.'[70] The force majeure event must have occurred after the contract was entered into, as the parties must be assumed to have factored conditions pre-existing the conclusion of the contract.[71] If the alleged force majeure event occurs in the context of challenging market conditions, it can be difficult to prove that the alleged event caused the failure to perform and not the deteriorating market.

In *Wheeling Valley Coal Corp. v Mead*, a case concerning the closure of a coal mine, the investor sought to justify the discontinuance of its mining operations based on new regulations increasing the cost of producing coal.[72] The U.S. Court of Appeals for the Fourth Circuit rejected this argument by ruling that the 'real cause' of the closure was the financial weakness of the operator. The regulatory measures 'were mere aggravating circumstances of a bad financial condition arising out of lack of sufficient operating capital and high operating costs.'[73]

There is no doubt that the COVID-19 pandemic contributed to further depressing energy prices (culminating in negative prices) and undermining the financial condition of energy market players. However, given pre-existing overproduction and a price war between the major oil producers,[74] the COVID-19 crisis may not be seen as the sole cause of the market collapse[75] and may even be seen as a 'mere aggravating circumstance' of an already bad situation.[76]

---

[67] Tribunals also tend to be careful in the application of the hardship clause to changes in price and market conditions. Hardship requires an unforeseeable and sufficiently significant change of the circumstances upon which the parties relied when concluding the contract. Given the known volatility of energy markets, it is difficult to argue that price fluctuations can cause hardship, unless the magnitude of the price change exceeded the parties' expectations considerably. For instance, a threefold increase of the price of oil in the context of global market turbulences was considered insufficient to justify withholding the delivery of oil and renegotiating the balance of the contract. See ICC Case No. 2508 (1976), in Jarvin and Derains, at 292-296. See also Final Award in Case 15051, ICC International Court of Arbitration Bulletin Vol. 25 No. 2, 2014, at 377; and Block (n 29) at 53; Firoozmand and Zamani (n 55) 409.

[68] *Seadrill Ghana Operations; Intertradex SA v Lesieur-Tourteaux SARL* (1978) 2 Lloyd's Reports 509.

[69] ibid; *Swift & Co. v Columbia R., Gas Electric Co.,* 17 F.2d 46, 1927 U.S. App. LEXIS 2902, *1-16, 51 A.L.R. 983 (4th Cir. S.C. January 11, 1927) Circuit Court of Appeals, Fourth Circuit; *Wheeling Valley Coal Corp. v Mead*, 186 F.2d 219, 1950 U.S. App. LEXIS 3685, *1-15, 28 A.L.R.2d 1007 (4th Cir. W. Va. December 20, 1950) United States Court of Appeals for the Fourth Circuit; *Berwind-White Coal Mining Co. v Solleveld*, 11 F.2d 80, 1926 U.S. App. LEXIS 2433 (4th Cir. Va. January 18, 1926) Circuit Court of Appeals, Fourth Circuit.

[70] *Seadrill Ghana Operations* (n 68).

[71] Final Award in Case 19149 (Extract) ICC Dispute Resolution Bulletin 2015 No. 2, at 353; Final Award in Case 11265 (Extract) ICC International Court of Arbitration Bulletin Vol. 20 No. 2.

[72] *Wheeling Valley Coal Corp. v Mead* (n 69).

[73] Ibid.

[74] International Energy Agency, 'Gas 2020' (n 11) (the 'Covid-19 pandemic hit an already declining gas demand'). See also B. Fattouh and A. Economou, 'Oil Supply Shock in the Time of the Coronavirus', Oxford Institute for Energy Studies (2020), <https://www.oxfordenergy.org/wpcms/wp-content/uploads/2020/03/Oil-Supply-Shock-in-the-time-of-the-Coronavirus.pdf> accessed 28 June 2021.

[75] *Seadrill Ghana Operations* (n 68).

[76] *Wheeling Valley Coal Corp.* (n 69).

VI. Disruption of unloading facilities as force majeure

Tribunals are unlikely to accept more expensive loading, transportation, and unloading as a force majeure event excusing non-performance of the contract if delivery of the energy remains possible. Insufficient storage capacity at the contractually agreed terminals is also unlikely to excuse the buyer from its obligation to take delivery. By contrast, the government-imposed lockdown measures provide a much stronger basis to suspend the performance of energy contracts under force majeure, if not the only basis for contracts with force majeure clauses excluding economic hardship.

A. Scarcity of storage and unloading capacity

Similarly to the 2020 energy crash, in *Classic Maritime Inc v Lion Diversified Holdings Berhad*, a steel company in Malaysia tried to obtain relief from its purchase obligation of iron ore following the collapse of global demand for steel in the wake of the 2008 economic crisis.[77] As the iron ore in the buyer's storage yards was not used up at the usual rate, there was insufficient storage capacity for new shipments. The force majeure clause explicitly covered the receiver's 'failure to discharge the cargo' resulting from any cause beyond the receiver's control. The steel company argued on this basis that, because its storage yards were full, it was impossible to discharge the vessel, preventing the performance of its obligation to take delivery. The High Court of England and Wales rejected this defence by emphasizing the absence of evidence of alternative options of taking the cargo out of the vessel. Full storage yards, as a result of lower steel production during the 2008 financial crisis, did not relieve the buyer from taking delivery of the shipment of iron ore, as the buyer did not demonstrate that there were no alternative options to taking the cargo out of the vessel 'for all forms of disposal, however uneconomic.' While it was understandable from a commercial perspective that the buyer wanted the cargo to be used for the intended purpose of steel production at its plants, all possibilities of discharging the cargo, 'albeit doubtless uneconomically and with resultant waste', had to be eliminated, before force majeure could be successfully triggered.[78] 'Impossibility of storage, even if proved, does not establish impossibility of discharge.'[79]

Similarly, in the context of the 2008 crisis, a coal trader unsuccessfully invoked the unavailability of storage capacity to escape the purchase obligations it undertook before the crisis.[80] The trader's stockpile capacity was full because market conditions depressed demand and its buyers were not taking all the coal they had contracted to purchase. The definition of force majeure in the mining lease included the 'refusal, failure or inability of any customer(s) to receive and purchase quantities of coal mined which such customer(s) had committed to receive and purchase.'[81] However, the U.S. court refused to accept that this broad definition covered the storage problems that resulted from the precipitous drop in the

---

[77] *Classic Maritime Inc v Lion Diversified Holdings Berhad* [2009] EWHC 1142 (Comm) [62].
[78] Ibid.
[79] Ibid.
[80] *Miller Bros. Coal, LLC v Consol of Ky., Inc. (In re Clearwater Natural Res., LP.)*, 421 B.R. 392, 2009 Bankr. LEXIS 3934 (Bankr. E.D. Ky. December 11, 2009).
[81] Ibid.

price of coal and the resulting failure to secure new contracts to sell the coal, as the agreement did not protect the buyer from such market risk.

Force majeure clauses in energy contracts can address disruptions specifically related to the technical operations of loading and unloading facilities.[82] However, unless energy sale-purchase agreements explicitly mention the scarcity of storage capacity as force majeure, buyers of oil and LNG are unlikely to be able to invoke full storage as a force majeure event excusing performance of their obligation to take delivery.

B. Government-imposed lockdown as force majeure

Force majeure clauses in energy contracts can include industrial disturbances, such as a strike or a 'lockout',[83] i.e. measures by an employer preventing workers from entering their place of work until they agree to particular employment conditions.[84] Tribunals have recognized strikes as force majeure events preventing the performance of energy contracts, including oil production and the loading of oil to tankers.[85] For instance, in *Phillips Petroleum Co Iran v The Islamic Republic of Iran*, the tribunal found that in the context of the Iranian revolution, the affected party had been forced 'to reduce and ultimately to cease production because of strikes ... which prevented oil from being loaded onto tankers'.[86] However, health-related 'lockdowns', based on government orders, have not explicitly been included in the definition of force majeure in the major energy contracts publicly available, and it is possible that the COVID-19 crisis will trigger a revision of force majeure clauses to include this disturbance.

The common requirement in force majeure clauses that the affected party took all reasonable measures to avoid and remove its inability to perform could possibly be interpreted as requiring opposition to lockdown measures.[87] In *Karaha Bodas Company v Pertamina and PLN*, for instance, the arbitral tribunal ruled that the government's decision to delay the construction of a power plant did not provide force majeure relief to the state-owned electricity company, as the latter 'fail[ed] to do its best efforts to reverse the Governmental decision, although it ... [was] in a position to efficiently intervene.'[88] In the context of COVID-19, requiring energy companies to oppose lockdown measures would raise serious legitimacy concerns, taking into account the importance of these measures in combating the pandemic.

---

[82] See e.g. Trafigura Master LNG SPA; GIIGNL Master LNG SPA; AIPN Master LNG SPA.

[83] See e.g. Art 15, BP Master LNG SPA; Art 18.2.1, Long-term Sale and Purchase Agreement between Pakistan State Oil Company Limited and Qatar Liquified Gas Company Limited, 10 February 2016.

[84] 'Lockout', Cambridge Dictionary, <https://dictionary.cambridge.org/dictionary/english/lockout>.

[85] Firoozmand and Zamani (n 55) at 402.

[86] See e.g. *Phillips Petroleum Co Iran v The Islamic Republic of Iran et al.*, Award No. 425-39-2 (29 June 1989). See, however, *Caltex Oil (Australia) Pty Ltd v Howard Smith Industries Pty Ltd (The 'Howard' Smith)* (1973) 1 Lloyd's Re 544.

[87] See e.g. K.-H. Böckstiegel, 'Enterprise v. State: the New David and Goliath?' (2007) 23(1) Arbitration International, 102, arguing that acts of state cannot be considered as force majeure if 'available remedies against the act were not exhausted.'

[88] *Karaha Bodas Company L.L.C. v Perusahaan Pertambangan Minyak Dan Gas Bumi Negara ('Pertamina') and PT.PLN (Persero) ('PLN')*, Final Award, 18 December 2000, [2001] (16) Mealey's International Arbitration Report C2-C17, para 64. See also *Jordan Investments Ltd v Soiuznefteksport*, discussed in Firoozmand and Zamani (n 55) 405; MD Aubrey, 'Frustration Reconsidered – Some Comparative Aspects' [1963] ICLQ 1183.

Contracts can seek to mitigate the risk of governments adopting regulations aiming to ex-cuse the performance of contracts that are no longer profitable by limiting force majeure to acts of government 'which are discriminatory towards' the other party.[89] In *Krupp-Koppers GmbH v Kopex*, the arbitral tribunal ruled that 'unilateral and specific interference of the State with contracts already entered into, by which the contracting parties are discharged of their contractual obligations is unacceptable under the principle of good faith.'[90] In *Okta Crude Oil Refinery AD v Mamidoil-Jetoil Greek Petroleum Company*, a 2003 case concerning the processing of crude oil and its supply to the Former Yugoslav Republic of Macedonia, it appeared that the national oil company persuaded the government to issue an order not to perform an oil supply agreement that became too expensive.[91] Although the agreement recognized as force majeure 'acts or compliance with requests of any government authority', the tribunal refused to accept that the government's order was 'beyond the control' of the oil company as there was evidence that the order was adopted at its request.[92] By contrast, in *Jordan Investments Ltd. v Sojuznefteksport*, a case concerning the export of oil to Israel in the context of the 1956 Israel–Egypt war, the tribunal accepted that the opposition of the Soviet government to the export transaction constituted a force majeure event that justified the Soviet state-owned enterprise to terminate the contract.[93] Although the government intervened with a specific transaction, its decision was not driven by financial concerns but pursued more general geopolitical purposes, in particular 'to impress Arab countries with the prohibition of oil deliveries to Israel.'[94]

Applied to COVID-19, state-owned enterprises will most likely have no difficulty proving that the lockdown measures that prevented the unloading of LNG were taken in the pursuit of a general consideration, in particular, to combat the virus. Although the state-owned enterprise—and thus indirectly the government—had an interest in withdrawing from un-profitable LNG purchase obligations following the collapse of LNG prices, lockdown meas-ures did not just affect the state-owned entities but applied to all economic players. The widespread use of lockdowns over the world to combat the virus supports this conclusion.

VII. Force majeure in the peak oil era:
essons from the 2020 energy market crash

Peak oil no longer refers to concerns of oil scarcity but now reflects the expectation that de-carbonization will cause the demand for fossil energies to drop and prices to collapse.[95] As

---

[89] Art 18.2.1, Long-term Sale and Purchase Agreement between Pakistan State Oil Company Limited and Qatar Liquified Gas Company Limited, 10 February 2016. See also Art 13, AIPN Master LNG Sale and Purchase Agreement 2012.

[90] *Krupp-Koppers GmbH v Kopex* (1983) International Council for Commercial Arbitration, Yearbook, Commercial Arbitration IX (1987), Kluwer Law International, at 74.

[91] *Okta Crude Oil Refinery AD v Mamidoil-Jetoil Greek Petroleum Company Sa and another* (2003) EWCA Civ 1031 Court of Appeal (Civil Division) 17 July 2003.

[92] Ibid.

[93] *Jordan Investments Ltd. v Sojuznefteksport (1958)* 53 AJIL (1959) 800–806.

[94] M. Domke, 'The Israeli-Soviet Oil Arbitration' (1959) 53 American Journal of International Law 187, 800.

[95] See e.g. S. Dale and B. Fattouh, 'Peak Oil Demand and Long-Run Oil Prices' (2018) Oxford Institute for Energy Studies <https://www.oxfordenergy.org/publications/peak-oil-demand-long-run-oil-prices> accessed 28 June 2021. See also J. Baffes et al, 'The Great Plunge in Oil Prices: Causes, Consequences, and Policy Responses' (2015) World Bank Group Policy Research Note<http://pubdocs.worldbank.org/en/339801451407117632/PRN01Mar2015OilPrices.pdf> accessed 28 June 2021.

the 2020 energy market crash 'serves as a warning for the industry of what is to come' in the peak oil era,[96] the above analysis provides elements of answer on the question of force majeure relief from carbon-intensive obligations in the peak oil era.

Force majeure clauses do not relieve an energy buyer from its purchase obligations in cases where prices and demand for energy collapse, unless the definition of force majeure under the applicable contract specifically included economic hardship. Problematically, the parties are required to perform their obligations, even if this results in wasteful behaviour. In *Classic Maritime Inc v Lion Diversified Holdings Berhad,* for instance, the buyer had to eliminate all possibilities of discharging the cargo, 'albeit doubtless uneconomically and with resultant waste'.[97] Supply of energy at depressed prices, and the obligation to take delivery of energy even when there is no longer sufficient demand, incentivizes irrational energy use and is thus incompatible with decarbonization.

A severe regulatory interference preventing a party from taking delivery of energy, such as a government-imposed lockdown measure neutralizing all unloading facilities can excuse that party from its contractual obligations, provided the contract includes 'acts of government' in the definition of force majeure. Similarly, in the peak oil era, stringent decarbonization regulation (e.g. a ban on coal or emission limits that leave inefficient installations no other choice but to close) could in principle qualify as 'acts of government' excusing the performance of long-term fossil energy agreements.

However, the condition that force majeure has to be beyond the control of the affected party can raise legitimacy concerns if it requires resistance to the adoption and implementation of government regulations. Given the urgency to act on climate change, energy companies, including state-owned entities, should be encouraged to cooperate with ambitious decarbonization efforts and not dig in their heels.

---

[96] Sheppard (n 7); McCormick (n 7).
[97] *Classic Maritime Inc.* (n 77).

14

Extreme Natural Event Impacts on the Energy Sector and its Regulation

Canada and North America

Alastair R. Lucas

I. Introduction

The Canadian energy sector plunged during the spring 2020 COVID-19 first wave of infections. Oil production declined precipitously, particularly in the key oil sands sector, as pandemic closure orders took effect.[1] As elsewhere, vehicle and aircraft use decreased significantly. Pipeline space opened and large-scale rail shipping, implemented only months before when pipelines were full, shrank to insignificance. This, with oil and gas, recovering from a pre-pandemic price shock that saw oil prices fall to negative levels[2] as commodity prices fell and financial markets tumbled. Yet four months later, Canadian and U.S. financial markets not only began to recover but by August 2020 were in full bull market mode. The Toronto Stock Exchange (TSX) moved beyond pre-pandemic levels, while the U.S. Dow Jones index hit record levels.[3] However, in the longer term, this must be tempered. Both the Canadian Energy Regulator and the International Energy Agency (IEA) in studies discussed below conclude that Canadian oil production will grow but is unlikely to recover to pre-pandemic growth levels.

This chapter assesses energy sector resilience in the face of extreme natural events, particularly the COVID-19 pandemic. The focus is the responses and approaches of Canadian oil and gas regulatory agencies, as well as direct government action. What legal and policy tools were marshalled? What investigative and decision processes were used? Can resilience features be identified? The chapter's scope takes into account the North American scale energy integration, including oil and gas markets and pipeline and powerline infrastructure. A case study is developed around the 2020–2021 COVID-19 pandemic.

In November 2020, Tiff Macklem, Bank of Canada Governor, speaking in a panel discussion on COVID-19 and Canadian competitiveness, said:

> These issues are taking on an increased urgency... Today's pandemic seems to have focused the public's attention on extreme global risks and the value of resilience...How well

---

[1] M. Refaei et al, 'Economic Recovery Pathways for Canada's Energy Industry: Part 2 - Canadian Crude Oil and Natural Gas', Canadian Energy Research Institute, (Calgary, AB, Study No. 192B, 2020) 3–4 <https://ceri.ca/assets/files/Study_192B_Full_Report.pdf> accessed 18 March 2021 (hereafter CERI 2020).

[2] Ibid.

[3] Tim Shufelt, 'Resources Rising: Metals, Energy Power TSX Rebound from Lows' *Globe and Mail* (Toronto 7 August 2020).

Alastair R. Lucas, *Extreme Natural Event Impacts on the Energy Sector and its Regulation* In: *Resilience in Energy, Infrastructure, and Natural Resources Law.* Edited by: Catherine Banet, Hanri Mostert, LeRoy Paddock, Milton Fernando Montoya, and Íñigo del Guayo, Oxford University Press. © Alastair R. Lucas 2022. DOI: 10.1093/oso/9780192864574.003.0014

we address climate change is becoming a competitiveness issue for Canadian businesses, consumers, workers and investors increasingly care about the environmental footprint of the products they buy, of the companies they work for, and the businesses they invest in.[4]

These can be climate risks—storms, floods, wildfires, earthquakes, extreme cold, or public health events like 2020's COVID-19 pandemic. Resilience is all-important. The energy sector, operating in a closely integrated global environment, is particularly vulnerable.

II. Energy Regulation

Energy regulatory regimes are intended to facilitate and regulate exploration, development, production, upgrading, and transportation of energy resources in the public interest. The North American statutes establishing these regimes have their roots in the economic and social development values of 19th and 20th-century settlers.[5] In Canada (and the U.S.), economies were based on staples with intense resource development for national and global markets.[6] Natural resources, including energy resources, were to be developed vigorously by private capital interests that were assumed to meet fundamental societal needs. This legislation covered historic fields of human endeavour, including forestry, mining, waterpower, and eventually oil and gas. Energy as a distinct field emerged gradually with industrial, space heating, and transportation needs, including coal-powered nation-building railways in the 19th century.

Embedded in energy statutes is the idea of public interest. However, there has been no consensus on the meaning of this term.[7] Various definitions, including shared values, majoritarian, and economic performance versions, have been articulated. Courts have adopted approaches that balance public benefit and detriment, the latter focusing on environmental, social, and local, regional, and national economic factors.[8] But measurement was largely recognized as a matter for elected officials and their administrators because public interest could only be a matter of opinion to be formed and applied as a matter of legal discretion.[9]

In principle, the structured but discretionary nature of energy regulatory decisions left ample room for growth and change in response to changing societal values and expectations. But fundamental underlying issues, such as recognition (particularly in Canada) of indigenous rights and land claims in a broader process of reconciliation, presented extreme regulatory challenges.[10] Another set of problems was revealed by the 2020–2021 COVID-19 pandemic: how to respond to the immediate and longer-term impacts of extreme natural public health and climate events? This takes us to ideas about vulnerability, impact, and resilience.

---

[4] David Parkinson, 'Climate Change Risks 'Taking on Increased Urgency' Macklem Warns' Globe *and Mail* (Toronto, 18 November 2020) B-1.

[5] E. Hughes, A. Kwasniak, and A. Lucas, *Public Lands and Resources Law in Canada* (Irwin Law 2016) 103.

[6] Ibid.

[7] See Jodie L. Hierlmeier, 'The "Public Interest": Can it Provide Guidance for the ERCB and NRCB?' (2008) 18 JELP 279.

[8] Cecilia Low, 'The "Public Interest" in Section 3 of Alberta's *Energy Resources Conservation Act*.' CIRL Occasional Paper #36, September 2011.

[9] See *Sumas Energy 2 Inc. v Canada (National Energy Board)*, 2005 FCA 377.

[10] See *Athabasca Tribal Council v Amoco Canada* [1981] SCR 699.

A Canada Energy Regulator study released in November 2020 found that the COVID-19 pandemic had significantly impacted the Canadian energy system, with energy use falling by 6 per cent and crude oil production decreasing by 7 per cent year over year.[11] Under assumptions described by the Regulator as the 'Evolving Scenario', oil and gas production increases, peaking around 2040. However, while fossil fuel consumption will decline ultimately, it still accounted for 60 per cent of Canada's fuel mix in 2020.

A. Provincial and federal energy regulation

The next three sections provide context by briefly reviewing the legal powers and duties of the Canadian federal government and the province of Alberta (the energy sector heart) and identifying legal authority particularly relevant to sudden unexpected energy sector impact responses. This leads to the assessment of the resilience of these regulatory bodies and their governments in the face of these crises.

In Canada's distributed federal system, it is the provinces that own and have powers to regulate development, production, and marketing of energy resources as well as necessary facilities in the provinces, while federal powers are limited mainly to interprovincial and international facilities (particularly pipelines and powerlines) and energy trade.[12] Federal environmental powers, particularly environmental impact assessment, in relation to energy are also significant.[13]

B. The Alberta Energy Regulator

Alberta's Energy Regulator (AER) is the modern version of the oil and gas regulator established in 1935.[14] At that time, facilitating new economic development was the core objective. It was a joint industry–government endeavour that accelerated after the pivotal Leduc oil discovery in 1949. The industry was the driver; the government collected royalties but provided fiscal and regulatory stability. Decision making was largely left to the Regulator, which developed as a surprisingly independent public service enclave.[15] This changed, particularly in the 2000s, with energy development decision power shifting to the Alberta Cabinet, culminating with the enactment of the Responsible Energy Development Act in 2012. The Act abolished the Energy Resources Conservation Board and replaced it with the Alberta Energy Regulator.

The AER says that it 'oversees all aspects of energy activities in accordance with government policies; "reviews" energy project applications and makes decisions on them; "inspect[s]" energy activities to ensure that requirements are met; "penalize[s]" non-compliant companies; holds hearings on proposed projects; and "look[s]" for ways to improve

[11]   Canada Energy Regulator, 'Canada's Energy Future 2020' (November 2020) 6 (hereafter CER November 2020).
[12]   *Constitution Act, 1867*; *Friends of the Oldman River Society v Canada (Minister of Transport)*, [1992] 1 S.C.R. 3 (hereafter *Oldman River*); see Martin Olszynski, 'Testing the Jurisdictional Waters: The Provincial Regulation of Interprovincial Pipelines' (2018) 23 Rev. Const. Stud. 91.
[13]   *Oldman River* (n 12).
[14]   David Breen, *Alberta's Petroleum Industry and the Conservation Board* (University of Alberta Press 1993).
[15]   Ibid, 544.

our regulatory system so that it is efficient, adaptive to the global market and technology changes that affect the industry and demonstrates Alberta's competitiveness'.[16] Note the language of change, efficiency, adaptation, and economic competitiveness. This largely tracks its mandate under the Responsible Energy Development Act.[17]

However, the website blurb does not acknowledge the Regulator's powers under environmental and water statutes over matters concerning energy facilities. This still controversial melding of energy and environmental powers dates from the AER's creation in 2012.

It is necessary to go to the Regulations to identify factors that the Regulator must consider in assessing energy facility applications (though the Act mentions the interests of landowners).[18] Factors that shall be considered are:

> (a) the social and economic effects of the energy resource activity, (b) the effects of the energy resource activity on the environment, and (c) the impacts on a landowner as a result of the use of the land on which the energy resource activity is or will be located.[19]

The Regulator's specific powers are under the energy resource enactments that govern the development of oil and gas, oil sands, coal, and pipelines in the province. Here, the purposes sections are more traditional. For example, the Oil and Gas Conservation Act's purposes section focuses on the 'economic, orderly, efficient and responsible development in the public interest of the oil and gas resources of Alberta', and 'conservation' of oil and gas resources—that is, maximizing ultimate economic recovery—all in the 'public interest'.[20] Empowering provisions such as those under the Oil and Gas Conservation Act concerning approval of oil and gas wells[21] and under the Oil Sands Conservation Act concerning approval of oil sands recovery schemes[22] make it clear that final authority rests with the provincial Cabinet.[23]

C. The Canada Energy Regulator

The Canada Energy Regulator (CER), established in 2019 by the Canadian Energy Regulator Act (CERA),[24] replaced the National Energy Board that had served as the federal Regulator for over 60 years. It regulates interprovincial and international oil and gas pipelines and electricity transmission lines, import of oil, gas, and electricity, as well as oil and gas exploration, development, and production in parts of the Canadian Arctic. Under the CERA, the overall regime for approval and regulation of these major energy facilities remained broadly similar to that under the predecessor National Energy Board Act.[25]

[16] Alberta Energy Regulator, 'How does the AER regulate energy development in Alberta?' <How does the AER regulate energy development in Alberta? | Alberta Energy Regulator> accessed 13 December 2021.

[17] SA 2012, C. R-17.3, s 2(1).

[18] Ibid, s 15.

[19] Responsible Energy Development General Regulation, Alta Reg 90/2013, s 3.

[20] Oil and Gas Conservation Act, RSA 2000, s 6.

[21] Ibid, s 18(2).

[22] RSA 2000, c O-7, s 18(2).

[23] Ibid, s 18 (2) (when the Regulator has refused a well licence, the provincial cabinet may review and direct the Regulator to issue the licence).

[24] SC 2019, c 28, s10 (hereafter CERA 2019).

[25] Nigel Bankes, 'Pipelines and the Constitution: a Special Issue of the Review of Constitutional Studies (2018) 23 Rev Const Stud 1, 21.

For new pipelines and powerlines, the Regulator determines whether a certificate should be granted, 'taking into account whether the pipeline 'is and will be required by the present and future public convenience and necessity ... '[26]and makes recommendations to the federal Cabinet accordingly. It must take into account explicit factors, including environmental effects, health, safety and security of persons, protection of property, constitutional rights of indigenous peoples, availability of oil or gas to the pipeline, available markets, and the proponent's financial resources. Other significant factors are, impact on government climate change commitments, relevant environmental assessments, and any public interest that the Regulator considers may be affected.[27]

The Regulator has the power to attach conditions to pipeline certificates concerning a range of matters, including economic, environmental, social, and security matters.[28] This includes potential effects on indigenous peoples and their lands. Operationally, it establishes rates, tariffs, and tolls for the transport of oil, gas, and electricity. It also monitors Canadian energy supply and demand and provides regular, publicly available studies and projections, often in the form of alternate scenario analysis. There is also the power to carry out public inquiries on energy matters and make recommendations to the responsible minister[29].

D. The regulators and their governments—vulnerability and resilience

Resilience in this context is characterized as 'the capacity of a system to absorb disturbance and reorganize while undergoing change so as to still retain essentially the same function, structure, identity, and feedbacks'.[30] This and earlier definitions were developed in the context of natural ecological systems.[31] However, the 'natural' qualifier is problematic. Even pandemic diseases like COVID-19 become catastrophic events only through human vectors. It has been observed that 'There's nothing natural about disasters ravaging the earth'.[32] Further, this ecological system's definition must be broadened to capture the resilience of socio-economic systems to unforeseen disturbances.[33] From a Canadian perspective, the U.S. industry and government is implicated because of the close North American oil and gas (and electricity) industry integration. This chapter focuses on the period just prior to and just after the beginning of the 2020–2021 COVID-19 pandemic when federal and provincial (and state) governments began to roll out policy and legal initiatives.

For energy regulators, sudden extreme events create four sets of issues. First, particular events may involve direct damage to regulated facilities such as pipelines and consequential damage to persons and property.

---

[26] CERA 2019, s 183 (1) (n 24).
[27] CERA 2019, s 183 (2) (n 24).
[28] CERA, s 183 (1) (b) (n 27).
[29] CERA, ss 80–83 (n 27).
[30] Brian Walker, C. S. Holling, Stephen R. Carpenter, and Ann Kinzig, 'Resilience, Adaptability and Transformability in Social–ecological Systems' (2004) 9 Ecology and Society 4, 5.
[31] E.g. C.S. Holling, 'Resilience and Stability of Ecological Systems' (1973) 4 Annual Review of Ecology and Systematics 14, 23.
[32] Elizabeth Renzetti, 'There's Nothing Natural about Disasters Ravaging the Earth' *The Globe and Mail* (Toronto, 10 September 2020)
[33] Fiona Miller et al, 'Resilience and Vulnerability: Complementary or Conflicting Concepts?' (2010) 15(3) Ecology and Society 11, 13 (hereafter Miller, 'Resilience and Vulnerability').

Second, where the economic consequences of extreme events are spread widely in the sector and the broader economy, regulators' concern must extend to the economic health of the sector and impacts in regional, provincial, and national economies. This may relate directly to statutory decision powers and criteria. For example, in inter-jurisdictional pipeline applications, a pipeline's economic feasibility, the existence of markets, financial resources, and financial responsibility of applicants are all factors required by section 183 (2) of the CERA to be taken into account.

Third, the financial strength of operating companies will affect their ability to address new statutory requirements such as those concerning climate change, designed to meet longer-term government policy goals.[34] Each of the regulators has public information and government advice powers. They can undertake studies and investigations on their own initiative or at the request of their governments. They are uniquely qualified to carry out investigations, consult appropriately, and provide policy advice to the governments. This is apparent where the issues concern proposed government response to unexpected events that damage the energy sector directly, such as catastrophic weather impacts on energy infrastructure. But they also have relevant expertise where sudden unexpected events, such as the COVID-19 pandemic, inflict serious damage to public health and welfare and prompt government responses that inflict short- and medium-term economic harm.

Finally, national and regional economic impacts may adversely affect the financial capacity of the regulators themselves to monitor, plan, make rules, and enforce regulatory requirements. This is particularly true for agencies like the AER and the CER, whose operating budgets depend on oil and gas production levies and other fees.

III. Sudden Extreme Events—Vulnerability and Resilience

When sudden extreme natural events occur, the public economic and regulatory environments may already be in a weakened condition. This was the pre-COVID-19 state of oil in 2019 as a result of the Russia–Saudi Arabia price dispute that saw oil markets decline sharply. Prices for oil futures dropped to minus values as oil flooded markets.[35] There had been only partial market recovery when the COVID-19 pandemic struck. Moreover, the lack of offshore export pipeline facilities meant that Canadian heavy oil already sold at a discount in United States markets. The subsections below take a closer look at the phenomenon of sudden extreme events, the vulnerabilities they affect in energy systems, and the potential resilience that may arise.

A. Sudden extreme events

Sudden extreme weather events—hurricanes, floods, and major wildfires—can create a significant economic loss. These events also underline developing climate change and affirm

---

[34] E.g. Canada, Prime Minister Justin Trudeau, 'Prime Minister announces Canada's strengthened climate plan to protect the environment, create jobs, and support communities', 11 December 2020 < Prime Minister announces Canada's strengthened climate plan to protect the environment, create jobs, and support communities | Prime Minister of Canada (pm.gc.ca)> accessed 7 June 2021.

[35] CERI 2020 (n 1) 7.

increasing global public concern. This concern is reflected in evolving government green agendas[36] and green investment community influence. The result in Canada has been a pivot from long-standing oil supply security concerns focused on market dynamics and political circumstances to a greater emphasis on the natural environmental risks presented by climate change. Government policies (particularly at the federal level) have shifted to emphasize vigorous GHG emission targets premised on hydrocarbon emissions reduction.

Energy emergencies caused by weather events including, wildfires, earthquakes, floods, and unseasonable cold, have not been uncommon in North America. An extended 2013 blackout covering a large area in Ontario, Quebec and the eastern United States was reportedly triggered by falling tree branches.[37] Recently, large wildfires in California, some caused by electricity transmission lines sparking in drought conditions, resulted in extensive damage and mass evacuations. Electric utilities have resorted to precautionary power shut off affecting large areas.[38] In February 2021, an unprecedented cold snap left large parts of Texas without power for as long as one week. The state's deregulated electricity market and unwinterized infrastructure coupled with its lack of interstate power interconnection combined to cause a system-wide failure.[39]

Alberta's Energy Regulator has emergency cleanup and shut down powers in relation to oil and gas facilities based on statutory legal authority, as well as conditions attached to facility licences initially and on approved transfer.[40] There are also preventive measures such as well integrity requirements for shale formation wells. Federally, the Canada Energy Regulator has similar powers and has developed a series of plans and protocols for emergency events, including floods, earthquakes, marine pollution prevention, and urban area protection.[41]

B. Vulnerability and resilience

Energy systems will never be free of vulnerability. Because they operate in global markets, and because they may be subject to various financial markets, economic conditions in different jurisdictions, various climate conditions, and actions of other national governments and regulators, they will never be immune to the impacts of rapid, significant disruptions. The rebalance aspect of resilience comes into play; so does the idea of adaptation if a longer-term perspective is taken. Energy regulators' public interest mandates require that they monitor the sector, actively monitor their regulatees, and respond as effectively as possible. Thus, there is an interplay between the ideas of vulnerability and resilience.[42] The former

---

[36] Ibid.
[37] 14 August 2003: A massive electrical blackout hits the eastern seaboard, sending Toronto into chaos: 'Blackout: The Power Outage That Left 50 Million W/o Electricity' | Retro Report | *New York Times* (14 August 2003).
[38] Christopher Weber, 'California Wildfire Risk High Amid Unpredictable Winds, Dry Conditions' *Globe and Mail* (Toronto, 3 December 2020) A22.
[39] Rachel Adams-Heard et al, 'The Blackout Blame Game' *The Herald* (18 February 2021) B2.
[40] Alberta Energy Regulator, Liability Management <Liability Management | Alberta Energy Regulator (aer.ca)> accessed 13 December 2021; Directive 071, Emergency Preparedness and Response Requirements for the Petroleum Industry <Emergency Planning, Preparedness, and Response Fact Sheet (aer.ca)> accessed 13 December 2021.
[41] Canada Energy Regulator, Emergency Management <CER – Emergency Management (cer-rec.gc.ca)> accessed 7 June 2021.
[42] See Miller, 'Resilience and Vulnerability' (n 33).

may precede the latter, creating the conditions calling for resilience. From another perspective, vulnerability and resilience may be viewed as antagonistic or even as opposites.[43]

It is significant that government action is not confined to that of the regulators. It can also take the form of government assistance delivered by targeted programs or under broader pandemic response legislation. This can take the form of assistance for laid off or furloughed employees, assistance to corporations, and assistance related to industry obligations, including environmental protection, as shown below.

Another perspective is presented by the rapid development of renewable energy. Renewable supplies—particularly wind and solar—have increased rapidly, driving construction costs down to or even below those of oil and gas. This has been impacted by the COVID-19 pandemic. There are, of course, inherent vulnerabilities associated with renewable energy, including intermittency and land requirements. But energy supply landscapes have nevertheless changed. This presents new regulatory issues posed by renewable electricity generation. It may also affect relations among regulatory agencies with hydrocarbon and electricity production typically divided between oil and gas regulators and public utility electricity regulators.

Below, resilience, as defined above,[44] will be used as a criterion to identify and assess energy regulators' actions in response to sudden extreme events. The focus below is on the COVID-19 pandemic. Vulnerability may be viewed as a negative factor in assessing the resilience demonstrated by regulators' strategies and actions. The next section is a case study that tests the resilience shown by the CER and AER in the face of the COVID-19 pandemic that began to affect Canada in early 2020.

IV. COVID-19 Case Study

For the Energy sector, the COVID-19 pandemic has been a classic significant unexpected disruption with extreme effects. Its impact on the global and Canadian energy sectors has been described above. The consequences in Canada include sudden, rapid energy production cuts resulting from sharp demand drops; initial rapid price decreases, particularly for oil; and COVID-19 outbreaks, particularly at oil sands production facilities.[45] In the paragraphs below, the context is discussed in more detail, along with the government's financial assistance. Then the impact on federal climate policy and energy futures is considered.

A. The context

The coronavirus was identified in December 2019, with cases appearing in China. Within three months, the virus had spread globally. In response, governments (including the Canadian federal and provincial governments) undertook measures to protect citizens' health. These included travel bans, distancing requirements, and closing businesses.

---

[43] Ibid.

[44] '[T]he capacity of a system to absorb disturbance and reorganize while undergoing change so as to still retain essentially the same function, structure, identity, and feedbacks', including general resilience of socio-economic systems to unforeseen disturbances (Section III.D).

[45] Emma Graney, 'Oil Sands Struggling to Keep Virus at Bay' *Globe and Mail* (Toronto, 4 December 2020) A6.

The impact of these actions has been extreme. According to the International Energy Agency:

> The energy sector is … severely affected by this crisis, which has slowed transport, trade and economic activity across the globe. Our latest analysis of daily data through mid-April… shows that countries in full lockdown are experiencing an average 25% decline in energy demand per week and countries in partial lockdown an average 18% decline.[46]

Canadian GDP declined in March and April 2020 by 19 per cent. The decline for 2020 was 5.4 per cent, the steepest since data were recorded in 1961.[47] Air travel and ground commuting were particularly hard hit.

For the Canadian energy sector, the sharp reduction in demand for gasoline, diesel, and jet fuel was felt immediately.[48] Globally, crude oil demand fell by 30 per cent. As noted, this accelerated the oil price decline already caused by increased Russian and Saudi Arabian production. Canadian gasoline and diesel demand (and retail prices) fell by 35 per cent. Refineries reduced output, and Canadian producers scaled back production and cut capital budgets to an unprecedented degree. Major Canadian hydro and wind electricity generation projects under construction were suspended.[49] Uncertainties suddenly appeared for Canada's long-term energy picture. According to the CER:

> The COVID-19 pandemic has clearly added an additional layer of uncertainty to any future projection or scenario. In the near term, key questions include the path of future infection rates, the timing and effectiveness of governments and vaccines, and the evolution of policy measures in response to the pandemic. In the longer term, there may be questions on how this experience will shape future social, work, and travel trends.[50]

IEA views on global energy systems COVID-19 impact recovery evolved quickly. In November 2020, its uppermost concern was resilience to support energy security.[51] By March 2021, in its Fuel Report, it saw earlier peak oil demand with no necessary return to normal in a post-COVID world. More governments were contemplating sustainable recoveries with emphasis on clean energy, thus creating a dilemma for oil-producing countries.[52] This set the stage for the IEA's May 2021 report, which saw a halt to new oil and gas development investment if a global net-zero GHG emissions goal is to be reached.[53]

---

[46] International Energy Agency, 'COVID-19: Exploring the impacts of the Covid-19 pandemic on global energy markets, energy resilience, and climate change' November 2020 < COVID-19 – Topics - IEA> accessed 7 March 2020 (hereafter IEA November 2020).

[47] Statistics Canada, The Daily < The Daily — Gross domestic product, income and expenditure, fourth quarter 2020 (statcan.gc.ca) > accessed 7 June 2021.

[48] Ibid 17–19.

[49] IEA November 2020 (n 46) 19.

[50] IEA November 2020 (n 46) 20.

[51] Ibid.

[52] International Energy Agency, Oil 2021, Analysis and Forecast to 2026, Fuel Report, March 2021 < Oil 2021 – Analysis - IEA > accessed 20 March 2021 (hereafter IEA March 2021).

[53] International Energy Agency, 'Shaping a secure and sustainable energy future for all' (18 May 2021) <IEA – International Energy Agency> accessed 6 June 2021.

Canada is among these dilemma-contemplating producer countries as it faces significant producer company project delays, particularly for new pipelines, along with major federal government clean energy development policies and plans.

The next section focuses on resiliency, both in Canada's energy system and, more specifically, in the key energy regulators—the Alberta Energy Regulator and the Canada Energy Regulator. The following qualitative factors will guide the review: (i) directness and potential impact of government and regulatory agency pandemic response actions; (ii) energy system short-term recovery time, (iii) longer-term energy system stability, and facilitation of green energy values.

B. Government financial assistance

The pandemic led to requests for energy sector-wide federal and provincial government aid. Ideally, this would be direct financial assistance. It extended to confirming and increasing government support for new pipelines. This would follow previous government support that in 2018 saw the federal government purchase the Trans Mountain Pipeline that extends from Alberta to BC tidewater, and the Alberta government provide a $(Can)1.2 billion loan guarantee to support the Keystone XL project designed to augment Alberta oil transportation to the U.S. gulf coast. The latter occurred in April 2020 during the pandemic.

General federal pandemic relief programs provided benefits to the oil and gas industry, valued in total at nearly $8 billion.[54] These programs were aimed at employees and companies. Among the nine most significant programs, the Canada Emergency Wage Subsidy (CEWS) and the field reclamation programs discussed next, provided the most short- and medium-term benefits.[55]

C. Contaminated oil and gas field cleanup funding

In April 2020, following energy sector lobbying, the federal government announced a $1.7 billion program to clean up orphan or abandoned oil and gas wells in Alberta, Saskatchewan, and Manitoba.[56] Orphan wells are those whose corporate owners can not be found, are bankrupt, or lack the financial resources to remediate well sites properly. Alberta has approximately 70,000 abandoned wells and 95,000 inactive wells.[57] The federal government also revealed a $750,000 fund aimed mainly at methane reduction and continued credit support for medium-sized energy companies. This is not the broader unconditional financial assistance the energy sector had lobbied for.

---

[54] CERI 2020 (n 1) 11.
[55] CERI 2020 (n 1) 11–13, 17–19.
[56] Drew Anderson, '$1.7B to Clean Up Orphaned and Abandoned Wells Could Create Thousands of Jobs' *CBC News*, <$1.7B to clean up orphaned and abandoned wells could create thousands of jobs | CBC News> accessed 13 December 2021.
[57] Alberta Energy Regulator, 'Orphan Energy Sites' <Orphan Energy Sites | Alberta Energy Regulator (aer.ca)> accessed 7 June 2021.

The federal site cleanup funds took the form in Alberta of direct grants to oil and gas service companies. While the climate change community was supportive, landowner response was that this amounts to a subsidy to industry:

> [T]he Alberta government is bailing out oil and gas companies that have profited from our public resources, but now refuse to adequately fund their own cleanup, ...[58]

This is a direct and timely benefit to the Alberta energy industry. The problem is that the private financial benefits are at the expense of a cooperative federal–provincial environmental remediation program that was underway. More specifically, as the quotation above suggests, it can be perceived as avoidance of industry responsibilities—a failure of the polluter pays principle. An established federal-provincial-industry program was destabilized.

D. Property tax breaks

Alberta oil and gas industry financial assistance in the face of the COVID-19 industry slow-down included a three-year municipal tax break program beginning in 2021. New oil and gas wells and pipelines receive a property tax exemption, and assessments for less productive wells will be lowered. The existing tax on well drilling equipment[59] will be eliminated. The problem is that because wells are assessed at replacement cost, not market value, conditions of reduced commodity prices, capital access, and share prices result in inequitably high valuations.

While these changes do address the financial concerns of many energy companies, there is pushback from rural municipalities. The Alberta Rural Municipalities Association, though understanding, has expressed concern about 'devastating impacts' on municipal facilities and services given the existing incidence of tax non-payment by some companies and inability to recover from bankrupt companies.[60] Tax revenue from oil and gas producers makes up a substantial portion of many rural municipal budgets.

E. Suspending oil sands environmental monitoring

Another indirect industry benefit is the federal–provincial administrative agreement of 7 July 2020 to cut previously agreed upon environmental monitoring of Alberta oil sands operations. This was done by removing approximately 25 per cent of the program's annual budget that supports fieldwork downstream from the oil sands to monitor seepage from tailings ponds. According to federal officials, the cuts are intended to protect workers from

---

[58] Kyle Bakx, 'Alberta Unveils Process for Paying out $1 billion in Oilfield Cleanup Grants' *CBC News*, <Alberta unveils process for paying out $1 billion in oilfield cleanup grants | CBC News> accessed 13 December 2021.

[59] Well Drilling Equipment Tax Rate Regulation, Alta Reg 293/2020.

[60] Lauren Stelck, 'Alberta Announces Three-Year Property Tax Breaks for Energy Industry' *Norton, Rose, Fulbright*, 23 October 2020,<Alberta announces three-year property tax breaks for energy industry | Canada | Global law firm | Norton Rose Fulbright> accessed 13 December 2021.

COVID-19. However, notwithstanding scientific criticism and questions, there was no information on the COVID-19 risks said to be addressed.[61]

Similarly, the Alberta Energy Regulator suspended oil and gas industry environmental reporting, part of its compliance and enforcement program, though data collection must continue.[62] Direct, responsive action was taken by three First Nations directly affected by Alberta oil sands operations. The Mikisew Cree, Fort McKay, and Athabasca Chipewyan Nations launched an appeal to the Alberta Energy Regulator, challenging the suspension decision. Grounds include a lack of rational connection between specific monitoring activities and COVID-19 risks, particularly since oil sands production activities were permitted to continue. The First Nations also alleged a lack of prior consultation, resulting in 'undermin[ing] the entire statutory regime for energy development in the province.'[63]

F. Regulatory hearing procedures during the pandemic

Energy regulators, including the CER, the AER and the Alberta Utilities Commission (AUC), the latter exercising renewable energy jurisdiction, moved to online disclosure and hearing processes during the pandemic. In principle, written and electronic processes are within the powers of these regulators. This is based on specific statutory authority[64] and the common law procedural fairness notice, hearing, and impartial decision-maker principles.[65] The latter include the decision-maker's choice of procedures as a factor in assessing procedural fairness. Here, the broader circumstances of the pandemic and government lockdown responses would be significant in justifying such innovations as virtual stakeholder engagement, and written or electronic hearings, including written information requests rather than cross-examination.[66]

Overall, while there have been complaints about less effective hearings with the demeanour of witnesses no longer relevant, less complete hearing inputs by parties, and muting control difficulties in electronic hearings, there has been no litigation. However, hearing delays have been common.[67]

G. COVID-19, federal climate policy and energy industry futures

It may be adaptation in the face of COVID-19, or it may be changes already underway prior to the pandemic. It may even be policymaking under pandemic cover. But, as 2021–2022

---

[61] Bob Weber, 'Alberta, Ottawa Reduce Oil Sands Environmental Monitoring Budget due to COVID-19 Pandemic', *The Globe and Mail*, 4 August 2020, A8 <Alberta, Ottawa reduce oil sands environmental monitoring budget due to COVID-19 pandemic - The Globe and Mail> accessed 13 December 2021.

[62] Alberta Energy Regulator, Bulletin 2020-10 and ministerial letter, 30 March 2020 <Bulletin 2020-10 | Alberta Energy Regulator (aer.ca)> accessed 7 June 2021.

[63] Carrie Tait and Ian Bailey, 'First Nations Appeal Halt on Oil Patch Environmental Monitoring' *Globe and Mail* (Toronto 9 June 2020) A6.

[64] Responsible Energy Development Act, SA 2012, c R-17.3 and Regulations.

[65] See *Baker v Canada (Minister of Citizenship and Immigration)* [1992] 2 SCR 817.

[66] See Alberta Utilities Commission, Bulletin 2020-06, 12 March 2020 < Bulletin (auc.ab.ca) > accessed 7 June 2021.

[67] Indra Maharaj, 'COVID-19, Procedural Fairness and Energy Regulation in Alberta', Canadian Institute of Resources Law, SMALS Program, 3 October 2020.

begins, a consensus appears to be emerging that the Canadian federal government is serious about a 2050 net-zero greenhouse emissions goal. This means major short- and long-term impacts on Canada's energy system. It is significant that the CER, in its December 2020 Report, began its energy futures analysis with pandemic impacts on short- and long-term energy supply and demand before moving to two scenarios that serve as a basis for assessing the potential shape of the Canadian energy system over the next 30 years. It also acknowledges that over 80 per cent of total Canadian GHG emissions are energy-related.[68]

The Canadian Net Zero Emissions Accountability Act (discussed in Section IV.I below), introduced in Parliament in November 2020, lays out a high-level legal plan for carbon price increases necessary to achieve the Paris Agreement GHG emission goals and go beyond net-zero conditions. This is the first time that the government has been explicit in laying out these long-term goals. It is also the first time that the CER has—scenario approach notwithstanding—acknowledged the likelihood of a new carbon-constrained future, particularly for the oil and gas sector.

H. Accelerated climate measures and energy

The CER proposes two scenarios over the period 2020–2050: (i) a 'reference scenario' in which climate change actions are limited to existing measures, with 'modest' technological development and existing market conditions; and (ii) an 'evolving scenario' that assumes increasing climate change action through the projection period, continuing climate policy commitment, and continued low carbon technology development.

For the latter scenario, assumptions are: carbon pricing by provinces and the backstop federal Greenhouse Gas Pollution Pricing Act; coal-fired electricity generation phase-out; energy efficiency regulation; electric vehicle promotion; and renewable energy requirements.[69] These assumptions are based on expectations that carbon prices will rise to '$125 in 2019 real terms by 2050' and that regulations will require significantly reduced emission intensity.

As its first key finding, the Report confirms that the COVID-19 pandemic has impacted the Canadian energy system significantly.[70] Because of pandemic response actions, energy use in 2020 was expected to fall 6 per cent, and crude oil production will decrease by 7 per cent, both compared to 2019. The short-term market impacts identified become elements of the Regulator's 'evolving scenario'. They provide a kind of kickstart. However, the CER assumption is that these COVID-19 effects add great uncertainty to the longer term, though they are expected to dissipate over the next two-three years.[71] Alberta Energy Regulator data, however, projects that Canadian oil production recovery may be more robust, with oil sands production reaching record levels in November 2020.[72]

[68] CER, Canada's Energy Future November 2020 (n 11) 9.
[69] CER November 2020 (n 11) 26.
[70] CER November 2020 (n 11) 6.
[71] CER November 2020 (n 11) 20.
[72] Alberta Energy Regulator, November 2020 data, reported 6 January 2021; see Nia Williams, 'Canada's Oil Sands Hit Record High Production' Commodities News, *Reuters* (6 January 2021) <Canada's oil sands hit record high production - gov't data | Reuters > accessed 7 June 2021.

After the COVID-19 shock, total Canadian crude oil production is expected to rise until 2030, then decline to 2050. Oil Sands production is likely to follow the same trend.[73] In the 'evolving scenario', no additional export pipeline capacity would be necessary, including the federal government-owned Trans Mountain pipeline, with its TMX Expansion Project now under construction.[74] While fossil fuel use declines by 2050, it is still expected to make up over 60 per cent of Canada's energy mix.[75] Electricity will become more competitive with fossil fuels, including for passenger vehicles, serving 27 per cent of total energy demand by 2050.[76]

I. Net-zero emissions

The Report goes on to discuss the implications of moving beyond the 'evolving scenario' to reach a national net-zero GHG emissions position and what is needed from the energy sector to achieve this goal. The Regulator does not attempt to provide a plan. However, it emphasizes that significant emission reduction action by the energy sector will be necessary. This is underlined by the continued fossil fuel reliance shown in the 'evolving scenario'. The focus is on three case studies: oil sands, personal transportation, and remote and northern communities. The net-zero discussion is necessarily speculative, amounting to a kind of 'further research needed' section at the end of the Report.

The CER Report does not address two developments that occurred at the time of or immediately before its release. One is the federal Plan for meeting Canada's targets under the Paris Agreement. Central is carbon prices under the Greenhouse Gas Pollution Pricing Act that will reach $170 per tonne by 2030.[77] This is more aggressive than the $125 by 2050 assumed by the Regulator in its 'evolving scenario'. Border carbon adjustments are to be explored, and a clean fuel standard will be introduced.

The second development is the 2020 Canadian Net-Zero Accountability Act.[78] The Preamble makes the overall goals clear. It recites the risks posed by climate change, a global problem requiring immediate action by all Canadian governments and industry; that Canada has ratified the Paris Agreement with its 1.5-degree global temperature increase limit goal; that this goal requires net-zero emissions; and that Canada has committed to developing a plan to achieve net-zero by 2050. In late June 2021, the Bill was still before the House of Commons.

Central to the Act is the net-zero emissions target, and that the Environment Minister must set a national emissions target for each 'milestone year'—2030, 2035, 2040, and 2050. Emissions reduction plans must be set, with appropriate public participation, for 2030 within six months of the Act coming into force and for subsequent milestone years with at least five years lead time. Plans must include emissions targets for the specific years, 'a description of the key emissions reduction measures . . . ' to achieve the plan, and a description

---

[73] CER 2020 (n 11) 41.
[74] CER 2020 (n 11) 14.
[75] CER 2020 (n 11) 15.
[76] CER 2020 (n 11) 10.
[77] John Paul Tasker, 'Ottawa to Hike Federal Carbon Tax to $170 a tonne by 2030' *CBC News* (11 December 2020) <Ottawa to hike federal carbon tax to $170 a tonne by 2030 | CBC News> accessed 13 December 2021.
[78] House of Commons, Bill C-12, First Reading November 19 2020.

of 'relevant sectoral strategies'.[79] It is significant that these measures are 'measures of the government of Canada', thus excluding a basis for influencing provincial actions.[80] Progress and assessment reports are required. The latter are linked to Canadian submission of its greenhouse gas inventory reports as required by the Framework Convention on Climate Change. The Act requires Ministerial reasons if targets are not met.[81]

The Act amounts to a declaration of government policy. It adds clarity and gives legislative weight to earlier government policy declarations. However, while it states that it is binding on the government[82], this is necessarily limited to the setting of plans containing the specified content items. Specific quantified emissions limits are yet to be established. These are the limits of potential judicial enforcement, and even the emission targets can be extended[83] and amended.[84] The Act could be otherwise amended or even repealed by subsequent parliaments.

Judicial enforcement action is unlikely, as shown by the Federal Court's decision in *Friends of the Earth v Canada*[85], an unsuccessful 2008 action to enforce the Kyoto Protocol Implementation Act (KIPA).[86] The court reasoned that in the KIPA, as in Bill C-12, Parliament intended only to authorize a government-managed process, not to lay down specific legally enforceable requirements. There were, said the court, 'policy-laden' considerations.[87]

Nevertheless, Bill C-12 does provide coherence for Canadian federal climate policy. It represents statutory linkage to international climate change commitments and to the Strategic Assessment on Climate Change[88] under the new federal Impact Assessment Act.[89] As noted, provincial roles are excluded as the Supreme Court of Canada in early 2021 deliberated on a provincial constitutional challenge to the federal Greenhouse Gas Pollution Pricing Act.[90]

Another federal climate initiative with an energy sector impact that had been in progress also emerged during the pandemic. This is the Clean Fuel Standard,[91] established under the Canadian Environmental Protection Act 1999.[92] It is intended to gradually limit GHG emissions from fuels (gasoline, diesel, and home heating oil) by requiring suppliers to reduce the carbon intensity of fuels. There is an investment fund to promote cleaner hydrocarbon fuels, including biofuels. A carbon market (particularly aimed at refiners) requires

---

[79] Ibid, s 10 (1).
[80] See David Wright, 'Bill C-12, *Canadian Net-Zero Emissions Accountability Act*: A Preliminary Review' (ABlawg, 23 November 2020) < Bill C-12, Canadian Net-Zero Emissions Accountability Act: A Preliminary Review | (ablawg.ca)> accessed 7 June 2021 (hereafter Wright ABlawg).
[81] Ibid, ss 14, 15, 16.
[82] Ibid, s 3.
[83] Ibid, s 9(3).
[84] Ibid, s 12.
[85] 2008 FC 1183, appeal dismissed 2009 FCA 297.
[86] SC 2007, c 30, repealed by the Harper government in 2012.
[87] Wright *ABlawg* (n 80).
[88] Government of Canada, 'Strategic Assessment of Climate Change, Revised October 20, 2020' < Strategic Assessment of Climate Change - Canada.ca.> accessed 7 June 2021.
[89] Ibid.
[90] Held constitutionally valid by the Supreme Court of Canada: Reference re Greenhouse Gas Pollution Pricing Act, 2021 SCC 11, following provincial court of Appeal decisions: Reference Re Greenhouse Gas Pollution Pricing Act, 2019 SKCA 40; 2019 ONCA 544; 2020 ABCA 74. (hereafter GGPPA Reference)
[91] 'Draft Clean Fuel Regulations and Regulatory Impact Analysis Statement', Canada Gazette, Part 1, Vol 154, 19 December 2020.
[92] SC 1999, c 33 (hereafter CEPA).

the creation or purchase of credits representing carbon intensity reduction, with excess credits marketable in future years. Though this will not apply to the upstream oil and gas sector, it aims at price-driven carbon energy reduction.

At the provincial level, Alberta released new, more stringent methane regulations that bring requirements to the level of earlier federal regulations.[93] This set the stage for a CEPA equivalency agreement[94] that will see the provincial regulations enforced in place of the federal equivalents.

J. COVID-19 recovery and federal environmental initiatives—the 'drafting' effect.

In early 2021 it is becoming clearer that the federal government has acted opportunistically during the pandemic to advance green energy and climate change goals. This is reflected in the CER scenario building and net-zero speculation discussed above. It can be described as 'drafting' in the sense of (think auto racing) using 'a pocket of air pressure behind a moving object'[95] to close the gap between moving objects, in this case, climate change and clean technology policy and legislation, and pandemic recovery measures.

There has been no direct federal legislative response to energy sector impacts and regulatory consequences of the pandemic, though there have been regulatory level actions (deferring or lightening environmental or fiscal requirements) and government spending program initiatives (contaminated well site cleanup), discussed in Section IV.C above. Federal legislative action has been limited to carbon pricing under the Greenhouse Gas Pollution Pricing Act, the Clean Fuel Regulations, and the Net Zero Accountability Act,[96] all discussed above. The former was enacted in 2018, prior to the pandemic but only in March 2021 was its constitutionality confirmed by the Supreme Court of Canada.[97] The Clean Fuel Regulations were published in the Canada Gazette Part I in 2020 while the pandemic was raging, triggering a 75-day comment period.

In a commentary on the oil market during the pandemic period, Peter Tertzakian likened the pandemic period to a 'thought experiment turned real'.[98] He noted that the scale of global oil use, which showed only a 20 per cent drop at the bottom of the pandemic-induced decrease in economic activity, is greater than we thought. There is extreme resilience. 'We just caught a glimpse [he says] of how painful it is to reduce significant volumes of oil consumption through forced behavioral change'. This reduction is comparable to IEA estimates that a 20 per cent reduction toward Paris Agreement goals would not be achieved until 2033.[99] The nature and pace of clean technology development are unclear, and in any event, there are specialized markets. Some oil products such as aviation fuel and asphalt will continue to have a high value.

---

[93] Marieke Walsh and Emma Graney, 'Province Toughens Methane Regulations' *The Globe and Mail* (12 May 2020) A6.

[94] Under CEPA (n 92) s10.

[95] Merriam-Webster Dictionary, 'draft' (Entry 3 of 3), <Draft | Definition of Draft by Merriam-Webster> accessed 7 June 2021.

[96] Net Zero Emissions Accountability Act, House of Commons Second Reading, 26 November 2020.

[97] GGPPA Reference (n 90).

[98] Peter Tertzakian, 'Lessons from crude's Year of Oblivion' *Calgary Herald* (4 March 2021) B1.

[99] IEA November 2020 (n 46).

This insight is consistent with the Canadian regulatory and governmental response to energy sector pandemic impacts. The resilience shown was not simply a restorative matter; the markets took care of that even though recovery of the energy sector and its regulators has been uneven. Natural gas, for example, showed little decline through the pandemic, and oil sands production remained surprisingly strong in comparison to the U.S. shale sector.[100] What was observed was dynamic resilience—the response of the energy sector and its regulators to the clean technology shift that has picked up momentum during the pandemic.[101]

K. Case study conclusions

Despite the pressure from the energy industry—particularly the oil and gas sector—the Canadian federal and provincial governments resisted calls for direct industry-specific open-ended financial assistance. Instead, federal assistance was primarily earmarked for orphan well remediation. This had become an increasingly urgent liability for the sector, particularly in Alberta. There were also federal methane reduction funds, with federal regulations designed to mesh with Alberta requirements and provide the basis for a federal-provincial equivalency agreement. The latter confirmed recognition of Alberta's authority concerning methane management. Federal and provincial environmental monitoring suspensions also provided some industry financial relief, as did Alberta's municipal property tax deferrals.

In early 2021, there is already evidence that the energy and particularly hydrocarbon sector recovery has been rapid. Subject to caution concerning lower long-term demand, there has been considerable oil price and production recovery, with oil sands performance particularly strong in terms of national GDP contribution. The natural gas industry also shows a recovery, having suffered a less severe downturn. Broadly, the same is true for the electricity sector. In all cases, while government programs, both industry-specific and general federal corporate and employee recovery programs, have played a role, sector recovery has been a consequence of global market advances.

Energy system and regulator recovery has been surprisingly fast. Initial recovery occurred in a few months, not the extended period that seemed more likely in 2020.

This has set the stage for a longer-term shift toward greener government and energy regulatory policies and actions as clean technology legislation is implemented and refined, and energy sector outlook and actions adapt accordingly.

Notably, government pandemic assistance, particularly that of the federal government, was linked to environmental policy objectives. Most of these environmental policy and regulatory initiatives predated the pandemic and then became part of the mix that informed government pandemic responses. Federal greenhouse gas emission pricing and clean fuel standard legislation have moved forward during the pandemic, benefitting from a 'drafting' effect in relation to pandemic energy and broader economic recovery measures.

[100] CERI 2020 (n 1) 13–14.
[101] See Miller, 'Resilience and Vulnerability' (n 33) 14.

V. Conclusions

Long experience with emergency response has positioned Canadian national and provincial regulators to address sudden specific events such as weather impacts on energy systems. In the face of the broader-based threat posed by the COVID-19 pandemic, federal and provincial governments and their energy regulators marshalled a combination of targeted spending and legislative and regulatory actions. Regulators, particularly the Alberta Energy Regulator, used specific powers to lighten regulatory burdens. The major federal spending program was targeted to major pre-existing facilities remediation facing the oil and gas industry. However, oil and gas and other energy subsectors also benefitted significantly from general federal wage and business support and recovery programs. There was no broad-based energy sector economic support program. This was a consequence of the surprising resilience shown by the energy sector. Oil and gas sector recovery was not complete in the spring of 2021, but recovery of the sector's national GDP contribution after a sharp drop that preceded the pandemic was significant. Resilience was also shown by the natural gas and electricity subsectors, which felt a less severe pandemic disturbance.

Perhaps the most surprising development is the federal success in linking, at least implicitly, several major green energy initiatives, particularly greenhouse gas pollution pricing and clean fuels initiatives, to energy sector pandemic recovery measures.

15

Creating a Framework that Supports Resilient Renewable Energy Generation

LeRoy Paddock

I. Introduction

Electricity generation in the United States has been rapidly evolving over the last 15 years driven by deployment of renewable energy generation, closing of several coal-fired power plants and a few nuclear power plants, and an emphasis on demand response and energy efficiency. This evolution has been stimulated by new legal mechanisms encouraging deployment of both utility-scale and distributed renewable energy generation, significant reductions in the cost of wind and solar deployment, new energy efficiency and battery storage technologies, growing support for demand-response programs, and public pressure to close old coal-fired power plants.

These changes are occurring in the context of growing concerns about the impacts of climate change highlighted by weather extremes including intense rainfall events and flooding, historic drought-intensified forest fires, extreme hot and cold weather events, more frequent and stronger hurricanes, unusual high wind and tornadic events, and rising sea levels. The changes and the events have raised critical questions about the resiliency of electrical grid in the U.S. This concern is perhaps most clearly emphasized by the February 2021 Texas blackout that resulted from the shutdown of almost half of the state's generating capacity caused by a polar vortex. The extreme cold froze natural gas supply lines, wind turbines, and coal piles causing system operators to shut down generating facilities to prevent system collapse. The event was responsible for over 100 deaths and economic damages in the range of US$200 billion.

In addition, over the past year equity concerns have been in the spotlight in the U.S. in a variety of contexts including in the generation and access to energy. Experience with the COVID virus has demonstrated the important role of pre-existing health conditions in mortality, including the impacts of emissions from fossil fuel energy generators that can impair lung capacity. The Texas blackout also showed the disproportionate impact that outages can have on underserved communities who have fewer options to deal with outages and who are least able to afford dramatic price spikes caused by shortages.

Cumulatively, these issues point to the need for a more resilient and adaptable energy generation mix that dramatically reduces greenhouse gas emissions to mitigate climate change, assures adequate energy supplies, is able to accommodate major economic shifts such as the growing electrification of transportation and buildings, provides reliable and affordable energy, avoids the health impacts of fossil fuels, and more equitably allocates the burdens and benefits of energy generation. Because fossil fuel electricity generation still

LeRoy Paddock, *Creating a Framework that Supports Resilient Renewable Energy Generation* In: *Resilience in Energy, Infrastructure, and Natural Resources Law.* Edited by: Catherine Banet, Hanri Mostert, LeRoy Paddock, Milton Fernando Montoya, and Íñigo del Guayo, Oxford University Press. © LeRoy Paddock 2022. DOI: 10.1093/oso/9780192864574.003.0015

contributed 27 per cent of U.S. greenhouse gas emissions in 2018[1]—about 1,800 million metric tons—a resilient electricity system must involve a transition to no or very low carbon sources of generation to meet the country's needs.

This chapter will examine these resiliency issues in the context of the United States electricity system with a specific focus on the legal issues that arise as the country moves towards a low carbon economy. It will begin by briefly outlining the evolution of the U.S. electricity generation system in the past 15 years. It will look at the legal measures and other factors that have been driving the shift to more renewable generation. The chapter will then examine the impact of climate change on the energy generation network noting resilience-related concerns about both continued reliance on fossil generation and about the rapid shift to wind and solar generation. The chapter will conclude with observations about how the system needs to continue to evolve to provide a resilient national electrical generation system.

II. The Changing Nature of the U.S. Grid

The Government Accountability Office (GAO) notes that the U.S. has 'over 10,000 power plants, more than 642,000 miles of high-voltage transmission lines, and 6.3 million more miles of distribution lines'.[2] GAO found that the average power plant is 30 years old and that 70 per cent of the transmission lines and transformers are at least 25 years old.[3] The grid is operated by a combination of private companies referred to as 'investor-owned utilities' or 'IOUs', publicly owned utilities operated by federal, state, or local government, and electricity cooperatives that are member-owned, non-profit organizations primarily serving rural areas and smaller cities.[4] For most purposes, states are the primary utility regulator. In the 23 states that are 'deregulated'[5], energy providers establish customer rates and make decisions on construction of new generation. In states that have not deregulated electric companies, the government primarily through 'public utility commissions' has the authority to set retail electricity rates that typically assure a 'reasonable rate of return' on investment for investor-owned utilities and to approve utility investments in generation and distribution facilities.[6] In some states, generation has been 'unbundled' from transmission and distribution and in other states utilities remain vertically integrated.

The Federal Energy Regulatory Commission (FERC), however, regulates wholesale energy prices—the price of energy bought and sold among utilities—to assure the rates are 'just and reasonable'. FERC is also responsible for overseeing voluntary grid operator networks, known as regional transmission operators (RTOs), that manage and operate regional networks of electric transmission lines and operate wholesale electricity markets to buy and sell services and maintain a reliable grid.[7] RTOs cover about two-thirds of the U.S. In regions without an RTO, the utilities serve as the grid operator.

---

[1] See <https://www.epa.gov/ghgemissions/sources-greenhouse-gas-emissions> accessed 21 March 2021.
[2] Government Accountability Office, 'Electricity Grid Resilience' (March 2021), 8.
[3] Ibid.
[4] Ibid, 10.
[5] See <https://paylesspower.com/blog/deregulated-energy-states/> accessed 30 March 2021.
[6] GAO, 'Electricity Grid Resilience' (n 2) 10.
[7] Ibid, 11

Electric systems in most of the United States and much of Canada are interconnected to provide a more resilient, flexible network. Most of Texas, however, operates independently from the two major interconnections allowing the state to avoid federal regulations in some contexts.

Electric reliability in most of the United States and Canada is overseen by the North American Reliability Corporation (NERC). In its original form, NERC was a utility industry voluntary organization. However, Congress in the Energy Policy Act of 2005 authorized the formation of a new, self-regulatory Electric Reliability Organization that would span North America and whose standards would be mandatory and enforceable.

The United States government, through tax incentives including investment tax credits and production tax credits, has encouraged the growth of wind and solar energy production in the United States for most of this century. Federal law also requires that federal agencies use renewable energy for at least 7.5 per cent of their energy needs annually.[8] Several states have been even more aggressive in promoting renewable energy than the Federal government with 29 states adopting mandatory 'renewable portfolio standards' (RPS) requiring electric generating companies to include renewable energy sources in their generation portfolio. Laws in 14 states require 50 per cent of energy generation portfolios come from renewable sources.[9] By one estimate, these standards have driven half of the growth in renewable energy in the country since the early 2000s, a US$64-billion market.[10] States have also frequently provided tax incentives for renewable energy generation.

Further, the cost of solar and wind generation has been reduced to the point that they are now often the least cost sources of new utility-scale energy generation. In 2019 half of the new renewable energy added was less costly than the cheapest coal generation and that trend is increasing.[11] Between 2011 and mid-2020, 95 gigawatts of coal generation have been closed in the United States and another 25 gigawatts are expected to close by 2025.[12] Coal now produces less than 20 per cent of U.S. electric energy, slightly less than nuclear energy and renewables (including wind, solar, hydro power, and biomass).[13] This is a remarkable reduction from 2005 when coal produced 50 per cent of U.S. electricity. The reduction of coal generation has important equity and environmental justice implications since coal plants are disproportionately located near underserved communities.[14] Renewables continue to be the fasting growing sources of new generation in the U.S. Solar energy generation expanded by 20.7 per cent during the first third of 2020 compared to the same period in the previous year. Solar also generated 3.0 per cent of energy capacity generated from all sources in the U.S. during the period. Wind energy generation grew by 12 per cent and accounted for more than 9.3 per cent of total generation during the first third of 2020.[15]

---

[8]   Energy Policy Act of 2005, s 203, 42 USC s 15852(a).
[9]   National Conference of State Legislatures, 'State Renewable Portfolio Standards and Goals' 4 January 2021 <https://www.ncsl.org/research/energy/renewable-portfolio-standards.aspx> accessed 9 March 2021.
[10]   Ibid.
[11]   International Renewable Energy Agency, 'Renewable Energy Generation Costs in 2019' (June 2020) <https://www.irena.org/publications/2020/Jun/Renewable-Power-Costs-in-2019> accessed 9 March 2021.
[12]   See Energy Information Agency, 'As U.S. Coal-Fired Capacity and Utilization Decline, Operators Consider Seasonal Operation' (1 September 2020) <https://www.eia.gov/todayinenergy/detail.php?id=44976> accessed 8 March 2021.
[13]   Energy Information Agency, 'Frequently Asked Questions'. <https://www.eia.gov/tools/faqs/faq.php?id=427&t=3> accessed 8 March 2021
[14]   Brett Israel, 'Coal Plants Smoother Communities of Color' (Scientific American 16 November 20212).
[15]   See <https://www.smart-energy.com/renewable-energy/us-renewables-outpace-coal-and-nuclear-says-eia-renewables/> accessed 21 March 2021.

III. The Resilience Threats

In a report focusing on 'Resilient Power',[16] the authors noted that 'Prominent threats to utilities, especially extreme weather events, are common and increasing. For utilities and their stakeholders, understanding likely impacts from these events is key to protecting the energy infrastructure, ensuring critical systems are able to function during and after an event, and supporting community resilience'.[17] The report identified several grid vulnerabilities including sea level rise, warming temperatures, extreme storms, and wildfires.

Extreme storm events including very intense rainfall and flooding, very high winds associated with tornados or derechos, and historic cold-weather events have steadily increased. Billion-dollar disasters more than doubled in the 2010s as compared to the previous decade.[18] Since most transmission and distribution infrastructure is above ground, these facilities are particularly vulnerable. The polar vortex in Texas resulted in 4 million residents losing power. Hurricane Irma also in Texas resulted in 4.2 million customers losing power.[19] Wildfires caused by wind driven sparking of electrical lines also have serious consequences for utilities. Pacific Gas and Electric, one of California's largest electric utilities, was forced into bankruptcy as a result of forest fires caused by their power lines. Part of the bankruptcy settlement was a nearly US$7 billion settlement with victims of forest fires caused by the company's power lines.[20]

The growing percentage of intermittent generation sources on the grid has also raised resilience concerns. These intermittent resources include utility-scale solar and wind generation as well as distributed, often small-scale generation, primarily in the form of solar panels. NERC has pointed out that U.S. has 21 gigawatts of distributed solar generation and is expected to have over 49 gigawatts by 2029.[21] The organization noted that:

> Asynchronous resources (those that are not physically synchronized with the BPS [bulk power system]) use a power electronic interface (i.e., inverters) to connect to the ac power grid. The system was largely designed around synchronous generating resources, and technical challenges and innovative solutions have emerged as the penetrations of inverter-based resources has continued to increase across many areas of North America. Some inverter-based resource performance issues have been significant enough to result in grid disturbances that affect the reliability of the BPS, such as the tripping of a number of BPS-connected solar PV generation units that occurred during the 2016 Blue Cut fire and 2017 Canyon 2 fire disturbances in California.[22]

Reliability issues are not limited to distributed renewable generation. NERC also observed that:

---

[16] Judsen Bruzgul and Neil Weisenfeld, 'Resilient Power: How Utilities can Identify and Effectively Prepare for Increasing Climate Risks' (ICF Consulting, 3 March 2021) https://www.icf.com/insights/energy/resilient-power-utilities-prepare-climate-risks accessed 21 March 2021.

[17] Ibid, 1.

[18] Ibid, 5.

[19] Ibid.

[20] See <https://www.pge.com/en/about/newsroom/newsdetails/index.page?title=20200701_pge_emerges_from_chapter_11> accessed 21 March 2021.

[21] North American Electric Reliability Corporation, '2020 State of Reliability (July 2020) 48.

[22] Ibid, 49.

With increasing levels of variable renewable generation in the resource mix, there is a growing need to have resources available that can be reliably called upon on short notice to balance electricity supply and demand if shortfall conditions occur. Flexible resources that can include responsive generators with assured fuel or energy and demand response are necessary in some areas today to ensure resource adequacy and meet ramping needs. ERCOT [the Texas grid operator] and California rely on the output from wind and solar generation to meet projected peak demand.… Should solar and wind output fall below expectations during peak conditions, these areas may need to draw on unanticipated resources or additional imports from outside of the area to maintain balance between load and generation. Additionally, the high levels of solar PV resources in these areas cause the daily load shape to change such that greater amounts of flexible resources are needed to match steep ramping conditions during times when the change in wind or solar output changes rapidly.[23]

By flexible resources, NERC means generation that can be rapidly ramped up to meet demand which typically means gas-fired generation, in some instances utility-scale battery power, or sufficient demand response to cover the anticipated generation shortage.

Finally, grid resilience will be challenged by new demands on the grid. Several automobile manufacturers including Ford and General Motors have now committed to electrification of their fleets. GM expects to have 30 EV models by 2030[24] and Ford plans 16 full electric and 24 plug-in electric vehicles by 2022.[25] While a 2019 report concluded that the grid with careful planning could accommodate rather rapid growth of EVs, it did identify key challenges that could impact grid resilience including:

- Distribution capacity expansion could present additional costs. Areas that should be assessed are: (a) high power charging of light-duty EVs (at 150kW and above), (b) high-power charging of medium- and heavy-duty vehicles (potentially at over 1 MW), (c) legacy infrastructure constraints in dense urban areas, and (d) low-power charging of light-duty EVs on distribution systems.
- Transmission constraints must be assessed. It is acknowledged that transmission expansions must be deliberate as these investments in the U.S. power system are expensive and time consuming.
- Ramping capabilities of the generating fleet and spinning reserve requirements of the bulk power system should be considered for EVs at Scale.[26]

A related challenge is the need to electrify building heating, water heating, and cooking as part of deep decarbonization efforts to address climate change.[27] A few cities such as

---

[23] Ibid.

[24] See <https://www.caranddriver.com/news/a34730248/gm-accelerates-electrification-plans/> accessed 21 March 2021.

[25] See <https://www.reuters.com/article/us-autoshow-detroit-ford-motor/ford-plans-11-billion-investment-40-electrified-vehicles-by-2022-idUSKBN1F30YZ> accessed 21 March 2021.

[26] U.S. Drive, 'Summary Report on EVs at Scale and the U.S. Electric Power System' v (November 2019) <https://www.energy.gov/sites/prod/files/2019/12/f69/GITT%20ISATT%20EVs%20at%20Scale%20Grid%20Summary%20Report%20FINAL%20Nov2019.pdf> accessed 21 March 2021.

[27] See LeRoy Paddock and Caitlin McCoy, 'New Buildings' in Michael Gerrard and John Dernbach, *Legal pathways to Deep Decarbonization in the United States* (Environmental Law Institute 2018).

San Francisco have already begun to require electrification of new residential and commercial buildings beginning in 2021.[28] While estimates of the impact on the grid of electrification designed to reduce greenhouse gas emissions from natural gas are not as advanced as is electrification of transportation, similar challenges in transmission, congestion, and ramping are likely to be involved.

IV. The Biden Administration Focus of Renewables and Climate Change

The Biden Administration has emphasized expansion of renewable energy as a critical element of its plans to reduce the U.S. contributions to greenhouse gas emissions and to meet the country's commitments after re-entering the Paris Agreement. The President's 27 January 2021 Executive Order directs federal agencies to procure carbon-free electricity and zero emission vehicles, double renewable production from offshore wind by 2030, and to take climate justice into account in agency decision making.[29] The President has announced a goal of carbon-free electricity by 2035 and net-zero carbon emissions and 100 per cent clean energy by 2050. Finally, President Biden has named several climate advocates to his cabinet and announced an 'all of government' climate effort.

It is clear that for at least the next several years, energy resilience in the U.S. will have to take into account continued reliance on intermittent generation resources and will have to use tools such as demand response, energy efficiency, battery storage technology, energy management approaches including enhanced geographic diversity through new transmission lines, and better energy management systems that can take advantage of distributed resources such as electric vehicles and distributed energy storage, rather than on continued fossil-fuel generation to produce a resilient grid.

In the first half of 2020, COVID significantly disrupted the expansion of solar and wind generation. Energy demand worldwide in 2020 contracted by six per cent,[30] although the share of energy production from renewable sources increased significantly, as much as 40 per cent in the United States.[31] This likely occurred because renewable sources are often the lowest cost source of generation and therefore the first sources dispatched to meet demand.[32] Supply chains for wind turbines and solar panels were disrupted during lockdowns in the first few months of the pandemic, although construction had returned to near normal within about three months.[33]

Even more striking for renewable energy in the United States was the massive energy outage in Texas caused by a polar vortex that resulted in a prolonged period of well-below freezing temperatures in the state. At its peak, 46,000 megawatts of generating capacity,

---

[28] See <https://sfgov.legistar.com/LegislationDetail.aspx?ID=4584221&GUID=1DA24E52-38A0-4249-9396-270D0E9353BB> accessed 21 March 2021.

[29] Executive Order 14008 (27 January 2021).

[30] World Economic Forum, 'COVID-19 is a Game-Changer for Renewable Energy. Here's Why' https://www.weforum.org/agenda/2020/06/covid-19-is-a-game-changer-for -renewable-energy/ accessed 1 March 2021.

[31] Ibid.

[32] Ibid.

[33] See International Energy Agency, 'Renewables 2020' <https://www.iea.org/reports/renewables-2020> accessed 1 March 2021.

about half of the states total generating capacity,[34] was shut down with 28,000 of that total being thermal plants and the remaining 14,000 coming from wind and solar. The cascading shut down of power generating facilities forced a rolling blackout to be instituted by the system operator—the Electric Reliability Council of Texas or ERCOT—which in some cases persisted for several days. The President of ERCOT has said that the blackouts were necessary because the systems was 'seconds and minutes' from catastrophic system failure that would have persisted for several weeks.[35] Blame for the blackout was cast in several directions early as the event unfolded with several more conservative voices pointing to the large number of wind turbines that froze up during the cold snap. Later analysis, however, found that about two-thirds of the generating facilities that closed were thermal generators, many of them natural gas plants where either onsite pipelines or natural gas supply lines were interrupted because of gas line or wellhead freezing.

V. Building a Resilient Renewable-Based Energy Grid

A resilient grid in the U.S. will require a wide range of initiatives. This section suggests a number of changes that will be needed to create a resilient, extremely low carbon, affordable, and equitable electricity grid in the U.S. given the pressures discussed above.

A. Accelerate the percentage of renewable energy sources on the grid

There is no doubt that the percentage of renewable energy on the grid must be dramatically increased to mitigate climate change both by reducing emissions from energy generation and reducing GHG emissions from other sectors such as transportation. Without this change resilience challenges will only increase as climate-related events continue to disrupt the grid. As a result, resilience measures must be assessed in the context of a grid that likely will include at least half of the generation coming from intermittent sources.

Currently, about 7.3 per cent of the U.S. energy is produced by hydroelectric facilities in the U.S. and in Canada. Another 1.4 per cent comes from biomass and 0.5 per cent from geothermal. These numbers have been fairly stable since 1990. Wind energy accounted for 8.4 per cent of energy production and solar 2.3 per cent in 2020. About 1 per cent of the energy used in the U.S. comes from hydroelectric facilities in Canada[36] At least three new cross-border transmission lines are planned including one between Montana and Alberta for wind generation in the region, one in Minnesota to connect to Manitoba Hydro and one from Quebec to New York to access Quebec hydro resources.[37] Over 30 power transmission lines currently connect the two countries.[38] These efforts may add some more hydroelectric

---

[34] Comptroller of Texas, 'Texas' Electricity Resources' (August 2020). <https://comptroller.texasv/economy/fiscal-notes/2020/august/ercot.php> accessed 1 March 2021.

[35] See Erin Douglas, 'Texas was "seconds to minutes" away from catastrophic months long blackouts, officials say' The Texas Tribune (Austin, 18 February 2021).

[36] See Energy Matters <https://www.enbridge.com/energy-matters/energy-school/hydroelectric-power-in-north-america> accessed 23 March 2021.

[37] Energy Information Agency, 'U.S.-Canada Electricity Trade Increases' https://www.eia.gov/todayinenergy/detail.php?id=21992 accessed 23 March 2021.

[38] Ibid.

energy to the U.S. mix but are not likely to dramatically alter the renewables contribution of hydroelectric generation. As a result, and absent breakthrough nuclear or other non-fossil fuel electric generation, the largest area of growth to meet the goal of decarbonizing the electric grid by 2050 will fall to intermittent sources of generation, wind and solar. The U.S. Energy Information Agency projects that over 35 per cent of electricity generation will be from wind and solar installations by 2050.[39] Others have predicted an even higher percentage which would be required to meet President Biden's goal of a decarbonized grid by 2050. The National Renewable Energy Laboratory (NREL) has noted that a simulation analysis:

> Indicates that estimated U.S. electricity demand in 2050 could be met with 80% of generation from renewable electricity technologies with varying degrees of dispatchability, together with a mix of flexible conventional generation and grid storage, additions to transmission, more responsive loads, and changes in power systems operations.
>
> . . . .
>
> This transformation of the electricity system, involving every element of the grid, from system planning through operation, would need to ensure adequate planning and operating reserves, increased flexibility of the electric system, and expanded multi-state transmission infrastructure, and would likely rely on the development and adoption of technology advances, new operating procedures, evolved business models, and new market rules.[40]

The NREL report noted that this scenario would allow electricity supply and demand to be balanced 'in every hour of the year in each region ... including nearly 50% from variable renewable generation.'[41]

While achieving 80 per cent renewables on the grid is possible, the caveat in the NREL report is critical—the system must be more flexible, use a variety of tools to meet demand and be better able to share resources. The North American Electric Reliability Corporation has warned that 'Sufficient flexible resources are needed in areas with high levels of variable generation to avoid short-falls when variable resource output is insufficient to meet demand.'[42]

A flexible, renewables-reliant grid will require creating stronger incentives to build resilience into energy systems, new transmission lines that cross both state lines and national borders, better integration of distributed generation, significantly enhanced energy storage, continuing focus on energy efficiency to reduce demand to help offset electrification of transportation and buildings, stronger demand-response programs, and maintaining some rapid ramping capacity that can respond to generation interruptions.

---

[39] Energy Information Agency, 'EIA projects renewables share of U.S. electricity generation mix will double by 2050' <https://www.eia.gov/todayinenergy/detail.php?id=46676> accessed 23 March 2021.

[40] U.S. Department of Energy, National Renewable Energy Laboratory 'Renewable Electricity Futures Study; Executive Summary' 2.

[41] Ibid, 3.

[42] North American Electric Reliability Corporation, '2020 Long-Term Reliability Assessment' 25 (December 2020).

B. Mandate that public utilities identify and plan for climate vulnerabilities including sea level rise and extreme weather events such as heat, cold, wind, drought, and flooding

In 2016, the U.S. Department of Energy observed that:

> Across the country, energy systems and infrastructure are already increasingly required to operate outside of the conditions for which they were designed. Appropriate and proactive planning and investment are needed to reduce our energy infrastructure's critical vulnerabilities to climate and extreme weather and to ensure that electric power systems can continue to deliver clean, affordable, and reliable energy with a high level of performance.[43]

The Department urged that electric utilities conduct assessments of the climate change impacts on their operations.

> Vulnerability assessments help utilities to determine where and under what conditions their systems may be vulnerable to rising temperatures and sea levels, changing precipitation patterns, or more frequent and severe episodes of extreme weather. Resilience plans, which are informed by the findings of the vulnerability assessments, identify solutions and prioritize climate resilience actions and investments. By completing the key steps in this Guide, utilities will develop planning-level documents that identify specific actions for managing or mitigating climate change risks.[44]

A recent study by the Sabin Center for Climate Change Law at Columbia Law School and the Environmental Defense Fund found that:

> Most electric utilities are, however, yet to integrate climate considerations into system planning, design, operation, and other decisions. Indeed, only a handful of electric utilities have conducted a comprehensive assessment of where and under what conditions their systems are vulnerable to the impacts of climate change, and fewer still have identified and implemented measures to reduce those vulnerabilities.[45]

The authors argue that electric utilities already have a legal obligation to plan for and address reasonably foreseeable climate vulnerabilities under both public utility law and tort law.[46]

Whether or not an obligation already exists to plan for and address climate vulnerabilities, it is increasingly clear that electric companies should be required to do so. At least for the bulk power system, the GAO has noted that:

---

[43]   U.S. Department of Energy, 'Climate Change and the Electricity Sector: Guide for Climate Change Resilience Planning' 1 (September 2016).

[44]   Ibid, i.

[45]   Romany M. Webb, Michael Panfil, and Sarah Ladin, 'Climate Risk in the Electricity Sector: Legal Obligations to Advance Climate Resilience Planning in the Electricity Sector' 2 (2020) <https://climate.law.columbia.edu/sites/default/files/content/Full%20Report%20-%20Climate%20Risk%20in%20the%20Electricity%20Sector%20-%20Webb%20et%20al.pdf> accessed 30 March 2021

[46]   Ibid.

According to FERC's strategic plan, one of FERC's core functions includes protecting and improving the reliable and secure operation of the bulk-power system by identifying reliability and security risks; overseeing the development, implementation, and enforcement of mandatory reliability standards; and promoting the resilience, reliability, and security of the bulk-power system.[106] However, according to FERC staff, FERC has not taken steps to identify or assess climate change risks to the grid or planned a response because the Commission has not directed staff to do so. By taking steps to identify and assess climate-related risks and plan a response, including identifying the actions needed to enhance the resilience of the grid to climate change, FERC could better manage such risks and achieve its objective of promoting resilience.[47]

Among other things, FERC could direct NERC to develop mandatory reliability standards for climate risks that go beyond the NERC 'Generating Unit Winter Weather Readiness' standard that NERC has been working on over the past few years.[48] States could then model their own climate resilience requirements to match.

Careful advanced planning for the potential impacts of climate change, particularly when conducted in consultation with important stakeholders, can play a critical role in anticipating and preparing for the increasing and evolving impacts of climate change thereby enhancing resilience. This type of planning could help justify rate changes that may be needed to finance climate adaptation measures.

C. Incentives to build resilience into the grid

Reasons to invest in resilience can come from either market signals of from regulatory requirements. As the recent Texas blackout indicated, there was insufficient incentive built into the grid financial model to take steps to protect the system from extreme cold weather events even though an incident a decade earlier indicated the possibility of crippling shortages due to cold weather. Proven technology is available that would have prevented both wind turbines and many fossil plants from having to shut down.[49] However, most utilities chose not to invest in the technology since cold weather events are rare in Texas.[50]

Texas has long been a deregulated electricity market with the incentive to invest in reserve capacity largely coming from the prospect of collecting high or even very high variable rates in times of supply shortage. Even though those incentives can be very high in Texas where variables rates can reach US$9,000 per megawatt hour, they failed to incentivize weatherization of gas, coal, and wind generation facilities. This situation indicates that incentives must be directly related to addressing the resilience threat—encouraging resilience costs to

---

[47] GAO, 'Electricity Grid Resilience, (n 2) 57.

[48] See North American Electric Reliability Corporation, 'Reliability Guideline: Generating Unit Winter Weather Readiness—Current Industry Practices—Version 3'. <https://www.nerc.com/comm/OC_Reliability_Gu idelines_DL/Reliability_Guideline_Generating_Unit_Winter_Weather_Readiness_v3_Final.pdf> accessed 30 March 2021.

[49] See <https://thehill.com/changing-america/sustainability/energy/539460-sweden-tells-texas-how-to-keep-turbines-spinning-in> accessed 28 March 2021; <https://energycentral.com/news/frigid-weather-no-problem-ne-minnesota-wind-turbines> accessed 28 March 2021.

[50] See <https://spectrumlocalnews.com/tx/san-antonio/news/2021/02/19/gov--abbott-calls-for-mandatory-winterization-of-power-plants--proof-blackout-was-imminent> accessed 25 March 2021.

be directly build into tariffs—which does not align well with a free-market economics approach to market regulation, or that essential resilience issues must be dealt with through legislation or regulation. With market incentives failing to drive investment needed to assure a resilient grid, the Governor of Texas is now calling for a winterization mandate for energy generating facilities.[51] For wind generators this can be an expensive proposition, adding as much as US$400,000 (five to ten per cent of the total cost) to a 2.5-megawatt wind turbine. While the cost is high and may add to consumer costs raising equity concerns, it must be weighed against the cost of energy during shortages, the economic disruption, prolonged outages in underserved communities, the loss of life that resulted from the blackout, and the potential that climate change will result in cold weather events becoming more common. Resilience has a significant cost just as the absence of resilience has a significant cost.

D. Geographically diverse sources of energy generation and adequate transmission

Professor Alexandra Klass has observed that deep decarbonization of the U.S. economy 'will require a doubling of U.S. electricity generation as well as a significant expansion of the U.S. electric transmission and distribution grid, particularly since onshore renewable energy resources are dispersed widely throughout the country and are often located far from population centers.'[52] She describes a variety of efforts to speed siting of new transmission lines and barriers to accomplishing this task. In addition to the importance of building out the transmission network to meet decarbonization goals, both the recent Texas blackout and previous grid disruptions demonstrate the need for access to geographically diverse sources of generation and the transmission facilities to support a resilient very low carbon grid.

Texas provides a unique example of the risk of grid isolation. Texas utility operators chose after the passage of the Federal Power Act in 1935 to maintain an almost entirely intrastate grid. This allows Texas to avoid many of the Federal regulatory requirement that apply to interstate flows of electricity.[53] This isolation and independence came back to haunt Texas in the February blackout because the state did not have access to interconnected transmission lines to bring that energy into the state. Resilience discussions are now raising the possibility that Texas should build interconnections to one of the two regional grids that serve the remainder of the country.

While illustrative of the importance of interconnections to resilience, the Texas example is far from the only issue of geographic diversity and transmission that needs to be addressed to deal with expanded intermittent resources. By integrating geographically diverse intermittent sources the problems of intermittency can be significantly reduced. To accomplish this result, the National Academies has recommended that the U.S. create a 'National Transmission Policy' to rely on high-voltage transmission lines to support 'energy diversity,

---

[51] See <https://gov.texas.gov/news/post/governor-abbott-declares-power-system-winterization-related-funding-as-emergency-items-provides-update-on-winter-weather-response> accessed 28 March 2021.
[52] Alexandra B. Klass, 'Transmission, Distribution, and Storage: Grid Integration' in Michael Gerrard and John Dernbach, *Legal Pathways to Deep Decarbonization in the United States* (Environmental Law institute 2019).
[53] Richard C. Cuhady, 'The Second Battle of the Alamo, the Midnight Connection' [1995] 10 Natural Resources & Environment 57.

energy security, and the nation's equitable transitions to low carbon energy economy.[54] The National Academies also recommended that the Federal Energy Regulatory Commission require transmission companies and regional transmission organizations to analyse and plan for 'electric system reliability; efficient dispatch of the bulk power system, taking into account economics, environment, and equity; and economical opportunities to expand the interstate electric system to open up access to and development of renewable resources and connect these regions with areas of high electricity demand.'[55]

Transmission capacity may be able to be increased using new grid-enhancing technologies that allow more energy to be transmitted over existing transmission lines. These technologies include advanced power flow controls, dynamic line ratings, and topological optimization (which can reroute energy flows around congestion).[56] These technologies may double the amount of renewables to be integrated into existing transmission capacity.[57]

E. Integrating distributed generation

Distributed solar energy generation produced about 24,000 megawatt hours of energy in the U.S. in 2020.[58] This number is expected to double by 2050 accounting for seven per cent of the total electricity generation in the U.S.,[59] with NERC estimating even more rapid growth.[60] Because of its growing size, distributed generation could play an important role in system resilience both by reducing load on the distribution grid and by supplying energy into the grid. This latter role is currently limited by grid management systems that make much of this distributed generation invisible to system operators and by rate structures that may not provide adequate incentives for distributed generators to provide resources at times of system shortages.

In addition, it is important that siting of distributed generation be coordinated wherever possible with electric utilities since poor placement of distributed generation can increase line congestion while optimal placement can play an important role in relieving grid congestion.[61] Both because of concerns about congestion and for safety reasons, new distributed generation facilities can require expensive interconnection studies. However, some states including California through the California Public Service Commission have adopted rules that authorize the use of Integrated Capacity Analysis (ICA) mapping to expedite authorization of distributed generation.[62]

[54] National Academies of Sciences, Engineering and Medicine, 'The Future of Electric Power in the United States (2021)' 10, (National Academies Press 2021).

[55] Ibid.

[56] See Brattle, 'Unlocking the Queue with Grid-Enhancing Technologies' 5 (1 February 2021), https://watt-transmission.org/wp-content/uploads/2021/02/Brattle__Unlocking-the-Queue-with-Grid-Enhancing-Technologies_ _Final-Report_Public-Version.pdf90.pdfaccessed 28 March 2021.

[57] Ibid, 8.

[58] See <https://www.publicpower.org/policy/electricity-generation> accessed 28 March 2021

[59] U.S. Energy Information Administration, 'Annual Energy outlook 2021' 13 (U.S. Department of Energy February 2021).

[60] NERC, '2020 Long-Term Reliability Assessment' (n 42) 39.

[61] See Greening the Grid, 'Distributed Generation' <https://greeningthegrid.org/integration-in-depth/distributed-generation> accessed 28 March 2021.

[62] California Public Utility Commission, Rule 21.

Integration Capacity Analysis (ICA) ... is a process of modeling conditions on the distri-bution grid that impact where additional distributed energy resources (DERs), like solar or energy storage, can be added without the need for costly upgrades and/or lengthy inter-connection studies. The resulting maps can be critical tools for enabling more efficient and cost effective deployment of clean energy and energy storage.[63]

The Interstate Renewable Energy Council observed that the ICA

can be useful both for showing where new generation (such as rooftop solar) can be added to the grid, as well as where new *load* (i.e., electricity demand, such as electric vehicle char-ging stations) can be accommodated.[64]

Distributed generation is now large enough to disrupt the bulk energy system in some cir-cumstances. As a result, new planning work is underway by NERC to develop a reliability standard addressing inverter-based distributed generation.[65] While the potential for grid disturbance needs to be addressed, the scaling up of distributed generation can in coordin-ation with other tools contribute to the resilience of the grid.

F. Expanded energy storage and EVs as a grid resource

Resilience of a grid that increasingly relies on intermittent generation requires more en-ergy storage. Utility scale battery storage (one megawatt or more) in the United States has quadrupled since 2014, increasing from 214 MW to 899 MW in 2019. That number is pro-jected to increase to 2,500 MW by 2023. In 2019 California alone had over 225 MW of en-ergy storage due in part to a state mandate in 2017 which required the three major IOUs in the State to install up to 166.66 MW of distributed energy storage systems.[66] Another way that variability is being addressed through battery storage is combining PV and wind plants with battery storage which is becoming more price competitive. These plants include ap-proximately four hours of storage which allows the plants to compete in capacity markets increasing the return on investment.[67]

FERC has also encouraged battery storage in order 841 issued in February 2018 that re-quires regional system operators to remove barriers to the participation of electric storage in the capacity, energy, and ancillary services markets thereby significantly enhancing the incentives to deploy battery storage. The FERC order was upheld by the D.C. Circuit Court of Appeals.[68] In addition, six states now have energy storage mandates or targets.[69]

---

[63] Interstate Renewable Energy Council, 'CPUC Ruling Improves a Key rid Transparency Tool for Siting Renewables, Energy Storage' (2 February 2021) https://irecusa.org/2021/02/cpuc-ruling-improves-a-key-grid-transparency-tool-for-siting-renewables-energy-storage/ accessed 31 March 2021.

[64] Ibid.

[65] NERC, '2020 Long-Term Reliability Assessment' (n 42) 37.

[66] California Public Utilities Commission, Decision 17-04-039.

[67] See National Academies of Sciences, Engineering and Medicine, 'The Future of Electric Power in the United States (n 54) 178.

[68] National Association of Regulatory Utility Commissioners v. FERC, No 19-1142 (D.C. Cir Ct of Appeals, 10 July 2020).

[69] See U.S. Energy Information Administration, 'U.S. Battery Storage Market Trends' 24 (July 2020) Small scale battery storage is also increasing rapidly, especially in California, and could play a role in demand-response programs. Ibid 21–22.

One of the most significant battery resources for the grid is expected to be electric vehicles (EVs). While EV uptake has been rather slow to date, a flurry of recent announcements by automobile companies and support from the Biden Administration is expected to drive a rapid increase in EVs over the next few years. Electrification of transportation will add significant new load to the grid, complicate grid planning as new charging stations come online, and potentially create new flexibility for the grid as EV batteries become accessible to grid operators to meet load demands. One pilot project conducted by BMW and Pacific Gas and Electric concluded that charging of EVs can be managed as a flexible grid resource that has the 'potential to result in cost savings associated with operating and maintaining the grid as well as owning an electric vehicle'.[70]

G. Expanded demand-response programs

Demand response (DR) programs can also play an important role in flexibility. The previous example related to EVs is just the latest in a variety of existing and potential demand-response opportunities that can provide grid operators with addition resources by quickly curtailing demand. FERC defines demand response as 'a reduction in the consumption of electric energy by customers from their expected consumption in response to an increase in the price of electric energy or to incentive payments designed to induce lower consumption of electric energy'.[71] DR typically includes two separate forms. The first is peak-load reduction or 'peak shaving' designed to reduce demand at times of high energy usage. Absent demand response, energy suppliers would have to build additional generation capacity, utilize often older, less-efficient power generating plants (that may produce higher levels of pollution), or buy power from other generators that can be very expensive during periods of high energy demand. The second, involves contributing to efficient operation of the distribution network. DR can help alleviate transmission line congestion and can provide ancillary serves such as frequency regulation that may be particularly important as more intermittent resources such as wind and solar are added to the generation mix.

The U.S. National Action Plan for Demand Response describes two forms of peak-load reduction:

> Demand response can be both dispatchable and non-dispatchable. 'Dispatchable demand response' refers to planned changes in consumption that the customer agrees to make in response to direction from someone other than the customer. It includes direct load control of customer appliances such as those for air conditioning and water heating, directed reductions in return for lower rates (called curtailable or interruptible rates), and a variety of wholesale programs (...) that compensate participants who reduce demand when directed for either reliability or economic reasons. This direction to reduce load can be in response to acceptance of the consumer's bid to sell its demand reduction at a price in an organized market (a wholesale price-responsive demand response) or to a retail provider.

---

[70] American Public Power Association, 'EVs Can Be Flexible Grid Resource, Say BMW and PG&E' (27 June 2017).
[71] 18 CFR s 35.28(4).

'Non-dispatchable demand response' refers to programs and products in which the customer decides whether and when to reduce consumption based on a retail rate design that changes over time. This is sometimes called retail price-responsive demand and includes dynamic pricing programs that charge higher prices during high-demand hours and lower prices at other times.[72]

A DR study noted 'The ability of storage-type demand response that can ramp in both directions to both reduce load and also absorb excess generation is a new and developing area of demand response that has proven reliable for balancing services (regulation and load-following) at a small scale'.[73]

DR in the U.S. has been encouraged, incentivized or required at the federal, regional, and state level and has evolved in waves over the past four decades. DR is currently recognized at all levels of government as a means of both improving grid reliability and saving costs.[74] The Regional Transmission Operator that covers portions of 13 states in the Mid-Atlantic and Midwest, and the District of Columbia, known as PJM,[75] provides a good example of how DR is dealt with in some jurisdictions. PJM aggregates DR using Curtailment Service Providers (CSPs).[76] These 'aggregators' provide consumers two ways to utilize DR. End-users can participate in Pre-Emergency and Emergency DR, which 'represents a mandatory commitment to reduce load or only consume electricity up to a certain level' in response to emergency conditions to avoid brownouts or blackouts.[77] PJM treats users who participate in this type of DR like generators, expecting them to perform and penalizing users who fail to comply.[78] Secondly, users can participate in economic DR, in which users voluntarily reduce load when the wholesale energy market price exceeds the net benefits price, which is the price at which 'the benefits incurred by a reduction in the wholesale price from the economic [DR] will exceed the cost to pay for it.[79]

DR programs will likely further expand as smart grid and smart appliance technologies are increasingly deployed across the country.

H. Continuing focus on energy efficiency to reduce demand

Energy efficiency in the United States has been an important element in managing energy demand for the past 30 years. Energy intensity—energy used per dollar of GDP declined

---

[72] FERC Staff, 'U.S. National Action Plan for Demand Response' 3 (FERC 2010) <https://www.energy.gov/sites/prod/files/oeprod/DocumentsandMedia/FERC_NAPDR_-_final.pdf> accessed 1 April 2021.

[73] Doug Hurley, Paul Peterson and Melissa Whited, 'Demand Response as a Power System Resource: Program Designs, Performance, and Lessons learned in the United States' viii (Regulatory Assistance Project, Synapsis Energy Economics 2013) <http://www.raponline.org/wp-content/uploads/2016/05/synapse-hurley-demandresponseasapowersystemresource-2013-may-31.pdf> accessed 1 April 2021.

[74] Portions of this section are derived from LeRoy Paddock and Charlotte Youngblood, 'Demand Response and Infrastructure Development in the United States' in Martha M. Roggenkamp et al (eds), *Energy Networks and the Law: Innovative Solutions in Changing Markets* (Oxford University Press 2012), 161–162.

[75] PJM, 'Who We Are' <http://www.pjm.com/about-pjm/who-we-are.aspx accessed 1 April 2021.

[76] PJM, 'Curtailment Service Providers' <http://www.pjm.com/markets-and-operations/demand-response/csps.aspx> accessed 1 April 2021.

[77] PJM, 'Demand Response and Why It's Important' (2018) 2-3 <http://www.pjm.com/-/media/markets-ops/dsr/end-use-customer-fact-sheet.ashx?la=en> accessed 30 June 2021.

[78] Ibid.

[79] Ibid.

by more about 40 per cent between 1990 and 2019. Energy intensity is expected to be less than 50 per cent of the 2005 energy intensity by 2050.[80] The Biden Administration has indicated that it will reverse the trend of the last four years by placing significant more focus on energy efficiency. Its day 1 Executive Order on 20 January 2021, required the Department of Energy to re-examine a series of appliance efficiency standards promulgated during the Trump Administration that would have eased efficiency requirements.[81] In addition, the Administration has proposed a variety of energy efficiency initiatives as part of its plans to address climate change.

Several states have also taken actions to drive energy efficiency. For example, California's latest building code which went into effect in January 2020 requires newly constructed residential and commercial buildings to use a combination of energy efficiency and renewable energy to meet 100 per cent of their annual energy needs—referred to as Zero Net Energy Buildings.[82] Several states and cities require energy use disclosure for commercial and large residential buildings so that prospective purchasers can assess the energy efficiency of the buildings. One of these jurisdictions, the City of Minneapolis, in February of 2013 adopted ordinance 47.190 requiring commercial buildings 50,000 square feet and over and city-owned buildings 25,000 square feet and over to annually benchmark their energy consumption and report this information to the City.[83] Several states now require electric utilities to create 'public benefit funds' to provide money for carrying out energy efficiency projects.[84] Finally, a few states have required their electric utilities to achieve specific energy efficiency improvements each year. The strongest Energy Efficiency Resource Standard requirements are in Rhode Island and Massachusetts where the states require 2.6 per cent and 2.93 per cent annual peak demand incremental savings respectively.[85]

An enhanced focus on energy efficiency can contribute significantly to resiliency by reducing overall demand allowing the grid to accommodate electrification more easily. Studies indicate that cost-effective energy efficiency measures could reduce demand by about 16 per cent of the estimated energy use in 2035.[86]

---

[80] U.S. Energy Information Administration, 'EIA projects U.S. energy intensity to continue declining, but at a lower rate' <https://www.eia.gov/todayinenergy/detail.php?id=42895> accessed 28 March 2021.

[81] Executive Order 13920, 20 January 2021.

[82] See Jake Richardson, 'First Zero Net Energy Community in California Announced' *CleanTecnica* (28 April 2015) <https://cleantechnica.com/2015/04/28/first-zero-net-energy-community-california-announced/> accessed 31 March 2021.

[83] City of Minneapolis, 'Minneapolis Climate Action Plan' <http://www.minneapolismn.gov/sustainability/climate-action-goals/climate-action-plan> accessed 31 March 2021.

[84] American Council for an Energy Efficient Economy, 'Energy Efficiency Programs for Utility Customers' <https://aceee.org/topics/energy-efficiency-programs-utility-customers> accessed 31 March 2021.

[85] American Council for an Energy Efficient Economy, 'State Energy Efficiency Resource Standard (EERS) Activity' (9 January 2017). <https://programs.dsireusa.org/system/program/detail/4507> accessed 31 March 2021.

[86] U.S. Department of Energy, 'Energy Efficiency: Savings Opportunities and Benefits' <https://www.energy.gov/eere/slsc/energy-efficiency-savings-opportunities-and-benefits> accessed 28 March 2021.

I. Maintain nuclear generation where feasible and some well-targeted natural gas rapid ramping capability preferable with carbon capture and sequestration

Nuclear power still provides 20 per cent of the country's generation and makes important contribution to base load power. Operating nuclear power plants has been uneconomical in some locations in the country as a result of the expansion of lower cost natural gas, wind and solar generation. To keep these plants running, nuclear power plants in Ohio, New York, New Jersey, Connecticut, Pennsylvania, and Ohio have all received government-authorized zero emission subsidies recognizing their value in avoiding greenhouse gas emissions.[87] These state subsidies of nuclear power plants were challenged as being beyond the authority of state government but have been upheld by the U.S. Second Circuit Court of Appeals in *Coalition for Competitive Electricity v Zibelman*,[88] and in the 7th Circuit Court of Appeals in *Electric Power Supply Ass'n v Star*.[89] At least in the near term, nuclear power plants are an important aspect of avoiding GHG emissions even though the waste disposal problem has not been solved. In the longer term, next generation nuclear power generation may be feasible to help bridge the intermittency issues with wind and solar, however given the time frame for authorizing new nuclear generation, the anticipated high cost of nuclear generation and the time needed to permit and site a nuclear generating plant, it is unlikely this new source of generation will be available within the next decade. Of course, other forms of power generation could emerge in the form of hydrogen fuels or carbon free produced methane but those sources are also still far from deployment.

As a result, some rapid ramping capability is likely to be needed to assure a resilient grid at least until electricity storage options are sufficiently robust to provide more than a few hours of backup generation or the new sources of carbon-free generation are available. Rapid ramping reserves will be a significant factor throughout the country as the percentage of intermittent generation increases and as the impacts of climate change create more extreme events that can disrupt generation. However, rapid ramping reserves may be particularly important for locations such as California, where solar energy provides a very significant portion of the power, to deal with a phenomenon referred to as a 'duck curve'. On hot days, peak demand occurs in the evening when solar power is declining. This requires regular ramping up of other sources of power to meet the evening demand. Some of this can come from imported hydropower but supplies from this source were not adequate to meet demand during the summer of 2020 resulting in occasional blackouts in California.

Currently, in most markets this ramping capacity is provided primarily by natural gas-fired power plants. However, to meet climate goals, greenhouse emissions from natural gas must be phased out beginning in the mid-2030s. As a result, it is important that carbon capture and sequestration development continue so that gas-fired power generation needed for ramping can utilize the technology to minimize carbon emissions. Planning for locating carbon capture and sequestration facilities should be coordinated with areas that will need rapid ramping gas facilities to meet resiliency needs. Both Congress[90] and the Biden

---

[87] Congressional Research Service, 'Staying Nuclear": Legal Challenges to State Subsidies for Aging Nuclear Power Plants and Related FERC Actions' (26 March 2021) 2.

[88] 906 F3rd 41 (2018).

[89] 904 F3rd 518 (2019).

[90] See Congressional Research Services, 'Carbon Sequestration Legislation in the 116th Congress' (21 February 2020) <https://crsreports.congress.gov/product/pdf/IF/IF11345>accessed 1 April 2021.

Administration[91] have proposed increased funding to advance carbon capture and sequestration technology that could allow nature gas power plants to operate without contributing to climate change.

VI. Conclusion

Creating a resilient electrical grid is a critical issue in the U.S. as demonstrated by a series of blackouts and service disruptions over the last decade that have caused very large economic losses and resulted in a number of deaths. This effort, however, must be pursued in the context of transitioning to a very low or zero carbon electric generating network to mitigate even more serious climate related extreme weather events and sea level rise. At least in the next decade and perhaps the next two decades this will require dramatically increasing the percentage of intermittent sources such as wind and solar energy. This situation requires a diverse set of tools that can contribute to resilience. These tools include better planning for extreme weather events and sea level rise, providing incentives for investing in grid resilience such as winterization, building transmission capacity to access more geographically diverse generation, better integrating distributed generation into the grid, expanding energy storage including through electric vehicles, expanding demand-response programs, accelerating energy efficiency programs, and providing continued access to nuclear generation and other flexible generation such as natural gas generation coupled with carbon capture and sequestration.

---

[91] MIT Technology Review, 'Here's Biden's plan to reboot climate innovation' (11 February 2021) <https://www.technologyreview.com/2021/02/11/1018134/heres-bidens-plan-to-reboot-climate-innovation/> accessed 1 April 2021.

PART V

STRATEGIC FINANCING AND ECONOMIC RESPONSES TO DISRUPTION

16

Transnational Energy Law Regimes and Systems Dynamics

Calibrating Finance Mechanisms of the International Renewable Energy Agency and the Energy Charter Treaty

*Nadia B. Ahmad**

I. Introduction

This chapter considers the transnational energy law regimes that have proliferated in response to climate change adaptation measures through the lens of the International Renewable Energy Agency (IRENA). While international treaties and agreements have formed the basis of energy law regimes, the growth of transnational intergovernmental organizations offers an additional dynamic beyond state actors in formation of energy governance systems. This chapter delves into the rise of green energy finance and renewable energy incentives for building better transnational energy systems and networks by understanding the functioning and finance mechanism put in place by IRENA and the Secretariat of the Energy Charter Treaty (ECT). IRENA as an intergovernmental organization and the ECT as an agreement are two ways to leverage capital to build more resilient energy systems. Considering the underlying mechanisms of these institutions provides a window to see how the idea of systems dynamics will be significant for building sustainable and reliable energy infrastructure worldwide. One of the key observations made is that when taking into account ongoing natural resource scarcity, high rates of joblessness, and market shocks, the transnational energy law regimes show promise in adapting to worsening climate change conditions and economic constraints. These variables can be understood through system dynamics, which is a part of systems theory, to understand and appreciate the dynamic approach to complex systems. Seeing the forces at play of systems dynamics in finance mechanisms shows how these relationships can build resiliency. Chapter 2 of this book covers resilience and systems theory in more depth.

While some may consider understanding systems dynamics a theoretical framework for management, it is also essential for the development and deployment of renewable energy resources and technologies, especially for emerging technologies, which may be hindered

* Much appreciation extended to the research assistance of Melissa Bryan. Thanks to Nicholas Robinson, Richard Ottinger, Jason Czarnezki, Katerina Kuh, Smitha Nrula, Michael Pappas, Justin Pidot, Brigham Daniels, Jessica Owley, Victor Flatt, Jonathan Rosenblum, Sharon Jacobs, Shi-Lin Hsu, Josh Galperin, Anastasia Teletsky, Nilmini Silva-Send, and Lee Paddock for advice, comments, and feedback. Thanks to the library assistance of Jason Murray, Diana Botluck, and Louis Rosen. A note of gratitude to Akmal, Senan, Hanan, Jihan, my parents, and my siblings for their unyielding love and support. To a world without fossil fuels. Reprint permission granted by *San Diego Journal of Climate and Energy*.

Nadia B. Ahmad, *Transnational Energy Law Regimes and Systems Dynamics* In: *Resilience in Energy, Infrastructure, and Natural Resources Law*. Edited by: Catherine Banet, Hanri Mostert, LeRoy Paddock, Milton Fernando Montoya, and Íñigo del Guayo, Oxford University Press. © Nadia B. Ahmad 2022. DOI: 10.1093/oso/9780192864574.003.0016

by lack of capital, finance, technical expertise, trouble-shooting, and supply chain issues. Systems dynamics offers the theoretical framework for accelerating the targets of the Paris Agreement to the United Nations Framework Convention on Climate Change (UNFCCC) as well as overcoming hindrances of the ECT. The Paris Climate Agreement set benchmarks, but it also included a means to accelerate benchmarks on emissions. It offered guidelines for lowering carbon emissions, but IRENA as an institution is what can provide the mechanisms and the systems for achieving the Paris targets through specialized knowledge and expertise on renewable energy governance and systems dynamics. The Paris Agreement is the 'what' needs to happen and IRENA and ECT provide the 'how' to achieve more resilient energy systems.

In Section II of this chapter, I explain how IRENA can overcome the shortcomings in the ECT for capacity building for more resilient systems. Then I consider reformulating systems dynamics for energy governance and resilience in Section III. The investment frameworks of the ECT will be analysed in Section IV to show how resiliency as a concept was underdeveloped. Then in Section V I argue ways that the Paris Agreement provides new guidance on how to build resiliency through stronger finance mechanisms.

II. The Capacity Building for Finance Mechanisms Through IRENA

No coincidence that the preparatory meetings for IRENA occurred following the Global Financial Crisis of 2008, which precipitated the Arab Spring of late 2010.[1] The pounding of protests and the unnerving possibility of toppling monarchies were not a desert mirage. These threats to power had to be neatly in the rearview. The Middle East drillers needed enough development to put people at ease, not enough to sway the balance of power. IRENA was simultaneously the aspiration of the Global South to answer for the insurgent extractive capitalism, which powered the Global North. People turned their noses on Doha, Qatar for its high per capita use of energy, but ignored the per capita use of energy in placed like Houston, Miami, or Los Angeles. A new movement was afoot, and the United States became more and more irrelevant in the climate change conversation.[2]

Even with a small budget and technical mandate, IRENA is becoming a key player in energy governance.[3] Two of IRENA's accomplishments include the Global Atlas and the Renewables Readiness Assessment. These online tools work to democratize the process of obtaining energy access for regions and countries that may not have information tools to determine metrics.[4]The IRENA Global Atlas initiative seeks to narrow 'the gap between countries that have access to the necessary data and expertise to evaluate the potential for renewable energy deployment in their countries and those that lack these elements.'[5]

[1] Johannes Urpelainen and Thijs Van de Graaf, 'The International Renewable Energy Agency: a Success Story in Institutional Innovation?' (2015) 15 International Environmental Agreements 159–177 DOI 10.1007/s10784-013-9226-1 (hereafter, Urpelainen and Van de Graaf, 'IRENA: a success story').
[2] John Allen, 'American Climate Leadership Without American Government' (Planet Policy, 14 December 2018), https://www.brookings.edu/blog/planetpolicy/2018/12/14/american-climate-leadership-without-american-government/.
[3] Urpelainen and Van de Graaf, 'IRENA: a success story,' (n 1).
[4] Nadia Ahmad, 'Unearthing Clean Energy' (TEDxOcala, 5 November 2016), <https://www.youtube.com/watch?v=QP39lio396s> accessed on 11 May 2021.
[5] Global Atlas, IRENA, <https://www.irena.org/globalatlas/> accessed on 11 May 2021.

IRENA's Renewables Readiness Assessment (RRA) is a tool for measuring the suitability of conditions in various nations for the development and deployment of renewable energy as wells as necessary conditions to achieve those results in the short- and medium-term.[6] The RRA is created as a country-led, collaborative instrument to widen the span of stakeholders under five main themes: 'national energy policy and strategy; institutions and markets; resources and technologies; the establishment of a business model; and the capacity needed to scale-up renewables.'[7]

Renewable energy has failed to reach it full potential, not because of the lack of technology, but because of bottlenecks of finance mechanisms. IRENA supports countries through the RRA to provide a toolkit for finance mechanism based on current needs and local generation and renewables capacity. Previous Director-General Adnan Amin realized the benefits of combining regulatory frameworks with targeted government intervention.[8] This process would seek to decrease investment risks and increase leverage through public–private partnerships.[9] IRENA further sought to develop capacity and financial strategy through the targeting of project developers, finance institutions, and public officials.[10]

Amin praised the electricity sector shift for renewables, arguing that the shift has become unstoppable.[11] He added, 'Globally, more renewable energy capacity has been installed than new fossil fuel and nuclear capacity combined, for four years running.'[12] Under the leadership of current IRENA Director General Francesco La Camera, membership for IRENA is approaching near-universality. As economies seek to recover from massive unemployment resulting from the coronavirus pandemic, a climate-centred recovery response has been gaining more traction. Not only are countries seeking to rebuild, they want to build better and not only build back. All recent major models of the future energy system from IRENA show Europe running on between 80–100 per cent renewable energy in 2050.[13] Even the International Energy Agency predicts higher use of renewables with its

---

[6] IRENA, 'Renewable Readiness Assessment' <https://www.irena.org/rra> accessed 11 May 2021.

[7] Ibid. 'While IRENA produces RRA reports to disseminate valuable country-level knowledge, the ultimate goals of the RRA process are to inspire new initiatives, refine policies and regulations to establish an enabling environment, and identify capacity-building measures and requirements.' Ibid.

[8] IRENA, Financial Mechanisms and Investment Frameworks for Renewables in Developing Countries (2012), <https://www.irena.org/-/media/Files/IRENA/Agency/Publication/2013/IRENA-report---Financial-Mechanisms-for-Developing-Countries.pdf> accessed 5 July 2021.

[9] Ibid, 11.

[10] Ibid, 11.

'Renewable energy investors in developing countries include governments, banks, equity firms, insurance companies, pension funds, industry bodies, clean energy companies, and start-up project developers. In some developing countries, such as India and Brazil, there is a growing appetite for RE investment, in particular among local pension funds and insurance companies. In the aftermath of the financial crisis, public institutions played an especially critical role in providing capital that was otherwise unavailable from private sources.

The RE investment functions performed by banks include corporate lending, project finance, mezzanine finance, and refinancing. Debt finance is usually provided by banks, whereas equity finance is often provided by equity, infrastructure and pension funds, either into companies or directly into projects or portfolios of assets. Different types of investors will engage depending on the type of business, the stage of technology development, and the degree of associated risk.'

Ibid, 17.

[11] Adnan Z. Amin, 'Remarks by Mr. Adnan Z. Amin at the 9th Session of the IRENA Assembly the Geopolitics of Energy Transformation' (IRENA) <https://www.irena.org/-/media/Files/IRENA/Agency/Speech/20190112-The-Geopolitics-of-Energy-Transformation.pdf> accessed 11 May 2021.

[12] Ibid.

[13] Remi Gruet, 'Recovery packages must make clean-energy a cornerstone of the new global economy' (Recharge, 11 May 2020) <https://www.rechargenews.com/circuit/recovery-packages-must-make-clean-energy-a-cornerstone-of-the-new-global-economy/2-1-805945> accessed 11 May 2021.

long-used modelling that underestimates renewable markets, with conservative estimates. In other parts of the world, the future share of renewables is anticipated to be well above 50–60 per cent, as deployments increase. The European Commission recommends a two-track approach to realize the more aggressive renewable energy targets. Most importantly, established renewables like wind power and solar will produce the majority of low-cost, emissions-free energy. Alongside those established renewables, the second-generation of renewables, such as wave, tidal, and OTEC (ocean thermal energy conversion), or SWAC (sea water air conditioning) should also be deployed at a larger scale. Amidst the carnage of the coronavirus, it is possible to imagine a new world for renewables. Looking back at this moment, history will judge us for taking decisive action to halt climate change impacts or for doing nothing and ignoring the lessons of inaction.

III. Reformulating Systems Dynamics for Energy Governance and Resilience

In this section, I propose two interventions. First, systems dynamics can offer a framework for assessing developing renewable energy governance models. Second, I argue that replying primarily on Western legal tools for renewable energy law governance overlooks other possibilities, such as indigenous and Third World legal modalities. Respecting and implementing such other approaches works to increase equity and reduce conflict over natural resource scarcity.

Complexity theory research considers systems and organizations function.[14] Cheryl Sullivan notes, 'Organizations are no longer believed to be simple, linear, independent systems tightly controlled to ensure stable environments.'[15] Complexity theory suggests that systems which are evolving continuously, are noted by 'partial order, and lie between the extremes of very rigid and highly chaotic organization.'[16] The ways that the law works to move, evolve, and change can be understood through complexity theory and systems dynamics.[17] This theoretical framework is significant because it offers a modality that has been successful in other business and entrepreneurial settings, including hydrocarbon development,

---

[14] Cheryl G. Sullivan, 'Exposure to Complex Environmental Health Challenges: Agent Orange and Sodium Dichromate' (2020) 17 Indiana Health Law Review 153, 155–156 (hereafter Sullivan, 'Exposure to Complex Environmental Health Challenges: Agent Orange and Sodium Dichromate'). Jeffrey Goldstein, an editor launching the journal, *Emergence: Complexity and Organization (E:CO)* in 2004, claims that 'complexity research has decidedly demonstrated that thriving organizations are better understood as complex[sic], nonlinear, far-from-equilibrium, and in vital contact with multiple environments.' Jeffrey Goldstein, Peter Allen, and David Snowden 'Editors' Introduction' (2004) 6 Emergence: Complexity and Organization v (hereafter Goldstein, Allen and Snowden, 'Editors' Introduction')

[15] Sullivan, 'Exposure to Complex Environmental Health Challenges: Agent Orange and Sodium Dichromate' (n 14). In linking complexity theory to capabilities of changing organizations, researchers concluded that '[c]ontinuously changing organizations are likely to be complex adaptive systems with semi-structures that poise the organization on the edge of order and chaos and links in time that force simultaneous attention and linkage among past, present, and future.' Ibid, citing Shona L. Brown and Kathleen M. Eisenhardt, 'The Art of Continuous Change: Linking Complexity Theory and Time-Paced Evolution in Relentlessly Shifting Organizations' (1997) 42 Administrative Science Quarterly 1, 32

[16] Sullivan, 'Exposure to Complex Environmental Health Challenges: Agent Orange and Sodium Dichromate' (n 14).

[17] Jeffrey Rudd, 'J.B. Ruhl's "Law-and-Society System": Burying Norms and Democracy Under Complexity Theory's Foundation' (2005) 29 William & Mary Environmental Law & Policy Review 551, 569 (hereafter Rudd, 'J.B. Ruhl's "Law-and-Society System": Burying Norms and Democracy Under Complexity Theory's Foundation')

and can thus be successful in the setting of renewable energy. Yet the changes and the potential for change require a fluid understanding of how the law operates versus an absolute linear understanding of the progression of the law. Resilience in the energy sector includes the ability to respond to shocks to the system whether they are slow-onset or sudden-onset. Resilience can also be understood as a way to move forward beyond adversity from natural disaster to political and economic upheaval. For example, one step forward may lead to four steps backward. These nonlinear progressions of the law can be seen in the instances in which President Donald Trump rolled back environmental regulations in a bid for runway deregulation of environmental laws. Evolutionary explanations relying upon a historical discussion of human choices 'fail to convey an essential characteristic of the process—law can only move in one direction along its path of change.'[18]

This forward movement of the law is characteristic of the concept of resiliency. Understanding resiliency requires multiple pathways for reconciliation and recalibration in the space of energy law and renewable energy deployment. The space of energy law is developed for oil and gas development. The space of the law is geared toward profit maximization of shareholders with limited regard for natural resource preservation. Meanwhile, renewable energy deployment requires a shifting of the legal landscape, especially for international agreements and international institutions. Resilience seeks to reconcile the impact 'under dynamic environments and across multiple time frames by supplementing traditionally static system performance measures to consider behaviors under changing conditions and complex interactions among physical, information and human domains.'[19]

Law professor J.B. Ruhl was the first to consider systems dynamics in the context of sustainable development and environmental law. He observed that 'Systems cope with their couplings to other systems' evolutions through strategies of cooperation, competition, and conflict.'[20] This Darwinian notion of evolutionary biology was based on the idea of natural resource scarcity and the prevalence of competition among and between species. Ruhl argues that the competition may involve conflict, but would not necessarily entail mortal combat over the same morsel of food. Competition systems could be able to resolve their conflicts through 'tacit or explicit compromises may assure two systems' mutual survival instead of each risking its own demise in all-out warfare.'[21] Ruhl argued that 'systems locked in co-evolutionary relations adopt shifting blends of cooperation, competition, and conflict to maintain fitness in a constantly changing evolutionary environment.'[22]

For example, in looking at the concerns surrounding pipeline siting, property and environmental rights can impact energy projects on tribal lands and on former tribal lands ceded to the United States. This problem may not appear as significant unless the broader issues of tribal lands are considered in the United States.[23] Consider though that 50 million

[18] Rudd, 'J.B. Ruhl's "Law-and-Society System": Burying Norms and Democracy Under Complexity Theory's Foundation' (n 17). Rudd notes, 'Law's evolution is not described solely in terms of the rules of motion— "laws ... on the law side, and social mores and ethics, on the society side," nor exclusively as an incremental historical process resulting primarily from normative choices.'
[19] Paul E. Roege, Zachary A. Collier, James Manchillas, John A. McDonagh, and Igor Linkov, 'Metrics for Energy Resilience' (2014) 72 Energy Policy 249.
[20] J. B. Ruhl, 'The Co-Evolution of Sustainable Development and Environmental Justice: Cooperation, Then Competition, Then Conflict' (1999) 9 Duke Environmental Law & Policy Forum 161, 169–170.
[21] Ibid.
[22] Ibid.
[23] Nadia Ahmad, 'Trust of Bust, Complications with Tribal Trust Obligations and Environmental Sovereignty' (2017) 41 Vermont Law Review 799, 802.

acres of Indian trust lands exist in the United States. At the same time, thousands of miles of easements traverse tribal lands for various purposes as crucial fragments of the national infrastructure. Significant swaths of tribal lands lay within the path of major energy infrastructure projects. American Indian communities experience an imbalanced proportion of environmental degradation on account of the mineral development in North America. Without improved tribal consultations and more robust treaty claims, the updated rights-of-way regulations in Indian Country will lead to a steady and blatant encroachment of tribal lands. Moreover, this will also affect all future development of energy easements, including lands of the White Earth Band of Ojibwe in northwestern Minnesota, Navajo Nation in Texas and New Mexico, and the Seminole Tribe of Florida's Big Cypress Reservation. Through a systems dynamics understanding of energy law regimes, the issue is not only about extracting crude oil and transporting it, but also respecting the tribal lands and corresponding tribal treaties, which will be at odds with tribal environmental sovereignty.

The concern of tribal land claims and environmental sovereignty for indigenous lands is repeated across the world for energy projects. Renewable energy projects are not immune from competing land claims and disputes about natural resources. For example, solar energy and wind energy, which may have zero carbon emissions, require rare earth minerals like lithium, which are located in vulnerable communities. Further concerns for life cycle analysis of hydrocarbon and renewable energy projects will require analysis followed by assurances of the actual carbon footprint of such projects. This life cycle analysis, which would consider environmental externalities, could benefit from an analysis of systems dynamics.

Wild Law attorney Thomas Berry argues that contemporary societies should consider indigenous practices as: '[D]ialogue with native peoples ... throughout the world is urgently needed to provide the human community with models of a more integral human presence to the Earth.'[24] The indigenous notions of land have the simultaneous existence of obligations and rights that are place-specific to the land.[25] Irene Watson argues, 'Ownership is not exclusive. And it does not define the owned object as a commodity: instead it defines it as the concern of a limited group of people who stand in a particular relationship.'[26] Watson rejects the formal native title system, arguing that it erodes and subverts native identities.[27] As such, she contends that '[n]ative title does nothing to help us care for country,' and she observes the law of people outside formal legal mechanisms.[28] This framework clarifies the consequence of vernacular law.[29] The official legal recognition of 'both ecocentric and indigenous descriptions of private property are related and there is the potential for great benefit from a dialogue and shared learning from both perspectives.'[30]

The thinking of law as centred around nature is crucial for seeing the connections for resiliency in energy systems. The systems of land title and systems of law are designed for wealth maximization and aggregate behind the principle of shareholder primacy to

---

[24] Thomas Berry, *The Great Work: Our Way into the Future* (2nd edn, Crown Press 1999) 180.

[25] Peter D. Burdon, *Earth Jurisprudence: Private Property and the Environment* (Routledge 2015) 121 (hereafter Burdon, *Earth Jurisprudence*).

[26] Ibid. (quoting Irene Watson, 'Buried Alive' (2002) 13 Law & Critique 253 (hereafter Watson 'Buried Alive')).

[27] Watson 'Buried Alive' (n 26). Watson is an elder among the Tanganekald-Meintangk peoples, who are the custodians of an area in Southeastern Australia, known as the Coorong.

[28] Ibid.

[29] Burns H. Weston and David Bollier, *Green Governance: Ecological Survival, Human Rights, and the Law of the Commons* (2013).

[30] Burdon, *Earth Jurisprudence* (n 25) 122.

effectuate capital accumulation. The idea of resilience runs counter to the notion of wealth maximization, because at its core, resilience is building equilibrium. Resilience thinking developed from physics, psychology, ecology, and urban planning and into the energy law space. Resilience brings balance. Ayyoob Sharifi and Yoshiki Yamagata argue that initial study of resiliency failed to consider the multiple components of the energy system including supply, transmission, and distribution.[31]

Indigenous conceptualizations of land are more akin to the Anglo–American governance model with property as a bundle of sticks. Indigenous frameworks for land preservation, environmental sovereignty, and natural resource conservation can aid a systems dynamics framework for conceptualizing energy governance and the deployment of renewables. Having an earth centred approach to systems dynamics is crucial for its development and deployment along with the scale up of such approaches. Along with indigenous frameworks, Third World Approaches to International Law (TWAIL) offers another legal modality for considering the formulation and implementation of energy governance.[32] For far too long, Eurocentric values of law and governance have usurped constructions of the law. When the Anglo–American and Indian notions of property clash, the Eurocentric configuration of property supersedes. Recognizing the legal modalities and sovereignty of the host nations and host sites of materials, supply chains, factories, labourers, and other raw materials is important. Insisting upon Western legal modalities and Western influence in energy governance is unfair, but also tactically negligent, because doing so underestimates the concerns of those involved. Reimaging the laws of host nations and indigenous groups will limit conflict of energy governance. Viewing humans as stewards of the Earth, instead of as its tillers and cultivators, is not complex to understand or nuanced in any way.[33] This idea is also captured with an Earth-centred approach to jurisprudence and contrasts with an anthropocentric perspective against the onslaught of overdevelopment.[34]

The next section analyses the Energy Charter Treaty and why it is important as a framework for renewable energy development, but also as hurdle in more rapid deployment of renewable energy systems. Yet the Energy Charter Treaty can be helpful also for understanding systems dynamics in the energy context with lessons for renewable energy development and deployment.

IV. The Investment Framework of the Energy Charter Treaty

Formed at the heels of the Soviet collapse, the ECT sought to establish a cooperative framework for energy investment, exploration, production, and transport.[35] The impetus behind

---

[31] Ayoob Sharifi and Yoshiki Yamagata, 'A Conceptual Framework for Assessment of Urban Energy Resilience' (2015) 75 Energy Procedia 2904, 2906.

[32] At its core, the phenomenon of Third World Approaches to International Law (TWAIL) asserts that international law is illegitimate, and its conceptualization can be traced back to a response to decolonization and the surrender of direct European control over non-Europeans. Makau Matua, 'What is TWAIL?' (2000).

[33] Nadia Ahmad, 'Energy for Metropolis' (2018) 72 University of Miami Law Review 258, 268–269.

[34] Judith E. Koons, 'Earth Jurisprudence: The Moral Value of Nature' (2008) 25 Pace Environmental Law Review 263, 263–265.

[35] 'Energy Charter Treaty (ECT)' (1994), <https://energycharter.org/process/energy-charter-treaty-1994/energy-charter-treaty/> accessed 11 May 2021 (hereafter 'ECT').

the ECT was to promote energy efficiency and mitigate environmental degradation.[36] Net-exporting nations would achieve a means to attract investment, protect their natural resources, and ensure reliable transportation for their energy exports.[37] The ECT essentially sought to mitigate 'political risk' for the Western companies which were investing in former Soviet countries.[38] What the ECT sought to do was create a mechanism for neutral arbitration to support a fair legal system for foreign investors from the possibilities of corruption and weak judiciaries.[39] While the impetus seemed fair enough, the treaty also gave foreign investors a bit of an upper hand in the negotiating and arbitration as presumably the foreign investor nations would draw out the legal principles.

Like other international agreements which strive for justice and equality, the ECT relied on a power imbalance for securing provisions. In other words, the investor countries are seen as having more sophisticated laws and tools for negotiations against corrupt and weak rule of law. This basic assumption underlies international law more broadly and is emblematic of the weakness of the rule of law generally in the global context, which allows transnational corporations to possess heavy-handedness in all aspects of deal-making, negotiating, dispute resolution, and litigation. Energy regulation and international trade expert Natasha Georgiou writes about the ECT:

> By facilitating synergy with the [World Trade Organization] rather than fragmentation, the ECT thus serves as a complementary forum in addressing the complexities of energy regulation in international trade. The ECT can therefore be said to be strengthening the rule of law and in so doing, providing a legally ordered institutional international environment in the energy sector. In this respect, the ECT's multilateral provisions that purport to advocate and constitute a model of good governance validate the assertion that there is to date no better alternative in the current global and interdependent energy world.[40]

Energy-importing nations would obtain protection for their outward energy investments and mechanisms to encourage supply security. Among the body of international laws, the ECT is the only set of international rules and regulations designed specifically for the energy sector, and it encompasses a diverse range of countries across Eurasia, including energy producers, consumers, and transit countries.[41] Fifty-four European and Asian

---

[36] 'The Protocol on Energy Efficiency and Related Environmental Aspects (PEEREA)' (International Energy Charter, 9 April 2015) <https://energycharter.org/process/energy-charter-treaty-1994/energy-efficiency-proto col/> accessed 11 May 2021 (hereafter 'Protocol on Energy Efficiency').

[37] Andreas Goldthau and Jan Martin Witte, 'The Role of Rules and Institutions in Global Energy: An Introduction' in Andreas Goldthau and Jan Martin Witte (eds), *Rules and Institutions in Global Energy* (Brookings 2016) 8–9 <https://www.brookings.edu/wp-content/uploads/2016/07/globalenergygovernance_chapter.pdf> accessed 11 May 2021 (hereafter Goldthau and Witt, 'Rules and Institutions').

[38] Volodymyr Ponomarov, 'The Energy Treaty 2.0 - What Does It Mean for the European Green New Deal' (Georgetown Environmental Law Review Online, 13 October 2020) <https://www.law.georgetown.edu/enviro nmental-law-review/blog/the-energy-treaty-2-0-what-does-it-mean-for-the-european-green-new-deal/>   accessed 11 May 2021 (hereafter Ponomarov, 'Energy Treaty 2.0').

[39] Ibid.

[40] Natasha Georgiou, 'A Rule Based Architecture for the Energy Sector, The WTO and the ECT' (*Energy Charter Secretariat, Occasional Paper Series,* 16 December 2016) <https://www.energycharter.org/what-we-do/knowle dge-centre/occasional-papers/a-rule-based-architecture-for-the-energy-sector-the-wto-and-the-ect/> accessed 11 May 2021 (hereafter Georgiou, 'Rule Based Architecture').

[41] Goldthau and Witt, 'Rules and Institutions' (n 37). See also Yulia Selivanova, 'Trade in Energy: Challenges for International Trade Regulation' (World Trade Organization, 11 June 2010) <https://www.wto.org/english/res_e/ publications_e/wtr10_forum_e/wtr10_11june10_e.htm> accessed 11 May 2021 (hereafter Selivanova, 'Trade in

countries have signed or acceded to the ECT.[42] With its current membership, the ECT has a natural focus on the evolving Eurasian energy market, including the Mediterranean region, the Middle East, and North Africa. Since Pakistan, China, Korea, Iran, and Association of South-East Asian Nations have all taken on observer status in recent years, the ECT's role will become increasingly significant in Asia. Yet without reconceiving the negotiation and dispute resolution rules to account for North-South and South-South frameworks for international legal norms, the ECT will also lack regional and international authority and legal effectiveness.

The ECT is a crucial model and organizing tool for IRENA. Seeing the potential synergies between the ECT and IRENA is another way that systems dynamics can be integral for rapidly deploying renewable governance systems. Overlooking the connections between these two instruments, systems, and bodies shows the problem of not using systems dynamics in the discussion of renewables. On the one hand, fossil fuels will have to be phased out. Hydrocarbon infrastructure will become a stranded asset. On the other hand, renewables will require accelerated deployment and have to penetrate the markets previously dominated by fossil fuels. Seeing the links and interrelations between the international energy and environmental agreements is essential.

The ECT sought to move past prior economic division in the energy sector.[43] The prospects for mutually beneficial cooperation became clear in the energy sector, which led to the idea of working toward a commonly accepted foundation for reorienting energy cooperation among Europe and Asia.[44] The interdependence of net energy exporters and net energy importers led to a recognition that 'multilateral rules can provide a more balanced and efficient framework for international cooperation than is offered by bilateral agreements alone or by non-legislative instruments.'[45] The ECT has a significant role in establishing the international framework for energy security through 'the principles of open, competitive markets and sustainable development.'[46]

Even though the ECT, created in 1994, is a young, multinational agreement, it is quite extensive. Article 2 states that ECT 'establishes a legal framework in order to promote long-term cooperation in the energy field, based on complementarities and mutual benefits, in accordance with the objectives and principles of the Charter.'[47] The ECT promotes investment liberalization through the establishment of an international legal order which ensures

---

Energy'). ECT General Secretariat Yulia Selivanova observes two major questions to consider in the context to energy trade work.

[42] Energy Charter Treaty, 'Energy Charter Treaty, Signatories/Contracting Parties' (Energy Charter Secretariat, 18 February 2019) <https://energycharter.org/process/energy-charter-treaty-1994/energy-charter-treaty/signatories-contracting-parties/> accessed 11 May 2021 (hereafter, ECT, 'ECT Signatories').
[43] Energy Charter Treaty, 'Energy Charter Treaty Process Overview' (Energy Charter Secretariat, 5 August 2015) <https://energycharter.org/process/overview/> accessed 11 May 2021 (hereafter, ECT, 'ECT Overview').
[44] Ibid.
[45] Ibid.
[46] Ibid. ('The Energy Charter Treaty and the Energy Charter Protocol on Energy Efficiency and Related Environmental Aspects were signed in December 1994 and entered into legal force in April 1998. The Treaty was developed on the basis of the 1991 Energy Charter. Whereas the latter document was drawn up as a declaration of political intent to promote energy cooperation, the Energy Charter Treaty is a legally-binding multilateral instrument.') Ibid.
[47] Energy Charter Treaty (open for signature on 17 December 1994, entered into force 24 April 1998) 2080 UNTS 100 (hereafter ECT).

a level playing field and respect for the rule of law.[48] By providing a dispute resolution mechanism before international tribunals, investor confidence has increased through the ECT by investors and the financial community and ensures the investment and trade flows, which lead to economic growth.[49] The ECT was designed 'to meet the need for multilateral rules for international cooperation on investment protection, which is required by the increasing globalization of the world's economy, the interdependence of the energy sector, and the long-term and highly capital-intensive nature of energy projects.'[50] To solidify and enhance the ECT's rulemaking bodies, investment protection measures, and dispute resolution mechanisms require further collaboration and cooperation by current observer nations and the loosening of the reins by its founding members. The move to cede power to achieve power will be the driver for change for the ECT's international energy investment protections. The ECT states its primary aim 'is to strengthen the rule of law on energy issues, by creating a level playing field of rules to be observed by all participating governments, thereby mitigating risks associated with energy-related investment and trade.'[51] The ECT fills gaps in global energy governance through energy sector specific rules.[52]

A number of critics assert that the ECT allows for large transnationals to sue countries that pass laws reducing fossil fuel emissions to meet their Paris Agreement obligations.[53] Many of the ECT disputes relate to fossil fuel investment conflicts.[54] At its core, the ECT is intended for investment protection for fossil fuel development, which is in many ways incongruous with efforts at reduction of greenhouse gas emissions.[55]

Belgium has sought clarification to the Court of Justice of the European Union (CJEU) regarding intra-EU investment dispute provisions relating to Article 26 of the ECT.[56] Even though, the ECT is undergoing modernization processes, the ECT may not be able to change for the demands of the Paris Climate Agreement and other efforts at accelerating reductions in carbon emissions.[57] Researcher Stefanie Schacherer argues, 'If the CJEU finds the draft to be incompatible with the EU Treaties, the European Commission will have to remediate the content of Article 26 ECT and must subsequently convince the other ECT contracting parties.'[58] Such an opinion of incompatibility would impact approximately 40

---

[48] Energy Charter Treaty, 'The Role of the Energy Charter Treaty in Fostering Regional Electricity Market Integration: Lessons Learnt from the EU and Implications for Northeast Asia' (Energy Charter Secretariat, June 2015) <https://energycharter.org/fileadmin/DocumentsMedia/Thematic/Northeast_Asia_Study_EN.pdf> accessed 11 May 2021 (hereafter, ECT, 'Fostering Electricity Market Integration').

[49] ECT (n 35).

[50] Edna Sussman, 'The Energy Charter Treaty's Investor Protection Provisions: Potential to Foster Solutions to Global Warming and Promote Sustainable Development' in Marie-Claire Cordonier Segger, Markus W. Gehring, and Andrew Paul Newcombe (eds), *Sustainable Development in World Investment Law* (Wolters Kluwer 2010) 517 (hereafter Susssman, 'ECT's Investor Protection Provisions').

[51] ECT (n 35).

[52] Selivanova, 'Trade in Energy' (n 41).

[53] Ponomarov, (n 38).

[54] Ibid.

[55] Ibid.

[56] *Slowakische Republik v Achmea BV*, ECJ, Case C-284/16, EU:C:2018:158 (hereafter *Slowakische v Achmea*).

[57] Aikaterini Florou, 'ECT Modernisation Perspective: The Energy Charter Treaty and EU Law – A Cherry-Picking Relationship?' (Kluwer Arbitration Blog, June 26, 2020) <http://arbitrationblog.kluwerarbitration.com/2020/07/26/ect-modernisation-perspectives-the-energy-charter-treaty-and-eu-law-a-cherry-picking-relationship/> accessed 5 July 2021. EU want to reform of the ECT's investor-State arbitration mechanism to fit the EU's work related to multilateral reform process in the United Nations Commission on International Trade Law (UNCITRAL). Ibid.

[58] Stephanie Schacherer, 'The uncertain future of the Energy Charter Treaty: Belgium asks the European Court of Justice to rule on the compatibility of the modernized ECT with EU law' (Investment Treaty News, 23 March 2021) <https://www.iisd.org/itn/en/2021/03/23/the-uncertain-future-of-the-energy-charter-treaty-belg

pending ECT intra-EU arbitrations, which could then be challenged through domestic courts.[59] Such conflicts would limit the efficacy of the ECT and international energy agreements. The Achmea decision could effectively end international arbitration as it is known.[60] The decision would impact 'investment arbitration clauses in investment contracts with the EU Member States, the future intra-EU investment court system, the EU Member States' with third countries, the investment court system (ICS) contained in the Comprehensive Economic and Trade Agreement (CETA) and the currently discussed multilateral investment court (MIC).'[61]

In September 2021, the EU's top court issued a decision clarifying that that companies cannot use the Investor-State Dispute Settlement in intra-EU disputes.[62] Through its ruling, the court confirmed that this mechanism 'must be interpreted as not applicable to disputes between a member state and an investor from another member state concerning an investment made by the latter in the first member state.'[63] The court added that the 'preservation of the autonomy and the particular nature of EU law precludes the same obligations under the ECT from being imposed on member states.'[64] This legal development is significant because the majority of ECT disputes (some 60 per cent) occur between members of the EU.[65] The *Komstroy* decision extend the scope of the previous *Achmea* decision, which declared that EU law precludes intra-EU arbitrations based on bilateral investment treaties between two EU Member States (*intra-EU BITs*), also to the ECT.[66]

Critics are saying that that the ECT limits climate action. Nathalie Bernasconi-Osterwalder argues that the 'ECT attracted little public attention as a legal instrument and remains largely unknown.'[67] In a 2018 report, the Corporate Europe Observatory and the Transnational Institute described the ECT as 'The One Treaty to Rule Them All,' allowing lawsuits against government and multi-million dollar payouts to energy firms with taxpayer

---

ium-asks-the-european-court-of-justice-to-rule-on-the-compatibility-of-the-modernized-ect-with-eu-law-stefa nie-schacherer/> accessed 5 July 2021.

[59] Ibid.

[60] Anna Bilanová and Jaroslav Kudrna, '*Achmea*: The End of Investment Arbitration as We Know It?' (2018) 3 European Investment Law and Arbitration Review Online 261 (hereafter Bilanová and Kudrna, 'End of Arbitration').

[61] Ibid.

[62] Judgment of the Court (Grand Chamber), Case C-741/19, *Republic of Moldova v Komstroy, a company the successor in law to the company Energoalians*, ECLI:EU:C:2021:655, 2 September 2021.

[63] Ibid.

[64] Ibid.

[65] Elena Sanchez Nicholas, Court exempts intra-EU disputes from energy treaty, EU Observer, Sept. 6 <https:// euobserver.com/climate/152818> accessed 5 July 2021.

[66] Gibson Dunn, Intra-EU Arbitration Under ECT is Incompatible with EU Law According to the CJEU in Republic of Moldova v. Komstroy, Sept. 7, 2021, https://www.gibsondunn.com/intra-eu-arbitration-under-the- ect-is-incompatible-with-eu-law-according-to-the-cjeu-in-republic-of-moldova-v-komstroy/#_ftn1.   'This should not have a major impact on the current status of intra-EU ECT arbitrations brought under the auspices of the International Centre for the Settlement of Investment Disputes (*ICSID*), which are in principle not affected by EU law and its developments. Yet, the *Komstroy* decision may further decrease the chances of successful enforcement of any resulting award within the EU; Non-ICSID intra-EU ECT arbitrations seated in the EU are, on the other hand, more likely to be affected by this development either in the course of the arbitration itself or in subsequent annulment proceedings.'

[67] Nathalie Bernasconi-Osterwalder, 'How the Energy Charter Treaty Could Have Costly Consequences for Governments and Climate Action' (International Institute of Sustainable Development, 19 June 2018) <https:// www.iisd.org/library/how-energy-charter-treaty-could-have-costly-consequences-governments-and-climate-act ion> accessed 11 May 2021 (hereafter, Bernasconi-Osterwalder, 'How the ECT Could Have Costly Consequences').

funds.[68] The Corporate Europe Observatory and the Transnational Institute report argues that the ECT 'can be used to lock countries into the use of climate-wrecking fossil fuels, shield disastrous energy projects from public opposition, and cement the power of big business over our energy systems.'[69] The report further warns that the ECT 'is in the process of expansion, threatening to bind even more countries to corporate-friendly energy policies.'[70] The Paris Agreement, however, serves as a counterweight toward resilience as well as a complementary instrument to the ECT, which does not account fully for resilience and sustainability frameworks. The next section considers the legal mechanisms of the Paris Agreement for the more widespread deployment of renewables.

V. Moving the Paris Agreement Beyond the Status Quo

Investment agreements have been designed primarily to protect the status quo. Conversely, compliance with the objectives of the Paris Agreement will require radical change: a future in which governments have met the collective goal of keeping below the 2°C guardrail is a future without fossil fuels.
— Kyla Tienhaara, Australian National University[71]

Climate action is not a burden, but an unprecedented opportunity. Decreasing our dependence on fossil fuels will build more inclusive and robust economies. It will save millions of lives and slash the huge healthcare cost of pollution.
— Erik Solheim, Head of UN Environment Programme (UNEP)[72]

The Paris Agreement is not precisely a treaty, but is instead built upon an existing treaty developed in 1992: the UNFCCC.[73] Key elements of the Paris Agreement[74] include notably: providing and establishing progressively ambitious, and the obligation to elaborate and communicate Nationally Determined Contributions (NDCs) in five-year increments.[75] Environmental law scholar Elizabeth Burleson notes, '[t]he requisite funding and the facilitative nature of five-year review/stock taking cycles remain broad brush rather than clearly

---

[68] Corporate Europe Observatory (CEO) and the Transnational Institute (TNI), *The One Treaty to Rule Them All: The ever-expanding Energy Charter Treaty and the power it gives corporations to halt the energy transition* (Transnational Institute, 2018) <https://www.tni.org/files/publication-downloads/one_treaty_to_ruled_them_all.pdf> accessed 11 May 2021 (hereafter, CEO and TNI, 'One Treaty to Rule Them All'),
[69] Ibid.
[70] Ibid, 10.
[71] Kyla Tienhaara, 'Regulatory Chill in a Warming World: The Threat to Climate Policy Posed by Investor-State Dispute Settlement' (2017) 3 Transnational Environmental Law 229, 250 (hereafter, Tienhaara, 'Regulatory Chill in a Warming World')
[72] Manuel Elias, 'US decision to withdraw from Paris climate accord a "major disappointment" – UN' (UN News, 1 June 2017) <https://news.un.org/en/story/2017/06/558562-us-decision-withdraw-paris-climate-accord-major-disappointment-un> accessed 11 May 2021 (hereafter Elias, 'US decision to withdraw').
[73] James Zimmer, 'Pulling Out of Paris and Following Connecticut: Aggressive State Energy Policy in the Trump Era' (2019) 34 Connecticut Journal of International Law 255, 258 (hereafter, Zimmer, 'Pulling Out of Paris').
[74] Conference of the Parties' Twenty-first Session, U.N. Framework Convention on Climate Change, *Paris Agreement*, U.N. Doc. FCCC/CP/2015/L.9/Rev.1 Dec. 12, 2015 (hereafter the Paris Agreement). The *Paris Agreement* went into effect on Nov. 4, 2016.
[75] Paris Agreement, Art 14 (n 74).

defined, yet a transparency framework is expected to help ratchet up implementation.'[76]At the core of the Agreement, parties will submit their updated plans, the so-called NDCs, every five years in a process that seeks to ratchet up climate ambition.[77] Not only governments, but also many corporations supported the Paris Agreement.[78] U.S. leadership on climate change adaptation was crucial for the success of the Paris Agreement. Under the Trump administration, and in the absence of federal government leadership, individual states and transnational corporations have worked towards achieving renewable energy targets and emissions reductions. Law professor Uma Outka observes, 'This context of federal policy reversal creates an environment in which companies' counterposing renewable energy goals stand out.'[79]

In November 2016, the United States issued a document titled United States Mid-Century Strategy for Deep Decarbonization with the objective to build a low-emission economic system to reduce climate change.[80] The Trump administration undid 'many of President Barack Obama's environmental initiatives, withdrawing the U.S. from the Paris Agreement, rolling back regulations like the Clean Power Plan and most recently ending California's authority to set its own stricter fuel emission standards.'[81] The head of the U.N. Environment Programme (UNEP), Erik Solheim, has said, 'the U.S. decision to leave the Paris Agreement in no way brings an end to this unstoppable effort.'[82] Solheim added, 'The success of the Paris Agreement is in "the achievement of the inherent synergy of [three] pillars": diplomatic, legal, and economic.'[83] Under the Biden administration the commitments to the Paris Agreement have been recalibrated and accelerated.

Investments in transmission grids and electrification will lead to more opportunities to include renewables. Attorney Ryan Suit notes, 'Investment into those projects would improve renewable energy technology, and renewable resources such as wind and solar power would become increasingly viable.'[84] The capital-intensive nature of renewable power generation technologies and the fact that fuel costs are low, or often zero is considered with 'the weighted average cost of capital... used to evaluate the project' and its impact.[85]

[76] Elizabeth Burleson, 'Climate-Energy Sinks and Sources: Paris Agreement & Dynamic Federalism' (2016) 28 Fordham Environmental Law Review 1, 3 (hereafter Burleson, 'Climate-Energy Sinks').

[77] Ibid.

[78] Uma Outka, '"100 Percent Renewable": Company Pledges and State Energy Law,' (2019) 2019 Utah Law Review 661, 674–675 (hereafter, Outka, '100 Percent Renewable')

[79] Ibid.

[80] Bob Lambrechts, Navigating the Change in Climate Change Regulation in Kansas and Beyond, (April 2017) Journal of Kansas Bar Association 42, 422 (hereafter, Lambrechts, 'Navigating the Change in Climate Change').

[81] Emily Tillett, 'Trump drops by United Nations Climate Summit' (CBS News, 13 September 2019) <https://www.cbsnews.com/news/un-climate-summit-trump-drops-by-climate-meeting-at-start-of-united-nations-general-assembly/> accessed 5 July 2021. 'Under the terms of the Paris agreement, the U.S. withdrawal will not be final until November 4, 2020, the day after the U.S. presidential election.' Ibid.

[82] Elias, 'US decision to withdraw' (n 72).

[83] Rafael Leal-Arcas and Antonio Morelli, 'The Resilience of the Paris Agreement: Negotiating and Implementing the Climate Regime' (2018) 31 Georgetown Environmental Law Review 1, 4 (hereafter Leal-Arcas and Morelli, 'Resilience of the Paris Agreement')

[84] Ryan Suit, 'Charging Forward with NERC: An International Approach to Solving North America's Grid Problem (2018) 24 Richmond Journal of Law & Technology 3, 36 (hereafter, Suit, 'Charging Forward with NERC').

[85] Ben N. Reiter, 'Blowing It: Why Is Wyoming Failing to Develop Wind Energy Projects?' (2019) 19 Wyoming Law Review 45, 85, citing IRENA, 'Renewable Energy Technologies: Cost Analysis Series 3' (IRENA, June 2012), <https://www.irena.org/documentdownloads/publications/re_technologies_cost_analysis-wind_power.pdf>, accessed 11 May 2021.

The Paris Agreement also will struggle with being able to have meaningful participation in international norms relating to climate assessment. For example, the climate assessment norm has grown in international acceptance from once domestic efforts to also encapsulate climate assessments in environmental assessments.[86] The idea of climate assessment is to analyse the impacts on climate change on multiple sectors, including environmental, public health, and the economy. Underpinning the idea of climate assessment is that all countries must contribute to climate change adaptation. If the developed nations, who are the primary contributors of greenhouse gases (GHG) emission and negative impacts, establish more robust frameworks for climate assessments, GHGs and negative climate impacts would decrease for all countries.[87] The problem is that many corporations are against significant climate reductions commitment. The political will in developed nations is also lacking. Jessica Rizzo observes, 'Because staving off or alleviating the effects of climate change will require national and international coordination, we will likely be confronted with more top-down policy intervention than many Americans would be comfortable with under normal circumstances.'[88] Even U.S. Climate Envoy John Kerry recognizes that climate risk disclosure standards need to be harmonized globally, requiring international discussion and cooperation.[89] The window to coordinate has closed as now there is only a window for rapid investment and technological investment. Without immediate deployment, as a population we are doomed.[90]

Since the 1992 Earth Summit in Rio de Janeiro, U.S. foreign policy has recoiled from its 1972 position to fortify the global environmental rule of law at the Stockholm Summit on the Human Environment.[91] The United States is often viewed as an inactive leader in environmental conservation.[92] Samuel Brown recognized the crucial moment to solve the climate crisis. 'We find ourselves at a multigenerational inflection point on climate change, transitions in energy and transportation, and the status and role of the United States in

---

[86] Katie Lindsay, 'The Climate Responsibility Norm Ensuring Meaningful Participation in A Budding International Norm' (2021) 27 Hastings Environmental Law Journal 177, 199 (hereafter Lindsay, 'The Climate Responsibility Norm').

[87] Ibid.

[88] Jessica Rizzo, 'The Children's Hour: Climate Change, Law, and the Family' (2021) 27 Hastings Environmental Law Journal 79, 81–82.

[89] Andrea Shalal, 'Climate-risk disclosure requirements will spark huge investments – U.S. official (Reuters, 7 April 2021 <https://www.reuters.com/business/sustainable-business/climate-risk-disclosure-requirements-will-spark-huge-investments-us-official-2021-04-07/> accessed 5 July 2021.

[90] Chloe N. Kempf, 'Why Did So Many Do So Little? Movement Building and Climate Change Litigation in the Time of *Juliana v. United States*' (2021) 99 Texas Law Review 1005, 1015.

[91] Nicholas Robinson, 'Transnational Perspectives on the Paris Climate Agreement Beyond Paris: Redressing American Defaults in Caring for Earth's Biosphere' (2021) 1 Comparative Environmental Law & Regulation § 2B:3.

[92] Ibid. 'The United States has been lagging behind in climate leadership for decades, not just during the Trump administration. China has raced ahead with new renewable technologies. The United States has been leading the rhetoric, but China has been making the economic investments and leading technological innovation. U.S. environmental leaders will be the first to admit the technological and political gaps'.

'As John C. Cruden noted in his December 10, 2018, presentation about the Secretary General's Report at the UN, the United States was indeed once the world's leader in developing environmental law, with adoption of the National Environmental Policy Act of 1969, and the public consensus expressed in the first Earth Day, as well as each annual Earth Day celebration since 1970. Along with France and Senegal, which embrace the right to a healthy environment nationally, the United States respects the environmental rule of law at home. Even in governments with markedly different legal systems, such as China, norms for protection for the environment have taken on an urgency in the face of acute pollution. Realizing, like the United States did in 1969, that it takes years to abate pollution and remediate its effects, China has responded positively, developing norms and policies, as well as practices for "ecological civilization." In China, investment in anti-pollution measures has seen a significant increase. Where gaps exist in environmental protection, grass-roots organizations can help close these gaps in the future, as they do today and have done in the past. Some States will lag while others advance'.

world affairs, and a mutual focus on decarbonization and sustainability is an ideal vehicle to cement the U.S.-EU relationship.'[93]

The Paris Agreement in Article 7 urges for the 'long-term global response to climate change to protect people, livelihoods and ecosystems.'[94] The global goal on adaptation seeks to improve adaptive capacity and resilience along with reduce vulnerability.[95]

VI. Conclusion

Financial crises have opened the possibilities to innovation as well as investment to combat uncertainty and volatility within energy markets. Further concerns about energy prices have been balanced with concerns of price increased on consumers. At the same time, investors have leveraged financing mechanisms to create more stability within the markets. For example, banks have sought to invest in renewable energy projects through corporate lending, project finance, mezzanine finance, and refinancing.[96] Financial policies will improve based on stronger national and subnational renewable energy policies for resilience and sustainability. The Paris Agreement as a multilateral agreement can be used to fill in deficiencies of other international trade and energy agreements, namely the ECT. The limitations of investment arbitration should be seen as a hurdle instead of a barrier to financing renewable energy.

---

[93] Samuel Brown, 'Transatlantic Green Agenda' (Spring 2021) Natural Resources & the Environment, at 64.

[94] U.N. Conference of the Parties, Rep. of the Conference of the Parties on Its Twenty-First Session, at 26, U.N. Doc. FCCC/CP/2015/10/Add.1 (Jan. 29, 2016). 'The Rio Declaration on Environment and Development, the 2030 Agenda for Sustainable Development, and the Paris Agreement all highlight that "social and economic development depends on the sustainable management of [the] planet's natural resources" and that the proper protection of biodiversity, ecosystems, and wildlife is needed.' Jankovic, see note 74, citing G.A. Res. 70/1, Transforming our World: The 2030 Agenda for Sustainable Development, at 9 (25 September 2015).

[95] UNFCC, New elements and dimensions of adaptation under Paris Agreement (Article 7) <https://unfccc. int/topics/adaptation-and-resilience/the-big-picture/new-elements-and-dimensions-of-adaptation-under-the-paris-agreement-article-7> accessed on 5 July 2021.

[96] IRENA, Financial Mechanisms and Investment Frameworks for Renewables in Developing Countries (2012), <https://www.irena.org/-/media/Files/IRENA/Agency/Publication/2013/IRENA-report---Financial-Mechanisms-for-Developing-Countries.pdf> accessed 5 July 2021.

17

How Strong Can You Stand If You're on Your Knees? Financing Crises in Africa

Implications for the Natural Resource and Energy Sectors

Hanri Mostert, Chris Adomako-Kwakye, Kangwa-Musole Chisanga, and Meyer van den Berg[*]

I. Introduction

Beginning as a health crisis, the COVID-19 pandemic seamlessly transitioned into a globally disruptive and spectacularly disastrous socio-economic predicament, particularly for those countries already struggling with climate-related disasters, by the first quarter of 2020.[1] It has been testing individuals', communities', businesses', and governments' resilience like no other phenomenon in our lifetime. And it could not have struck Africa at a worse time.[2]

The continent was already facing several challenges: in West Africa and the Sahel region, security concerns were burgeoning in the face of increased terrorism.[3] Southern Africa was already dealing with the fallouts of extreme weather shocks, which were causing drought, floods, and cyclones.[4] In East Africa, a severe locust outbreak was jeopardizing agricultural production.[5] Crises and disasters such as these are exacting a heavy, barely affordable toll on

---

[*] The chapter was written with the financial support of the DST/NRF South African Research Chairs Initiative. Opinions and errors are the authors' own and should not be attributed to any of the institutions mentioned. The research assistance of SARChI: MLiA postdoctoral fellow, Dr Richard Cramer, and doctoral researcher, Kennedy Chege, is gratefully acknowledged.

[1] See Danielle N. Poole, Daniel J. Escudero, Lawrence O. Gostin, David Leblang, and Elizabeth A. Talbot, 'Responding to the COVID-19 Pandemic in Complex Humanitarian Crises' (2020) 19(14) International Journal for Equity in Health, 1.

[2] Matthew Cummins and Paul Quarles van Ufford, 'Africa's Children are Paying for COVID-19 with their Futures' (*UNICEF*, 15 May 2021) <https://www.unicef.org/esa/stories/africas-children-paying-for-covid-19-with-their-futures> accessed 8 May 2021; Afke Zeilstra, 'Covid-19 Aggravates Sub-Saharan African Debt Problems: Atradius Regional Economic Outlook' *Atradius Regional Report SSA* (October 2020) <https://group.atradius.com/publications/economic-research/covid-19-aggravates-sub-saharan-african-debt-problems.html> accessed 11 April 2021, 2 (hereafter Zeilstra, 'Debt Problems').

[3] Sampson Kwarkye, 'Breaking Terrorism Supply Chains in West Africa' *ISS Today* (8 June 2020) Institute for Security Studies <https://issafrica.org/iss-today/breaking-terrorism-supply-chains-in-west-africa> accessed 2 August 2021.

[4] Samuel N. A. Codjoe and D. Yaw Atiglo, 'The Implications of Extreme Weather Events for Attaining the Sustainable Development Goals in Sub-Saharan Africa' *Frontiers in Climate* (10 December 2020) <https://doi.org/10.3389/fclim.2020.592658> accessed 21 June 2021.

[5] Madeleine Stone, 'A Plague of Locusts has Descended on East Africa. Climate Change May Be to Blame' *National Geographic* (14 February 2020) <https://www.nationalgeographic.com/science/article/locust-plague-climate-science-east-africa> accessed 27 March 2021; Samuel Okiror, 'Second Wave of Locusts in East Africa Said to be 20 Times Worse' *The Guardian* (13 April 2020) <https://www.theguardian.com/global-development/2020/apr/13/second-wave-of-locusts-in-east-africa-said-to-be-20-times-worse> accessed 3 March 2021.

Hanri Mostert, Chris Adomako-Kwakye, Kangwa-Musole Chisanga, and Meyer van den Berg, *How Strong Can You Stand If You're On Your Knees? Financing Crises in Africa* In: *Resilience in Energy, Infrastructure, and Natural Resources Law*. Edited by: Catherine Banet, Hanri Mostert, LeRoy Paddock, Milton Fernando Montoya, and Íñigo del Guayo, Oxford University Press. © Hanri Mostert, Chris Adomako-Kwakye, Kangwa-Musole Chisanga, and Meyer van den Berg 2022. DOI: 10.1093/oso/9780192864574.003.0017

African economies. They are pushing low- and middle-income countries into debt crises, which in turn affects countries' propensity for climate change adaptation, resilience, and mitigation, especially in the Global South."[6]

Most African countries already have severely restricted fiscal policy spaces, with high debt and major structural budget deficits.[7] The COVID-19 pandemic hit those economies dependent on tourism and the export of commodities such as oil and metals particularly hard.[8] Commodity price volatility in energy, agriculture, and mineral resources has been especially detrimental to Africa, because of its dependence on these types of exports.[9] The deterioration of revenues from these sectors resulted in large external imbalances, putting pressure on currencies.[10] It quickly became clear that such states would need external financial assistance to weather the crisis.[11] However, borrowing costs have risen alongside expectations that inevitable widespread defaults will cause credit markets to freeze.[12]

Opportunities for financing developing countries' responses to crises, disasters, or pandemics present as offerings from various international financing agencies (such as the International Monetary Fund (IMF) or the World Bank), from other states, and from other development bank institutions.[13] Thereby, patterns of debt accumulation that recommenced in Africa since 2010 will become entrenched. These were already being followed with concern, as sovereign lending patterns are shifting: apart from the traditional multilateral lending institutions, countries have also been borrowing from commercial lenders and new actors, such as China, often at higher interest rates.[14]

Accepting such offers resign developing states to adopting the financiers' terms and conditions, which may be contrary to those states' development goals, or which may lead to debilitating national debt. Financing resilience from external sources thus could have the effect of reducing countries' ability to build resilience from within, and lead to a peculiar kind of codependency at the international level.

This chapter interrogates the recourse taken in South Africa, Namibia, Zambia, and Ghana to close the financial gaps where crises affect the natural resource and energy sectors in particular, and their societies more generally. Chosen courses of action are invariably backed by the laws in those systems, but the legal provisions are not our main interest. We consider these examples specifically in the context of the debt created at the country level. What interests us, is how such debt, created to address the resilience of developing countries

---

[6] Tunicia Phillips, 'Debt Crisis May Be Good for Africa' *Mail & Guardian* (9 April 2021) <https://mg.co.za/africa/2021-04-09-debt-crisis-may-be-good-for-africa/> accessed 21 August 2021 (hereafter Phillips, 'Debt Crisis').

[7] Palesa Shipalana, Alexander O'Riordan, and Cyril Prinsloo, 'The Macroeconomic Impact of Covid-19 on Africa' (*South African Institute of International Affairs*, 2020) <https://www.jstor.org/stable/resrep28262> accessed 8 July 2021 (hereafter Shipalana et al 'Macroeconomic Impact').

[8] Sharp declines in export revenues were observed in South Africa, Botswana and Zambia; and especially oil exporting countries such as the Republic of Congo and Angola suffered severe blows. See Zeilstra, 'Debt Problems' (n 2) 3.

[9] Shipalana et al 'Macroeconomic Impact' (n 7) 4.

[10] Zeilstra, 'Debt Problems' (n 2) 4.

[11] Government of France, 'Summit on the Financing of African Economies, Paris, 18 May 2021: Declaration' (News and Press Release, 18 May 2021) <https://www.elysee.fr/admin/upload/default/0001/10/8cafcd2d4c6fbc57cd41f96c99f7aede6bd351f1.pdf> accessed 22 June 2021, 1 (hereafter Government of France, 'Financing of African Economies').

[12] Shipalana et al 'Macroeconomic Impact' (n 7) 3.

[13] Government of France, 'Financing of African Economies' (n 11) 1.

[14] Justin Sandefur and Divyanshi Wadhwa, 'Chart of the Week: A New African Debt Crisis?' (*Center for Global Development*, 2 March 2018) <https://www.cgdev.org/blog/chart-of-the-week-new-african-debt-crisis> accessed 9 July 2021.

to the types of crises mentioned, may achieve the opposite. By casting light on this phenomenon, we hope to show the importance of sound policy choices and coherent economic
strategies for any legal reforms needed to enable more resilient responses on the political,
economic, and humanitarian levels.

Section II examines the effects of crises and disasters in the mentioned countries. The
COVID-19 pandemic forms the backdrop of the inquiry, and Ghana and South Africa
are the case studies in assessing economic responsiveness in the wake of the global havoc
wreaked by the pandemic. For Zambia and Namibia, the context is further complicated by a
predating El Niño weather effect: the drought of 2017–2018. The result has been a clustering
of crises, each rendering the building of resilience from within harder to achieve.

Section III then interrogates responses to such recent crises. By surveying the four countries' responses to the COVID-19 crisis against their finance policy choices (IIIA), we focus
on the repercussions such responses have had on country debt. We then draw a series of inferences (IIIB) about the position of these countries—and others like them—in negotiating
deals and loans that may finance resilience in the longer term.

Section IV considers various financing options and approaches available to debt-
strapped African countries in the aftermath of the latest cluster of crises. The purpose is to
find the points at which shifts are still possible: shifts that could assist countries dealing with
the spectre of unsustainable debt in choosing policy approaches that maximize resilience
and minimize dependency on the international world. The African continent's resource
wealth of African states may play a significant role in this respect.

Our chapter concludes with some overarching observations in Section V.

II. Clustering of Crises and their Economic Consequences

Topography, climate, and location render Southern Africa dependent on seasonal rainfall patterns, and vulnerable to climate anomalies, such as those resulting from an El Niño
phase in the southern oscillation cycle, which may cause or worsen drought in the region,[15]
and aggravate food insecurity.[16] Both Zambia and Namibia were extremely hard hit by the
three-year-long regional droughts between 2017 and 2019. It left an estimated 25 per cent
of the Zambian[17] and 20 per cent of the Namibian[18] population likely to face ongoing crisis
levels of food insecurity.[19] And in South Africa, anaemic rainfall over three consecutive

---

[15] Madeleine C Thomson, Kobi Abayomi, AG Barnston, Marc A Levy, and M Dilley, 'El Niño and drought in
Southern Africa' (2003) 361 The Lancet 437. Clever Mafuta, Leonissah Munjoma, and Stanley Mubako, 'Southern
Africa Environment Outlook' (*Southern African Development Community (SADC) and partners,* 2008) <https://
www.sardc.net/books/SAEO/SAEO.pdf> accessed 23 April 2021.

[16] European Commission, 'Southern Africa | Drought Situation' (*Emergency Response Coordination Centre
(ERCC) – DG ECHO Daily Map,* 29 January 2019) <http://www.gdacs.org/contentdata/maps/daily/DR/1012728/
ECDM_20190129_Southern_Africa_Drought.pdf> accessed 25 May 2021.

[17] 1.73 million people.

[18] 440 000 people.

[19] IPC, 'Democratic Republic of Congo: Integrated Food Security Phase Classification Snapshot' (*Integrated
Food Security Phase Classification,* March 2021) <https://reliefweb.int/report/democratic-republic-congo/dem
ocratic-republic-congo-integrated-food-security-phase> accessed 12 May 2021; IPC, 'Southern Africa: Drought
2018-2021' (OCHA) <https://reliefweb.int/disaster/dr-2018-000429-zwe> accessed 25 May 2021. Reliefweb,
'GIEWS Country Brief: Namibia' (*FAO,* 30 April 2021) <https://reliefweb.int/report/namibia/giews-country-
brief-namibia-30-april-2021> accessed 25 May 2021.

winters brought the city of Cape Town to the verge of 'Day Zero'.[20] It was averted only because of a 'barrage of efforts', involving reallocation of water earmarked for agriculture to
urban consumption, the ramping up of the city's conservation efforts and tariffs, and a
clamping down on non-essential usage.[21] And the rain gods pulling through, just in time.

Food and water security in the face of climate change and drought is one issue. Another
complication is energy access and efficiency.[22] As it is, across Africa, the need for electricity far
outstrips the current capability of supply.[23] For Zambia, which relies heavily[24] on hydropower
for its electricity needs, the recent drought affected the operation and future development of
thermal and hydropower plants. When water levels of major rivers,[25] dropped so significantly,
existing hydropower plants had to be ramped down to as low as 25 per cent of rated capacity.[26]
Others were earmarked for shutdown where water dried up.[27] The Namibian energy sector
came under similar stress. The drought debilitated supply from the Ruacana Hydro Power
Station,[28] which contributes the bulk[29] of Namibia's domestic energy generating capacity.

The drought had further knock-on effects. In Namibia, for instance, the worst drought
in 90 years, between October 2018 and May 2019,[30] devastated[31] many individuals and
economic sectors, not only agriculture.[32] The severity of the drought's economic impact
manifested, for instance, in Namibia's subsequent credit rating downgrades from Moody's
Investor Service and Fitch Ratings.[33] The economic hardship resulting from the 2018/
2019 drought lingers in Namibia and Zambia, even after a wet season in 2020, which in

---

[20] The dreaded 12 April 2018 was expected to become 'the largest drought-induced municipal water failure in
modern history.' Christian Alexander, 'Cape Town's 'Day Zero' Water Crisis, One Year Later' (*Bloomberg, CityLab*,
12 April 2019) https://www.bloomberg.com/news/articles/2019-04-12/looking-back-on-cape-town-s-drought-
and-day-zero accessed 11 July 2021.

[21] Ibid.

[22] Rebekah Kates Lemke, 'The Effects of Climate Change in Zimbabwe' (*CRS*, 20 September 2016) <https://
www.crs.org/stories/power-climate-change-zimbabwe> accessed 2 May 2021 (hereafter Lemke, 'Climate Change
in Zimbabwe').

[23] Yinka Omorogbe, 'Universal Access to Modern Energy Services: The Centrality of the Law' in Yinka
Omorogbe and Ada Okoye Ordor (eds), *Ending Africa's Energy Deficit and the Law: Achieving Sustainable Energy
for All in Africa* (Oxford University Press 2018) 5–6.

[24] 21 per cent of the region's electricity supply is from hydropower. The rest is made up of charcoal.

[25] The Zambezi, Kunene, and Vaal rivers.

[26] United Nations Economic Commission for Africa (UNECA), 'Energy Crisis in Southern Africa: Future
Prospects' (*UNECA*, 2018) <https://repository.uneca.org/bitstream/handle/10855/41827/b11925668.pdf?seque
nce=1&isAllowed=y> accessed 19 May 2021, vi, 11 (hereafter UNECA, 'Energy Crisis').

[27] There were indications that Kariba power station (both the north and south banks) may have had to be shut
down in the second half of 2016 for lack of water. Lemke, 'Climate Change in Zimbabwe' (n 23).

[28] Godwin Norense Osarumwense Asemota, 'Electricity Use in Namibia: Developing Algorithms to Encourage
More Efficient Consumer Behaviour and Motivate More Environmentally Friendly Utility Practices' (iUniverse,
Incorporated 2013) 22–23.

[29] Around 350MW.

[30] Resulting from its driest rain season in 38 years. See Rosemary N. Shikangalah, 'The 2019 Drought in
Namibia: An Overview' (2020) 37 Journal of Namibian Studies, 50 (hereafter Shikangalah, '2019 Drought');
African Development Bank (AfDB), 'Proposal for a Grant of US$ 1 Million for Humanitarian Emergency
Assistance to Mitigate the Effects of the 2018/2019 Drought' (*AfDB*, August 2019) <https://www.afdb.org/en/
documents/namibia-humanitarian-emergency-assistance-mitigate-effects-2018-2019-drought-emergency-and-
special-assistance-grants> accessed 24 May 2021, 1 (hereafter AfDB, 'Humanitarian Emergency Assistance')

[31] Water supply for agricultural, domestic and industrial purposes was in crisis. Around 257,383 people (almost 10 per cent of the entire Namibia population) was without adequate food. African Development Bank,
'Humanitarian Emergency Assistance' (n 30).

[32] Annual agricultural output dropped below 50 per cent in 2019. Shikangalah, '2019 Drought' (n 30) 38.

[33] See Calle Schlettwein, 'Statement On the 2019 Fitch Credit Rating Opinion on Namibia' (Ministry of Finance,
01 October 2019) <https://mof.gov.na/documents/35641/36580/01092019+++Ministry+of+Finance+Statem
ent+on+2019+Fitch+Rating+Action.pdf/9584ce56-87ea-3992-a0f2-f814249dafc9> accessed 22 June 2021, 3.

Zambia caused flooding in isolated parts.[34] Acute food insecurity persisted into 2021 and is forecasted to deteriorate further,[35] because of COVID-19 induced adverse impacts on income-generating activities.[36]

These countries, as many others in Africa, have seen a downturn in economic outlook, due to the COVID-19 pandemic. Government-introduced lockdowns, physical distancing requirements, closing of borders, and bans on educational and religious activities and travel, to contain the spread of the virus, visited unprecedented hardship on many economies: loss of employment, disruption in the financial sector, and health sector complexities are but a few. Across Africa, the COVID-19 pandemic alone caused an economic contraction of 4.6 per cent in 2020, because of its disruption of trade and travel, and the concomitant drop in commodity demand and prices on the continent.[37] By the end of 2020, only Ethiopia, Rwanda, Mali, Burundi, and Guinea were not in recession.[38]

III. Country Survey of Crisis Responses

Countries' different reactions to crises and disasters invite a range of consequences to be visited on their national economies, health systems, and energy and resource sectors. For instance, some governments suspended mining activities, partially or fully, pursuant to the COVID-19 crisis, while others allowed their sectors to remain operative.[39]

A. Country responses

Ghana's approach is mentioned as an example of policy choice to repurpose resource revenue (among others) to deal with the immediate crisis. This channelled resources for creating resilience and long-term prosperity away from their initial purpose. In the process, those goals become less attainable. South Africa's approach had been to re-budget and to supplement with loans, to reach as broad a possible base of the poor segment of society. New debt thus incurred will have to be serviced, which will leave the country vulnerable in

---

[34] RFIC, 'Zambia: Drought Operation Update Report 2, Emergency Appeal n°: MDRZM012' (*OCHA*, 9 March 2021)   <https://reliefweb.int/report/zambia/zambia-drought-operation-update-report-2-emergency-appeal-n-mdrzm012> accessed 31 March 2021 (hereafter RFIC, 'Zambia: Drought Update 2').

[35] RFIC, 'Zambia: Drought Update 2' (n 34).

[36] In Zambia, this crisis placed strain on the provision of both water and electricity (from hydropower). RFIC, 'Zambia: Drought Update 2' (n 34). In Namibia, water shortages have directly impacted local industry, creating a rise in unemployment. Coupled with chronic depression of prices of minerals such as uranium—an all-important source in Namibia—the mining industry suffered specifically. AfDB 'Africa Economic Outlook 2021: Namibia Economic Outlook' <https://www.afdb.org/en/countries/southern-africa/namibia/namibia-economic-outlook> accessed 5 August 2021; Robert McGregor, Cheryl Emvula, and Rowland Brown, 'Beneficiation in Namibia: Impacts, Constraints and Options' (IPPR Research Report, 2017) 37–39 <https://www.ippr.org.na/wp-content/uploads/2017/11/BeneficiationFINAL_WEB.pdf> accessed 21 August 2021.

[37] Zeilstra, 'Debt problems' (n 2). See also Shawn Donnan et al, 'A Covid-19 Supply Chain Shock Born in China Is Going Global' (Bloomberg, 20 March 2020) <https://www.bloomberg.com/news/articles/2020-03-20/a-covid-19-supply-chain-shock-born-in-china-is-going-global> accessed 20 August 2021.

[38] Zeilstra, 'Debt problems' (n 2) 3.

[39] Lee Corrick et al, 'Mining Tax Policy Responses to Covid-19' (Intergovernmental Forum on Mining, Minerals, Metals and Sustainable Development, April 2020) <https://www.iisd.org/system/files/publications/mining-tax-policy-covid-19-en.pdf> accessed 14 March 2021, 2 (hereafter Corrick et al, 'Mining Tax Policy Responses').

terms of building resilience. Zambia, still grappling with high sovereign debt in the wake of the drought exemplifies how options become increasingly limited as resources dwindle. Contrast this with Namibia: although also hard hit by both the drought and COVID-19, its response to crisis-clustering seems to have been less harried because it was economically in a much better starting position than any of the other countries in the study.

Ghana

Ghana's Finance Minister summarized the economic impact of COVID-19 well when stating that it was the country's most severe external shock since independence. After Ghana's Minister for Health announced the first two cases on 12 March 2020, emergency legislation[40] was passed,[41] which led to a series of legislative instruments[42] crafting the government's response.

Although mines remained operative[43] during the lockdown,[44] communities and individuals were nonetheless affected.[45] Pandemic-related restrictions reduced incomes of 77.4 per cent of Ghanaian households.[46] For mining companies, COVID-19 restrictions lead to increased production costs (due to stockpiling necessities) and affected mining companies' tax obligations. In 2020, Ghana's estimated Gross Domestic Product (GDP) target, set at 6.8 per cent, plummeted to around 2.6 per cent.[47] An estimated shortfall in import duties stood at nearly USD 139 million.[48]

By the end of 2020, Ghana's stimulus package to reduce the harsh consequences of the COVID-19 pandemic had already cost around USD 2.5 billion.[49] A disbursement of USD 1 billion from the IMF's Rapid Credit Facility went towards covering part of the costs. The Ghanaian government used part[50] of the Ghana Stabilisation Fund (GSF), which exists under the Petroleum Revenue Management Act (PRMA)[51] to cushion the impact on public

---

[40] The Imposition of Restrictions Act, 2020 (Act 1012).
[41] As per Art 21(4)(c)–(e) of Ghana's 1992 Constitution.
[42] EI 63: 'Establishment of Emergency Communications System Instrument' (2020) gazetted on 23 March 2020; EI 64: 'Imposition of Restrictions (Coronavirus Disease (COVID-19) Pandemic) Instrument' (2020) gazetted on 23 March 2020; EI 65: 'Imposition of Restrictions (Coronavirus Disease (COVID-19) Pandemic) (No.2) Instrument' (2020) gazetted on 30 March 2020; E.I. 66: 'Imposition of Restrictions (Coronavirus Disease (COVID-19) Pandemic) (No.3) Instrument' (2020) gazetted on 3 April 2020.
[43] Interview: Oxford Business Group, 'Eric Asubonteng, Managing Director, AngloGold Ashanti (Ghana); and President, Ghana Chamber of Mines' (Ghana | Energy, 15 May 2020) <https://oxfordbusinnesgroup.com/covid-19-economic-impact-assessment> accessed 23 October 2020 (hereafter Interview: OBG 'Eric Asubonteng').
[44] The partial lockdown affected parts of Accra and Kumasi, and not the mining towns. See further Corrick et al, 'Mining Tax Policy Responses' (n 39) 2.
[45] The government indefinitely closed universities, schools, churches, mosques, and banned public gatherings on 15 March 2020. On 21 March 2020, the government ordered the closure of the country's land, sea, and air borders. Accra and Kumasi's partial lockdown followed on 27 March 2020, and the government lifted it on 19 April 2020 and implored Ghanaians to observe safety protocols. The worst effects were in the private and educational sectors, the hospitality industry, and support and auxiliary workers.
[46] Ghana Statistical Service 'Household and Job Survey' <https://statsghana.gov.gh/searchread.php?searchfound=MTY2MjY1OTQ4My43MTk1/search/qoq66r703n> accessed 20 August 2021.
[47] See Deloitte Ghana, 'Economic Impact of COVID-19 Pandemic on the Economy of Ghana: Summary of Fiscal Measures and Deloitte views' (Deloitte, April 2020) <https://www2.deloitte.com/content/dam/Deloitte/gh/Documents/about-deloitte/gh-economic-Impact-of-the-Covid-19-Pandemic-on-the-Economy-of-Ghana_03012020.pdf > accessed 5 November 2020 (hereafter Deloitte Ghana, 'Economic Impact').
[48] GHC 808 million. Deloitte Ghana, 'Economic Impact' (n 47).
[49] GHC 11.2 billion. Ernest Addison, 'Pandemic, The Economy and Outlook' University of Ghana Alumni Lecture by the Governor, Bank of Ghana (17 December 2020) <https://www.bis.org/review/r201223k.pdf> accessed 24 August 2021.
[50] See section 23(3), Petroleum Revenue Management Act (PRMA) 2011 (Act 815).
[51] Petroleum Revenue Management Act 2011 (Act 815).

expenditure capacity during periods of unanticipated petroleum revenue shortfalls.[52] The Ghanaian government also wanted to amend the PMRA to access the Ghana Heritage Fund, to meet the increased expenditures incurred due to the COVID-19.[53] Parliament[54] and Civil Society Organisations, however, resisted the Ghanaian Government's attempt to amend the PRMA; and the idea to use the Heritage Fund to cover costs has not been seriously revisited again.[55] The Government intends to amend the Bank of Ghana Act to limit the amount the government can borrow from the Central Bank if tight domestic financing market conditions remain.[56]

Amid financial constraints, with private sector donations and collaboration,[57] Ghana's government crafted its response: it set up the Ghana COVID-19 National Trust Fund to alleviate the pandemic's effects, and create capacity to treat the disease.[58] The Ghanaian government further introduced financial stimulus packages, including the injection of over USD 344 million[59] by the Bank of Ghana into the economy to help pharmaceutical, hospitality, and manufacturing sectors with a 2 per cent reduction in interest rate.[60] Consumers of electricity and water received some reprieve, with the government absorbing three months' cost of electricity, partially for most, but fully for lifeline consumers.[61] Collaborating with the National Board for Small Scale Industries Business and Trade Associations, and selected Commercial and Rural Banks, the Government rolled out a USD 102,852,540.00 soft loan with a one-year moratorium and two-year repayment period for Small, Medium, and Micro

---

[52] GhanaWeb, 'Government to Utilize USD 200 Million from Stabilization Fund' (GNA, 3 April 2020) <https://www.ghanaweb.com/GhanaHomePage/business/Government-to-utilize-US-200-million-from-stabilization-fund-913069> accessed 30 October 2020 (hereafter GhanaWeb 'Stabilization Fund'). The Finance Minister stated that the government intended to lower the cap on the Ghana Stabilisation Fund (GSF) from the current USD 300 million to USD 100 million in accordance with the PRMA. According to him, the measure would enable the excess amount in the GSF to be transferred into the Contingency Fund (Art 177(1) of Ghana's Constitution creates the Contingency Fund to receive monies and utilize the same to meet unplanned and unforeseen expenditures) to meet unplanned expenditures. See section 23(3) and (4), PMRA. The USD 200 million transferred into the Contingency Fund would fund the COVID-19 through the Coronavirus Alleviation Programme (CAP).

[53] See GhanaWeb 'Stabilization Fund' (n 52). The Ghana Stabilisation Fund and the Ghana Heritage Fund exist under the PRMA as amended. The object of establishing the Ghana Stabilisation Fund is to cushion public expenditure during shortfalls in petroleum revenue. The Ghana Heritage Fund is to supply an endowment to support development for future generation upon depletion of the oil reserves.

[54] Members of Parliament of the ruling government had no problem with the announcement to use the Ghana Stabilisation Fund and amend the PRMA to use the Heritage Fund as well to finance the cost associated with COVID-19. The minority members agreed with the use of the Ghana Stabilisation Fund but disagreed with the amendment to use the Ghana Heritage Fund. According to the minority members, the fund exists to cater for development for generations yet unborn.

[55] See GhanaWeb, 'Stabilization Fund' (n 52).

[56] See Ministry of Finance, 'Statement to Parliament on Economic Impact of the COVID-19 Pandemic on the Economy of Ghana' (Minister of Finance, 30 March 2020) <https://www.mofep.gov.gh/sites/default/files/news/MOF-statement-to-parliament_20200330.pdf> accessed 14 October 2020 (hereafter Ministry of Finance 'Statement to Parliament').

[57] Michael Danquah, Simone Schotte, and Kunal Sen, 'Covid-19 and Employment; Insights from sub-Saharan African Experience' (2020) 63(Suppl 1) Indian Journal of Labour Economics 28.

[58] Under the Covid-19 National Trust Fund Act (CNTF), 2020 (Act 1013). Several institutions contributed to this fund.

[59] GHC 3 billion.

[60] See Ministry of Finance 'Statement to Parliament' (n 56).

[61] I.e. persons who consume zero to fifty-kilowatt hours a month. James Dzansi, Minki Kim, David Lagakos, and Henry Telli, 'Real-Time Economic Impacts of COVID-19 in Ghana' (*IGC Policy brief* GHA-20071, March 2021) 5 <https://www.theigc.org/wp-content/uploads/2021/04/Dzansi-et-al-March-2021-Policy-brief.pdf> accessed 22 August 2021. Water consumers received the same relief. After June 2020, the government continue to absorb the utility bills of lifeline consumers and discontinued that of customers outside that threshold.

Enterprises (SMMEs).[62] The government further introduced measures to cushion the vulnerable in the areas affected by the partial lockdown, among others through the provision of food parcels.[63] The government of Ghana has withdrawn USD 218 million from the GSF and further borrowed almost USD 2.3 billion from the Bank of Ghana.[64]

Ghana's natural resources sectors, particularly the mining sector, has been more resilient than other sectors, but that was because the partial lockdown affected Accra and parts of greater Kumasi, but not the mining towns. The situation allowed the mining companies to operate without significant challenges.[65] Nevertheless, the mining companies were compelled to stockpile raw materials, which tended to increase production cost. This affected mining companies' tax obligations.[66]

The AFDB indicates that Ghana's economic outlook now is good in the short to medium term, contingent on an increase in demand for its exports, improved business confidence, and successful implementation of the Ghana COVID–19 Alleviation and Revitalization of Enterprise Support program. It projects growth of around 4 per cent in 2021 and 4.1 per cent in 2022.[67] Yet, COVID-19's severe economic implications compelled Ghana's government to external borrowing, and according to the IMF, Ghana continues to be classified at high risk of debt distress.[68] The following loans were made to address Ghana's many commitments:

(i) The World Bank made available USD 100 million for COVID-19 pandemic-related short-, medium- and long-term support.[69] The facility supported the government to improve the response systems by preventing, detecting, and responding to the pandemic to slow its transmission.

(ii) The International Monetary Fund has granted Ghana USD 1 billion under the Rapid Credit Facility.[70] The credit facility seeks to address urgent fiscal and balance-of-payments needs resulting from the pandemic.[71]

(iii) The African Development Bank Group, through its concessional member, African Development Fund (ADF) has approved USD 69 million in July 2020 as 'Crisis Response Budget Support.'[72] The grant, termed 'Crisis Response Budget Support,'

---

[62] GHC 600 million. See International Monetary Fund, 'Policy Responses to COVID-19' (IMF, 2021) <https:www.imf.org/en/Topics/imf-and-covid19/Policy-Responses-to COVID-19#G> accessed 20 September 2020 (hereafter 'IMF, Policy Responses').

[63] Danquah et al, 'Covid-19 and Employment' (n 57).

[64] GHC 10 billion. See IMF, 'Policy Responses' (n 62).

[65] Interview: OBG 'Eric Asubonteng' (n 43).

[66] Corrick et al, 'Mining Tax Policy Responses' (n 39) 2.

[67] African Development Bank Group, 'Ghana Economic Outlook' <https://www.afdb.org/en/countries/west-africa/ghana/ghana-economic-outlook> accessed 22 August 2021.

[68] International Monetary Fund, 'IMF Executive Board approves a USD 1 billion disbursement to Ghana to address the COVID-19 Pandemic' (Press Release No. 20/153, 13 April 13, 2020) <https://www.imf.org/en/News/Articles/2020/04/13/pr20153-ghana-imf-executive-board-approves-a-us-1-billion-disbursement-to-ghana-to-address-covid-19> accessed 22 August 2021 (hereafter IMF, 'Disbursement').

[69] The World Bank, 'World Bank Group Supports Ghana's COVID-19 Response', (Press Release, 2 April 2020) <https://www.worldbank.org/en/news/press-release/2020/04/02/world-bank-group-supports-ghanas-covid-19-response> accessed 12 November 2020.

[70] IMF, 'Disbursement' (n 68)

[71] IMF, 'Disbursement' (n 68).

[72] African Development Bank Group, 'African Development Bank Group supports Ghana's COVID-19 response plan with $69 million grant', (AfDB, 24 July 2020) <https://www.afb.org/en/news-and-events/press-releases/african-development-bank-group-supports-ghana's-covid-19-sponse-plan-69-million-grant-37028> accessed on 12 November 2020 (hereafter AfDB, '$69 million grant').

i.e. increases the population tested and provides intensive care treatment and facilities.[73]

These interventions, necessitated by the pandemic, increased Ghana's external debt, which pre-pandemically, in 2019, stood at almost USD 27 billion.[74] Additional unplanned spending in the health sector certainly had a negative impact on fiscal deficit.[75] Deloitte Ghana forecasts that, if COVID-19 persists for much longer, Ghana may suffer from a significant decline in government revenue, international trade, and reserves, because the nation is an import-driven economy. Also, prolonged struggles to contain COVID-19 will further slow down economic development.[76]

The African Development Bank's assessment was that the COVID–19 pandemic significantly curtailed Ghana's economic growth momentum. The pandemic-induced oil-price slump and weakened global economic activity, decelerated Ghana's real GDP growth from 6.5 per cent in 2019 to 1.7 per cent in 2020.[77] Even so, it's outlook is not quite as dismal as some of the other examples in the survey. Also, it remains committed to 'policies consistent with strong growth, rapid poverty reduction, and macroeconomic stability over the medium-term.'[78]

South Africa

South Africa's economy was on its knees[79] even before COVID-19 hit.[80] It had been plagued with what has become known as the 'evil triplets' of poverty, unemployment, and inequality.[81] In 2019, almost half (49.2 per cent) of the population was already classified as poor;[82] more than a quarter (29.1 per cent) was unemployed.[83] South Africa is also notorious for being one of the most unequal societies in the world.[84]

---

[73] AfDB, '$69 million grant' (n 72).

[74] World Bank Group, 'External debt stocks, total (DOD, current US$) – Ghana', <https://data.worldbank.org/indicator/DT.DOD.DECT.CD?locations=GH> accessed 22 August 2021.

[75] Deloitte Ghana, 'Economic Impact' (n 47).

[76] See Deloitte Ghana, 'Economic Impact' (n 47)

[77] AfDB, '$69 million grant' (n 72).

[78] IMF, 'Disbursement' (n 68).

[79] Good Governance Africa 'COVID-19 – A GGA Response: The Likely Impact of Covid-19 on the Extractive Industries and its Governance Implications' (GAA May 2020) 5. <https://media.africaportal.org/documents/The_likely_impact_of_COVID-19_on_the_extractive_industries.pd> accessed 12 March 2021. Wim Naudé and Martin Cameron 'Failing to Pull Together: South Africa's Troubled Response to COVID-19', IZA Discussion Paper No. 13649 (August 2020) 7 (hereafter Naudé and Cameron 'Failing to Pull Together'.

[80] Margaret Chitiga-Mabugu, Martin Henseler, Ramos Mabugu and Hélène Maisonnave, 'Economic and Distributional Impact of Covid-19: Evidence From Macro-micro Modelling of The South African Economy' (2021) 89:1 South African Journal of Economics, 83 (hereafter Chitiga-Mabugu et al 'Macro-micro Modelling').

[81] Phrase attributed to a 2011 speech of former South African Mineral Resources Minister, Susan Shabangu, in a 2011 speech referred to the 'evil triplets' of the mining sector as poverty, inequality and unemployment. See for example, Sekai Chiwandamira and Tiyani Majoko, 'South Africa: The Evil Triplets and the Mining Industry' (*Routledge Modise*, 2 February 2012) <https://www.mondaq.com/southafrica/mining/163204/the-evil-triplets-and-the-mining-industry > accessed 17 December 2020. See also Sekai Chiwandamira and Tiyani Majoko, 'The Evil Triplets and the Mining Industry' (2011) 11 Without Prejudice 53–55.

[82] Victor Sulla and Precious Zikhali, 'Overcoming Poverty and Inequality in South Africa: An Assessment of Drivers, Constraints and Opportunities' (International Bank for Reconstruction and Development / The World Bank, March 2018) <http://documents.worldbank.org/curated/en/530481521735906534/> accessed 30 April 2021, xii.

[83] Department: Statistics South Africa, 'Quarterly Labour Force Survey: Quarter 3' 2019 (Statistical Release P0211, 2019) <https://www.statssa.gov.za/publications/P0211/P02113rdQuarter2019.pdf> accessed 4 April 2021.

[84] Sulla and Zikhali, 'Overcoming Poverty and Inequality' (n 82) 42. South Africa's Gini coefficient was 0.63, one of the highest inequality rates in the world, in 2014. The World Bank, 'Gini index (World Bank estimate) -

And the government's general external debt was estimated at USD 76.10 billion in 2019.[85]

The restriction of economic freedoms under COVID-19 regulations has aided further rises in these statistics.[86] As a first response, the South African government declared a national state of disaster[87] and adopted severe containment measures[88] that were gradually relaxed. When the new Beta variant of the virus was identified in South Africa towards the end of 2020, restrictions that had meanwhile been relaxed, were tightened again.[89]

The hard lockdown severely impaired the economy[90] resulted in many distressed businesses—even ones that before the pandemic had been doing fine, financially.[91] South Africa is export-dependent, and so its challenges have been influenced by the economic situation in trading partner countries (e.g. China, the US, and Europe,[92]) whose economies also experienced COVID-19-related slowdowns. Some 30 per cent of South Africa's total exports come from the minerals sector (coal, gold, and manganese specifically).[93] Consequently, this sector was particularly hard hit in terms of profitability, with a concomitant effect on labour and a rise in unemployment.[94]

Before the COVID-19 pandemic set in, the mining industry was still dubbed the 'Sunrise Industry'[95] for its potential to contribute to the country's job market and economic outlook,

---

South Africa' <https://data.worldbank.org/indicator/SI.POV.GINI?locations=ZA> accessed 15 February 2021. Statistics South Africa, 'Inequality Trends in South Africa: A Multidimensional Diagnostic of Inequality' <http://www.statssa.gov.za/?p==12744> accessed 22 August 2021. Anton van Dalsen and Charles Simkins, 'Does Gini Index really show SA as most unequal society in the world?'(Politics Web, 13 June 2019) <https://www.politicsweb.co.za/opinion/does-the-gini-index-show-that-sa-is-the-most-unequ> accessed 17 February 2021.

[85] World Bank Group, 'Present Value of External Debt (Current US$) - South Africa' <https://data.worldbank.org/indicator/DT.DOD.PVLX.CD?locations=ZA> accessed 22 August 2021.

[86] Benjamin Fogel, 'There Is No Silver Lining to South Africa's Zuma Insurrection' *Jacobin* (15 July 2021) <https://jacobinmag.com/2021/07/jacob-zuma-south-africa-looting-riots-kwazulu-natal> accessed 16 July 2021; Jonathan Katzenellenbogen, 'Business Warns of "Economic Ruin", via Covid-19 Lockdown' *BizNews* (14 May 2021)   <https://irr.org.za/media/business-warns-of-2018economic-ruin2019-via-covid-19-lockdown-biznews> accessed 24 August 2021.

[87] Jiska De Groot and Charlotte Lemanski, 'COVID-19 Responses: Infrastructure Inequality and Privileged Capacity to Transform Everyday Life in South Africa' (2021) 33(1) International Institute for Environment and Development (IIED) 259.

[88] Under the Disaster Management Act 57 of 2002, amended to cater for responses to deal with the infestation of the coronavirus, and a host of regulations, a hard lockdown, extensive travel bans, school closures, and closures of beaches and public parks were instituted. A full list of the applicable laws are available on the South African Government's website under <https://www.gov.za/covid-19/resources/regulations-and-guidelines-coronavirus-covid-19#dma> accessed 22 August 2021.

[89] Houriiyah Tegally, Eduan Wilkinson, Tulio de Oliveira et al, 'Detection of a SARS-CoV-2 Variant of Concern in South Africa' (2021) 592 Nature 438.

[90] See Chris Hattingh, 'South Africa's Lockdown Is Especially Severe' (*Foundation For Equal Education*, 24 May 2020) <https://fee.org/articles/south-africas-lockdown-is-especially-severe>accessed 11 February 2021.

[91] Chris Bateman, '"It's such a botch:" SA's Vaccine Delays and Covid Lockdown Proved Deadly – Prof Alex van den Heever' *Daily Maverick* (28 March 2021) <https://www.dailymaverick.co.za/article/2021-03-28-its-such-a-botch-sas-vaccine-delays-and-covid-lockdown-proved-deadly-prof-alex-van-den-heever/> accessed 26 June 2021 (hereafter Bateman, 'Botch').

[92] Wilma Viviers and Peet DF Strydom, 'Global Value Chains: A New Era for South Africa's Foreign Trade' (2015) 12(2) Africagrowth Institute 10.

[93] Chitiga-Mabugu et al 'Macro-micro Modelling' (n 80) 87.

[94] Ibid. Even as early as June/July 2020, while SA was still in partial lockdown, the CCMA was already dealing with mass retrenchment processes involving a number of around 6,713 retrenchments from mines nationwide.

[95] Government Communications (GCIS) 'Highlights of the State of the Nation Address' <https://www.gov.za/sites/default/files/gcis_documents/SoNA201hHighlights_0.pdf> accessed 22 August 2021.

despite seeing a steep decline over the previous three decades.[96] At first, the economic consequences of trying to keep the South African people out of harm's way during the pandemic made its mining sector very infirm. The responses needed to contain and suppress the spread of the virus jeopardized livelihoods dependent on the mining sector:[97] the stringent 2020 lockdown[98] brought many mining operations to an abrupt halt.[99] Coal production was one exception: even under the harshest (level-5) lockdown, it could proceed, because of the need to service Eskom, the national electricity provider (who still bases its energy generation largely around fossil fuels).[100] Coal producers were also permitted gradually to scale up to full employment.[101] Other mining operations were dialed back significantly. They were only permitted a phased restart later in the year, when the mining sector was declared an 'essential service'[102] and the COVID-19 alert levels were lowered. This was conditional upon a reduced employment capacity of 50 per cent and, concomitantly, presented limited possibilities of production.[103] Many mining companies (especially SMMEs) found themselves in distress,[104] while the pandemic induced mass retrenchments also in the mining sector.[105]

The congregate nature of working underground put miners—and by extension mining-affected communities—at particular risk of contracting and spreading COVID-19, as the Labour Court judgment in *Association of Mineworkers and Construction Union (AMCU) v Minister of Mineral Resources and Energy*[106] highlighted, when positioned to pronounce on implementing non-pharmacological, contain-and-suppress strategies in the mining sector. The reopening of the sector hence necessitated a mandatory code of practice for compliance with COVID-19 safety guidelines for mines.[107]

---

[96] The contribution of South Africa's mining sector to the GDP had waned significantly, from over 20 per cent in the 1980s to just about 7 per cent to 8 per cent over the past decade. See Ana Monteiro and Felix Njini, 'Gold Street Is Where South Africa's Mining History Goes To Die' *Bloomberg Quint* (20 June 2018) <https://www.bloombergqu int.com/business/gold-street-is-where-south-africa-s-mining-history-goes-to-die> accessed 31 March 2021.

[97] John Basquill, 'Shafted: Covid-19 Devastates South Africa Mining Industry' *Global Trade Review* (7 August 2020) <https://www.gtreview.com/supplements/gtr-africa-2020/shafted-covid-19-devastates-south-africa-min ing-industry/> accessed 22 August 2021 (hereafter Basquill, 'Shafted').

[98] Zindoga Mukandavire, Farai Nyabadza, Noble J. Malunguza, Diego F. Cuadros, Tinevimbo Shiri, Godfrey Musuka, 'Quantifying Early COVID-19 Outbreak Transmission in South Africa and Exploring Vaccine Efficacy Scenarios' (*Plos One*, 4 July 2020) <https://doi.org/10.1371/journal.pone.0236003> accessed 22 August 2021.

[99] Shabir Ahmed, 'The Impact of COVID-19 on the Mining Sector' (*SAP*, 31 March 2021) <https://news.sap. com/africa/2020/03/the-impact-of-covid-19-on-the-mining-sector/> accessed 10 June 2021.

[100] Jan van Heerden and Elizabeth Louisa Roos, 'The Possible Effects of the Extended Lockdown Period on the South African Economy: A CGE Analysis' (2021) 89 South African Journal of Economics, <https://doi.org/ 10.1111/saje.12273> accessed 23 August 2021, 101–102.

[101] Ibid.

[102] On 16 April 2020, when the National Command Council announced amendments to the regulations for the mining sector. Section 11J and 11K, amendments to Regulations in Schedule to the Disaster Management Act 57 of 2002, as announced on 16 April 2020, R. 465 Government Gazette No. 43232.

[103] Basquill, 'Shafted' (n 97).

[104] Shakeel Kalidas, Nomfanelo Magwentshu, and Agesan Rajagopaul, 'How South African SMEs can Survive and Thrive post Covid-19' (McKinsey & Company, 10 July 2020) <https://www.mckinsey.com/featured-insig hts/middle-east-and-africa/how-south-african-smes-can-survive-and-thrive-post-covid-19> accessed 23 August 2021.

[105] Gaopalelwe Mathiba, 'The looming coronavirus-induced mass retrenchments: At the crossroads of MPRDA & LRA' (Mineral Law in Africa, 29 April 2020) <http://www.mlia.uct.ac.za/news/looming-coronavirus-induced-mass-retrenchments-crossroads-mprda-lra> accessed 27 June 2021.

[106] (2020) 41 ILJ 1705 (LC).

[107] Department of Mineral Resources and Energy, 'Guidelines for a Mandatory Code of Practice on the Mitigation and Management of Covid-19 Outbreak', 18 May 2020 Government Gazette No. 43335.

As Bhorat and Köhler observe,[108] South Africa had spent 'enormous amounts of money to get the country back on its feet.'[109] Already in April 2020, it made available a USD 26 billion[110] fiscal emergency response—one of the most substantial fiscal response packages among developing countries globally, to limit the economic fallout of the pandemic.[111] Equating to 6.5 per cent of South Africa's GDP,[112] the package included a Social Relief of Distress Grant.[113] Support allocations were largely determined by a pro-poor distribution policy, under the government's Economic Reconstruction and Recovery Plan (ERRP), aimed at restoring the South African economy.[114] The stimulus package[115] provided financial support through specific initiatives, as the pandemic raged. The COBRA (COVID-19 Business Rescue Assistance) initiative[116] and the support program of the Unemployment Insurance Fund / COVID-19 Temporary Employer-Employee Relief Scheme (UIF/TERS)[117] are two noteworthy interventions that assisted companies and workers who were affected by the lockdown. Temporary tax breaks and temporarily increased social grants for the most vulnerable were further initiatives.[118] Food parcel distribution was also increased.[119]

As the pandemic progressed, the South African government allocated additional funds for public works programs and made available funds to assist distressed SMMEs[120] and to support sectors that were particularly hard hit.[121] The government also introduced an official loan guarantee scheme, which assisted businesses who needed to fund operational expenses during the pandemic.[122] A solidarity fund[123] was created, and with allocations made by the government and donations by private parties, these funds were directed towards combating the spread of the virus, and supporting municipal provision of emergency water supply, increased sanitation in public transport, and food and shelter for the homeless.[124]

---

[108] Haroon Bhorat and Tim Köhler, 'Lockdown Economics in South Africa: Social Assistance and the Ramaphosa Stimulus Package' (*Brookings*, 20 November 2020) <https://www.brookings.edu/blog/africa-in-focus/2020/11/20/lockdown-economics-in-south-africa-social-assistance-and-the-ramaphosa-stimulus-package/> accessed 27 June 2021 (hereafter Bhorat & Köhler, 'Lockdown Economics').

[109] See further Gracelin Baskaran, Haroon Bhorat, and Tim Köhler, 'South Africa's Special COVID-19 Grant: A Brief Assessment of Coverage and Expenditure Dynamics' (Development Policy Research Unit (DPRU) Policy Brief 2020/55, November 2020) 1.

[110] ZAR 500 billion.

[111] National Treasury South Africa, *Supplementary Budget Review 2020* (National Treasury, 24 June 2021) (hereafter National Treasury, *Supplementary Budget Review*) 'Chapter 1: Building a Bridge to Recovery Beyond COVID-19', 3–4.

[112] Haroon Bhorat, Tim Köhler, Morné Oosthuizen, Ben Stanwix, François Steenkamp, and Amy Thornton, 'The Economics of Covid-19 in South Africa: Early Impressions" *DPRU Working Paper* 2020/54 (June 2020, DPRU, University of Cape Town) 1.

[113] National Treasury, *Supplementary Budget Review* (n 111) 'Chapter 2: Revisions to In-Year Spending Plans and the Division of Revenue', 8.

[114] Bhorat & Köhler, 'Lockdown Economics' (n 108).

[115] Ibid.

[116] See <https://cobra.org.za> accessed 23 August 2021.

[117] Department of Employment and Labour Notice (215 of 2020) 'Covid-19 Temporary Employee / Employer Relief Scheme (C19-TERS) 26 March 2020' Government Gazette No. 43161.

[118] Ndangwa Noyoo, 'South Africa's Social Policy Response to Covid-19: Relief Measures in an Unequal Society' CRC 1342 Global Dynamics of Social Policy, *Covid-19 Social Policy Response Series*, No. 21 (Bremen University, 2021)<https://nbn-resolving.org> accessed 23 August 2021, 6.

[119] IMF, 'Policy Responses' (n 62).

[120] National Treasury South Africa, *Budget 2021: Budget Review*' (National Treasury, 24 February 2021) 157 (hereafter 'National Treasury, *Budget 2021*').

[121] E.g. a ZAR 1.2 billion Tourism Equity Fund was announced in late January 2021.

[122] National Treasury, *Budget 2021* (n 120) 88.

[123] See <https://solidarityfund.co.za> accessed 23 August 2021.

[124] Juliet Nyasulu and Himani Pandya, 'The Effects of Coronavirus Disease 2019 Pandemic on the South African Health System: A Call to Maintain Essential Health Services' (2020) 12(1) Afr J Prm Health Care Fam Med a2480, <https://doi.org/10.4102/phcfm.v12i1.2480> accessed 23 August 2021.

Scholars have commended the significant reach of the social assistance component,[125] calculated at having supported almost two-thirds of the country's population.[126] Indeed, the scale of support has been massive, but it came at the expense of a similarly massive rise in the fiscal deficit.[127] General Government debt remained around at USD 76.1 billion in March 2021, while the country's Gross External Debt amounted to USD 164 billion.[128] South Africa is on the brink of fiscal unsustainability.[129]

The COVID-19 induced overall reduction in South Africa's GDP has been estimated between 10.3 per cent and 14.14 per cent.[130] The country is said to be 'on the cusp of an economic breakdown'[131] with a projected 15 to 20 per cent fiscal deficit, and an almost 80 per cent debt to GDP ratio; with unemployment rates soaring.[132] Its already dismal pre-pandemic growth record of 1.4 per cent over the past decade, fell to -8 per cent in 2020.[133] The even higher numbers of people living below the poverty line had further effects on the capabilities of the government, who remains responsible, through its rudimentary social welfare and social healthcare systems, for an ever-growing body of need.[134]

Initial optimism[135] over the South Africa's handling of the pandemic soon dissipated,[136] as the press and civic society became vocal about mismanagement of the non-pharmaceutical intervention (lockdown) strategy.[137] A damning analysis emphasized how South Africa

---

[125] Haroon Bhorat, Morné Oosthuizen, and Ben Stanwix, 'Social Assistance Amidst the Covid-19 Epidemic in South Africa: An Impact Assessment' (DPRU, University of Cape Town, June 2020) 2–4.

[126] Bhorat & Köhler, 'Lockdown Economics' (n 108).

[127] Ibid.

[128] Trading Economics 'South Africa Total Gross External Debt' <https://tradingeconomics.com/south-africa/external-debt> accessed 23 August 2021.

[129] Bhorat & Köhler, 'Lockdown Economics' (n 108).

[130] Chitiga-Mabugu et al, 'Economic and Distributional Impact' (n 80) 89.

[131] Greg Mills, 'Is South Africa Descending into Failure?' (*The Brenthurst Foundation*, 13 August 2020) <https://www.thebrenthurstfoundation.org/news/is-south-africa-descending-into-failure/> accessed on 27 February 2021 (hereafter 'Mills, Failure').

[132] See e.g. the 2020 Covid-19 Economics & Human Rights Fact Sheet #2: Institute for Economic Justice, Section 27 and Center for Economic and Social Rights, 'Unemployment and Precarity During Covid-19: The Right to Work and the Right to Just and Favourable Conditions of Work' <https://iej.org.za/wp-content/uploads/2020/10/IEJfactsheet-Work-and-COVID19-1.pdf> accessed 23 August 2021.

[133] Mills, Failure (n 131).

[134] Where the economic effects of Covid-19 impoverish communities, robbing them of their livelihoods, they become more dependent on municipalities. And where such communities have been overly dependent on mines, their economic strategies for resilience tend to be limited. Many municipalities therefore now also must take care of a growing number of people who are living hand to mouth. See Modimowabarwa Kanyane, 'Exploring Challenges of Municipal Service Delivery in South Africa (1994–2013)' (2014) 2(1) Africa's Public Service Delivery and Performance Review 90, 99.

[135] Andrew Harding, 'South Africa's Ruthlessly Efficient Fight Against Coronavirus' *BBC News*, 3 April 2020 <https://www.bbc.com/news/world-africa-52125713> accessed 23 August 2021; Christopher Vandome, 'Covid-19 in South Africa: Leadership, Resilience and Inequality' (*Chatham House*, 7 May 2020) <https://www.chathamhouse.org/2020/05/covid-19-south-africa-leadership-resilience-and-inequality> accessed 23 August 2021. Guy Oliver, 'Six ways COVID-19 is Changing South Africa' (*The New Humanitarian*, 28 May 2020) https://www.thenewhumanitarian.org/feature/2020/05/28/South-Africa-coronavirus-positive-changes accessed 23 August 2021.

[136] Bateman, 'Botch' (n 91).

[137] Amid police brutality in the enforcement of a lockdown that rapidly degenerated into a system of irrational, illogical policies (such as a blanket ban on alcohol and tobacco sales and controversial guidelines which did not permit open-toe shoes to be sold online) the government failed to prevent large-scale corruption in the allocation of COVID-19 relief funding. Ferial Haffajee, 'Ramaphosa Calls 11 Lockdown Deaths and 230,000 Arrests an Act of 'Over-Enthusiasm' - Really!' (*Daily Maverick*, 1 June 2020) <https://www.dailymaverick.co.za/article/2020-06-01-ramaphosa-calls-11-lockdown-deaths-and-230000-arrests-an-act-of-over-enthusiasm-really accessed 23 August 2021>; Pieter-Louis Myburgh, 'Ace Magashule's sons each bag a Free State Covid-19 contract' (Daily Maverick, 31 July 2021) <https://www.dailymaverick.co.za/article/2020-07-31-ace-magashules-sons-each-bag-a-free-state-covid-19-contract/> accessed 23 August 2021; Naledi Shange, 'Cigarettes 'Exported' from SA During Lockdown

had 'lost its first battle against COVID-19' because of problematic responses to the pandemic both on the side of the government and the business sector.[138] Some critical voices, concerned about the potential exploitation of the indigent during the pandemic,[139] pointed out that the Government's COVID-19 support system failed to recognize the importance of the informal sector in poverty alleviation.[140] Some commentators observed that it had taken a crisis of the scale of COVID-19 to jumpstart the government into doing no more than its job—providing the kinds of services that had been needed all along.[141] The crushing final analysis is that the COVID-19-induced economic contraction would have been far less debilitating 'if South Africa had better provision of social security and health insurance, broader, better and more equal access to digital infrastructure to work and school from home, better-equipped hospitals, a more diversified economy and better governance to limit corruption.'[142]

To complicate matters, even before the pandemic, South Africa became subject to a series of downgrades from credit rating agencies which cumulatively affected the government's borrowing costs and caused increasing capital flight and currency weakness.[143] During the pandemic, the country found itself descending ever further into 'junk' status,[144] so much so that the Minister of Finance identified 'an urgent need for government and its social partners to work together' to maintain 'the sanctity of the fiscal framework and implement much-needed structural economic reforms to avoid further harm to [the] sovereign rating.'[145] Further, the IMF reports that, although initial currency depreciation could be reversed, South Africa's net non-resident portfolio outflows (bonds and equities) have amounted to around USD 14 billion (4.5 percent of GDP) since the pandemic commenced.[146]

Never Got Out: Report' (*TimesLive*, 7 October 2020) <https://www.timeslive.co.za/news/south-africa/2020-10-07-cigarettes-exported-from-sa-during-lockdown-never-got-out-report/> accessed 23 August 2021.

[138] Naudé and Cameron 'Failing to Pull Together' (n 79) 2–10.
[139] Suraya Scheba, 'Covid-19 and the Virulence of Global Capitalism – The Poor are on the Frontline' *Daily Maverick* (30 March 2020) <https://www.dailymaverick.co.za/article/2020-03-30-covid-19-and-the-virulence-of-global-capitalism-the-poor-are-on-the-frontline/> accessed 27 June 2021.
[140] Katlego Ramantsima, 'Dancing on the Spot: Covid-19 in the Low-Income Economy' *Daily Maverick* (27 May 2020) <https://www.dailymaverick.co.za/opinionista/2020-05-27-dancing-on-the-spot-covid-19-in-the-low-income-economy/> accessed 27 June 2021.
[141] Mafaniso Hara, Bongani Ncube, and Darlington Sibanda, 'Water and Sanitation in the Face of Covid-19 in Cape Town's Townships and Informal Settlements' Institute for Poverty, Land and Agrarian Studies (PLAAS) (8 April 2020) <https://www.plaas.org.za/water-and-sanitation-in-the-face-of-covid-19-in-cape-towns-townships-and-informal-settlements/> accessed 27 June 2021; Estelle Ellis, 'Covid-19: Exposing a water crisis in the making' Daily Maverick 14 May 2020) <https://www.dailymaverick.co.za/article/2020-05-14-covid-19-exposing-a-water-crisis-in-the-making/> accessed 27 June 2021.
[142] Naudé and Cameron 'Failing to Pull Together' (n 79) 13.
[143] Daniel Francois Meyer and Lerato Mothibi, 'The Effect of Risk Rating Agencies Decisions on Economic Growth and Investment in a Developing Country: The Case of South Africa' (2021) 14(288) Journal of Risk and Financial Management <https://doi.org/10.3390/jrfm14070288> accessed 16 June 2021, 14.
[144] Fitch Rating: BB- (negative outlook) <https://www.fitchratings.com/entity/south-africa-80442220>; Moody's Rating: Ba2 <https://www.businesslive.co.za/bd/economy/2021-05-08-moodys-holds-off-on-sa-credit-rating-review/>. Standard & Poor's Rating: BB- <https://www.spglobal.com/marketintelligence/en/news-insights/latest-news-headlines/s-p-global-ratings-downgrades-south-africa-on-economic-impact-of-pandemic-58364224> (all websites accessed on 18 August 2021).
[145] National Treasury, 'Government's Response to the Rating Actions of S&P Global Ratings (S&P), Fitch Ratings (Fitch) and Moody's Investors Service (Moody's)' *Media Statement* (21 November 2020) <http://www.treasury.gov.za/comm_media/press/2020/20201121%20Media%20Statement%20-%20Response%20to%20Ratings%20Agencies.pdf> accessed 22 June 2021. See also Paul Wallace, 'The Price SA will Pay for Being Downgraded to Junk' *BusinessLIVE* (30 March 2020) <https://www.businesslive.co.za/bd/e conomy/2020-03-31-the-price-sa-will-pay-for-being-downgraded-to-junk/> accessed 23 August 2021.
[146] IMF, Policy Responses (n 62).

The compounded effect of such experiences and the critiques arising therefrom, is the 'predictable ... massive erosion of trust' in a government that was already in a precarious position vis-à-vis the public before the pandemic-induced crisis of governance.[147] Internal conflicts within the South African government's ruling party, the African National Congress, who is trying to come to terms with the insidiousness of the politics of corruption that have plagued South African society for over a decade,[148] compound the problem. Public protest actions have increased eightfold over the past three years,[149] and business confidence levels fell to their lowest in 45 years.[150] The South African government was also criticized for many of its decisions,[151] and for dragging its feet in the rolling out of a vaccination strategy,[152] which the mining sector desperately needed to get back on track.[153]

At the massive scale of the COVID-19 crisis response and given the already distressed fiscal situation in South Africa, the government's response needed external financing. The South African government received a USD 288 million 'crisis response budget' support from the African Development Bank[154] and was also granted emergency assistance from the IMF under the Rapid Financing Instrument, equivalent to USD 4.3 billion.[155] This was to 'support the authorities' efforts in addressing the challenging health situation and severe economic impact of COVID-19.' At about 1.1 per cent interest over 20 months, this is a relatively cheap funding source.[156] It also seems that the conditions attached were not too far out of line with what the government was planning to do in any event: (i) stabilizing the country's finances by cutting government spending to reduce its need to borrow (most like through austerity in public sector wages and funding for state-owned enterprises); (ii) improving the governance of state owned enterprises, and (iii) introducing reforms

[147] Badri Zolfaghari, 'Why we Need to be Able to Trust Our Government in a Time of Crisis' *Mail & Guardian* (17 April 2020) <https://mg.co.za/article/2020-04-17-why-we-need-to-be-able-to-trust-our-government-in-a-time-of-crisis/> accessed 23 August 2021.

[148] Benjamin Fogel, 'There Is No Silver Lining to South Africa's Zuma Insurrection' *Jacobin* (15 July 2021) <https://jacobinmag.com/2021/07/jacob-zuma-south-africa-looting-riots-kwazulu-natal> accessed 16 June 2021.

[149] Lizette Lancaster and Godfrey Mulaudzi, 'Rising Protests are a Warning Sign for South Africa's Government. *ISS Today, Institute for Security Studies* (6 August 2020) <https://issafrica.org/iss-today/rising-protests-are-a-warning-sign-for-south-africas-government> accessed 23 August 2021.

[150] Prineshna Naidoo, 'South Africa Business Confidence Drops to Record Low on Lockdown' *Bloomberg* (10 June 2020) <https://www.bloomberg.com/news/articles/2020-06-10/south-africa-business-confidence-drops-to-record-low-on-lockdown> accessed 23 August 2021.

[151] E.g. Duncan Mcleod, 'Allowing unfettered e-commerce would be seen as "unfair"' Patel' (*Tech Central*, 25 April 2020) <https://techcentral.co.za/allowing-unfettered-e-commerce-would-be-seen-as-unfair-patel/97636/> accessed 23 August 2021. More generally also Naudé and Cameron 'Failing to Pull Together' (n 79) 2–10.

[152] Bateman, 'Botch' (n 91).

[153] Christi Nortier, 'Going Underground: When and From Where Will Miners Get Their Promised Covid-19 Vaccines?' *Daily Maverick* (15 June 2021) <https://www.dailymaverick.co.za/article/2021-06-15-going-underground-when-and-from-where-will-miners-get-their-promised-covid-19-vaccines/> accessed 27 June 2021.

[154] Newsletter: African Development Bank 'South Africa: African Development Bank approves first ever crisis response budget support of R5 billion to fight COVID-19' (African Development Bank, 22 July 2020) <https://www.afdb.org/en/news-and-events/press-releases/south-africa-african-development-bank-approves-first-ever-crisis-response-budget-support-r5-billion-fight-covid-19-36964> accessed 23 August 2021.

[155] International Monetary Fund, 'IMF Executive Board Approves US$4.3 Billion in Emergency Support to South Africa to Address the COVID-19 Pandemic' (Press Release No. 20/271, 27 July 2020) <https://www.imf.org/en/News/Articles/2020/07/27/pr20271-south-africa-imf-executive-board-approves-us-billion-emergency-supp ort-covid-19-pandemic> accessed 27 June 2021 (hereafter IMF, 'US$4.3 Billion'). This funded, among others, the increased measures needed in the health sector.

[156] Danny Bradlow, 'The IMF's $4 bln Loan for South Africa: The Pros, Cons and Potential Pitfalls' *The Conversation* (28 July 2020) <https://theconversation.com/the-imfs-4bn-loan-for-south-africa-the-pros-cons-and-potential-pitfalls-143553> accessed 23 August 2021 (hereafter Bradlow, 'IMF's $4 bln Loan').

to stimulate a growing and inclusive economy, potentially with measures to improve competition.[157]

Zambia

Zambia's economy was also already in crisis even before the COVID-19 outbreak. This was due to large fiscal imbalances, a narrow tax base, unsustainable expenditure levels, and rapidly rising public debt.[158] The COVID-19 pandemic had a further adverse impact on the Zambian economy in that the local currency depreciated sharply, yields on public debt increased, and the economy was disrupted by lockdowns in trading partners.[159]

So far, Zambia has suffered through three waves of the COVID-19 pandemic.[160] Its early response, suppress-and-contain measures, included closure of schools and universities, bars, cinemas, and casinos; suspension of non-essential foreign travel; mandatory quarantine for all foreign travellers; delivery and take-out only regime for restaurants; restricting sports activities, and public group gatherings to no more than 50; a temporary lockdown on the towns of Kafue and Nakonde; and a partial closure of the border with Tanzania.[161] Restrictions were eased after the first wave, and some of them were reintroduced later, in anticipation of the second and third waves.

The COVID-19 pandemic caused Zambia's economy to fall into a deep recession, with 'unprecedented deterioration in all the key sectors of the economy.'[162] Real GDP contracted by an estimated 4.9 per cent in 2020, nearly completely undoing the modest growth of the prior two years.[163]

Because COVID-19-related restrictions on movement affected mineral exports, and in turn mineral royalty payments charged at the point of export,[164] after the initial wave of COVID-19 infections, the government's Economic Recovery Program aimed to prioritize the recovery of the mining sector.[165] For instance, import duties on mineral concentrate and export duties on precious metals were suspended to support the mining sector.[166] Zambia's second[167] and third[168] waves only worsened the outlook, hitting the mining sector

---

[157] IMF, 'US$4.3 Billion' (n 155); Bradlow, 'IMF's $4 bln Loan' (n 156).

[158] Government of the Republic of Zambia, 'Economic Recovery Programme 2020-2023: Restoring Growth and Safeguarding Livelihoods through Macroeconomic Stability, Economic Diversification and Debt Sustainability' (Ministry of Finance & Ministry of National Development and Planning, 2020) 16 (hereafter Zambia, 'Economic Recovery 2020-2023').

[159] IMF, 'Policy Responses' (n 62).

[160] The first between March and August 2020, a second between mid-December 2020 and January 2021, and a third wave commencing at the end of May 2021. IMF, 'Policy Responses' (n 62).

[161] Ibid.

[162] African Development Bank, 'Zambia Economic Outlook' (AfDB, 2020) <https://www.afdb.org/en/countries-southern-africa-zambia/zambia-economic-outlook> accessed 23 August 2021.

[163] 4.0 per cent in 2018 and 1.9 per cent in 2019.

[164] Reuters, 'Zambia Mining Revenues Drop 30% due to COVID-19, Chamber of Mines says' (*Thomson Reuters*, 18 June 2020) <https://www.reuters.com/article/us-zambia-mining-idUSKBN23P1NB> accessed 31 March 2021.

[165] Zambia, 'Economic Recovery 2020-2023' (n 158) 2.

[166] IMF, 'Policy Responses' (n 62).

[167] Policy Monitoring and Research Centre, 'Zambia's Second Wave of Covid-19: A Call to Collective Action' (Press Statement, 22 January 2021) <https://pmrczambia.com/wp-content/uploads/2021/01/Press-Statement-Zambia%E2%80%99s-Second-Wave-of-COVID-19-A-Call-to-Collective-Action.pdf> accessed 6 February 2021.

[168] Zambia National Public Health Institute, 'Zambia COVID-19 Statistics Daily Status Update (9 June 2021) <https://www.zawya.com/mena/en/press-releases/story/Coronavirus__Zambia_COVID19_Statistics_Daily_Status_Update_09_June_2021-AFPR0906202114847/> accessed 4 May 2021.

particularly, because of how heavily Zambia's export earnings depend on the sector,[169] and how few linkages there are between mining and other economic sectors.[170]

To finance COVID-19 related expenses, including health spending, arrears clearance, grain purchases, and a recapitalization of a non-bank financial institution (NATSAVE), the Zambian government issued bonds amounting to 2.3 per cent of the GDP.[171] In its 2021 Budget, it then further envisioned tax breaks, e.g. for tourism, but also a permanently lower corporate income tax rate, and suspended import duties and fees.[172]

While Zambia tried to address pressure to finance the crisis through measures that would facilitate investment attractiveness, it also responded to the COVID-19 crisis in a manner typical of resource nationalism.[173] The latter is evidenced particularly in recent developments in the mineral and energy sectors: by taking over mining companies and incorporating new ones to take on new ventures, the Zambian government is seeking more control over its mineral resources. Even so, these acquisitions come at a cost, the financing of which requires government lending. For instance, the Government acquired Mopani Copper Mines after preventing the company from placing its mines on care and mainten- ance during the COVID-19 pandemic.[174] This acquisition required the company to obtain a loan of $1.5 billion; pushing the country further in debt. The Government's mining invest- ment holding company, Zambia Consolidated Copper Mines Investment Holdings Limited incorporated a subsidiary to operate in the gold mining sector.[175] The stated aim of entering the gold mining sector is to enable the sale of bullion to the Bank of Zambia, Zambia's cen- tral bank.[176]

The same is true of the energy sector. The Minister of Energy in 2020 took over the trans- mission lines of the Copperbelt Energy Company ('CEC').[177] CEC is the bulk supplier of electricity to the mines and so the acquisition of these powerlines gave the government greater control over both the energy and mining sector. When this action was taken for judicial review, the High Court reversed the Minister of Energy's decision.[178] The Minister has taken the matter to appeal. The actions of the Government in the mineral and energy sectors prove that Zambia is taking resource nationalistic stances and this needs to be moni- tored in further research into resilience.

Zambia's experience with the climate-change induced three-year drought made it clear that it is not the best strategy to have an electricity system supplied almost entirely from

---

[169] PN Osakwe, 'COVID-19 and the Challenge of Developing Productive Capacities in Zambia' (UNCTAD Research Paper No. 63, April 2021) 18 (hereafter Osakwe, 'Developing Productive Capacities').

[170] Osakwe, 'Developing Productive Capacities' (n 169) 22.

[171] USD 884 million (ZMW 8 billion).

[172] IMF, 'Policy Responses' (n 62).

[173] The term 'resource nationalism' here refers to efforts by the government to shift economic and political con- trol over their extractives sector. See Ian Bremmer and Robert Johnston, 'The Rise and fall of Resource Nationalism' (2009) 51(2) Survival: Global Politics and Strategy 149.

[174] Economist Intelligence Unit (EIU) 'Country Report: Zambia Generated on March 30th 2021' (*EIU*, 2021) 46-47 (hereafter EIU, 'Zambia'); Nicola Woodroffe, 'Force Majeure and Other Coronavirus-Era Legal Challenges: Lessons for Resource-Dependent Countries from the Glencore-Zambia Dispute' *Natural Resource Governance Institute (NRGI)* (13 May 2020) <https://resourcegovernance.org/blog/force-majeure-coronavirus- legal-challenges-resource-dependent-zambia-glencore> accessed 27 June 2021.

[175] ZCCM-IH, 'ZCCM-IH and Its Investment Strategy in the Gold Sector in Zambia' (*ZCCM-IH Press Statement*, 24 May 2020) <https://www.zccm-ih.com.zm/2020/05/26/zccm-ih-and-its-investment-strategy-in- the-gold-sector-in-zambia/> accessed 28 June 2021.

[176] Zambia, 'Economic Recovery 2020-2023' (n 158) 35.

[177] See Electricity (Common Carrier) Regulations Statutory Instrument No. 57 of 2020.

[178] See application for judicial review in *The People v Attorney General & Energy Regulation Board* [2020] HP 0575.

hydropower in a region afflicted by extreme water shortage. Absent an adequate energy supply, socio-economic progress and development are inconceivable. Zambia's response to the drought was to consider the addition of nuclear energy[179] to its energy mix.[180] As a developing-country signatory to the Paris Agreement,[181] however, Zambia is obliged to mitigate environmental impact and develop its plans for a low-carbon future.[182] These obligations coupled with the high cost of setting up nuclear power plants render forthwith implementation of a nuclear programme in Zambia unlikely. In the latest Economic Recovery Program, Zambia instead recommitted to completing pending hydro-electric projects.[183]

In its Economic Recovery Program, Zambia's government admits that the country's debt is unsustainable.[184] Leveraging the country's mineral wealth is listed among the short-term resource mobilization measures to finance the economic recovery program.[185] It is in this regard that the Central Bank will purchase gold bullion to build gold reserves as a measure to address debt unsustainability. The government also committed itself to enhance debt transparency to reduce the pace at which government accumulates debt.[186] Public scrutiny of the national debt is to come through publication of quarterly reports detailing public debt and loans. Copies of these public debt reports are available on the website of the Ministry of Finance.[187] At an estimated USD 12 billion in 2021, Zambia is highly indebted.[188] It has defaulted on paying back its Eurobond and other foreign obligations, which accounts for its low credit ratings.[189]

Zambia is now seeking a debt restructuring.[190] Virtual talks with the IMF around securing a bailout loan drew attention to the burdensome, opaque terms of Zambia's agreements with China.[191] The loans Zambia could secure (USD 1.4 million 'to improve

[179] Nuclear power currently accounts for only 3 per cent of total energy output of the Southern African region as opposed to the 60 per cent output from coal and 20.9 per cent output from hydro-electric. UNECA, 'Energy Crisis' (n 26) 9.

[180] Kangwa-Musole George Chisanga, 'Energy Justice and Nuclear Power: Considerations for Zambia Atomic Agency' (2020) 19 SI *Centre Annual Review* 18.

[181] 2015 (entered into force on 4 November 2016). Zambia is a signatory and has submitted plans for its contribution to achieving the Paris Agreement accordingly. See United Nations Climate Change, 'Zambia' (2021) <https://unfccc.int/node/61237> accessed on 27 January 2020. See also United *Nations, 'Zambia's Intended Nationally Determined Contribution (INDC) to the 2015 Agreement on Climate Change' (2016) <https://www4.unfccc.int/sites/ndcstaging/PublishedDocuments/Zambia%20First/FINAL+ZAMBIA%27S+INDC_1.pdf> accessed 28 June 2021.

[182] Paris Agreement 2015, Art 4.4, 4.6.

[183] Zambia, 'Economic Recovery 2020–2023' (n 158) 33.

[184] Ibid, 16.

[185] Ibid, 17.

[186] Ibid, 20.

[187] Ministry of Finance 'Public Debt Reports' <https://www.mof.gov.zm/?page_id=5252> accessed 19 May 2021. (Information last updated in 2016).

[188] Alexandra Wexler and Nicholas Bariyo, 'After Default, Zambia's Outsized Bet on Copper Could Play Into China's Hands' *Wall Street Journal* (27 April 2021) <https://www.wsj.com/articles/after-default-zambias-outsized-bet-on-copper-could-play-into-chinas-hands-11619514520> accessed 24 August 2021.

[189] Fitch Rating: RD (https://www.fitchratings.com/entity/zambia-90269061). Moody's Rating: Ca (https://www.spglobal.com/marketintelligence/en/news-insights/latest-news-headlines/moody-s-downgrades-zambia-s-ratings-57907548). Standard & Poor's Rating: SD (https://www.spglobal.com/marketintelligence/en/news-insights/latest-news-headlines/s-p-downgrades-zambia-to-selective-default-on-debt-payment-freeze-60858913#:~:text=S%26P%20Global%20Ratings%20lowered%20its,debt%20service%20payments%20to%20creditors) (all websites accessed on 18 August 2021).

[190] EIU, 'Zambia' (n 174) 7.

[191] Soshana Kedem, 'IMF Seeks China Loan Transparency in Zambia Talks' *African Business* (12 February 2021) <https://african.business/2021/02/economy/imf-seeks-china-loan-transparency-in-zambia-talks/> accessed 24 August 2021.

household food security in wake of COVID-19'[192] and USD 450,000 to help communities acquire goods[193]) seem like drops in a leaking bucket.

Policy trends towards resilience in Zambia will likely be heavily influenced by the debt owed to China. This is because other international lenders such as the IMF consider Zambia's current debt levels unsustainable, to the extent that they are unwilling to lend to the country.[194] However, China remains heavily invested in the Zambian mining sector and has Chinese contractors carrying out numerous infrastructural works.[195]

It is thought that Zambia's negotiating position could improve given recovery in international demand for copper has raised prices.[196] This may well result in a current-account surplus; provided that the country puts in measures to resume payments on defaulted debts, and that potential impediments to global economic recovery from the pandemic will not stifle the demand for copper.[197] Limited government infrastructure investment — owing to the sovereign debt crisis — will cause exports to outweigh imports by a considerable margin.[198]

Namibia

In Namibia, a national emergency had to be declared in 2019[199] because of the drought. Later that year,[200] the Namibian government appealed to development partners (the private sector, diplomatic missions, humanitarian institutions, the United Nations, civil society, and international organizations) for emergency assistance to mitigate the impacts of the drought.[201]

Namibia was initially lauded by governments and the WHO for its quick and efficient response to the COVID-19 crisis. Shortly after the first two COVID-19 cases were reported on 13 March 2020, a state of emergency was declared and the country placed in lockdown. All international borders, schools, universities, and business were closed.[202] The initial measures taken, however, proved ineffective against the mutating COVID-19 virus, the rise in infections, the unavailability of medical resources and infrastructure (including hospital beds, ambulances and oxygen), and a slow vaccine uptake. These factors, amongst others, 'has led Namibia to the perfect storm in which it finds itself.'[203]

---

[192] African Development Bank Group, 'Zambia: African Development Bank approves $1.4 million grant to improve household food security in the wake of Covid-19' (*AfDB Newsletter*, 16 June 2021) <https://www.afdb.org/en/news-and-events/press-releases/zambia-african-development-bank-approves-14-million-grant-improve-household-food-security-wake-covid-19-44187> accessed 24 August 2021.

[193] African Development Bank Group, 'Zambia: The Bank helps cushion the impact of COVID-19 with livestock and aquaculture projects' (*AfDB Newsletter*, 16 June 2021) <https://www.afdb.org/en/success-stories/zambia-bank-helps-cushion-impact-covid-19-livestock-and-aquaculture-projects-42458> accessed 24 August 2021.

[194] EIU, 'Zambia' (n 174) 7.

[195] Peter Kragelund, 'Knocking on a Wide-open Door: Chinese Investments in Africa' (2009) 36(122) Review of African Political Economy 479–497

[196] https://www.afdb.org/en/countries-southern-africa-zambia/zambia-economic-outlook. Copper prices are expected to rise to levels not seen in recent history (predicated on electric vehicle demand).

[197] https://www.afdb.org/en/countries-southern-africa-zambia/zambia-economic-outlook

[198] EIU, 'Zambia' (n 174) 11.

[199] On 6 May 2019.

[200] On 4 June 2019.

[201] AfDB, 'Humanitarian Emergency Assistance' (n 30).

[202] World Health Organization (WHO), 'Namibia praised for its quick and efficient response to COVID-19' (*WHO Newsroom*, 16 June 2020) https://www.who.int/news-room/feature-stories/detail/namibia-praised-for-its-quick-and-efficient-response-to-covid-19> accessed 24 May 2021. Namibia's response also included educating outbreak preparedness and response teams and staff from public and private health facilities.

[203] Michaela Clayton, 'Namibia is facing Covid-19's "perfect storm"' *Daily Maverick* (29 June 2021) <https://www.dailymaverick.co.za/article/2021-06-29-namibia-is-facing-covid-19s-perfect-storm/>, accessed 28 August 2021.

For Namibia, as profound as the impact of the COVID-19 pandemic has been on the country's economy by large, its effects on mining had been particularly harsh. As a cornerstone of the Namibian economy, mining contributes on average around 11 per cent to the GDP.[204] Containment measures against the spread of the coronavirus resulted in a three-week cessation of mining activities.[205] The subsequent global economic slowdown further contributed to the extreme consequences: Debmarine Namibia, a 50–50 joint venture diamond-mining company between De Beers and the Namibian government, reported a 13 per cent drop in production in 2020.[206] Many other Namibian mining companies had to scale down operations, institute temporary mine closures, and implement cost-cutting measures.[207]

The economic outlook of Namibia during 2020 was bleak, as this country, too, succumbed to the spread of the coronavirus.[208] National containment and suppression measures between March and September 2020[209] contributed to an estimated contraction of Namibia's real GDP of between 7 per cent and 8 per cent,[210] the largest annual decline since Independence in 1990.[211] Real GDP growth is projected to increase to 2.7 per cent in 2021 and 3.3 per cent in 2022, partly because of estimated better growth prospects for diamond mining, agriculture, and transport.[212] The Bank of Namibia expects improved growth rates in 2021 and 2022 in the primary sectors, including diamond mining and metal ore sectors. Secondary sectors, such as the electricity and water sectors, are also expected to turn positive. However, low international prices for some of Namibia's export commodities (such as uranium) and unpredictable climate changes remain risks for domestic growth.[213] The

---

[204] From 2000 to 2018, uranium contributed 1.8 per cent to GDP, while diamond mining contributed 7.6 per cent. Victoria Nambinga, 'The Impact of Mining Sector to the Namibia Economy: Assessing Socio-economic and Environmental Effects' (*Namibia National Planning Commission*, October 2019) <https://www.npc.gov.na/downl oad/Researches_by_NPC/The-Impact-of-Mining-sector-to-the-Namibia-economy-FINAL.pdf> accessed 24 May 2021, 4.

[205] From 28 March 2020 to 16 April 2020. Reuters, 'Namibia Suspends Mining Operations as coronavirus Lockdown Takes Effect' *Thomson Reuters* (28 March 2020) <https://www.reuters.com/article/health-coronavi rus-namibia/namibia-suspends-mining-operations-as-coronavirus-lockdown-takes-effect-idINL8N2BL0CW> accessed 24 May 2021.

[206] Reuters, 'Namibia's Marine Diamond Miner's Production Hit by COVID-19, Drops 13% in 2020' *Thomson Reuters* (8 March 2021) <https://www.reuters.com/article/namibia-mining-idUSL8N2L63YL> accessed 24 May 2021.

[207] Fabian Shaanika, 'Opinion – Unearthing Social Responsibility in Namibia's Mining Sector' (The Namibian, 11 December 2020) <https://neweralive.na/posts/opinion-unearthing-social-responsibility-in-namibias-mining-sector> accessed 12 January 2021.

[208] First cases reported on 13 March 2020. As of 25 May 2021, Namibia has reported 53,432 cases (49,550 recoveries) and 779 deaths. See Worldometer, 'Namibia Coronavirus Cases' (2020) <https://www.worldometers. info/coronavirus/country/namibia/> accessed 25 May 2021; Ralph Marenga and Job Shipululo Amupanda, 'The Coronavirus and Social Justice in Namibia' (2021) 48(2) Politikon: South African Journal of Political Studies, 214 (hereafter Marenga et al, 'Coronavirus and Social Justice').

[209] The President declared a state of emergency on 17 March 2020. (Declaration of State of Emergency: National Disaster (COVID- 19) Proclamation 7/2020, published in Government Gazette 7148 of 18 March 2020), which was followed by various stages of state of emergency regulations. The state of emergency and the lockdowns eventually ended in September 2020. Marenga et al, 'Coronavirus and Social Justice' (n 208) 215.

[210] Sources vary, the IMF indicating a figure of 7.2 per cent and the AFDB a figure closer to 7.9 per cent, while the Bank of Namibia puts the contraction at 7.3 per cent. IMF 'US$270.83 Million' (n 215); 'African Development Bank Group, Namibia Economic Outlook' *AfDB* <https://www.afdb.org/en/countries/southern-africa/namibia> accessed 24 August 2021 (hereafter AfDB, 'Namibia Outlook'); Bank of Namibia, 'Economic Outlook Update - February 2021' (2021) <https://www.bon.com.na/CMSTemplates/Bon/Files/bon.com.na/02/028351bb-556d-4917-ba74-45e97e0f1374.pdf> accessed 24 May 2021, 4 (hereafter Bank of Namibia, 'Economic Outlook 2021').

[211] Bank of Namibia, 'Economic Outlook 2021' (n 210) 4.

[212] Ibid, 4.

[213] Ibid, 4–6.

African Development Bank expects the Namibian economy still to face substantial risks and challenges in the short to medium term.[214]

The IMF granted Namibia a disbursement of USD 270.83 million to provide an 'urgent balance of payment and fiscal financing stemming from the COVID-19 pandemic'.[215] To mitigate the effects of COVID-19 on the Namibian economy, the Government put in place an economic stimulus package[216] of USD 544 million[217] (4.25 per cent of GDP).[218] The package supported once-off emergency income grants for those affected and not otherwise eligible for social grants.[219] Another mitigation measure was a National Employment and Salary Protection Scheme by the Social Security Commission and the Ministry of Finance (N\$320 million, or USD23 million) that consisted of an Employer Wage Subsidy Program to motivate employers in the construction, tourism, and aviation sectors not to retrench employees in the short term, and an Affected Employee Program to provide support for individuals who have suffered a loss of income as a result of the COVID-19.[220] The Bank of Namibia also reduced the repurchase (repo) rate with 100 basis points to 5.25 per cent to alleviate COVID-19's impact on the economy. Various other mitigation measures were also put in place.[221] On 23 August 2021, the IMF also allocated special drawing rights worth N\$3.8 billion to Namibia, 'almost rebuilding the country's depleted borrowing capacity from the fund',[222] although the Ministry of Finance has not indicated whether the treasury plans to borrow from the fund.

B. Inferences

COVID-19 has had a huge impact on African economies. As was shown, the lockdown strategies it necessitated radically reduced fundamental income sources in some of the countries discussed. Income generated from natural resource extraction was severely affected in at least three of the four countries discussed. The damage—the 'years of economic and social progress' which has come undone—will leave 'lasting scars on the region's economies.'[223]

---

[214] AfDB, 'Namibia Outlook' (n 210).

[215] International Monetary Fund, 'IMF Executive Board Approves US\$270.83 Million Disbursement to Namibia to address the COVID-19 Pandemic' (*IMF Press Release 21/95*, 31 March 2021) https://www.imf.org/en/News/Articles/2021/04/01/pr2195-namibia-imf-executive-board-approves-disbursement-to-address-covid-19-pandemic> accessed 24 August 2021 (hereafter IMF 'US\$270.83 Million').

[216] On 1 April 2020. Iipumbu Shiimi, 'Economic Stimulus and Relief Package: Impact of COVID19 on the Economy and Households' Namibian Ministry of Finance (Media Statement, 1 April 2020).

[217] N\$ 8.1 billion.

[218] Marenga et al, 'Coronavirus and Social Justice' (n 208) 215; Barry Maher and Gracelin Baskaran, 'Southern Africa: Why Risk Financing is Critically Important During COVID-19 recovery' (*World Bank Blogs*, 1 September 2020) <https://blogs.worldbank.org/africacan/southern-africa-why-risk-financing-critically-important-during-covid-19-recovery> accessed 24 May 2021.

[219] Comprising a N\$750 (US54) once-off payment available to unemployed persons between the age of 18 and 60 years who do not receive any other social grants. Marenga et al, 'Coronavirus and Social Justice' (n 208) 216.

[220] Social Security Commission, 'National Employment and Salary Protection Scheme for Covid19', (SSC, 2020) <https://www.ssc.org.na/resources/STIMULUS_PACKAGE_INFORMATION.pdf> accessed 24 May 2021.

[221] Marenga et al, 'Coronavirus and Social Justice' (n 208) 218–221.

[222] Lazarus Amukeshe, 'IMF gives Namibia special drawing rights worth N\$3.9b' (*The Namibian*, 27 August 2021) <https://www.namibian.com.na/104757/read/IMF-gives-Namibia-special-drawing-rights-worth-N\$39b> accessed 28 August 2021.

[223] The number of people in sub-Saharan Africa living in extreme poverty is projected to have increased by more than 32 million in 2020; the number of missed school days is more than four times the level in advanced economies; and employment fell by around 8.5 percent in 2020. In terms of livelihoods, per capita income has returned to 2013 levels. Abebe Aemro Selassie and Shushanik Hakobyan, 'Six Charts Show the Challenges Faced by

The above survey of crisis responses show that, when faced with a crisis of the epic proportions created by the COVID-19 pandemic, countries' abilities to bounce back depends on various factors. Five that are relevant for purposes of this analysis, are:

(i)   The extent to which such countries are already weakened by a clustering of crises, be they of natural or of socio-political origin, may affect their ability to respond to crisis. The drought in Southern Africa broadly is an example of a natural phenomenon that already had Namibia and Zambia's economies on their knees. The problems caused by overspending and mismanagement of public funds and alleged graft during former South African President Jacob Zuma's nine-year rule[224] is an example of the type of economic weakening that is more governance-oriented.

(ii) Where, in times of relative prosperity, countries have tried putting long-term policies in place to foster financial resilience, and epic crisis might still bring them to the precipice of destitution, although they might be better positioned to keep themselves from going over the brink. Ghana's Stabilisation and Heritage fund initiatives over the past decade certainly have placed it in a healthier starting position to weather the COVID-19 crisis.

(iii) The economic outlooks in the countries studied obviously raise concerns about debt sustainability levels. If their economies are not already in the high-debt distress category, they are heading that way. For all of the countries in this discussion, the economic situation is bound to worsen before it improves.[225] In the face of an epic crisis, or crisis clustering, countries sometimes must make rather ruinous fiscal and policy decisions. Crisis borrowing and spending may harm the economy.[226] At least some of the countries in this study (South Africa and Zambia) now find themselves with unsustainable debt levels. In desperate times, it is far more difficult to make policy choices that will lead to long-term sustainability. This may lead countries down a negative policy spiral that certainly does not foster resilience, but instead sabotages what resilience may be left in a system. For countries finding them in such unenviable positions, it would be important to approach future policy choices around development and lending negotiations with great care.

(iv) In resource-dependent countries, mine closures—even if temporary or partial—can have a devastating effect on the economy on two fronts. First, it can deny the state revenue in the form of royalties, corporate tax, and taxes from employees. This may dilute whatever reserves of resilience a particular state can rely on in times of crisis. Secondly, the continued closure of mines due to COVID-19 may lead to job losses exacerbating the unemployment problems. This may place increased pressure on

---

Sub-Saharan Africa' <https://www.imf.org/en/News/Articles/2021/04/12/na041521-six-charts-show-the-challen ges-faced-by-sub-saharan-africa> accessed 23 August 2021 (hereafter Selassie et al 'Six Charts').

[224] Tom Wilson, 'Graft under Jacob Zuma Cost South Africa $34bn, says Ramaphosa' *Financial Times* (14 October 2019) <https://www.ft.com/content/e0991464-ee79-11e9-bfa4-b25f11f42901> accessed 24 August 2021. Thomas A Koelble, 'Globalization and Governmentality in the Post-Colony: South Africa under Jacob Zuma', Discussion Paper No. SP V 2018-103 (Wissenschaftszentrum Berlin für Sozialforschung (WZB), Berlin, 2018) <http://hdl.handle.net/10419/190803> accessed 24 August 2021.

[225] See III.B. above

[226] Nafi Chinery, 'Ghana: Initial Assessment of the Impact of the Coronavirus Pandemic on the Extractive Sector and Resource Governance', (NRGI Briefing, 26 May 2020) 3.

such a state for a crisis response, which is bound to affect resources available for re-silience building. The scale of the crisis will impact on the extent to which existing resources get depleted.

(v) Governments' capacity to respond has also been affected by their ability (or willingness) to access finance to meet the additional cost of COVID-19 and to finance future fiscal stimulus. Both in Ghana and South Africa,[227] the governments were criticized[228] for heavy-handed responses to curb the spread of COVID-19 infection. However, the governments' financial resources probably did not allow for more nuanced, sophisticated strategies.[229] Indeed, state coffers were stretched beyond imagination, as the above-mentioned debt-to-GDP ratios suggest.

At the time of writing, all four the countries in this analysis found themselves with more sovereign debt than at the beginning of the COVID-19 pandemic. For some (Ghana, Namibia), the situation is not yet as dire as it is for others (Zambia, South Africa). The bottom line, though, is that responses to future crises, looming as the earth moves ever closer to overstepping yet more of the planetary boundaries, can only be as strong as these countries' resources (human, fiscal, natural) allow.

IV. The Spectre of Unsustainable Debt

Economists emphasize that limited fiscal space is a major factor contributing to Africa's vulnerability in recovering from crises such as the COVID-19 pandemic.[230] Already in 2018, before the pandemic immersed the continent in crisis, they pointed out that for most African countries, the 'cost of borrowing exceeded the rate of growth.' They also cautioned that 'debt dynamics' were already adverse, because of 'widening primary deficits, slowing growth, and rising interest rates.'[231] Analysts forecasted that Africa could lose up to 30 per cent of its fiscal revenue,[232] which could trigger inabilities to service debt or even defaults. They indicate that sovereign credit rating downgrades in the wake of declining fiscal

---

[227] See section III.A.2 above.

[228] For Ghana, see Maame Efua Addadzi-Koom, 'Quasi-State of Emergency: Assessing the Constitutionality of Ghana's Legislative Response to Covid-19' (2020) 8(3) The Theory and Practice of Legislation 2; Kwadwo Appiagyei-Atua, 'Emergency without a State of Emergency: Effect of Imposition of Restrictions Act, 2020 on Rights of Ghanaians, cited by Addadzi-Koom, A. Kwasi Prempeh, 'Executive Powers and Domestic Response to Coronavirus Pandemic: Is the Imposition of Restriction Bill Necessary?', Ghana Law Hub. For South Africa, see Christopher Vandome, 'COVID-19 in South Africa: Leadership, Resilience and Inequality' (*Chatham House*, 7 May 2020) <https://www.chathamhouse.org/2020/05/covid-19-south-africa-leadership-resilience-and-inequality> accessed 26 June 2021 (hereafter Vandome, 'Leadership').

[229] Vandome, 'Leadership' (n 228).

[230] Shipalana et al 'Macroeconomic Impact' (n 7) 5.

[231] Indermit Gill and Kenan Karakulah, 'Sounding the Alarm on Africa's Debt,' (*Brookings, Future Development*, 6 April 2018) <https://www.brookings.edu/blog/future-development/2018/04/06/sounding-the-alarm-on-africas-debt/> accessed 8 July 2021 and Giovanni Faleg 'What If...Sub-Saharan Africa Is Hit By A Continental Debt Crisis?' in Florence Gaub (ed), *WHAT IF...? Scanning the Horizon: 12 scenarios for 2021* (European Union Institute for Security Studies (EUISS) 2019) <https://www.iss.europa.eu/content/what-if-scanning-horizon-12-scenarios-2021> accessed 8 July 2021.

[232] AU, 'Impact of the Coronavirus (COVID-19) on the African Economy: Report' (Addis Ababa, AU Commission, 2020) <https://www.tralac.org/news/article/14483-impact-of-the-coronavirus-covid-19-on-the-african-economy.html> accessed 24 August 2021. Shipalana et al 'Macroeconomic Impact' (n 7) 5.

revenues and foreign exchange receipts alongside widening fiscal deficits and rising debt-to-gross domestic product (GDP) ratios[233] worsen the outlook.

The point is that African countries generally did not have the financial luxury of 'doing all it would take' to contain the spread of COVID-19.[234] The fiscal packages the continent could afford on average were only about a third of what advanced economies could spend, measured as a percentage of GDP.[235]

The IMF estimates that sub-Saharan Africa needs about USD 425 billion between now and 2025, if it is to address the costs of the pandemic and reduce poverty.[236] It has hence scaled up its lending capacity to Africa thirteenfold over the past year.[237] But many African countries entered the COVID-19 crisis with elevated debt vulnerabilities and less scope for incurring expenses.[238] Many of them are now reeling under precarious debt burdens that worsened during the pandemic.[239] In general, by the end of 2020, public debt in sub-Saharan Africa had increased to its highest level in almost 15 years, owing largely to declining revenues and output.[240] As African countries take on more debt to allay economic repercussions of crises such as the drought and the COVID-19 pandemic, the situation gets more concerning.

The IMF estimates that 17 African countries (generating 25 per cent of the region's GDP) are either already debt distressed, or will be soon.[241] By September 2020, Ghana's public debt had reached 71 per cent of the Gross Domestic Product.[242] Government debt to GDP in Ghana is expected to reach 82 per cent by the end of 2021 and projected to rise to 83 per cent in 2022 and 84 per cent in 2023.[243]

South Africa's Government Debt to GDP ratio increased to 83 per cent in 2020 from 62.20 per cent the previous year.[244] Its public debt levels are expected to exceed 100 per cent of GDP by 2025, and to rise to almost 114 per cent by the end of this decade.[245]

---

[233] Shipalana et al 'Macroeconomic Impact' (n 7) 3.

[234] Christopher Adam, Mark Henstridge, and Stevan Lee, 'After the Lockdown: Macroeconomic Adjustment to the COVID-19 Pandemic in Sub-Saharan Africa' (2020) 36(S1) Oxford Review of Economic Policy 338–358.

[235] For African countries, fiscal packages averaged at 2.6 per cent of GDP in 2020, compared to the 7.2 per cent of GDP for advanced economies over the same period. Selassie et al 'Six Charts' (n 223).

[236] The number of people in sub-Saharan Africa living in extreme poverty have increased by more than 32 million in 2020: Selassie et al 'Six Charts' (n 223).

[237] Georgieva, 'Road Ahead' (n 240).

[238] Selassie et al 'Six Charts' (n 223).

[239] Haroon Bhorat and Gracelin Baskaran, 'From Stimulus to Debt: The Case of South Africa', Brookings, Foresight Africa, 2 February 2021 <https://www.brookings.edu/blog/africa-in-focus/2021/02/02/from-stimulus-to-debt-the-case-of-south-africa/> accessed 24 August 2021.

[240] Kristalina Georgieva, 'The Road Ahead for Africa—Fighting the Pandemic and Dealing with Debt' Speech delivered to the African Development Bank Annual Meeting, 23 June 2021 <https://www.imf.org/en/News/Articles/2021/06/23/sp062321-the-road-ahead-for-africa-fighting-the-pandemic-and-dealing-with-debt> accessed 24 August 2021 (hereafter Georgieva, 'Road Ahead').

[241] Selassie et al 'Six Charts' (n 223).

[242] Deloitte Ghana, 'Economic Impact' (n 47).

[243] Trading Economics 'Ghana - Economic Forecasts' <https://tradingeconomics.com/ghana/forecast> accessed 27 August 2021.

[244] Trading Economics, 'Government Debt to GDP in South Africa increased to 83 percent in 2020 from 62.20 percent in 2019' (South African Reserve Bank, 2020) <https://tradingeconomics.com/south-africa/government-debt-to-gdp> accessed 18 December 2020 (hereafter Trading Economics 'Government Debt').

[245] According to a document presented by Finance Minister, Tito Mboweni and reported on in Antony Sguazzin and Prinesha Naidoo, 'South Africa Sees Debt Topping 100 per cent of GDP in 2025' (Bloomberg, 20 June 2020) <https://www.bloomberg.com/news/articles/2020-06-20/south-africa-sees-government-debt-at-113-8-of-gdp-in-2028-29> accessed 26 June 2021.

In Namibia, the increase, over one year, was from 54.80 per cent to an all-time high of 69.60 per cent in 2020.[246] Government debt in Namibia is expected to reach USD 7502 million[247] by the end of 2021 and in the long term, the Namibia government debt is projected to trend around USD 7702 million[248] in 2023, according to econometric models.[249]

In Zambia, between 2019 and 2020, the debt-to-GDP ratio increased from 94.5 per cent to 117.8 per cent.[250] It is projected to increase to approximately 145.04 per cent by 2025. In 2020, Zambia became the first African country to default on its debt,[251] and it is projected to go bankrupt by 2025 if the issue of debt is not properly handled by the government.[252]

Beyond the countries under discussion here, several other regions in Africa have been suffering spirals of dwindling or negative growth, over-indebtedness, and downgraded credit ratings. It is clear that Africa urgently needs to deal with its growing debt burden. Unsustainable debt levels represent a risk to recovery, and have implications.[253] For one, the larger a country's public debt levels, relative to GDP, the greater the risk of default will be. Moreover, when budget and resources have to go to servicing impossible debt levels, a country's ability to respond to crises may become impaired and implementation of policies supporting long-term sustainability may be difficult.[254] This leaves law and policymakers on the African continent with the challenge of imagining different kinds of policy responses to their reality: responses that could improve economic resilience and climate and energy transformations.[255]

V. Policy and Contractual Options to Finance Crisis Management and Resilience

The African continent cannot go its struggle with crisis clustering and concomitant rising debt alone. The help of the international community is needed to strengthen Africa's recovery and resilience. It will require new ways of thinking to go into legislating, negotiating, and differentiating between options available. How such interventions are to be approached is a highly politicized question. The following paragraphs look at the viability of some of the policy and contract options available.

---

[246] Trading Economics 'Government Debt' (n 244).

[247] NAD 112,000 million.

[248] NAD 115,000.00 million.

[249] See Trading Economics, 'Namibia Government Debt' (2021) <https://tradingeconomics.com/namibia/government-debt> accessed 2 June 2021.

[250] Knoema, 'Zambia - General Government Gross Debt in % of GDP' (*World Data Atlas*, 2020) <https://knoema.com/atlas/Zambia/topics/Economy/Financial-Sector-General-Government-finance/Government-debt-percent-of-GDP> accessed 8 February 2021.

[251] Phillips, 'Debt Crisis' (n 6).

[252] See Bwalya Chanda, 'Opinion: Zambia may go bankrupt by 2025' (*ZambiaNews365*, 30 November 2020) <https://zambianews365.com/opinion-zambia-may-go-bankrupt-by-2025/> accessed 26 June 2021.

[253] Justin Joy and Prasant Kumar Panda, 'An Empirical Analysis of Sustainability of Public Debt among BRICS Nations' (2021) 21 J Public Affairs <https://doi.org/10.1002/pa.2170> accessed 20 August 2021, 1–3.

[254] Mthuli Ncube and Zuzana Brixiová, 'Public Debt Sustainability in Africa: Building Resilience and Challenges Ahead' (2015) 33(5) Development Policy Review 558, 561.

[255] See e.g. Dunia Prince Zongwe, 'First Impressions on the First Negotiations for the First-Ever EU Sustainable Investment Facilitation Agreement' (*Afronomics Law*, 5 July 2021) <https://www.afronomicslaw.org/category/analysis/first-impressions-first-negotiations-first-ever-eu-sustainable-investment> accessed 21 August 2021 (hereafter Zongwe, 'First Impressions').

A. IMF policy approaches and friction points

From the quarters of the IMF, the policy approach is to encourage economic growth and transformative reforms: improvement of public service, strengthening of governance through radical transparency, and a boosting of domestic revenue mobilization. It has also been suggested that carbon offsets could become a new source of finance for distressed countries.[256]

From the IMF's latest allocation of Special Drawing Rights (SDRs) of USD 650 billion—the historically largest amount ever—just about USD 33 billion was made available to boost the reserves and liquidity of African member states. Such funds may help address emergency needs,[257] especially on the still largely under-vaccinated continent,[258] but may not be able to stretch far enough to encourage a better bounce-back. In fact, commentators are critical about the IMF's decision to allocate 60 per cent of the SDRs to 'the rich countries that do not need them.'[259] Munevar and Mariotti provide a sobering perspective by pointing out that the SDRs allocation envisaged for sub-Saharan Africa is about USD 22 billion, while merely servicing the total public debt of that region would amount to USD 37 billion.[260]

The IMF has indicated that sub-Saharan Africa's interest payments in 2020 amounted to 20 per cent of the tax revenue for the whole region and exceeded one-third of revenue in some countries.[261] Such obligations render it difficult to prioritize development projects.[262] Affordability issues, for instance, is what made Zambia abandon its intention of introducing nuclear power, which it considered a more viable alternative to hydropower. Steering away from hydropower would have been sensible, given the region's vulnerability to drought. However, inability to afford alternatives have now compelled Zambia to revert to completing ongoing hydropower projects.[263]

During the COVID-19 pandemic, the IMF worked with its more affluent members to get them to reallocate their SDRs to help poorer countries. The recently announced G7 initiative that 'Development Financing Institutions and multilateral partners intend to invest at least USD80 billion into the private sector in Africa over the next five years',[264] taps into this

---

[256] Georgieva, 'Road Ahead' (n 240).

[257] Georgieva, 'Road Ahead' (n 240).

[258] The IMF acknowledges that lower access to vaccines, slower vaccine rollouts, and prohibitive costs of vaccinations are holding back the recovery in sub-Saharan Africa. It indications that sub-Saharan Africa accounts for 15 per cent of the global population, but as of April 2021, only 0.5 per cent of all administered doses globally were in sub-Saharan African countries. Selassie et al 'Six Charts' (n 223).

[259] Danny Bradlow, 'How Africa Can Seize the Moment and Start Resetting its Relationship with the IMF' *The Conversation* (19 August 2021) <https://theconversation.com/how-africa-can-seize-the-moment-and-start-resetting-its-relationship-with-the-imf-166302> accessed 24 August 2021; Daniel Munevar and Chiara Mariotti, 'The 3 Trillion Dollar Question: What Difference will the IMF's New SDRs Allocation Make to the World's Poorest?' (*Eurodad*, 7 April 2021) < https://www.eurodad.org/imf_s_new_sdrs_allocation> accessed 20 August 2021 (hereafter Munevar et al, 'Difference').

[260] Munevar et al, 'Difference' (n 259).

[261] Georgieva, 'Road Ahead' (n 240).

[262] Justin Joy and Prasant Kumar Panda 'Sustainability of public debt among BRICS nations' (n 253) 2–3.

[263] See above III.A.3.

[264] African Development Bank Group 'G7 Development Finance Institutions and Multilateral Partners to Invest over $80 Billion into African Businesses over the Next Five Years' (AfDB Newsletter, 14 June 2021) <https://www.afdb.org/en/news-and-events/press-releases/g7-development-finance-institutions-and-multilateral-partners-invest-over-80-billion-african-businesses-over-next-five-years-44133> accessed 24 August 2021 (hereafter AfDB, 'G7 Development Finance Institutions').

strategy.[265] Such investments are expected, i.e. to 'tackle both COVID-19 and accelerate the green transition in Africa.'[266] However, despite the IMF's steps to make more funds available to deal with the immediate crisis caused by the COVID-19 pandemic, pre-pandemic concerns about the effects of IMF-administered rescue programs continue to dominate discourse.[267] Taking recourse to the IMF's Poverty Reduction and Growth Trust, for instance, remains controversial because of the conditionalities it attaches to concessional financing for low-income countries,[268] which have historically 'cohered around four central principles to neoliberalism: economic stabilisation, liberalisation, deregulation, and privatisation.'[269] Even the IMF's ostensible shift towards 'pro-poor' policies in the 1990s is criticized for having changed rhetoric, but otherwise little of practical significance.[270]

There are strong voices from Africa (and further afield) discouraging the dependency on the IMF's options.[271] IMF bailouts, it is said, lead to prolonged periods—sometimes decades—of debt dependency.[272] And debt dependency, it is argued, 'undermines a country's sovereignty and integrity of domestic policy formulation.'[273] Hence the IMF policy choices, enveloped in its offering of structural adjustment programs to developing countries (of which sub-Saharan Africa remains the region with the largest take-up)[274] have met with consistent condemnation.[275] The conditionalities attached to such funding (e.g. cutting government borrowing and spending, lowering taxes and import tariffs, raising interest rates, privatizing state owned enterprises, and deregulating key industries) have effects that can be ill-afforded by developing countries: commentators report on how such actions beget 'further suffering, poorer standards of living, higher unemployment as well as corporate failures.'[276]

Regional development banks (the Asian, African, and Inter-American Development Banks) are criticized for following the precedent set by the IMF and World Bank.[277] The African Development Bank (AfDB) was initially intent on maintaining 'an African character' and 'solving the continent's problems internally,'[278] but was compelled to adjust its lending policies away from project lending and more towards structural-adjustment lending after oil price hikes in the 1970s eroded its capital and massive debt arose among

---

[265] Bradlow 'How Africa can seize the moment' (n 259).

[266] AfDB, 'G7 Development Finance Institutions' (n 264) quoting Werner Hoyer, President of the European Investment Bank.

[267] Christina S. Kingston, Godspower Irikana, Victory Dienye, and Kato Gogo Kingston, 'The Impacts of the World Bank and IMF Structural Adjustment Programmes on Africa: The Case Study of Cote D'Ivoire, Senegal, Uganda, and Zimbabwe' (2011) 1(2) Sacha Journal of Policy and Strategic Studies 110–130; Michael Thomson, Alexander Kentikelenis, and Thomas Stubb, 'Structural Adjustment Programmes Adversely Affect Vulnerable Populations: A Systematic-Narrative Review of Their Effect on Child and Maternal Health' (2017) 38(13) Public Health Reviews, DOI 10.1186/s40985-017-0059-2 (hereafter Thompson et al 'Structural Adjustment Programmes').

[268] Bradlow 'How Africa can seize the moment' (n 259).

[269] Thompson et al 'Structural Adjustment Programmes' (n 267) 3.

[270] Ibid, 3–4.

[271] Misheck Mutize, 'Why South Africa shouldn't turn to the IMF for help' The Conversation (8 August 2017) https://theconversation.com/why-south-africa-shouldnt-turn-to-the-imf-for-help-82027> accessed 24 August 2021 (hereafter Mutize 'South Africa').

[272] Ibid.

[273] Ibid.

[274] Thompson et al 'Structural Adjustment Programmes' (n 267) 4.

[275] See the sources quoted in n 268 above. Also Aramide Odutayo, 'Conditional Development: Ghana Crippled by Structural Adjustment Programmes' (E-International Relations, 1 March 2015) <https://www.e-ir.info/2015/03/01/conditional-development-ghana-crippled-by-structural-adjustment-programmes/> accessed 24 August 2021.

[276] Summarized in Mutize 'South Africa' (n 271).

[277] Thompson et al 'Structural Adjustment Programmes' (n 267) 3.

[278] Ibid, 4.

its member nations.[279] Now the IMF and World Bank 'co-finance some 90% of AfDB loans' and the AfDB's lending terms are very similar to those institutions' terms.[280]

B. Alternative multilateral development finance

Meanwhile, countries' options for obtaining international financing are diversifying. In the multipolar world order of today, the IMF 'no longer [has] the resources or bargaining power to drive the global response to a financial crisis [as it did during the sovereign debt crisis of the 1980s]'.[281] Reforms and developments in global multilateral financing have started offering other opportunities:[282]

Contributing to the development of a new 'global financial architecture', modelled upon a 'loose set of multilateral agreements and understandings ... among a core group of powerful capitalist states',[283] the BRICS[284] block founded the New Development Bank (NDB) in 2013. The NDB's work is intended to complement the existing efforts for global growth and development of multilateral and regional financial institutions.[285] The specific intent was to create a multilateral development bank to mobilize resources and provide technical assistance for infrastructure and sustainable development projects in BRICS and other emerging economies and developing countries,[286] also in Africa. South Africa has so far drawn on this option twice (during June 2020 and April 2021) to the tune of USD 2 billion in total for a COVID-19 Emergency Program Loan.[287]

The NDB's purpose includes 'complementing the existing efforts of multilateral and regional financial institutions for global growth and development'.[288] However, its focus is on sustainable development and resources for infrastructure, whereas the regional development banks all lean clearly towards accelerating the process of economic development within their member states.[289]

Building a 'robust and diversified portfolio of sustainable infrastructure projects', the NDB focuses on the national priorities of the BRICS countries, for instance the development of the human capital through education, health care and social security, agriculture, infrastructure, public management, environmental and energy efficiency, and innovation.[290] It

---

[279] Ibid.
[280] Ibid.
[281] Bradlow 'How Africa can seize the moment' (n 259).
[282] African Forum and Network on Debt and Development 'BRICS Development Bank: A New Model for Africa' (Policy Briefing, October 2013) 2 (hereafter AFRODAD, 'New Model').
[283] A. Morozkina, 'The New Development Bank in the Global Financial Architecture' (2015) 10(2) International Organisations Research Journal 68 (hereafter Morozkina, 'New Development Bank').
[284] Brazil, Russia, India and China, and South Africa.
[285] AFRODAD, 'New Model' (n 282) 1–2.
[286] NDB *NDB's General Strategy: 2017–2021*, 20–21 <https://www.ndb.int/wp-content/uploads/2017/08/NDB-Strategy.pdf> accessed 2 September 2021 (hereafter NDB *Strategy*).
[287] See New Development Bank 'Projects' at <https://www.ndb.int/covid-19-emergency-program-sa/> and <https://www.ndb.int/covid-19-emergency-program-loan-for-supporting-south-africas-economic-recovery-from-covid-19/> both accessed 2 September 2021.
[288] BRICS 'BRICS and Africa: Partnership for Development, Integration and Industrialisation' (eThekwini Declaration, Durban, 27 March 2013) <http://www.brics.utoronto.ca/docs/130327-statement.html> accessed 25 August 2021; BRICS 'Agreement on the New Development Bank' (Fortaleza, Brazil, 15 July 2014) <http://www.brics.utoronto.ca/docs/140715-bank.html> accessed 25 August 2021.
[289] Morozkina, 'New Development Bank' (n 283) 69.
[290] Ibid.

is also reported to be more intent on involving internal capacity—experts and equipment from the BRICS countries—rather than resources from the global North. The latter may often be compelled inclusions in projects financed by the IMF or the World Bank, which usually deploy resources from western countries.[291]

The NDB's mandate is pursued through utilizing the proven financial model of multilateral development banks.[292] The initial focus is on infrastructure, but the intention (set out in NDB's mandate) is also at a later stage to pursue the funding of sustainable development projects, including projects in areas of critical concern, such as natural resource depletion, climate change, sustainable land use and biodiversity conservation, and / or pollution.[293]

There are three main features that set NDB-led loans apart from other typical IMF and regional development bank loans. First, NDB-led loans are not normal 'business-as-usual' loans, but instead commit to the principle of sustainable development.[294] Furthermore, the NDB is a development bank created by the Global South to meet its own development needs. The intention is to ensure the provision of development financing free of political conditionalities.[295] Finally, all five BRICS governments holds one-fifth of the ownership of the NDB, thus ensuring equal decision making.[296]

C. China and resources for infrastructure (R4I) contracts

A modality that offers another alternative to multilateral lending against unfavourable conditionalities, is the mechanism of the resource-for-infrastructure (R4I) investment contract. This option relies on the principles of contract and property: through a contractual arrangement with another nation, the host nation trades its natural resources for major infrastructure works.[297] It is favoured by China in its engagements on the African continent.[298]

China's foreign direct investment into Africa over the past decade or two has been intense.[299] It is explained by an observed natural 'economic complementarity' between China's need to feed its massive, globally competitive construction industry with natural resources, and resource-rich Africa's hunger for infrastructure.[300]

R4I contracts can provide a substantial boost for a host nation's economy if the contract is properly negotiated and designed. The R4I-contract mechanism contemplates using

---

[291] Ibid.

[292] NDB *Strategy* (n 286) 3.

[293] NDB *Strategy*, 20–21.

[294] Supriya Roychoudhury and Karin Costa Vazquez, 'What is new about the BRICS-led New Development Bank?' (*Devex*, 9 May 2016) <https://www.devex.com/news/what-is-new-about-the-brics-led-new-development-bank-88126> accessed 28 August 2021.

[295] Ibid.

[296] Ibid.

[297] Dunia Prince Zongwe, 'How Africans trade their riches for roads and bridges: Three stories' in Olga Bialostocka (ed), *Agenda 2063: Culture at the Heart of Sustainable Development* (HSRC Press 2018) at 36–37.

[298] Dunia Prince Zongwe 'Ore for Infrastructure: The Contractual Form of Economic Complementarities Between China and Africa' (July 2009) 42 China Monitor: China's Growing Relationship With Francophone Africa 7.

[299] Magnus Ericsson, Olof Löf and Anton Löf 'Chinese control over African and global mining — past, present and future' (2020) 33 Mineral Economics 153–181 <https://doi.org/10.1007/s13563-020-00233-4> accessed 21 August 2021.

[300] Dunia Prince Zongwe, 'The Competitive Edges of China's Resource-for-Infrastructure Investment Contracts in Africa' (2010) 2 Peking University Journal of Legal Studies 227.

revenues generated from the extraction of minerals and hydrocarbons to finance major infrastructural works.[301] In essence 'barter trade agreements' or 'exchanges of wants and needs', R4I contracts do not involve direct money transfers. Thus the risk of funds misappropriation, associated with the conditionalities typically attached to international financing, do not arise.[302] These mechanisms hence also may become attractive options where unsustainable debt renders further borrowing from international lenders impossible or unfavourable.[303]

The R4I mechanism itself is controversial in the African context, because of the perception that they are predatory. Also, the stabilization clauses common in these type of agreements can be seen as hindering domestic policies aimed at fostering sustainable development.[304] China's investment in Africa has furthermore been linked to many controversial issues—especially in the natural resources sector—such as environmental degradation, corruption, health and safety risks, poor wages and labour relations, and product quality concerns.[305] Zongwe stresses,[306] therefore, that African states must negotiate these contracts with care, as they normally find themselves in the weaker bargaining positions. But he indicates that there is room for applying this mechanism to the benefit of African countries, provided African governments have appropriate investment policy responses in place to require such Chinese initiatives for foreign direct investment to support state building and economic prosperity. These investment policies must also incorporate mechanisms addressing issues of environmental protection and sustainable development, combating of corruption, proper labour relations, and good governance.[307]

R4I contracts can be designed in a sustainable manner, integrating environmental, social, and governance factors, setting it apart from bilateral investment treaties.[308] The sovereignty of the host nation should also be maintained, so clauses affecting sovereignty (such as stabilization clauses) should be approached and designed carefully. A balance needs to be struck between ensuring the optimum benefit for the host nation, while maintaining an attractiveness for foreign investment.

D. The IMF's Prospective Resilience and Sustainability Trust

There is also talk of a new mechanism being created by the IMF: the Resilience and Sustainability Trust,[309] which may be set up to deal better with crises in the developing world, considering specifically the relevant needs. While this space is still being negotiated, scholars see room for the developing world to influence the agenda:

In the IMF's reduced leverage power at the global scale, Bradlow sees opportunities for developing countries to shape the agenda for future financing options.[310] One suggestion is

---

[301] Zongwe 'Ore for Infrastructure' (n 298) 7.
[302] Zongwe 'Competitive Edges' (n 300) 242–243.
[303] Ibid.
[304] Zongwe, 'First Impressions' (n 255).
[305] Zongwe 'Competitive Edges' (n 300) 243–234.
[306] Ibid.
[307] Ibid.
[308] Zongwe, 'First Impressions' (n 255).
[309] Marc Jones and Andrea Shalal, 'Backing Grows for New IMF Covid and Climate Fund' *Reuters* (24 June 2021) <https://news.trust.org/item/20210624025043-g0beh/> accessed 2 September 2021.
[310] Bradlow 'How Africa can seize the moment' (n 259).

for Africa to call for 'reforms that will make the Poverty Reduction and Growth Trust more responsive to African needs and more accountable to Africans.'[311] Practical adjustments that would go some way in achieving this would be, first, to convince the IMF to instate a third African chair on its board of executive directors, where Africa is still underrepresented in matters of policy decision making. A second adjustment would be to move for transparency in the applicable operational policies, especially where considerations around climate, inequality, and gender have begun influencing budgeting decisions. A third suggested adjustment is for a mechanism for independent oversight, such as an ombudsman, to ensure policy compliance and serve the interests of procedural justice.[312]

V. Conclusion

As the world starts recovering from the effects of the COVID-19 pandemic—demonstrated by increased trade, higher commodity prices, and a resumption of capital inflows—recovery in sub-Saharan Africa is expected to lag,[313] according to a 2021 IMF report.[314] This report further forecasts that African economies that are *less* resource intensive will recover *better*.[315] Clearly, recovery depends on many factors, among others the availability of COVID-19 vaccines, the cost of which may be prohibitive for some countries, and the distribution of which could be hampered by lacking infrastructure. The bottom line from the discussion of crisis responses of all four countries studied above, is that, where internal resources are depleted, states have no choice but to turn to lending.

The country studies above show that, in Africa, the imperative to respond to clusters of crises is leading to debilitating national debt and potentially also the further risk of defaulting on sovereign debt. But for countries such as these, who were already on their knees in economic terms before the COVID-19 health pandemic struck, it is impossible to deal with the economic fall-out of this latest crisis cluster without external funding support. On taking up offers from multilateral funding agencies, developing states often have to resign themselves to adopting the financiers' terms and conditions, which may be contrary to development goals within the states. The alternative options are to engage in resources-for-infrastructure arrangements, in which such countries are at risk of agreeing to unfavourable terms, because of real or perceived imbalances in bargaining power. Either way, their strategic choices will have a significant impact on the extent of their resource dependency in years to come.

Where countries have high debt, it might create a spiral of incapacity to craft resilience by 'building back better', because the majority of revenue generated will have to go to servicing country debt, and not enough will remain for the crafting a more resilient fiscal space. In cases where a country's natural resources are bartered for the acquisition of important infrastructure or energy solutions, it may keep such countries from harnessing their resources more favourably to generate wealth through trade. Either way, financing resilience

---

[311] Ibid.

[312] Daniel David Bradlow, 'Operational Policies and Procedures and an Ombudsman' in B. Carin and A. Wood (eds), *Accountability of the International Monetary Fund* (IDRC/Ashgate 2005).

[313] Georgieva, 'Road Ahead' (n 240).

[314] Selassie et al, 'Six Charts' (n 223).

[315] Ibid.

by raising unsustainable debt levels, or by overcommitting valuable natural resources, may ultimately reduce countries' ability to build resilience from within. It may also lead to debt dependencies or resource commitments that are hard to shake: a country that is on its knees, financially, will struggle to stand strong in the face of further crises requiring resilience.

The implications of a continental debt crisis in Africa should not be underestimated, especially because it is now riding on the back of a cluster of natural and health disasters. Sovereign debt default risk is now a reality in some African economies.[316] As African countries' financing opportunities and its debt composition diversify, the international mechanisms for preventing and resolving debt crises must be carefully monitored. More research is needed to understand not only the economic parameters for resilience-fostering policymaking, but also the political, security, and humanitarian imperatives, if Africa's progress towards meeting the Sustainable Development Goals, is not to come undone.

To deal with the economic fallouts of crises such as drought and health pandemics, especially the debt distress that seems to follow in the wake of crises responses in African countries, such governments may want to strategize stimulating economic recovery. Economists suggest that at least three key responses will be needed: strengthening global confidence in the country's ability to adhere to a fiscal consolidation path; improving the efficiency of expenditures; and strengthening revenue mobilization.[317] Equally important is the agency required from the affected countries' governments to deal with crises and disasters.[318] To deal appropriately with the complexity of all the moving parts that need to make up any response to a crisis such as the one elicited by the COVID-19 pandemic or the sweeping droughts in Southern Africa, a government needs a sufficiently nuanced and sophisticated strategy, providing for better social security and health insurance and better-equipped hospitals, enabling equal access to digital infrastructure where work- and school-from-home are unavoidable, fostering economic diversification, and improving governance to limit corruption. Putting these in place will take time and it will cost money. But they are necessary, if also African countries are to become more resilient in the face of further future pandemics or similar global economic shocks.

---

[316] Shipalana et al 'Macroeconomic Impact' (n 7) 4.

[317] Haroon Bhorat and Gracelin Baskaran 'From stimulus to debt: The case of South Africa' (Brookings, Foresight Africa, 2 February 2021) <https://www.brookings.edu/blog/africa-in-focus/2021/02/02/from-stimulus-to-debt-the-case-of-south-africa/> accessed 22 August 2021.

[318] Minister of Finance 'Statement to Parliament' (n 56).

18

Natural Damage Insurance

An Instrument for Economic Resilience

Hans Jacob Bull

I. Introduction

Around 03.30 on 30 December 2020, a large quick clay landslide hit the little town Ask in the municipality Gjerdrum, near Oslo. The landslide destroyed a large number of dwelling houses and left others inhabitable; hit and destroyed private and municipal infrastructure, with roads disappearing and water and electricity supply broken; and killed 10 people, while others were rescued by helicopters in pitch darkness from their destroyed homes. Many people were evacuated for fear that the landslide might widen and threaten more homes, as well as schools, kindergartens, and institutions for elderly people.

In early February 2021, with about 800 persons still evacuated, the area considered to be safe was enlarged and 600 persons were allowed to return home. As of July 2021, 150 persons are still awaiting decisions from relevant authorities on the pending question: will their homes ever be regarded as safe again?

The government has appointed a fact-finding commission to establish why the landslide happened and to examine the decisions made by relevant authorities and private developers to approve and undertake housebuilding in an area with known quick clay underground.

The Gjerdrum disaster forms the background for the questions discussed in this chapter: is private insurance a viable tool to provide the necessary economic resilience to persons, private entities, and municipalities to withstand the effects of natural disasters and to recover quickly and easily after such a misfortune? Or should both preventive measures to protect private investments against natural disasters and economic compensation when such investments have been damaged or destroyed, be seen as a public responsibility?

The discussion has a Norwegian angle, primarily. Norway has chosen a complex and extensive solution to the questions posed (Section II), with a semi-compulsory insurance scheme playing a central part (Sections III and IV). Contrasting the Norwegian system with prevailing solutions in other countries shows the advantages, but also some of the challenges, of a complete and combined system with a semi-compulsory insurance scheme at the centre (Section V).

II. The Norwegian System: An Over-All Picture

To understand the different elements of the Norwegian compensation system, we have to look at the historical context. Up until 1979, the State was in charge of implementing and

Hans Jacob Bull, *Natural Damage Insurance* In: *Resilience in Energy, Infrastructure, and Natural Resources Law*. Edited by: Catherine Banet, Hanri Mostert, LeRoy Paddock, Milton Fernando Montoya, and Íñigo del Guayo, Oxford University Press. © Hans Jacob Bull 2022.
DOI: 10.1093/oso/9780192864574.003.0018

financing measures for the prevention of natural perils and for the compensation sought by those who had suffered loss or damage from such perils.[1] In 1979, the compensation system was to a large extent 'privatized', with a semi-compulsory insurance system established as the main source for compensation for natural damage.[2] Fire insurance taken out on buildings or (most types of) movable property situated in Norway will automatically give compulsory cover against damage caused by natural perils as well. The concept 'natural perils' is not all-inclusive but comprises landslides, storms, flooding, storm surge, earthquakes, and volcanic eruptions. A solidarity principle forms the basis for the scheme, as the premium rate charged for the natural perils cover is the same for all policyholders and for all insurance companies. Consequently, the premium charged will not reflect the risk for natural damage encountered by the individual policyholder.

However, the State did not leave the compensation scene completely.[3] Where loss or damage to private property falls outside the natural damage insurance system because the property in question cannot be covered by ordinary insurance,[4] the private party is legally entitled to claim compensation from the State,[5] as long as the loss has been caused by one of the six natural perils included in the natural damage insurance scheme.[6]

Since neither the natural damage insurance scheme nor the state compensation scheme for natural damage is all-inclusive, natural damage caused by risks other than the six enumerated perils is not included. Urban flooding caused by heavy rain is probably the best example. The ordinary insurances on private property offered by the main Norwegian insurance companies will provide cover for most of these risks. However, the insurance cover and the premium rates are risk-based and on competitive terms, with the effect that both the extent of coverage and the rates may vary between the separate companies and depending on who the insured parties are and where their property is situated.

Movable property like ships, aeroplanes, cars, and cargo under transport, as well as equipment used in petroleum-extraction activities, fall outside both the Norwegian natural damage insurance scheme and the state compensation scheme. However, the all-risks policies offered by Norwegian insurance companies for most of such property would include damage caused by natural perils as part of their ordinary cover.

III. The Natural Damage Insurance Scheme

A. The history

When the previous State scheme for compensation of natural damage was partly 'privatized' in 1979, the purpose of setting up an alternative insurance scheme for natural damage

---

[1] See Act 9 June 1961 no. 24 on protection against and compensation for natural damage.
[2] Details of the system are set out in Sections III and IV below.
[3] See Act 15 August 2014 no. 59 on compensation for natural damage (the natural damage compensation act) (hereafter NDCA).
[4] Private infrastructure, such as private roads, and farmland are examples of property included under the state compensation system.
[5] Compensation for natural damage to property and infrastructure owned by a municipality falls outside the legally founded state compensation scheme (n 3). However, the state may offer financial assistance on a case-by-case basis to municipalities that have had their infrastructure damaged or destroyed due to natural perils, see Prop. 105 S (2019–2020) (Kommuneproposisjonen 2021) pp 32–33.
[6] On average, the yearly compensation amounts to NOK 100 million.

was twofold: first, to secure a more extensive economic cover for those who had suffered a loss due to a natural peril; and second, to relieve the State of substantial parts of its commitment to cover the economic consequences of natural damage. Demand for state compensation had shown a steady increase over the years. Simultaneously, greater investment in preventive measures was seen as both necessary and important to avoid or soften the effects of natural perils. It seemed like a viable compromise to leave the costs of compensating those affected to a privately-financed insurance scheme and concentrate the State's financial contribution on efforts to avoid the damaging effects of natural perils.[7]

Originally, the natural damage insurance scheme was incorporated in the Insurance Contract Act 1930.[8] When this Act was repealed in 1989,[9] the sections on natural damage insurance were repeated almost verbatim in a new Act 16 June 1989 no. 70 on natural damage insurance (hereafter NDIA). Since 1989, this Act has undergone several alterations. The material significant changes are commented upon below.[10]

From 1979, a total amount of NOK 18.7 billion has been paid out in compensation under the natural damage insurance scheme. The years with the largest total amount paid were 1992 (NOK 1.3 billion) and 2011 (NOK 2.5 billion). Of the total amount, storms have accounted for NOK 9.9 billion and floods for NOK 5.4 billion. The highest amount ever paid out in a single year for storm damage was in 2011 (NOK 1.5 billion) and for flood damage in 1995 (NOK 0.9 billion).[11]

B. The cover

1. A semi-compulsory cover
Natural damage insurance in Norway is organized as a semi-compulsory cover through its linkage to the insurances against fire. In principle, all property covered against the risk of fire under any set of insurance policy will automatically be covered against natural perils as well. Although persons or companies are under no duty to take out fire insurance, experience shows that owners of most buildings and relevant movable property will do so.

2. Natural perils covered
NDIA defines natural damage as being damage 'directly caused by a natural peril, such as landslide, storm, flooding, storm surge, earthquake and volcanic eruptions'.[12] The definition of 'landslide' (*skred*) would also cover the collapse of part of a mountain and an avalanche. The quick clay landslide that hit Gjerdrum in December 2020 (above Section I) clearly falls within the categories mentioned in the act.

Given the way the text is formulated, with the words 'such as' placed in front of the listing, a pertinent question is whether the list of perils should only be seen as relevant examples, enabling the inclusion under the insurance scheme of damage caused by other natural perils

---

[7] See NOU 1974: 9 Erstatning for naturskader p 10.
[8] See Act 6 June 1930 no. 20, which had sections 81a–81d added to it by Act 8 June 1979 no. 46.
[9] See the new Act 16 June 1989 no. 69 on insurance contracts (the insurance contracts act).
[10] Of the Decrees authorized by NDIA, the Decree 21 December 1979 no. 3420 on instructions for the Norwegian Natural Perils Pool (hereafter 'Decree on instructions') is the most important.
[11] The numbers are taken from statistics provided by Finans Norge Forsikringsdrift, see <https://www.naturskade.no/statistikk> accessed 10 December 2021.
[12] See NDIA section 1 first paragraph second sentence.

as well. However, the preparatory works make it clear that the listing should be regarded as exhaustive.[13] Consequently, damage due to heavy rain is not covered by the scheme unless it results in the flooding of rivers, etc., which again causes damage to property.[14]

To be covered, the damage suffered must be 'directly caused' by the natural peril. The state compensation scheme uses the same term, but the insurance companies construe the term in NDIA less strictly than what is the situation under the state scheme.[15]

3. Property covered

'Property in Norway that is insured against damage caused by fire, is also insured against damage caused by natural perils ...'[16] The concept of 'property' covers both real property (buildings, industrial plants, etc.) and movable property. It is irrelevant whether the property is covered under a separate and independent fire insurance policy or as part of a combined real property insurance policy. Such combined insurance would include several different perils, with the cover against fire constituting an element. 'In Norway' would encompass both mainland Norway and Svalbard.[17]

Since the introduction of the scheme in 1979, there have been two extensions in terms of property covered. Both extensions relate to the situation where the property insured is a residential or recreational house. The first extension, from 2004,[18] incorporated natural damage to gardens, yards, and access roads of such houses into the insurance scheme.[19] The second extension, from 2017,[20] gave owners of such residential and recreational houses[21] the right to claim the value of the site[22] in addition to the house itself.[23] One precondition for the extended coverage is that the house was completely destroyed or incurred damage due to a natural peril or that the ground under the building became unstable due to a natural

[13] Ot.prp. no. 46 (1978–79) p 33. In Norway, statements found in the preparatory works, such as the Government's proposal to the Storting (the Norwegian Parliament), play an important role in the interpretation of the act. It is interesting to note that the state compensation scheme, which uses exactly the same wording, is supposed to be understood differently, see NDCA section 4 first paragraph and the comments made in Prop. 80 L (2013–2014) p 58.

[14] As already mentioned in Section II above, as a general rule, damage to property caused by water flooding into a building due to heavy rain ('urban flooding') will be covered by the insurance companies' ordinary combined insurance policy on buildings, see, as an example, the insurance company If's insurance conditions for buildings (2020) section 4.4 bullet point no. 4.

[15] See, as an example of the strict interpretation under the state compensation scheme, the Court of Appeal case LF-2014-49538: damage to a fence caused by trees falling over it during a heavy storm not considered directly caused by the storm. Under the insurance scheme, such a damage would have been covered, see the *Handbook on Handling Damage*, issued by the Norwegian Natural Perils Pool (below Section IV).

[16] NDIA section 1 first paragraph second sentence.

[17] The concept 'Svalbard' is defined in Act 17 July 1925 no. 11 on Svalbard section 1 second paragraph, and includes more than just the Spitsbergen islands.

[18] See Act 17 December 2004 no. 98, which added a new third sentence to NDIA section 1 first paragraph. The area covered by this extension is limited to five dekar (about a quarter acre).

[19] The state compensation scheme previously covered such natural damage.

[20] See Act 21 April 2017 no. 17, which added a new third paragraph to NDIA section 1.

[21] Owners of factories and other industrial buildings are not granted the same right. However, if their buildings are lost or damaged due to a natural damage, they may claim a total loss compensation for the building, in case the municipality declines their application to rebuild or repair the building out of fear for future natural damage to the building. In the Gjerdrum case (above Section I), owners of damaged farmhouses like barns may be eligible for such a compensation.

[22] The size of the site is limited to five dekar (about a quarter acre).

[23] NDIA section 1 had a fourth paragraph added to it by the Act mentioned in n 20. The paragraph offers the insurance company an alternative. Instead of compensating the insured owner according to the third paragraph, the insurance company may choose to secure the property at their own cost. The insurance companies have claimed that the conditions set in the provision do not make the alternative a viable solution. In the Gjerdrum case (above Section I), the insurance companies did not make use of the alternative.

peril. A second precondition is that the municipality is unwilling to grant the owner the ne-cessary permission to rebuild or repair the house at the former location due to the risk of future natural damage.[24]

On the other hand, there are some important limitations regarding property included in the cover. First, the scheme will not cover natural damage already covered by another in-surance policy.[25] Second, there is an express exclusion for certain specific types of property, whether or not another insurance scheme will, in fact, cover the property.[26]

4. Parties protected

The relevant rules under the natural damage insurance scheme do not impose any limita-tions on class of owner of the relevant property, provided fire insurance covers the property. Consequently, as insured parties under a fire insurance policy, private persons, companies, municipalities, etc., will be eligible for cover under the scheme.[27]

5. The assessment of claim

The insurance conditions of the company that has provided the insured party's fire insur-ance will form the basis for the assessment of the insured party's claim in the event of natural damage. Broadly speaking, the insured party will be treated in the same way as if the prop-erty had suffered loss or damage due to a fire. Repair costs are covered in case of damage, as are the costs of rebuilding a new house where the house is a total loss.

Differences in the extent of the cover may occur between the insurance companies. However, this does not create practical problems when it comes to the distribution of nat-ural damage costs between the insurance companies. The rules of the Norwegian Natural Perils Pool, see Section IV.D below, establish to what extent a claim incurred by an insurance company may be accepted for distribution and equalization under the pool arrangement. If

---

[24] In the Gjerdrum case (above Section I), the interpretation of these preconditions may turn out to be prob-lematic. For houses lost in the landslide, the preconditions are clearly fulfilled and their owners will be entitled to a total loss compensation both for the house and for the site. For houses that have suffered damage, but are still standing on their original site, the crucial question will be whether the municipality will grant the necessary per-mission to reconstruct or repair the house considering the risk of a future natural damage. If such permission is denied, the insured party may claim total loss compensation for the house and for the site. The most intricate ques-tions arise for houses that have not been damaged, but where the ground under the house is considered unstable as a consequence of the natural damage. If the municipality issues a ban on possible future work on the house due to the risk of prospective natural damage, the owner of the house will be able to claim a total loss compensation for both the house and the site.

[25] See NDIA section 1 first paragraph first sentence (last part of the sentence). The 'all risks' insurances men-tioned in Section II above are examples of relevant insurance schemes.

[26] See NDIA section 1 second paragraph. As examples of property falling under this exclusion, mention is made of cars, airplanes, ships, and goods under transport, as well as equipment used in the petroleum industry. Accordingly, cars lost or damaged in the Gjerdrum case (above Section I) will not be covered under the natural damage insurance scheme, whether or not they are insured. For such excluded property, 'all risks' insurances are often available in the insurance markets, see Section II above.

[27] In contrast, the state compensation scheme excludes municipalities and companies owned by them from cover, with the effect that there is no cover for damage to the municipalities' infrastructure (roads, bridges, etc.) under either of the two established schemes. As mentioned above in n 5, the State offers financial assistance, on a case-by-case basis, to municipalities that have had their infrastructure damaged or destroyed due to natural perils. In the Gjerdrum case (above Section I), the municipality of Gjerdrum will have cover under its natural damage insurance for buildings destroyed or damaged by the landslide. On the other hand, the legal-based insurance and compensation schemes will not apply to destroyed or damaged infrastructure owned by the municipality, like roads and water and electricity supply. For the necessary repair and reconstruction costs, the municipality will have to rely on the State's case-by-case compensation arrangement for (partial) cover. As of July 2021, the munici-pality has received NOK 20 million under this arrangement.

an insurance company has given its policyholders better conditions than those decided by the pool rules, the insurance company will have to bear the extra costs itself.

In addition, relevant provisions of the Insurance Contract Act 1989 and the NDIA may come into play. NDIA prescribes a reduction in the insured party's compensation in the event of inadequate construction or maintenance of the property.[28] Expenses incurred for preventive and safeguarding measures will not be covered, even if they may contribute to reducing the risk of future natural damage to the property.[29]

The insured party will have to bear a deductible for each natural damage occurrence.[30] Today, the deductible amounts to NOK 8,000.

The natural damage insurance scheme operates with an absolute limit for all claims made after a single natural catastrophe.[31] The relevant amount today is NOK 16 billion.

IV. The Organization

A. The Norwegian Natural Perils Pool

The Norwegian Natural Perils Pool (*Norsk naturskadepool*) was set up in 1980 as part of the enactment of the natural damage insurance scheme.[32] The pool has central functions as a coordinator of different elements in the scheme.[33]

According to NDIA, '[a]ll non-life insurance companies that indemnify natural damage according to section 1 shall be members of a common claims pool.'[34] All insurance companies providing cover against fire in Norway are thus obliged to be members of the pool,

---

[28] See NDIA section 1 sixth paragraph. An outside body, the Appeals Board of the state compensation scheme, may decide whether reduction of the compensation meets with the relevant criteria, see NDIA section 2 first paragraph first sentence. The Appeals Board may also decide whether the criteria for natural damage provided for by NDIA section 1 first paragraph are in fact met. The right to reduce the compensation in case of inadequate construction or maintenance has not played an important role under the natural damage insurance scheme. In the Gjerdrum case (above Section I), there is little reason to believe that the insurance companies will invoke the rules.

[29] See Decree on instructions section 3 second paragraph. NDCA section 5 fifth paragraph prescribes the same solution for the state compensation scheme.

[30] See NDIA section 3 first paragraph, which gives the King (in reality the Ministry of Justice and Public Security, see Decree 15 December 1989 no. 1241) the right to stipulate the amount in a decree, see Decree 15 December 1989 no. 1335 section 1, last amended 11 February 2005 no. 125. Under the state compensation scheme, the deductible is considerably higher and assessed in a more complicated way, see NDCA section 9 and Decree 7 July 2016 no. 904 sections 12 and 13.

[31] See NDIA section 3 second paragraph, with authorization for the King (in reality the Ministry of Justice and Public Security, see n 30) to stipulate the amount. The authorization has been used in Decree 15 December 1989 no. 1335 section 2, last amended in Decree 23 November 2017 no. 1828. It follows from NDIA section 3 fourth paragraph that the Appeals Board (see n 28) has the authority to make the final determination on whether one or several natural disasters have occurred. If the relevant claims exceed the stipulated amount, the parties insured will have to accept a proportional reduction in their claims, see NDIA section 3 fifth paragraph. The state compensation scheme has formally no absolute limit for the relevant amount payable, but NDCA section 10 states that compensation may be reduced if Parliament does not grant the means necessary to cover the claims forwarded after an extensive natural damage situation.

[32] In December 2017, the Ministry of Justice and Public Security appointed a Law committee to look into certain aspects of the natural damage insurance scheme, inter alia, the Norwegian Natural Perils Pool. The committee presented its report (NOU 2019: 4 Organisering av norsk naturskadeforsikring – Om Norsk Naturskadepool, hereafter NOU 2019: 4) in February 2019. The Ministry had not acted upon the reform proposals presented in the report by December 2021.

[33] See NDIA section 4 second paragraph second sentence.

[34] See NDIA section 4 first paragraph first sentence, and Decree on instructions section 1.

regardless of where they have their head office.[35] Today the pool has around 100 members. Membership will automatically begin when the insurance company starts signing contracts for fire insurance in Norway and will end when the company is no longer liable for the claims and costs incurred under the natural damage cover.[36]

The legislator has considered it important to ensure that a (foreign) insurance company can only enter into a fire insurance contract in Norway where it is a member of the pool. If an insured party enters an insurance contract with a non-member of the pool, he 'shall pay a fee to the pool', which 'is determined on the basis of the sum on the fire insurance coverage'.[37] Payment of the fee does not provide the insured party a right to claim compensation from the pool for natural damage incurred.[38]

B. Premium

An important element in the natural damage insurance scheme is that the premium rate charged for the cover is the same for all the participating insurance companies and for all relevant insured parties, regardless of the individual risk for suffering natural damage.[39] This solidarity principle forms an important element in the current structure of the scheme. The board of the pool stipulates the rate, 'taking into account that the total premiums shall over time correspond to the NPs[40] and the individual company's amount of loss and damage and administrative expenses'.[41] Today's rate is 0.065 per mille (per thousand) of the sum of insurance for the relevant property under its fire insurance. Over the years, the rate has varied considerably from 0.25 per mille to 0.065 per mille.[42] The individual insurance company will collect and retain the premium payable by each separate insured party.

C. Reinsurance

Reinsurance is arranged through the pool. The board makes the necessary reinsurance arrangements in accordance with the reinsurance principles approved by the annual meeting.[43] The reinsurance program has seen a considerable expansion over the years. As of

---

[35] See NDIA section 4 first paragraph second sentence. Consequently, both Norwegian and non-Norwegian insurance companies are obliged to be members.

[36] See NOU 2019: 4 section 11.2.2 for further details.

[37] See NDIA section 4a first paragraph, which was inserted by Act 24 June 1994 no. 40. The provision is supplemented by Decree 25 November 1994 no. 1026.

[38] The provisions in NDIA section 4a on fees do not seem to have played a central role in practice. In NOU 2019: 4, the commission proposed to maintain the present solution, see proposed Decree chapter 10.

[39] See Decree on instructions section 11 second paragraph first sentence.

[40] I.e. The Norwegian Natural Perils Pool.

[41] See Decree on instructions section 11 first paragraph. In NOU 2019: 4, the commission's majority found (see section 4.3.4) that premium charged over the years had been higher than necessary to achieve the targets indicated, providing the insurance companies who had been members of the pool from its start with a considerable profit and a resulting huge natural damage account, see Section III.E and n 58 below. The commission's majority suggested a more transparent manner for calculating future premiums, based on detailed parameters laid out in a revised Decree on instructions, see chapter 8 for the discussion and section 8-6 for the proposal.

[42] The rate 0.065 per mille was set in 2019 and has been constant since then. The present rate is—for all practical circumstances—consistent with a calculation based on the parameters suggested by the commission's majority in NOU 2019: 4, see n 41.

[43] See NOU 2019: 4 section 10.2.1.

1 January 2021, the program offers coverage for NOK 16 billion in two layers, with retention of NOK 1.5 billion. The first layer gives cover between NOK 1.5 billion and NOK 3.5 billion, and the second between NOK 3.5 billion and NOK 16 billion. The total reinsurance premium paid in 2018 under these two layers amounted to NOK 87 million and NOK 151 million, respectively, with a 100 per cent reinstatement premium.[44] The reinsurance program must be placed with reputable companies with an acceptable rating, with the board stipulating the minimum rating requirements.[45] As of 1996, member companies of the pool have had the opportunity to act as reinsurers under the program, with a share equal to their share in the pool, provided they satisfy the rating requirements.[46] Over the years, reinsurance has been called upon very seldom. A preliminary assessment of the compensations due after the Gjerdrum incident (above Section I) seems to indicate that the costs will not hit the reinsurance arrangement.[47]

D. Settlement of claims

As pointed out in Section III.B.5 above, each insurance company regulates and settles the natural damage claims reported by its own policyholders.[48] The terms and conditions agreed in the individual insurance contract form the basis for the settlement.

Having settled the claims with the insured parties, the insurance company reports the claims to the pool.[49] The pool has a separate set of standard conditions for use between the member companies and the pool.[50] These conditions will decide to what extent a member company may equalize in the pool claims settled between itself and the insured parties.[51]

The pool will handle jointly all claims pertaining to a single calendar year (the claim year).[52] The relevant amount to be equalized is the total allowable compensation paid by all the member companies for natural damage claims under a claim year, including interest and settlement costs,[53] together with the administrative costs of the pool itself. The costs of the reinsurance program administered by the pool (see Section IV.C above), and possible reinsurance settlements received from the reinsurers are also taken into consideration when assessing the relevant amount for claim equalization.[54]

---

[44] See NOU 2019: 4 section 10.1.1.

[45] See NOU 2019: 4 section 10.2.1.

[46] In NOU 2019: 4 chapter 10, the commission's majority supported a continuation of the present reinsurance arrangement, rejecting a proposal to leave the placing of reinsurance to the individual member company. The full commission gave its approval to continue the present solution with members of the pool accepted as reinsurers.

[47] Compensations due under the natural damage insurance scheme have been assessed on a preliminary basis (as per July 2021) to NOK 800 million.

[48] See Decree on instructions section 4 first paragraph.

[49] This is done on a monthly basis, see Decree on instructions section 5.

[50] Terms for settlement through the Natural Perils Pool, to apply from 1 January 2019, revising the terms that applied from 1 January 2016, as revised 1 January 2018.

[51] The previous terms from 1 January 2012, named the common terms and conditions for all insurance cover against natural damage, applied as an independent set of insurance terms and served as a minimum cover for the insured party.

[52] See Decree on instructions section 6.

[53] See Decree on instructions section 10, with detailed provisions on the types of settlement costs covered.

[54] See Decree on instructions section 7.

The basis used for the settlement between the member companies (the distribution formula) is the aggregated sum insured for fire insurance across all the member companies as of 1 July of the relevant claim year.[55] The claims settlement for each separate claim year is made on a quarterly basis, based on the payment statements received from the member companies.[56] When calculating the annual settlement in January, the amounts already paid in the quarterly settlements will be adjusted according to the distribution formula for the relevant claim year.

E. Allocations

The NDIA rules regulating how possible future claims for natural damage are to be allocated in the insurance companies' accounts fall into two categories. First, each insurance company is required to allocate 'in the normal manner' its proportionate share of the overall claims reserve for unsettled claims to be regulated through the pool, as well as an ordinary premium reserve based on the natural damage insurance premium.[57] Second, if the accrued premium exceeds the company's share of the compensation payments to be made through the pool *and* the claims reserve allocated for unsettled claims, the difference must be allocated to a special natural damage account within the member company.[58] This natural damage account belongs to the company,[59] and its use is restricted to cover future natural damage claims.[60]

---

[55] See Decree on instructions section 8.

[56] See Decree on instructions section 9.

[57] See Decree on instructions section 11 third paragraph. During the period 2010–2017 these allocations varied considerably, from NOK 5 million in 2010 to NOK 400 million in 2017, see NOU 2019: 4 p 78 n 2. The large allocation amount in 2017 was due to several unsettled claims from extensive flooding late in the year.

[58] See Decree on instructions section 11 fourth paragraph. In NOU 2019: 4 section 3.7, the total allocations on the companies' natural damage accounts by the end of 2017 were estimated to about NOK 8, 5 billion. The amount was spread unevenly between the companies, with four companies being in possession of about 89 per cent of the total. The distribution was also uneven between 'old' and 'new' companies, with newcomers to the fire insurance market in Norway only having a small or no natural damage account. In case of a deficit in a claim year on the natural damage insurance business, companies with a natural damage account could use the amount on the account to cover the loss, whereas companies with a small or non-existent natural damage account would be forced to draw on their equity base. In NOU 2019: 4, the commission's majority, recognizing the negative effect on competition of the unfairness in the present system, proposed a different solution. A possible surplus on the natural damage insurance business is placed on a separate account in the pool. In case of a deficit in a claim year, all the companies are entitled to draw on this account, see the proposed new Decree sections 7-3 and 7-4 and the corresponding discussion in section 7. In a transitional period, until the pool's natural damage account had reached an amount of NOK 4 billion, the majority proposed a slight modification. In case of a deficit, companies with their own natural damage account should be obliged to draw on that account to cover their share of the deficit, whereas companies with no or insufficient natural damage account were allowed to draw on the pool's account, see proposed new Decree section 7-5.

[59] The Decree on instructions section 11 fourth paragraph had a new last sentence added to it by Decree 19 February 2016 no. 163, which expressly stated that the natural damage account belongs to the member company.

[60] The Decree on instructions section 11 fifth and sixth paragraphs provide rules for the situations where a member company either transfers its fire insurance business to another company or else ceases operations. Whereas, in the first instance, the accumulated natural damage account will be transferred to the other company, in the second instance the account will be transferred to the pool without compensation being paid, for onward distribution among the other member companies.

F. The internal organization

The pool's highest authority is the annual meeting.[61] At the annual meeting, each member company of the pool has voting rights corresponding to the distribution formula explained in Section IV.D above. This leaves the four biggest non-life insurance companies operating in Norway[62] with a dominating position in the annual meeting, provided they advocate a shared view. The annual meeting adopts the pool's annual report and accounts, elects the board and its chairperson and deputy chairperson, as well as the auditor, and deals with other matters on the agenda.[63]

The board[64] consists of eight members with personal deputies. Members serve for a period of two years. The four largest member companies of the pool always have representatives on the board. The companies' policyholders or the public at large are not represented on the board.[65] The board stipulates the yearly premium rate and enters into reinsurance treaties. As for claims settlement, the board has a supervisory function.

The board appoints the claims committee,[66] consisting of five members, each serving for a period of three years.[67] The committee shall perform the necessary review of the claims submitted by the member companies for distribution. It shall also take necessary initiatives to coordinate the treatment of large claims, where more than one company and/or the state natural damage compensation scheme are involved. The claims committee is responsible for the ongoing contact between the pool and the state natural damage compensation scheme.[68] To deal with matters where a common interest exists, a special liaison committee with three members from each party meets at least every four months.

The general manager of the pool is Finans Norge,[69] the Norwegian financial services association.[70] The general manager has responsibility for the day-to-day management of claims.

---

[61] See Decree on instructions section 14.

[62] See NOU 2019: 4 section 3.7 tables 3.1 (2009) and 3.3 (2017). Of the four, two are Norwegian-owned and two foreign-owned.

[63] In NOU 2019: 4, the commission suggested several rules to strengthen the influence of the smaller insurance companies and the policyholders. Most of the suggestions had the support of the full commission. As for the annual meeting, the suggestion was to continue most of the present rules, see proposed new decree section 2-2.

[64] See Decree on instructions section 15.

[65] In NOU 2019: 4, the majority of the commission suggested that the board should consist of six members, with two members representing the policyholders and one member the smaller insurance companies, see proposed new decree section 2-3. The majority also gave the board members representing the policyholders a blocking vote on questions pertaining to the premium rate, the reinsurance arrangements, and the management of the pool's natural damage account. The annual meeting would not be allowed to reassess the board's decision on these questions, see proposed new directive section 2-2 first paragraph.

[66] See Decree on instructions section 17.

[67] In NOU 2019: 4, the commission suggested that the policyholders and the smaller insurance companies should appoint one member each to the claims committee, with three members left for the larger insurance companies, see proposed new decree section 2-5. In other committees, like the reinsurance committee and the investment committee, the policyholders were entitled to appoint a member, se proposed new decree section 2-6.

[68] See Decree on instructions section 18.

[69] See Decree on instructions section 16.

[70] In NOU 2019: 4, the commission suggested to uphold Finans Norge's position as general manager, see proposed new decree section 2-4. A novelty is the commission's proposal to secure transparency and publicity regarding the activities of the pool, see proposed new directive section 2-9.

V. Discussion and Conclusions

A. The Norwegian system is a successful and internationally unique economic resilience response

Natural damage-related disasters constitute a challenge to persons, companies, municipalities, and states. To overcome the problems such challenges create for the investments they have made in buildings, plants, and infrastructure, an economically resilient response is needed. The Norwegian system offers a successful, complex, and multifaceted solution, involving both the State and private insurance companies. A semi-compulsory insurance scheme forms the central part of the compensation system, with the State incorporating the rules for the scheme through legislation, leaving the day-to-day business to the insurance companies. The basis for the scheme is a principle of solidarity, both for the insured parties and for the insurance companies involved. The same premium rate and the same deductible applies for all insured parties, regardless of the risk involved. All losses are distributed and equalized between the companies, based on their market share in fire insurance and regardless of the losses suffered by the individual company. A state-financed compensation scheme complements the insurance scheme where a natural peril hits private property or infrastructure that insurance against fire cannot cover. Risk-based private-company insurance schemes add to the system where either the natural peril involved falls outside the natural damage insurance scheme, urban flooding due to heavy rain being the best example, or where separate all-risks insurances are available for specific purposes.

The Norwegian system is not unique in an international setting.[71] France has a similar system, and other countries have at least parallel elements in their cover.[72] On the other side, many countries leave the question of compensation for natural damage to voluntary private insurances. Here, risk-based premium ratings and deductibles are set in competition between the insurance companies.[73] This is not surprising. It is difficult to imagine a solution in a competitive private insurance market where the 'price'—i.e. the rate level and the size of the deductibles—will not reflect the calculated risk involved in the natural damage market.

B. Critical factors in the Norwegian system

The Norwegian system is far from perfect. Some critical factors in the system are discussed below.

---

[71] The subsequent information is taken from Prop. 80 L (2013–2014) Lov om erstatning for naturskader chapter 4 and Sandberg, Økland, Tyholt, *Natural perils insurance and compensation arrangements in six countries*, Klima 2050 Report no 21E—Trondheim 2020 (ISBN 978-82-536-1673-5).

[72] Iceland, Spain, and Switzerland are examples of countries where the state plays a more active role in securing compensation for natural damage.

[73] Sweden, Finland, Germany, Great Britain, Canada, and United States are examples of countries where private risk-based insurances form the core of the economic response to natural damage. Apparently, Finland has changed recently from a state–private compensation system to a private insurance scheme, whereas Canada is said to contemplate a move from a private insurance system to a state–private compensation system. The reason for such a potential move is apparently that the public seems to have problems finding insurance companies that are willing to offer the necessary natural damage insurances.

The system is complicated. The involvement of several different compensation schemes, with their specific criteria for cover, makes it difficult to obtain a full and complete insight and understanding of the overall system. The historic development provides a fair explanation of the complex situation. Both economically and politically, it was seen as a viable solution to reduce the State's former involvement in the compensation of natural damage, while upholding the State's social responsibility to secure the public's need for economic resilience in case of natural disasters. Private insurance companies have been given the practical task of fulfilling central parts of the State's continued effort through a pool arrangement based on solidarity.

The concept 'natural damage' encompasses six specific types of peril in both the natural damage insurance scheme and the state-financed compensation scheme. The chosen perils are a follow-up of the relevant perils under the state's compensation scheme prior to 1979. They include earthquakes and volcanic eruptions, perils that are irrelevant in Norway. On the other hand, heavy local rainstorms and the consequential urban flooding, which seem to be important consequences of the climate change with severe economic implications,[74] are not included in the concept today. Traditionally, they are left for ordinary risk-based insurances to cover, although the disastrous effects would make it more natural to include them in the two natural damage schemes.

A novelty introduced in the natural damage insurance scheme in 2017[75] enabled owners of residential buildings to claim the value of the site in addition to the house itself in cases where the house is destroyed (constructive total loss). The solution ensured the owner the financial ability to rebuild the house in a secure area. As an alternative, the insurance companies were given the opportunity to implement and pay for safety measures to safeguard the original site. Unfortunately, a proposition to expand the solution and include other buildings like factories or industrial plants in the new set-up was not adopted.[76] Also, the insurance companies have found conditions stipulated under the alternative mentioned unacceptable, with the effect that the alternative is not used.

The above presented insufficiencies should be seen in conjunction with another important restriction in the present regulation under both natural damage schemes. Restoring damaged buildings, plants, etc. is restricted to the previous standard, with no cover for extra costs needed to achieve a higher standard of resistance against future natural damage.[77]

The natural damage insurance scheme in particular has been criticized for its lack of elements to implement precautions to prevent natural damage.[78] The critics have suggested various solutions. One would be to reformulate the compensation rules just described and increase the compensation paid to cover money spent on preventive and safeguarding measures to reduce the risk of future natural damage to the property.[79] Another solution

---

[74] Statistics from Finans Norge Forsikringsdrift (see n 11 above) illustrate the huge amounts paid in compensation by risk-based insurances over the last 10 years to cover the economic effects of such rainstorms, compared with the total sums paid in natural damage compensation.

[75] See Section III.B.3 at nn 20–24 above.

[76] See Prop. 36 L (2016–2017) Endringer i naturskadeforsikringsloven p 11–13.

[77] See Section III.B.5 at n 29 above.

[78] See as examples of such criticism NOU 2010: 10 Tilpasning til et klima i endring (Adapting to a changing climate), p 153, NOU 2015: 16 Overvann i byer og tettsteder (Urban flooding in cities and densely populated areas), p 226 and NOU 2018: 17 Klimarisiko og norsk økonomi (Climate risk and the Norwegian economy), pp 130–131.

[79] In Hans Jacob Bull, Cecilie Flyen, and Christian Riis, *Forslag til finansierings- og forsikringsordninger for kommunal infrastruktur*, Report 19 June 2017 to the Norwegian Association of Local and Regional Authorities, the authors proposed a natural damage insurance arrangement for infrastructure owned by the municipalities, with a solution along the lines indicated in the text.

might be to differentiate the premium rate or the deductible amount dependent on the risk for the individual insured party of future natural damage. However, a solution along these lines would in effect mean the abandonment of the present solidarity principle and the transition to an ordinary risk-based insurance scheme. A third solution could be to strengthen the prevention efforts by using part of the premium paid by the insured parties for collective preventive measures, initiated by the State or by the municipality. A recent report suggests the adoption of the solution found in France through the so-called Barnier fund.[80] This state-organized fund is an offshoot of the French natural damage insurance scheme CATNAT, financed by a part of the premium paid by the French public for their compulsory damage insurance. The Barnier fund receives yearly about 200 million euro from CATNAT, which is earmarked for financing preventive measures against natural damage.

C. Does the Norwegian system provide the necessary economic resilience for the energy, natural resources, and infrastructure sectors?

Economic resilience for the energy and natural resources sector is not a stated objective of the Norwegian system. Rather, the system has been formulated with the aim of offering compensation for natural damage to individuals, companies, and municipalities on a general basis and according to specified criteria. As long as investments in the energy and natural resources sector match the formulated criteria, the investments will be treated in the same way as investments made in any other sector. Consequently, as a general rule, loss of or damage to movable property, buildings, factories, and infrastructure in the energy and natural resources sector will have cover, one way or another.[81]

One particular energy sector, the petroleum sector, has been expressly excluded from cover under the natural damage insurance scheme and the state-financed compensation scheme.[82] In Norway, the petroleum resources are located on the continental shelf, but part of the produced petroleum is brought ashore to the Norwegian mainland through pipelines or by ships. The exclusion would apply to production facilities and pipelines offshore, as well as onshore. The justification for the exclusion seems to be that including these costly petroleum facilities would have serious economic implications for the two schemes, and completely undermine their foundation and the solidarity principle. The exception for the petroleum sector has a general bearing on the expediency of adapting the Norwegian system in an international energy and natural resources setting. Investments in industrial plants in these sectors will tend to reach huge amounts, and will easily have a negative effect on the willingness to accept them in a collective insurance system based on solidarity.

---

[80] See NVE report no 9/2021 *Naturfareforum – Insentiver til og finansiering av forebygging mot naturfare.* The Barnier fund is presented in the Klima 2050 report mentioned in n 71 above.

[81] As an example, a fire-insured hydropower plant will be protected against the economic consequences of natural damage under the natural damage insurance scheme, whereas natural damage to the infrastructure of the plant, such as the penstock, will be compensated by the state-financed compensation scheme.

[82] Interestingly enough, the exclusion is formulated differently under the two schemes. NDIA section 1 second paragraph first sentence uses the expression 'equipment for the exploitation of oil, gas and other natural resources on the seabed', whereas NDCA section 2 fifth paragraph excludes the petroleum extraction activity from the scope of the act. Neither of the expressions are particularly precise, but they do not seem to have caused problems in practice.

Another important factor to be taken into account is the socio-economic background for the schemes established in Norway and in some other European countries. In these countries, the State has played a central role in providing the public with the necessary economic resilience against natural damage. Replacing the state-supported system is politically acceptable if the public may be guaranteed the same economic resilience and social security through the introduction of an insurance scheme based on solidarity. In countries where the State has not played such an active role in providing economic resilience, there would hardly be the same political pressure to resist an insurance scheme with a risk orientation and risk-based insurance premiums.

19

Public–Private Partnership in the Reconstruction of the Energy Sector

The Case for EV Buses in Thailand

Piti Eiamchamroonlarp

I. Introduction

Acknowledging energy as a key factor behind greenhouse gas emissions and being a party to the United Nations Framework Convention on Climate Change (UNFCCC), Thailand has stimulated investment in renewable energy industries.[1] Conventional electricity and renewable resourced electricity will contribute to the security of supply. The Bangkok Mass Transit Authority's (BMTA) deployment of electric buses to replace 4,000 diesel buses for public transportation presents challenges to Thailand's electricity system and electricity regulation. A question arises as to determine the capability of the electricity sector, which is primarily regulated by the Energy Industry Act B.E. 2550 (2007), to cope with the rising electricity demand because of the development in the transportation sector while still promoting utilization of renewable resources. The capability of the electricity regulatory regime in responding to a decline of electricity demand will also be tested by potential bus service disruption due to unforeseen events such as a pandemic outbreak. Hence, in addition to energy security, it appears reasonable to address and analyse the capability of Thailand's electricity regulatory regime to withstand increasing participation of renewable resources as well as electricity demand variation.

The electricity licensing regime and the third party access (TPA) right, as guaranteed by the Energy Industry Act B.E. 2550 (2007), can contribute to energy resilience as they serve as legal bases permitting utilization of an energy system storage system as well as peer-to-peer electricity trading. Furthermore, electricity from renewable resources allows the electricity system to be flexible to cope with electricity demand variation. In explaining these findings, this chapter begins by analysing the interaction between Thai electricity law and energy. Further, it explains how the deployment of BMTA electric buses could trigger challenges to energy resilience and how the electricity regulatory regime can simultaneously contribute to the security of the electricity supply and energy resilience. The third section discusses how the Energy Industry Act B.E. 2550 (2007) can help overcome challenges stemming from the intermittent nature of renewable resources.

---

[1] Office of Natural Resources and Environmental Policy and Planning, 'Thailand's Intended Nationally Determined Contribution (INDC)' (*UNFCC*, 1 October 2015) <https://www4.unfccc.int/sites/ndcstaging/PublishedDocuments/ Thailand%20First/Thailand_INDC.pdf> accessed 1 June 2021.

Piti Eiamchamroonlarp, *Public–Private Partnership in the Reconstruction of the Energy Sector* In: *Resilience in Energy, Infrastructure, and Natural Resources Law*. Edited by: Catherine Banet, Hanri Mostert, LeRoy Paddock, Milton Fernando Montoya, and Íñigo del Guayo, Oxford University Press. © Piti Eiamchamroonlarp 2022. DOI: 10.1093/oso/9780192864574.003.0019

II. Interaction between an Electricity Law and Energy Resilience

Uninterrupted electricity supply at reasonable prices is a key objective of an electricity system.[2] In achieving these goals, electricity law, a kind of energy law, serves as rules supporting and regulating electricity operational activities, including generation, transport, distribution, and marketing. However, like other industries, the electricity industry can be negatively affected by misfortune, shock, and unexpected events. Therefore, in addition to contributing to the security of electricity supply, electricity law must contribute to a power system's ability to withstand initial shock and rapidly recover from disruptive events. This section addresses and analyses the capability of Thailand's Energy Industry Act 2007 to contribute to energy resilience, especially in transitioning towards renewable energy.

A. Aims and function of an electricity law: the Energy Industry Act B.E. 2550 (2007)

Human physical and social needs rely heavily on electricity.[3] Therefore, electricity must be made available to the consumer reliably at affordable prices. Availability is the ability of consumers to secure the energy that they need.[4] Reliability reflects the extent that supply is protected from disruption.[5] Affordability implies that the electricity consumer price is reasonable.[6] When one applies a concept of energy security to electric vehicle usage, an electric vehicle user, for example, an EV bus service provider, must be capable of continuously securing electricity at a reasonable price. Hence, this chapter analyses how the Energy Industry Act 2007 can contribute to the security of the electricity supply.

Electricity generation, networks (transmission and distribution systems), electricity supply, and electricity system operator are licensable activities under the Energy Industry Act 2007.[7] An operator, private or state, desiring to carry out these operational activities shall obtain electricity licences from an independent energy regulator called the Energy Regulatory Commission (ERC).[8] Apart from issuing electricity licences, the ERC is vested with powers to regulate tariffs for energy industry operation,[9] establish standards and safety in the energy industry operation,[10] and regulate access and operation of energy network systems.[11] In addition, the ERC is vested with public powers to ensure an electricity operator's right of access to electricity networks owned by another operator—the third party access regime.[12]

---

[2] B.W. Ang, W.L. Choong, and T.S. Ng, 'Energy security: Definitions, Dimensions and Indexes' (2015) 42 RSE Rev 1077, 1078.

[3] Marina Mola, Maksims Feofilovs, and Francesco Romagnoli, 'Energy Resilience: Research Trends at Urban, Municipal and Country Levels' (2018) 147 Energy Procedia 104.

[4] Ruven Fleming, *Shale Gas, the Environment and Energy Security: A New Framework for Energy Regulation* (Edward Elgar 2017) 35.

[5] Benjamin K. Sovacool (ed), *The Routledge Handbook of Energy Security* (Routledge 2011) 9.

[6] Leigh Hancher and Sally Janssen, 'Shared Competences and Multi-Faceted Concepts – European Legal Framework for Security of Supply' in B. Barton et al (eds), *Energy Security: Managing Risk in a Dynamic Legal and Regulatory Environment* (Oxford University Press 2004) 93.

[7] Energy Industry Act B.E. 2550 (2007), s 47.

[8] Ibid.

[9] Ibid, Division 3: Part 2.

[10] Ibid, Division 3: Part 3.

[11] Ibid, Division 4: Part 4.

[12] Ibid.

Despite the Energy Industry Act 2007, the Electricity Generating Authority of Thailand (EGAT), the Metropolitan Electricity Authority (MEA), and the Provincial Electricity Authority (PEA), which are state-owned enterprises, have dominated Thailand's electricity industries. Electricity producers can apply for an electricity generation licence from the ERC. EGAT is the largest power producer in Thailand and, as the only electricity system operator,[13] is responsible for purchasing bulk electricity from Independent Power Producers (IPPs), which are large-size power producers with generation capacity exceeding 90 MW,[14] Small Power Producers (SPPs) with generation capacity from 10 MW to 90 MW[15], and neighbouring countries. EGAT then transmits the electricity through its transmission grids to MEA and PEA for distribution. Under this industry structure, IPPs cannot freely sell their electricity to the wholesale electricity markets. Still, they must enter into a long-term power purchase agreement (PPA) with EGAT under ERC power purchasing rules.

Very Small Power Producers (VSPPs) with generation not exceeding 10 MW, for example those generating from renewable resources and a household wishing to sell electricity generated from their rooftop photovoltaic systems, can sell their electricity to MEA and PEA under the ERC power purchasing rules announced by the ERC.[16] Alternatively, they can choose to directly sell their electricity to their consumers without the need for intermediaries like MEA and PEA under a peer-to-peer (P2P) model.[17] These power producers can transport or wheel their electricity through electricity networks owned by MEA and PEA.

BCPG Public Company Limited launched the first P2P renewable energy trading project in Thailand in 2018. BCPG's P2P platform will rely on rooftop solar systems with a total capacity of 635 kW deployed across four participating entities and co-located battery storage, which should cover 20 per cent of the community's overall electricity needs.[18] The trading transaction will be settled through a blockchain trading platform.[19]

B. Ability of the Energy Industry Act B.E. 2550 (2007) to ensure energy resilience

The concept of resilience originated in psychology and physics or engineering.[20] Psychological resilience can be referred to as ability to bounce back from negative emotional experiences and by flexible adaptation to the changing demands of stressful experiences.[21] A person can suffer adversity and need to bounce back from adversity and go on with their

[13] Energy Regulatory Commission, 'List of a system operator' (*ERC*, July 2021) < http://app04.erc.or.th/ELicense/ Licenser/05_Reporting/504_ListLicensing_Columns_New.aspx?LicenseType = 5> accessed 14 June 2021.
[14] Electricity Generating Authority of Thailand, Operation Code (*EGAT*, July 2017) <https://www.sothailand.com/gridcode/operationcode.pdf> accessed 4 July 2021, 4.
[15] Ibid.
[16] For example, see Regulation of the Energy Regulatory Commission re: Electricity Purchasing from Very Small Power Producers (Community-Based Power Plant) B.E. 2563 (2020).
[17] IRENA, *Innovation landscape brief: Peer-to-peer electricity trading* (IRENA 2020) 6.
[18] IEEFA, 'Blockchain energy trading pilot planned in Thailand' (*IEEFA*, 15 October 2018) <https://ieefa.org/blockchain-energy-trading-pilot-planned-in-thailand/> accessed 6 June 2021.
[19] Ibid.
[20] Marina Mola et al, 'Energy resilience: research trends at urban, municipal and country levels' (2018) 147 Energy Procedia 104, 105.
[21] Michele M. Tugade and Barbara L. Fredrickson, 'Resilient Individuals Use Positive Emotions to Bounce Back From Negative Emotional Experiences' (2004) 86(2) J Pers Soc Psychol. 320.

life.[22] In the context of physics or engineering, resilience concerns the ability of one system capacity to bounce back into shape or position.[23] A system can be negatively affected by an external shock and needs to recover from a shocking event.[24] Resilience is now understood as a process that the observed system undergoes in response to a disruption quantified in terms of a measure of system performance and its evolution during the system response time after an event.[25] It is generally referred to as the ability to cope with misfortune, shock, and the unexpected.[26] In power systems, the concept of resilience can be broadly defined as the ability of a power system to withstand initial shock, rapidly recover from a disruptive event, and adapt to mitigate the impact of future similar events.[27] Resilience, therefore, extends the definition of energy security beyond frequency and severity by accounting for the ability to recover quickly and adapt to new operating conditions.[28]

1. The COVID-19 pandemic: electricity demand variation

The COVID-19 pandemic resulted in a new operating condition with potential adverse impact on the ability of the Thai electricity industry, which is regulated by the Energy Industry Act 2007 and is mainly state-owned enterprises, to ensure reliable and available electricity. The disruption of economic activity has led to a decline in demand for energy.[29] Power load is mainly residential, commercial, and industrial.[30] According to the International Energy Agency, electricity demand fell significantly due to lockdown measures, with knock-on effects on the power mix.[31] Electricity demand fell by 20 per cent or more during full lockdown in several countries. Demand drop depended on measures adopted, their severity, and duration.[32] Therefore, it is key to determine the ability of the electricity system and the country's electricity regulatory regime to respond or withstand the decline in demand for industrial and commercial electricity.

Under power purchase agreements between EGAT and IPPs, EGAT is bound by minimum-take obligations to take all electricity IPPs produce as long as the output does exceed the contracted capacity.[33] In exchange, these power producers receive availability payment (AP) and energy payment (EP) from EGAT.[34] The former aims to compensate

---

[22] Janyce G. Dyer and Teena Minton McGuinness, 'Resilience Analysis of the Concept' (1996) 10(5) Archives of Psychiatric Nursing 276, 277.

[23] Andrea Gatto and Carlo Drago, 'A Taxonomy of Energy Resilience' (2020) 136 Energy Policy 1, 1; B.W. Smith, E.M. Tooley, P.J. Christopher, and V.S. Kay, 'Resilience as the Ability to Bounce Back from Stress: A Neglected Personal Resource?' (2010) 5(3) Journal of Positive Psychology 166.

[24] Anna Bozza, Domenico Asprone, and Francesco Fabbrocino, 'Urban Resilience: A Civil Engineering Perspective' (2017) 9 Sustainability 103.

[25] Patrick Gasser et al, 'A Review on Resilience Assessment of Energy Systems' (2019) 6(5) Sustainable and Resilient Infrastructure 273, 275.

[26] Marina Mola et al (n 20) 105.

[27] Ibid.

[28] Patrick Gasser et al, 'Comprehensive Resilience Assessment of Electricity Supply Security for 140 Countries' (2020) 110 Ecological Indicators 1, 2.

[29] Imlak Shaikh, 'Impact of COVID-19 Pandemic on the Energy Markets' [2020] Economic Change and Restructuring 1, 2.

[30] Rajvikram Madurai Elavarasan et al, 'COVID-19: Impact Analysis and Recommendations for Power Sector Operation' (2020) 279 Applied Energy 1, 4.

[31] IEA, 'Global Energy Review 2020 Abstract the impacts of the Covid-19 crisis on global energy demand and CO2 emissions' (*IEA*, 28 April 2020) <https://iea.blob.core.windows.net/assets/7e802f6a-0b30-4714-abb1-46f21 a7a9530/ >Global_Energy_Review_2020.pdf accessed 10 June 2020, 3.

[32] Ibid.

[33] International Energy Agency, 'Thailand Power System Flexibility Study' (*IEA*, 4 June 2021) < https://iea.blob. core. windows.net/assets/19f9554b-f40c-46ff-b7f5-78f1456057a9/ThailandPowerSystemFlexibilityStudy.pdf> accessed 4 July 2021, 57.

[34] Regulation of the Energy Regulatory Commission re: Standard for Power Producer (EGAT) B.E. 2559 (2016).

a power producer that makes electricity available for transmitting; the latter compensates for the electricity transmitted to the grid. Therefore, even if demand decline meant that the available electricity was not transmitted, the power producer who made it dispatchable or available will be compensated. This compensation mechanism increases operational costs, but, simultaneously, contributes to electrical supply reliability and security. These costs will eventually pass on to MEA and PEA electricity consumers.

However, the COVID-19 pandemic can adversely impact the financial position of state-owned electricity operators. Lower demand and end-consumer payment stresses are constraining the ability of distribution operators MEA and PEA to make payments to power producers like EGAT.[35] One may argue that electricity operators can gain more income from the increase in demand for residential electricity. However, residential consumption increases do not compensate for drastic reductions in industrial, commercial, and tertiary activities.[36]

In addition to the availability and reliability of electricity, affordability is also one element of energy security. Unfortunately, the ability of electricity users to pay for power has also been negatively impacted by the COVID-19 pandemic, thus reducing the revenue for electricity operators.[37] Regardless of actual usage and lower ability to pay for electricity, electricity users have to pay for increasing operational costs resulting from minimum-take obligations under a firm power purchase agreement between EGAT and IPPs.

Responding to an affordability challenge, the ERC exercised its regulatory power by announcing exemptions on minimum charges for certain electricity users such as medium and large business operators and non-profit organizations.[38] These exempted electricity users are required to pay only for the demand charge.[39] The minimum charge exemption reflects the flexibility and resilience of the Energy Industry Act 2007 since it allows the ERC to adjust the electricity tariff due to the change in economic and social conditions.[40]

The above discussion reveals the ability of electricity industries, dominated by state-owned electricity enterprises and regulated by the ERC, to withstand electricity demand variation. On the one hand, despite the decline in electricity demand, power producers can still earn revenue from making electricity available through long-term power purchase agreements. On the other hand, responding to the limited ability to pay for electricity, the ERC is vested with the public power to adjust the electricity tariff.

2. Renewable resources: a more resilient way forward

Electricity generated from renewable resources can enhance the resilience of electricity systems.[41] Reliance on distributed energy resources, such as renewable resources, can

[35] Tonci Bakovic et al, 'The Impact of COVID-19 on the Power Sector' (*IFC*, June 2021) <https://www.ifc.org/wps/wcm/ connect/f73f9cf3-3abd-4378-b5b6-c8eb8c4c1b45/IFC-Covid19-PowerSectorfinal webrev.pdf?MOD= AJPERES& CVID=n9.O4sQ> accessed 12 June 2021, 3.

[36] Ettore Bompard et al, 'The Immediate Impacts of COVID-19 on European Electricity Systems: A First Assessment and Lessons Learned' (2021) 14 Energies 96, 98.

[37] Michael Boulle and Anthony Dane, 'The impacts of Covid-19 on the Power sector in sub-Saharan Africa, and the Role of the Power Sector in Socioeconomic Recovery' (*KAS*, 15 July 2020) <https://www.kas.de/docume nts/   282730/   8327029/Covid_Energy_SSA_publication.pdf/efc74763-8f85-39c6-53e4-de16cb75f71d?t= 1594778811782> accessed 12 June 2021, 2.

[38] Notification of the Energy Regulatory Commission re: Exemptions of Minimum Charge (March 2020).

[39] Ibid.

[40] Energy Industry Act B.E. 2550 (2007), s 68.

[41] Mario Pagliaro, 'Renewable Energy Systems: Enhanced Resilience, Lower Costs' (2019) 7(11) Energy Technology 1, 1.

stimulate more participation of new entrants, including household producers in electricity industries.[42] Importantly, renewable resources are more dispersed and available at smaller scales. Resilience can be improved because the consequences of a disruptive event can be reduced.[43] Unlike a large-scale power plant that contributes to electricity availability and reliability based on supply-on-demand, renewable projects rely on 'capture-when-available' and 'store-until-required' approaches.[44] For example, a household electricity consumer may choose to install a solar photovoltaic system (PV) rooftop to generate electricity for house-hold consumption and, consequently, need less electricity from MEA and PEA. However, due to the intermittent nature of renewable resources, especially sunlight and wind, these consumers may still need access to electricity grids owned by MEA and PEA and purchase electricity from the grid.

Given potential contributions of renewable resources to more resilient electricity sys-tems, an issue arises as to the capability of the Energy Industry Act B.E. 2550 (2007) to promote utilization of renewable resources. Generating and supplying electricity from photovoltaic solar panels are licensable activities. If the generation capacity is lower than 1,000 Kilovolt-Amps (kVA), a power producer is exempted from obtaining a power gener-ation licence.[45] Like the exemption of generation activity, electricity supply capacity lower than 1,000 kVA is exempted from obtaining a power generation licence.[46] When an oper-ator is exempted from obtaining the licence, the operator must notify the ERC Office about details of its operation.[47] The aforesaid regulatory requirements reveal an attempt of the Energy Industry Act B.E. 2550 (2007) to allow small-scale renewable projects in Thailand.

In addition to the licensing regime, third party access, as guaranteed by the Energy Industry Act B.E. 2550 (2007), can contribute to utilization and commercialization of re-newable resources in Thailand. Under the electricity TPA regime, EGAT, MEA, and PEA, as licensees who own and operate electricity networks, shall allow other licensees or energy business operators to use or connect to its energy network system, under the regulations prescribed and announced by them.[48] EGAT, MEA, and PEA must operate their electricity networks fairly and must refrain from unjust discrimination.[49] Unfair or discriminatory electricity network operation practices of EGAT, MEA, and PEA are subject to the regula-tory power of the ERC.[50]

A private renewable operator may enter into a transmission or distribution service agree-ment with EGAT, MEA, or PEA to transmit or distribute its electricity to the buyer under a private power purchase agreement. This private power purchase agreement will allow the producer to directly collect electricity charges from the customer, while using the electri-city network owned by EGAT, MEA, or PEA. A private power purchase agreement can be structured in a way that a power producer can collect energy payment for actual electricity

[42] Raphael J. Heffron, 'A Treatise for Energy Law' (2018) 11 Journal of World Energy Law & Business 34, 46–47.
[43] Ibid.
[44] Geoff O'Brien, 'Vulnerability and Resilience in the European Energy System' (2009) 20(3) Energy & Environment 399, 403.
[45] Royal Decree re: Types, Size, and Characteristic of Energy Businesses that are Exempted from Obtaining Energy License B.E. 2552 (2009), s 3(1).
[46] Ibid, s 3(3).
[47] Energy Regulatory Commission Notification re: Notification Requirement for the Exempted Activities B.E. 2552 (2009), cl 3 and cl 4.
[48] Ibid, s 81 para 1.
[49] Ibid, s 80.
[50] Ibid, ss 82–84.

usage, not for making electricity available. The producer is responsible for paying transmission or distribution service fees, transmission or distribution charges, connection charges, imbalance charges, and ancillary charges under a transmission or distribution service agreement.[51]

Wheeling charges are assessed and collected when electricity leaves or enters the electrical distribution grid.[52] Due to the intermittent nature of renewable resources, a prosumer may transmit more or less electricity than the contracted capacity. In this situation, EGAT, MEA, and PEA, being electricity network operators, need to balance the generation and consumption of electricity.[53] Balancing refers to the process through which a system operator manages the physical equilibrium between grid injections (generation) and withdrawals (consumption).[54] In exchange for providing the balancing service, network operators can collect imbalances charges from users. However, these charges are deemed service fees for energy business operation and subject to ERC approval.[55]

Electricity licensing and electricity TPA regimes under the Energy Industry Act B.E. 2550 (2007) likely contribute to energy reliance as they serve as legal bases supporting renewable projects that offer flexible electricity supply sources compared with conventional power plants. However, this theoretical finding—readiness of the electricity regulatory regime to ensure energy reliance—will be tested by deploying electric buses for public transport service in Bangkok. Such deployment could trigger practical challenges to energy resilience, especially from electricity demand variation caused by ridership fluctuation.

III. Electric Bus Deployment

The resilience of Thai electricity systems will face challenges arising from uncertainty caused by several factors such as driving behaviour, battery efficiency over life, and fluctuation of ridership level.[56] Responding to the demand rise for electric buses, electricity operators, both state and private, can rely on electricity from EGAT, MEA, and PEA networks. However, the traditional electricity networks have limited capability to ensure flexibility for the likely uncertainty of electric bus electricity consumption.

A. Roles of a state-owned enterprise

Established in 1976 as a state-owned enterprise,[57] BMTA is responsible for mass transit in the Bangkok area or to conduct related businesses.[58] Since its establishment, BMTA has

---

[51] See, for example, SMUD, 'Sacramento Municipal Utility District's Rate Policy and Procedures Manual re: Distribution Wheeling Service' (*SMUD* 1 July 2017) <https://www.smud.org/-/media/Documents/Going-Green/PDFs/ Distribution-Wheeling-Service-Policies-and-Procedures.ashx> accessed 1 February 2021.

[52] Ibid, 8.

[53] European Network of Transmission System Operators for Electricity, 'Development Balancing Systems to Facilitate the Achievement of Renewable Energy Goals' (*ENTSOE*, November 2011) <https://eepublicdownloads.ent soe.eu/ clean-documents/pre2015/position_papers/111104_RESBalancing_ final.pdf> accessed 12 March 2021, 4.

[54] Ibid.

[55] The Energy Industry Act 2007, ss 65 and 66.

[56] Gamal Alkawsi et al, 'Review of Renewable Energy-Based Charging Infrastructure for Electric Vehicles' (2021) 11 Appl. Sci. 3847, 1; Jari Vepsäläinen et al, 'Energy Uncertainty Analysis of Electric Buses' [2018] E 11 3267.

[57] Royal Decree on Establishment of the Bangkok Mass Transit Authority B.E. 2519 (1976), s 4.

[58] Ibid, s 6.

been a wholly-owned state-owned enterprise of the Thai government and an administrative agency under the Thai legal system.[59] In April 2020, BMTA reported using 2,516 diesel buses, which have been in operation for more than 20 years.[60] Only 489 natural gas buses are in operation through a procurement agreement with a private operator.[61]

Relying on diesel buses, BMTA faces increasing operational costs associated with increasing gasoline/diesel oil prices. Its rehabilitation plan anticipates the price of diesel rising from THB 25.89 in 2018 to THB 32.28 in 2027.[62] However, it noted that compressed natural gas (CNG) and electricity would become more economical choices. One kilogram of CNG, THB 14.62 in 2018, was already cheaper than a litre of diesel in the same year, whereas one kilogram of CNG is expected to cost THB 21.43 in 2027.[63] The cost of electricity seems to be the most economical compared with diesel and CNG. One kWh of electricity for an EV bus was THB 3.13 in 2018 and is expected to be THB 4.49 in 2027.[64]

In addition to operational costs, public buses must be fully equipped with state-of-the-art supporting equipment. According to the BMTA Rehabilitation Plan, an e-ticket system shall be installed on each public bus to allow the passenger to make payments electronically.[65] Moreover, a global positioning system (GPS) and a Wi-Fi system shall be made available on each bus to enhance efficiency in monitoring and safety of the service.[66]

To acquire fully equipped electric buses for public bus service in the Bangkok area, BMTA plans to rent 2,511 electric buses from a private contractor for a 14-year term. However, to promote electric vehicle industries in Thailand, the buses to be delivered under a rental agreement must be locally assembled and contain at least 50 per cent of the value of locally manufactured material and equipment.[67] In addition to the electric bus rental arrangement, BMTA may choose to enter into a service agreement requiring a private contractor to provide public bus service by relying on fully equipped buses.

Apart from economic reasons, electric bus deployment can be justified on the ground of environmental protection. Air pollution has become a serious environmental and health issue for those residing in the Bangkok area and the country. Bangkok Metropolitan Environmental Office's environmental plan (2021) notes that emissions from transportation, especially from internal combustion engine vehicles, significantly contribute to air pollution in Bangkok.[68] Responding to this air quality crisis, the Pollution Control Board suggested the deployment of low-carbon buses.[69] The Ministry of Transport instructed

[59] The Act on Establishment of Administrative Courts and Administrative Court Procedure 1999, s 3.
[60] Bangkok Mass Transit Authority, 'Rehabilitation Plan of Bangkok Mass Transit Authority (revised version)' (*BMTA*, 23 April 2019) <http://www.bmta.co.th/sites/default/files/files/about-us/rehabilitation-plan-april63.pdf> accessed 20 February 2021, 9.
[61] Ibid.
[62] Ibid, 11.
[63] Ibid.
[64] Ibid.
[65] Ibid, 20.
[66] Ibid.
[67] Ibid, 15.
[68] Bangkok Metropolitan Environmental Office, 'The Environmental Plan (2021)' (*Bangkok Metropolitan*, 2021) < http://www.bangkok.go.th/upload/user/00000231/data/plan64/plan2564.pdf> accessed 15 June 2021, 2.
[69] Pollution Control Board, 'Meeting Resolution No.6/2562' (*OIC*, September 2019) <http://www.oic.go.th/FILEWEB/CABINFOCENTER3/DRAWER056/GENERAL/DATA0001/00001565.PDF> accessed 15 June 2021.

BTMA, being the key public bus service provider in the Bangkok area, to procure new effi-cient buses with low pollution emissions and promote eco-friendly vehicles.[70]

B. Collaboration with private operators

For electric bus rental agreements and electric bus service agreements, BMTA must comply with procurement procedures under the Public Procurement and Supplies Administration Act B.E. 2560 (2017). In the bidding process, BMTA is required by the public procurement law to use a general solicitation notification method to invite proposals from the private sector fairly and competitively.[71] The selected bidder must enter into a rental agreement and/ or a service agreement—two types of agreement recognized by the Civil and Commercial Code of Thailand.

Under a rental agreement, the private party lessor delivers electric buses to BMTA for transport services in the Bangkok area. In exchange for the delivery, the private party has a right to a rental fee from the BMTA. BMTA has typically relied on performance-based met-rics in determining the rental fee. This metric shifts emphasis from specifications stressing supplier inputs (e.g. staff and equipment) and service processes to specifications empha-sizing service outputs (e.g. availability and reliability).[72] Applying this method, BMTA can pay the rental fee based on the availability and reliability of the delivered electric buses and related equipment.

Under the service agreement, the private sector does not deliver the electric bus to BMTA but instead use the electric bus to provide transport service, thus becoming a service pro-vider.[73] In exchange for the delivered bus service, BMTA pays the service provider a service fee. Like a rental agreement, the service fee can be calculated on a performance basis. When a private operator performs its obligations, either delivering electric buses or operating bus services, BMTA will be responsible for compensating such performance under the agreed performance-based basis, regardless of ridership levels.

It can be argued that an electric bus rental and an electric bus service agreement, which are based on the performance-based basis for remuneration determination, put BMTA at risk associated with variation of ridership level due to a lockdown. If ridership level drops due to a pandemic situation, BMTA, which is bound by the procurement agreement to compensate the performance achieved by the private party, is then at risk.

Responding to the demand risk stemming from a lockdown, BMTA may choose to enter a public–private partnership (PPP) contract instead of a rental and a service agreement. Under the Public–Private Partnership Act B.E. 2560 (2017), BMTA can delegate its re-sponsibilities,[74] namely delivering transport service, to a private party. This delegation can be done through a bus service concession. Under this arrangement, the private party will

---

[70] Jaee Nikam, 'Air quality in Thailand: Understanding the Regulatory Context' (*Stockholm Environment Institute*, 12 February 2021) <https://cdn.sei.org/wp-content/uploads/2021/02/210212c-killeen-archer-air-qual ity-in-thailand-wp-2101e-final.pdf> accessed 15 June 2021, 37.

[71] Public Procurement and Supplies Administration Act B.E. 2560 (2017), s 55(1).

[72] Kostas Selviaridis and Andreas Norrman, 'Performance-Based Contracting for Advanced Logistics Services: Challenges in Its Adoption, Design and Management' (2015) 45(6) International Journal of Physical Distribution & Logistics Management 592, 594.

[73] The Civil and Commercial Code, s 575.

[74] Royal Decree on Establishment of the Bangkok Mass Transit Authority B.E. 2519 (1976), s 6.

become a service provider and collect bus fares from passengers. In this case, the private operator will gain financial benefits from the bus services it delivered, rather than rental fees or service fees from BMTA. A user-payment PPP contract can be structured so that revenue accruing from the bus service will be shared by BMTA and the private operator. If the ridership level drops, both parties' revenue shall accordingly be affected.

C. The need for energy resilience

Deployment of electric buses under a PPP arrangement will inevitably trigger challenges for electricity systems. To ensure continuity of the bus service, electricity operators, including EGAT, MEA, PEA, and private power producers, must be ready to supply continuously electricity for buses. However, it can be argued that electricity from renewable resources can help minimize the consequences of disruptive events faced by centralized electricity systems and be more adaptive to electricity demand variation caused by an unforeseen event such as a pandemic outbreak.

1. Security of electricity supply from distributed electricity generation

Regardless of the ability of BMTA to economically withstand an event negatively affecting ridership level, a challenge from an energy resilience perspective arises for electricity operators. Any electric bus operator will need a reliable electricity supply for uninterrupted electric bus operation. The deployment of electric buses will pose a demanding challenge to Thai electricity systems in Thailand. Electric bus operation inevitably means more electricity demand for the deployed electric buses. Given this electricity demand forecasting, EGAT can ensure the security of electricity supply through its generation capacity or purchasing electricity from private power producers.

Electricity from renewable resources may be a solution to challenges posed by the deployment of electric buses. Instead of relying on electricity from electricity networks, the electric bus can rely on electricity generated from renewable resources by households in Bangkok. More participants and more reliance on distributed energy resources can help improve the resilience of electricity systems since it helps to diversify sources of electricity and thus reduces the consequences of disruptive events faced by centralized electricity systems. Since the Energy Industry Act B.E. 2550 (2007) serves as a legal basis of the ERC to authorize distributed electricity generation, hopefully, the electricity regulatory regime helps to contribute to the security of electricity supply and, simultaneously, energy resilience.

The reliance on electricity generated from conventional resources such as fossil fuels can be criticized for negative environmental impacts to the people residing in the generation areas.[75] Therefore, in addition to minimizing risks associated with a centralized electricity system, fuelling electric buses with electricity generated from renewable resourced electricity helps overcome the criticism of pollution caused by electricity generation.

---

[75] Allen Saylav, 'Economic and Social Benefits of Electric Public Transport Vehicles' (*Parliament of Victoria*, 7 April 2016) <https://www.parliament.vic.gov.au/images/stories/committees/SCEI/Electric_Vehicles/Submissions/ S2-AVASS_GROUP-ATT1.pdf> accessed 14 June 2021.

2. Electricity demand variation

An unforeseen event such as a pandemic outbreak can directly lead to a drop in the number of passengers using bus service. This ridership reduction contributes to electricity demand fluctuation. For example, a lockdown will restrict people's movement in a city. Less bus service will be required and, consequently, less electricity will be needed. The government may lift the lockdown if the pandemic situation improves. More people's movement in the city after the lifting means more electricity consumption for electric buses. However, a seemingly improving pandemic situation may also suddenly worsen again, and the lockdown may be reinstated. These uncertainties cause electricity demand variation and, inevitably, challenges to electricity systems.

Electricity generated from renewable resources is based on capture-when-available and store-until-required strategies.[76] People residing in the Bangkok area may apply for electricity generation and distribution licences to generate and supply electricity to electric bus charging stations through electricity networks owned by MEA under the electricity TPA regime under the Energy Industry Act B.E. 2550 (2007). This electricity system is more adaptive to demand variation since the self-generated electricity from renewable resources is supplied to the networks only when there is electricity demand, for example, when a lockdown is lifted and the bus operation is needed. When demand for residential electricity rises in a sudden lockdown, the self-generated electricity will be used for lockdown activities. So, an electricity system that relies on renewable resources appears to be more adaptive to change in operating conditions than traditional electricity, especially for electricity demand variations.

IV. Enhancing Energy Resilience through Renewable Resources

The availability and reliability of electricity systems based on renewable resources can be undermined by the intermittent nature of renewable resources. Given this challenge, this section analyses how the electricity licensing and the electricity TPA regimes under the Energy Industry Act B.E. 2550 (2007) cope with the intermittent nature of renewable resources and, ultimately, support the availability and reliability of electricity systems for electric buses.

A. Energy storage system: licensable activity?

To ensure the availability of electricity for electric buses, a charging station operator can legally obtain an electricity generation licence from the ERC. Upon obtaining an electricity generation licence, the operator can generate electricity from a solar resource through a photovoltaic system and utilize its self-generated electricity for electric vehicles. Furthermore, it may choose to sell this self-generated electricity to others upon receiving an electricity supply licence. However, a critical challenge concerns the intermittent nature of renewable energy resources. More rapid and less predictable fluctuations characterize

---

[76] O'Brien (n 44) 403.

solar power.[77] This intermittent nature of solar power can cause difficulties to a public bus service that needs the supply to be continuous and reliable. Therefore, despite contributing to energy resilience, reliance on renewable resources triggers a challenge to the security of electricity supply.

Unlike the conventional approach, a renewable producer does not rely on a supply-on-demand approach but 'capture-when-available' and 'store-until-required' strategies.[78] Due to the intermittent nature of renewable resources, a renewable energy producer can generate electricity when the renewable resources are available and may need to store the generated electricity until it is needed. This means that, apart from generating electricity, a charging station operator may store the self-generated electricity in an electrical energy storage system (ESS). ESS is a process of converting electrical energy from a power network into a form that can be stored for converting back to electrical energy when needed.[79] With this technology, a power producer can convert and store solar resources the photovoltaic system receives in the daytime. The stored resource can be converted back to electrical energy at night when electric buses are not in operation. From an energy resilience perspective, maintaining an energy source for electric buses that is not grid reliant can help reduce the impact minor power outages have on charging capacity.[80]

Moving away from the centralized electricity mode, renewable resources for electricity generation can contribute to energy resilience but need to be supported by disruptive energy technologies such as an ESS. Therefore, the capability of the electricity regulatory regime can be determined by its ability to allow for the deployment of the ESS for renewable projects. All types of electricity operational activities are regulated by the ERC under the Energy Industry Act B.E. 2550 (2007). ESS is yet to be recognized as an operational activity under the Royal Decree regarding: Types, Size, and Characteristic of Energy Businesses that are Exempted from Obtaining Energy License B.E. 2552 (2009).

Not being recognized as a licensable operation activity under the by-law does not mean that ESS is prohibited. The ERC recognizes the potential roles of an ESS in supporting renewable resources electricity generation systems. For example, the ERC explicitly refers to ESS in its regulation on electricity purchasing from VSPPs (Community-Based Power Plant) B.E. 2563 (2020).[81] Under the aforesaid regulation, a power producer who produces electricity from renewable resources with a generation system having capacity not exceeding 10MW, can use an ESS to support a generation system for supplying electricity to MEA and PEA.[82] The electricity regulatory regime under the Energy Industry Act B.E. 2550 (2007) has acknowledged the contribution of the ESS to renewable technologies. This acknowledgement contributes to the security of electricity supply, especially when more electricity is generated from renewable resources.

---

[77] Elaine K. Hart, 'The Potential of Intermittent Renewables to Meet Electric Power Demand: Current Methods and Emerging Analytical Techniques' (2012) 100(2) Proceeding of the IEEE 322, 323.

[78] O'Brien (n 44) 403.

[79] Haisheng Chen et al, 'Progress in electrical energy storage system: A critical review' (2009) 19(3) Progress in Natural Science 291, 291.

[80] Lauren Bailey, 'Planning for a Climate Resilient Electric Bus Fleet' (*TSTC*, 30 October 2020) <http://www.tstc.org /wp-content/uploads/2020/09/09-29-2020_Resiliency-Report.pdf> accessed 15 June 2021, 9.

[81] Regulation of the Energy Regulatory Commission re: Electricity Purchasing from Very Small Power Producers (Community-Based Power Plant) B.E. 2563 (2020), cl 3.

[82] Ibid, cl 18.

B. A third party access of the prosumer and P2P electricity trading

Despite the potential use of ESS to store electricity generated from renewable resources, a charging station operator may obtain electricity from other electricity producers that generate electricity from renewable resources in the Bangkok area to ensure electricity availability. This alternative is possible under the concept of the prosumer. A household electricity consumer that generates renewable electricity for its consumption and who may store or sell self-generated renewable electricity is deemed a 'prosumer'.[83] As such, a legal question arises to determine whether a charging station operator can purchase electricity from prosumers who can generate electricity from renewable energy resources.

As licensable activities, rights to generate and sell electricity are recognized by the Energy Industry Act B.E. 2550 (2007). However, prosumers who do not have their electricity network and wish to transport their electricity to a charging station will need access to the electricity grid. In the Bangkok area, most electricity networks are owned and operated by MEA. MEA is required by the Energy Industry Act B.E. 2550 (2007) to allow other licensees to utilize or connect to its energy network system in a non-discriminatory manner.[84] MEA is vested with a power to announce its connection, operation, and service codes.[85]

A right of access to the electricity grid, or the so-called third party access,[86] serves as a crucial element that physically links prosumers to a charging station operator. A prosumer is not compelled to sell its self-generated electricity to MEA but can use the MEA's grid to transmit its self-generated electricity to a charging station operator. In this case, MEA is not a power purchaser but a wheeling service provider responsible for transmission service that enables the delivery of electricity between a buyer and seller.[87] MEA can gain revenues from the delivered wheeling service under a wheeling service agreement using wheeling charges.

The third-party access to electricity networks under the Energy Industry Act B.E. 2550 (2007) reveals a possibility of the Bangkok prosumers' roles in contributing to the availability and reliability of electricity supply for electric bus charging stations. On the one hand, they are users of public bus services; on the other hand, they may earn additional revenue from selling self-generated electricity to charging station operators. This can help to lessen dependency on coal-fired electricity from the grid. Importantly, it helps to ensure the ability of a power system to withstand the intermittent nature of renewable resources by offering additional electricity supply from distributed energy resources, thus contributing to energy resilience. Moreover, electricity generated from renewable resources can be purchased on a non-firm basis. Under a non-firm power purchase agreement, there is no contracted capacity to be delivered by the power producer. On the other hand, the power purchaser does not have minimum-take obligations. Therefore, electricity users like charging stations are bound to pay only for actual electricity usage without a responsibility to pay for availability charges.

---

[83] Directive (EU) 2018/2001 of European Parliament and the Council of 11 December 2018 on the promotion of the use of energy from renewable sources, Art 2(14).

[84] The Energy Industry Act B.E. 2550 (2007), s 80.

[85] Ibid, s 81.

[86] Kim Talus, *Introduction to EU Energy Law* (Oxford University Press 2016) 19.

[87] Jenny Heeter et al, 'Wheeling and Banking Strategies for Optimal Renewable Energy Deployment: International Experiences' (*NREL*, March 2016) <https://www.nrel.gov/docs/fy16osti/65660.pdf> accessed 11 March 2021, 2.

V. Conclusion

An electricity licensing regime, as well as the third-party access right as guaranteed by the Energy Industry Act B.E. 2550 (2007), can contribute to energy resilience, which is the ability of a power system to withstand initial shock, rapidly recover from a disruptive event, and apply adaptation measures for mitigating the impact of similar events in the future. Renewable resources are more dispersed and available at smaller scales. Resilience can be improved because the consequences of a disruptive event can be reduced. Since the electricity regulatory regime can serve as a legal basis permitting and incentivizing electricity generation from renewable resources, it can contribute to energy resilience.

Referring to electric bus deployment by BMTA as an example, this chapter examines how the electricity regulatory regime contributes to the resilience of the electricity systems when facing electricity demand variation, especially when facing a decline in electricity demand due to an unforeseen event such as a pandemic outbreak. Moreover, it finds that BMTA may contractually allocate risks associated with dropping ridership levels to a private contractor or jointly bear such risks if not fully allocated. When the ridership levels drop, a user-payment PPP contract will allow both BMTA and its partner, a private contractor, to share this demand risk.

Regardless of BMTA's ability to allocate the demand risk to a private PPP contractor, the electricity system and electricity operators, such as charging station operators, will face challenges arising from electricity demand variation, especially when the ridership levels drop. From an energy resilience perspective, electricity generated from renewable resources should help ensure the availability and reliability of electricity for electric bus operations by diversifying sources of electricity, thus reducing the consequences of disruptive events faced by centralized electricity systems. However, given their intermittent nature, the electricity regulatory regime that supports energy resilience must support disruptive energy technologies such as ESS. The electricity regulatory regime under the Energy Industry Act B.E. 2550 (2007) has acknowledged the contribution of the ESS to renewable technologies and, simultaneously, energy resilience. More participants and more reliance on distributed energy resources can help improve the resilience of electricity systems since it helps to diversify sources of electricity and thus reduces the consequences of disruptive events faced by centralized electricity systems.

In addition to contributing to the utilization of the ESS technology, the Energy Industry Act B.E. 2550 (2007) can help ensure the resilience of electricity systems through the TPA regime. Despite its willingness to utilize renewable resources, charging station operators must have adequate and reliable electricity for electric buses. One possible way forward is to rely on the prosumer and the TPA regime under the Energy Industry Act B.E. 2550 (2007). Under this regulatory framework, the energy resilience of a charging station operator can be achieved by purchasing electricity from prosumers in Bangkok through MEA-owned electricity networks. Moreover, electricity generated from renewable resources can be purchased on a non-firm basis. On this basis, no availability payment will be passed on to electricity users.

PART IV

MANAGING DISRUPTION
AND RESILIENCE
AT CONSUMPTION LEVEL

Access to Energy, Demand Response, Equity

20

Building Resilience from the Ground Up

Local Supply and Demand Management with Renewables, Prosumers, Energy Efficiency, Critical Minerals, and the Circular Economy

Barry Barton

I. Introduction

Can we reduce the extent to which we are hurt by disruptions if we source our energy and materials from nearer at hand, and become able to get by with less of them? An examination of this question allows us to explore resilience on the demand side of the energy and natural resources equation rather than the supply side, and to see what the users and buyers of energy and mineral resources can do to manage their use and demand, and source it locally, in order to reduce their vulnerability to disruption. Consumers and consumer countries can make active choices in the origins of what they use, and how much they need; and legal consequences can flow from those choices. Interestingly, in broad terms the same questions can be asked for both energy and mineral resources. We therefore turn first to the local production of energy as a form of resilience, followed by energy efficiency as another, and then to minerals, first to policy for the sourcing of minerals and materials, and then to recycling and the circular economy.

The chapter is a forward-looking or even speculative inquiry, but it attempts to bring together strands of thinking and research that have long been part of the literature and are the subject of considerable law and policy effort. The challenges that we face—climate change, the pandemic, and the continuing imperative of addressing poverty—call on us to look at everything afresh. Some of the disruptions that test our resilience have long been with us— storms, earthquakes, civil unrest, international coercion, war—but new weather risks are posed by climate change, and cybercrime is a new kind of disruption.[1] In addition, many of our social and economic systems have become more complex and globalized than ever.

II. Energy Resilience in Closer Supply and Efficiency

A. Energy security traditionally

What we must now think of in terms of resilience in the energy sector has sometimes been thought of as energy security. The author and some of the other contributors to this volume,

---

[1] Benjamin Monarch, 'Black Start: the Risk of Grid Failure from a Cyber Attack and the Policies Needed to Prepare for it' (2020) 38 Journal of Energy and Natural Resources Law (hereafter JERL) 131.

Barry Barton, *Building Resilience from the Ground Up* In: *Resilience in Energy, Infrastructure, and Natural Resources Law.*
Edited by: Catherine Banet, Hanri Mostert, LeRoy Paddock, Milton Fernando Montoya, and Íñigo del Guayo, Oxford University Press.

in a predecessor study, defined energy security as 'a condition in which a nation and all, or most, of its citizens and businesses have access to sufficient energy resources at reasonable prices for the foreseeable future free from serious risk of major disruption of service.'[2] The International Energy Agency (IEA) defines it as 'the uninterrupted availability of energy sources at an affordable price'[3] and notes that it has both long-term and short-term aspects.

For crude oil, security and resilience has long been a matter of geopolitical importance. The supply crisis of 1973–1974 led to the Agreement on an International Energy Program of 1974 which commits signatory countries to hold emergency oil stocks equivalent to at least 90 days' net oil imports (60 days until 1976).[4] Oil continues to be a special concern as the energy backbone of the modern economy although over time oil exporters have not been able to use oil as a weapon in international affairs.[5] Natural gas is more broadly distributed that oil, but pipelines as the main means of transporting it expose it to threats whether from natural hazards or political developments. Coal is even more diversified in its supply. However the energy transition now under way opens up a set of resilience challenges that are different from those that have affected oil and other fossil fuels for many years.

B. The energy transition and the localization of supply

The enormous transition under way in energy is largely driven by climate change, but also by the emergence of new energy technologies at a scale and at a low enough cost that they appear likely to displace much use of oil and gas and coal. The transition has the potential to increase local supply, and to reduce the length, complexity, and vulnerability of energy supply chains. In turn we consider the roles of renewables, electrification, and distributed generation.

1. Renewables
Renewable energy is one of the fundamentals of the energy transition and has been growing rapidly in significance. Under its Stated Policies Scenario, which envisages less change than its other scenarios, the IEA sees that renewable sources of electricity will rise two-thirds between 2020 and 2030, and that by 2025 renewables will overtake coal as the primary means of producing electricity.[6] Hydroelectricity continues to be the largest renewable source of electricity, but wind and especially solar photovoltaic generation is growing massively and no longer needs direct financial support to be commercially viable. Renewable fuels outside the electricity sector (solid biomass, liquid biofuels, and biogases) continue to grow, but rely on policy support.[7]

---

[2] B. Barton, C. Redgwell, A. Rønne, and D. Zillman (eds), *Energy Security: Managing Risk in a Dynamic Legal and Regulatory Environment* (Oxford University Press 2004), editors' Introduction.

[3] International Energy Agency (hereafter IEA), 'Energy Security', <https://www.iea.org/topics/energy-secur ity> accessed 17 June 2021.

[4] Agreement on an International Energy Program (with annex) (adopted 18 November 1974, entered into force 19 January 1976) 1040 UNTS 272; R Scott, *The* (5 vols), https://www.iea.org/about/history accessed 10 December 2021; Mason Willrich and Melvin A. Conant, 'The International Energy Agency: An Interpretation and Assessment' (1977) 71 Amer J of International Law 199. The Agreement is related to the IEA but was established separately from the IEA's origins in the OECD.

[5] IEA, *World Energy Outlook* (2020) 258; OPEC plus Russia produces less than half of the world's oil.

[6] IEA, *World Energy Outlook* (2020) 214, 222.

[7] IEA, *World Energy Outlook* (2020) 285.

The increasing role of renewable energy, especially in electricity generation, has the potential to increase the resilience of energy systems, although the picture has a good deal of variation in it and we should be cautious of going too far with generalizations. Certainly, hydro and geothermal power generation must be located where the resource is to be found and may therefore require long transmission lines to bring the power to cities and other load centres. Wind farms and solar installations can be located closer to load centres, although ideal sites may be further away, and for high rates of penetration the quality of the transmission network is an important factor.[8] So too is the overall configuration of the system in its ability to handle the variable qualities of wind and solar. Solid biomass (such as wood chips or biogas) and methane from waste are invariably sourced locally.

But even taking all due care about the contribution that renewables can make to resilience, we must bear in mind that the comparison is with fossil fuels, oil and gas and coal. Whether renewable energy sources are used directly or through the medium of electricity or hydrogen, they are less likely to depend on international trade to be brought to consumers. In addition, wind, sunlight, and water (usually) are free so renewables are not subject to fuel prices that may be commercially unpredictable or politically volatile. However the question is not well explored, and empirical research would be desirable to more fully understand the resilience benefits of renewable energy that are likely to accompany their value in reducing greenhouse gas emissions.

2. Electrification

Electricity is gaining on other means of providing energy to consumers,[9] and it offers the prospect of greater resilience in the form of more localized production. It is a kind of fuel switching and occurs for example where a natural gas furnace is replaced with a heat pump, or where an internal combustion engine is replaced with an electric vehicle. Electrification is central to emissions reduction efforts, even though it is not viable for some energy uses; shipping, aviation, heavy-duty trucking, cement making, and steel making will need low-carbon fuels or carbon capture systems for some time to come.[10] Electrification is already a global trend, especially in light industry and household consumption, and indeed the growth of electricity demand in recent years is consistently running at around twice the pace of overall energy demand growth.[11] The IEA expects that the trend will continue, and that under its Sustainable Development Scenario, where heat pumps, electric vehicles, and electrolytic hydrogen take off, electricity would move even more dramatically to the centre of the energy stage.[12]

Electrification can tend to produce higher levels of local supply of energy. One should not overstate the possibility, recognizing that the circumstances of different countries and regions will produce very different results. But on a global scale electricity is less traded

---

[8] IEA, *Net Zero by 2050: A Roadmap for the Global Energy Sector* (2021) 180 (hereafter IEA, *Net Zero*).

[9] The global source share of energy total final consumption held by electricity was 9.4 per cent in 1973, 19.3 per cent in 2018: IEA, *Key World Energy Statistics 2020*, 34.

[10] IEA, *World Energy Outlook* (2020) 159; IEA, *Net Zero* (n 8) 14.

[11] IEA, *World Energy Outlook* (2020) 36, 216.

[12] In the Stated Policies Scenario electricity demand growth globally outpaces all other fuels and meets 21 per cent of global final energy consumption by 2030 and 24 per cent by 2040. The Sustainable Development Scenario sees electricity's share reaching 24 per cent by 2030 and 31 per cent by 2040. IEA, *World Energy Outlook* (2020) 213, 216, and 221–226.

internationally than oil, natural gas, or coal.[13] Much oil is traded in elaborate international supply chains. Natural gas may be supplied from domestic sources, but if it is in international trade it depends on either pipeline systems and a complex web of commercial and political relationships, or (for liquefied natural gas) elaborate maritime supply chains. Compared with them, electricity supply chains—although complex in their own way—are less vulnerable to the far-off disasters that may affect oil and gas fields, refineries, ports, and shipping, and less vulnerable to global political and security problems. Globally, most electricity is produced domestically. Electric vehicles in the writer's home jurisdiction of New Zealand demonstrate the resilience benefits; buying one is a shift from petroleum as the fuel, mostly imported, to electricity, mostly produced from domestic renewable resources, and a shift to a fuel priced in local currency, reducing exchange risks.[14]

3. Distributed generation and prosumers

Distributed generation is another element of the energy transition that increases resilience. It allows electricity to be generated closer to where it is required and allows the system to be managed locally.[15] A more decentralized system with shorter supply chains has more ability to ride out disruptions such as natural disasters or cyber attacks. Improvements in transmission and hardware are accompanied by digitalization so as to create a 'smart grid'.[16] In another chapter in this book Louis de Fontanelle points to the benefits of this decentralization in energy citizenship and as a guard against global risks, and discusses its implications for energy industry structure.

Distributed generation has taken different forms. Some of the first departures from highly centralized systems were sparked in the United States by the Public Utility Regulatory Policies Act 1978 which gave priority to 'qualifying facilities' that had to be either solar, wind, or co-generation, and which obliged the conventional utility companies to buy their output.[17] Co-generation often led to significant improvements in energy efficiency, such as where a heat plant installed a gas turbine to generate electricity before using the hot gases to heat its boilers. Alternatively distributed generation can simply be small generation units that allow utilities or users to manage outages or peak demand periods. Regulatory reform has generally been necessary to enable such decentralization to occur.

The most spectacular recent form of distributed generation are the rooftop solar photovoltaic arrays that allow consumers even at the household scale to generate some or all of their electricity needs. A household can become both a producer and consumer of electricity, a 'prosumer'.[18] When solar arrays or other power sources are connected to storage batteries, electric vehicles, and smart appliances, then a household, company, or institution can achieve a high level of autonomy in meeting its energy needs. The user will often want to retain the advantages of a connection to the electricity distribution network, and at that point

---

[13] Globally, the percentage of energy sources produced that are imported by one country from another are: crude oil 48 per cent, natural gas 24 per cent, coal 17 per cent, electricity 14 per cent: IEA, *Key World Energy Statistics 2020*, 13–33.

[14] B. Barton and P. Schütte, *Electric Vehicle Policy: New Zealand in a Comparative Context* (Research Report, Centre for Environmental, Resources and Energy Law) 2015.

[15] Frederick R. Fucci, 'Distributed Generation' in M. Gerrard (ed), *The Law of Clean Energy* (ABA Publishing 2011) (hereafter Fucci).

[16] IEA, 'Smart Grids Tracking Report' (2020)< https://www.iea.org/reports/smart-grids>accessed 17 June 2021.

[17] Fucci (n 15).

[18] Yael Parag and Benjamin Sovacool, 'Electricity Market Design for the Prosumer Era' (2016) 1 Nature Energy 1; Daniela Aguilar Abaunza, 'Getting Ready for the Future' [2018] NZLJ 292.

the matter becomes considerably more complex, in law and regulation, in the relationship of the user with the distribution operator, retailers, and the electricity market generally. The distribution network and transmission network are not obsolete but they change their roles significantly. For all that change and complexity, the prosumer dimension of the energy transition offers substantial increases in energy system resilience.

C. Energy efficiency

The demand side of energy policy is at least as important as the supply side, in thinking about energy resilience as much as anything else. Demand-side management (demand flexibility or demand response) is deployed more and more in electricity systems to reduce load and deal with fluctuations such as variable renewable energy supply. It mainly addresses short-term peaks in demand, but it can also provide a degree of short-term resilience when a disaster strikes, especially if it can be provided locally.[19] However one probably needs to turn to energy efficiency for long-term resilience.

Energy efficiency is the level of energy consumption to provide a given service; how many kilowatt-hours to light up a building, or how many litres of fuel to drive a vehicle 100 kilometres.[20] Energy efficiency has long been known to offer great economic benefits, advantages in moderating the need to build more energy infrastructure, and progress in alleviating energy poverty by increasing the benefits that a customer receives such as in the form of a warm house to live in. It is one of the key elements of any climate change strategy. A common general indicator of energy efficiency is energy intensity, a country's total energy supply in relation to its gross domestic product, and globally energy intensity has decreased by 36 per cent between 1990 and 2018; in China the reduction was 70 per cent.[21] However these energy efficiency gains have slowed down since 2015, which is troubling; the IEA's Sustainable Development Scenario relies on efficiency to deliver more than 40 per cent of the reduction of energy-related greenhouse gas emissions over the next 20 years.[22]

Energy efficiency can lead directly to resilience. It reduces the degree of dependence on fuels or energy sources to deliver the services required, and in particular it can reduce the reliance of a country or a company on imports of oil, gas, and coal. Efficiency gains can have enormous effects. In IEA and other major economies, efficiency gains since 2000 avoided the need for over 11 exajoules (EJ) of fossil fuel imports in 2017, which would have been 20 per cent more.[23] Energy efficiency can often produce these gains in a cost-negative manner in that the improvements often pay for themselves even before the benefits in energy security and risk reduction are taken into account. Energy efficiency also reduces the likelihood of supply interruptions: 'the only energy source that cannot be interrupted is the energy that is not used.'[24] Efficiency measures can also play a role after a disaster, along with

---

[19] IEA, 'Demand Response' (Tracking Report, June 2020) <https://www.iea.org/reports/demand-response> accessed 17 June 2021. The chapter by Louis de Fontanelle in this book gives detailed consideration to demand-side flexibility in the European Union.
[20] IEA, *Spreading the Net: the Multiple Benefits of Energy Efficiency Improvements* (Insights Series 2012) 9.
[21] IEA, *Energy Efficiency 2020* (2020); IEA, *Energy Efficiency Indicators Highlights 2020* (2020) 2.
[22] IEA, *Energy Efficiency 2020* (2020) 10; IEA, *Net Zero* (n 8) 14.
[23] IEA, 'Multiple Benefits of Energy Efficiency' (2019) online report <https://www.iea.org/reports/multiple-benefits-of-energy-efficiency> accessed 17 June 2021 (hereafter IEA, Multiple Benefits).
[24] IEA, Multiple Benefits (n 23).

emergency conservation actions, as was demonstrated in the response to the Great East Japan Earthquake in 2011.

Curiously, energy efficiency is often downplayed as a policy option. For example, American public utility regulation, as Inara Scott shows, imposes restrictions on energy efficiency measures, such as a cost-effectiveness test, that it does not impose on renewable energy measures.[25] An undue preoccupation with renewables or new technology can produce a policy discussion, even among progressive voices, that pushes for increases in the renewables proportion of energy supply without stopping to think of what total supply is actually needed and how we might do something to modify it.[26] Certainly, energy efficiency is a debated concept,[27] especially because it involves analysis from different disciplinary perspectives and at different scales.[28] What is clear is that more than in most fields of energy policy it concerns human behaviour, and that makes for a complexity that requires transdisciplinary research efforts to understand.[29] Also clear is the role that legal analysis must play in formulating policy that seeks to shift human behaviour.[30] Resilience and security stand out as strong reasons for legal and policy action to accelerate energy efficiency.

III. Minerals

Having considered the localization of supply and efficient use as contributors to resilience in the context of energy, we can proceed to consider the comparable contributions in relation to mineral resources. The parallels are striking.

Over the last 50 years, the countries that produce the most minerals and the countries that consume the most of them have drifted into separate groupings. The historical industrialization of Europe and North America was based largely on mineral raw materials produced locally, but after decades of globalization the domestic mining industries of many advanced economies have shrunk back in the face of cheaper mineral imports from distant countries. Industrialization has taken place in countries with limited domestic resources, especially in Asia, and mineral production has grown most in regions without the same levels of industrial activity; Australasia, Latin America, Africa, and Asia excluding Japan and China. In 1960 the world's major consumer countries supplied 82 per cent of their own iron ore, 78 per cent of their nickel, and 52 per cent of their copper; by 2010 the proportions had fallen to 35 per cent, 38 per cent, and 27 per cent; about half of what it had been.[31] The

---

[25] Inara Scott, '"Dancing Backwards in High Heels": Examining and Addressing the Disparate Regulatory Treatment of Energy Efficiency and Renewable Resources' (2013) 43 Environmental Law 255.

[26] Barry Barton, 'The Denominator Problem: Energy Demand in a Sustainable Energy Policy' (2013) 9 Policy Quarterly 3.

[27] Horace Herring, 'Energy Efficiency – A Critical View' (2006) 31 Energy 10 voices the view that energy efficiency gains are usually swallowed up by a rebound effect where demand increases. Elizabeth Shove, 'What is Wrong with Energy Efficiency?' (2018) 46 Building Research & Information 779 questions the relationship with energy sufficiency.

[28] Tian Goh and B.W. Ang, 'Four Reasons Why There is so Much Confusion about Energy Efficiency' (2020) 146 Energy Policy 111832.

[29] Janet Stephenson et al, 'Energy Cultures: a Framework for Understanding Energy Behaviours' (2010) 38 Energy Policy 6120; Felix Creutzig et al, 'Towards Demand-Side Solutions for Mitigating Climate Change' (2018) 8 Nature Climate Change 260. The IEA emphasizes the role of behaviour changes in its Sustainable Development and Net Zero Emissions 2050 Scenarios: IEA, World Energy Outlook (2020) 142.

[30] M. Eusterfeldhaus and B. Barton, 'Energy Efficiency: A Comparative Analysis of the New Zealand Legal Framework' (2011) 29 JERL 431.

[31] David Humphreys, The Remaking of the Mining Industry (Palgrave Macmillan 2015) 175.

consequence is that a greater proportion of mineral inputs are in international trade, and the supply chains are longer and more complex. Some minerals are produced in countries that struggle with poverty, corruption, and weak governments; some are beset by periodic bouts of resource nationalism—all of which are threats to supply. In addition, some mineral supplies are very concentrated, as the example of rare earth elements below will show; and the non-fuel minerals are very diverse and some of them do not have easy substitutes. As a result there are more reasons to be concerned about the disruption of mineral supplies than for many other commodities. But it is only recently that these concerns have drawn the attention of policymakers.

A. Minerals required for electrification

One of the main reasons why policymakers have recently begun to examine the resilience of mineral supplies is the enormous change under way in how we produce and use energy, driven by climate change concerns but also driven by changing technology costs. The trend towards renewable energy and electrification changes the mix of metals and other minerals required to manufacture equipment and products of all kinds, as the IEA explains.[32]

> Copper, lithium, cobalt and platinum are at the core of the energy transition: copper is needed for transmission and distribution lines; lithium and cobalt for the currently prevailing lithium-ion battery designs; and platinum in fuel cells. The material with the most fragile supply chain is cobalt, which has highly geographically concentrated mining and processing facilities. The supply chain risks were made clear by a very sharp price hike in 2018, which provided a strong incentive for battery producers to reduce the cobalt content of battery chemistries: several chemistries are now being developed that do not require cobalt, although their timescales are uncertain. Lithium currently has a more stable supply chain, but it is likely to keep its status as a critical material because its physical properties make it nearly non-substitutable in the production of high energy density batteries.

The technologies of the low-carbon future are often more material-intensive than traditional fossil-fuel-based systems, because of the extra effort required to use energy sources that are less energy-dense than oil, gas, and coal. Solar power requires more copper than does thermal power, and electric vehicles require three times as much as conventional vehicles.[33] Indeed electric vehicles require a more exotic mix of materials than do internal combustion vehicles, which mainly need steel. Non-energy products often have similar needs for diverse materials; computers and information technology devices are examples.

A new study by the IEA emphasizes that the rising importance of minerals in decarbonization requires energy policymakers to expand their horizons: 'Concerns about price volatility and security of supply do not disappear in an electrified, renewables-rich energy system.'[34] The study suggests that by 2040 total mineral demand from clean energy

---

[32] IEA, *Energy Technology Perspectives 2020*, 98; also World Bank, *The Growing Role of Minerals and Metals for a Low Carbon Future* (2017).

[33] Takuma Watari et al, 'Analysis of Potential for Critical Metal Resource Constraints in the International Energy Agency's Long-Term Low-Carbon Energy Scenarios' (2018) 8 Minerals 156 (hereafter Watari).

[34] IEA, *The Role of Critical Minerals in Clean Energy Transitions* (2021) 5, 50 (hereafter IEA, *Critical Minerals*). Also see Florencia Heredia, Agostina L. Martinez, and Valentina Surraco Urtubey, 'The Importance of Lithium

technologies (excluding steel and aluminium) double in the Stated Policies Scenario and quadruple in the Sustainable Development Scenario; and that lithium sees the fastest growth rate, with demand growing by over 40 times in the latter Scenario. It recommends a number of actions to improve the resilience, reliability, and diversity of mineral supply chains.

B. Critical minerals strategies

An awareness that the flow of important materials could be vulnerable has come to the attention of many policymakers. The European Union has been developing its materials resilience policy since 2008,[35] looking ahead to the needs of new electric technology and the underlying fact that it is between 75 per cent and 100 per cent reliant on imports for most metals. It listed its critical raw materials using a methodology that identified the factors of economic importance and supply risk. The list is a factual tool to support policy, for example in trade negotiations and research funding. The 2020 version deleted helium and added bauxite, lithium, titanium and strontium, and proposed a four-point action plan.[36] The first point was to develop resilient value chains for raw materials for EU industrial ecosystems, adjusting the lending policies of the European Investment Bank and mobilizing support for compliant exploration, mining, and processing projects for critical raw materials. The second was to reduce dependency through the circular use of resources, under the Action Plan that will be discussed below. The third was to strengthen sourcing from within the EU, developing territorial just transition plans and examining the obstacles that make it difficult to bring new mines into operation; but without, one notices, actually declaring a policy of encouraging more mines. The fourth is diversified sourcing from third countries, removing distortions in international trade and building partnerships with developed mining countries like Canada and Australia, integrating the Western Balkans and other near regions into EU supply chains, and developing relations with key countries in Africa and Latin America.

As a Communication this does not have the legal status in the EU of a directive, regulation, decision, or even a policy, but it may have legal effect as a formal statement of aspirations that decision-makers can properly take into account. For instance a company with a rare earth elements mining project at Norra Kärr in Sweden seized on the Commission's plan as a reason why the project should go ahead. The company's opponents in the district worry that the plan could cause authorities to wave the project through despite legal doubts: 'Legally, it should not have an impact, but I am afraid it will, because the judges and the people at the Mining Inspectorate are only people, so if they get those kinds of signals from the EU, of course that might influence them.'[37] The proper weight to give to such signals would be an issue in many legal systems.

for Achieving a Low-Carbon Future: Overview of the Lithium Extraction in the "Lithium Triangle" ' (2020) 38 JERL 213.

[35] European Commission, 'Raw Materials Initiative – Meeting our Critical Needs for Growth and Jobs in Europe' Communication COM (2008) 699 final, 4 November 2008.
[36] European Commission, 'Critical Raw Materials Resilience: Charting a Path towards Greater Security and Sustainability' Communication COM(2020) 474 final, 3 September 2020.
[37] Charlie Duxbury, 'Sweden's Ground Zero for the EU's Strategic Materials Plan' *Politico* (20 November 2020) quoting Högberg Björck, lawyer for NGOs and local residents.

In the United States, concern about the supply of critical minerals has often been framed as a matter of national security and protection against disruption by a foreign adversary. An executive order in 2017 declared a policy of reducing this vulnerability.[38] A second order in 2020 declared a national emergency to deal with the threat posed by the nation's undue reliance on critical minerals from foreign adversaries, and to enhance its domestic mining and processing capacity.[39] Relevant agencies were to prioritize the expansion of the domestic supply chain for minerals, and to accelerate the issuance of permits and the completion of projects for that purpose—all as appropriate and consistent with applicable law. Through the Development Finance Corporation the Government took a US$25 million stake in a battery metals miner with a nickel–cobalt project in Brazil to reduce the country's reliance on China.[40] Another order by the incoming Biden administration called for a wider evaluation of supply chain resilience in the face of pandemics, cyber attacks, climate shocks, terrorist attacks, and geopolitical and economic competition, with a special focus on semiconductor manufacturing, advanced packaging, high-capacity batteries, rare earth elements, and pharmaceuticals.[41] In 2021 the US Senate passed a bill authorizing a grant program to finance pilot projects for the domestic development of critical minerals and called for work by the US Trade Representative on rare earth minerals.[42]

Policymakers in other countries have been re-examining their manufacturing needs in relation to their mineral inheritance.[43] Australia launched a Critical Minerals Strategy in 2019,[44] giving critical minerals extra emphasis in exploration funding, government research, and geological spending, led by a Critical Minerals Facilitation Office. In early 2021 it launched a Resources Technology and Critical Minerals Processing roadmap.[45] Canada has a list of critical minerals[46] and emphasizes its mutual interest with the United States in improving critical mineral security, and its role as a dependable supplier of minerals. A joint action plan has been announced.[47] However the Canadian Minerals and Metals Plan of 2019 said little about supply resilience or critical minerals,[48] and an update did not address them either.[49]

For their part, mining companies ask how should they position themselves to survive these struggles between states, and how to avoid being sacrificed on the altar of national

[38] Executive Order 13817, *A Federal Strategy to Ensure Secure and Reliable Supplies of Critical Minerals*, 20 December 2017, 82 Federal Register 60835; Department of the Interior, *Final List of Critical Minerals 2018*, 83 Federal Register 23296.

[39] Executive Order 13953, *Addressing the Threat to the Domestic Supply Chain from Reliance on Critical Minerals from Foreign Adversaries*, 30 September 2020, 85 Federal Register 62539.

[40] Cecilia Jamasmie, 'U.S. Grabs Stake in Battery Metals Miner to Fight Chinese Control' *The Northern Miner* (Toronto October 2020) 12–25, 16.

[41] Executive Order 14017, *America's Supply Chains*, 24 February 2021, 86 Federal Register 11849.

[42] United States Innovation and Competition Act of 2021, 117th Congress 1st Session S. 1260.

[43] Rajesh Chadha, *Skewed Critical Minerals Global Supply Chains post-COVID-19: Reforms for Making India Self-Reliant* (Brookings India, discussion note, 2020).

[44] Government of Australia, 'Australia's Critical Minerals Strategy' (2019).

[45] Government of Australia, 'Using our Resources Strengths to Grow Manufacturing' (media release, Scott Morrison, Prime Minister, 4 March 2021).

[46] Natural Resources Canada, 'Canada Announces Critical Minerals List' (news release, 11 March 2021).

[47] Natural Resources Canada, 'Canada and U.S. Finalize Joint Action Plan on Critical Minerals Collaboration' (news release, 9 January 2020). It is not clear whether the Plan exists as a document separately from the press release.

[48] Government of Canada, 'Canadian Minerals and Metals Plan' (2019).

[49] Government of Canada, 'Canadian Minerals and Metals Plan: Update to Action Plan 2020.'

interest.[50] For example a miner producing a critical material may find itself restricted in the sale of its product and forbidden from selling its output overseas. Such restrictions could put companies in a legally difficult situation where long-term offtake or streaming agreements are in place as part of a mine's financing.[51]

C. Rare earth elements and cobalt

The story of rare earth elements over the last 15 years is instructive although we have to be careful generalizing from it. This group of elements or materials is not as rare as its name might suggest, but viable deposits are few, and new supply is slow to appear.[52] Their unique chemical properties make them valuable even in trace quantities in a number of applications, but it is in electronics, permanent magnets, and batteries that they are essential for modern technology and in particular advanced wind turbines and electric vehicles. Demand for them began to surge in the mid-2000s. China has a near-monopoly on rare earth production and processing, and in 2008 it began to consolidate the industry, cracking down on informal mines, and imposing environmental controls, export taxes, production quotas, and export quotas.[53] Exports declined and international prices rose dramatically. Although controls were justified to clean up the industry, the restrictions were also used to exert diplomatic pressure on Japan. The United States was concerned about the supply of materials for its defence industry and other manufacturing. Both countries took counter-measures to diversify supply, open or reopen rare earth mines, and fund mineral exploration. They and other countries initiated dispute proceedings at the World Trade Organization (WTO), arguing that China's actions on rare earths (and tungsten and molybdenum) contravened provisions of the General Agreement on Tariffs and Trade that prohibited restrictions on exports, and contravened the terms on which China had acceded to the WTO. The WTO panel and the Appellate Body ruled in favour of the claimants, and in 2014 the Chinese Government abolished the export quotas and replaced the export tax with a set of ad valorem royalties.[54] The threat to international security did not last long.

Jeffrey Wilson argues convincingly that there were three reasons why the Chinese Government was not able to wield rare earths as a strategic weapon. First, demand was very sensitive to price movements; manufacturers in importer countries proved to be good at reducing the amounts of rare earth minerals they needed. Secondly, the Chinese Government did not have the institutional capacity to enforce its export controls and prevent the massive smuggling that took place to avoid them. Thirdly, its monopoly on current production

---

[50] For example, Fasken Martineau DuMoulin, 'Critical Minerals in the COVID-19 Era: Supply Chain and Survival' (webinar 1 March 2021) <https://www.fasken.com/en/faskeninstitute/2021/03/pdac-critical-minerals> accessed 12 March 2021.

[51] Barry Barton, *Canadian Law of Mining* (2nd edn, LexisNexis 2019) 904 (hereafter Barton, *Canadian Mining*).

[52] Nimila Dushyantha et al, 'The Story of Rare Earth Elements (REEs): Occurrences, Global Distribution, Genesis, Geology, Mineralogy and Global Production' (2020) 122 Ore Geology Reviews 103521 (hereafter Dushyantha).

[53] Jeffrey Wilson, 'Whatever Happened to the Rare Earths Weapon? Critical Materials and International Security in Asia' (2018) 14 Asian Security 358 (hereafter Wilson); Nabeel Mancheri, 'World Trade in Rare Earths, Chinese Export Restrictions, and Implications' (2016) 46 Resources Policy 262.

[54] World Trade Organization, *China – Measures Related to the Exportation of Rare Earths, Tungsten, and Molybdenum*, WT/DS431/AB/R, WT/DS432/AB/R, WT/DS433/AB/R, 7 August 2014 (Reports of the Appellate Body AB-2014-3, AB-2014-5, AB-2014-6).

did not translate into control of future supply because the mining industry could react to high prices by finding new mines, reopening old mines, and reopening old processing facilities. The conditions necessary to use rare earths as an instrument of coercion were absent, and Wilson goes on to suggest that no other mineral, even oil, is likely to be usable in that way either.[55] Even cobalt, which attracts advocacy similar to rare earth elements, might be difficult, despite the concentration of more than half of production and reserves in the Democratic Republic of Congo and of more than half the refining capacity in China.[56]

D. The role for critical minerals policies

What role do we see, then, for critical minerals policies and other efforts to increase the resilience of supply chains? If international rivals cannot use rare earths and other minerals as coercive weapons, and if the market will provide, what need is there for resilience initiatives from the government? Certainly there are difficulties with these initiatives. Policymakers need to be careful with the abundant opportunities the issue presents for industries to play on national security fears and lobby for subsidies, import protection, easier mineral exploration access to public lands, funding for research, and tax breaks for domestic mineral exploration and production.[57] As for the market, it is certainly true that the mining industry is versatile in reacting to price signals; it is engaged in a constant process of evaluation and re-evaluation of mineralizations and assets. Mineral explorationists may be searching new ground in order to find a mine, or, more typically, they are learning more about a mineral occurrence that is already known but only partly understood. Often they are trying to look at it in a new way, such as with a new geological theory, to unlock possibilities that others have not seen. Even the operators of existing mines can re-evaluate their geology and milling operations in order to recover mineral values that had not been considered previously. Experts in extractive metallurgy may find opportunities to extract newly-valuable materials from old tailings deposits. Policymaking is also complicated by the fact that mineral resources are imperfectly known; it is rather difficult for a government to strategize about a mineral resource when it does not know what quantities of it might be found within its jurisdiction.

For all that these difficulties exist, we can identify several factors that may make critical minerals strategies worthwhile. War, internal conflict, cybercrime, and catastrophic storms can cut supply chains as much as strategic competition; we should not let the rare earths example dominate our thinking about resilience. There will be other pinch points in supply lines for the many materials that are necessary for the modern economy. In addition, supply and demand sometimes take years or decades to adjust, because the mineral exploration and development process is a long one.[58] New supply may emerge years after it is called for, so prices of mineral commodities are notoriously cyclical, and the boom-and-bust cycles

[55] Wilson (n 53) 370 points out that OPEC's efforts to use oil as a diplomatic weapon have not been effective. Only network-reliant resources, such as natural gas supplies from Russia to Europe, may provide leverage, at least in the short term.
[56] IEA, *World Energy Outlook* (2018) 59; also IEA, *Critical Minerals* (n 34) 32, 90.
[57] For examples, see Congressional Research Service (US), 'An Overview of Rare Earth Elements and Related Issues for Congress' (R46618, B Tracy, 24 November 2020).
[58] Some of these characteristics are described in Barton, *Canadian Mining* (n 51) 4, 797.

can hurt manufacturers. Further, there are growing non-financial reasons for mineral-importing countries and mineral-using companies to pay attention to the sources of their supplies, and be aware of the hazards of corruption, human rights abuses, environmental damage, and carbon footprint that may attend distant mineral operations.[59] Arguably, then, there are substantial benefits in resilience to be had from strategic planning for minerals and raw material supplies. Countries are not helpless in the face of international market forces; they can plan for different contingencies and decide what activities they want to support, within and beyond their borders, in order to strengthen and diversify their lines of supply. Increased domestic mineral production may encounter resistance in developed countries where mining has become unfamiliar, even though opponents face an ethical problem if in effect they argue that mineral needs should be met from mining in distant developing countries.

E. Demand side-measures: the circular economy

Protecting the sources of supply of materials, and diversifying them, is one way of building resilience, but another is managing demand; the amount of materials that we need. Substitution of one material for another in the design of a product is a form of demand management that we noted in the context of rare earth elements, and so is design that can simply reduce the amount of a material that is required to produce the finished product.

A more general approach to these matters is the concept of a circular economy that is an alternative to the traditional extract-produce-use-dispose model of materials flows in the economy. In a circular economy, materials, components, and products are kept at their highest value for as long as possible, by using cyclical materials flows, renewable energy sources, and cascading energy flows.[60] True circularity goes beyond recycling and waste management and involves all elements of the value chain, to include the re-use of materials, re-manufacturing, and the design of products so that they can be disassembled, repaired, and re-purposed. It seeks 'cradle-to-cradle' flows of materials, rather than 'cradle-to-grave' flows that produce waste. It builds on well-established insights into our relationship with the natural world such as the frontier economy of taking and discarding resources and the need to change to thinking of a 'spaceship' economy where humanity takes care of its life-supporting systems.[61] There are now many approaches to the concept and debate about its relationship with sustainable development; it can be seen as an implementation of Sustainable Development Goal 12, ensuring sustainable consumption and production patterns.[62] It has

---

[59] Steven Van Bockstael, 'The Emergence of Conflict-free, Ethical and Fair Trade Mineral Supply Chain Certification Systems: A Brief Introduction' (2018) 5 The Extractive Industries and Society 52.

[60] Jouni Korhonen, Antero Honkasalo, and Jyri Seppälä, 'Circular Economy: the Concept and its Limitations' (2018) 143 Ecological Economics 37.

[61] K.E. Boulding, 'The Economics of the Coming Spaceship Earth' in H Jarrett (ed), *Environmental Quality in a Growing Economy* (Resources for the Future, 1966).

[62] Julian Kirchherr, Denise Reike, and Marko Hekkert, 'Conceptualizing the Circular Economy: an Analysis of 114 Definitions' (2017) 127 Resources, Conservation & Recycling 221; Neal Millar, Eoin McLaughlin, and Tobias Börger, 'The Circular Economy: Swings and Roundabouts?' (2019) 158 Ecological Economics 11.

attracted a great deal of interest and commitment from the business world and in environ-mental and economic policy.[63]

However, behavioural change to improve material handling, both in commerce and in households, is often difficult to bring about, and so is the establishment of new busi-nesses and industries that can be run profitably on circular economy principles. Technical change is necessary too; the small traces of diverse metals in electronic equipment are dif-ficult to separate economically, the recycling of rare earth elements from electric and elec-tronic waste is in its infancy, and technical innovation is necessary to better exploit mine tailings and other secondary sources.[64] One study suggests that primary metal demand for low carbon energy technology could be reduced by 20 per cent to 70 per cent by 2060 with recycling.[65]

What has this got to do with resilience? Circularity improves resilience by reducing de-pendency on fresh raw materials, and that is accompanied by a reduction in dependency on complex processing and transport systems, with their associated greenhouse gas emis-sions. Even a partial increase in circularity means that an industry or an economy is more able to find its inputs nearby, with less importing, less reliance on global transport chains, and fewer concerns about commercial and political instability. Circularity and recycling are a form of local provision. Thus the European Commission identifies the benefits of a more circular use of critical raw materials as ensuring security of supply, reduced energy use, and reduced water use; and there may also be less harm to the biosphere and less waste produced per tonne of material obtained.[66] The European Union has committed itself to the concept of the circular economy in ways that are significant for materials supply resili-ence. It has formulated a Circular Economy Action Plan as one of the key components of its industrial strategy and its European Green Deal strategy.[67] The Plan emphasizes that circu-larity is an integral part of the transition to a low-carbon economy.

Elements of the mining industry are looking ahead to a circular economy. An industry leader at a symposium in 2021 said that companies initially see the circular economy as 'anti-mining' but are increasingly building circular concepts into their strategic planning and modelling.[68] The CEO of Anglo American spoke of the strong rationale to engage with the circular economy; in the past the company saw itself as a mining company, in the pre-sent sees itself as a metals and mining company, and tomorrow may well characterize itself as a materials solutions company.

Materials circularity is not the whole answer to climate change or any other sustainability problem, any more than is energy efficiency; but both are hugely important parts of the so-lution and should be the subjects of substantial policy and law reform effort.

---

[63] World Economic Forum, *Towards the Circular Economy: Accelerating the Scale-up across Global Supply Chains* (2014); Ellen MacArthur Foundation, *Universal Circular Economy Policy Goals: Enabling the Transition to Scale* (2021).

[64] Dushyantha (n 52).

[65] Watari (n 33), 156.

[66] European Commission, *Report on Critical Raw Materials and the Circular Economy* (2018).

[67] European Commission, *A New Circular Economy Action Plan for a Cleaner and More Competitive Europe* (Communication COM (2020) 98 final). It comes after earlier policy work, in particular European Commission, *Closing the Loop – An EU Action Plan for the Circular Economy* (Communication and Action Plan COM(2015) 614). Also European Commission, *Critical Raw Materials Resilience: Charting a Path towards Greater Security and Sustainability* (COM(2020) 474 final) 9.

[68] 'The Circular Economy Set to Transform the Mining Industry, says Panel at the Global Mining Symposium' *The Northern Miner* (Toronto, 25 February 2021) quoting Andrew Cheatle and Mark Cutifani.

IV. Discussion

The two themes that we have explored, local provision (or more locally-controlled provision), and managing or reducing demand through prudent use, are broad ones, and to discern them we have had to pull some very different threads together. But it is striking how the two themes both appear in energy and in minerals; the two sectors have a good deal in common.

Local provision and management of demand clearly have significant contributions to make to improving resilience and reducing the effects of disruption. Local provision in energy takes the form of distributed energy supply, prosumer participation, renewables, and electrification; and in minerals, critical minerals policies seek to reduce dependence on distant sources especially when supply of a mineral is concentrated. Management of demand in energy takes the form of energy efficiency and demand response; and in minerals, the emerging concept of the circular economy. Consumers of energy and consumers of minerals, both on the demand side, can take a role in reducing and modifying their dependence on external sources of supply.

The opportunities for significant gains in resilience seem to be substantial. Suitable legal measures can enable nations, companies, and people to reduce their dependence on complex national or global networks and supply chains (even if they cannot discard them altogether), and thereby reduce their risks, increase their autonomy, and improve their ability to withstand unexpected shocks. Empirical analysis of the opportunities would be very desirable. Also calling for closer examination is the line between localism and insularity; we see resilience value in local supply, autonomy, shortened supply chains, and self-sufficiency, but we can distinguish that from xenophobia and protectionism. The benefits of resilience need to be weighed against those of international cooperation.[69] Certainly there is no call for an end to international cooperation, or trade; what is called for, rather, is for consumers (at the national, corporate, or individual level) to make active choices in deciding where to get their energy and resources, and how much they need.

It is striking that local provision and demand management can produce many benefits other than resilience. Energy efficiency, distributed generation, renewables, and circularity are well recognized as vital elements of a transition to address climate change, reduce poverty, and improve economic performance. They contribute to a just and effective transition, rather than being in tension with it, which is enormously important because resilience can never be an excuse for going light on sustainability or mitigation. The reason why they contribute rather than detract is that they are mainly on the demand side of the energy and minerals equation rather than the supply side. Because of their multiple benefits, policy and law reform processes must give them substantial attention and avoid a framing of resilience policy as a matter of simply strengthening supply.

The law reform agenda, as our final point, seems to be different for energy and minerals, notwithstanding the similarities we have discussed. Renewable energy, electrification, distributed energy, prosumers, and energy efficiency are already the subject of legal and regulatory action in many countries, but it seems desirable to add resilience to the list of objectives or purposes which regulators are to pursue in promoting them. As to minerals

[69] IEA, *Net Zero* (n 8) 187.

and materials, a foreseeable problem is the legal significance to be given to critical minerals strategies. At the present they are usually policy statements, not made in a specific legal framework, and without specified legal consequences. It will be a live question in many legal systems whether a strategy can or should be taken into account in making statutory decisions about mineral development, as in the Swedish case we noted in Section III.B. Similarly, should mining companies prepare for restrictions on international sales of their products because of resilience concerns? Will circular economy initiatives produce regulatory action in primary and secondary markets for raw materials? New measures localizing supply and managing demand seem very promising in order to promote resilience but are sure to create new legal questions.

21

Increasing the Resilience of the Energy System Through Consumers

Towards Decentralized, Interconnected, and Supportive Ecosystems

Louis de Fontenelle

I. Introduction

The COVID-19 pandemic crisis we are experiencing shows how our systems are interconnected and how vital cooperation is. The situation requires cross-cutting responses. Today, we face a health crisis, an economic, and social crisis, all in the context of the climate crisis. This complex equation needs to be solved with a new paradigm based on short- and long-term responses to rethinking the energy model.

In this perspective, the resilience of the energy system could be achieved through increased decentralization of energy systems in which the consumer would have a crucial role. In this particular context, united consumers within energy communities could become the essential cells of energy systems, producing, storing, and sharing energy at the local level.

What does a crisis look like for the energy sector? It could be a nuclear incident or accident, a conflict that threatens supply, or extreme weather events. The current situation is very illustrative. The pandemic has revealed multiple problems, for the agents themselves, affected by the disease, for consumption, which is being modified, and for investments, which are being redirected.[1] In other words, the entire system is affected. In its 'World Energy Outlook' report, published on 30 April 2020, the International Energy Agency estimates that with the COVID-19 pandemic, the global energy system is experiencing 'its biggest shock in more than seven decades', with a significant drop in consumption, particularly of fossil fuels—a 'great lockdown'[2]—but at the same time with a correlative decline in energy-related CO_2 emissions.

From a general point of view, our legal systems can deal with crisis. There are rules and mechanisms in national constitutions and laws, and during the current health crisis, States have proved their ability to put in place 'tailor-made' emergency legislation very quickly.[3] At

---

[1] Oxford Energy Forum, *COVID-19 and the Energy Transition* (Issue 123, 2020)

[2] Caroline Kuzemko et al, 'Covid-19 and the Politics of Sustainable Energy transitions' (2020) 68 Energy Research & Social Science.

[3] In France, for example, this was the case with Law No. 2020-290 of 23 March 2020 1 to deal with the Covid-19 pandemic. This was a new mechanism known as the 'state of public health emergency' (CSP, Art 3131-12), which can be decreed by the Council of Ministers, and which gives the Prime Minister responsibility for taking the administrative police measures required by the situation, in the event of 'a public health disaster endangering, by its nature and gravity, the health of the population'.

Louis de Fontenelle, *Increasing the Resilience of the Energy System Through Consumers* In: *Resilience in Energy, Infrastructure, and Natural Resources Law*. Edited by: Catherine Banet, Hanri Mostert, LeRoy Paddock, Milton Fernando Montoya, and Íñigo del Guayo, Oxford University Press. © Louis de Fontenelle 2022. DOI: 10.1093/oso/9780192864574.003.0021

the level of the European Union (EU), EU authorities have perceived the energy sector as strategic during the health crisis and administrations have reacted to ensure continuity of activity. Of course, there were some differences between States,[4] and public authorities have responded differently.[5] However, as a general rule, States have adapted their legal frame-work during the crisis to encourage operators to focus on the performance of their core tasks and provide otherwise for flexibility and solidarity by, for example, postponing tax or social payment deadlines during the health emergency period. From the very beginning of the crisis, some actors voluntarily activated their national crisis cell as a preventive measure.

Each operator defined the perimeter of its essential missions concerning its public service obligations and the economic and technical realities. Their business continuity plans (BCPs)[6] included the evaluation of consumption and production, the balancing of supply and demand, the correct routing of electricity and gas to consumption, the maintaining of the electricity and gas transmission and distribution networks (especially urgent work), and the proper functioning of IT tools and services enabling the company to adapt its operations (remote access, secure teleworking). In addition, economic actors have sometimes, on their own initiative, put in place solidarity measures.[7] To sum up, the various stakeholders acted to ensure the continuity of activity and solidarity.

However, this was only a quick and immediate response to a sudden problem. Today, the issue is the convergence of problems in a time of combined economic, environmental, health, and climate crises, which reveal a problematic recomposition of our environment, not least because of the long time frame in which these problems and their solutions arise. The reality of the global context is well known: climate disruptions are accelerating, in-equalities are increasing as needs grow (on a worldwide scale, a large part of the population is deprived of access to energy and therefore to what it offers in terms of health, transport, food, etc.).

In this context, the term 'crisis' seems inappropriate. Even defining the events we are experiencing as a 'crisis' is questionable, given their long-term nature. However, if we agree that a crisis is a sudden and intense event of limited duration that can lead to harmful consequences, we will agree that what we are experiencing is more akin to a crisis than a prob-lematic recomposition of our social-economic climate environment. This also explains why we must adapt our tools to this overall recomposition. We cannot stop rising water with a dam. We are learning to live on water, which requires adaptation to this broad change and choices, including shared values and policies.

In this context, the resilience of the energy system is crucial. Resilience is not a legal concept.[8] We find this notion in the physics of materials, where it is defined as 'the resistance of a material to impact'. This notion is also in common use, where it is understood to mean

---

[4] Sarah Wolff and Stella Ladi, 'European Union Responses to the Covid-19 Pandemic: Adaptability in Times of Permanent Emergency' (2020) 42(8) Journal of European Integration 1025–1040.

[5] EFELA, *How EFELA'S 13 countries coped with the coronavirus pandemic* (2020)

[6] In France, for example, these consisted of the public administrations: National Energy Ombudsman, the Energy Regulatory Commission, the National Agency for Radioactive Waste Management and Nuclear Safety, and private operators: Engie, RTE, Enedis, EDF, Téréga, GRTgaz, EpexSpot, Nordpool, local distribution companies, etc. (BCPs).

[7] For example, widening the scope of beneficiaries of the energy bill deferral, requiring the immediate payment of invoices from suppliers and subcontractors in difficulty even if the legal or contractual deadlines have not expired, donating personal protective equipment for employees, masks, freezers, etc., to other companies in the sector or to their suppliers or subcontractors.

[8] See Chapter 2 of this book.

'moral strength; the quality of someone who does not become discouraged or disheartened'. The concept of resilience has also been used in academic work on ecological systems.[9] However, the notion of resilience is interesting in the context of energy transition.[10] In this framework, the law can help a system to be resilient, i.e. to withstand and overcome crises. This is the originality of the energy system. This system was built to work in the event of a crisis by structuring it in such a way as to avoid service interruptions. In other words, the energy system is structurally designed to be resilient. The aim is for the system to function continuously, regardless of the crisis.

The energy transition itself, i.e. the transformation of the energy sectors, is based on adapting to the climate and environmental crisis. Energy systems are therefore being restructured in such a way that no crisis will affect them. Indeed, in Europe, the energy transition is based on a set of common objectives defined by the EU throughout various successive energy packages, and lately the Clean Energy Package,[11] which must be transposed, with some differences depending on the model, into the laws of the Member States.[12] According to this model, the aim of energy transition is thus to reconcile the security and sustainability of supply, the competitive nature of the market, compliance with environmental protection, and the fight against global warming, in particular through the development of renewable energies and the reduction of fossil fuels, energy decentralization, intelligence and digitalization of networks, and the democratic challenge of the appropriation of the system by the citizenry. The objective of the EU is therefore to conduct this energy transition model while designing it in such a way that it is crisis-resistant.

In the traditional system, resilience is in the hands of the supply side. But we will see that citizens can contribute more or less directly to crisis resolution. However, we are interested in the citizens' changing role because we can assume that a large part of the system's resilience will be in their hands in the long term.

These citizens' contributions question an aspect that this study has the advantage of highlighting, which is that, contrary to what we sometimes hear, the fight against climate change is not only a physical problem, it also raises social, cultural, economic, geographical, and legal issues,[13] particularly on the question of commitments, identities, individual and collective values. This requires interdisciplinary and sometimes even transdisciplinary approaches, involving sociology, psychology, spatial sciences, law, economics, humanities, and communication sciences.

In this perspective, we will consider the forms that these citizen contributions take (II). Then, we will look at what shapes citizen energy identities (III). Finally, we will consider

---

[9] Stanley Holling Crawford, 'Resilience and Stability of Ecological Systems' (1973) 4(1) Annual Review of Ecology 1–24.

[10] See Chapter 2. Adde B. J. Jesse, H. Heinrichs, and W. Kuckshinrichs, 'Adapting the Theory of Resilience to Energy Systems: A Review and Outlook' (2019) 9 (27) Energy Sustainability and Society.

[11] Based on Commission proposals published in 2016, the package consists of eight new laws (Energy Performance of Buildings Directive 2018/844; Renewable Energy Directive (EU) 2018/2001; Energy Efficiency Directive (EU) 2018/2002; Governance of the Energy Union and Climate Action (EU) Regulation 2018/1999; Risk-preparedness in the electricity sector—Regulation (EU) 2019/941; European Union Agency for the Cooperation of Energy Regulators—Regulation (EU) 2019/942; Internal market for electricity—Regulation (EU) 2019/943; Common rules for the internal market for electricity—Directive (EU) 2019/944)

[12] In France, these provisions are contained in Arts L. 100-1 et seq. of the French Energy Code.

[13] Donald Zillman, Lee Godden, LeRoy Paddock, and Martha Roggenkamp, *Innovation in Energy Law and Technology: Dynamic Solutions for Energy Transitions* (Oxford University Press 2018).

the impact of these citizen initiatives on traditional energy systems and the changes they imply (IV.).

II. Actions: Forms of Citizen Contribution to the Resilience of Energy Systems

Citizens can ensure the resilience of the energy system by participating in the energy re-composition which, as explained above, aims to be designed in such a way as to avoid what threatens it. Within the traditional paradigm, resilience was in the hands of supply, but in the future paradigm it will be in the hands of demand (demand response).

For this purpose, a distinction will be made between operational means of action (A) and more structural means of action (B).

A. Operational means for citizen-based crisis resolution

Energy consumers can provide various flexibility services to the networks, including service interruptibility, or variation in consumption according to peak periods. In doing so, they contribute to the promotion of a balanced and efficient supply, which means increased resilience.

In a future electricity system based on renewable energies, supply will be guaranteed by consumers themselves to an increased share, since new technologies will allow them to consume whenever it is most convenient for the rest of the system. These guarantees of the resilience of the system go through a certain number of mechanisms that ensure its functioning. In the following, we will address the issue of what is called demand-side flexibility in the electricity sector.

An electricity network must always be balanced between supply and demand, or there is a blackout. To ensure this balance, the network's mission consists of electricity balancing. It can be based on supply, by injecting more electricity, or on demand, by simply limiting or interrupting consumption. Within the European Union, the electricity transmission system operators (TSOs) have the task of ensuring that the electricity flow through the network is balanced at all times, and guaranteeing the safety, security, and efficiency of the network. They also have the task of certifying generation and erasure capacities under the terms of the capacity mechanism. Obviously, in times of crisis this balancing needs to be supported by resources. Initially, only the means of production were used in balancing, then demand-side flexibility was gradually introduced, which first of all involved the introduction of a tariff policy aimed at orienting the periods of electricity consumption by consumers.

For some years now, balancing by interruptible demand has been increasing, consisting of a momentary reduction or interruption in consumption. Over the last 10 years or so, the flexibility of consumers who are either electro-intensive, or small or medium-sized consumers (known as load management), and whose interruptible capacities can be aggregated,[14] has thus been promoted. Since then, the volumes of interruptible capacities have

---

[14] Cherelle Eid et al, 'Aggregation of Demand Side Flexibility in a Smart Grid: A Review for European Market Design' (2015) 12th International Conference on the European Energy Market 1–5.

grown considerably, and could develop further, at the same time as new technologies make it possible to remotely control energy consumption through storage means (electric vehicles, power-to-heat, power-to-hydrogen, etc.).

The use of demand-side flexibility has several advantages. On the one hand, it allows a better integration of renewable energy, which is almost entirely intermittent, which means that the electricity produced is not injected continuously. On the other hand, ensuring the flexibility of the system through consumption avoids oversizing the network. In addition, the demand response usually results in energy savings for whoever implements the mechanism. Finally, flexibility through demand makes it possible to increase the resilience of the network in the event of a consumption or production crisis, for whatever reason (extreme climatic event, conflict, health crisis, etc.).

From a technical point of view, the erasure of consumption will take place at the request of an aggregator or an electricity supplier to a consumer or a consumption site. This may involve electro-intensive industry or small consumers, either individuals or companies. Deletion consists of a temporary drop in the level of electricity withdrawal from the transmission or distribution networks. In concrete terms, a box is installed at the final consumer's home, connected to the electricity meter and various pieces of electrical equipment, which will enable the operator to remotely interrupt the use of this equipment.

From a legal point of view, this practice is authorized and regulated by law.[15] Erasure capacity targets are thus established in planning documents. Offers from operators are also regulated.

There are several difficulties, however. First of all, there is the relationship between erasure operators and suppliers, bearing in mind that in France, for example, a consumer can freely decide to use an aggregator rather than his/her supplier. This implies that the aggregator can market demand response on the energy markets via the NEBEF (Block Exchange Notification of Demand Response) system as if it had been produced or purchased without the supplier's authorization. However, in return, he/she will have to pay the supplier for the energy through a third party, in accordance with the independence principle. It is also necessary to ensure that the interruption or reduction has really occurred using a reference corresponding to the 'normal' consumption of the site without flexibility. NEBEF are not only valued on the demand response markets but also on other erasure channels like capacity mechanisms. These mechanisms have the advantage of ensuring that consumers' or suppliers' responses to TSOs receive a fixed premium, independently of this capacity being activated, in order to deliver energy.

B. Citizens' energy ecosystems: a structural factor in crisis resolution

What better way to guard against global risks than to set up local, sustainable, safe means of production, disconnected from the general network and its risks? This is what energy decentralization aims for, whose legal framework has gradually been established, first in the framework of individual or collective self-consumption, then in that of energy communities.

---

[15] Ex: in French Law, Code de l'énergie, Arts L271-1 et seq.

These local energy ecosystems are interesting to study from many aspects: from a scientific point of view because they are based on various innovative technologies, and from the point of view of social and human sciences because they involve environmental and spatial recompositions, as well as uses and behaviours.[16]

The legal concept of collective self-consumption has clearly prefigured energy communities from a legal point of view. This is a group of consumers and producers, located in geographical proximity, who join together within a legal entity in order to produce electricity by their own means, and consume it for their own needs, according to terms and conditions that they determine collectively. This is currently the most highly developed framework in European law. However, European legislative recognition is recent, through Article 21 of the 2018 Renewable Energy Directive.[17]

Participatory financing has also prefigured energy communities. In this case, it involves financial support from natural or legal persons for a given project. This practice is encouraged by the development of digital platforms, both generalist and specialized, whose aim is to bring together project leaders, the public, and the territories.[18] Obviously, in this case, citizen involvement depends on the type of funding involved, which may be donations, loans, investment in securities. Whether participatory financing or collective self-consumption is involved, the aim is to participate in the development of citizen and local participation and thus raise public awareness.

The essence of this approach now lies in the new concepts of renewable energy communities (RECs) and citizen energy communities (CECs), which can be brought together under the banner of energy communities. The concept of 'energy communities' comes from European Union law.[19] It translates into law a de facto reality that is part of the energy and environmental transition.[20] This concept refers to a group of public or private, natural or legal persons (citizens, local and regional authorities and their public establishments, small and medium-sized enterprises) which, within a given area (a building, a district, a commercial zone), will take charge of all or part of the production, transmission, distribution, and supply of energy and use this energy for different purposes, according to rules which they will establish among themselves.

Within the framework of the Clean Energy Package, the European Union establishes two concepts: the concept of 'renewable energy community', in the 2018 Renewable Energy directive, and that of 'citizens' energy communities', in the 2019 Electricity Directive of 5 June 2019. These directives are intended to be transposed into national law in order to adapt them to national specifics. In France, the first part of the provisions has been adopted under the Energy-Climate Act and the second part will be adopted under an ordinance (pursuant

---

[16] Marianne Ryghaug, Tomas Moe Skjølsvold, and Sara Heidenreich, 'Creating Energy Citizenship through Material Participation' (2018) 48(2) Social Studies of Science 283–303.

[17] Directive (EU) 2018/2001 of the European Parliament and of the Council of 11 December 2018 on the promotion of the use of energy from renewable sources (hereafter Directive RE 2018, Art 2)

[18] Titiana Petra Ertiö and Akshay Bhagwatwar, 'Citizens as Planners: Harnessing Information and Values from the Bottom-Up' (2017) 37(3) International Journal of Information Management 111–113.

[19] Directive RE 2018, Art 2—Directive (EU) 2019/944 of the European Parliament and of the Council of 5 June 2019 on common rules for the internal market for electricity and amending Directive 2012/27/EU (hereafter, Directive electricity market 2019)

[20] Marieke Oteman, Mark Wiering, and Jan Kees Helderman, 'The Institutional Space of Community Initiatives for Renewable Energy: A Comparative Case Study of the Netherlands, Germany and Denmark' (2014) 4(1) Energy, Sustainability and Society 1–17.

to Article 38 of the French Constitution) which reorganizes all applicable provisions around a chapter dedicated to 'energy communities'.[21]

The status of these communities is not predetermined by the European legislator. The Renewable Energy Directive specifies that 'Member States should therefore be able to choose any form of entity for their renewable energy communities'.[22] It is therefore conceivable that these legal entities could take the form of an association, a cooperative, a commercial company, or a public company.

From the point of view of participation, this is considered 'open and voluntary'. However, limits are set in the directives to ensure that the organization is designed in such a way as to avoid any stranglehold of traditional market players. Thus, CECs must be 'effectively controlled by members or shareholders who are natural persons, local authorities, including municipalities, or small enterprises' and 'members or a shareholder ... who are engaged in large-scale commercial activity or whose main field of economic activity is the energy sector may not, individually or jointly, have unilateral decision-making powers within that community'.[23] Similarly, the shareholders or members of RECs are 'natural persons, small and medium-sized enterprises or local authorities and their groupings'[24] with local proxies for energy projects and where an enterprise participates in a renewable energy community, such participation may not constitute its principal commercial or professional activity.[25]

With regard to their purpose, RECs may take over all or part of the activities of production/consumption/storage/sale of renewable energy. CECs will also be able to carry out other energy service activities (recharging, energy efficiency, etc.). The main purpose is to provide 'environmental, economic or social benefits'[26] to their shareholders or members, or in favour of the local territories in which they operate. In other words, they must not aim at profit. This is why an essential part of the community's activity must be carried out for its members or shareholders, or the territories in which it operates, and only an ancillary part may be carried out on the competitive market (e.g. sale of surplus electricity).

Finally, and this is an essential point, the Electricity Directive opened up the possibility for States to authorize CECs to set up 'closed distribution networks' in the form of microgrids. In France, this possibility was immediately ruled out because it was received with great reluctance. This hypothesis was ruled out by the main and delegated legislator, which wished to preserve the monopoly of the historic managers of the public electricity and gas networks. However, in any case, a link must be made between the communities and the network managers, who will have to allow access to the main network, under fair and transparent conditions.

In any case, energy communities can contribute to the resilience of energy systems. They could even eventually be the essential cells of energy systems, producing, storing, and sharing energy at the local level. These territorial ecosystems reflect the concepts of

---

[21] Loi n° 2019-1147 du 8 novembre 2019 relative à l'énergie et au climat - Ordonnance n° 2021-236 du 3 mars 2021 portant transposition de diverses dispositions de la directive (UE) 2018/2001 du Parlement européen et du Conseil du 11 décembre 2018 relative à la promotion de l'utilisation de l'énergie produite à partir de sources renouvelables et de la directive (UE) 2019/944 du Parlement européen et du Conseil du 5 juin 2019 concernant des règles communes pour le marché intérieur de l'électricité.

[22] Directive RE 2018, (71).

[23] Directive electricity market 2019, Art 2.

[24] Ibid.

[25] Ibid.

[26] Ibid.

decentralization and energy subsidiarity. In conjunction with technological developments (storage, microgrids, artificial intelligence, etc.), they could promote decentralized production and local flexibility and thus avoid supply and network balancing problems while reducing energy bills and raising the awareness of consumers, who are still passive concerning energy.

Of course, the success of these communities will largely depend on the various actors (citizens, communities) taking ownership of them. From this point of view, the law can promote the use of this practice, first by setting up an appropriate legal framework, then by establishing financial and fiscal support instruments (e.g. awarded through calls for tenders or with an electricity buy-back mechanism), but also by contributing to training and information. Of course, the most important thing will be the construction of a civic identity in the field of energy.

III. Identities: Energy Citizenship as a Resilience Factor

Citizens are actors in the energy transition, working alongside the other entities involved: national and international public actors (such as the State and its dedicated ministries, local authorities, etc.) and socio-economic actors (suppliers, transporters, distributors, aggregators, as well as associations and NGOs, etc.). A lot is expected of citizens. They are required to behave prudently to avoid health crises, to consume differently, to travel and build differently, in order to avoid climate crises, and they must have confidence in the economy and spend the money they have hoarded to fight the economic crisis. The citizen has multiple roles and responsibilities and the one that will interest us is that of an actor in the energy transition and the effect that this can have in overcoming and slowing down the crises.

Here, we consider the identity of the citizen. The notion of citizen is important in law. With regard to the energy transition, other terms could have been used (consumer, civil society, etc.). However, the notion of citizenship has a double relevance in the energy field, in that it reflects:

- a legal reality, because it is the citizen who is now directly targeted in European directives;[27]
- and a social reality, because it is in the name of citizenship that energy projects emerge.[28]

In the energy sectors, there has been a change in the role of individuals:[29]

---

[27] For example, Directive electricity market 2019, (4): 'The Commission Communication of 25 February 2015, entitled "A Framework Strategy for a Resilient Energy Union with a Forward-Looking Climate Change Policy", sets out a vision of an Energy Union with citizens at its core, where citizens take ownership of the energy transition, benefit from new technologies to reduce their bills and participate actively in the market, and where vulnerable consumers are protected'.

[28] It is particularly instructive to read the documentation of RESCoop, a European association that federates energy community projects and presents itself as 'the European federation of citizen energy cooperatives'.

[29] Lea Diestelmeier, 'Changing Power: Shifting the Role of Electricity Consumers with Blockchain Technology – Policy Implications for EU Electricity Law' (2019) 128(January) Energy Policy 189–196;Marie Lamoureux, *Droit de l'énergie* (LGDJ 2020).

- they were initially seen as users of public services or large national monopolies;
- then consumer law was forged throughout Europe: they became consumers;
- next, they were able to become active consumers, i.e. through their choices, indirectly directing the composition of the mix;
- they then became 'prosumers' (contraction of producer and consumer) in the legal and technical framework of self-consumption;
- the last stage will be the energy citizen, directly referred to in the European texts, notably through the concept of citizen energy communities.

This notion of citizen is obviously not neutral in legal terms. The notion of citizen traditionally has a precise legal definition, which does not fit well with other disciplinary approaches.[30] Citizenship from a legal perspective refers to the status of a person recognized by the law of a sovereign State. Therefore, the concept of citizenship refers only to natural persons and not to legal persons, and may differ from one State to another. Although the EU is not a sovereign State, the Maastricht Treaty of 1992 referred to the concept of European citizenship.[31] On the basis of this concept of citizenship, a citizen is basically an individual who has specific rights and duties in the territory of the State where he or she resides.

In the field of energy and the environment, this concept of citizen is referred to, for example, in the context of constitutional or international environmental law, in particular through the prism of the right to participate in environmental decision making. This is stipulated in the Aarhus Convention. In addition, citizens are also explicitly targeted in the text relating to the energy transition: they are invited to make participatory investment, self-consumption, and energy communities. In other words, the public authorities ensure that this citizenship can emerge.

An 'energy citizenship' would therefore emerge and it is in the name of this 'energy citizenship' that citizens, actors of the energy transition, could also play a role in crisis prevention, thus contributing to what is called the general resilience of the system.

This concept of 'energy citizenship' could leave a lawyer perplexed because traditionally we learn that citizenship is a coherent and global concept that is not broken down into areas of activity. One is either a citizen or one is not. Accordingly, there is no such thing as energy citizenship, environmental citizenship, digital citizenship, etc. A definition of the term is therefore essential. This is the heart of the problem because at least two concepts coexist.

First, energy citizenship can be defined, from a legal point of view, as the person who, in a democratic State, legally has the status of citizen (acquired by nationality) and consequently has the rights and duties that are attached to this status. In law, citizenship is indeed based on rights and duties; first and foremost the right and duty (whether or not sanctioned) to vote. In this framework, the link with energy is obvious: citizens, either by themselves or through their representatives, can express themselves on energy-related texts (laws, international treaties, administrative acts) and thus improve their knowledge, convictions, and even their commitments. Citizens also have many other rights and duties that may be directly or indirectly related to energy. Indirectly related rights include the precautionary principle, the

---

[30] Patrick Devine-Wright, 'Energy Citizenship: Psychological Aspects of Evolution in Sustainable Energy technologies' (2007) Governing technology for sustainability 63–86.

[31] Treaty on European Union, 1992, Title 1, Art B. EU citizenship is now established in Art 9 of the Consolidated Version of the Treaty on European Union (2016) and in the Art 20 of Consolidated Version of the Treaty on the Functioning of the European Union (2016).

right to a healthy environment and the right to demonstrate; rights more directly related to energy citizenship, such as the right to public participation in the development of energy policies and projects, or the right to energy supplies to meet basic needs. Rights directly related to energy include the obligation to contribute to the cost of public energy services, and to adapt to energy efficiency or conservation, to pay taxes or charges to support energy transitions and to combat global climate change. Thus, traditionally a link between citizenship and energy can be legally established in texts that set out the rights and duties of the citizen in concrete energy standards.

However, citizenship could also be seen as being defined not (only) by law but as the embodiment of the aspiration of individuals or collectives of individuals to influence the choices of human societies. This is done by claiming specific values in deed and in word with the aim that these values will be shared by the majority and incorporated into the norms of societies and organized institutions. In this case, the legal study of the citizen's identity is based on individual action and commitment to influence public policies.[32] The rights and obligations of citizenship are not set by law but by ethical or moral rules that the individuals concerned set for themselves. In this sense, energy citizenship is acquired through its practice.

These different perspectives are both linked to an individual's identity,[33] so they are not unconnected, but the processes by which this identity develops are very different. What seems to be the common goal is the necessary awareness of a citizenship which is expressed on the one hand through the exercise of rights and duties, and on the other through the implementation of individual or collective actions for changes deemed necessary.

Having said this, it seems that the two concepts are different and that this difference is due to the role of the State in each case.

In the first case, citizen identity is forged from above.[34] This stems from a 'statist' view of citizenship, where it is sovereign power that defines who is a citizen and what citizenship means. It is therefore the people—then defined as a coherent whole—who, through their representatives or by themselves (through referendums), establish the founding framework of citizenship. In this framework, energy citizenship is only an emanation, an offshoot of this citizenship whose conceptual framework is defined by the State. In this sense, the desire of the public authorities to build an 'energy' citizenship can be explained as their objective is energy transition, since energy communities promote renewable energies, accelerate the transitional process by multiplying the number of actors involved, and at the same time foster the social appropriation of the whole by the very fact of this involvement. To this end, the State sets up rules that favour citizen initiatives, for example through participatory investment, self-consumption, and energy communities.[35]

In the second case, citizen identity is specific to each individual and can intervene in collectives and communities. In this case, citizenship is no longer defined by the State but is understood as part of the individual's identity, which is in turn understood as an awareness

[32] Maarten Arentsen and Sandra Bellekom, 'Power to the People: Local Energy Initiatives as Seedbeds of Innovation?' (2014) 4(1) Energy, Sustainability and Society 1–12.

[33] Stefan Bouzarovski and Mark Bassin, 'Energy and Identity: Imagining Russia as a Hydrocarbon Superpower' (2011) 101(4) Annals of the Association of American Geographers 783–794.

[34] Breffní Lennon et al, 'Citizen or Consumer? Reconsidering Energy Citizenship' (2020) 22(2) Journal of Environmental Policy & Planning 184–197.

[35] Matthew J. Burke and Jennie C. Stephens 'Energy Democracy: Goals and Policy Instruments for Sociotechnical Transitions' (2017) 33 Energy Research and Social Science 35–48.

of belonging to a global ecosystem and of bearing individual responsibility and a willingness to act.

Of course, in reality things are more complex. These two concepts coexist and act reciprocally,[36] creating a dialectic. Fundamentally, there are ultimately also two opposing conceptions of the general interest, one is proactive and conceived as being at the initiative of the State, which decides transcendentally on individual interests. The other only involves the State as an arbiter of the various interests of citizens. In short, interactions are created and are at the root of the dialectical process. The State relies on citizen initiatives, supports them, and appropriates them, while collectives use this support to develop their own concept and thus influence the State's public policies. While this fruitful dialogue is verifiable, it is not on a significant scale at present. If we look at the figures, we can see, for example, that this civic identity is only in its infancy with regard to energy and has not led to an increase in commitments.

Whatever the situation, a citizen identity is never acquired or sudden. This is why both public authorities and citizens' groups, convinced of the need for the energy transition (or at least of their conception of the energy transition), are campaigning for the emergence of an energy citizen identity. This shows the determination and the limitations of the exercise: however attractive the vehicle, the important thing is that the citizen actually gets on board. In other words, citizen identity cannot be decreed. In order for citizen initiatives to multiply, citizen awareness must be developed.

So how is this citizenship forged? We can already see the ineffectiveness of simple injunctions to become a citizen. According to the most recent research, it would seem that citizenship is acquired only by exercising it, and that to exercise it one must have the means to do so.

On this basis, a complex interplay of actors is created involving some very interesting legal issues. It would seem that citizenship identity has two main vectors for forging itself. First, the means of appropriation, i.e. the means of informing, training, and convincing in order to forge at least opinions, at best convictions, so that people produce and consume green and local energy in individual or collective projects. Secondly, the means of action to foster citizen engagement. The idea is to have the public authorities and other actors support individual or collective projects so that they bring together individuals, communities, and companies as shareholders in local projects in the form of cooperatives or companies. This involves financial, administrative, or fiscal support.

Obviously, this citizen identity requires some minimum conditions to be met in order to be forged. It can therefore be assumed that energy poverty is a major obstacle to the construction of this identity.[37] This is one of the major challenges of the Clean Energy Package, which addresses these issues of support to enable the fastest possible implementation of local energy communities and energy decentralization through collective self-consumption and also the technologies that support it.

---

[36] Nicolien Van Aalderen and Lummina Geertruida Horlings, 'Accommodative Public Leadership in Wind Energy Development: Enabling Citizens Initiatives in the Netherlands' (2020) Energy Policy 138.

[37] Martha M. Roggenkamp and Lea Diestelmeier, 'Energy Market Reforms in the EU: A New Focus on Energy Consumers, Energy Poverty and Energy (in)Justice?' in Iñigo Del Guayo et al (eds), *Energy Justice and Energy Law—Distributive, Procedural, Restorative and Social Justice in Energy Law* (Oxford University Press 2020).

IV. Recomposition: The Positive and Negative Effects of Energy Citizenship on Traditional Energy Systems

There is significant potential for developing energy communities according to a recent study which shows that half of European citizens could produce their own renewable electricity by 2050, thus covering 45 per cent of the energy demand, in today's rather favourable context of constantly falling renewable energy prices and technological development (smart grids, electricity storage, electro-mobility). However, this favourable context will need to be reassessed in the light of the real impacts of the current COVID-19 health crisis, which are difficult to assess today.

There are certainly many advantages to citizen energy ecosystems: reduction of energy bills, securing production, reduction of environmental impact, optimization and intelligence in the use of networks, association and therefore awareness of energy issues among actors-consumers. However, there are also disadvantages to these communities, mainly in that they disrupt the organization and functioning of the current, highly centralized system, which could generate costs in terms of network reinforcement and possibly transfers of charges between users of these networks. The deployment of energy communities thus gives rise to legitimate fears on the part of existing players, whose customers could gradually become competitors. It also entails risks, if it were to emerge too abruptly, in terms of competition, or disparities between territories and populations. These communities would have to rely to a large extent on the production of renewable energies, dependent on wind or sunshine conditions, which would obviously favour the territories where these conditions are optimal, an additional advantage when transferring the load of the main networks from consumers who are members of a community to consumers who are not. All of these issues will have to be debated.

One of the most illustrative and crucial points is the option that the European legislator leaves to the Member States to decide. The Electricity Directive allowed the Member States to authorize citizen energy communities to set up 'closed distribution networks' in the form of microgrids. In France, this possibility immediately aroused strong reservations on the part of the network operators in particular. Thus, for the time being, this hypothesis has been excluded by the French legislator, which preserves the monopoly of the incumbent public electricity and gas network operators. However, the question will inevitably arise again with the development of these energy communities, which will undoubtedly claim management of their networks. This situation would raise two types of difficulties. First, such a hypothesis would imply structuring normative modifications to reconcile the existing with the new (in terms of ownership of the network or exclusivity of its management). Secondly, opening up infrastructure to competition would require extensive studies to demonstrate the benefits of running it competitively and its impact on public electricity service. Indeed, the 'autonomous' management of the networks would impact the national equalization of public network costs and, consequently, on solidarity between consumers.

The development of energy communities thus ultimately raises a crucial question at the heart of the political debate on the very future of the energy transition, including the way in which this transition is conceived. Energy communities embody a real paradigm shift that radically contrasts with the traditionally vertical vision of energy markets where, schematically, large energy companies produce gas or electricity, which are then transported and distributed across networks to final consumers.

They represent a new model characterized by energy decentralization, where some or all of the traditionally centralized functions of energy production, transmission, and distribution will be disconnected from the main grid to be taken over by these communities, with necessarily smaller mesh sizes and voltage levels.

The development of new local energy ecosystems therefore requires us to rethink our energy model. This opens up three challenges, to establish a reliable measure of the impact of this new model on the market (wholesale and retail trade, flexibility, over-the-counter market), on energy networks (access, pricing, impacts) and on solidarity mechanisms (territorial equalisation, aid, information, support, services of general interest). In addition, we need to rethink the legal model, which today is based on the idea of a universal service provided through public networks and the financing model attached to this service.

This is why the idea of transition should be at the heart of this process. It should therefore be a real transition and not too abrupt a break with the existing model. The idea is to favour the coexistence of the models and then, if necessary, discard the old model.

This notion of balance between centralization and decentralization has very concrete implications for production. For example, concerning French production, the 'ARENH' (Regulated Access to Historic Nuclear Electricity) mechanism was designed to allow the emergence and development of competition in the French electricity sector. Suppliers can buy energy from EDF, which is obliged to sell it to them at a price determined by the government. This notion of balance is also found in network matters. Everywhere in Europe tensions are rising around the monopolies of network management in a context of rapid evolution of the energy sectors. This is due to the interest of local and regional authorities and communities, which is growing as their expertise in this field increases, and to the development of energy decentralization, particularly in relation to local RE production. This movement is encouraging these new operators to demand that they be allowed to manage private and closed distribution networks. The Electricity Directive has clearly established the possibility for national legislators to open up this option. Resistance is strong, however. In France, for the time being, the legislator has excluded this possibility on principle, but for how much longer?

At the same time, we must question the very relevance of ending centralized network management. Beyond the legal aspects, more strategic elements of an economic, financial, or even political nature deserve to be taken into consideration. First of all, because the current crisis has proved the efficiency of network managers—including local operators—in ensuring the stability of the system. The introduction of competition for infrastructure would require in-depth studies to demonstrate the advantage in having them managed competitively, the impact that this would have on the public electricity service, and the question of the relevant local scale. This would be all the more important as nationalized management is not only based on a compilation of local networks but also on the pooled resources (human, financial, and structural) that have been established over time.

Finally, the problem today is that we want the law to resolve major political issues as if the law itself contained the essential truth. The real issue here is one of politics and civics.

V. Conclusion

The COVID-19 pandemic illustrates the need to ensure the resilience of energy systems in a future of increasing crises. Citizens can contribute to ensuring this resilience and even become key. They are already involved in the context of techniques such as load management. Energy communities, even more so, can increase this contribution. These communities reveal a new paradigm, with energy needs being covered on a local scale. However, the development of these consumer contributions depends to a large extent on the willingness of consumers to take them up. This is why the concept of citizenship is crucial. However, this concept covers different realities and definitions depending on whether one considers it top-down or bottom-up. These different conceptions are not insignificant because they reveal different approaches in terms of the organization, functioning, objectives, and purposes of energy communities. One of the main difficulties is the link these communities will have with the rest of the energy system. Indeed, if they were to develop, they would necessarily affect the classic functioning of energy networks which, for example, within the European Union, is based on a conception of public energy service, notably through national solidarity based on the sharing and equalization of network access costs. For all these reasons, decentralization must be carried out gradually, carefully, and reasonably.

PART VII
CONCLUSION

22

Conclusion—Managing Disruption and Reinventing the Future

Resilience as Requirement for Legal Frameworks

Catherine Banet, Hanri Mostert, LeRoy Paddock, Milton Fernando Montoya, and Íñigo del Guayo

I. Introduction

The chapters in this collection all demonstrate how resilience considerations are progressively gaining ground in law. As a notion emanating from the science of ecosystems, and further developed within systems theory,[1] resilience thinking has already entered the law and policy discourse, as this book shows. In the legal regulatory and policy context, resilience thinking is driven by the need to respond to and avoid the increasing occurrence and scale of nature-based disruptive events.[2] Such disruptions—their growing scope and increasing frequency—are challenging the deeper foundations of our legal regulatory and policy systems.

This book observes the transition from engineering-based concepts of resilience to the wider use of the term as a characteristic of social-ecological systems.[3] However, the 'legal translation of resilience' raises a series of challenges, and as lawyers, we must remain mindful that transplanting such concepts is not always straightforward, nor is it easy. As so many of the chapters in this book demonstrate, dealing with crises and building resilience through those experiences occur in a precise legal context. To appraise the effects of applying resilience thinking to a particular context, it is crucial to understand the applicable legal framework itself as a complex and interlinked system.

This chapter does three things. It contextualizes, the concept of resilience for legal work, both practical and theoretical in nature. It draws broader inferences from the many examples represented in the chapters we have collated here. And finally, it begins to formulate a set of structural resilience principles for Energy, Infrastructure, and Natural Resources Law that may serve us better in years (and crises) to come.

---

[1] Chapter 2 by Bankes, Godden, and del Guyao.
[2] Chapter 1 by Banet, Mostert, Paddock, Montoya, and del Guayo.
[3] Chapter 2 by Bankes, Godden, and del Guyao.

Catherine Banet, Hanri Mostert, LeRoy Paddock, Milton Fernando Montoya, and Íñigo del Guayo, *Conclusion—Managing Disruption and Reinventing the Future* In: *Resilience in Energy, Infrastructure, and Natural Resources Law.* Edited by: Catherine Banet, Hanri Mostert, LeRoy Paddock, Milton Fernando Montoya, and Íñigo del Guayo, Oxford University Press. © Catherine Banet, Hanri Mostert, LeRoy Paddock, Milton Fernando Montoya, and Íñigo del Guayo 2022. DOI: 10.1093/oso/9780192864574.003.0022

II. Contextualizing Resilience in the Law

This section draws the concept of resilience into legal discourse by offering a definition. It demonstrates how important the concept is in crafting legal, regulatory, and policy frameworks for the future. It encourages integrative thinking about legal systems: the law as ecosystem, within a global context, based on social-ecological thinking. Systemic interdependency is presented as an important hallmark for the future—in law as much as in ecosystems. The section also contemplates the possibilities and limitations offered by the urgent need to shift our thinking around resilient legal and policy frameworks.

A. Defining resilience in law

Resilience is progressively appearing as a new paradigm, entering law and policy frameworks. Across all of the chapters, however, it becomes clear that the notion has being introduced into law and policy in a haphazard, inconsistent, and reactive manner. Often, it is the very experience of crisis that instigates the shift towards resilience. The chapters reveal that, although thoughts converge on the need to introduce resilience into legal, policy, and regulatory frameworks in a more comprehensive and consistent manner, the actual approaches to implementing the idea in law and policy making are multiple and diverse.

Indeed, even our various understandings of resilience are not consistent, judging by the legal and policy frameworks that have already been influenced by resilience thinking. Some neighbouring concepts are already enshrined in laws and policies: security of supply, disaster risk reduction, flexibility, resource adequacy, reliability, deliverability, durability, adaptation, climate resilience, vulnerability reduction. These concepts, and their related frameworks and implementation mechanisms, all address a part of resilience, but have different meanings and functions. A more comprehensive engagement with the meaning of resilience must surely assist legal and policy frameworks to respond to—or, better yet, avoid—disruptions, and minimize the impact of disasters while building resilience.

This realization grows from several of the chapters arguing for better recognition of the concept of resilience in legislation. Reactions to past shocks have often resulted in defining new overriding policy objectives in the legislation, which could make its systems more resilient to future upsets. An example is the reactions to energy supply shortage and the promotion of security of supply. However, a system that develops based on reactions from case to case may ultimately suffer from poor construction. This is why we hope this work will promote discourse about resilience in the law as a common objective in and even requirement for developing future legal frameworks. Our grand hope, and the call encompassed in this book, is for a definite and deliberate change in approach.

Promoting resilience in legal and policy frameworks requires that the term to be given a precise meaning. Indeed, we now often refer to the concept of resilience, but we have not yet done the fundamental work of defining it in the legal context. Not having a single overarching definition of the concept is convenient, allowing for consensus building and flexibility, but as a strategy, it has major shortcomings and it complicates implementation.

The different understandings of resilience lead to divergent approaches to disaster preparedness and recovery, with shortfalls in terms of sustainability, cost-efficiency, and equity.[4] In addition, one should acknowledge that energy, infrastructures, and natural resources systems are complex and evolving. This means that where a risk or disruption needs to be addressed,[5] careful analysis will always be needed. Even so, such caution does not preclude framing resilience as steering concept.

A first working definition of resilience in legal context could then be:

the ability of our social-ecological ecosystems[6] to resist and adapt to disruptions, and to pursue sustainable development and equity in an inclusive and nature-based manner.

B. The importance of legal, regulatory, and governance systems

This book does not deal with the *resilience of the law* as such, but rather with the creation of *legal frameworks for resilience*. In pursuing this analysis, we need to acknowledge the role played by the different types of legal systems and legal traditions within which resilience-supporting legal frameworks are to be developed. This applies to the value embodied by legal rules and the manner legal rules are developed and implemented, but also to different governance approaches.[7]

Resilience can be built into legal frameworks at the normative level, as several of the chapters affirm. Existing features of the legal system may enable such a shift. Legal traditions will orientate countries towards a certain use of legal mechanisms or tools, especially when they are already widely used (e.g. in planning frameworks).[8] At other times, mechanisms more broadly available may facilitate the shift. The interaction between international law and national legal orders may be relevant here, as may be the ability of binding and soft international instruments to change and evolve in response to disrupting events.[9] In addition to treaty law, soft law can help build resilience into the norm-creating process. In developing a normative framework within which resilience can drive law and policy, one may also want to be open to the possibilities offered beyond the known or widely accepted avenues for value embodiment.[10] One can also question whether the more nature-centred approach that indigenous practices take in their thinking about the law could serve as inspiration for the shaping of resilience legal frameworks.[11] At the regional level, the European Union legal order enables streamlining and even harmonizing legal responses to resilience issues between Member States.[12] At a more practical level, some common legal approaches and solutions to resilience will be required as a direct consequence of the need to collaborate in managing shared natural resources or infrastructures.

The regulatory and governance system in place will greatly influence the response to resilience. And there is a complex interplay of legislation, policy, institutional arrangements

---

[4] Chapter 8 by Godden and Chapter 4 by Banet.
[5] Chapter 8 by Godden.
[6] Be it a group of individuals, a natural ecosystem, a city, an infrastructure, a country, a sector, or an economy.
[7] Chapter 7 by Zhang.
[8] Chapter 4 by Banet.
[9] Chapter 3 by Redgwell.
[10] Ibid.
[11] Chapter 16 by Ahmad.
[12] E.g. in the context of European Union harmonized legislation. See Chapter 5 by Roggenkamp and Chapter 4 by Banet.

which must be appraised when addressing resilience. Particular tensions and risks of inefficient or inconsistent approaches to resilience are related to the structure of the state, and notably the repartition of competences between different government levels. This is both the case for federal states and for unitary systems with a high degree of decentralization.[13] Where shifts towards resilience in a legal system are necessary as part of an immediate crisis response, the avenues for financing such responses may also have an influence on the legal system's ability to move towards resilience-supporting frameworks. In the developing world, this may well have a significant influence on the trajectories of development, especially where externally funded initiatives come with strings attached.[14]

In some circumstances, such as in Mexico[15] or recently in the United States with more conservative-led governments, there may be tensions between resistance of the political governance structure in place and the need to act on resilience. In these cases, political institutions and governments may hamper building the appropriate legal framework. Counter-powers will play a crucial role, notably the judiciary in preserving rights and principles defined in constitutions and other laws. The same can be observed as to the respect of international environmental treaties or agreements (e.g. Paris Agreement) and trade treaties (World Trade Organization regime, Energy Charter Treaty), although the enforcement mechanisms tend to be weaker. This leads to the conclusion that building resilience also requires a resilient governance structure.

C. Regulatory ecosystem approach and interlinkages

The book shows that certain types of assets are given central attention in the legislation on risk preparedness and security of supply. Such is the case for infrastructures like energy, water, heat, transport, or IT that are essential in the functioning of societies and in the supply of essential services. The legislative frameworks often put emphasis on the need to protect them and define a regime for 'critical infrastructures'.[16] This need is only reinforced by the increasingly digitalized nature of infrastructures, and the spread of distribution networks due to the decentralization of energy generation.

Although some isolated disruption risks can be addressed by single measures under a single legal framework, the complexity of resilience issues will often need to activate several frameworks at the same time. As an example, and as noted in the book, dealing with the energy price volatility in the MENA region 'will require a legal, fiscal and institutional reform agenda' aimed at mainstreaming disaster risk reduction and resilience measures into energy law and policy across the MENA region.[17]

The different legal and regulatory frameworks are closely interlinked, and streamlining resilience building indeed requires one to apply a transversal, coordinated (if not integrated) approach.[18] Reform in one sector can foster or delay resilience building in another one. Several chapters take the example of market design rules in the energy sector, the

[13] Chapter 8 by Godden, Chapter 7 by Zhang, Chapter 12 by Smith and Zillman, and Chapter 14 by Lucas.
[14] Chapter 17 by Mostert, Adomako-Kwakye, Chisanga, and van den Berg.
[15] Chapter 11 by González Márquez and Chapter 12 by Smith and Zillman.
[16] Chapter 5 by Roggenkamp, Chapter 8 by Godden, Chapter 6 by Klass and Foote, and Chapter 15 by Paddock.
[17] Chapter 9 by Olawuyi.
[18] Chapter 4 by Banet.

effects of liberalization reforms, and the unbundling and third party access regimes,[19] with the underlying question of the effects of chosen energy market design model on resilience management. Ownership models—public or private—may also influence response to disruption. Inspired by system theories, these interlinkages argue in favour of applying a regulatory ecosystem approach to the design of resilience framework.

D. Social-ecological resilience and new regulatory models

The legal literature has started to call for a critical look at the current legal system applying to environmental protection and natural resources. For example, L. J. Kotzé and R. Kim, applying earth system governance thinking to juridical systems, argue in favour of moving towards 'earth system law'.[20] T. Stephen, considering that the world is entering the Anthropocene, is calling legal scholars to re-examine and re-imagine international environmental law's objectives.[21]

Many chapters in this volume refer primarily to social-ecological theory that posits the synergy between physical and social systems, as well as a 'fundamental interdependency' between social and environmental sub-systems.[22] Following a social-ecological approach sets some pre-conditions to the development of a legal framework modelled on resilience. It will have effects on the planning process for resilience response, on the choice of mitigation instruments, and on the diversity of actors to be involved. One example is the manner in which 'community resilience' can support resilience of the whole society.[23] A second example is the increasing focus put on nature-based solutions in addressing resilience.[24]

E. The demands of urgency

In many ways, it is striking to see how quickly the response to COVID-19 has been, with immediate lockdowns and recovery packages, while the response to climate change and biodiversity loss still lags behind. As emphasized by the Intergovernmental Panel on Climate Change,[25] we have little time left to act. This raises questions around the urgency of action demanded and the choice of law and policy approach to resilience.

Many regulatory agencies are only beginning to address how to define and implement resilience[26] and indeed, we are still in an early phase of legal action on resilience in many

---

[19] Chapter 2 by Bankes, Godden, and del Guayo, Chapter 4 by Banet, Chapter 5 by Roggenkamp, Chapter 6 by Klass and Foote, Chapter 8 by Godden, Chapter 14 by Lucas, Chapter 15 by Paddock, Chapter 16 by Ahmad, Chapter 19 by Eiamchamroonlarp, and Chapter 21 by de Fontenelle.
[20] L. J. Kotzé, R. E. Kim, 'Earth System Law: The Juridical Dimensions of Earth System Governance' (2019) 1 Earth System Governance 100003.
[21] T. Stephens, 'What is the Point of International Environmental Law Scholarship in the Anthropocene?' in O.W. Pedersen (ed), Perspectives on Environmental Law Scholarship: Essays on Purpose, Shape and Direction (Cambridge University Press 2018) 121–139.
[22] E.g. Chapter 2 by Bankes, Godden, and del Guayo, and Chapter 8 by Godden.
[23] E.g. Chapter 21 by de Fontenelle.
[24] Chapter 8 by Godden, Chapter 4 by Banet, and Chapter 20 by Barton.
[25] 'Climate Change 2021: The Physical Science Basis', Contribution of Working Group I to the Sixth Assessment Report of the Intergovernmental Panel on Climate Change.
[26] Chapter 6 by Klass and Foote.

parts of the world. The speed of change is also very different from sector to sector.[27] This calls for a diversity of legal responses, with a combination of hard and soft law, legal rules, and good practice.[28] At the international level, international treaty systems can provide a useful source of flexibility, necessary to adapt the law to unexpected disruptions and so promote resilience. A dynamic interpretation of framework treaties, supported by the work of bodies like Conference of the Parties or other subsidiary bodies, has proven to be effective mechanisms.[29]

III. Lessons Learned From Legal Responses to Resilience and Resilience Building

From the chapter contributions one can infer several lessons. From the typical legal inquiry of who is at fault for a particular disaster or crisis, a resilience-supporting framework shifts to questions about response-ability: who must and can respond. From observing this broad shift, the discussion below moves to acknowledging the wide diversity in regulatory approaches already prevalent in legal systems around the world. It observes the role that finance—and the ability to access funding—plays in enabling resilience. The discussion below also recognizes that there are fundamental questions of coordination that deserve attention, and that inability or unwillingness to act on the need to build resilience may have considerable impacts on equity. Finally the discussion below highlights some insights into the moment of the system 'flip'—when change becomes inevitable.

A. Responsibility allocation in resilience building

When asking who is responsible for ensuring resilience, there is no obvious answer. Or, the answer may be that everyone is responsible. But from the legal perspective the allocation of responsibilities needs a more refined answer. Indeed, there is a complex interplay between actors and considerations that needs to be weighed.

Risk and liability allocation is a classical issue for contracts[30] and insurance regimes,[31] and juxtaposes with other questions about responsibility. One chapter in the book asks whether both preventive measures to protect private investments against natural disasters and economic compensation when such investments have been damaged or destroyed, should be seen as a public responsibility.[32] In another facet of the questions around responsibility, one chapter concludes that there must be 'a sharing of responsibility for resilience across the public and private sectors and the community'. Such partnership models are evident in much of the adaptation planning in Australia.[33]

---

[27] Ibid.
[28] Chapter 3 by Redgwell, Chapter 4 by Banet, Chapter 16 by Ahmad, Chapter 17 by Mostert, Adomako-Kwakye, Chisanga, and van den Berg, and Chapter 18 by Bull.
[29] Chapter 3 by Redgwell.
[30] Chapter 13 by Boute.
[31] Chapter 18 by Bull.
[32] Ibid.
[33] Chapter 8 by Godden.

In circumstances where resilience requires actions by multiple actors, there must be a clear role allocation for certain aspects of resilience. International law points in the direction of states, where for example, in 2016, the International Law Commission produced a set of draft Articles on Protection of Persons in the Event of Disasters. Draft Article 9 in particular recognizes the obligation for the states to reduce the risk of disasters, including assistance of the international community 'where appropriate and necessary'.[34] The Sendai Framework for Disaster Risk Reduction 2015–2030 also points in the direction of states and the need to support their planning efforts.[35]

At national level, much depends on sector regulation. In the energy sector, transmission and distribution system operators are often the ones identified as responsible for system reliability, and responsible for planning and coordination.[36] Consumers and communities are increasingly given a bigger role through regimes such as demand response and energy communities.[37] They can be active participants in resilience planning and building.[38] The international climate regime also encourages community resilience and advocates for pursuing community-based adaptation planning as bottom-up planning approach.[39] Consumers can play a more active role, including in the management of natural resources such as critical minerals.[40]

When defining resilience as a goal or requirement in legislation and identifying responsibility in ensuring resilience, one also should raise the question of litigation risk. This has not yet been theorized, but one could wonder whether institutions, states, local entities, or companies could be sued for lack of preparedness or lack of action on resilience, as observed in the field of climate litigation. What our authors have considered are the litigation grounds relating to contracts and insurance, as well as the financial risks that may arise.[41] They also consider the matter of liability for the maintenance of electricity infrastructures that can cause bushfires—as has already been illustrated by law suits in Australia and the United States.[42]

Beyond the allocation of responsibilities, dealing with and building resilience raises some fundamental questions of coordination between institutions. Due to the large scope of action needed to ensure resilience, there is a need for increased coordination between entities having their own area of responsibility. In addition to the risk of *regulatory fragmentation*[43] due to sectoral approaches, there is also a risk of *institutional fragmentation*.[44] This is sometimes seen as a consequence of liberalization reforms, but mechanisms can and have been developed to address these risks. Mandatory consultation, a duty to cooperate, consultation procedures, and coordination entities are among the solutions adopted.[45]

---

[34] Chapter 3 by Redgwell.
[35] Chapter 9 by Olawuyi.
[36] Chapter 5 by Roggenkamp, Chapter 4 by Banet, Chapter 6 by Klass and Foote, Chapter 8 by Godden, Chapter 14 by Lucas, and Chapter 15 by Paddock.
[37] Chapter 15 by Paddock and Chapter 21 by de Fontenelle.
[38] Chapter 8 by Godden.
[39] E.g. UNFCCC Adaptation Committee, 'Opportunities and options for enhancing adaptation planning in relation to vulnerable ecosystems, communities and groups', Technical paper, FCCC/TP/2018/3.
[40] Chapter 20 by Barton
[41] Chapter 13 by Boute on contracts and Chapter 18 by Bull on insurance (and see further Section II.C below)
[42] Chapter 8 by Godden.
[43] Chapter 7 by Zhang and Chapter 6 by Klass and Foote.
[44] Chapter 8 by Godden.
[45] Chapter 4 by Banet.

B. Financing resilience and effects on project development

Considering climate-related risks to the financial systems and the economy in general is be-coming common in many jurisdictions by, for example, public pension funds and sovereign welfare funds, but also for companies.[46] Taxation frameworks should also be aligned with the same policy objectives.[47] The role of publicly owned companies can also be questioned, as powerful instruments in channelling green finance and promoting public private part-nership to de-risk certain projects.[48]

A common observation is that revenue diversification strengthens resilience of the economy and the society as a whole, with direct social benefits. Stimulating entrepreneur-ship and investments across diverse underdeveloped sectors can also play a crucial role in building resilience in the face of disruptive events.[49] However, the financing models for assets and infrastructures deemed essential to society and its resilience (and so subject to expansion or reinvestment) must be scrutinized. Legal and policy frameworks can be powerful tools in incentivizing investments in the 'right' infrastructures, supporting, for example, more investment in renewable energy generation or more adaptive infrastructure, but it can also disincentivize investments that create disruptions, for example, fossil fuels.[50] Lessons can be drawn from the manner COVID-19 recovery packages have been designed. Recovery packages have increasingly integrated a resilience dimension. However, where governance frameworks are weak, the financial response provided to the pandemic has not been as useful as expected, and has even been counterproductive.[51]

The ability of contracts to deal with the COVID-19 pandemic's effects carries valuable lessons for the ability to deal with other types of disruption. As pointed out in some chap-ters, failure to effectively introduce risk mitigation techniques and hedging clauses that deal with unexpected changes—such as oil price collapses—could have a significant impact on the resilience of a country.[52] Here, much attention should be paid to the drafting of review and force majeure clauses during the contract negotiation.[53] However, those contractual flexibility mechanisms, although they help adjusting to disruptions, may also contribute to locking parties in their long-term obligations and continuing a non-sustainable model.[54]

C. Just resilience

This book follows our previous volume, which was dedicated to energy justice.[55] Between the work for these two volumes the contributors can draw essential lines between energy

---

[46] Chapter 9 by Olawuyi, Chapter 12 by Smith and Zillman, Chapter 14 by Lucas, Chapter 16 by Ahmad, and Chapter 17 by Mostert, Adomako-Kwakye, Chisanga, and van den Berg.
[47] Chapter 9 by Olawuyi.
[48] Chapter 19 by Eiamchamroonlarp.
[49] Chapter 9 by Olawuyi.
[50] Chapter 6 by Klass and Foote, Chapter 7 by Zhang, Chapter 9 by Olawuyi, Chapter 10 by Montoya and Aguilar Abaunza, Chapter 14 by Lucas, Chapter 15 by Paddock, Chapter 16 by Ahmad, Chapter 17 by Mostert, Adomako-Kwakye, Chisanga, and van den Berg, and Chapter 19 by Eiamchamroonlarp.
[51] Chapter 17 by Mostert, Adomako-Kwakye, Chisanga, and van den Berg.
[52] Chapter 9 by Olawuyi and Chapter 13 by Boute.
[53] Ibid.
[54] Chapter 13 by Boute.
[55] I. del Guayo, L. Godden, D. Zillman, M. F. Montoya, and J. J. González (eds), *Energy Justice and Energy Law: Distributive, Procedural, Restorative and Social Justice in Energy Law* (Oxford University Press 2020).

justice and resilience. Several chapters address equity issues as part of resilience frameworks.[56] Notably, the lack of action on resilience may have considerable impacts on equity, where the weakest ones tend to suffer most of the consequences of natural disruptions. This can take the form of environmental refugees, property loss, deteriorated health conditions, and energy poverty. Law and policy frameworks that support resilience can advance energy and extractive justice in myriad ways. The following points bear mention.

First, the involvement of affected communities in the resilience building process will enable these communities to bring their insights into finding solutions and be invested in new resilience approaches. In many circumstances this involvement could improve living conditions and provide useful resilience services to the rest of the society.

Second, legal regimes relevant to address resilience often contain reference to solidarity. Responding to disruptions may require support from neighbouring communities, countries, or the international community. Increasingly, the legal framework has been defining solidarity requirements such as in case of natural disasters (e.g. insurance coverage)[57] or security of energy supply shortages (e.g. EU principle of solidarity).[58] At the international level, this is, however, challenged by recent return to protectionism, which weakens the ability to advance collectively on resilience.[59]

Third, information management is seen as an important part to resilience management framework, with benefits in terms of risk reduction.[60] Procedural rights during public consultation processes on plans or projects strengthening resilience also contribute to reinforcing more justice outcomes.[61]

Finally, the regimes promoting the status of active consumers and demand response contain a strong element of energy justice. The consumers' role moves from being passive to becoming active players. Empowerment of consumers through prosumer regime is one illustration of this legal development.[62] The legislative recognition of the status of renewable energy communities and citizen energy cooperatives is another one.[63]

D.   System flips, or the moments of change and new states of regulatory stability

The tension between resistance and resilience has been pointed out above, in the context of political governance resistance. The legal framework itself may resist the need to act in a resilient way. The critical issue is at which moment does the tension between the legal framework in place and the need to act on resilience be so high that there will be a system change, a 'flip', towards a new 'stability region' consisting of a new legal framework where resilience considerations are better addressed and social-ecological resilience plays a central role.[64]

---

[56] Chapter 6 by Klass and Foote, Chapter 9 by Olawuyi, Chapter 10 by Montoya and Aguilar Abaunza, Chapter 17 by Mostert, Adomako-Kwakye, Chisanga, and van den Berg, Chapter 15 by Paddock, Chapter 19 by Eiamchamroonlarp, and Chapter 21 by de Fontenelle.

[57] Chapter 18 by Bull.

[58] Chapter 3 by Redgwell and Chapter 5 by Roggenkamp.

[59] Chapter 11 by González Márquez and Chapter 12 by Smith and Zillman.

[60] Chapter 20 by Barton.

[61] Chapter 4 by Banet.

[62] Chapter 2 by Bankes, Godden, and del Guyao and Chapter 19 by Eiamchamroonlarp.

[63] Chapter 21 by de Fontenelle.

[64] Chapter 2 by Bankes, Godden, and del Guyao.

C. J. Holling's research pioneered this theory, where resilience is part of an evolutionary model. There is a particular level of disturbance a system could absorb before the ecosystem is 'flipped' to a new set of characteristics, i.e. another 'stability domain'.[65]

The regulatory ecosystem may 'flip' because of the weakness of the legal framework. But a system flip may also shift those ingrained weaknesses and offer opportunities for renewal and improvement. The question is then how the law can and should accompany and enable the shift towards a new stability domain, and what 'legal directions' would support the shift.[66]

III.   Final Word: Structural Principles of Energy, Infrastructure and Natural Resources Law in the Forthcoming New Era

The growing recognition of resilience-thinking within the legal field challenges us to design and elaborate new principles that could structure legal frameworks for resilience.[67] The reflection is just starting, but several chapters in this book have already identified some structuring principles either already existing and in need of reinforcement, or new principles.

In terms of existing principles, the sustainable development principle is getting a wider consideration in the context of resilience, with the idea of moving to another stability region and continuation of development, but in a different manner, on a different basis. The solidarity and equity principles get reinforced in a resilience context because of the closer interactions disruption response and resilience building require from a social-ecological perspective (between human activities and natural systems).

The principle of energy justice is also gaining a new dimension. Notably, a resilient social-ecological system can have many benefits from other actors and interests, such as the delivery of resilience services. Resilience services could take the form of, for example, new green, blue, or energy infrastructures that contribute to fostering resilience to natural disasters.

New principles are also beginning to be defined, such as integration principle in energy system and natural resources planning.[68]

Finally, the studies in this book have shown us that the time has come to think in more integrative ways about the system of which we all are a part. In a global system such as ours, one which expects to see more disruptions, even at the massive scale of the COVID-19 pandemic, the interrelatedness of societies and interests can no longer be denied or ignored. The need to think and act more in terms of social-ecological ecosystems is stark. Resilience provides a different frame within which to evaluate the roles, functions, and even sources of law.

---

[65] C. S. Holling, 'Resilience and Stability of Ecological Systems' (1973) 4 Annual Review of Ecology and Systematics 17–19. Chapter 2 by Bankes, Godden, and del Guyao and Chapter 8 by Godden.

[66] Chapter 2 by Bankes, Godden, and del Guyao.

[67] See also B. Bohman, *Legal Design for Social-Ecological Resilience* (Cambridge University Press 2021).

[68] Chapter 4 by Banet.

Index

For the benefit of digital users, indexed terms that span two pages (e.g., 52–53) may, on occasion, appear on only one of those pages.